FIGHTER BOYS
AND
BOMBER BOYS

ALSO BY PATRICK BISHOP

NON-FICTION

The Winter War (with John Witherow)

The Provisional IRA (with Eamon Mallie)

The Irish Empire

Famous Victory

3 Para

Battle of Britain

Ground Truth – 3 Para: Return to Afghanistan

Target Tirpitz

Wings

The Reckoning

NOVELS

A Good War

Follow Me Home

PATRICK BISHOP

FIGHTER BOYS

AND

BOMBER BOYS

Saving Britain 1940–1945

**WILLIAM
COLLINS**

William Collins
An imprint of HarperCollins*Publishers*
1 London Bridge Street
London SE1 9GF

WilliamCollinsBooks.com

This omnibus edition first published by William Collins in 2017

1

Fighter Boys: First published in Great Britain by Harper*Press* in 2003
Copyright © Patrick Bishop 2003

Bomber Boys: First published in Great Britain by Harper*Press* in 2007
Copyright © Patrick Bishop 2007

Patrick Bishop asserts the moral right to be
identified as the author of this work

Plans of Halifax and Lancaster bombers © Copyright The National Archives.
Plans of Stirling, Mosquito and Wellington bombers © Crown Copyright RAF Museum

Maps of Cologne and Berlin © Copyright Royal Geographical Society

Maps of Bomber Command Stations, Targets in Europe, Germany,
and the Ruhr Valley by John Gilkes

While every effort has been made to trace the owners of copyright
material reproduced herein, the author and publishers would like
to apologise for any omissions and will be pleased to incorporate
missing acknowledgements in any future editions.

A catalogue record for this book is
available from the British Library

ISBN 978-0-00-826198-6

Printed and bound by
CPI Group (UK) Ltd, Croydon, CR0 4YY

MIX
Paper from
responsible sources
FSC
www.fsc.org   **FSC™ C007454**

This book is produced from independently certified FSC paper
to ensure responsible forest management.

For more information visit www.harpercollins.co.uk/green

FIGHTER BOYS

PATRICK BISHOP

FIGHTER BOYS

Saving Britain 1940

**WILLIAM
COLLINS**

To Kelly and Bill

Contents

List of Illustrations

Preface

This book is an attempt to answer a question that has fascinated me since I was a child. I grew up in Kent and London in the late 1950s and early 1960s, when the Second World War was still a real presence. There were daily reminders of it in the weed-choked gaps between houses where German bombs had fallen and the muddy Anderson shelters that could still be found in suburban back gardens.

My first years were spent in the village of Charing. One of my earliest memories is of walking with my father, mother and sister through a ground mist of bluebells in Long Beech woods on the ridge above the village, close to the Pilgrim's Way. Not long before the skies overhead had been a battleground. Occasionally my playmates and I found cartridge cases rusting underneath the ferns that we imagined had tumbled from the heavens during the fighting. Later I learned that a fighter pilot had crashed in flames into Long Beech after being shot down in the autumn of 1940.

We boys knew all about the Battle of Britain from small, square comic books, describing the great events of the war, that we bought eagerly as soon as they appeared in the village newsagent. They were our first history books. There, for the first time, we met heroes other than our fathers. It was the fighter pilots who hijacked our imaginations. We acted out their deeds in our games and dreamed about being them when we grew up. Their style and dash made them much more glamorous than the earthbound drudges of the infantry. Adults seemed to think so too.

The Battle of Britain was mythologised before it was even over and those who took part in it were bathed in the glow of the legend.

At adolescence you shed your old heroes and get a new set. For a while it was slightly embarrassing to recall the passion that the silhouette of a Hurricane or the smudged snapshot of a young pilot once provoked. The grown-ups also seemed to have moved on. This was the Sixties. Men in uniform were now the targets of mockery.

Then, in the funny way that the recent past becomes suddenly almost as remote as the Dark Ages, the pilots slipped into history. There were plenty of books about the battles they fought and their crucial importance to the twentieth century. But they themselves grew obscure, blurred and monochrome like the photographs they took of each other, always smiling, as they hung about at dispersal, waiting to take off.

In the pages that follow I have tried to colour in the picture and to answer the question: What were the Fighter Boys really like? My researches have been helped by the generosity of many people. I am particularly grateful to Malcolm Smith of the Battle of Britain Fighter Association for pointing me to the veterans whose reminiscences enrich this story and answering many queries with his celebrated kindness, good humour and patience. The survivors are men of their time. Everyone I approached was unfailingly courteous, helpful and hospitable. Meetings were invariably a pleasure. The Fighter Boys retain their *joie de vivre*. The contribution of individuals is made clear in the text, and to each of them I give my thanks. Without them the book could not have been written. I would like to make special acknowledgment to Group Captain Billy Drake, Air Commodore Peter Brothers and Air Chief Marshal Sir Christopher Foxley-Norris for the repeated calls I made on them. Group Captain John Cunningham, Hugh Heron, Squadron Leader Jocelyn Millard, Group Captain Anthony O'Neill, Wing Commander Harbourne Stephen and Flight Lieutenant William Walker were also generous with their time.

I was fortunate to be given access to several unpublished texts. Among them was Tim Vigors's splendid autobiography, which has yet to appear in print, a situation which I hope will soon be rectified. I am also grateful to the Beaumont family for allowing me to see S. G. Beaumont's

Reminiscences, to the Fenwick family for sending me Charles Fenwick's account of a young pilot's life, *Dear Mother*, and to Michael Butterworth for enabling me to see Group Captain Frank Carey's personal history. Squadron Leader Dennis Armitage supplemented his talk with me with his written account of the summer of 1940. Edith Kup was kind enough to spend a wintry afternoon filling in some of the gaps in the story of her love affair with Denis Wissler and to allow me to see his letters. Valerie Preston shared with me some of her souvenirs of the White Hart and Robin Appleford has allowed me to reproduce some glimpses of off-duty life in 66 squadron.

I would also like to thank Mrs Lesley Kingcome, her mother Sheila, her daughter Samantha and her son Gavin for their hospitality in Devon and for their memories of the late Brian Kingcome, as well as for permission to reproduce the photographs that appear here and to quote from his memoir, *A Willingness to Die*. I am grateful, too, to Sarah Quill for talking to me about her father Jeffery and for showing me letters from the family archive, and to Yvonne Agazarian for sketching in some details of her brother, Noel.

Our understanding of the ethos of Fighter Command has been helped greatly by the work of the Imperial War Museum, which more than 20 years ago set out to record the testimony of many of those engaged in the air battles of 1940 and preserve them in its sound archive. These interviews have provided much fascinating material and I am grateful for permission to reproduce extracts. The staffs of the Sound Archive, Department of Documents and Printed Books, Photograph Archive and Film and Video Archive were always helpful and efficient. I also want to thank Gordon Leith and his team at the Department of Research and Information Services at the RAF Museum, Hendon and the staff of the Public Record Office in Kew for their patience and the hard work they did on my behalf. Jean Buckberry was a gracious guide to the Royal Air Force College, Cranwell and its library. The staff of RAF, Benson, provided me with the records of the Oxford University Air Squadron in the interwar years.

In another, very different, area of research, I would like to thank Rod

Dean, himself a former RAF fighter pilot, for taking me through the basic manoeuvres of a dogfight in a Harvard trainer in the skies above Tangmere and for explaining the principles of air fighting.

My task would have been much more difficult if it were not for the work done by several aviation historians of the period. I am indebted to Ken Wynn for the definitive research contained in *Men of the Battle of Britain* and to Christopher Shores and Clive Williams for the wealth of detail found in their two-volume *Aces High*. The chronology was greatly aided by reference to Francis K. Mason's *Battle Over Britain*. The writings of Norman Franks, H. Montgomery Hyde, John James, Dr Tony Mansell, Dilip Sarkar, Richard C. Smith and John Terraine were always illuminating.

Thanks are due to the Grub Street team, who continue to ensure that the voices of those who fought the Second World War are heard, for permission to quote from Dennis David's *My Biography*, and *Shot Down In Flames* by Geoffrey Page, to Hutchinson for extracts from *Flying Start* by Hugh Dundas, reprinted by permission of the Random House Group Ltd, who also allowed me to use passages from Alan Deere's memoir *Nine Lives*. Wing Commander Paddy Barthropp allowed me to make use of his autobiography *Paddy*. I am also grateful to Cassell Military for letting me reproduce parts of Paul Richey's classic, *Fighter Pilot*.

Franziska Thomas put me in touch with German Luftwaffe veterans and was a skilful translator of my talks with them. My friend Sophia Coudenhove was a model researcher, a shrewd and indefatigable toiler in the archives and a source of cheer. Nick Farrell, Harry de Quetteville and Hugh Schofield gave encouragement and ideas when the going got heavy. Charles Moore, Editor of the *Daily Telegraph*, and Alec Russell, Foreign Editor, were generous and understanding bosses, and my colleague Ian Jones took the author photograph. My gratitude is due to Leslie Bonham Carter for providing a wonderful working environment at Bussento at a crucial stage of writing.

In closing I would like to mention my late father, Ernest Bishop, himself an RAF man, in whose endlessly-leafed through wartime photograph albums the germ of this project perhaps lies. It would have lain dormant, however, were it not for the intervention of my agent David Godwin, who devoted his great talent and energy to getting *Fighter Boys* airborne. The process was helped enormously by the professionals at Harper-Collins. I would like to thank Michael Fishwick for his enthusiasm and backing, Kate Johnson for her intelligent appreciation of the subject, Mary Ore and Peter Ford for their meticulous editing and Melanie Haselden for the care she took over the picture selection.

The last acknowledgement should really have come first. My eternal gratitude, Marie darling, for your support and – how shall I put this? – *tolerance*. Now it is your turn.

Group 13

Group 12

Group 11
see inset

Group 10

Wick
Inverness
Dyce
Aberdeen
Kirkwall
Orkney
Islands
Grangemouth
Edinburgh
Glasgow
Drem
Turnhouse
Berwick
Usworth
Acklinton
Newcastle
Middlesbrough
Catterick
Church
Fenton
York
Leeds
Leconfield
Hull
Manchester
Liverpool
Kirton-in-Lindsey
Tern Hill
Watnall
Digby
Nottingham
Birmingham
Wittering
Coltishall
Coventry
Cambridge
Norwich
Duxford
Pembrey
Cardiff
Filton
Oxford
Bristol
Colerne
Box
Middle
Wallop
Boscombe Down
Southampton
Exeter
Exeter
Warmwell
Portsmouth
Hastings
St. Eval
Roborough
Weymouth
Brighton
Plymouth
London
Dover

NORTH SEA

N

Shetland
Islands
Sumburgh

ENGLISH CHANNEL

NETHERLANDS
Amsterdam
The Hague
Soesterberg
Rotterdam
GERMANY
Dunkirk
Ostend
Antwerp
Cologne
Ghent
Brussels
Wissant
BELGIUM
Lille
Liège
Arras
LUXEMBOURG
Amiens
Luxembourg
Dieppe
Laon
Verdun-
Sur-Meuse
Cherbourg
Beauvais
Berry-au-Bac
Metz
La Havre
Reims
Caen
Bar-Le-Duc
Flers
Falaise
Paris
Brest
Dinard St. Malo
Villacoublay

FRANCE

Coquelles

0   50 miles

Inset: Group 11

Group 11

FC

High
Street
Dunwich
Martlesham
Debden
Stapleford
Bawdsey
Bromley
North Weald
Walton
Northolt
Hendon
Canewdon
Rochford
Uxbridge
Hornchurch
London
Gravesend
Croydon
Detling
Dunkirk
Foreness
Kenley
Manston
Biggin Hill
West
Malling
Hawkinge
Portsmouth
Tangmere
Eastchurch
Dover
Southampton
Brighton
Hastings
Lympne
Rye
Dover
Lee-on-Solent
Fairlight
Gosport
Thorney
Island
Truleigh
Pevensey
Beachy Head
Ventnor
Ford
Poling
Westhampnett

▲ Basic (Chain Home) Radar Stations
△ Low Flying (Chain Home Low) Radar Stations

FC   RAF Fighter Command Headquarters
□   RAF Group Headquarters
■   Sector Airfields
□   Other fighter Airfields
——— RAF Group Boundaries
——— Sector Boundaries
▪▪▪▪▪ Luftwaffe Boundary

Prologue: The White Hart

At 9 p.m. on Thursday, 15 August 1940, in a low-beamed, tile-hung pub in the Kentish village of Brasted, the conversation faded as a radio was switched on and the familiar pulse of the electronic time signal counted down the seconds to the main BBC news broadcast of the evening.

The voice of the announcer was calm but the events he described could not have been more dramatic. Throughout the day huge formations of German bombers, protected by large numbers of fighter escorts, had been crossing the Channel unloading cargoes of high explosive on military and industrial targets across south-east England.

The report was heard in silence until the newsreader revealed the day's score. At least 182 enemy aircraft had been destroyed, he claimed, against British losses of only 34 fighters. There was a burst of cheering and a surge to the bar for celebratory drinks. As the radio was switched off the noise in the pub's stone-flagged bars climbed back up to its normal convivial level.

Most of the men in the White Hart Hotel that evening were pilots from the fighter station at Biggin Hill, seven miles away through ragged, dusty-green lanes, across wheat fields ripened to the colour of wet sand. Watching them was an American journalist who had driven down from London that afternoon. In his report he wrote that he 'found it incredible that these noisy youngsters were in fact front-line troops, even then in the thick of battle'.

It was true. The boisterous young men, tankards and cigarettes in hand, the top buttons of their slate-blue uniform tunics undone to show the world they were fighter pilots, had been on duty since the first light of what had been an unusually misty summer morning. Some had been in action three times.

The day had seen the most intense air fighting in history. The pilots had won a remarkable victory, though not as great a one as the official figures suggested. In fact seventy-eight German aircraft had been knocked down. It was less than half the number claimed, but there was no doubt that the Luftwaffe had been made to suffer.

Half of the men were from 32 Squadron. At the centre of the crowd was the new commander, Flight Lieutenant Michael Crossley, thin and dark-haired, with deep-set humorous eyes, who at six foot two was half a head taller than the other pilots. Before leading the men off, as the dusk thickened, for pints of the warm sudsy Page & Overton bitter that the White Hart's landlady Kath Preston served from wooden casks, he had recorded the events of the day.

> Down to Hawkinge 1 p.m. and from then on had a remarkably blitzy afternoon. Chased something up to Harwich and got mixed up with 109s going home. Got none. They got Grubby Grice instead who descended into the sea . . . back to Biggin to refuel. Off to Portsmouth and attacked thousands of 88s and 110s, got three. Refuel again and attack thousands of 17s who were beating up and bombing Croydon. Slapped down seven. 'Polly' Flinders took training flight out and he and Humph slapped down one each. Day's bag twelve.[1]

The 109s mentioned in this laconic entry were the Messerschmitt fighter escorts shepherding the fleets of raiders that arrived in successive waves from late morning. The '88s' were Junkers 88s, twin-engined medium bombers. The '110s' were Messerschmitt 110s, twin-engined fighters, and '17s' were Dornier 17s, another medium bomber. The Germans had come in unprecedented numbers, launching attacks across an 800-mile front that reached from Edinburgh to Exeter in an effort to overwhelm Britain's air defences and prepare the way for invasion.

The main engagement of 32 Squadron came late in the day. Shortly after 6 p.m., as the sun slipped westward, a force of Me 110s and 109s crossed the Kent coast near Dungeness and raced towards what they thought to be the RAF base at Kenley, a vital station in the RAF defensive system. A mistake in navigation meant they dropped their bombs on Croydon aerodrome instead. The effect was devastating. The bombs crashed between buildings. The blast rolled back and forth to maximum destructive effect. The passenger terminal, which before the war had been a symbol of all that was hopeful and positive about the new world of aviation, was wrecked. Sixty-eight people were killed, all but six of them civilians. There had been no warning. The air-raid sirens sounded fifteen minutes after the attack began.

The streets around the aerodrome were full of people. Newspapers had warned that morning that the air fighting of the previous few days had been only a prelude to the real battle. Invasion fears were excited by the discovery of parachutes scattered across the Midlands and Scotland – but no parachutists. The sight of the bombers sent people running to the earth-and-corrugated-iron shelters they had dug in their back gardens. Others were too absorbed in the drama to take cover. Mr H. J. Edgerton of Couldson watched the Messerschmitts flash past, seemingly only a few feet over the roof of his mock-Tudor home, as 'about 20 Hurricanes and Spitfires streaked after them. Our fellows attacked them from below and roared up under them in terrific power climbs.' It was strangely exciting. The engines were 'screaming deafeningly'. The aeroplanes flew perilously close to each other and 'time after time I thought the RAF were going to ram the bombers but they swept past them'.[2]

On leaving, the Luftwaffe raked its nails across Croydon's homely, lower-middle-class face. Bombs tumbled into the streets, ripping up tarmac, blowing out windows and tearing off roofs. A woman emerged from her shelter to find nappies drying on the line shredded by machine-gun bullets. A doomed bomber piled into a row of semis, peeling away the walls, putting on display the modest lives being lived inside.

The Hurricanes of 32 Squadron and Spitfires of 610 Squadron had been unable to block the attack, though they shot down several of the raiders as they ran for home. Despite the deaths and the devastation there were few recriminations about the lack of warning or the level of protection the anti-aircraft defences and the air force had been able to provide. On the contrary, there was intense pride in the sight of the fighters charging in to attack. It seemed to Mr Edgerton that the British pilots had deliberately held their fire for several minutes, 'because of the danger of bringing the bombers down on the thickly populated district'.

In fact no such restraints were imposed either by the controllers directing the defences or by the pilots themselves. The assumption of selflessness was revealing. Already, after only a few weeks of the air war over Britain, the pilots of Fighter Command were bathed in the light of nobility. The organization was just four years old. Before the spring of 1940 fighter pilots were known as a small, vaguely glamorous élite. Their role in the fighting in France had been peripheral, and, in the great drama of the Dunkirk evacuation, somewhat contentious. Now, with Britain facing possible extinction, they were at the centre of the national consciousness, turning day by day into the heroes of a salvation legend. When people spoke about them it was in an increasingly proprietorial way touched with familial affection. First they were 'our boys'. Then, by midsummer, they were 'fighter boys'. The name conveyed everything: their youth, their job, their dash – and the warm regard in which they were held. 'Stuffy' Dowding, the pilots' austere commander, was the first to use it officially, writing in June a letter of congratulation to his 'dear Fighter Boys'.

By the end of the summer everyone in Britain was in love with them. The air battles of 1940 were intimate affairs. Unlike any external war Britain had been engaged in in the previous thousand years, this one was fought in the sight of the inhabitants of the island, over the territory the pilots were giving their lives to defend. Combat took place above the monotonous roofs of London suburbs, the old market towns and villages of Kent, Sussex and East Anglia, the fields and orchards of the Home Counties. Those below had only to look up to see an unprecedented spectacle: huge masses of bombers and fighters skidding across the cerulean summer sky, scribbling white vapour trails on its placid surface and stitching the blue with the red and gold of cannon and tracer. It was thrilling, and from a distance beautiful and unreal. Then a Heinkel would falter, stagger out of formation, slide into a stricken dive; a Hurricane would spurt flame, roll on to its back and spin down in frantic spirals, and with a final flash and boom the violence reached earth in an ugly tangle of scorched metal and roasted bodies.

The pilots fighting the battles lived among those they were defending. At 6.40 p.m. that Thursday, just outside Sevenoaks, Michael Crossley caught up with one of the Me 110s that had raided Croydon and set it on fire, sending it crashing down near the pleasant village of Ightham. Two hours later he was accepting drinks from locals in the pub, a few miles from where workers were clearing the wreckage and retrieving the corpses of the dead.

The Battle of Britain had many of the characteristics of a siege. Everyone inside the enclave, active or passive, soldier or civilian, was a defender. The closeness this engendered could sometimes be almost unbearable. The girlfriend of Flying Officer Douglas Grice, the 'Grubby' of Crossley's report, was a Waaf at Biggin Hill. The buzz that her man had 'gone in' reached her in a break between driving pilots out to their aircraft. Grice was badly burned but recovered. There were much worse stories. On a later occasion another Waaf, Edith Heap, who worked in the Debden control room, froze as a voice over the Tannoy reported 'Blue Four' was falling into the sea in flames. She knew, without waiting for confirmation, that the man she loved and was about to marry was dead.

Looking up at the wheeling Spitfires and Hurricanes, ordinary people imagined their own sons or brothers at the controls. Sometimes it was true. The mother of Tim Elkington, a young pilot with 1 Squadron, watched from the balcony of her flat on Hayling Island as he was shot down, baled out and drifted perilously over the sea before finally landing safely.

But you did not need ties of blood or romance to feel a particular bond with the Fighter Boys. The backgrounds of the few thousand pilots flying Hurricanes and Spitfires in the summer of 1940 reflected the social composition of the nation, a point that was emphasized by official and

5

unofficial propagandists. 'The most striking thing about the fighter pilots is their ordinariness,' wrote a war artist who spent months among them. 'Just you, I, us and co.; ordinary sons of ordinary parents from ordinary homes.'[3] Fighter Command was perhaps the most motley élite ever to exist in the British military. In 32 Squadron, Crossley had been at Eton. John Proctor had left school at fourteen to become an RAF apprentice. Many of those standing in the pub had been in the RAF reserve before the war, training in their spare time from their often mundane jobs. Oliver Houghton had been a fitter in a Coventry factory. William Higgins was a teacher in a Derbyshire village school.

Their interests and attitudes were as broad as their backgrounds. Fighter pilots might be philistines or intellectuals, bon vivants or ascetics, pious or godless, cynical or trusting. There were some whose dominant trait of recklessness or aggression or amiability made them stand out, but most were too ordinarily complex to be pigeonholed. Fighter squadrons were collections of individuals. The nature of the fighting made it so. Once combat began, a pilot was usually on his own, beyond the control of his commander and making fateful decisions alone.

There were, though, strong affinities and common characteristics that bound the bunch together. The most potent was a love of flying. Speaking about flying, and when occasionally they wrote about it, the pilots dropped their usual clipped understatement for the language of passion. It was an obsession and an addiction and aeroplanes were far more than simply machines. They had quasi-human qualities. They could be brutish and heavy or beautiful, fragile and sensitive. If it was love, it was nearly always love at first sight. The pilots' reminiscences are full of lyrical memories of the first encounter, when the flying circus arrived in town or a mysterious figure floated out of the sky to land in the field next door.

Charles Fenwick was a little boy in the Kentish village of Harbledown when Sir Alan Cobham's troupe of itinerant flyers passed through. His aunt took him to see them.

'Would you like to go for a flip?'

What a stupendous question! I was on my way to the plane as fast as

I could go. I was small for my age and flopped into the rear cockpit. The plane was an early Avro, an aerial marvel quite beautiful to behold. Well, my idea of beauty, all struts and wires and canvas with that intoxicating smell compounded from dope and fuel and hot oil. But to beat it all she was alive. She was roaring like a lion and rattling. I was heading for heaven.[4]

Flying requires courage. Going solo in any aeroplane is alarming. Most aviators never lose a faint feeling of insecurity, no matter how great their experience. Flying with an instructor for the first time in a light aircraft, trainees noted queasily how thin the fuselage seemed, how flimsy the wings, how easy it might be to tip out in a turn. The sensations got more alarming as they progressed to more powerful machines. The Harvard trainer, whose 600-horsepower engine provides only half the thrust of the Merlins of the Hurricanes and Spitfires, is disconcerting enough. Clamping into a tight turn, the most basic manoeuvre of dog-fighting, G forces drag your guts to the sump of your stomach and press your head down on your chest as if you are being crushed by a giant hand. A simple half-roll sends the world spinning incomprehensibly, earth and sky alternating in a blur.

When I experienced this as a passenger, fear never felt far away. It is hard to imagine how pilots were able to fling their aeroplanes around in this way without succumbing to disorientation or panic. It is harder still to understand how they could shoot at, and hit, other aeroplanes while they were doing so. To have the reflexes and eyesight needed to do these things you had to be young. Most pilots were aged between nineteen and twenty-six. They tended to be young in their outlook as well. They liked the latest music, films and fashions and spiced their talk with Americanisms, creating a Hollywood-meets-public-school slang.

The Fighter Boys belonged firmly to contemporary Britain, ideal warriors in what was being shaped as a people's war. To the public it seemed that their technological skill was, comfortingly, fused to old values and traditions. The pilots' fathers had fought and died in a war that had traumatized Europe and stimulated a wave of pacifist, and then defeatist, feeling. Yet the sons were accepting their duty willingly, almost cheerfully, and confronting the horror again.

On that August night, as the blackout shutters were fitted into the leaded windows of the White Hart, as last orders were called and the banter and laughter subsided, unwelcome thoughts of tomorrow edged in. The fighting of the day had brought only an interim victory, one that would have to be won over and over again. No one present, airman or civilian, was now in any doubt that they were in the middle of a struggle which would determine whether or not Britain would survive as a free country. Winston Churchill had set the stakes even higher. The battle, he said, would decide the fate of the civilized world. Many elements were involved in determining the outcome. Chief among them was the skill, morale and courage of the Fighter Boys. It was an extraordinary responsibility. Not since classical times had such a tiny band of warriors been asked to bear such a heavy burden. It was the pilots, though, who seemed the least concerned as they finished the dregs from their pewter mugs and stepped out into the cool, hop-scented Kent night.

I

Sportsmen and Butchers

In the summer of 1940 the art of air fighting was only twenty-six years old. In that time, aeroplanes had moved from the extreme periphery to the centre of modern warfare. The invention of aircraft made air wars inevitable. Innovators moved with depressing speed to fit guns to flying machines. The air shows at Hendon, Brooklands and Rheims held before the First World War emphasized the potential destructive power of the thing they were celebrating, with aviators dropping flour bombs on the outlines of warships traced in chalk on the ground. Writers frightened readers with stories of airships bombarding cities, a prophecy whose accuracy was soon to be confirmed.

For the military, though, it was the information-gathering potential of aeroplanes that first attracted interest. The first aircraft were used as observation platforms. In the war game played in September 1912 at the annual British army manoeuvres, Red Force and Blue Force were each equipped with a supporting air component. Early on, two airborne officers from Blue Force spotted a concentration of opposition troops and correctly guessed their direction. The information helped their side to win.

The victorious commander, Lieutenant-General Sir James Grierson, drew an important conclusion from the exercise. 'So long as hostile aircraft are hovering over one's troops,' he wrote, 'all movements are likely to be seen and reported. Therefore the first step in war will be to get rid of hostile aircraft.'[1]

This was how combat in the air was to develop in the four years of the Great War. The essential role of aeroplanes was to lift the roof off the battlefield, allowing commanders to peer into the enemy's territory, detecting his movements and trying to divine his intentions. At the same time, spotters hovering perilously over the front lines helped to direct the artillery barrages that occupied much of the effort of both sides.

The rival pilots, from the outset, tried to kill each other. One of the first recorded encounters took place on 25 August 1914. Lieutenant C. E. C. Rabagliati of the Royal Flying Corps was cruising with an observer on a reconnaissance mission over northern France when they came across a lone German aeroplane. Rabagliati's aircraft was unarmed, but he had with him a .303 service rifle. The German carried a Mauser pistol, fitted with a wooden shoulder stock. The two machines approached each other and circled, coming within feet of colliding. Rabagliati fired a hundred rounds without success. Then, he reported afterwards, 'to my intense joy, I saw the German pilot fall forward on his joystick and the machine tipped up and went down'.[2]

Such encounters were to be repeated thousands of times in the following years. Technological advances, accelerated by the demands of warfare, meant that the aircraft became faster, more nimble and more sturdy, and the weapons they carried more deadly. But the purpose of aerial fighting remained the same. No bomber heavy enough to make a significant difference on the battlefield or in the rear had emerged by the end of the war. The main function of military flying remained observing the enemy, and trying to prevent the enemy from observing you.

These activities grew to be increasingly important as the war progressed. The RFC went to France with sixty-two aircraft. In April 1918 it became, together with the Navy's air arm, a service in its own right, the Royal Air Force. It finished the war with 1,799 aeroplanes. This transformation was presided over by a particularly forceful and energetic commander, Hugh Trenchard. There were others who played a crucial part in the creation of a separate air force, but Trenchard's passion made him stand out. He became known as 'The Father of the RAF', a label he claimed to detest. The designation had some truth in it, though. He loved the air force with the fierce love of a father; a Victorian father who would not flinch from sending his boy to his death if duty demanded it.

Trenchard combined nineteenth-century mores with a twentieth-century appreciation of the new. He was born on 3 February 1873 in the West Country, and had a difficult childhood. His sister died of diphtheria, his solicitor father was bankrupted and he failed several attempts to enter military schools before scraping a commission as a second-lieutenant in the Royal Scots Fusiliers and being posted to India. He spent the first decade of the new century in southern and western Africa. In October 1900 he was shot in the chest while trying to capture Boers and was expected to die. Trenchard, who 'hated sick people', pulled through, recovering in characteristic fashion by hurtling down the Cresta run at St Moritz.

He was tall, bony, with mournful eyes that seemed to search for faults and slights. His personality was similarly angular: quarrelsome, morose and dissatisfied, ill at ease in the genial atmosphere of mess and gym-khana club. By 1912 it was clear that his career was going nowhere. He was approaching forty, unmarried and not much loved. His salvation came in a letter from one of his few friends, Captain Eustace Loraine, who was learning to fly at the RFC aviation school on Salisbury Plain. 'You've no idea what you're missing,' Loraine wrote excitedly. 'Come and see men crawling like ants.'[3]

Trenchard was not a natural pilot. His tall, long-legged frame looked ridiculous crammed into the narrow seats of the primitive Blériots and Farmans that were used to give instruction to trainees. What fascinated him was not flying itself, but its potential. He sensed he had finally made his rendezvous with destiny and joined the RFC. Three years later, in August 1915, he became its commander.

Trenchard tried to make the RFC indispensable, straining to satisfy every demand made on it by the army no matter how unreasonable, or how limited his resources. The aim was to obtain and maintain control of the air over the trenches. The balance of power shifted constantly as the technological and tactical advantage swung back and forth between the sides. The level of fighting was kept high. The RFC's main business was reconnaissance. Trenchard decided early on that the best way of defending the spotter aircraft and ensuring a steady flow of intelligence to the army was to go on the offensive, reaching over the lines into enemy air space. This was, at best, a logical response to the three-dimensional nature of aerial warfare in which there were no fixed lines to defend and to wait for the enemy to attack was to cede a moral advantage. At times, though, it could seem like an echo of the numb thinking of the terrestrial generals, who, literally stuck in the mud, threw more and more troops into futile attacks because they could think of nothing better to do.

Trenchard did not hesitate to sacrifice men to fulfil the RFC's obligations to the army and maintain the momentum of aggression. The losses among pilots during the great offensives of 1916 and 1917 came close, in proportionate terms, to matching those on the ground. During the Battle of the Somme pilots were in the air for five or six hours a day. The gaps were often filled by novices coming straight from flying school. Cecil Lewis, eighteen years old, was asked by a senior officer when he arrived at No. 1 Aircraft Depot at St Omer how many hours' flying experience he had.

'Fourteen hours.'

'Fourteen! It's absolutely disgraceful to send pilots overseas with so little flying. You don't stand a chance . . . Another fifty hours and you might be quite decent; but fourteen! My God, it's murder.'[4]

The aeroplanes which carried the war to the Germans became known as fighters. The machines were constantly being refined and improved. These efforts produced steady rather than startling increases in performance. The Bristol Scout, in service in 1915, had a top speed of 86.5 m.p.h. at 10,000 feet, to which level it could climb in twenty-one minutes. The Sopwith Camel, one of the most ubiquitous types in the closing stages of the war, could in ten minutes reach 10,000 feet, where it could travel at 112 m.p.h. Aircraft armaments similarly became heavier and more accurate as interrupter devices were refined to allow bullets to pass through the arc of the propeller.

Fighter pilots came to exemplify the character and spirit of the new air force, even though their role was essentially secondary. They were a godsend to propagandists charged with conjuring romance out of the horror of mechanized warfare. They operated in the clean medium of the air, detached from the vileness of the trenches. The nature of their work made it inevitable that they would be linked to an older, nobler fighting tradition. Some aviators believed this themselves, at least at the beginning. 'To be alone,' wrote Cecil Lewis, fresh from flying school, 'to have your life in your own hands, to use your own skill, single-handed against the enemy. It was like the lists in the Middle Ages, the only sphere in modern warfare where a man saw his adversary and faced him in mortal combat, the only sphere where there was still chivalry and honour.'[5]

What was true was that to be a successful fighter pilot required differ-ent qualities from those that made a good infantry officer. In the air you were on your own. The business was entirely new. There was no one to teach it, no textbooks to refer to. To survive, the pilot had to make his own decisions and develop his own tactics. The new air service attracted men who were independent-minded, adventurous, often unusual, some-times to the point of eccentricity. Among the first to emerge on the British side was Albert Ball, in whom the values of the playing field jostled unhappily with the neurosis of the battlefield. Ball was brought up in a middle-class home in Nottingham where his father hauled himself up the class ladder, starting his working life as a plumber and ending up mayor of the city. He was educated at a local fee-paying school, founded to promote Anglican principles and a sense of patriotic duty. There were cold baths, perpetual exercise and an emphasis on technology.

Like tens of thousands of other young men, he joined up as soon as he was able, and was posted to the infantry. Frustrated at the delay in being sent to the front he took private flying lessons to improve his chances of entering the RFC. Ball fell instantly in love with flying, despite the hazards. 'It is rotten to see the smashes,' he wrote in one of his frequent letters home. 'Yesterday a ripping boy had a smash and when we got up to him he was nearly dead. He had a two-inch piece of wood right through his head and died this morning.' He added, without apparent irony, that he would be 'pleased to take you up any time you wish', if his parents felt like a flip.[6]

He arrived in France, now a lieutenant in the RFC, in time for the great Somme offensive. He flew a French Nieuport, one of the new generation of single-seater scouts. His methods marked him out immediately. He would fly straight into packs of enemy aircraft, getting in as close as he could, firing off a Lewis gun at point-blank range, breaking off an inconclusive attack only to change the ammunition drum and bore in again. It was simple, effective and desperately dangerous. He would return from sorties with his machine shredded by enemy fire.

On the ground his behaviour struck his fellow officers as odd. At his first base, Savy Aubigny aerodrome, north-west of Arras, he turned down a billet in the village, preferring first a tent, then a wooden hut he built for himself at the edge of the airfield, two miles from the squadron mess. He sent home for packets of seeds to plant marrows, lettuce, carrots, cress and flowers. He spent hours in the hangars, chatting with the riggers and fitters, making constant adjustments to his aeroplane to improve its capabilities, yet he seemed less interested in flying for its own sake than as a means of fighting. The camaraderie of the mess held little interest for him. Nor did women.

His main relaxation was the violin, which he would play after dinner while walking around a red magnesium flare. Another fellow pilot, Roderic Hill, described him sitting outside his hut, playing his gramophone and brooding. 'He had but one idea: that was to kill as many Huns as possible, and he gave effect to it with a swiftness and certainty that seemed to most of us uncanny. He nearly always went out alone; in fact he would not let anyone fly with him, and was intolerant of proffered assistance.'[7]

For all his oddness, he was respected. A young New Zealander pilot, Keith Caldwell, saw him as 'a hero . . . and he looked the part too; young, alert, ruddy complexion, dark hair and eyes. He was supposed to be a "loner", but we found him to be friendly . . . One felt that it could only be a matter of time before he "bought it", as he was shot about so often.'[8]

Looking now at the photographs of Ball, at the thick, glossy hair and the black eyes set in the taut, uncreased skin, one senses fatalism behind the easy smile. Almost from the beginning the mild bragging in the letters home is matched by disgust at what duty had led him into. By the end of August he was yearning for home. 'I do so want to leave all this beastly killing for a time,' he sighed in a letter.[9] Yet even when complaining of nerves he would still take every possible opportunity to get airborne.

In October his superiors ordered him back to England for a rest and a new posting as an instructor. He was already famous, the most successful pilot in the RFC, with an MC, DSO and bar. The prime minister, Lloyd George, invited him to breakfast. He went to Buckingham Palace, where King George V presented him with his medals.

Despite the peace and the nearness to family that he had yearned for when in France, he was restless and unhappy and soon agitating to go back. The pressure worked. In February he was posted to 56 Squadron, which was being formed as an elite unit to fly the new SE5 fighters against the best of the German air force. While waiting he fell in love, with an eighteen-year-old florist called Flora Young, who an old friend had brought with him when he drove over to visit him at the base. The attraction was instantaneous. He offered to take her up in an aeroplane and she gamely accepted. That night he was writing to thank her for 'the topping day I have had with you. I am simply full of joy to have met you.'[10] On 7 April 1917 the squadron left England. Ball's tour was supposed to be for a month only. He sent daily letters to Flora detailing his successes and setting himself a target. Once he had overtaken the German champion Oswald Boelcke, he would come home.

At 5.30 p.m. on Monday, 7 May, he lead a squadron of SE5s on an offensive sweep aimed at seeking out enemy fighters, believed to be led by the German ace Manfred von Richthofen, who were operating in the Arras area.

Cecil Lewis described the chocolate-coloured fighters flying into a 'May evening ... heavy with threatening masses of cumulus cloud, majestic skyscrapes, solid-looking as snow mountains, fraught with caves and valleys, rifts and ravines'.[11] Suddenly, high over the Cambrai–Douai road, out of these clouds came the Albatross D111 scouts they were looking for. Richthofen was not among the pilots, but his brother Lothar was. The formations rounded on each other in a confused mêlée of individual combats. Lewis described how Ball 'flew straight into the white face of an enormous cloud. I followed. But when I came out the other side, he was nowhere to be seen.' Four German officers on the ground heard aircraft engines and looked up to see Ball's machine slip out from low cloud upside down with its propeller stopped and trailing black smoke. It disappeared behind a stand of trees and crashed into a shoulder of farmland. By the time the officers reached the wreckage a young Frenchwoman had pulled the pilot clear. There were no marks on the fresh features, but Ball was dead.

Lothar von Richthofen claimed the victory, though no one on the British side believed him. The most likely explanation was that Ball became disoriented inside the cloud – a common hazard – and emerged to find he was flying upside down too low and too late to correct the error.

'The mess was very quiet that night,' Lewis wrote. They held a sing-song in a nearby barn to try and raise morale. The squadron band played and the men sang the hits of the time: 'There's a Long, Long Trail', 'Way Down upon the Swanee River', 'Pack Up Your Troubles'. Then Lewis sang the Robert Louis Stevenson 'Requiem'.

> Under the wide and starry sky,
> Dig the grave and let me lie.
> Glad did I live and gladly die,
>   And I laid me down with a will.

A month after Ball's death the *London Gazette* announced the award of a posthumous VC, noting that 'in all Captain Ball has destroyed forty-three

German aeroplanes and one balloon and has always displayed most exceptional courage, determination and skill'.

A new hero was already emerging from the ranks of the RFC by the time of Ball's demise, a man of very different background and character. Edward 'Mick' Mannock had been in France for just over five weeks when Ball crashed. He knew all about him. Ball's exploits, read about in the newspapers, had been one of the reasons he had applied to transfer to the RFC from the Royal Engineers. By the time he arrived at the main depot in St Omer he was already twenty-seven, oldish to be a pilot. He had reached the air force by an erratic route. He was born on 21 May 1889 to Irish parents. His father had been a non-commissioned officer in the Second Inniskilling Dragoons, who drank, beat his wife and dis-appeared, leaving her with two sons and two daughters who she brought up in poverty in Canterbury. Mannock left school at fourteen to work as a clerk. His hard early life converted him to socialism and throughout his military career he enjoyed alarming conventional comrades with his views about class and privilege. He was also an Irish nationalist.

When the war came he was working as a labour supervisor in Turkey with a cable-laying company. He was interned until the Red Cross inter-vened, returned to England and, with his technical background, ended up in the Royal Engineers with an ambition to be a tunnelling officer. But the training bored him and he was irritated by his fellow officers and their talk of cricket, girls and dances. No one was sorry when he applied for the RFC and went off to learn to fly, managing to bluff his way through the medical despite being blind in one eye from a childhood illness.

By the summer of 1917 the brief period of air superiority the RFC had enjoyed during the Somme offensive, when it had been operating with greater numbers of aircraft and using better tactics, was over. Once again the Germans had taken the technological lead with a new breed of Albatros aircraft grouped into Jagdgeschwaders tasked with achieving control of the sky in whichever sectors commanders selected. Richthofen lead Jagdgeschwader 1. The leading pilots painted their machines in glar-ing colours – blood red for Richthofen – and decorated them with ancient symbols and devices, including the swastika, which had yet to lose its innocence. Some advertised their identity in huge letters on the top wing. One had inscribed underneath his name, *Kennscht mi noch?* – 'Don't you remember me?'

On 7 June Mannock was helping to escort a bombing mission over Lille when 'we met Huns. My man gave me an easy mark. I was only ten yards away from him so I couldn't miss! A beautifully coloured insect he was – red, blue, green and yellow. I let him have sixty rounds at that range, so there wasn't much left of him. I saw him go spinning and slipping down from fourteen thousand. Rough luck but it's war and they're Huns.' On 19 August he ran into one of the leading German pilots, Leutnant von Bartrap, a holder of the Iron Cross. 'He came over for one of our balloons . . . and I cut him off going back . . . The scrap took place at two thousand feet up, well within view of the whole front. And the cheers! It took me five minutes to get him to go down and I had to shoot him before he would land. I was very pleased that I did not kill him.'[12]

On other occasions he was less considerate. Caldwell remembered watching Mannock chasing a German two-seater trying to reach the safety of its own lines. 'The Hun crashed but not badly, and most people would have been content with this – but not Mick Mannock. He dived half a dozen times at the machine, spraying bullets at the pilot and observer, who were still showing signs of life . . . On being questioned as to his wild behaviour after we had landed, he heatedly replied, "the swines are better dead – no prisoners for me!"'[13]

Mannock was full of such contradictions, mixing vindictiveness with bouts of remorse. He seemed to genuinely enjoy air fighting, writing about it unabashedly as 'fun' and 'sport' in the manner of the day. But he also worried constantly that he was going to crack up. Towards the end he became convinced his death would be a fiery one. It was a common sight to see an aeroplane plunging earthwards, trailing an oily wake of smoke. Fifty-five of eighty machines shot down by Richthofen were registered as *gebrannt* (burned). On most aircraft the fuel tank was fitted in the nose, close to the engine. In the event of fire the backwash from the propeller blew the flames into the pilot seated behind. Once an aircraft was alight there was no escape. Efficient parachutes existed but pilots were not allowed to have them. The staff view was that possession of a parachute might weaken a pilot's nerve when in difficulties so that he abandoned his valuable aeroplane before he had to. Anyway, one general reasoned, aeroplanes went down so swiftly there was really no time to jump.[14]

Mannock carried a revolver in the cockpit 'to finish myself as soon as I see the first sign of flames'.[15] The sight of his victims catching fire upset him – 'a horrible sight and made me feel sick', he confided to his diary after shooting down a BFW biplane on 5 September. But he referred to the victory in the mess as 'my first flamerino'.[16] 'Flamerinoes' became an obsession. One day after shooting down his fourth German in twenty-four hours he arrived back in high spirits. 'He bounced into the mess shouting: "All tickets please! Please pass right down the car. Flamerinoes – four! Sizzle-sizzle wonk!" '[17] It seemed to be a case of making light of that which he most feared. In London on leave in June 1918 he fell sick with influenza and spent several days in bed in the RFC club, unable to sleep because of the nightmares of burning aircraft that swamped in every time he closed his eyes. He visited friends in Northamptonshire. When he talked about his experiences he subsided into tears and said he wanted to die.

He returned to France as commander of 85 Squadron. On the evening of July 25 he bumped into a friend from 74 Squadron, Lieutenant Ira Jones, who asked him how he was feeling. 'I don't feel I shall last much longer, Taffy old lad,' he replied. 'If I'm killed I shall be in good company. You watch yourself. Don't go following any Huns too low or you'll join the sizzle brigade with me.'[18]

The following day he set off at dawn with a novice pilot, Lieutenant Donald Inglis, who had yet to shoot anything down, to show him how it was done. They ran into a two-seater over the German lines. Mannock began shooting, apparently killing the observer, and left the *coup de grâce* for his pupil, who set it on fire. Instead of climbing away as his own rules demanded, Mannock turned back over the burning aircraft, flying at only

200 feet. Inglis 'saw a flame come out of the right hand side of his machine after which he apparently went down out of control. I went into a spiral down to fifty feet and saw the machine go straight into the ground and burn.'[19]

Mannock's self-prophecy had been fulfilled. The bullets that brought him down appear to have come from the ground, a danger he had constantly warned against. He was credited with destroying seventy-four German aircraft by the time he died, nearly reaching the eighty victims recorded by his German opposite number, Richthofen.

Where Mannock and Ball manifested in their own separate ways certain facets of Britishness, Manfred von Richthofen was, to the point of caricature, a paradigm of Prussian maleness. He explained himself with jovial arrogance in an autobiography, *The Red Air Fighter*, which appeared in 1917. The von Richthofens were aristocrats, though not particularly martial ones. Manfred joined the 1st Regiment of Uhlans after cadet school and was twenty-two when the war broke out. Stationed on a quiet sector of the Western Front, he got bored and applied to join the flying service. After a mere fortnight's training he was sent to Russia, flying as an observer. By March 1916 he had qualified as a pilot and began operating over Verdun before being transferred back to Russia, where, he confessed, 'It gave me tremendous pleasure bombing those fellows from above'.[20]

Richthofen impressed Boelcke, who was on a visit to the Eastern Front looking for candidates for the new Jasta fighter units, and brought him back to the West. On 17 September 1916 he claimed his first English victim, flying in 'a large machine painted in dark colours. Apparently he was no beginner, for he knew exactly that his last hour had arrived at the moment I got at the back of him.' Richthofen was 'animated by a single thought: "the man in front of me must come down whatever happens".

At last a favourable moment arrived. My opponent had apparently lost sight of me. Instead of twisting and turning he flew straight along. In a fraction of a second I was at his back with my excellent machine. I gave a short burst with my machine-gun. I had gone so close that I was afraid

I might dash into the Englishman. Suddenly I nearly yelled with joy, for the propeller of the enemy machine had stopped turning. Hurrah! I had shot his engine to pieces.'

He had also mortally wounded the two occupants. Richthofen 'honoured the fallen enemy by placing a stone on his beautiful grave'.[21]

So Richthofen's memoir continues, like the reminiscences of some grotesque big-game hunter, constantly noting his score, always on the lookout for opportunities to increase the bag. He was a 'sportsman' by nature rather than a 'butcher'. 'When I have shot down an Englishman, my hunting passion is satisfied for a quarter of an hour,' he wrote. 'Therefore I do not succeed in shooting two Englishmen in succession. If one of them comes down I have the feeling of complete satisfaction. Only much later have I overcome my instinct and have become a butcher.'

As a sportsman he was keen on trophies and the mess of his 'Flying Circus' was hung with the debris of his victims' aircraft. It was a habit he shared with Mannock, another inveterate crash-site scavenger. In keeping with the hunter's philosophy, he admired his prey and had strong ideas about what quarry was worthy of him. Between the 'French tricksters' and 'those daring fellows, the English', he preferred the English, though he believed that frequently what the latter took to be bravery 'can only be described as stupidity'. Richthofen, of course, subscribed to the courtly view of air fighting – 'the last vestige of knightly individual combat'. But he was sensible about how it should be practised. 'The great thing in air fighting is that the decisive factor does not lie in trick flying but solely in the personal ability and energy of the aviator. A flying man may be able to loop and do all the tricks imaginable and yet he may not succeed in shooting down a single enemy. In my opinion, the aggressive spirit is everything.'[22] It was an observation that was to prove equally valid when the two sides met again in the air twenty-three years later.

Richthofen's caution meant that in a long fighting career he sustained only one injury before the end. It came on 21 April 1918 when his red Fokker triplane crashed into a beet field at Vaux-sur-Somme. As with Mannock and Ball, the exact circumstances of his death are confused.

The credit for it was contested. Captain Roy Brown of 209 Squadron plausibly claimed to have been shooting at Richthofen when he went in. So, too, did an Australian machine-gun battery in the vicinity. The body was removed from the wreckage and taken to Poulainville airfield fifteen kilometres away. Richthofen was laid out in a hangar on a strip of corrugated metal, staring upwards, in unconscious imitation of the effigy of a medieval knight. In the night soldiers and airmen came in and rifled his pockets for souvenirs.

The notion of 'aces' placed Richthofen, Mannock, Ball and perhaps a dozen others at the pinnacle of their weird profession. Beneath them were thousands of other aviators who, though mostly anonymous, none the less regarded themselves as special. The faces that look back from the old RFC photographs are bold and open. The men have modern looks and modern smiles. Unlike the army types, whose stilted sepia portraits require an effort of imagination to bring to life, you can visualize the flesh and blood. The images pulse with confidence.

Unorthodox, even louche, though the pilots seemed to the military establishment, the ethos of the RFC was public school. Cecil Lewis, on applying to join, was interviewed by a staff officer, Lord Hugh Cecil.

'So you were at Oundle?'

'Yes, sir.'

'Under the great Sanderson?'

'Er – yes, sir.'

'Play any games?'

'Yes, sir. I got my school colours at fives, and I captained the house on the river . . .'

'Fives, you say? You should have a good eye, then.'

After a brief discussion as to whether his six foot three inches would be a major handicap, Lewis was in.[23]

But there were plenty of pilots who knew nothing of the school close or the college eight. James McCudden, one of the RFC's greatest pilots, started his career as a boy bugler in the Royal Engineers before transferring to the RFC as a mechanic. Once inside, though, class was always waiting to pounce. John Grider, an American serving with 85 Squadron, recounted how his fellow pilots objected to having McCudden as their commanding officer, 'because he was once a Tommy and his father was a sergeant-major in the old army. I couldn't see that that was anything against him but the English have great ideas of caste.'[24] The technical ability that flying demanded meant that the RFC could not afford to be exclusive, even though some of the attitudes struck by the pilots seemed in the spirit of a cavalry regiment of another, more raffish time.

The airmen liked alcohol and women, though there were notable exceptions. Ball was teetotal, and had no girlfriend until his meeting with Flora. Mannock drank little and seems to have shown a courtly restraint towards females. Like Ball, he was planning marriage before his death, to a Sister Flanagan who was nursing in France. For Lewis and many like him, though, the bar and the brothel provided fun and relief after the appalling strain. Their playful attitude was summed up in a 1915 drinking song, describing the finale to a day in which the squadron has only narrowly escaped a mauling by an Albatros Jasta.

But safely at the 'drome once more, we feel quite gay and bright.
We'll take a car to Amiens and have dinner there tonight.
We'll swank along the boulevards and meet the girls of France.
To hell with the Army Medical! We'll take our ruddy chance!

In the cafés of Amiens there seemed to be a large supply of young women happy to entertain Allied pilots who were undeterred by the risk of a dose of clap. Then, as later, wings on a tunic exercised a strong attraction, as Lewis discovered (describing the incident rather coyly in the third person) when he removed his greatcoat after returning with an eighteen-year-old to her room and its vast black iron-and-brass bed.

'Ah! Tu es pilote! Que j'aime les pilotes!'
'Yes?'
'Yais! Yais!' she imitated, deftly catching a handful of his hair and

tugging at it. 'Tue es beau, tu sais.' She was on his knee again, and under her open blouse the hollow of her young shoulder seemed infinite in its promise.[25]

Squadrons would lay on spectacular 'drunks' at which the participants sucked on a sponge soaked in a cocktail of whisky and champagne, mixed in a bucket. It was drinking to forget. Insouciance was obligatory. Each death in Mannock's diary is recorded in the same carefully offhand way – 'poor old Shaw went West', 'We've lost poor old Davis', etc. Trenchard had a policy of 'no empty chairs at breakfast' to discourage brooding, replacing pilots instantly, often with greenhorns who were themselves propelled straight to death. During the bad times, the mess at nightfall could be a very melancholy place.

> In such an atmosphere you grew fatalistic, and as time went by and left you unscathed, like a batsman who has played himself in, you began to take liberties with the bowling, [Lewis wrote]. You took unnecessary risks, you volunteered for dangerous jobs, you provoked enemy aircraft to attack you. You were invulnerable: nothing could touch you. Then, when one of the old hands, as seemingly invulnerable as yourself, went West, you suddenly got cold feet. It wasn't possible to be sure – even of yourself. At this stage it required most courage to go on – a sort of plodding fatalism, a determination, a cold-blooded effort of will. And always alone! No friends right and left, no crowd morale.[26]

Crack-ups were routine. Pilots got to recognize the signs in each other and were sympathetic. Mannock, who was hard on anyone he suspected of hanging back, was kindly towards those he saw were reaching the end of their tether, and in contrast to the trenches a certain humanity seems to have guided posting policy so the bad cases were sent to less arduous duties.

Whatever their personal dreads, the pilots were always grateful they were not on the ground. They looked down at the 'poor little maggoty men' toiling in the churned and polluted earth below and blessed their luck. From time to time, they saw the lines at close quarters and the reality was sickeningly brought home. The 20th of July 1917 was a bad day for Mannock. Having shot down a two-seater, he went to inspect the wreckage and discovered a 'little black and tan terrier – dead – in the observer's seat. I felt exactly like a murderer. The journey to the trenches was rather nauseating – dead men's legs sticking through the sides with putties and boots still on – bits of bones and skulls with the hair peeling off, and tons of equipment and clothing lying about. This sort of thing, together with the strong graveyard stench and the dead and mangled body of the pilot (an NCO), combined to upset me for a few days.'[27]

By the last two years of the war, whatever faint notions of nobility and romance may have clung to the business of air fighting had faded. The headlong style of Ball had given way to cold stalking tactics. The general slowness of the aircraft and the narrowness of the speed margins meant that the attacker approached gradually, leaving plenty of time to reflect on what he was doing as he overhauled his prey.

The most successful pilots spent hours synchronizing their guns and sights. McCudden would seek out the sluggish two-seaters on reconnaissance and, taking great care not to be seen, approach slowly to attack from the blind spot behind the enemy plane, finishing the job with a single carefully aimed burst. 'My system was always to attack the Hun at his disadvantage if possible,' he wrote before his death in a crash.[28]

Mannock dinned into his pilots a basic rule of survival: always above; seldom on the same level; never underneath. The huge tactical advantage of invisibility, gained by having the sun at your back, was quickly understood by both sides, but all light conditions carried their advantages and disadvantages. Allied pilots would lurk in the dusk falling in the east to catch Germans on their way home.

Richthofen, despite his fantasies of knightly combat, made sure he had every advantage possible when he went out to deliver death, protected by his fellow pilots when the odds were in the German favour, allowing him to attack without fear of ambush and breaking off if he felt his opponent was getting the upper hand.

It was all a long way from Rabagliati's gentlemanly airborne duel in

August 1914. Yet when the end came the survivors felt a sort of regret at the passing of what they already saw as aerial warfare's heroic era. Cecil Lewis was in a village near Ypres when the news of the Armistice came through. 'So it was over. I confess to a feeling of anticlimax ... when you have been living a certain kind of life for four years, living as part of a single-minded and united effort, its sudden cessation leaves your roots in the air, baffled and, for the moment, disgruntled. But the readjustment was rapid and soon we began to explore the possibilities of peace. Where should we go? What should we do?'[29]

2

Fighters *versus* Bombers

The possession of an air force the size of the RAF was an affront to the peacetime mood of economy and war-weariness. Under Trenchard it had grown huge. By the end of the war it had 30,122 officers, 263,410 men and 188 combat squadrons.[1] Shortly after the Armistice a decision was taken to prune back the service to a modest force of thirty-three squadrons. The Northcliffe press and air-power enthusiasts in Parliament denounced the myopia of the policy and warned that German quiescence was only temporary. But hardship, public disgust with war and a belief in Britain's ability to rise to the occasion in a future crisis ensured, until the rise of Hitler forced a change of mind, that a frugal attitude to air spending was maintained. In August 1925, the belief that there was no war on the horizon became official policy with the Cabinet's adoption of the 'ten-year rule', which stated that, in revising defence estimates, it should be assumed that the Empire would not be involved in a major conflict for a decade.

Trenchard was put in charge of supervising the new incarnation. He was philosophical about the new restraints. In his brisk memorandum setting out the post-war organization of the RAF he compared the force to 'the prophet Jonah's gourd. The necessities of war created it in a night, but the economies of peace have to a large extent caused it to wither in a day, and we are now faced with the necessity of replacing it with a plant of deeper root.'[2]

The RAF needed roots if it was to resist the grasping hands of the army and navy, who were once again eager now that the war was over to snatch back control of air assets so they could apply them to their own particular needs. They maintained this covetous attitude throughout the inter-war period. Trenchard fought a canny and tenacious defensive campaign. As Chief of the Air Staff, he limited himself to providing 'the vital essentials of a skeleton force while giving way on every possible detail on which he felt expense could be spared'.[3] He reined in his obstreperous nature and tried to make the best use of the tiny resources available. He needed institutions that would provide the foundations of the new force and establish it as an independent reality, and to arrange the limited manpower at his disposal in the most efficient and flexible way.

In this delicate job he had the backing of Winston Churchill, Secretary of State for War and Air, who had, predictably, been enthusiastic about flying since its inception, even trying to qualify as a pilot and almost killing himself in the process. None the less Churchill's support could be fickle and his resolve slacken when faced with the opposition of strong vested interests.

In a paper written for Churchill, Trenchard concluded that the future could be approached in two ways. The first was 'to use the air simply as a means of conveyance, captained by chauffeurs, weighted by the navy and army personnel, to carry out reconnaissance for the navy or army, drop bombs at places specified by them . . . or observe for their artillery'. The other choice was 'to really make an air service which will encourage and develop airmanship, or better still, the air spirit, like the naval spirit, and to make it a force that will profoundly alter the strategy of the future'.[4]

He argued his case for the latter in front of the prime minister, Lloyd George, and the Cabinet, who accepted, with some financial restraints, his and Churchill's main points. The proposals were set out in a 7,000-word White Paper. The document stated that 'the principle to be kept in mind in forming the framework of the Air Service is that in the future the main portion of it will consist of an Independent Force, together with

Service personnel required in carrying out Aeronautical Research'. With that established, the RAF was saved from assimilation by its hungry older rivals, though Trenchard threw them a scrap by allowing that smaller units within it would be specially trained for cooperation work with the army and navy and would probably be absorbed into their organizations in future.

Starved of money, he planned a small versatile service. Twenty squadrons were to be deployed overseas, ready to react rapidly to local unrest. Four squadrons would be held at home in reserve. All the rest of the RAF's resources would be concentrated on training officers and men to provide a pool of expertise which could be drawn on when a crisis arose. New training establishments would have to be set up. Trenchard had rejected the suggestion of the generals and admirals that the RAF should use existing army and navy facilities. The 'air spirit' could only be fostered in places the RAF could call its own.

To solve the problem posed by the youthful nature of military flying, which meant there were many junior officers and comparatively few senior ranks, he proposed a novel system. Only half the officers at any time would hold permanent commissions. Of the rest, 40 per cent would be short-service officers, serving for four or six years with another four on the reserve. The other 10 per cent would be on secondment from the army and navy.

The permanent officers were to be supplied mainly by an RAF cadet college, the air force equivalent of Sandhurst or Dartmouth, and also from the universities and the ranks. Once commissioned, they would be posted to a squadron. After five years they were required to adopt a specialization, such as navigation, engineering or wireless.

The new air force needed a steady supply of first-class mechanics, riggers and fitters. Most of the thousands of skilled tradesmen who had manned the workshops and hangars on the Western Front and at home bases during the war had returned to civilian life. Trenchard's Jesuitical solution was to recruit 'boys and train them ourselves'. They would serve three-year apprenticeships before joining the ranks. There were also plans for a staff college, at Andover, to train future commanders, and centres for research into aircraft development, armaments, wireless and aerial photography.

Cranwell, in Lincolnshire, was chosen for the cadet college. Halton Park, in Hertfordshire, was selected for the main apprentice school. Cranwell was flat, windy and had a large existing airfield. Trenchard liked the fact that it was a long way from London. He hoped that, 'marooned in the wilderness, cut off from pastimes they could not organize for themselves, they would find life cheaper, healthier and more wholesome'. This, he reckoned, would give them 'less cause to envy their contemporaries at Sandhurst or Dartmouth and acquire any kind of inferiority complex'.[5]

Halton, on the other hand, was chosen for the apprentices – 'Trenchard brats', as they became known – because of its proximity to the Smoke. Homesick adolescents would be in easier reach of their metropolitan parents and there were dance halls and cinemas nearby to keep them entertained when the working day was over.

Cranwell is scoured in the winter by freezing winds that race in from the Wash, sunny in the summer. It had been a training base for the Royal Naval Air Service. With the amalgamation of the RNAS and the RFC it had passed into RAF ownership. It opened as the Royal Air Force College in February 1920, the first military air academy in the world. The entrance examination was essentially the same as that for the Sandhurst and Woolwich army cadet colleges, testing applicants on a broad range of subjects, including English, history, languages ancient and modern and sciences – though you could be selected without tackling a science paper.

In the bleak late winter it was a dispiriting place. The first fifty-two cadets arrived, one of them wrote afterwards, to a 'scene of grey corrugated iron and large open spaces whose immensity seemed limitless in the sea of damp fog which surrounded the camp'.[6] The new boys lived in single-storey wood and iron huts, scattered on either side of the Sleaford road, linked by covered walkways to keep off the rain and snow. It was not until 1929 that money was available to start work on the main college building, which was specially designed to look old and respectable.

Despite its ramshackle origins, the college was confident from the beginning that it would be great. Writing in the first issue of the college magazine in September 1920, Churchill set the tone.

> Nothing that has ever happened in the world before has offered to man such an opportunity for individual personal prowess as the air fighting of the Great War. Fiction has never portrayed such extraordinary combats, such hairbreadth escapes, such an absolute superiority to risk, such dazzling personal triumphs . . . It is to rival, and no doubt to excel these feats of your forerunners in the Service that you are now training yourselves and I, for one, look forward with confidence to the day when you who are not at the College will make the name of the Royal Air Force feared and respected throughout the world.[7]

The RAF thought hard about the sort of boy it was looking for. In 1919 a committee chaired by Lord Hugh Cecil, the staff officer who had waved Cecil Lewis into the RFC on the basis of his fives prowess, was set up to try and define the educational and human qualities needed for the officer corps. The architects of the new service accepted, in theory at least, that it should be open to all talents. It had been clear since the end of the previous century that social exclusivity was ultimately incompatible with the technological competence modern warfare required. The first senior military figure to understand this was Admiral Fisher, who insisted all his officers had a degree of technical understanding, a move that challenged the class structure of the Navy.[8]

The Cecil Committee decided that all officers must be able to fly, though the qualification was not so rigid as to exclude good technicians who were poor aviators. It wanted boys who exhibited 'the quality of a gentleman'. It was careful, though, to emphasize that by this they meant 'not a particular degree of wealth or a particular social position but a certain character'.[9] Even so, the new cadet college must have seemed to any ambitious lower-class boy and his parents as cold and daunting as the old ones. Air Ministry officials set out to recruit people like themselves. They wrote to public-school headmasters, advertising the benefits of a service career and claiming that flying training was not the hair-raising activity it had been in the war years (though this was far from the truth and accidents at the college were frequent).[10] An Old Etonian officer was dispatched to the Alma Mater to act as a liaison officer.

Unlike the public schools, few state schools had the resources to provide coaching for the entrance exam. Fees were prohibitive. Parents were expected to pay up to £75 a year plus £35 before entry and £30 at the start of the second year towards uniform and books; this at a time when a bank manager earned £500 a year. Despite the Cecil Committee's wish that selection should be 'free of the suspicion of partiality in favour of either individuals or classes', most cadets in the interwar years were public schoolboys.

The curriculum at the beginning was a mix of academic and practical subjects interspersed with drill and PT. In the first year there was little flying, though much time was spent in the workshops and hangars. Cadets lived five to a hut until their fourth, senior, term, when they got their own cubicles. They received £2 15s. (£2.75) a week and each day was packed with activities from reveille at 6.45 a.m. to dinner in the mess. Sports were a fetish, particularly rugby, which Trenchard considered 'the best game for making an officer and a gentleman out of any material'.[11] Keenness on boxing was admired. The life was clean, spartan, boisterous. Women were nowhere to be seen, except at the end-of-course dance, and the limited delights of Sleaford, the local town, were out of bounds. Cadets were allowed motorcycles but not cars and the lanes round about buzzed with souped-up Broughs and Rudges.

Fun was bruising. First-termers were forced to sing a song for the other cadets. Failure to perform well earned a punishment called 'creeping to Jesus'. The victim was stripped almost naked, blindfolded and forced to sniff his way along a pepper trail that ended at an open window, where he was tipped outside and drenched in cold water.[12] The first commandant, Air Commodore C. A. H. Longcroft, was a hunting man and cadets were encouraged to ride to hounds, though a shortage of mounts meant beagling was more practical. The college had its own pack.

Intellectual activity was limited. There was encouragement from an early teacher, S. P. B. Mais, who left Tonbridge School to become Professor of English at Cranwell. He felt cadets should be treated as undergraduates and founded a play-reading circle and a debating society. The response was initially hesitant. The cadets had gone to Cranwell to fly. Yet at the outset, at the end of their two-year courses, this was something they were still not fully qualified to do. A shortage of aircraft and the demands of the curriculum meant graduates left without their wings, or even a high standard of airmanship. One cadet spent less than nine hours in an aeroplane in his first year, and then only as a passenger. The Avro trainers were equipped with a compass and a bubble indicator like a spirit level to show whether they were flying straight. Navigation was primitive and many flights consisted of simple hops to neighbouring airfields. Cranwell cadets were awarded their wings after leaving once they had satisfied their first squadron commanders that they could indeed fly.

But Cranwell succeeded from the start in generating an air force spirit. The cadets knew what was wanted. Aerial warfare, they understood, had created the need for a hybrid warrior who combined mastery of the latest technology with the mental bearing of a classical champion. It was a new military caste and Cranwell was its spiritual home.

The same aspiration to excellence was encouraged at Halton. Five thousand applicants responded when the scheme was announced. They were mostly boys from the lower middle and upper working classes who saw the RAF as a means of advancement and a gateway to the intoxicating world of aviation. The entrance exam tested applicants on mathematics, experimental science and English. To pass, boys were essentially expected to be up to school certificate level, a tough examination taken at sixteen that qualified the successful candidate for higher education. It was also the entry requirement for Cranwell. Many of those who sat for entrance to Halton and its sister technical schools therefore, had parents who were sufficiently comfortably off to keep them on past the normal school-leaving age of fourteen. Or sufficiently self-sacrificing. In January 1921 a photographer was present as 300 new recruits set off from a

London terminus to begin their course. The boys are cheering. Many wear shabby suits and flat prole hats that make them seem miniature versions of their fathers. The caption notes that 'the variety of class of boys was very striking, many of them having quite an imposing kit, whilst not the least pleased with the whole proceedings were those whose belongings were kept within bounds in brown paper parcels'.[13]

The high standard at entry meant that many of the mechanics servicing the aeroplanes would be educationally equal, and superior in mechanical skill, to the men flying them.[14] RAF other ranks showed less deference to their officers than was customary in the army, where most privates and NCOs came from the uneducated working class. In the RAF, the path from the Naafi to the officers' mess was wider and more frequently trodden than in any of the other services, and many a rigger and fitter ended up a pilot. The system was constructed to allow, if not exactly encourage, the process. The best three apprentices each year were offered a cadetship at Cranwell, with the expectation, frequently fulfilled, that this would lead to the highest reaches of the service. A new class of airman pilots was announced in late 1921 that offered flying training to outstanding candidates from the ranks. They served for five years before returning to their own trade, but kept their sergeant's stripes gained by being in the air. The policy meant that by the time the war started about a quarter of the pilots in RAF squadrons were NCOs – a tough, skilful difficult-to-impress élite within an élite.[15]

There were 300 places in the first intake. The regime followed the same hardworking lines as at the cadet college, with classes and workshop sessions from Monday to Friday and Wednesday afternoons off for games. Discipline was milder than in the army or navy, but firm none the less. Only over-eighteens were allowed to smoke, and then when off-base. Trenchard was as proud of Halton as he was of Cranwell. He was aware that by engineering a new class of educated other ranks, the first in British military history, he was doing something radical, almost revolutionary.

Cranwell and Halton formed the human nucleus for the new air force, but the manpower they provided fell far short of requirements. The short-service commission scheme helped reduce the deficit. It started in 1924 when the Air Ministry advertised for 400 young officers for flying duties. It wanted British-born men of pure European descent[16] who would serve up to six years and spend four more on the reserve list. Despite the lack of long-term career security, there were many takers. The universities seemed another promising recruiting ground. The idea started with RFC veterans, who went up to Cambridge after the war to study engineering, and was encouraged by Trenchard during a visit in 1925. It spread to Oxford, and later to London.

Trenchard had raised the notion of a territorial air force of weekend fliers in his 1919 proposals. Churchill rejected it. It won the backing of the subsequent air minister Sir Samuel Hoare. A bill to set up an Auxiliary Air Force (AAF) was brought in by the short-lived Labour-led government which came to power in January 1924. The first four squadrons were formed in October 1925: No. 600 (City of London), No. 601 (County of London), No. 602 (City of Glasgow) and No. 603 (City of Edinburgh). The pilots were amateurs who flew in their own time on aeroplanes supplied and maintained by the RAF, and the units were intended to have a strong local character. Trenchard considered they would be a success 'if it was looked upon as as much of an honour to belong to one . . . as it is to belong to a good club or a good university'.[17]

This suggested a degree of social exclusivity. There was a strong snobbish tinge to some of the first formations. Flying had always been fashionable and rich amateur airmen were numerous. The Auxiliary Air Force provided an opportunity for some of them to band together in a patriotic cause, with friends from club, links and office. No. 601 Squadron was, according to its own legend, founded in White's, the grandest address in Clubland, on the initiative of the son of the first duke of Westminster. Lord Edward Grosvenor, after Eton and a spell in the French Foreign Legion, had served as a pilot in the RNAS in the First World War. Like several forward-looking grandees he believed air power would decide future conflicts. Auxiliary squadrons, he felt, would allow men to go to war surrounded by comrades with whom they shared ties of place and friendship. Seriousness of purpose was overlaid with thick layers of upper-class fun. He recruited from his own circle. The squadron historian noted that he 'chose his officers from among gentlemen of sufficient presence not to be overawed by him, and sufficient means not to be excluded from his favourite pastimes – eating, drinking and White's'.[18] Candidates were invited to his home in Eaton Square and sluiced large glasses of port. If they passed muster it was on to the club bar for gin and tonics. The squadron's town headquarters were at 54 Kensington Park Road, in Notting Hill. They were furnished and equipped to cavalry regiment standards with silver, military prints on the walls, costly vintages and rich food. The gatherings echoed to the sound of broken glass. After dinner it was customary for diners to try and circumnavigate the room without touching the floor. Another game involved persuading some visiting dupe to 'calibrate the table'. One of the company would lie on his back with his legs hanging over the edge of a large oval table while other squadron members tilted it back and made a show of measuring the angle between wood and limb. Then it was the victim's turn. Once he was helpless, his ankles were grabbed, the table was tipped back and tankards of beer poured down his trouser legs.

Members held an annual training camp at Port Lympne on the Kent coast. It was the summer home of their patron, Sir Philip Sassoon, who combined a wild enthusiasm for flying with almost total ineptitude as a pilot. Squadron pride was nourished by manufactured rivalries with other Auxiliary Air Force units, japes designed to annoy the regular RAF, and self-conscious displays of individualism such as the wearing of bright red socks with uniform.

The snobbery was in keeping with the times and provoked indulgent smiles. But this was not what Trenchard had had in mind. At Cambridge he had emphasized that in the AAF and university squadrons, there was room for everyone: 'the man of initiative and the man of action, the methodical man and even the crank. We open our ranks widely to all.'

Despite the gilded image, not all the auxiliary pilots were rich. Applicants to the AAF needed to be able to fly solo and hold an A licence and courses cost £100. It was a considerable investment. The Air Ministry recognized the reality, refunding tuition costs once a trainee had qualified. Altogether there were to be twenty-one auxiliary squadrons drawn from all over the country. From 1934 they were equipped with fighters instead of bombers. When the war came they made up a quarter of Fighter Command's front-line strength.

Trenchard retired at the end of 1929. His energy and advocacy had ensured the survival and growth of the RAF, albeit slowly and painfully. The RAF was undernourished. From 1921 to 1930 the annual expenditure estimates hovered between £19 million and £18 million. In 1923 the government had promised to build a metropolitan air force of fifty-two squadrons for home defence. Six years later, there were only twenty-five home-based regular squadrons in service, augmented by eleven auxiliary and reserve units, and no official hurry to make up the shortfall.

But the service had an existence and an identity. It had a sky-blue ensign, adorned with one of the red, white and blue roundels the First World War pilots had had painted on their aircraft to shield them from 'friendly fire'. It had its own slate-blue uniform and forage cap. It had a good motto – *Per Ardua ad Astra*. A system of squadron organization, evolved in the battlefields of France, had been established and an independent rank structure, painfully worked out in face of mockery from the army chiefs, that climbed from aircraftman to Marshal of the Royal Air Force. There was an apprentice school to ensure a steady flow of skilled technicians to maintain the aeroplanes and a cadet school and a short-service commission scheme to provide pilots and commanders.

Great energy and thought had gone into the work of creating the new service, comparatively little on defining its purpose. The RAF had men, machines, organization and identity. What it did not have as yet was a clear idea of its purpose. A post-war Marshal of the Royal Air Force Sir John Slessor once wrote that 'before 1939 we really knew nothing about air warfare'. It was a frank admission, but Slessor was in a position to know. Twenty years earlier, in May 1937, he had been promoted to the post of deputy director of plans at the Air Ministry and was appalled to discover how unfitted the RAF was to defend Britain.[19]

The state of the air force during most of the inter-war period was a reflection of a general unwillingness, found in every corner of society, to contemplate another bloodbath. Preparing for war seemed more likely to encourage than prevent it. There were clear political, economic and psychological reasons for Britain's reluctance to rearm. The aversion to doing so was reinforced by confusion as to what weapons were required. Everyone agreed that air power would be crucial. No one knew exactly why or how. If there was a consensus it centred on the belief that bombers and bombing would play a predominant role. Something of the effects of aerial bombardment was already known, from the British and German experiences in the First World War and from small wars that had flared up around the world subsequently. Many military and political analysts believed that hostilities would begin in the air and the results, particularly for civilians, would be horrible.

German Zeppelin airships, then Gotha and Giant bombers, had provided a glimpse of what could be expected, from their intermittent and haphazard bombing campaign on British cities and coastal towns that began in January 1915. Altogether, in 103 raids they killed 1,413 people, all but 296 of them civilians. They wounded between 3,400 and 3,900, the vast majority of them non-combatants.

What impressed was not the quantity of the violence but the quality. In one raid carried out in daylight on 13 June 1917, fourteen Gothas, each loaded with a 500-kilogram bomb, reached the centre of London. One bomb struck a school in Poplar, killing 18 children and maiming 27. Zeppelins excited particular terror. Their destruction provoked un-British displays of glee, with crowds clapping, singing and cheering in the streets as the airships sank to earth with their sixty-strong crews roasting in the flames.

Henceforth, civilians could expect to be in the front line and neither military nor political thinking placed much faith in their ability to endure the experience. As the overture wars of the 1930s established the themes of the great symphony of violence to come, it appeared more and more certain that civilian morale would be unable to withstand the coming ordeal. As early as 1925, the Air Staff were predicting casualties of 1,700 dead and 3,300 injured in London alone in the first twenty-four hours of hostilities, resulting in 'the *moral* [original italics] collapse of the personnel employed in the working of the vital public services'.[20] The Japanese bombing of Shanghai in 1932, the German Condor Legion's destruction of Guernica in April 1937, the Italian bombardment of Barcelona, all reinforced notions of aerial warfare's crucial, possibly decisive, importance.

There were two obvious approaches to countering the danger. One was to improve Britain's defences to a point where the enemy – always Germany, apart from a brief, fantastical moment in 1922 when France was identified as the threat – would be deterred from launching an attack or would suffer severely if it did. Proponents of this view believed that the war had shown that fighters mustered to defend British airspace were, after a slow start, competent to handle raiding airships and bombers. At the same time, the experience had accelerated the development of effective anti-aircraft gunnery and searchlights. The second approach was to concentrate on building up a strong offensive bomber force. That, too, would have a deterrent effect. But if deterrence failed, it left Britain with the means of striking back.

It was the second view that took hold, both in air force and political thinking, although never to the point where alternative reasoning was suppressed. The strategic debate of the inter-war years was dominated by two phrases. They were slogans rather than expressions of profound thought. One was the idea of the 'knock-out blow', which could bring victory in a single action. The other was the conviction that 'the bomber will always get through' – a phrase popularized by Baldwin in November 1932 in a Commons speech which sent a spasm of foreboding through the country. What that meant, he continued brutally, was that 'the only defence is offence . . . you have to kill more women and children more quickly than the enemy if you want to save yourselves'.[21]

The logic of this bleak conviction was that fighters would have only a secondary role to play. Despite the prevalence of these views, successive governments proved reluctant to invest in building up a bombing force that could both 'get through' and strike the 'knock-out blow'. Money was one problem. But the understandable miserliness of politicians trying to manage a vulnerable economy in shaky times was informed by less easily identifiable and more complex motives. Many of the public figures of the 1920s and 1930s had served in the war and knew its horrors at first hand. They shared the ordinary citizen's dread of a recurrence, and shrank away from consideration of the unpopular positions that a reasoned rearmament policy would have required.

The conduct of Britain's defence in the years from 1918 to 1936 looks now to have been extraordinarily negligent and foolhardy. It seemed so to some at the time. But among the victor nations the impulse was to seek idealistic alternatives, exemplified by the great disarmament conference of 1932–4 and the foundation of the League of Nations. Until the threat from Germany was naked and unmistakable, the RAF would lack the sort of carefully planned, sensibly timed and realistically funded programme it needed to develop properly. Progress was jerky and reactive and frequently triggered by panic. The original plan to create fifty-two squadrons for home defence was provoked by alarm at the news that France had an air fleet of 300 bombers and 300 fighters. When that chimerical threat evaporated, so, too, did the will to pursue the scheme.

The arrival of Hitler in 1933, and Germany's withdrawal from the League of Nations and the disarmament conference, produced another spurt of activity, resulting in what was known as expansion scheme A. It was officially announced in July 1934, the first of thirteen such schemes that appeared over the next four years, most of which never got beyond the proposal stage, as Britain tried to achieve some sort of rough parity with Germany. Scheme A was an interim measure designed to signal to Hitler that Britain was prepared to take to the starting blocks in an aerial arms race. It also created a structure to provide training, and the basis for a more ambitious expansion should the message be ignored. The planned level of home squadrons was increased from the original fifty-two to sixty-four. Scheme A also increased the proportion of fighter squadrons. There were to be twenty-five now, against thirty-nine bomber units compared to seventeen and thirty-five in the 1923 plan.

The shift was a political rather than an air force initiative. It was opposed by the Chief of the Air Staff, Sir Edward Ellington, who stuck to the view that a big bomber fleet was central to Britain's security. The well-publicized fact that the increased range of German bombers meant they could now reach well into the industrial north-east of Britain and the Midlands undermined this approach.

The argument that there was no real defence against bombers was being invisibly eroded anyway. Out of sight and far away from the committee rooms where military planners and government ministers and officials met, scientists and engineers worked with RAF officers to develop technologies that would greatly increase the vulnerability of attacking air forces. In the search for scientific means of combating attacking aircraft, attention had been given to a 'death ray' which would neutralize the ignition systems of aircraft, causing them to drop from the sky. Research under the direction of R. A. Watson-Watt, superintendent of the Radio Department at the National Physics Laboratory, suggested the scheme was impractical. However, the experiments confirmed the fact that aircraft interfered with radio waves and radiated a signal back. This suggested the possibility of a detection system that could reveal their position, height and direction. The huge importance of the discovery was recognized immediately and from February 1935 there was strong official backing for the development of what became known as radar.

The RAF's own thinking had been that if enemy aircraft were to fly at more than 200 m.p.h. at over 10,000 feet, and no warning was given of their approach before they reached the coast, it would be impossible to get aircraft airborne in time to prevent them from bombing London. Now radar could provide that warning, a development which, as one historian of the RAF observed, 'indicated the obsolescence of the RAF's whole existing theory of war'.[22] None the less the belief that bombers provided the best security would persist until the end of 1937. The change was led by government figures who were persuaded that there was no longer any hope of equalling the numerical strength of the Luftwaffe before war broke out.

Radar complemented important breakthroughs that were being made in aircraft design. The development of military aviation in Britain had been haphazard. The Air Ministry had no designers of its own and relied on private firms to answer specifications for new types. Perennial money problems made it difficult to establish long-term relationships with private manufacturers, hindering the development of an efficient system of procurement, research and development such as existed in Germany.

There were delays of up to six years between the issue of a specification, acceptance of a design, manufacture and entry into service. The progress of the Hurricane and the Spitfire from drawing board to the skies was quicker, but far from smooth. By the end of the 1920s it was obvious the biplane era was over. The most powerful machine in the RAF's hands, the Hawker Fury, could only manage 250 m.p.h. The 1929 Schneider Cup, a competition of speed and endurance between seaplanes, was won by the Southampton firm of Supermarine with an S6, a monoplane with a streamlined fuselage and metal wings, flying at an average of 328.63 m.p.h. In 1930 the Air Ministry issued specification F.7/30 for a new high-speed fighter, opening the competition to single wing designs. Monoplanes had been around from almost the beginning of aviation but were inferior in terms of manoeuvrability to biplanes, whose twin surfaces provided considerably more lift. Streamlining, metal airframes and new engines powerful enough to keep them airborne removed this restriction and delivered the future to the monoplane.

In August 1933 Sydney Camm, chief designer at Hawker Aircraft Limited, presented two designs to the Air Ministry for a biplane and a monoplane. Both were rejected as too orthodox – evidence of the presence of some radical and imaginative minds at important decision-making levels inside the air establishment. The board of Hawker decided to continue development anyway. When the Air Ministry issued a new specification the following year, Camm's design was close to their requirements, and a prototype, K5083, was ordered. The RAF wanted a fighter capable of 300 m.p.h. which could fly as high as 33,000 feet. To meet these demands the aircraft needed to be streamlined with an enclosed cockpit and a retractable undercarriage. It also had to be capable of bearing a battery of machine guns. Ballistics experts calculated that at the new high speeds an intercepting fighter would have only two seconds to shoot down an incoming bomber. Eight machine guns, each firing 1,000 rounds a minute, were needed to provide the required weight of fire.

The novelty of the project and the high demands of the specification meant that fundamental problems of physics, engineering and design arose at every stage. The crucial question of power had been answered by the appearance of the Rolls-Royce PV twelve-piston engine, later known as the Merlin. It developed 1,030 horsepower, more than twice that of the best engine of the First World War. The thrust it delivered made speeds of 330 to 340 m.p.h. possible – more than enough to satisfy the RAF's demands.

Camm's original design had been called the Fury monoplane, a name that conceded the fact that even after 4,000 blueprints the aircraft was only half-way evolved from its biplane origins. The frame was of metal tubes and wooden formers and stringers. The skin was fabric, heavily painted with dope to reduce drag, and stressed-metal wings were only added fairly late in the development. The outlines of the old Fury were certainly discernible in its profile. But it was definitely something else. They called it a Hurricane. It was not a new name, having belonged to a short-lived aircraft of the 1920s. But it conveyed a note of confidence and aggression that was infinitely more reassuring than the placid Harts, Flycatchers and Grebes of the previous generation.

The Hurricane made its first flight on 6 November 1935 at Brooklands in Surrey. Hawker's chief test pilot, George Bulman, a small, bald, ginger-moustached extrovert who had flown with the RFC in the war, was in the cockpit. The prototype had been developed in great secrecy. When the tarpaulins were stripped away and the hangar doors opened, there were murmurs of surprise. It was painted silver, which emphasized the sleekness of its low, humped lines and the sculptured way the rounded wings fitted beautifully flush to the fuselage below the neat, narrow cockpit. It was big, bigger than any existing fighter, and at more than 6,000 pounds very heavy. It seemed unlikely that a single engine could get it off the ground. Bulman, in overalls and flying helmet, approached the machine and vaulted into the cockpit watched by Camm and other Hawker executives, who stood at the edge of the damp field, smoking nervously. The Hurricane bumped away into the distance then turned into the wind. The rumble of the Rolls-Royce engine deepened into a roar. The machine moved forward, gathering speed, but slowly, so that some thought Bulman would not get airborne before he ran out of field. At the last moment the Hurricane left earth in an abrupt bounding movement and climbed steeply. The spectators watched the undercarriage retract and the muscular shape dwindle into the distance until it disappeared and the sound of the engine faded. Half an hour later the reassuring drone was heard again. Bulman performed a perfect three-point landing and taxied over to where Camm was waiting to report the flight had been 'a piece of cake'.[23]

The Spitfire, the first prototype of which flew in March 1936, was a more modern design, all metal with a monocoque fuselage and thin, elliptical wings, the more sophisticated offspring of the Supermarine C6. It had the same Merlin engine as the Hurricane and carried the same guns, but at 5,180 pounds it weighed 1,000 pounds less and went 30 m.p.h. faster. The name was proposed by the chairman of Vickers, Sir Robert McLean, whose company had taken over Supermarine. R. G. Mitchell, whose designs carried the machine through its various evolutions to become the most beautiful and efficient fighter of its era, was not impressed. 'Just the sort of bloody silly name they would choose,' he is reported to have said on hearing the decision.[24] But in the propaganda film of his life *The First of the Few*, which appeared in 1942, he is portrayed as devising the name himself: 'A curious sort of bird . . . a bird that spits out death and destruction . . . a Spitfire bird.'

The orders came quickly, with the Air Ministry ordering 600 Hurricanes and 310 Spitfires in the summer of 1936. The accelerated pace reflected alarm that the next war might come sooner than expected. Preparations at every level speeded up as successive intelligence reports, and the Germans' own boasts, suggested that Britain's reluctant rearmament programme was insufficient either to deter or defend.

The sense of urgency, and the rapid twists and turns of circumstance, were evident in the brevity of the shelf-lives of the schemes that succeeded Scheme A, as both government and the Air Ministry tinkered with the plan to take account of a situation that always seemed to be changing for the worst. Only one scheme, Scheme F, approved by the cabinet in February 1936, was implemented as planned, coming to fruition in March 1939.

But the expansion was real. From 1935 forty-five new air stations were ordered to be built, most of which were finished by the time war came. Scheme C, which was approved in May 1935, envisaged 123 home squadrons as opposed to the 76 designated in Scheme A. That meant recruiting 1,500 pilots in the next two years. Altogether the RAF was to increase fivefold between 1934, when there were 31,000 officers and men, and the outbreak of war, when the service had an actual strength of 118,000 backed by about 45,000 reserves.

The Air Minister, Lord Swinton, inherited Trenchard's system of short-service officers, who since the early 1920s had supplemented and outnumbered the cadre of permanent RAF officers. He intensified links with public schools, attracting 1,700 entrants. A further 800 pilots were found among RAF non-commissioned officers. Australia, Canada, New Zealand and South Africa were all asked to contribute men. The number of auxiliary squadrons increased from eight to twenty in the run-up to the war. But more radical measures were needed to satisfy the new demand and, equally important, to provide a reserve.

A pool of pilots would be essential to replace the dead and wounded once the fighting started. The Director of Training at the Air Ministry, Air Commodore A. W. Tedder, a Trenchard protégé who had inherited some of his briskness of thinking, conceived the idea of a 'Citizen Air Force'. It was to be democratic in character, and linked to a locality, but to the factories, offices and avenues and crescents of semi-detached homes in the new estates springing up around towns rather than to the shires to which the army's territorial units attached themselves. The Air Ministry added that the new force should be 'open . . . to the whole middle class in the widest sense of that term, namely the complete range of the output of the public and secondary schools'. Given its nature it was felt 'inappropriate to grade the members on entry in as officers or airmen according to their social class'. Everyone therefore started out the same, as airmen under training, with commissions being awarded later on ability and leadership qualities.[25] The Royal Air Force Volunteer Reserve, as it was christened, started in August 1936. It gave young men of between eighteen and twenty-five the chance to learn to fly, at no cost, in their spare time. They received £25 per annum and were expected to attend an annual fifteen-day flying course at one of the training centres set up around the country. The aim had been to take on 800 a year over three years, but the potential number of recruits was much greater and by the spring of 1939 there were 2,500 RAFVR pilots in training. When war broke out, 310 had already entered Fighter Command.

The second half of the 1930s saw the RAF transformed from a small, professional élite into a mass force with the potential to fight a major war. The question of how it would go about doing that was not finally resolved until the end of 1938, when the great strategic conundrum of bombers or fighters, offence or defence, was settled, at least for the first stage of the coming war. In December that year the balance shifted decisively in favour of fighters and 'close defence'. The change was initiated not by the air force itself but by the government. Despite radar and the advent of the Hurricane and Spitfire, the Air Ministry pressed for parity with the German bomber force. But the government decided this was no longer possible within the time available. The goal had always been unrealistic. Britain was a democracy, reacting wearily to the threat of a war it had no wish to fight. Rearmament had been late and grudgingly paid for, with the aircraft factories still operating at peacetime levels of production. Germany was a dictatorship, heading at full speed and with no concern for cost towards a conflict of its own making. Britain was not going to catch up before the war was launched. It was the minister in charge of defence coordination, Sir Thomas Inskip, who forced the air force to accept the change in strategic thinking. In a memo to Swinton of 7 December he stated the new thinking crisply:

I cannot take the view that our Air Force must necessarily correspond in numbers and types of aircraft with the German Air Force. I cannot, therefore, persuade myself that the dictum of the Chief of the Air Staff that we must give the enemy as much as he gives us is a sound principle. I do not think it is the proper measure of our strength. The German Air Force . . . must be designed to deliver a knock-out blow within a few weeks of the outbreak of war. The role of our Air Force is not an early knock-out blow – no one has suggested that we can accomplish that – but to prevent the Germans from knocking us out.[26]

The inference was clear. For the time being at least the emphasis would be on defence and making any German attack on Britain too painful to sustain. Despite the strenuous opposition of the Air Ministry and RAF senior staff, the Cabinet backed Inskip's view. The next years would belong to the fighters, and those who flew them.

3

'Free of Boundaries, Free of Gravity, Free of Ties'

The great RAF expansion gave thousands of young men the chance to realize an ambition that had seemed remote and probably unattainable when they first conceived it. That flying was possible was still a relatively novel idea. For most people in the world the thought that they would ever actually do so themselves was fantastical. The banality of aviation has hardened our imaginations to the fascination it excited in the years between the wars. Once, in Uganda in the 1980s, I was at a remote airstrip when a relief plane took some adolescent boys for a joyride. It was the first time they had been in an aeroplane. When they landed their friends ran out to examine them, as if they expected them to have been physically transformed by the experience.

So it was, or nearly so, in the inter-war years. 'Ever been up?' people would ask each other at the air displays that attracted hundreds of thousands in Britain in the 1920s and 1930s. Those who could say 'yes' were admired for their daring, their worldliness, their modernity. The men and women who flew the beautiful treacherous machines were exalted and exotic. In the eyes of many, their courage and skill put them at the apex of human evolution.

Aviators were as popular as film stars. Record-breaking feats of speed, distance and endurance filled the papers. Men were the most avid readers of these stories, young men and boys. Almost every pilot who fought in

Fighter Command in 1940 fell for flying early. Their interest flared with the intensity of a great romance. For some, the first magical taste came with a ten-minute flip in the rear cockpit of one of the rickety machines of the flying circuses that hopped around the country, setting up on racecourses or dropping in at resort towns. The most famous was led by Alan Cobham, a breezy entrepreneur who was knighted for pioneering flights across Asia. Billy Drake was sixteen years old, on holiday from his boarding school in Switzerland, when the circus arrived to put on a display close by his father's golf club near Stroud. It was half a crown to go up. Drake was already intoxicated with aviation, but his parents tried to dissuade him, partly because flying seemed a dead end for a middle-class boy, but also because they feared for his safety. The brief hop over the Gloucestershire fields was enough to set the course of his early life. 'When I got down,' he remembered many years later, 'I knew that this was it.'[1]

Pete Brothers watched aeroplanes in the skies around his home in Lancashire, where his family owned a firm supplying chemicals to the food and pharmaceutical industries. In his spare time he made model aeroplanes. His family were wary of his enthusiasm. In 1936, on his sixteenth birthday, he was given flying lessons at the Lancashire Aero Club in the hope that the draughty, dangerous reality of flying would cool his ardour. 'My father said, "You'll get bored with it, settle down and come into the family business." But I didn't. I went off and joined the air force.' He took his father flying and he, too, became 'flat-out keen'.[2]

Sometimes, unwittingly, parents planted the germ themselves. Dennis David was seven years old and on holiday in Margate when, 'as a special treat, my mother and I went up in an Avro 504 of the Cornwall Aviation Company. Though I was surprised by the din, this ... sowed a seed inside me.'[3]

Just the sight of an aeroplane could be enough to ignite the passion. James Sanders got up at five one morning, in July 1933, at the villa in Genoa where his wealthy archaeologist father had moved the family, to watch a formation of twenty-four Savoia Marchetti seaplanes, led by Italo Balbo, the head of the Italian air force, heading west on a propaganda visit to the United States, and felt two certainties. 'There was going to be a war, there was no question about it, and I was going to be in the air force.'[4]

Throughout the inter-war years, all around the country, many a flat, boring pasture was transformed into an airfield and became an enchanted domain for the surrounding schoolboys. On summer evenings Roland Beamont would cycle from his prep school in Chichester to the RAF station at Tangmere, climb on to his bicycle to see over the hedge and watch 11 Squadron and 43 Squadron taking off and landing in their Hawker Furies. From the age of seven, when he had been taken up by a barnstorming pilot, he had been entranced with flying. Watching the silver-painted biplanes, the sleekest and fastest in the air force, he decided he 'wanted more than anything else to be on fighters'.[5] Twelve years later he was in the middle of the Battle of Britain, flying Hurricanes from the same aerodrome.

First encounters with aeroplanes and airmen sometimes had the quality of a dream. Bob Doe, a shy schoolboy, was walking home after classes to his parents' cottage in rural Surrey when 'an RAF biplane fighter . . . force-landed in a field close to the road. I was able to walk around it, touch it and feel what was to me [the] beginning of the mystery of aviation.'[6] Thousands of miles away on the other side of the world, near the town of Westport in the Southern Alps of New Zealand, a small, restless boy called Alan Deere had experienced the same revelation. While playing near his father's farm he heard the note of an engine in the sky, looked up and saw a tiny silver machine. He had heard of aeroplanes but never seen one. 'The fact that one was now overhead seemed unbelievable. Where did it come from? Who was the pilot? Where was it going to land?' After the aircraft put down on a beach, he and his friends stood 'for long hours . . . and gazed in silent wonder at the aeroplane until eventually our persistence was rewarded by an invitation to look into the cockpit. There within easy reach was the "joystick" . . . the very sound of the word conjuring up dreams of looping and rolling in the blue heavens.' As he studied the instruments 'there gradually grew within me a resolve that one day I would fly a machine like this and perhaps land on this very beach to the envy and delight of my boyhood friends.'[7]

Almost all of these recorded episodes feel like encounters with fate. Brian Kingcome was making his languid progress through another term at yet another boarding school when, one sunny afternoon, 'there came the drone of an aero-engine overhead – not a common sound in the mid 1930s – and a small aircraft circled the school a couple of times at roof-top height. The whole school rushed out to watch spellbound as the tiny machine throttled back and, in that lovely, burbling, swooshing silence that follows the throttling back of an old fashioned aero-engine, glided in to land in the park in front of the house.' The pilot who emerged, nonchalant and romantic in flying helmet and silk scarf, was a young man, four years Kingcome's senior, whom he had known at one of the several previous schools his mother's whims had directed him to.

'Is there a Brian Kingcome here?' he asked. 'Have I come to the right place?'

He had, and there was. My stock soared . . . Basking in the gaze of many envious eyes, I climbed aboard and a moment later found myself for the first time in a world I had never dreamed could exist – a world free from the drag of earth's umbilical cord, free to climb, swoop and dive, free of boundaries, free of gravity, free of ties, free to do anything except stand still.[8]

Whatever their differences of background, all these boys were children of their time. Their enthusiasms were stoked by what they read in the illustrated papers, aimed at the youth market, that sold in millions. These, just as others would do a generation later, leant heavily on the preceding war for their material, and particularly on the doings of the heroes who had emerged from the RFC. The anonymous editors of the comics of the era, with their almost infallible comprehension of the young male psyche, recognized at once the charge that old-fashioned swashbuckling married to modern technology would carry. The example of the first fighter aces fixed itself in the imaginations of a generation being born just as they had met their deaths. Even at nineteen the thoughts of Geoffrey Page as he left his public school to go up to study engineering at London University 'were boyishly clear and simple. All I wanted was to be a fighter pilot like my hero, Captain Albert Ball. I knew practically all there was to know about Albert Ball; how he flew, how he fought, how he won his Victoria Cross, how he died. I also thought I knew about war in the air. I imagined it to be Arthurian – about chivalry . . . death and injury had no part in it.'[9]

Yet the most popular chronicles of the air war were remarkably frank about what was entailed. The deterrent effect appears to have been minimal. Perhaps Fighter Command's single most effective recruiting sergeant was Captain James Bigglesworth, created by W. E. Johns, who had flown with the RFC in the First World War and whose stories began to appear in *Popular Flying* magazine in 1932. The first novel, *The Camels Are Coming*, was published the same year. Biggles seems unattractive now; cold, driven by suppressed anger, a spoilsport and a bit of a bully. He was a devastatingly romantic figure to the twelve- and thirteen-year-olds who went on to emulate him a few years later. Johns introduced them to a

slight fair-haired, good-looking lad still in his teens but [already] an acting flight commander . . . his deep-set eyes were never still and held a glint of yellow fire that somehow seemed out of place in a pale face upon which the strain of war, and sight of sudden death, had already graven little lines . . . He had killed six men during the past month – or was it a year? – he had forgotten. Time had become curiously telescoped lately. What did it matter, anyway? He knew he had to die some time and had long ago ceased to worry about it.

Many of the stories were based on real events, some relating to Mannock, who appears disguised as 'Mahoney'. Johns made no attempt to hide the grisliness of the business, emphasizing the man-to-man nature of primitive air fighting. In one story he repeats with approval von Richthofen's maxim that 'when attacking two-seaters, kill the gunner first', and goes on to describe his hero doing just that. 'Pieces flew off the green fuselage, and as he twisted upwards into a half roll Biggles noticed that the enemy gunner was no longer standing up. "That's one of them!" he thought coolly. "I've given them a bit out of their own copy-book." '[10] In another, Biggles notes an 'Albatros, wrapped in a sheet of flame . . . the doomed pilot leaping into space even as he passed'.[11]

It is not only Germans who die. Getting killed is presented as almost inevitable. An important and enduring message, one the young readers took to heart, was that there was no point dwelling on it. 'One of the most characteristic features of the Great War,' Johns wrote in the Foreword to *Biggles in France*, 'was the manner in which humour and tragedy so often went hand in hand. At noon a practical joke might set the officers' mess rocking with mirth. By sunset, or perhaps within the hour, the perpetrator of it would be gone for ever, fallen to an unmarked grave in the shellholes of No Mans Land.'[12]

The Biggles stories are practically documentary in their starkness, as good a guide to the air war over the trenches as the non-fictional memoirs. Their audiences were absorbed and inspired by them. They changed lives. Reading them reinforced Pete Brothers's decision to seek a short-service commission in the RAF. He found them 'beautiful stories that enthralled me and excited me and made me want to emulate them'. At the Lancashire Aeroclub before taking up a short-service commission in January 1936, he had been pleased to find his instructor had been a Sopwith Camel pilot in the war.[13]

Cinematic portrayals of the air were equally frank. The most successful was *Dawn Patrol*, starring Errol Flynn, David Niven and Basil Rathbone, which came out in 1938. The 59th Squadron is based on a sticky sector of the Western Front. Sixteen men have gone in a fortnight. Replacements arrive, fresh from a few weeks at flying school. Orders to send them up against hardened Germans come by telephone from senior officers, comfortably quartered miles behind the lines. New names are chalked up on the duty blackboard to be wiped off within an hour. Kit-bags are returned home without ever being unpacked. The *Daily Express* praised the film's 'lack of false sentiment or mock heroics' and called it 'one of the best and bitterest melodramas about men and planes'. It was a box-office hit and was seen, often several times, by hundreds of the pilots who fought in 1940. No one was put off. It was the glamour, camaraderie and romance of flying that pulled them back to the local fleapits, not the message of waste and futility. By this time every young man in Britain was facing a prospect of early extinction. Dying in the air might be awful, but it was better than dying on the ground.

With the expansion programme, thousands of young men were now being given a choice in how they would fight the next war. Before it began, the RAF recruited annually about 300 pilots and 1,600 airmen. Between 1935 and 1938 the average RAF intake was 4,500 and 40,000 airmen and apprentices. Air Ministry officials appealed directly to schools for recruits and advertised in the flying magazines and popular newspapers the young men they were looking for might be expected to read. One that appeared on the front page of the *Daily Express*, adorned by a drawing of three Hurricanes, promised 'the life is one that will appeal to all men who wish to adopt an interesting and progressive career . . . leave is on a generous scale . . . applicants must be physically fit and single but no previous flying experience is necessary'. Pay, in cash and kind, was set at between £340 and £520 a year. A £300 gratuity was payable after four years' service, or £500 after six years. Age limits were set between seventeen and a half and twenty-eight. The educational qualification was school certificate standards, although 'an actual certificate is not necessary'.

Pat Hancock, a mechanically minded eighteen-year-old from Croydon, was at Wimbledon Technical College when he saw an advertisement in the *Daily Express*. 'The ministry – bless it – was offering commissions to suitable young gentlemen – four years, and at the end if you survived you got a magnificent lump sum of £300, which was really a lot in those days. I pounced on it and sweet talked my father and mother into allowing me to apply.'[14]

Parental permission was needed if the applicant was under twenty-one, and many pilots seem to have faced, at first at least, family opposition. Flying was undeniably dangerous. In an era when men chose a profession, trade or occupation and tended to stick with it for the rest of their working life, it offered a very uncertain career. Despite popular enthusiasm, commercial aviation had been slow to expand. Air travel was confined to the rich. RFC pilots who hoped to make their livings flying in peacetime were mostly disappointed. Arguments were needed to overcome the objections. Billy Drake misunderstood the terms and thought the RAF would pay him an annuity of £300, a detail which persuaded his parents to grant their approval.

Geoffrey Page's distant and authoritarian father summoned him to his London club when he heard of his plans to apply for Cranwell. Flying was the family business. Page's uncle ran Handley Page, a leading British aircraft manufacturer. Over tea his father told him he had 'spoken to your uncle at length about your desire to be a pilot and he has advised me strongly against it. Pilots, he tells me, are two a penny. Hundreds are chasing a handful of jobs.' He refused to pay for the 'stupidity' of pursuing an RAF career. Page's mother pleaded with him not to take up flying. Page rarely saw his father and resented the intervention strongly. Later he decided it had been motivated by concern. His father had lost a younger brother in the war, shot down and killed over the North Sea while serving in the Royal Navy Air Service.[15] Page eventually made his own way into the RAF, via the London University Air Squadron.

The RAF set out to be meritocratic in its search for recruits, and Tedder, as director of training, decided to cast the net wide in the search for the best candidates. The requirement to have reached school certificate level meant boys from poor families who could not afford to keep their children on until sixteen were theoretically excluded. The rules were not always strictly imposed and officials occasionally used their discretion.

Bob Doe's father was a gardener on the Surrey estate of the editor of the *News of the World*. Doe left school at fourteen without passing any exams and got a job as an office boy at the paper's headquarters in Bouverie Street. One lunchtime he walked over to the Air Ministry headquarters in Kingsway and announced he wanted a short-service commission. 'I was passed from office to office. They were very disapproving when they found I'd passed no exams. Then I found myself in front of this elderly chap with lots of braid on his uniform and he seemed to like me.'[16] When he discovered that Doe had already joined the RAFVR and done seventy-five hours' flying, any lack of formal education was forgotten. Doe sat the entrance exam, and with some coaching from his Air Ministry sponsor, got through. Doe's case was exceptional. Most entrants had passed their school certificate and had gone to fee-paying or grammar schools.

One obvious source for the sort of healthy, uncomplicated, modern-minded young men the RAF was seeking was the Empire. Senior officers were sent overseas to Australia, Canada, New Zealand and South Africa to supervise selection. The decision to leave home to cross the world at a time when war seemed to be stirring again in Europe was a dramatic one. Yet the populations of the colonies felt strong sentiments of loyalty and respect towards Britain. The RAF appeal offered broader horizons to ambitious and adventurous young airmen as well as touching a sense of obligation. The response was enthusiastic. On catching their first sight of the mother country, many of them wondered whether they had made the right choice. Alan Deere left Auckland in September 1937 aboard the SS *Rangitane* and arrived at Tilbury docks at the start of an English winter. 'The cold discomfort of the railway carriage and the flat, treeless acres of southern Essex were depressing reminders of the warmth and sunshine of far-off New Zealand. We stared in amazement at the grim rows of East End houses, pouring their smoke into the clouded atmosphere, and were appalled by the bustle and grime of Liverpool Street Station, so different from the luxurious gateway to the London of our dreams.'[17]

Despite the relative elasticity of the RAF approach, the selection process was thorough and demanding. After the written test and a strict medical, candidates were summoned to a board and questioned by a panel of officers. The examiners were looking for some technical knowledge and evidence of keenness. Enthusiasm for sports was usually taken as strong proof of the latter. At first, short-service entrants were sent off immediately to an RAF flying training centre, but the existing facilities could not cope with the wave of new recruits and Tedder decided to pay civilian flying schools to give *ab initio* instruction.

The new boys learned in two-seaters, Avro Tutors and de Havilland Tiger Moths. A first flight in the flimsy, thrumming trainers left an indelible impression, akin, as some would remember, to their first encounter with sex. Dennis David had his first lesson in a Blackburn B2 at the grandly named London Air Park, near present-day Heathrow. In reality it was a tiny grass field with a clump of trees in the centre, surrounded by houses. Many years later he 'still [found] it hard to find the words to describe my sheer delight and sense of freedom as the little biplane, seeming to strain every nerve, accelerated across the grass and suddenly became airborne'.[18]

Fantasizing about flying aeroplanes was no preparation for the reality. A few, not necessarily the best pilots, found it gratifyingly easy. Johnny Kent, an eighteen-year-old Canadian, had begun learning at the Winnipeg Flying Club, 'and was absolutely thrilled with the experience of actually handling the controls and I managed to cope with all the manoeuvres including an approach . . . at the end of this first lesson I knew I could fly'.[19] But many found flight in a small, sensitive aircraft unnerving. Bob Doe was 'petrified when I first went up. The side of the aeroplane was so thin that when you banked round I was afraid of falling through it. In no way did I have an affinity for it.'[20] On Hubert Allen's first flight as a new candidate for a short-service commission the instructor

> put the Tiger Moth into a bunt [loop] and I was sick. He shouldn't have
> done that, but perhaps he thought I was over-confident and needed
> cutting down to size. He was mistaken. I was under-confident so I
> probably acted the part of extrovert to conceal this. 'Good God,' he said,
> when after landing and turning off the magnetos he peered into my
> cockpit and noticed that I was covered in vomit. 'I hope you're not
> going to be one of those air-sick fellows . . . better give the rigger half a
> crown for cleaning up the mess.' . . . he strode off to the bar.[21]

Even those who had flown regularly as passengers discovered that the violent manoeuvres essential to military aviation differed dramatically from the pleasant sensations of straight and level flying. Tim Vigors, a sporting young man from a landed Irish family, had been taken flying by his godmother, who was an air enthusiast, and he liked it so much he applied to Cranwell. Starting flying training he felt fearful and nauseous. As the instructor put the aeroplane into a loop, a standard, elementary manoeuvre, a 'queasy feeling engulfed me . . . then the whole weight of my body fell on my shoulder harness as we turned upside down in a slow roll . . . fear of falling out of the cockpit eclipsed all other sensations'.[22]

Initial success did not mean that progress would then be steady. Robert Stanford Tuck was a confident young man whose long face, athletic build and pencil moustache made him look like Errol Flynn. He had lead an adventurous life in his teens, escaping the mundane horizons of Catford in south-east London for a career in the merchant navy before being accepted for a short-service commission. Tuck started off well. But he found it difficult to progress beyond basics and develop the instinctive ease of handling, the *feel* that was essential if one was to become a serious pilot. Tuck's cocky judgement after his first go at the controls was that flying was easy. So it is, if restricted to the basic manoeuvres of take-off, straight and level flight, shallow turns and landing. But after that the learning ladder is steep. Diving, looping and banking tightly are disorientating. Mistakes lead quickly to panic as the actions required to retrieve the situation are usually counter-instinctive. Tuck found he was the dud of his intake, snatching at the controls, over-correcting and suffering potentially fatal lapses of concentration. He began to fear that something he had come to love would be snatched away from him. It was only when he learned that flying did not require great physical effort that his performance started to improve. The secret lay in relaxation, avoiding sharp movements and settling oneself into the fabric of the machine so as to become part of its nervous system. You had to feel the aeroplane. For the fighter pilots of the First World War, buttocks had been an important sensory tool. Pilots felt they lost something when, in 1927, parachutes, which they were obliged to sit on, became standard equipment.

By the time war broke out the RAF was mass-producing officers. The privately run elementary flying training schools dotted around the country taught a basis in practical flying, with a grounding in navigation and gunnery, that prepared pupils for an advanced course at one of the RAF's own flying training schools. The idea was that, unlike in the previous war, when half-trained men were expected to learn while on squadron duty, pilots would now arrive at their units ready for operations.

The initial flying was done in biplanes. Pupils underwent twenty-two stages of instruction, starting with 'air experience' – the first flip – through to aerobatics during the eight- to twelve-week course. Emphasis was placed on learning to recover from a spin, and there was a compulsory practice every week. It was the only manoeuvre, apart from straightforward flying, that was taught previous to the first solo, which came half-way through the course. Most pupils got off alone after between eight and ten hours in the air. Alan Deere was so impatient to do so he forgot the last words of his instructor to fly for only ten minutes and to attempt only two landings. 'I was really straining at the leash by the time he had delivered these homilies and, thinking he had finished, banged the throttle open . . . and so into the air, solo at last. One, two, three landings, around again and again I went, the ten-minute limit completely forgotten in the thrill and excitement of this momentous occasion.'[23]

Aerobatics were promoted to give pupils complete confidence in their machines as well as preparing them for the stomach-churning reality of aerial combat. Flying blind, encased in a hood, relying only on the instruments, was also taught. Later this hair-raising method was replaced by means of an earthbound flight simulation trainer, the Link. The cost of elementary training was expensive at £5 per pupil per hour (double for advanced training) and those who showed little aptitude were weeded out early on. Those who finished the course successfully went on to a stint at the RAF Depot at Uxbridge for two weeks of drilling, physical training, familiarization with the limited administrative duties required of young officers and learning the niceties of mess protocol. During the fortnight, tailors arrived to kit out the fledgling officers and provide an opportunity for a laugh. Blond, raffish Paddy Barthropp remembered the response to the inevitable question, as they were measured up for their uniforms, which included mess kit with very tight-fitting trousers. 'When the cutters asked their customers which side they dressed the reply would come. "Just make them baggy around the kneecaps." '[24] The new officers were given £50 to cover everything, including uniforms, shirts, socks, two pairs of shoes and a cap – not enough if you went to the better outfitters.

Before candidates moved on to the next stage of training, the chief instructor at the elementary flying school made a recommendation as to whether a pupil's abilities best suited him to fighters or bombers. Flying anything required delicacy. Flying fighters required a particular softness of touch. Horsemen, yachtsmen and pianists, the prevailing wisdom held, made the best fighter pilots. The decision was made on the pilot's flying ability but also on his temperament. Success depended on a combination of discipline of the sort needed to maintain the flying formations beloved of the pre-war RAF, with the audacity and nerve inherent in the dazzling aerobatics which the service also prized as an indication of worth and quality.

The pilots themselves had a say in their fate. To some, like Dennis David, it seemed the choice was preordained, feeling from the outset that 'it was inevitable that I was to be a fighter pilot . . . from the start I was a loner. It was just me and my aeroplane hoping that neither of us would let the other down.'[25] Alan Deere felt the same certainty, 'had always determined to be a fighter pilot' and pressed his superiors to be posted to fighters.

Fighters were not the automatic choice for all young pilots. The strategic thinking of the previous two decades had its effect on ambitious trainees. Most of Deere's contemporaries thought bombers offered a better career and he was one of only four to go to a fighter squadron. But for the majority fighters offered a degree of freedom and individuality that was not available in a bomber crew – and, as was clear even before the war began, a greater chance of survival. Brian Kingcome, who after Cranwell was posted to 65 Fighter Squadron, considered that 'only a man brave beyond belief would ever want to go into bombers. Us cards all went into fighters.'[26]

After leaving the depot, the half-formed pilots moved on to one of the flying training schools to learn on service aircraft. In the early days of expansion, trainee fighter pilots started out on biplanes like the Hawker Hart or the Audax. These eventually made way for the Miles Master and the North American Harvard. The latter was a twin-seat, single-engined trainer with half the horsepower of the new breed of fighters, but which none the less gave a taste of what it would be like to handle a Hurricane or Spitfire when the time came.

The instruction was testing. Deere lost his temper after his teacher scolded him for his clumsy performance of the highly difficult manoeuvre of spinning a Hart, first one way, then the other, with a hood over his head to blot out vision. The tantrum nearly lost him his commission and he was told he had been given another chance 'only because the Royal Air Force has already spent so much money on your training'.[27] The pilots were taught set-piece attacks against bomber formations, each one numbered according to the circumstances. There was some gunnery practice, a small part of which involved using live ammunition on towed aerial drogues.

The student pilots lived in the mess and dressed for dinner each night in mess kit, dinner jacket or lounge suit, depending on the day of the week. Saturday was dress-down day, when blazer, flannels and a tie were permitted. After successful completion of the first half of the course, pilots received their wings, a brevet sewn over the tunic pocket that announced their achievement to the world. It was a great moment, 'the most momentous occasion in any young pilot's career', Dennis David thought. Al Deere felt a 'thrill of achievement and pride' as he stepped forward to receive the badge.

Finally, on completion of training, the new pilots were posted to a squadron. In the first years of expansion, units did their best to preserve what they could of the civilized atmosphere that had prevailed before the shake-up. At Hornchurch, where 65 Squadron was stationed, Brian Kingcome enjoyed 'a most marvellous life . . . if I wanted to take off and fly up to a friend of mine who had an airfield or station somewhere a hundred miles away for lunch, I would just go. It went down as flying training. I didn't have to get permission or [check] flight paths. I just went. If you wanted to go up and do aerobatics, you just went.'[28] Hornchurch was a well-appointed station, built, like many of the inter-war bases, in brick to a classically simple Lutyens design. The mess, where everyone except the handful of married officers lived, was separate from the main base across the road and in front of the main gates. It stood in its own grounds, with a large dining room and bedrooms. Kingcome found it 'luxurious beyond belief . . . the food was superb; you had your own batman and quarters. There was no bar in those days so you did all your drinking in the anteroom with steward service. The gardens outside the mess were beautifully kept with pristine lawns and flower beds.' There were also squash and tennis courts and a small croquet lawn. Pilot officers – the lowest commissioned rank – were paid fourteen shillings (70p) a day, from which six shillings (30p) went on the cost of mess living. That covered food, lodging, laundry and a personal batman.

The rest went on drink and cars, which the junior officers clubbed together to buy to visit country pubs and make the occasional trip to London, less than an hour away. The frequency of nights out depended on two considerations: the price of drink and the price of petrol. To initiate a pub crawl, Kingcome and three or four friends would each put half a crown (12½p) into the kitty. They would then board one of the jalopies (cost £10 to £25) held in loose collective ownership by the squadron. Petrol cost a shilling (5p) a gallon for the best grade, or tenpence (a little over 4p) for standard grade. After having downed several drinks costing eightpence (4p) for a pint of beer or a measure of whisky, they would still have some change over to share out at the end of the evening. Ten shillings (50p) would cover a trip to town, including train fare if no car was available, and the bill at Shepherd's, a pub in Shepherd's Market in Mayfair. It was run by a Swiss called Oscar and became one of Fighter Command's main drinking headquarters in London. For a pound the evening could be rounded off in a nightclub.

Biggin Hill, which like Hornchurch originated as a First World War station, was rebuilt in September 1932 to a similar design. It became home to two fighter units, 23 Squadron and 32 Squadron. Pete Brothers arrived in 1936 to a 'nice little airfield, a lovely officers' mess'. The station had a reputation for *joie de vivre*, and its members enjoyed, when they were not flying, a life of sport, of visits to London and being entertained at surrounding country houses. Because of the airfield's location, 600 feet above sea-level, unexpected visitors aboard civil airliners often dropped in when Croydon was closed by fog. One day in 1936 an Imperial Airways airliner landed carrying the American Olympic team, including Jesse Owens, fresh from his triumph at the Berlin Games. On another occasion a party of French models arrived after being diverted there on their way to a London fashion show. Churchill, whose home at Chartwell was only a few miles away, arrived unexpectedly one evening early in 1939. 'We were having a drink in the anteroom when the door opened and in walked Winston,' Brothers, who by then was a twenty-one-year-old flight commander with 32 Squadron, recalled. 'We all got up and said, "Good evening, sir, can we get you a drink?" The waiter brought him a dry sherry and he asked if we could turn the radio on so he could hear the news. We listened, then he said, "Are you enjoying your Hawker Spitfires?" We didn't like to say, "You've got it wrong, they're Hurricanes."' [29]

Behind the military briskness there lurked an atmosphere of fun. Jokes were not always in the best taste. In 1936, at the height of the war in Abyssinia, Biggin Hill, like every other station, put on a display for the annual Empire Air Day. To demonstrate bombing techniques a Hawker Tomtit dropped flour bombs on an old car carrying two 'native' figures. One, disguised in a black beard, dressed in a white sheet and wearing a pith helmet, was unmistakably supposed to represent Haile Selassie, the Emperor of Abyssinia who had lost his throne after the Italian invasion. The crowd loved it but the Air Ministry was not amused. There was jovial rivalry between the Biggin units. A new squadron, No. 79, was formed around a core of pilots transferred from No. 32 while Peter Brothers was there. 'There were games. We decided we'd have a contest to see who could do the shortest landing. We had to pack it up when some chap hit the hedge and turned his aircraft over and smashed it up.'

Tangmere, at the foot of the South Downs, was a particularly pleasant post. A dreamy, prelapsarian atmosphere seems to have permeated the place in the last years of peace. Billy Drake, arriving there aged nineteen in the summer of 1937 as a newly commissioned pilot officer, found life was sweet. The summer routine involved rising at six and flying until lunchtime in Hawker Furies. Afternoons were spent swimming or sailing at Bosham and West Itchenor. Then there would be a game of squash or tennis before dinner and bed. Social life centred on the mess, furnished like the lounge of a luxury liner, where Hoskins and Macey, the white-coated stewards, shuttled back and forth with silent efficiency. There were good pubs nearby; like the Old Ship at Bosham, where on a summer evening you could sit with fellow pilots or a girlfriend and watch the sun going down over the estuary. Conversation concerned aeroplanes, cars, sport and parties, rarely politics. What was happening in Abyssinia, Germany or Italy was hardly mentioned. If the drums of war were beating, the pilots affected not to hear them. Drake had barely considered the implications of his decision to apply for a short-service commission. 'I simply wanted to go flying,' he said. 'The fact that it might involve going to war never occurred to me until 1938 or 1939.'[30]

Life was not so congenial at every fighter base. Conditions around the country were variable. The fast rate of the expansion meant accommodation often lagged behind needs. Desmond Sheen, a nineteen-year-old Australian who joined the RAF on a short-service commission from the Royal Australian Air Force, arrived at 72 Squadron at Church Fenton in Yorkshire in June 1937 to be told he was living in a tent at the end of the airfield while the mess was being built. 'We stayed there until November when the fog and the mists drove us out and we moved into hangars until the building was completed.'[31] When Arthur Banham reported for duty to 19 Squadron at Duxford in Cambridgeshire after finishing his training in August 1936, he was put with nine other junior officers in a hut which acted as a dormitory. 'The whole place was a mess, with trenches all over the place where they were laying foundations for the new buildings. The officers married quarters weren't built and most officers lived out of the aerodrome altogether.'[32]

Arriving at their first posts, the newly qualified pilots learned quickly that henceforth everything would centre on the squadron. It became the focus of their professional and their social lives. Nothing could be more exciting than flying and no one could be more fun to be with than one's fellow fighter pilots. 'It was a wonderful time for most of us,' remembered John Nicholas, who joined 65 Squadron in December 1937. 'It was very pleasant to be with a number of young men of one's own age, most of whom believed in the same things.'[33] Some of the pre-expansion pilots had worried that the influx would dilute the clubby character of the old organization and dissolve its tenderly guarded *esprit de corps*. Peter Townsend, a sensitive, reflective career officer who had passed out of Cranwell as the Prize Cadet, returned to Britain to join 43 Squadron in June 1937 after a posting to the Far East, to find that 'gone were the halcyon days of "the best flying club in the world". Tangmere was now peopled by strange faces, different people with a different style. I resented the new generation of pilots who had answered the RAF's urgent appeal and found heaven-sent relief from boring civilian jobs.'[34] Townsend accepted, almost immediately, that these feelings were unworthy. In a subsequent *mea culpa* he admitted that 'my prejudices against them were ignoble, for they were soon to become the most generous-hearted friends, then, a little later, die, most of them, for England'. The reasoning was, anyway, wrong. At any time in the years before the run-up to the expansion programme, a majority of officers in the admittedly much smaller RAF were serving on short-service commissions.

The newcomers took to the existing traditions quickly, offering no serious challenge to the way things were done. Many were familiar with the routines of sport, joviality and boisterous high spirits from school days. Most of the short-service commission pilots entering in the expansion years had a public-school background of one sort or another. Roland Beamont was at Eastbourne College, Geoffrey Page at Dean Close, Cheltenham, Paddy Barthropp went to Ampleforth and Arthur Banham to the Perse School, Cambridge. Bob Tuck attended a small fee-paying day school, St Dunstan's at Catford, and Pete Brothers a similar establishment, North Manchester School. Billy Drake, James Saunders and John Nicholas were educated abroad. Pat Hancock went to a day school in

Croydon before moving to the technical college. Dennis David had been to a boarding school in Deal before changing to Surbiton County School. Of the Cranwellians, Tim Vigors had been at Eton and Brian Kingcome at Bedford.

Most of the entrants, even if they had not been to a proper public school, knew something of the ethos, if only from the pages of the *Magnet* and the *Gem*. Bob Doe, a secondary-school boy, felt out of place. Of his fellow short-service entrants he was 'probably the poorest of the lot. I hadn't done all the things other people had done. I felt very much an outsider. I was very shy as well, which didn't help. They were friendly enough but I always felt I was inferior.'[35] The barriers were lowered when he was invited to club together with three others to buy a Hispano-Suiza saloon for £20, this enabling them to go on occasional forays into Cheltenham, twelve miles from Little Rissington, where they were based.

The overseas entrants had little difficulty fitting in. Their status as colonials put them beyond the rigid categorizations of the British class system. Desmond Sheen's father was a plasterer, but he found at 72 Squadron that 'everyone got on, with a lot of hilarity and a lot of fun, extremely well. There was no conflict. There was a lot of taking the mickey out of each other, but it was all very friendly. They were all good sports.'[36]

Being a good sport was the essential quality in fitting in. Taken literally, it meant that athletic ability would count in a pilot's favour, a factor which benefited the outdoorsy arrivals from the Empire. Deere found that 'the natural reserve of all Englishmen gave way to a more friendly approach' after a game of rugby in which New Zealanders took on the rest, beating the English pilots by a colossal score. He was a boxer who had taken part in the New Zealand amateur championships. He was reluctant to don the gloves again, but was persuaded to do so by a senior officer who advised him it would be good for his career. The abbreviation of a first name, the bestowal of a nickname, signalled you were in. Alan quickly became Al.

Being a good sport, however, went beyond the observance of the conventions, attitudes and observances of middle-class males of the time.

A mood of tolerance prevailed so that individuality, even eccentricity, was prized. The business of aerial warfare meant that the type of military discipline applied to soldiers and sailors was not appropriate for airmen. Junior officers addressed their squadron superiors as 'sir' on the initial meeting of the day. After that it was first names. Once in combat in the air, everyone was essentially on their own and beyond the orders of a commander. Good pilots, anyway, succeeded by initiative and making their own decisions.

From the earliest days on the Western Front, pilots took a relaxed view of military conventions and often displayed a sceptical attitude towards senior officers, though seldom with their own immediate commanders if they had earned their respect. Pomposity was ruthlessly punished and shyness discouraged. Coy newcomers learned that a certain amount of leg-pulling and practical joking was the price of belonging. Deere, like all new arrivals, spent his first few weeks at 54 Squadron at Hornchurch doing dogsbody tasks like overseeing the pay and clothing parades. He was also required to check the navigation inventory and found to his concern that an item called the Oxometer was missing. On informing his flight commander, he was told that this was a very serious matter and the station commander might have to be notified if it was not found. It was some days before he 'realized that no such item of equipment existed and that it was a trick played on all new pilots and one in which everyone from the station commander down participated'.[37] The joke took on a further refinement when a particularly earnest pilot officer was told that the missing Oxometer had been found. A fake instrument was rigged up and the relieved officer invited to blow in it to check it was working, which resulted in him being sprayed with soot.

The boisterous and extrovert tone of squadron life disguised a level of consideration and fellow feeling that perhaps marked out the RAF from the other services. The testimony of survivors, and what little was written down by those who died, is imbued with an overwhelming affection for fellow pilots and for the units in which they served. The camaraderie that came with membership of a fighter squadron appears to have provided a degree of spiritual sustenance, augmenting the warmth of an absent family or making those with dislocated backgrounds feel they had arrived at a place where they belonged. The simple cheeriness that was the Fighter Boys' chosen style masked some complicated stories. Geoffrey Page's parents were separated. His father frightened him and he resented his miserly attitude toward his mother. Dennis David was brought up by his mother after his father, who drank and had financial troubles, abandoned the family when he was eight. Brian Kingcome's mother had returned to England with her children, leaving her husband to continue working in India. He returned only once every two and a half years. As Kingcome was at boarding school, he barely saw his son during his childhood and adolescence.

The modern assumption is that such experiences must leave a mark. Feeling sorry for oneself lay outside the range of emotions allowed to adolescents in Britain in the 1930s. Kingcome admired and respected his largely absent father. Paddy Barthropp's mother died in childbirth, a tragedy that meant his father 'resented my very existence almost up to the time of his own death in 1953. I never blamed him.' At Ampleforth one day in 1936 'a school bully approached me to say that it would be a good idea if I read page four of *The Times* in the school library. There it was for all to see – "In the High Court of Bankruptcy, Elton Peter Maxwell D'Arley Barthropp" . . . the fact that one was skint was not acceptable and carried a long-lasting social stigma . . . the next few days were the most embarrassing of my life.' He was farmed out to a step-grandfather, 'extremely rich and very nasty', among whose many possessions was the Gresford Colliery near Wrexham. On hearing that there had been a disaster at the mine killing 264 miners, the old man 'replied that he didn't want to be disturbed. He disgusted me.'[38] Barthropp eventually got an apprenticeship with Rover Cars in Coventry before deciding to join the RAF after a visit to the Hendon Air Display.

Barthropp was hopeless academically. He failed the school certificate five times, and only scraped through his RAF board by gaining 'a phoney pass' from a crammer. Roland Beamont also failed his school certificate and had to resort to coaching to get the qualification he needed to be eligible for a short-service commission. Denys Gillam, who joined the

RAF on a short-service commission in 1935, had been kicked out of his prep school, then his public school, Wrekin College, for drinking and exam irregularities. He later joined 616 Squadron and commanded two fighter squadrons. Against the wisdom of the pre-war days his preferred pilots were 'non-athletic men between the ages of eighteen to twenty-three', who had 'better resilience to stress than the successful rugger player or his equivalent . . . all the best pilots that I knew tended to be rather weedy, though there were exceptions. The best pilot were ones that hadn't had much success in other spheres and were determined to succeed.' Teaching a course to a class of wing commanders later in his career, he discovered that 'out of a group of twelve . . . four had been thrown out of their school before they left. This was, I think, fairly typical.'[39] Kingcome was to deliver the opinion later that, 'Fortunately for us, and, I believe, for the RAF in that generation, there were [no] . . . psychological and aptitude tests, which would have failed a majority of candidates for short-service and permanent commissions and I suspect might have cost us the Battle of Britain.'[40]

Expansion increased the flow of men from the lower reaches of the RAF into the ranks of the fliers as candidates were selected from among the ground crews to serve as sergeant pilots. Of the 2,500 pilots originally sought to man the new aircraft and squadrons, 800 were found from among those already serving as aircraftmen or non-commissioned officers. The RAF apprentice schemes allowed a trickle of fitters, riggers and other tradesmen to receive flying training, on the understanding that they would return to their trades after five years. There were also two places set aside for the top performers at Halton to go on to Cranwell to take up a cadetship. Many, perhaps most, apprentices had dreams of flying. Realizing them was difficult. There was an obvious necessity to maintain the supply of highly skilled, expensively trained ground staff to keep the service flying and prevent apprenticeships from turning into a back-door route to a career as a pilot. None the less, in the pre-expansion years, some of the keenest and most talented felt themselves baulked by what was supposed to be a system that worked on merit. George Unwin was brought up in South Yorkshire, where his father was a miner. His mother encouraged his education and he won a scholarship to Wath Grammar School, and aged sixteen passed his Northern Universities matriculation exam. There was no money for him to take up a place. The only work on offer was down the pit. When, a month before he was due to leave, his headmaster showed him an RAF recruiting pamphlet, he decided to join up.

Unwin chose the Ruislip administrative apprentice school rather than the technical school at Halton, as the course there was two rather than three years. It was a spartan life. The food was horrible. They seemed to live on gristly mutton rissoles, and food parcels from the outside world were eagerly received. They shaved in cold water and lived twenty to a billet. Unwin initially had no thoughts of flying, but the sights and sounds of the aerodrome kindled his ambition. After passing out in 1931 as a leading aircraftman, the minimum rank to qualify for pilot training, he applied, but discovered that 'only one per cent per six months was taken'.

He repeated the process twice a year without success. 'I was getting a bit fed up at not being accepted. I had everything else. I was playing for the RAF at soccer, and that was one of the things you had to be, to be very good at sport. I couldn't understand why I wasn't being selected. You went through a very, very tedious process. First of all you saw your flight commander, then your CO, and then your station commander. If you got past him you saw the air officer commanding. I'd reached the point when I was going to see the AOC and I was getting desperate. At the time it was Air Vice-Marshal J. E. A. Baldwin, who loved polo and kept his own polo ponies.' Unwin decided that when the inevitable question about hobbies came up at the interview, he would be prepared. 'I said "horse riding". He pricked up his ears and said, "Really?" I said, "Of course, I can't afford it down here, but the local farmer at home has a pony and lets me ride it." The only time I'd ridden a pony or anything on four legs was in the General Strike when the pit ponies were brought up and put in fields. I was thirteen and we used to catch them and jump on their bare backs and go haring down the field until we fell off.'[41]

It worked. He was on the next course. It was 1935, four years after he first applied. In August 1936 he was posted to 19 Squadron at Duxford as a sergeant pilot, where his flight commander was Flight Lieutenant Harry Broadhurst, an ex-army officer who had joined the RAF in 1926 and flew in the campaigns against unruly tribesmen on India's North-West Frontier. Broadhurst had played a large part in building the squadron's reputation for flying excellence, which had won it many trophies, and he was regarded as the best shot in the RAF.

Unwin, despite his background, fitted relatively easily into the squadron. His best friend was another ex-apprentice whom he had met on the flying course, Harry Steere, who had gone to Halton from his secondary school in Wallasey in 1930. The two were to fly together for six out of the next seven years. Unwin found that 19 Squadron's competitive streak was compatible with a relaxed approach to duty. 'You didn't fly Saturdays, ever. You could take an aeroplane away for a weekend any time you liked. You used to fly away for lunch. You were encouraged to do this because it helped your map-reading. There were no aids at all, so you [navigated] visually. Radio telephony wouldn't work more than three miles from the aerodrome and then the background noise was so terrific you couldn't hear anything anyone was saying.' On annual exercises at Catterick, Unwin would take his aircraft and buzz his home village of Bolton Upon Dearne.

Making the transition from ground to air was a hit-and-miss affair and required the patronage of an interested senior officer. Ronald Brown left Halton in 1932 to be posted to the RAF station attached to Cranwell, where he worked as a fitter overhauling the engines of the aircraft on which the cadets at the college were taught to fly. Every morning 'the instructors would have a ten-minute flight to check the aircraft was safe for the cadets, and as they were dual-control aircraft we were able to jump in the back or the front. Inevitably that meant we were allowed to fly the plane with them, and long before I went on a pilot's course I was looping and rolling aeroplanes to my heart's delight every morning.'

Brown played football for the RAF and the group captain commanding him was a keen sportsman. 'I had the opportunity of flying him around once or twice and I think that, plus my sporting activity, gave me the chance of being selected for pilot training.'[42] Brown was one of only two airmen to be given the opportunity to fly in the three years he spent at the base. Before he could begin his flying training he was, to his disappointment, posted as a fitter to No. 10 Bomber Squadron at Boscombe Down. When he complained to the CO, he was told he could not start the course until the football season was over and the squadron had won the RAF cup. He was sent to 111 Fighter Squadron at Northolt in February 1937.

Sporting prowess got an airman applicant noticed and pushed his name further up the list. George Bennions, from Stoke-on-Trent, arrived at Halton in January 1929. He was a keen boxer and believed that 'they preferred to recommend sportsmen to become sergeant pilots [as] one way of sorting out the wheat from the chaff because there were many, many people at Halton who could equally have done the job'. Bennions was put forward for a Cranwell cadetship, an offer that later fell through, though he did end up joining 41 Squadron as a sergeant pilot and was commissioned in the spring of 1940. Some of Halton's most successful products were outstanding athletes. Don Finlay, who left in August 1928, became a world-class hurdler, winning a silver medal for Britain at the 1936 Berlin Olympics. He was to take command of 54 Squadron in August 1940, during some of the heaviest fighting of the summer.

As the situation worsened and the demand for pilots grew, the process of transformation became easier. George Johns arrived at Halton in January 1934 as an aircraft apprentice and by the end of 1939 was a sergeant pilot with 229 Squadron. 'You immediately said to yourself: I'm working with these aeroplanes. I'm going to fly them some time. That was the attitude you found there.'[43] Airmen who rose from the ranks to become pilots were to play an enormously important part in the air fighting of 1940. Often they had spent more time in the service than the officers and gained more flying experience. Unlike many of the officers, they also had a deep knowledge of the aircraft they were operating. Pre-war conventions created a certain distance between officer and NCO pilots, but this faded with the intimacy brought by shared danger and death.

Boosting the short-service commission system and intensifying internal recruitment ensured the supply of pilots needed to man the new squadrons. But men were also needed to fill the places of those who would be killed and badly wounded in the initial fighting. The Volunteer Reserve (VR) had been created to fill that gap, though this was not how it was presented to the men who turned up at the centres that sprang up around the country to process applicants. There were many of them. The target figure set in 1936 of 800 a year for three years was reached quickly, and in the spring of 1939 there were 2,500 volunteers under training. By then there were thirty-five flying centres, with eight in and around London and three near Bristol, while Manchester and Birmingham were served by two each.

Tedder had decreed that this should be a 'Citizen Air Force', modern and democratic, attracting 'air-minded' young men from factory, shop and office, and this was how it turned out. Frank Usmar was a postman's son from West Malling in Kent, who left school at fourteen to work in an office and spent his evenings studying accountancy at night school. In 1938 the RAF opened a recruiting office in Rochester. Usmar's interest in flying had stemmed from seeing *Dawn Patrol*. He applied, was accepted and thereafter spent two nights a week attending lectures at the VR Hall in Rochester and weekends flying at a local airfield, for which he was paid a shilling an hour. After nine and three quarter hours dual flying on an Avro Tutor, he went solo. The part-time nature of the training meant that it took much longer to get new pilots up to standard, and it was a year before he moved on to service aircraft like the Hart, Hind and Audax.

But the system did identify pilots showing great potential who could be brought to operational level quickly when the time came. Charlton Haw would never have got into the RAF under normal peacetime conditions. He left school at fourteen to become an apprentice in a lithographic works in York, and as soon as he was eighteen applied for the RAFVR. 'I'd always wanted to fly, from when I was a small boy. I never wanted to do anything else, really, but I just didn't think there would ever be a chance for me. Until the RAFVR was formed, for a normal schoolboy it was almost impossible.'[44] Haw went solo in four hours forty minutes, at a time when the average was eight to ten hours, and was considered a natural pilot by his instructor. Not that a slow start necessarily denoted incompetence. There was a school of thought that said that the longer the apprenticeship, the better the pilot.

The reserve offered an escape from dreary jobs in stifling offices. John Beard was working in the Midland Bank at Leamington when a circular arrived saying that employees who joined the VR would be granted an extra week's holiday to allow them to train. Beard began flying at Ansley aerodrome at weekends and going to lectures in Coventry on navigation, meteorology and elementary engineering and aeronautics a few evenings a week. Ron Berry left school at sixteen and got a job as a clerk at an engineering works in Hull. He stayed eighteen months before moving on to the city treasurer's department. Early in 1938 he saw an advertisement for the RAFVR in a local paper and realized how 'keen I was to try something like that'. To prepare for the medical he ran round the local park every morning at seven o'clock. He was interviewed by an impressive squadron leader in a uniform displaying an Air Force Cross. 'He made me feel strongly about doing something other than clerical work in the city treasurer's office.'[45]

The RAFVR also gave young men a say in their own fate, a chance to choose which branch of the services they would be absorbed into before the inevitable seeming processes of conscription took the decision for them. In January 1939, Robert Foster was working at Shell headquarters in London. 'I thought there was going to be a war and I didn't particularly want to be in the army, or a conscript. I never really thought about the problems of being in the air force, but that seemed a better way to fight a war than as a common soldier.'[46]

The RAF seemed to offer a relatively clean way of fighting the coming war. Many of those who joined had fathers who had served in the First World War and whose experiences had left a strong and disturbing impression. Christopher Foxley-Norris, who was commissioned in the RAFVR after leaving the Oxford University Air Squadron, remembered that undergraduates, when 'sitting around in the evening having a beer . . . used to discuss our ability to survive trench warfare. We'd all read

All Quiet on the Western Front and those sort of things. My father was gassed at Loos in 1915. He died after the war in 1923, of cancer. I think most of us doubted we could stand it.'[47]

The expansion programme also brought an influx of new pilots – many originating from further up the social scale than the young men flocking to the RAFVR – into the Auxiliary Air Force (AAF) and University air squadrons buttressing Trenchard's design for the air force. After February 1936 eight new auxiliary units were created and four existing special reserve squadrons were transferred to the AAF. By the beginning of 1939, fourteen squadrons, most of which had started out equipped with bombers, had been redesignated as fighter units, though the aeroplanes for them to fly were often slow in coming. By the time the great air battles began in July 1940, there were twelve auxiliary squadrons operating as day fighters and two as night fighters – a quarter of Fighter Command's strength.

Among the new creations was 609 (West Riding) Squadron, formed in February 1936. Its first commanding officer was Harald Peake, an old-Etonian businessman from a local coal-owning family who had been chairman of large concerns like Lloyds Bank and London Assurance, and a keen amateur flier who took his private aeroplane on summer tours of the Continent. Peake had long been eager to raise auxiliary squadrons in the county when further units were required, and as soon as he was given the go-ahead began recruiting from among the sons of the big industrial and landowning families of Yorkshire. Stephen Beaumont, a junior partner in his family's law firm, which had Peake as a client, was one of the first to join. He was a thoughtful and dutiful man with a strong social conscience. With Hitler's arrival in power he felt a growing conviction that war was inevitable and he decided to fight in it as a pilot. He began flying at the West Riding Aero Club at Yeadon near Leeds, and when he heard that a new squadron was being formed, offered his services to Peake.

Beaumont found Peake 'very capable. He was about thirty-seven and had held commissions in the Coldstream Guards at the end of the First World War and later in the Yorkshire Dragoons Yeomanry. Perhaps because of our professional relationship I was somewhat in his confidence. He wanted officers who were no more than twenty-five, of public-school and university backgrounds and unmarried.' Beaumont was twenty-six and engaged to be married but was accepted none the less. Peake could afford to be choosy. By 8 June he had vetted 80 applications for commissions and 200 for posts as airmen. Despite this response, actual recruitment was slow, only speeding up as war approached. The squadron had a sprinkling of officers from aristocratic and county backgrounds. They included Peter Drummond-Hay, a textile executive who insisted on the use of both barrels of his Scottish name. He was discontented with his work in the cloth trade. Beaumont wrote that 'he liked to give the impression that he would be better employed as the owner of a large country estate, where he would know all the county, and indeed in North Yorkshire he did know a great many of that section of society. Somewhat caustic about and dismissive of most Yorkshiremen, he was very courteous to women.'[48] Dudley Persse-Joynt was an oil executive from an old Anglo-Irish family, and the first auxiliary adjutant was the Earl of Lincoln, who later became the Duke of Newcastle. But most of the members came from families who had prospered in the reign of Victoria and whose wealth was founded on coal and cloth.

Philip Barran's family were textile and coalmining magnates from Leeds. Joe Dawson's father, Sir Benjamin Dawson, was a power in the cloth trade and a baronet. A later recruit, John Dundas, was related to two Yorkshire grandees, the Marquess of Zetland and Viscount Halifax, and was a cousin of Harald Peake. He was academically brilliant, winning scholarships to Stowe and Oxford and taking a first in modern history before going on to study at Heidelberg and the Sorbonne. He had joined the staff of the *Yorkshire Post*, specializing in foreign affairs, and was sent to report from Czechoslovakia at the time of Munich and accompanied Chamberlain and his own kinsman Halifax to Rome. Barran, always known as Pip, was stocky, boisterous, a rugby player, a trainee mining engineer and the manager of a brickworks owned by his mother's family. His commanding officer eulogized him as 'the very best type of AAF officer, a born leader who communicated his enthusiasm to others'.[49] It was he who came up with the nicknames that adorned the members of 609 as they prepared for war.

The last auxiliary squadron to be formed was 616, which officially came into being on 1 November 1938 in Doncaster, South Yorkshire, as an offshoot of 609. Hugh Dundas had left Stowe in the summer of that year and was hoping to follow his brother John to Oxford. His father, however, insisted on him going into the law and he ended up being articled to a firm of Doncaster solicitors. Dundas applied to join 616 Squadron, but mysteriously failed the medical exam three times before finally being passed fit by an ex-Ireland rugby international RAF doctor after 'the most perfunctory examination', for which Nelsonian oversight he was eternally thankful.

Dundas finally joined in the last summer before the war. His CO was the Earl of Lincoln, who had moved on from 609, and other squadron members included Teddy St Aubyn, a Lincolnshire landowner who had moved into the AAF after being forced to resign his commission in the Grenadier Guards following his marriage to Nancy Meyrick, daughter of Kate 'Ma' Meyrick, who presided over the Forty-Three, a nightclub in between-the-wars London whose liveliness shaded into notoriety.

Dundas spent his time divided between Bawtry, the home of his aunt and her husband Bertie Peake – a lakeside house where the décor and routines had not changed since the 1890s – and the mess at the squadron station at Doncaster, where he also had a room and a batman. It was there that he acquired his nickname. 'I was sitting by the fireplace in the mess one evening before dinner. On the wall at my side was the bell button. Teddy St Aubyn and others were there. Teddy felt the need for further refreshment and decided that I was conveniently placed to summon the mess steward. "Hey you," he said pointing at me. "Hey you – Cocky – press the bell." I promptly did his bidding. But why had he described me as "Cocky"? What had I done? Nervously I asked him.' St Aubyn replied that he had forgotten his name, but that Dundas, an elongated figure with a shock of hair, reminded him of a 'bloody great Rhode Island Red'. The name stuck to him for the rest of his life.

He spent the summer days learning to fly in an archaic dual-control

Avro Tutor, probably one of the last RAF pilots ever to do so. Some difficult manoeuvres came quite easily, 'But slow rolls I hated and had great difficulty in achieving. I felt quite helpless when the machine was upside-down and I was hanging on my straps, dust and grit from the bottom of the cockpit falling around me. Again and again, when inverted, I instinctively pulled the stick back, instead of pushing it forward and so fell out of the roll in a tearing dive.'[50]

The search for new pilots also meant an increase in the strength of the university air squadrons. In May 1938 there were three, Oxford, Cambridge and London, which had been set up three years previously. That month they each increased the number of available places from seventy-five to a hundred. It had been hoped that the squadrons would provide a practical link between the air force and aeronautical research, particularly at Cambridge. The Oxford University Air Squadron (OUAS) operations book records its primary object as being 'to provide at the university a means by which interest in the air generally and in particular in the Royal Air Force can be stimulated'. Its second function was to 'provide suitable personnel to be trained as officers for the Royal Air Force in the event of war'. In practice, for most of its life the squadron functioned primarily as a flying club, for which the government paid.

Christopher Foxley-Norris went up to Oxford from Winchester in 1936 and was encouraged to join the OUAS by his brother, who was already a member. The prospect of the £25 gratuity paid on being accepted was also attractive. He wanted to buy a car, which he believed to be a crucial accessory if he was ever to get a girlfriend. OUAS members cut a dash. They were chauffered to their station at RAF Abingdon in two old Rolls-Royces, nicknamed Castor and Pollux, hired from a local firm. Once qualified, one was entitled to wear the squadron blazer with crest and gold RAF buttons. Foxley-Norris regarded it as 'a *corps d'élite*. It was very difficult to get into because there were some very outstanding people. It was a glamorous sort of club to be in, but not like the Bullingdon or something upmarket like that.'

The most immediately noticeable member was Richard Hillary, whose harsh wit, self-regard, good looks and ability as an oarsman made him stand out in a society not short of distinctive characters or large egos. Foxley-Norris met Hillary through friends who had been with him at Shrewsbury, his old school. 'I came across him when we were out on pub crawls and that sort of thing and I got to know him quite well. He was extremely arrogant and conceited.'[51] Hillary was also a poor learner, and his progress was not helped by the amount of time he spent on the river. 'This member proved very difficult to get off solo,' noted his instructor. 'He would not relax on the controls, he just held on like a vice.' Once flying alone, however, he 'improved rapidly'. The chief flying instructor judged that he 'lacked keenness . . . I do not consider that he has any real interest in flying'.[52]

Hillary was to have a powerful effect on British and international perceptions of the character and motivations of the pilots of 1940 through his book *The Last Enemy*, which appeared in 1941 after he had been shot down and badly burned, and became a best-seller in Britain and the United States. It is a book as much about friendship as flying, and those closest to him in the last years of his short life were all products of the University Air Squadrons. Among them was Noel Agazarian, the third son of an Armenian father and a French mother who had bought an old Sopwith Pup biplane and parked it in the garden of the family's Georgian house in Carshalton, Surrey, for the boys to clamber over. Agazarian went from his public school, Dulwich, to Wadham College, Oxford, in 1935, leaving three years later with a boxing blue and a law degree. He joined the air squadron and was commissioned into the RAFVR in January 1939. He was a brilliant linguist, funny and disrespectful. He was also good looking and when it came to attracting women was a match for Hillary, who seems to have rather resented his easy and natural charm. 'We called him Le Roi Soleil,' said his adoring young sister, Yvonne. 'He was always laughing and clowning. Noel was very much loved by everyone who met him.'[53] Peter Pease and Colin Pinckney, both old Etonians, had also joined the Cambridge University Air Squadron and both had been commissioned in the RAFVR by the end of 1938. They met Hillary during training and their subsequent intense and poetic triangular relationship was to be celebrated in the book.

The great variety of backgrounds and schools, the wide divergences of rank, wealth and privilege, made Fighter Command perhaps the most socially diverse élite ever seen in the British military. In a country where minutely defined social gradations conditioned the reactions of human beings to each other, the mingling of the classes caused some discomfort. The situation was described in a condescending *bon mot*: 'Auxiliaries are gentlemen trying to be officers. Regulars are officers trying to be gentlemen. VRs are neither trying to be both.' It was a last, snobbish gasp from a disappearing world. Very soon the distinction would not matter. It was true that many of the men in Fighter Command came from backgrounds that were 'ordinary'. But that did not mean that they themselves were so; and they were about to do extraordinary things.

4

The Fatal Step

The new pilots had been recruited to fly a new generation of fighter aeroplanes, but the machines were painfully slow in reaching the squadrons. The first Hurricanes did not appear in service until January 1938, when 111 Squadron became the first unit to receive them. It was August, and the eve of the Munich crisis, before 19 Squadron took delivery of the first Spitfires. At the end of the year most fighter squadrons were still flying biplanes.

Ronald Brown, the ex-Halton boy who had been selected for flying training, was a sergeant pilot at Northolt with 111 Squadron when the Hurricanes arrived. The squadron commander and flight commanders were the first to test them. Then it was the turn of the junior pilots. They were told to keep the undercarriage lowered in order to reduce speed. The great power of the Merlin engine, twice as potent as anything they had previously known, would take time to adjust to, it was thought. Brown, even though it was the first time he had handled a monoplane, in fact found it 'quite an easy plane to fly'.[1] Most pilots' accounts of their experience of the Hurricane, however, reveal a mixture of trepidation and elation. Roland Beamont remembered 'a feeling of exhilaration with all this power and being able to get up to 300 miles an hour on the air-speed indicator very easily in a shallow dive at any point in your flight. This was a great experience for an eighteen-year-old.'[2] The Gloster Gauntlets and Gladiators, which represented the zenith of biplane fighter design and served as a stopgap with many fighter squadrons while the new monoplanes were brought in, could manage only 230 and 255 m.p.h. respectively.

For pilots used to biplanes, the Hurricane seemed to take a long time to get airborne. Initially it had a fixed-pitch, twin-bladed propeller that only allowed one setting. With variable-pitch propellers, which were soon to come in, the pilot put the airscrew in 'fine' for take-off. This provided less speed but more power, giving maximum thrust – the equivalent in motoring terms of first gear. Once aloft, the pilot changed to 'coarse', altering the angle of the propeller blade so that it was taking bigger bites out of the air, generating less power but more speed. Later both types would be fitted with constant-speed governors that adjusted the blade angles automatically. Beamont thought flying a Hurricane was 'simple, straightforward'. Christopher Foxley-Norris found it reassuring. 'You get into an aircraft and it gives you confidence. You get into another one and it doesn't . . . [The Hurricane] was very stable but at the same time manoeuvrable. If you didn't want it to do a turn it was absolutely rock stable. If you did turn it was very manoeuvrable.'[3]

The Hurricane was slower than a Spitfire but could turn more tightly. Its wide-legged undercarriage, which opened outwards, planting the aeroplane firmly on the ground, made it 'very forgiving', another advantage over the Spitfire, which balanced on a narrow wheelbase. The initial canvas-and-girder construction of the fuselage meant bullets and cannon shells could go straight through it without bringing the aircraft down, and its sturdy wings provided solid bracing for the eight Brownings. It was, everyone said, an 'excellent gun platform', better, in fact, than the Spitfire. The machine guns were arranged in two groups of four, as close in to the fuselage as they could be placed to clear the propeller. The Spitfire's armament was spread out, with the outboard gun a third of the way in from the wing-tip; then a group of two, then an inboard gun on each wing, which could cause some flexing when the guns fired, making them less accurate. The Hurricane was fast and nimble but honest. It was not quite perfect. Pete Brothers discovered 'it could fall out of the air if you mistreated it trying to be too clever'.

The arrival of the new fighters aroused the fervent interest of newspapers and newsreel companies. Brown remembered them making 'an absolute meal of the Hurricane. We were wonderboys, travelling at vast speeds, pulling all this G [the heavy gravitational force exerted when turning]. We were getting constant visits from the press and staff colleges who wanted to see these things in action.'[4] Having appeared before the Spitfire, the Hurricane was the first to plant itself in the public imagination, though its primacy did not long survive the arrival of its more beautiful sister. The public perception that it represented a battle-winning technical advance was encouraged by a government and military establishment anxious to reassure citizens that the criticisms of the rearmament lobby were unfounded. Some pilots, used to the fixed wheels, open cockpits, broad flying surfaces and manageable speeds of the old types, wondered whether they would be able to cope. The difficulties which 111 Squadron had in making the transition were not reassuring. Some pilots simply could not adjust. Several were killed. One Australian pilot took off without realizing the wheel brakes were engaged. He only avoided crashing on take-off and landing because the field was so muddy the aeroplane slithered through the grass. When he made a subsequent landing without lowering the undercarriage, he was rapidly posted away.

Pilots liked the Hurricane's chunky lines and solid profile. The lean, curved elegance of the Spitfire inspired something more profound. There was never 'a plane so loved by pilots', wrote Hugh Dundas.[5] 'Everybody wanted to fly a Spitfire,' said Jeffrey Quill. 'Most pilots used to want to fly the best. It certainly was the best.' Quill knew the quality of the machine better than anyone. He was a test pilot at Supermarine and had taken the Spitfire through the most difficult stages of its development, as the design team struggled to overcome profound technical problems that were preventing it from making the evolutionary transition from being a very good aeroplane to a great one.

Quill was intelligent, shrewd and popular in both air force and civilian aviation circles, as much for his good nature as his superb abilities as a pilot. His father was Irish, an engineer who among other things had built Sierra Leone's water system before retiring to Littlehampton in Sussex.

He died in 1926 when Jeffrey was thirteen and a schoolboy at Lancing. As a young boy he watched the aeroplanes at the RFC base at Ford, near the family home. He decided early on to go into the air force, but he was the youngest of five children and there was little money. He had to forgo Cranwell, where his family would have had to support him for two years, and applied instead for a short-service commission. His first posting was to 17 Squadron, flying Bulldogs. Then he joined the Meteorological Flight at Duxford, which made daily sorties to take weather-forecasting readings, dangerous work that was given only to very good pilots. He hoped for a permanent RAF commission. But even in 1935, with expansion under way, his prospects were not sure and with some misgivings he accepted an offer to join Supermarine as an assistant to its chief test pilot, Mutt Summers, working on the Spitfire.

Progress was fitful. The prototype could not reach the 350 m.p.h. expected of it, only scraping up to 335 m.p.h. The propeller was one problem. It had been supplied by an outside contractor. A new one was designed by the Supermarine team and added an extra 13 m.p.h. Then the body surface was not smooth enough. Sinking rivets into the skin of the airframe would have brought better aerodynamic efficiency, but doing so would take much time and money. The team stuck split peas on the prototype to simulate round-headed rivets, which were much simpler to punch, then progressively removed them during aerodynamic tests to see which surfaces absolutely required flush rivets and which did not.

Failure to solve these problems and reach the performance levels Mitchell had claimed for his design could have meant the Spitfire never going into service. Quill and the rest of the team knew what was at stake. Later he revealed how close the decision had been. 'A lot of people felt that the Spitfire, although it had a very good performance . . . had been bought at too high a price. In terms of ease of production it was going to be a much more expensive and difficult aeroplane to mass produce. In terms of the ease of maintenance it was going to be a much more complicated aeroplane to look after and service . . . For instance, you could lower the undercarriage of a Hurricane and take the wings off because the undercarriage was in the centre section . . . You could take the wings off, put the tail up on a three-ton lorry and tow it along the road. You couldn't do that with a Spitfire. If you took the wings off . . . it took the undercarriage off as well . . . There were a lot of people who were against the Spitfire for those practical considerations. Therefore if we had not been able to show a really definite advantage over the Hurricane, it probably wouldn't have been ordered. We were well aware of that.'

A final, crucial question had to be settled. In May 1936 a prototype was sent to the RAF Aircraft and Armament Establishment at Martlesham for trials by the service's test pilots. Before the programme was complete, the research and development representative on the Air Council, Wilfred Freeman, asked the establishment's flight commander Flight Lieutenant Humphrey Edwards-Jones, whether the Spitfire could be flown with relative ease by ordinary squadron pilots. 'Old "E.-J." quite rightly said, "Yes, it can," ' Quill said later. On the strength of this judgement, before any performance testing had taken place, the decision to order was made. Quill reckoned there would have been 'an awful delay if he'd hedged about that. It was one of the best things ever done.'[6]

No. 19 Squadron had been chosen as the first unit to receive the Spitfire because of its record of superlative flying, demonstrated at displays around the country by an aerobatic team which performed such impressive but not necessarily militarily useful stunts as flying in rigid formation tied together with ropes. The five pilots selected to put the Spitfire through a 500-hour series of tests included two sergeants, George Unwin, the Ruislip apprentice, and his best friend Harry Steere. Unwin was particularly struck by the sensitivity of the controls. 'There was no heaving or pulling and pushing and kicking, you just breathed on it. She really was the perfect flying machine. She hadn't got a vice at all. She would only spin if you made her and she'd come straight out of it as soon as you applied opposite rudder and pushed the stick forward . . . I've never flown anything sweeter.' The Spitfire's engine note was instantly recognizable to those who had flown it, and distinct from that of a Hurricane, even though they both had the same Merlin power unit. Many years later Unwin was coming out of Boots in Bournemouth with his wife when he heard 'that peculiar throaty roar . . . I said to her, "There's a Spitfire somewhere." A taxi driver was standing there and said, "There she is, mate." It is a noise you will never forget.'[7]

Brian Kingcome believed 'it had all the best qualities an aircraft could have. It was docile, it was fast, it was manoeuvrable, it was gentle . . . it did everything you asked of it.'[8] John Nicholas of 65 Squadron accompanied Kingcome to the Supermarine airfield at Eastleigh, Southampton, where Jeffrey Quill showed them the controls. He warned them that 'everything was sensitive . . . it was so light on the controls, index finger and thumb would fly it'.[9]

There were disadvantages, too, the first of which was immediately obvious at take-off. The undercarriage hydraulics were manual and the wheels had to be pumped up by lever with the right hand. There was a natural tendency to waggle the control column back and forth during the manoeuvre, and new pilots were recognizable by the way they pitched and yawed after they got airborne. This problem disappeared with the fitting of a power pump. It was easy to forget the propeller adjustments that had to be made to the Spitfire, the same as they did to the Hurricane. Brian Considine, a trainee executive with Unilever who joined the RAFVR at nineteen, had only flown fixed-pitch propeller biplanes when he was sent to join 238 Squadron at Tangmere. He was given one short trip in a single-wing Master trainer as preparation for his Spitfire debut. He 'took off in fine pitch and promptly forgot to put it back into coarse pitch, and did a few circles round the field thinking how marvellous it was . . . I made a nice landing and as I taxied in I could see the CO jumping up and down like a monkey in a rage. When I got out he told me I had wrecked the thing. I hadn't, but it was all covered in oil.'[10]

The Spitfire had a very long nose, which allowed the pilot virtually no forward vision when tilted on the back wheel in the taxiing position. To see ahead it was necessary to swing the aircraft from side to side. The centre of gravity was also unusually far forward, so a heavy foot on the brakes would tip the machine on to its propeller. But these, the infatuated pilots believed, were foibles not faults. The Spitfire was certainly a better aeroplane than the Hurricane and at least the equal of its German rival, the Messerschmitt 109. The former it could out-climb and out-dive. The latter it could out-turn. It was still in service in its Mark XII incarnation at the end of the war when the Hurricane had been phased out and replaced by the Typhoon. Brian Kingcome judged that 'the Hurricane was already more or less at the peak of its operational and design potential when it first came into service . . . its future was strictly limited by its rugged, uncouth airframe . . . The Spitfire, by contrast, possessed a unique capacity for development.'[11]

None the less the competitive spirit that the RAF, and particularly Fighter Command, fostered meant that the Hurricane pilots were loyal to their machines, maintaining to the last that they would not have swapped them for a Spitfire if given the choice. No. 111 Squadron pilots had had to endure some mockery at the time it took them to master the new fighters and finish the 500 hours of testing. George Unwin remembered that, as soon as they could muster twelve aircraft, the first thing they did was to come down to 19 Squadron at Duxford to 'beat up' the aerodrome, as the RAF called the practice of flying low and fast over bases to impress their rivals – or show off to girlfriends. Once 19 Squadron was able to do so, it flew over to Northolt and returned the compliment.

The re-equipment programme went slowly, moving at the limited pace that peacetime industrial capacity allowed. By the late summer of 1938 it seemed alarmingly out of step with events. The Munich crisis of September 1938 showed how swiftly the RAF might be called upon to act, and how unprepared it was to do so. As it broke, there were just six squadrons equipped with Hurricanes, only half of which were combat-ready. No. 19 Squadron had only three Spitfires, which were armed with machine guns but lacked gunsights. The remaining sixteen operational squadrons had Gladiator, Gauntlet, Demon and Fury biplanes to oppose the sleek, modern might of the Luftwaffe.

As the crisis deepened, officers of 1 Squadron and 43 Squadron joined aircraftmen in the hangars to cover the gleaming silver paint that usually decorated the Furies – to show them to their best advantage in formation flying and aerobatics – with dismal shades of camouflage green and brown. Billy Drake and his comrades were ordered to sleep in the hangars, next to the aircraft to be at full readiness. No one knew quite what to expect. 'I think we had an idea that they would go for us on the airfields, but nobody really seemed to have any strategy in mind – not at our level anyway.'[12]

At Biggin Hill, 79 Squadron was recalled from leave and on 27 September the auxiliaries of 601 Squadron were summoned to move from Hendon to the station, which had been designated their wartime base. At Hornchurch, 54, 74 and 65 Squadrons were called to immediate readiness and some pilots slept in crew rooms close to the aircraft. No. 74 Squadron had to abandon a gunnery practice camp at Sutton Bridge in Lincolnshire and return home, where they obliterated the squadron badges and tiger stripes adorning the fuselages of their Gauntlets and Gladiators, mixing up the paint from the colours available in the stores when the green and brown ran out. Al Deere, now with 54 Squadron, found it 'a heartrending operation having to desecrate one's beautiful Gladiator'. With the return of Chamberlain, waving his assurance from Hitler, the crisis fizzled out. The sigh of relief that gusted across Britain was not shared by all. 'It is callous and wrong to say it, but when "peace in our time" was agreed, I was horribly disappointed,' Deere admitted later.[13]

The likelihood of the Luftwaffe bombing Britain in the early autumn of 1938 was small, but the scare the crisis engendered was real and had the useful effect of speeding up the delivery of Hurricanes and Spitfires. The episode also blew away the last wisps of complacency that clung to the air force about what the future held. Politicians might maintain that this time Hitler could be trusted and a cataclysm had been averted rather than simply postponed. But many of the young pilots, and those who commanded them, now believed that a clash with the Luftwaffe was inevitable.

By the end of 1938 the Furies disappeared from Tangmere and Hurricanes took their place. Paul Richey arrived there in March 1939. He was in his twenty-third year and had been brought up in Switzerland, France and Albania, where his father, a veteran of the trenches, had helped to organize King Zog's gendarmerie. He was commissioned in 1937 and already knew Tangmere from visits during training. Posted there to join No. 1 Squadron, he noted the new atmosphere.

> Half the pilots in each squadron now had to be permanently available on station in case of a German attack. Gone were the carefree days when we would plunge into the cool blue sea at West Wittering and lie on the warm sand in the sun, or skim over the waters in Chichester harbour, in the squadron's sailing dinghy, or drive down to the Old Ship at Bosham with the breeze in our hair and knock it back under the oak rafters. Our days were now spent in our Hurricanes at air drill, air firing, practice battle formations and attacks, dogfighting – and operating under ground control with the new super-secret RDF (the name then given to radar).[14]

It was the same for everybody. The pleasant old arrangements of no flying after 4 p.m., and weekends and Wednesday afternoons off, were dropped and the tempo of practice and training quickened. The activity was intense but lacked direction and seemed curiously disconnected from the realities of aerial warfare as had been demonstrated by the German and Italian air forces in the skies over Spain. The preparations also seemed to lack consistency, with different squadrons following different programmes. It would soon become clear that some skills vital for success and survival in the changed conditions of air fighting were miserably under-taught and in some cases ignored altogether.

Tactical training before the war was based on two premises that would turn out to be fatally mistaken once the conflict began. The first of these was that close, tight formation flying concentrated force in such a way as to make fighters both more destructive and more secure. The second was the expectation that they would be facing fleets of bombers arriving in waves, capable of defending themselves with onboard guns but unprotected by escorting fighters. The logic of the assumption was that the Luftwaffe would be confined to its German bases and its Me 109s would not have the range to accompany the bombers.

Those who survived the war complained that the RAF had a drill-hall mentality, exalting the sort of flying discipline exemplified by 19 Squadron's aerial rope trick. There was a useful point to close formation flying. It helped groups of aeroplanes to move through cloud without colliding or losing contact with each other. But good formation drill was also seen as the basis of good tactics. Al Deere wrote later that 'the majority of our training in a pre-war fighter squadron was directed at achieving perfection in formation with a view to ensuring the success of the flight and squadron attacks we so assiduously practised'. These were known as Fighter Area Attacks, and were numbered from one to five, depending on the fighters' line of approach and the number of bombers. Thus, No. 1 involved a section of three or a flight of six fighters attacking one after the other a single bomber from astern. In No. 2, two or more fighters attacked a single bomber in line abreast, and No. 3 envisaged three fighters coming at a single bomber simultaneously from rear, beam, and rear quarter. It was all very theoretical and, as it turned out, of little use. But theory was all there was to go on.

'The order to attack was always preceded by the flight commander designating the number of the attack, viz. "FAA attack No. 5 – Go!"' Deere wrote later. 'These attacks provided wonderful training for formation drill, but were worthless when related to effective shooting. There was never sufficient time to get one's sights on the target, the business of keeping station being the prime requirement.'[15] Pete Brothers and the rest of 32 Squadron at Biggin Hill prepared for war by following rigid scenarios that proposed set responses to set situations, practising on 'enemy bombers' that flew stolidly on, disdaining to take any evasive action. 'If there was a small number of bombers your twelve aircraft would be divided up into sections of three. Then three of you would have a go at one bomber, one after the other. If there was a large number, you would spread out into echelon starboard [diagonally] setting it all up and giving them plenty of warning you were coming. It must have been all theoretical because no one had actually fought in these conditions before.'[16]

The tactics taught to George Unwin in 19 Squadron were 'more suited to the Hendon air display' than the realities of war. When put into practice for the first time over Dunkirk, the results were to be disastrous. The severe limitations of the pre-war tactical approach was to become apparent almost immediately, but this did not stop it being taught well into the war. Roger Hall, a young, pre-war professional soldier who transferred to the RAF, was posted to 152 Squadron at the height of the fighting in September 1940 after only a week's operational training. He remembered during his instruction being 'briefed on how to attack a bomber, but it was so perfunctory really that it was almost ludicrous.' Three pilots were designated to take off in their newly acquired Spitfires and 'attack' a Wellington which was playing the role of an enemy bomber. Green though he was, Hall knew that 'when you attack a hostile bomber they try to get out of the way. But this particular one was simply flying straight and level . . . The drill was to get above the bomber and the first Spitfire would come down and shoot its port engine and then it would break away. The next one would come and shoot the starboard, then that would break away. Then the third one would come down and shoot the body of the machine and then break away, but all the time the Wellington was just going straight and level, just asking for it . . . I used to laugh about that.'[17]

Brian Kingcome recalled that 'fighter *versus* fighter wasn't really envisaged or catered for', and the assumption was that if they did take place they would be 'pretty much as they were in the First World War except that you had faster, better aircraft and the huge advantage of a parachute'. None the less individual pilots did get in unofficial practice, going off in pairs to chase each other around the sky.[18]

The pilots who went into action for the first time in 1939 and 1940 might have known a lot about flying. They knew little, though, about how to fight in the air and less about how to shoot. Aerial gunnery was supposed to be taught as part of training and each regular fighter squadron was expected to go to an annual camp at one of the armament training stations for practice with live ammunition, shooting at drogues towed behind other aircraft, or at ground targets. This was occasionally supplemented by the use of camera guns, from which theoretical scores could be deduced. It was all a long way from reality.

In retrospect the amount of time spent on what was a fundamental air skill would seem desperately inadequate. 'Looking back,' Al Deere wrote afterwards, 'I can see how dreadfully we neglected gunnery practice, live or by means of cine-films, and what an important part it plays in the part of a successful fighter pilot ... squadron morale carried us safely through the early fighter battles of the war, not straight shooting.'[19]

Some pilots never fired at an aerial target before going into action. Tony Bartley, the son of a colonial service judge, who was awarded a short-service commission after leaving Stowe school, did his training before the war. Yet the first time he aimed his guns at a flying object was when he shot at an Me 109 in May 1940. George Unwin was fortunate in having Harry Broadhurst, an outstanding shot, as his flight commander. 'Training in shooting was nonexistent. No one ever taught you how to shoot. But he did.' Broadhurst emphasized 'that the key to shooting was to get in close and the closer you got the more chance you had of hitting'. Unwin, who became a gunner instructor later in his career, found that one of the biggest weaknesses among fighter pilots at the beginning of the war was their inability properly to calculate how far they were from the aircraft they were attacking, often opening fire long before they reached what combat experience would teach was the optimum range of 250 yards. In the pre-war days, when aircraft were still equipped with a simple ring sight, Broadhurst taught his charges to work out the distance of the target by measuring it against the diameter of the circle. At 400 yards a bomber the size of a Wellington exactly filled the sight. At 250 yards, the ring was just outboard of the two engines. It was simple and effective, but according to Unwin never taught systematically.

The apparent explanation for the lack of firing practice was that, with tight financial restraints on the expansion programme, the Air Ministry had decided that spending money on the aircraft and pilots needed to man and equip the new squadrons took priority over new ranges, and so allowances for practice ammunition were cut to a minimum. There was no such excuse in 1940. By then shortage of time was to blame for a continuing failure to teach raw pilots how to shoot before throwing them into battle. When Archie Winskill, a softly spoken RAFVR volunteer from Cumberland, reached 72 Squadron at Biggin Hill on 4 October 1940, he was 'well-schooled in formation flying and tactics but regrettably with no air-firing experience. I'd only fired my guns once into the sea off Liverpool . . . We knew nothing about deflection shooting.'[20]

What was needed to attack successfully was the skill to manoeuvre into a favourable position, the ability to judge the correct range to open fire, and finally, and usually equally importantly, the knowledge of how to angle the shot so it stood the best chance of hitting the enemy aeroplane. The latter was deflection shooting. In all but full-on frontal or rear attacks, shooting in a straight line was useless. To strike the target required 'laying off', in the same way that a game shooter aims ahead of the pheasant so that the bird flies into the spread of pellets. The principle was recognized in the clay pigeon range installed at pre-war Tangmere and copied later in the war at many fighter bases. Some of the most deadly pilots, like Bob Tuck and Adolph Malan, attributed at least some of their success to their skill with shotguns. The importance of deflection shooting was obvious. Winskill was not to learn it until he was sent off to a gunnery course long after the 1940 crisis had passed.

The pilots of Fighter Command also went into the war with little idea of what they would be shooting at. George Unwin 'didn't know a thing' about the Germans' strengths, aircraft types and likely *modus operandi* before he met them in the air. At the time of Munich, the British air attaché in Berlin made a tour of squadron bases and delivered a lecture about the Luftwaffe. But detailed intelligence briefings on the enemy were never given on an organized basis before the fighting began, and during the battles of 1940 pilots were seldom allowed a glimpse of the bigger picture. Their knowledge was confined to what had happened to them and their companions on the base, or what they heard on the radio. These shortcomings in training and preparation would only become fully apparent when revealed by the stresses of combat.

The approach of the cataclysm forced the pilots to think about the future. That the crisis was coming to a head seemed surprisingly comforting to some. Watching Europe's tottering, somnambulistic progress once more towards the precipice induced feelings of restlessness and a desire to get the inevitable over with. Peter Townsend, who at the time of the Abyssinian war had been sickened by the thought of the effects of bombs on men, found the sight of the enemy, clear and unambiguous, was a liberation. 'A complete change of mind and heart had by now come over me . . . My pacifism of the previous year had evaporated; I was becoming rather bellicose – at least as bloody-minded as every other Englishman felt towards the swaggering, bullying Germans.'

Townsend also noticed that the imminence of danger broke down whatever barriers remained between the new and the old RAF inside 43 Squadron, so that 'in the growingly tense atmosphere, I was discovering that those parvenu pilots I had once so resented were really the warmest, most generous friends . . . genuine 'fighter boys', who lived for the shining hour, who did not take themselves seriously.'[21]

The attitude cultivated by fighter pilots from the first days on the Western Front had been hedonistic, light-hearted, little concerned with events outside their world. This was to some extent genuine, to some extent affectation. Nobody now could be indifferent to what was happening in Europe. A number of the pilots had first-hand knowledge of the rise of fascism from time spent on the Continent. James Sanders, who was brought up in Italy, had once at the age of nine sung, with the school choir, the slaves' chorus from Verdi's *Nabucco* in front of Mussolini himself. This encounter had induced no sentiments of respect. Later he got into trouble at school for using squares of newspaper, bearing the Duce's photograph, as lavatory paper. Billy Drake had been sent by his father, first to a German-speaking, then to a French-speaking school in Switzerland in preparation for a career in the hotel business. In the first establishment, 'I was the only English boy and all my classmates were Germans or Italians. I got a bit fed up with their sniping at the British Empire all the time. I spoke to the housemaster and told him what was happening and told him I intended to challenge them to a boxing bout every time it happened with him as the referee. And so I was knocked down about twelve times.'[22]

Pat Hancock was sixteen when, in 1935, he went to stay with a family near Hanover and attended the local school. 'I saw enough of the German youth movement to know how strictly disciplined they were and how confident they were that they had a great role to play in the world.' In the streets of Hanover he saw formations of troops marching everywhere. 'They were cock of the walk . . . everything glistened. I thought, my goodness, these are people who are going to have a go, given an opportunity.'[23]

During an air tour of Europe in the spring of 1935 Jeffrey Quill had stopped at Berlin. He wrote to his mother that he had arrived at Templehof 'in the middle of a sort of Hendon Air Display – they shot red lights at us to stop us landing but I was hanged if I was going to float round the sky waiting for their air display to finish, so I landed in the middle of it. They were a bit annoyed at first, but as I couldn't understand what they were saying I just laughed and they soon quietened down. They are much too serious up here.'[24]

Tony Bartley decided to visit Germany after being told by the captain of his rugby team, an RAF officer, that war was inevitable. After leaving Stowe school he had joined a City accounting firm to learn the profession, but left after a year. What he saw in the Reich impressed him profoundly. In Frankfurt-on-Main, staying with acquaintances of his parents, he came across a middle-aged man with a shaven head in the city's botanical gardens. He learned he was a distinguished Jew who had just been released from a concentration camp. He told him of his experiences and invited him home to meet his family. When Bartley informed his hosts, they were horrified and told him to sever the new friendship or return to Britain. When he asked for a reason, he was told that 'their son, a Hitler Youth, would denounce his father to the Gestapo for harbouring a Jew fraternizer'.[25]

Ben Bowring, who joined 600 Auxiliary Squadron in 1938, met Germans in Switzerland, where he was at school, and in America, where his father travelled for business, and later through friends in Britain. He 'absolutely loathed them. I knew them socially and they were always asking me to fly over to Germany and one thing and another. I knew perfectly well by their attitude that they were a very cruel type of people . . . [They] had quick tempers and they thought they were masters of everything. Since I was something of an athlete, if I beat them at a game they were quite upset and quite likely they wouldn't talk to you for a day or so. Or else if you beat them very badly they would come cringing to you on their knees (like) bullies, having been very unpleasant to you beforehand.'[26]

The same unsporting tendencies were to strike Richard Hillary when he went with an Oxford boat crew to compete in Germany in July 1938 in the 'General Goering Prize Fours' at Bad Ems. The team's attitude to the race appeared languid, an approach which annoyed their hosts.

> Shortly before the race we walked down to the changing-rooms to get ready. All five German crews were lying flat on their backs on mattresses, great brown stupid-looking giants, taking deep breaths. It was all very impressive. I was getting out of my shirt when one of them came up and spoke to me, or rather harangued me, for I had no chance to say anything. He had been watching us, he said, and could only come to the conclusion that we were thoroughly representative of a decadent race. No German crew would dream of appearing so lackadaisical if rowing in England: they would train and they would win. Losing this race might not appear very important to us, but I could rest assured that the German people would not fail to notice and learn from our defeat.

The Oxford crew won, by two fifths of a second, and took home the cup, a gold shell-case mounted with a German eagle. 'It was certainly an unpopular win,' Hillary wrote afterwards. 'Had we shown any enthusiasm or given any impression that we had trained they would have tolerated it, but as it was they showed merely a sullen resentment.'[27]

Hillary subsequently saw the race as a metaphor for the coming conflict, a 'surprisingly accurate pointer to the course of the war. We were quite untrained, lacked any form of organization and were really quite hopelessly casual'. This was a particularly British piece of mythologizing that was some distance from the truth. Hillary was fiercely competitive on the river, and the pilots of Fighter Command would turn out to be just as aggressive as their Luftwaffe counterparts. As for training, they had prepared for the war as hard as anybody. The problem was that much of the effort had been misdirected.

It was a question of image. The Fighter Boys, like the rowers, wanted to win, and took their superiority for granted. They would rather, though, that victory was attained without too much obvious exertion. The picture was of amused, easy-going Britons triumphing over robotic Germans. It was the view the pilots had taken of themselves and it was the way they wished to be seen. This, very soon, would come to pass.

It was true, however, that deep political thinking, let alone ideological conviction, was rare among the pilots. All the services had a tradition in which political enthusiasms were regarded as both unprofessional and socially undesirable. The RAF was different in that the majority of its members, the tradesmen and technicians, were from the ambitious upper working class or lower middle class and more inclined to question authority than their counterparts in the army. Junior officers could also be vocal about decisions by higher authority, especially where life-or-death matters concerning equipment or tactics were concerned, and the general conduct of the war would later sometimes be criticised.

At Cranwell, the debating society provided a formal arena for political discussion. In November 1938 the motion was that, 'This House considers that an agreement with Germany is in the best interests of Great Britain and of the world at large.' It was only narrowly defeated by thirty-six to thirty-four votes, after an intervention by a cadet who pointed out that 'the persecution of the Jews precluded any decent-minded people from having anything to do with the Germans'.[28]

Among the squadron pilots, though, domestic and international politics and the details of each crisis appear to have excited little interest. Billy Drake and the Tangmere pilots 'bought a newspaper to look at the sporting events, that's all. We didn't read it to find out what Hitler was doing. The attitude in the mess was that the war was inevitable, so why talk about it?'[29] Geoffrey Page's recollection was that 'pre-war and all through the war one never really discussed politics at all. It wasn't an issue . . . Two subjects were taboo in an officers' mess. You never talked politics and you never talked about the opposite sex.' The first prohibition was more strictly observed than the second.[30]

At Oxford, the University Air Squadron appears to have been gripped by the general sense of inexorability. By 1939 its members all assumed they were going to have to fight, despite the continuing optimistic noises being made by Chamberlain and his supporters. Individual political beliefs, where they were held at all, had become irrelevant. Richard Hillary was contemptuous of his bourgeois left-wing contemporaries and impressed but unconvinced by heartfelt pacifists. He and his contemporaries were perceived, he wrote, as superficially 'selfish and egocentric without any Holy Grail in which we could lose ourselves'. The war, by offering up an unmistakable and worthwhile enemy, had provided it. Now they had 'the opportunity to demonstrate in action our dislike of organized emotion and patriotism, the opportunity to prove to ourselves and the world that our effete veneer was not as deep as our dislike of interference, the opportunity to prove that, undisciplined though we might be, we were a match for Hitler's dogma-fed youth'.[31]

These were more complex sentiments than were felt by most of the pilots. Stephen Beaumont, notably decent and intelligent, was probably nearer the feelings of the majority when he reflected on the motives that had pushed himself and his upper middle class Yorkshire comrades to join the auxiliaries. 'Old-fashioned patriotism? Desire to give back to the community something for their – at least in some cases – admittedly favoured social background? Dismay, turning to acute dislike even hatred of the bullying they came to see in Germany? A desire to fly? Probably all these things.'[32]

The overseas pilots were moved by a simple sense of duty that must have seemed slightly anachronistic even in 1939. Asked later what he had been fighting for, Al Deere replied: 'In my generation, as schoolboys, we always thought of [Britain] as the home country, always referred to it as the Mother Country. That was the old colonial tie . . . There was no question that if this country was threatened, New Zealanders wouldn't go to war for Britain.'[33] It was the same for Adolph 'Sailor' Malan, a South African ex-merchant navy officer who settled in Britain in 1935 and applied for a short-service commission. Malan's voyages with the Union Castle line had taken him to Hamburg, where he 'spent a lot of time talking to German harbour officials, sailors and civilians. Their attitude made me realize that war was inevitable.'[34]

The pilots were joined by men who had no strong bonds natural with Britain, such as Billy Fiske, an upper-class American sportsman, captain of the US Olympic bobsled team, who volunteered two weeks after the outbreak of war. Several recruits came from Ireland. The fact that Eire was officially neutral and just emerging from a bitter independence struggle with Britain had made no difference to 'Paddy' Finucane, whose father had taken part in the 1916 Easter Rising, nor to John Ignatius 'Killy' Kilmartin, black-haired and sleekly handsome, who was to fight almost from the first day of the war to the last.

Acceptance, resignation, a certain thrilled apprehension seem to have been the predominant attitudes and emotions as the last days of peace slipped away. Not everyone answered the call of duty. In 609 Squadron one pilot decided to defect. He was, Stephen Beaumont recalled, 'not a particularly attractive man . . . We felt no loss at his going.' The squadron structure and the overwhelming importance of *esprit* meant that only the dedicated were welcome.

At Hornchurch, aircraft were now dispersed away from their hangars and along the far side of the airfield and tents put up to house the ground crews. A readiness system was introduced so that one shift of pilots was always dressed and ready to fly at short notice. It was to last until 1943 when the Luftwaffe no longer posed any serious threat to the country in daylight. Al Deere and the other pilots spent summer days stripped to the waist, filling sandbags to build the walls of U-shaped blast-protection pens that shielded their Spitfires. At Tangmere 1 Squadron and 43 Squadron skimmed their Hurricanes over the Channel waves, firing at splash targets with volleys from their Brownings that kicked up jagged white plumes and churned the water. The effect seemed devastating to old-timers brought up on the spindly fire-power of a single Lewis gun. 'The noise is not so much a rat-a-tat as a continuous jarring explosion,' wrote an RFC veteran.[35] By night they climbed into the Sussex skies, suspended between the stars and the street lighting that provided bearings and allowed them to keep station in the pre-blackout era. On landing, the ground crews would pounce to rearm and refuel in minutes, practising the rapid turnarounds that would prove crucially important in the fighting to come.

It was not all work. Squadron Leader Lord Willoughby de Broke arrived with the other members of 605 Auxiliary Squadron at Tangmere and entertained at Tangmere Cottage, opposite the base. The pilots, Peter Townsend remembered, 'spent wild evenings, drinking, singing, dancing to romantic tunes', with 'These Foolish Things', the hit of the day, revolving eternally on the gramophone.

All around, though, the peacetime landscape was changing. The whitish aprons and parade grounds of Biggin Hill were covered in chippings in a vain attempt to disguise the station from the air. On several nights, the lights of London were extinguished in a trial to test the efficiency of the blackout. A pilot reported that the ground 'looked like space inverted, just space with a few pinpricks of light like stars'. Barrage balloons wallowed in the air over town and suburb. The skies themselves were filled with ominous noises. In August, 200 bombers, fighters and reconnaissance aircraft appeared over London, Liverpool, Bristol, Birmingham, Manchester and Oxford, where they attracted the attention of RAF fighters and searchlight units. The aircraft were French, and the exercise intended as a test of Britain's air defences, but few could have looked up without a *frisson* of apprehension.

Death moved a little closer. The Oxford University Air Squadron and RAFVR summer camp at Lympne in July was overshadowed by a mid-air collision in which Pilot Officer David Lewis, an experienced pilot who was flying solo in a Hawker Hind, crashed into a Gipsy Moth carrying a pupil and instructor from the Kent Flying School. All three were killed. It was, the OUAS log recorded 'the first fatal accident in the squadron since it formed'.

Accidental deaths were commonplace, however, elsewhere in the air force, as pilots stalled, spun in, or flew into 'clouds with a hard centre' – hills obscured by fog. On one murky night at Biggin Hill, Flying Officer

Olding was sent up to report on the state of a practice blackout in the Greater London area. Soon after take-off his engine seemed to cut out, then the pilots in the mess heard an explosion. A fire tender was ordered out, but fearing it would never be able to locate the wreckage in the foul weather, Flying Officer Woolaston took off, intending to drop a magnesium flare near the crash site. A few minutes later a second explosion was heard. His Hurricane was found a hundred yards from Olding's, having flown into the top of Tatsfield Hill.

The effect of such events could be profound, but not necessarily lasting. Brian Kingcome was ordered to go and formally identify the body of a squadron pilot who crashed near Andover. He flew down and was met by a policeman who was concerned at the effect the sight of a mangled body might have on a healthy young man. 'The body had been quite badly battered, he warned me, and I braced myself for the worst. Gently he drew back the sheet . . . I looked at the broken body and felt curiously unmoved . . . On my way back to Hornchurch I briefly wondered whether there was not a lesson here: whether I ought to be more careful, stick more closely to the rule books . . .' The mood, though, 'was short-lived'.[36]

The number of fatal accidents inevitably increased as the 300 m.p.h. plus monoplanes, far harder to control than the biplanes, and in need of more room to recover if a mistake was made, were fed into the squadrons. At Tangmere, one pilot slid too slowly out of a turn and crashed in front of his comrades. Another time they watched as a pilot clipped the top of a tree coming in to land and burned to death before their eyes. Afterwards, Peter Townsend recorded 'we had our own methods of restoring our morale. In the early hours of that morning, in the mess, we mourned our lost comrade in our own peculiar way, which smacked somewhat of the ritual of primitive tribesmen. Fred Rosier took his violin and to the tune of the can-can from *Orpheus in the Underworld*, we danced hilariously round the mess.'[37]

Other atavistic instincts were stirring; the impulses to marry, or at least to have sex. The pre-war RAF discouraged officers from matrimony under the age of thirty. This was partly out of parsimony, partly out of considerations of efficiency and the desire to foster a mess-centred squadron spirit. What the service needed were single men free of family responsibilities, ready to move, at virtually no notice, where and when they were needed. Pilots had to seek the permission of their commanding officers before taking a wife. Failure to secure it meant no married quarters accommodation and no allowances. As the year wore on, the number of requests multiplied. On getting engaged to his girlfriend, Annette, Pete Brothers had to appear before Group Captain Dick Grice, the Biggin Hill commandant, who, 'fortunately . . . was a very charming chap. He was sitting behind a desk smoking a pipe, and he said, "You're very young" – I was just 21 – "what if I refuse?" I said in that case it would be very difficult to send him an invitation to the wedding.'[38] Grice, an immensely popular father figure with Biggin Hill pilots and staff, laughed and gave in.

Tim Vigors, on leave from Cranwell, took advantage of a trip to London to look up Kitty, a girlfriend who was staying in town with an aunt. They spent the evening dancing in a club off Regent Street, leaving at 3 a.m. Vigors daringly suggested that she come back for a drink. To his surprise she agreed and they repaired to the Regent Palace Hotel. He was prevented from taking matters further when a vigilant night porter blocked his path, protesting that Vigors had 'only booked a single and anyway she's far too young for those kind of tricks'. He 'tried to remain calm despite the fact that I had never felt so embarrassed in my life. "None of your business!" I retorted. "Come on Kitty, let's get inside and lock this bastard out!"' Kitty, however, burst into tears. Vigors gallantly drove her home and returned to the hotel 'feeling embarrassed, ashamed, angry and frustrated'.[39]

Senior officers, too, felt youthful stirrings as the great trial approached. Air Vice-Marshal Trafford Leigh-Mallory, the Air Officer Commanding No. 12 Fighter Group covering the Midlands and north, visited his pilots in 616 Squadron at their summer camp at Manston on the Kent coast. A dinner was laid on in his honour in one of the marquees. At the end of the evening the inevitable, well-lubricated games began. One involved climbing up the centre pole, squeezing through a ventilation flap, clambering over the ridge pole and re-entering the tent through the flap on the other side. Several pilots, including Hugh Dundas, did so without mishap.

> Then someone suggested that the AOC should have a go. Very sportingly, he agreed. But he was not really built for that kind of thing. In the course of the passing years his figure had thickened. He got up the pole all right. But he had a terrible job squeezing out through the ventilation flap. We stood below and cheered him on. At last he plopped through and his face, purple with exertion, disappeared out into the night. The tent swayed and the ridge-pole sagged as he struggled across the top. His legs reappeared on the other side. He got half-way and stuck.
>
> Shouting with laughter, we urged him on and his legs and buttocks wiggled and waggled as he fought his way through that canvas flap. Someone shinned up the pole and helped him with a few hearty tugs. He came out like a champagne cork, grabbed desperately at the pole and descended from a height of about ten feet in a free fall . . . He accepted a very large, very dark whisky and soda and left us hurriedly before we started playing something else.[40]

A few days later Dundas was sitting in the mess tent after a morning's flying when the news of the Molotov–Ribbentrop pact came through. 'Teddy St Aubyn, who was sitting opposite me, put down his soup spoon and said in a loud, clear voice: "Well that's . . . d it. That's the start of the . . . g war." ' Looking back, Dundas could not say why this pronouncement struck him with such force, given that, as he dryly remarked, 'Teddy . . . was not noted as a political pundit or a serious student of international affairs. But I heard his words and knew they were true.'

The announcement was finally made late on the morning of 3 September, a day that was generally remembered as being exceptionally warm, sunny and redolent of all the promise of young life. At fighter bases the length and breadth of the country the pilots gathered in the mess or clustered round portable radios rigged up at the dispersal areas to hear Prime Minister Chamberlain speak. At Tangmere, the pilots in Peter Townsend's flight were lying on the grass by their Hurricanes when they were told that 'the balloon goes up at 11.45'. They walked over to the mess, covered in pink creeper, and waited while the faithful stewards served drinks in pewter mugs. As the broadcast ended, 'the tension suddenly broke. The fatal step had been taken; we were at war.' Caesar Hull, a brilliant sportsman and aerobatic pilot who had joined the RAF on a short-service commission from South Africa, was the first to rejoice, repeating, 'Wizard!' over and over. He turned to another 43 pilot John Simpson, and laughingly prophesied: 'Don't worry, John, you'll be one of the first to be killed.' Simpson survived the war. Hull died a year and four months later while attacking a large formation of German bombers. That night, after being released, Townsend and his comrades raced to the Old Ship at Bosham. 'What a party we had; at closing time, we went out into the street and fired our revolvers into the air. Windows were flung open, people rushed from their houses, thinking the invasion had started.'[41]

At Cranwell, Tim Vigors and his fellow cadets were ordered to the ante-room to hear the broadcast. When the declaration of war came, 'a shout of excitement rose from all our throats. As one man we jumped to our feet cheering. There was not one amongst us who would not have been bitterly disappointed had the declaration of war not been made.' The same scene was taking place simultaneously in a classroom in Hull, where Charlton Haw and thirty of his fellow RAFVR pilots were gathered after being called up the week before. 'A tremendous cheer went out from all of us. We were very pleased about the whole thing. We didn't think about the danger. We all had visions of sitting in a Spitfire the following day. And then the disappointing thing was we were all sent home.'[42] In Romford, where he worked in the Ind Coope brewery, another reservist, William Walker, switched off the radio, put on his sergeant's uniform and walked out of his block of flats. A group of men were digging an air-raid shelter and he offered to help. 'They said: "No, not at all! You're in uniform. We can't let you do that sort of thing." '[43]

Charles Fenwick, who had recently joined the RAFVR, was one of the few to be surprised by the news. He was so buoyed up by happiness that he had refused to believe war could not be avoided. 'I was in love as only a twenty-year-old can be in love, I was all set for Cambridge, I owned a lovely little car and damn it I was enjoying life. Then this shit-head comes along and puts the lid on everything.' His first reaction was 'one of absolute shock, horrified shock . . . My second reaction was not long in coming. No bloody German was going to hurt those I loved and get away with it if I could stop him.'[44]

The pilots of 56 Squadron were sitting in small groups in the sun on the east side of the aerodrome at North Weald in Essex, listening to radios powered by outsize batteries. Earlier the squadron adjutant had distributed blue will forms to be filled in. 'There were great roars of laughter,' remembered Peter Down, a twenty-three-year-old who had joined eighteen months before. 'All we had to leave really were our golf clubs and tennis rackets and things. We had the odd car and there were shouts of, "Who wants my Lagonda?" or, "Who wants my clubs?" We left them to each other.'[45]

Not everyone was so light-hearted. Brian Kingcome was struck by the flatness of the address, devoid of drama or tension, 'just this, sorrowful defeated voice going on'. He looked around at his companions in the hangar office in Hornchurch, 'thinking to myself, probably the whole lot of us will be dead in three weeks . . . No sooner had Chamberlain finished his speech on the radio than we expected to hear the murmur of hordes of German bombers approaching and that became the norm at dispersal for a while.'[46]

5

Winter of Uncertainty

The war began in a flurry of false alarms. Air-raid sirens sounded almost immediately after Chamberlain's Sunday broadcast, sending civilians hurrying to the shelters. But no Germans came. The defenders were eager for action and trigger-happy. Three days after the declaration of war, a searchlight battery on Mersea Island in the Blackwater estuary spotted what was thought to be a hostile aircraft crossing the Channel coast. This exciting news was passed on to the Northolt headquarters of 11 Group, which covered the south-east of England. They, in turn, ordered the local sector controllers at North Weald to send up fighters to investigate. Hurricanes from 56 Squadron took off from North Weald aerodrome and climbed through the mist into the clear morning sky to hunt for the intruders. As they did so, their traces were picked up by the radar station at Canewdon, on the muddy tongue of Essex that sticks out between the Crouch and Thames estuaries. Even now, the cause of the tragic fiasco that followed is not entirely clear. Air Chief Marshal Sir Hugh Dowding, the Fighter Command chief, said later that the equipment was faulty and the baffle designed to block out electronic echoes from the landward side was not functioning, though this was disputed. To the operators it seemed they had located a big enemy formation coming in over the sea. More fighters were scrambled to deal with the apparent threat, and they in turn registered on the screen and added to the thickening confusion. Among them were twelve Spitfires from 74 Squadron at Hornchurch. 'A'

Flight, commanded by Adolph Malan, took off first. He led one section of three aircraft. Flying Officer 'Paddy' Byrne, an experienced, Irish-born pilot with a reputation for eccentricity, led another. In the adrenaline-charged atmosphere, chaos, then catastrophe, ensued.

Pilot Officer John Freeborn, barely out of Leeds Grammar School but well-freighted with Yorkshire obstinacy, was directly behind Byrne. 'It was a very misty morning but it was a beautiful day,' he said. 'I remember looking down and seeing we had cut a line through the haze where we had taken off. Malan was well in front . . . We saw these aircraft and Malan gave the order: "Number One attack – go!" They made an attack at these aircraft and then pulled away. And so we went and attacked.'[1]

The combat was only too successful. Freeborn, Byrne and the third man in the section, Sergeant Pilot John Flinders, swooped down in line astern. Freeborn and Byrne opened fire and saw two aircraft go down trailing smoke. Freeborn felt 'exhilarated' at their success. On the way back to Hornchurch he saw what he thought was a Luftwaffe bomber and was about to attack when Flinders yelled a warning on the R/T that it was in fact a friendly Blenheim. On landing he was met by his commanding officer, Squadron Leader George Sampson, and told that the aircraft he and Byrne had disposed of were Hurricanes from 56 Squadron. Pilot Officer Montague Hulton-Harrop was dead. He was nineteen years old, a newcomer to the squadron and 'tall, fair-haired and eager', according to Eric Clayton, a ground-crew member who maintained his machine. Pilot Officer Tommy Rose survived and showed up later in the day.[2]

Freeborn was appalled. He tried to find Malan, but he had 'done a bunk completely. Never saw him.' He and Byrne were put under arrest. 'I was sent to my room with a bloke from 54 Squadron to guard me . . . I was eighteen years old, frightened to bloody death.'[3] Coming soon after an incident when he had been severely reprimanded for landing with the undercarriage of his Spitfire up, Freeborn assumed his RAF career was over. The affair was particularly agonizing because, as squadron adjutant, he had previously distributed orders to the pilots telling them under no circumstances to shoot at single-engined planes. The instruction was based on the calculation that no Luftwaffe fighter had the range to reach Britain and that any single-engined machine was bound to be friendly. The speed with which Freeborn forgot the order was proof of the disorienting power of the heat of the moment. Al Deere, who was also scrambled that morning, had felt it too. 'We were all keyed up,' he said. 'You didn't think about the fact that a 109 could never have got as far as England from the then borders of Germany.'[4]

A general court martial was set for 7 October. Sampson, 'an absolute toff' according to Freeborn, put the pair in touch with Sir Patrick Hastings, an intelligence officer at Fighter Command HQ at Stanmore, who had been a leading QC in peacetime. Hastings agreed to act as prisoners' friend and told them to speak to Roger Bushell, another well-known figure at the London bar who was now commanding 600 (City of London) Auxiliary Squadron at Biggin Hill. Bushell, whose charm and indomitable nature made him one of the best-liked men in the air force, agreed to act as junior to Hastings. The proceedings were held at Stanmore and have never been made public. Freeborn claims Malan denied ever giving the order to attack. The defence argued that the case should never have been brought. After about an hour the four-man tribunal, led by the Judge Advocate, acquitted the two. It was the start of a long-running enmity in 74 Squadron. 'From then on,' Freeborn said, 'Malan and I never got on.'

'Sailor' Malan had already established himself as a formidable personality. He was short, with fair hair, blazing blue eyes and a square, impassive face and cleft chin. He was coming up to twenty-nine, considerably older than most of the other pilots. He had done much in a hard life, and spoken little. Adolph Gysbert Malan was born within sight of Table Mountain in Cape Province and brought up on a farm near the small town of Slent. As a child he roamed the veldt with a shotgun, developing a marksman's eye that would serve him well in the war. Aged fourteen he was sent off to a maritime college on board the training ship *General Botha*. The regime was spartan, the bullying institutionalized and the discipline harsh, bordering on the sadistic. Smoking was punished by six strokes of the lash. The victim was first certified as medically fit enough to withstand the punishment. He was ordered to strip to 'No. 1 Duck Trousers' – shorts – and given a rubber disc to bite on. Then he was stretched over a table in the recreation room and roped down to a ring bolt while the punishment was administered in public.

Malan once said: 'The first time I saw this punishment handed out it was to a big chap – an Old Salt (as the senior cadets were known). It was quite a shock to see him break down. Later on I understood why.' Freeborn had seen the scars from the whippings on Malan's back. His biographer wrote that 'in talks with Sailor, during which he described incidents infinitely more dramatic and perilous than anything that happened aboard the *Botha*, I never saw him more emotionally stirred than when he recalled the ceremony of being tied down and thrashed. The memory of it stayed with him vividly as a deed of outrage, an invasion of pride and privacy that helped to fashion a kind of stoicism that became an armour plating for the strenuous days to come.' The experience also made him reluctant, 'in later years, to join in the horseplay of RAF squadron initiating customs'.[5]

The 6 September débâcle was inscribed in RAF folklore as the Battle of Barking Creek, a reference to a nearby landmark which was a joke location beloved of music-hall comedians. It was one of several similar incidents, all efficiently hushed up (an official communiqué was not issued until seven months later), which revealed to the air force and the government the dangerous inadequacies of the country's air defences. On the same day as the 'Barking Creek' episode, Brian Kingcome was with 65 Squadron patrolling at 5,000 feet over the Thames. Every time they passed over the Isle of Sheppey, anti-aircraft guns opened up, even though the undersides of their Spitfires were painted black and white to identify them as friendly. A signal was sent to the batteries telling them to hold their fire, but it did not stop one aeroplane being hit in the wing and fuselage.

The basic problem was one of identification. The aircraft that sparked the panic on 6 September was, according to Dowding, carrying refugees from Holland. Other accounts say it was a Blenheim returning from a patrol over the North Sea, or an Anson from Coastal Command. Unless air traffic could be quickly and accurately recognized as friend or enemy, the potential for disaster was enormous. The problem had already been solved by a system called IFF (Identification Friend or Foe), a transmitter which sent back an amplified signal that established an aircraft's innocent intentions when picked up in a radar beam. But none of the Spitfires or Hurricanes chasing each other around the Thames estuary had yet been fitted with it. After the incident the installation programme was belatedly speeded up, so that by June 1940 it was standard equipment on every fighter.

The fiasco concentrated minds. Al Deere, who was with 54 Squadron at Hornchurch, noted that 'on five out of my next six training flights I was engaged on tactical exercises in cooperation with the control and reporting organization'. In retrospect he felt that some good had come out of 'this truly amazing shambles'. It was, he thought, 'just what was needed to iron out some of the many snags which existed . . . and to convince those who were responsible that a great deal of training of controllers, plotters and radar operators, all of whom had been hastily drafted in on the first emergency call-up, was still required before the system could be considered in any way reliable'.[6]

The mechanisms for identifying and reporting the approach of enemy aircraft, and the command and control structure to counter their attacks, would be refined and tested in the relative quiet of the winter and spring. Radar was at the heart of the system. It was based on the discovery that solid objects reflected radio waves. A projected radio signal, on encountering the metal skin of an aircraft, bounced back and registered as a blip on a cathode-ray tube. The military potential was obvious and the United States, Japan and, above all, Germany worked on applications throughout the 1930s.

Britain got radar late but it had recovered lost time and by the onset of the war was protected by two chains of transmitters covering the upper and lower airspace of the island's eastern and southern approaches. The twenty stations, with their mysterious 350-feet-high transmitters and 240-feet receivers, could locate aircraft a hundred miles away and give an approximate idea of direction, height and numbers. With radar, the historical defensive advantage given to Britain by the sea extended to the air. It was particularly effective over large expanses of water where there was no confusing 'clutter'. Even so it was to remain, for several years, an inexact science.

The electronic information pulsing on the cathode-ray tubes under the intense gaze of the Waafs, who were the most expert operators, was supplemented by the eyes and ears of the spotters of the Observer Corps. These were volunteers who squatted in sandbagged posts, equipped with binoculars, aircraft identification pamphlets and a crude altitude measuring instrument, trying to track enemy aeroplanes as they droned overhead. The blurred picture provided by the two was brought into sharper focus after passing through the filter room at Bentley Priory, an eighteenth-century Gothic mansion in Stanmore on the north-west edge of London, where Dowding and Fighter Command had their headquarters. There the reports were interpreted in the light of other data, and the distances of incoming aircraft reported by neighbouring radar stations subjected to a calculation known as 'range cutting' to provide a more accurate idea of their course.

The graded information was now transferred on to a map with red counters representing enemy aeroplanes and black counters friendly ones. The information was passed on to the operations rooms at each level of the chain of command – sector, group and Fighter Command HQ – where it was translated on to identical map tables. The development of a raid was watched by the controller and his staff from a balcony. The resources at hand to deal with the intruders were indicated on a large board rigged with coloured bulbs, which showed which squadrons would be available in thirty minutes, which were at five minutes' readiness, which were at two minutes' readiness and which were already in the air.

Fighter Command had a simple pyramid command structure, with Dowding, in Bentley Priory, at the top. One step down were the group commanders, each presiding over one of the four quadrants into which Britain's air defence had been divided. The south-west, and half of Wales, were covered by 10 Group, the middle segment of England and Wales by 12 Group, and Scotland and the far North by 13 Group. No. 11 Group, with responsibility for London and the south-east corner of England, was the busiest. Each group was subdivided into sectors that centred on a main fighter base, supplemented by a number of satellite aerodromes.

Raids fell naturally into one or another group's area of activity. When enemy aircraft were reported, the duty controller in the group operations room, in consultation with the group commander, decided which sector would deal with it and which aircraft would be 'scrambled'. Control of the fighters then passed to the sector controller, whose task was to manoeuvre his aircraft into the best position to intercept the raiders. He was helped in this by the IFF reports, which allowed him to keep track of his assets. The signal – 'Tally Ho!' – from the squadron or flight commander, meant that the enemy had been sighted and battle was about to be joined. At this point control of events passed to the pilots.

Orders and information were passed down the command chain and from pilot to pilot in a code that was very soon to enter public parlance and the popular imagination. The enemy were 'bandits' (the Germans called them *Indianer* – 'indians'). 'Angels' indicated altitude, so that 'Angels fifteen' meant 15,000 feet. 'Pancake' was an order to come back and land. 'Vector', plus a number indicating geometric degrees, gave the course a pilot was to steer. 'Buster' meant flat out. The trusty clock system – 'bandits at ten o'clock' – devised on the Western Front, provided an accurate fix on where the trouble was located.

The prevailing jumpiness of the first weeks of the war was partly because few of those involved in air defence had any clear idea of what to expect. The experience of Poland had suggested a blitzkrieg, sudden and pitiless, in which virtually everything was vulnerable. In fact the first German target was logical and conventional: the British Home Fleet, tucked away in the estuaries and anchorages of Scotland, from where it could menace Germany and its navy in relative security. On the morning of 16 October, twelve Junkers 88 fast bombers set off from Westerland on the Island of Sylt just off the Danish coast to attack shipping at the Royal Navy base at Rosyth on the north side of the Firth of Forth. The first group arrived at 2.30 in the afternoon, taking anti-aircraft gunners south of the Forth Bridge – just east of the base – by surprise. The main target was the battleship HMS *Hood*, but to the disappointment of the raiders it was in dry dock. Hitler, apparently anxious to avoid civilian casualties while there was still a chance of a settlement with Britain, had ordered that only ships on the water could be attacked.

Two targets presented themselves: the cruisers HMS *Southampton* and HMS *Edinburgh*, riding at anchor on the eastern side of the bridge. The Junkers were each carrying two 500-kg bombs. At 2,500 feet, several of them dived on the vessels and released their loads. Both ships were hit, but the bombs failed to do significant damage. Ten men were injured, none fatally.

The anti-aircraft batteries now opened up, joined by fire from the cruisers, which had previously been ordered to engage aircraft only if they proved hostile, presumably a precaution taken to counter the reckless gunnery of the first weeks. The action took place on the doorsteps of two RAF stations. Turnhouse, the home of 603 (City of Edinburgh) Squadron, just to the south of the Forth Bridge, and Drem, where 602 (City of Glasgow) Squadron was based. The raid was already several minutes old before Spitfires were in the air. As the bombers headed for home, they were chased out to sea. One was caught by three fighters from 603 Squadron, who opened fire, killing the rear gunner and shutting down the port engine. They were joined by another section from the squadron, who added to the fusillade battering the Junkers. 'He was responding with all his armaments; tracers were shooting past me, and I got a glimpse of a gunner behind twin guns,' one of the pilots, Patsy Gifford, said after the action. 'We went in again and gave him some more and I saw he was hit forward. Bits of fabric were dropping off and I thought I saw a red glow inside the fuselage.'[7] The Junkers hit the sea with bullets from the Spitfires stitching the water. The surviving three from the four-man crew were picked up by a trawler.

Another Ju 88 was shot down by 602 Squadron, also crashing into the sea. In both cases several pilots had been involved in their destruction. The official account recorded that this had been a team effort, but it singled out Gifford and two 602 pilots, George Pinkerton and Archie

McKellar, for special mention. They were identified not by name but by pre-war profession. The squadrons involved were auxiliaries. Gifford, like several others in 603 Squadron, was a solicitor; he spent his weekends driving a Frazer-Nash car very fast, shooting, fencing, taking out girls and flying. Pinkerton was thirty years old, and had left his wife, six-month-old daughter and fruit farm in Renfrewshire behind after the squadron was called up. McKellar was twenty-seven, short, aggressive and fit, and worked in his father's plastering business before joining the squadron full time. Gifford was to be killed the following spring, McKellar in the autumn.

The image they presented of social cohesion, of ordinary men from different walks of life coming together in the defence of their country, was naturally appealing to official propagandists. The fact that it was the amateurs of the auxiliary air force who had drawn first blood was given the maximum emphasis. 'Saturday Afternoon Airmen Shoot Nazi Bombers Down', was the headline in the *Daily Express*.

In other respects the Rosyth raid gave little reason for satisfaction. The fighters had not been able to prevent one of the raiders dropping an opportunistic bomb on a destroyer, HMS *Mohawk*, entering the Firth of Forth as the Luftwaffe was leaving, killing sixteen members of the crew, including the captain. Once again, the warning system had failed. Intelligence reports had predicted an attack, but from ten o'clock on the morning of the raid the local radar station was ineffective, due either to a power failure or a faulty valve. No sirens were sounded to alert the civilian population (though they were activated at military bases). Despite the rejoicing at the downing of two German bombers, the first raiders to be shot down, the Luftwaffe got off very lightly, given the superior speed and firepower of the attackers. That ten escaped was partly owing to the fact that the Spitfire pilots were under orders to go no closer than 400 yards, which was thought to be the most effective range for the Brownings. The pilots immediately recognized that getting in closer would produce more devastating results.

The bomber crews also benefited from a certain caution on the part of the defenders. When Hector MacLean, who had been training to be a solicitor in a Glasgow legal office before moving to Drem with 602 Squadron, was scrambled he 'couldn't believe it wasn't another mess-up because we'd been ordered off so often to intercept things and it had been a Blenheim or an Anson or something like that'. Spotting a bomber, he 'followed it gingerly thinking . . . I must not shoot one of our own fellas down, but there were the crosses so finally I had a go.' Having emptied his ammunition, he hurried back to rearm in preparation for a second wave that never came. Until the squadron moved south in August the following year, the only Germans he saw were 'mainly single aircraft sneaking over to take pictures and drop the odd bomb and attack convoys off the coast. It was easy to do. They could nip in, drop a few bombs around the boats and get out before we could get at them.'[8]

The same pattern of frustration and boredom settled over all the fighter squadrons in England and Scotland. Pilots spent their days at readiness, being ordered airborne to check out incursions by unidentified aircraft, 'X' raids as they were known, that almost always turned out to be friendly or else were too far off to intercept. Then there were the dreary convoy patrols, flying in circles over ships that were rarely attacked. There were occasional brushes with the enemy. On 20 November, 74 Squadron at Hornchurch recorded its first success when three pilots fastened on to a Heinkel 111 heavy bomber and shot it down over the Thames estuary. The following day two Hurricanes from 79 Squadron at Biggin Hill were patrolling over the south coast when they were ordered to investigate a radar sighting that turned out to be a Dornier 17 medium bomber on a weather reconnaissance. They found it, descended on it, opened fire and watched it explode as it hit the Channel.

On 3 February Peter Townsend took part in the destruction of the first German bomber to be shot down on British soil since the First World War, after 43 Squadron had exchanged bucolic Tangmere for the bleak surroundings of Acklington, high up on the north-east coast near Newcastle. He was leading his section on patrol over the sea, keeping at wave level to surprise any German aircraft, which tended to hug the clouds, when he saw a Heinkel. The crew saw nothing 'until the bullets began tearing into their bomber. Only then did red tracer come spurting from their rear guns, but, in the first foolish rapture of combat, I believed myself . . . invulnerable.' The Heinkel staggered over the cliffs at Whitby and crash-landed in snow behind the town. Townsend felt elated at the success – then, on hearing there were two survivors, a touch of remorse. He visited them in hospital. Then he returned to the mess to drink champagne. It was, he thought later, 'a horribly uncivilized way of behaving, really, when you have just killed someone. But an enemy bomber down was proof of our prowess, and that was a legitimate pretext for celebration. For the enemy crew, whom we had shot to pieces, we gave no thought. Young, like us, they had existed, but existed no longer. Deep down we knew, but dared not admit, that we had little hope of existing much longer ourselves. So, meanwhile, we made merry.'[9]

Death was more likely to come through accident than enemy action that winter. The need to have fighters on permanent standby around the clock meant that pilots were called on to do an increased amount of night flying, a skill to which insufficient attention had been paid before the war. George Bennions, now with 41 Squadron at Catterick, found it was 'automatically assumed that they would just send you off at night and there would be no problem'. The Spitfires they were flying were notoriously difficult to operate in a darkness which had deepened considerably with the introduction of the blackout. 'The long nose blotted everything out straight in front of you, and because the engine had very short stubs, all that you saw . . . was a great moustache of flame . . . The only thing you could do was to tuck your head back into the cockpit and take off on the instruments, which was all right for a trained pilot, but for new pilots who hadn't done any night flying, or very little, it must have been terrible.'

A Canadian pilot, Pilot Officer Overall, took off one night, circled round and flew straight into a house. Bennions protested at the stupidity of sending off pilots in pitch darkness without allowing them to first get familiarized in conditions of bright moonlight. A senior officer accused him of being afraid. His suggestion, though, was eventually adopted.[10]

Even the most skilful pilots found themselves in difficulties, especially when sensory deprivation was combined with incompetence on the part of those directing them on the ground. Al Deere nearly got killed while being guided back after a night patrol in total darkness by the Hornchurch controller, who vectored him straight into a clump of barrage balloons. It was no wonder that so many pilots hated and feared night flying.

The winter of 1939 is frozen in the memory of those who lived through it as the bitterest they ever endured. On many mornings, snow had to be shovelled off the aprons and runways and the Merlin engines of the fighters thawed out and run up before any flying could take place. The aircraft were often covered in a crust of ice and had to be scrubbed down with wire-bristle brooms. At Drem, the 'coldest spot on earth', the pilots sat in poorly insulated dispersal huts, clustered around a lukewarm stove, playing 'uckers' – a form of ludo – and waiting for the phone to ring. Very soon everyone could distinguish the tone of the 'ops' phone, announcing a scramble, from that of the 'admin' line. The bad weather would continue to make flying and life in general difficult well into the spring.

Conditions in the cosy brick messes and living quarters of the fighter station headquarters were bearable enough, but existence at the satellite stations could be miserable. The members of 32 Squadron, pilots and ground crew, had to move to Gravesend while Biggin Hill was temporarily closed so deep shelters could be dug and a concrete runway laid – part of a nationwide programme to replace the now embarrassingly anachronistic grass fields with all-weather surfaces. The squadron diarist recorded that 'the wretched troops lived in the utmost discomfort, sleeping on palliases on the floor and being fed from a cooking trailer . . . the NCOs also slept on the floor, and the less lucky of the officers.'

Great ingenuity was used in the pursuit of fun. When the well-connected sportsmen of 601 Auxiliary Squadron found themselves based briefly at Hornchurch around Christmas, the commanding officer, Max Aitken, son of the press magnate Lord Beaverbrook, used his show-business contacts to arrange for the cast of the Windmill Theatre to visit. The men loved the demure striptease for which the Windmill girls were famous. Several members of the Women's Auxiliary Air Force, the

'Waafs', who were now being posted to RAF stations around the country, walked out in protest, however.

For most pilots, though, life was spartan and uncertain, especially for the newcomers and those finishing their training. In letters home they recounted their daily routines, successes and setbacks in a tone of jaunty confidence that seemed designed to calm the fears of anxious mothers and fathers, brothers and sisters. Occasionally, though, a note of doubt or worry breaks through the surface of imperturbability, a reminder that behind the bravado were innocent young men, barely out of adolescence, green, apprehensive and homesick. Paddy Finucane, then at No. 8 Flying Training School at RAF Montrose, still sounds like a schoolboy in a letter to his younger brother, Kevin. 'How did you like *Robin Hood*? I saw it in London when I was at Uxbridge. It was on at the local fleapit and I enjoyed it immensely. The part I liked was when old Guy of Gisborne got a good twelve inches of cold steel in the bread basket. The fighting and shooting scenes were very good . . .'[11]

Noel Benson sent long, regular letters to his mother and doctor father at their house at Great Ouseburn, near York, throughout the winter of 1939 and 1940, detailing his progress. He had gone to Cranwell as a flight cadet in April 1938 after leaving Sedbergh public school. At the end of November 1939 he was with 145 Squadron at Redhill and Croydon and writing home to complain that the letters 'daddy' sends are not long enough. His main concern is the stinginess of the authorities in allocating petrol coupons, which may prevent him from getting home for leave. He seems to have spent much of his spare time quietly, visiting family and friends in the area for lunch and supper, dutifully negotiating the blackout to give lifts home to other guests. The news from the squadron was mostly domestic. A brother pilot was getting married and he would like to give him a dog as a present. A bitch in the Benson household had recently littered. Could they send photos of the pups so he can pick one out? Occasionally he vented his frustration at the inaction of the phoney war. One of his acquaintances was 'one of the lucky ones', who had been posted to one of the four fighter squadrons sent to France. On 11 December he was 'pretty fed up because there is absolutely nothing doing here. But the big bugs do such damn stupid things at times that it is enough to make anyone wild and fed up. If I try and say any more I shall probably choke with rage!!!'

Eleven days later he had been posted to 603 Squadron, now at Prestwick near Glasgow, and was 'busy from the word go. I started flying immediately which suited me fine.' At the end of the month he reported that he was 'having a very busy time here but like it very much. I am "on" from dawn to dusk, so you see I have not much free time. I am afraid there is no hope whatsoever of any leave for the next month or so.'

On the first day of the New Year, Benson was trained up and took his place as a fully operational member of the squadron. He found his comrades 'a very decent crowd', and liked the fact that, despite an influx of outsiders, the unit was still mostly composed of the pre-war amateurs. 'Being an auxiliary squadron they [all] had jobs before the war and this was really their hobby. So there is a lot of red tape brushed aside. The regulars in the squadron are quite often horrified at the irregular things that they do but I must say they get the job done.'

The squadron routine meant that time off was scarce. After three weeks' continual duty, he went with a friend to Glasgow, where they could 'hardly see a thing because just outside the city we ran into the smoke fog that hangs over the place, and although it was mid afternoon it looked like dusk. Everyone seemed to have long faces and I don't blame them if they are always in that muck.' There is no mention of girlfriends or even women. The boyish note, the thank-yous to uncle Reg for a cardigan and unknown donors for mittens to combat the hellish cold, gradually fades, edged out by a mounting confidence. For his birthday, he announced, he would like a car badge, 'in the form of a Spitfire. It must be a Spitfire, no other type will do.' On 8 February he reported 'we chased away another Hitlerite today, two in fact, but they nipped into the clouds before we got a smack at them'. Early in March he once again expressed his frustration, this time because the auxiliaries of 602 Squadron were seeing more action than his own unit. 'There is a good deal of friendly rivalry between us,' he wrote. 'We are rather annoyed because we have not seen any fun lately while this other squadron has been having all the fun.'[12] This fretting at not being in the thick of things earned him the nickname 'Broody', the commanding officer of 603 told Benson's father later, in a letter, 'because he was always so despondent if, for any reason, he was not allowed to fly'. He also 'had a habit of pondering over the many problems confronting him'.[13]

Noel Benson sounds from his letters to have been what was known as a 'keen type'. To be identified as such won a pilot official approval, but it invited mild, affectionate scorn from comrades who considered conspicuous effort to be slightly embarrassing. The truth was that almost everyone was keen. They were just reluctant to appear so.

Denis Wissler seems to have conformed more to the social norm. He was intelligent and warm-hearted to the point of vulnerability. His father was of Swiss origin, and came from the family that invented Marmite, whose London headquarters he ran. Denis joined the RAF on a short-service commission in July 1939 after leaving Bedford School, alma mater of a number of Fighter Command pilots. In January 1940, aged nineteen, he was in the middle of advanced training at 15 Flying Training School Lossiemouth, in the far north of Scotland. Wissler kept a journal, each evening recording the day's events, no matter how tired he was or how much beer had been taken, in a small red leather Lett's diary. It is a lively account: of days flying and fighting and evenings drinking, of flirtation burgeoning into romance. Sounding through it all is one dominant and recurring theme: his desire to succeed as a pilot and be worthy of the Fighter Boy camaraderie that he, like so many, felt with the force of love.

He began the course on 1 January, flying in the morning and 'feeling perfectly fit and quite at home in the air'. On 3 January he spent the day working on perfecting his rolls – the manoeuvre of rotating while flying straight and level. 'I did two and they were grand,' he recorded with satisfaction. 'I even gained height in the second.' Two days later he felt he 'had them taped now. My two best efforts were a roll at 1,000 feet then three rolls in succession'. The following week he had a flying test in which he was put through '(1) a spin (2) a slow roll (3) a loop (3) [sic] steep turns both ways to left and right (4) a forced landing (5) low flying

(6) slow low flying (7) and naturally a take-off and landing. The instructor said that it was quite good, but that my steep turns were split-arse (ragged and wild).' After a few days without flying, partly it seems because of restrictions imposed by the instructors, he was in the air again, but noted disconsolately that he 'flew very badly today, heavens knows why because I really felt on top of the world and was looking forward to flying again, but somehow it didn't just connect'. Despite the off days, Wissler was a good pilot. At one point he writes that he was asked if he would like to go on an armament course, which would mean rapid promotion and the chance of a permanent commission, but as it entailed a long course of lectures and exams and little or no flying, 'I said NO.'

The prospect of dying pointlessly, crashing into a hillside or misjudging a landing, was always present. On his second day he came back late from a session on a Harvard, an aircraft notoriously difficult to retrieve from a spin, to find that his fellow pupils had heard rumours of a crash and assumed 'I was a fried piece of meat . . . everyone was saying "poor old Wissler"'. A week later a pupil and instructor were killed after their aeroplane 'hit something, what, we don't know yet but it brought the plane down'.

Lossiemouth was an isolated spot, stranded on the chilly extremities of the Morayshire coast, but there were cinemas and pubs a few miles away in Elgin. Given the town's isolation, there seems to have been a variety of films to see. On 19 January Wissler and his friend 'Wootty' – Ernest Wootten, another short-service entrant – saw *The Ghost Goes West*, which he judged a 'grand film and really comes up to what everyone says about it'. In the next nine days he took in *Wuthering Heights*, *Jesse James*, *The Four Feathers* and *The Lion Has Wings*, a stirring story featuring Bomber and Fighter Command based on the raid on German warships in North Sea harbours at the beginning of the war, directed by Alexander Korda and starring Ralph Richardson. Sequences of it had been shot at Hornchurch using 'B' Flight of 74 Squadron the day after Barking Creek. The hard work in the air was supplemented by hearty drinking. On 2 February he wrote, 'we did no flying today as the weather wasn't good enough . . . In fact I did nothing until the evening when Wootty and I went out to the "Beach Bar" and met Sergeant Harman, one of the instructors in my flight, and I really got more drunk than ever before, so badly that I couldn't even stand.'

Despite the overall cheeriness that emanates from the faded ink, sometimes his mood faltered and dejection crept in. On 8 February he went down with German measles ('most unpatriotic'), came up in spots and was confined to bed. Four days later he was allowed out. 'I got up and walked down to flights. Wootty wasn't doing anything so he and I walked into Lossiemouth where I posted a letter home and bought a magazine to help while away the time this evening. Our dinner was quite uneatable tonight. Oh God what a hole this is and how glad I shall be to go.'

He was, it is clear, painfully homesick. The laborious procedures and long delays involved in making a trunk call, made worst by wartime restrictions, never deterred him from ringing home. After a night drinking strong ale mixed with draught bitter he none the less remembered his parents were waiting to hear from him and, after a lengthy wait for a line, 'carried on a small conversation. I could never have forgiven myself if I had missed one word Mummy or Pop had said.'

On Friday, 16 February, he and the rest of his class were given a leaving dinner in the mess and got appropriately drunk. The following day he learned he was going to St Athans in Wales to finish his training. He wrote the news in his diary on the train home to ten days' leave in wobbly writing, registering his delight. It meant that he was 'on fighters'.

It took several more weeks and another move to the operational training unit at Sutton Bridge in Lincolnshire before he finally took the controls of the aeroplane that would carry him through the rest of his war. 'I at last went solo in a "Hurricane",' he wrote on Wednesday, 20 March, 'and did five landings in fifty minutes. It is a grand aeroplane and not so very difficult . . . I can now wear the top button of my tunic undone, as is done by all people who fly fighters.'[14]

The remainder of Wissler's time at Sutton Bridge was spent on Harvards and Hurricanes, frequently practising the disciplined formation manoeuvres that were still considered to be the best training for air flying. In the evening there was snooker and darts in the mess or at the Bridge, a local hotel. The war was moving closer. At the end of March a request was made for volunteers to go to France to replace casualties in the four fighter squadrons based there. Wissler put his name forward, then reconsidered after worrying about the effect such a move would have on his parents.

At the end of April there was another flap when it appeared that one of the pilots was being posted to Norway. His order to move was cancelled at the last minute. It was a small example of the chaos surrounding an enterprise that was ill-organized and amateurish from start to finish. Dowding had been asked to provide fighter cover for an expedition to secure the iron-ore fields of northern Sweden and provide help for the Finns, who had been showing unexpectedly strong resistance to the Russian invaders in their 'Winter War'. Following the capitulation of the Finns to Moscow in March, the Germans had taken the opportunity on 9 April to seize ports and airfields in Norway as bases for an escalated war against Britain and the objective changed. The force was now charged with seizing them back and 263 Squadron was assigned to help them. The squadron had only been reformed six months previously and was equipped with Gladiators, which now had the look of museum pieces. It was facing 500 Luftwaffe combat aircraft, including 330 bombers. The pilots arrived near Trondheim on the evening of 24 April, having flown in from the aircraft carrier *Glorious*. Their base was to be on the ice of Lake Lesjaskog. The following morning the wheels of all the machines were frozen to the ice, the controls locked solid, and it was impossible to start the engines. To compound a hopeless situation, supplies supposed to have been waiting at a nearby port failed to arrive so there was no mobile radar, only two light guns for airfield defence and no petrol bowser or acid for the accumulators in the starter trolleys used to fire up the engines.

In the end these deficiencies were academic. The base was attacked by Heinkel 111s, which swept over, bombing and machine-gunning the Gladiators as they sat glued to the ice. The already demoralized ground crews, many of whom were new to the squadron, ran for the cover of the surrounding forest. By the end of the first day the squadron was reduced to five serviceable aircraft. By the end of the second day there were three, and on the third there were none. The squadron was withdrawn to re-form and re-equip. On 22 May it was back in Norway with its Gladiators as part of the force trying to capture Narvik, where it was joined by 46 Squadron, equipped with Hurricanes. This time it managed to operate on twelve days, flying 389 sorties and claiming to have shot down twenty-six enemy aircraft.

No. 46 Squadron also flew on twelve days and claimed eleven aircraft destroyed. It arrived in Norway from the *Glorious*, but had to return to Scapa Flow when the first airfield selected, near Harstad, turned out to be unusable. On their return they had to abandon a second base at Skaanland after two Hurricanes, including one flown by Squadron Leader Cross, ploughed into the soft ground and went tail-up, and the rest of the squadron was diverted to Bardufoss, sixty miles to the north. Flight Sergeant Richard Earp, who had gone to Halton from his Warrington grammar school before being selected for flying training, managed to land safely. He remembered Skaanland as 'nothing but a strip by a fjord. The troops had been working very hard out there and they'd covered the place with coconut matting and wire netting. Poor Cross came along to land on it and it just rolled up in front of his wheels.'[15] They washed in melted snow and lived six to a tent. 'All I had was a groundsheet and two blankets. You couldn't sleep. It was daylight all the time. It was terribly bloody cold.' As the decision was taken to abandon the campaign, the squadron was withdrawn.

Earp left on a fishing boat and was picked up by a destroyer that took him back to Scotland. When he returned to the base at Digby he found that 'there was hardly any of the rest of the squadron left'. On 7 June ten exhausted pilots of 46 Squadron managed to land their Hurricanes on the *Glorious*, despite the absence of arrester hooks, supposedly an impossible feat. No. 263 Squadron was already embarked. On the way back the carrier was sighted by the battlecruiser *Scharnhorst*, which opened fire at long range. The second salvo smashed into the ship, setting it ablaze. It sank within an hour, taking with it 1,474 officers and men of the Royal

Navy and 41 members of the RAF, including all but two of the pilots. It was the final disaster in a doomed campaign. From the cold perspective of Fighter Command, it was also a terrible waste of men and machines which would be badly needed in the months ahead.

6

Return to the Western Front

In Britain the Fighter Boys waited for the real battle to begin. Across the Channel a handful of pilots were getting a foretaste of what lay ahead. When, in September 1939, the British Expeditionary Force was sent to France, the air force inevitably went too. Four fighter squadrons were sent in the first week of the war to support the army and protect a small fleet of bombers, the Advanced Air Striking Force. This token deployment had been agreed earlier in the year. Dowding none the less protested, claiming he had been promised that no fighters would be sent until 'the safety of the Home Base had been assured'. His fear, justified as it was to turn out, was that once the war started in France, the RAF would be committed to providing more and more aircraft and pilots to fight someone else's battle, leaving the country's air defences fatally weakened when the Germans moved on to attack Britain.

The squadrons flew off to bases that would have been familiar to their RFC predecessors. Their daily patrols took them over shell-ploughed earth, splintered forests and shattered villages that were only just recovering from four years under the hammer of war. No. 1 Squadron arrived in high spirits in Le Havre, flying low over the town in a display of exuberance that impressed both the locals and the Americans crowding the port in search of a passage home. They spent their first night in a requisitioned convent, and their first evening drinking in the Guillaume Tell, the Normandie, the Grosse Tonne and La Lune. The latter was a brothel where the carousing could go on until dawn. The following day they blew away their hangovers with a choreographed 'beat up' of the town, looping and rolling in tight formation at rooftop height. While waiting to move to their forward base, the pilots spent the non-flying hours of the day playing football and writing letters home, and the evenings cruising the boulevards. 'We all felt that our first taste of service in France would probably be our last of civilization and peace for a long time and we wanted to make the best of it,' wrote Paul Richey, who had joined the squadron six months earlier. He took the opportunity to make his peace with God. The old *curé* at the church of St Michel heard his confession, 'giving me the strength and courage to face whatever was to come'.[1]

The No. 1 pilots had a rich variety of temperaments and backgrounds, typical of the established squadrons going into the war. The unit had served on the Western Front from 1915 and got through the inter-war years without suffering disbandment or amalgamation. Its leader was P. J. H. 'Bull' Halahan, whose Irish father had been an RFC pilot. His flight commanders were Peter 'Johnny' Walker from Suffolk, a member of the unit's acrobatic team at the 1937 Hendon Air Pageant; and Peter Prosser Hanks from York, who had been with the squadron since September 1936. There was an American, Cyril Palmer, known as 'Pussy'; a Canadian, Mark 'Hilly' Brown; an Australian, Leslie Clisby, who had been an RAAF cadet, and a New Zealander, Bill Stratton. There was also an Irishman, John Ignatius Kilmartin. 'Killy' was a romantic figure with black wavy hair and chiselled good looks who had been born in Dundalk in 1913, one of eight children of a forester. His father died when he was nine and he was dispatched to Australia under a scheme for orphans known as 'Big Brother'. As soon as he was old enough to work, he was sent to a cattle station in New South Wales, where he lived for five years. He moved on to Shanghai, where he had an aunt, and got a job as a clerk in the Shanghai gasworks. In his spare time he rode as a jockey for Sir Victor Sassoon. Seeing an advertisement offering short-service commissions, he applied, was summoned for an interview and made his way to London via the Trans-Siberian Railway in company with a group of Sumo wrestlers heading for the 1936 Berlin Olympics.

There were four sergeant pilots: Arthur 'Taffy' Clowes and Fred Berry, both of whom had begun their careers as aircraft apprentices in 1929 and volunteered for pilot training, and Frank Soper and Rennie Albonico. The best-known member of the squadron was to be Paul Richey, whose *Fighter Pilot*, based on his diaries and published in 1941, was one of the best books ever written about the experience and ethos of air fighting, and still rings with unalloyed authenticity. Richey was educated at the Institut Fisher in Switzerland and at Downside. He was intelligent and amusing and a good linguist. He was also tall, blond and strikingly good-looking. Cuthbert Orde, who had been a pilot in the RFC before he became a war artist, found him at first 'rather quiet, shy and serious minded', while acknowledging his enthusiasm for a party. Richey's comparative sophistication disguised a strong humanitarian streak and an unusual ability to analyse his feelings. He sympathized with the victims of the war, whoever they might be. It was a quality he shared with Billy Drake, another middle-class Catholic boy in 1 Squadron who displayed a marked sense of decency.

By the middle of October, after several moves, the squadron settled down at an airfield near Vassincourt, perched above a canal and a railway line amid lush and watery cow pastures near Bar-le-Duc where Champagne meets Lorraine. No. 73 Squadron was based not far away at Rouvres, on the drab Woevre plain, east of the heights of Verdun. Their duties were to protect the Advanced Air Striking Force, deployed around Reims and made up of Fairey Battle and Blenheim light bombers in support of the French army holding the Maginot Line along the Franco-German frontier.

To the north were 85 and 87 Squadrons, equipped with Hurricanes, who formed the fighter element of the air component of the British Expeditionary Force (BEF). They were joined on 15 November by two auxiliary squadrons, 607 (County of Durham) and 615 (County of Surrey), in response to persistent demands from the French government for British forces in France to be strengthened. They would have to make do with their Gladiators until Hurricanes arrived. The Hurricanes' wide undercarriage made them less likely to come to grief on the rough grass airfields of northern France than the Spitfire with its narrower wheelbase. There was also a strategic reason for the decision not to send Spitfires. Dowding's vision of a French campaign turning into an unstoppable drain on resources had made him determined not to risk his most valuable weapon in the enterprise.

The pilots of 1 Squadron were billeted in Neuville, a few miles from the airfield, a village accustomed to being washed by the tides of war, having been twice occupied by the Germans, in 1871 and 1914. The squadron flew patrols whenever the poor weather permitted. On a clear day the view from the cockpit was sublime, with the Rhine winding in the distance, beyond it the Black Forest, and way off, glittering on the far horizon, the white battlements of the Swiss Alps. As in Britain, friends were at first to prove more dangerous than enemies. Richey, mistaken for a German, was attacked by two French pilots in Morane-Saulniers, the relatively slow and underarmed standard fighter of the Armée de l'Air. Fortunately his Hurricane's superior performance allowed him to shake them off.

On the afternoon of 30 October 1939, a gloriously sunny day, the unfamiliar drone of bombers was heard high over the airfield, sending the pilots scrambling to get airborne and give chase. Ten miles west of Toul, Pilot Officer Peter 'Boy' Mould, an ex-Cranwell cadet who joined the squadron in June, caught up with a Dornier 17 cruising along at 18,000 feet. Mould approached from behind, hosing the bomber nose to tail with his Brownings. The Dornier, according to the squadron operations record book, 'appeared to have been taken by surprise as no evasive tactics were employed and no fire was encountered by PO Mould'. It caught fire immediately, plunged into a vertical dive and exploded into the French countryside. The only discernible remnants of the crew of four were five hands recovered from the wreckage, along with a mangled gun and an oxygen bottle with a bullet hole in it, which were taken off to the mess as trophies in an echo of old RFC practices. The human debris was buried with full military honours but Mould felt bad about his victory, getting very drunk that night and telling Richey: 'I'm bloody sorry I went and looked at the wreck. What gets me down is the thought that *I* did it.'[2]

For much of the time there was little to do, apart from patrol and practice attacks on 'enemy' Battles. The problem, from the fighter pilots' point of view, was not that there were too many Germans, but too few. When they did appear, usually flying high on cautious reconnaissance missions along the frontier defences, there was a rush to get at them that could produce moments of black farce. On 23 November, after weeks of fruitless patrols, bad weather and exercises, there was, for a change, plenty of activity. Between them 1 Squadron and 73 Squadron accounted for five Dorniers and a Heinkel 111. The Heinkel was heading home when it was spotted at 20,000 feet between Verdun and Metz by a section of three Hurricanes from 1 Squadron, who chased it over the German frontier. The effect of their repeated attacks was limited owing to the fact that at least eleven of the Hurricanes' guns were frozen because of the altitude, a fault later remedied when engine heat was fed to the gunports. The last bursts, which finally brought the Heinkel down, were fired by Taffy Clowes, the ex-Halton boy who was one of the squadron's most dogged and skilful pilots. As he was breaking away, six French Moranes rushed in, firing wildly. One of them smashed into his tail, destroying half the rudder and one of the elevators. The French pilot was forced to bale out and it was only by an extraordinary display of virtuosity that Clowes was able to nurse his machine back to Vassincourt, where he crash-landed. Richey noticed that, when he emerged from the cockpit, 'though he was laughing he was trembling violently and couldn't talk coherently'.[3]

Clowes's experience was one of several dramas on an eventful day. Earlier Pussy Palmer had led a section from 'A' Flight against a Dornier, setting it on fire. The rear gunner and navigator escaped by parachute, but the pilot flew on. As Palmer drew alongside, the German throttled back, causing the Hurricane to overshoot. Then he fastened on to Palmer's tail and opened up, hitting the aircraft thirty-four times. One round, which punctured the locker behind Palmer's head and smashed the windscreen, would surely have killed him if he had not put his machine into a dive.

With clouds of smoke issuing from the engine, he prepared to bale out, but when they dispersed, strapped himself in again and crash-landed with his wheels up. The others in the flight, Killy Kilmartin and Frank Soper, returned to the attack, and this time the Dornier went down. Miraculously the pilot seemed unharmed as he clambered out of his devastated machine, giving them a wave as they circled overhead.

The pilots were reluctant to abandon the notion that a trace of chivalry clung to the business of air fighting. That night, in a gesture the RFC would have recognized and applauded, 1 Squadron decided to honour the pilot who had fought so doggedly and well with dinner in the mess. By now he was in the hands of the French at Ste Menehould gaol, and Billy Drake, who like Richey spoke good French, was sent off to borrow him for the evening. His captors reluctantly let him go, on condition that he was accompanied by a gendarme and delivered to the citadel at Verdun when the evening was over.

His name was Arno Frankenberger, and he had been a glider pilot before the war, when he joined the Luftwaffe, volunteering for special reconnaissance duties. The pilots did their best to help him relax, removing trophies from the mess and insisting on first names. It was hard work. At first he stood up every time he was addressed by an officer. After a while he fell silent and put his head in his hands. Peter Matthews, a twenty-year-old pilot officer from Liverpool who had planned to follow in his father's footsteps and become a vet, but applied for a short-service commission instead, watched what happened next. 'He left rather hurriedly,' he said. 'When he came back in about five minutes' time he was full of beans. He said, "You know, I was told by my officers that the British air force were a bunch of swine, but you're all very nice chaps." '[4] In these improved spirits he boasted that the German maps of Britain were better than the ones of the German frontier the squadron had pinned up on the mess wall, and that the new variation of the Messerschmitt 109 was superior to the Hurricane.

The Hurricane pilots had yet to put this proposition to the test and would not come face to face with the Luftwaffe's most lethal fighter until the spring of 1940. The intervening months were spent patrolling, training and learning what they could from limited experience. Pussy Palmer's narrow escape had demonstrated the vital need for armour plating behind the pilot's back. In front, there was a bullet-proof windscreen insisted upon by Dowding in the face of the objections of cost-conscious Air Ministry officials. The engine block also gave forward protection. The squadron put in a request for steel plates to be fitted behind the seat. Hawker's were consulted, but again there were objections, this time on the grounds that the extra weight would upset the aeroplane's centre of gravity and impair its flying performance. Bull Halahan was not deterred. The bomber pilots had armour. He tracked down a wrecked Battle and had the steel plating removed and fitted on a Hurricane. The squadron record book noted that 'although this alters the flying characteristics . . . to some extent, it most certainly adds to the pilot's confidence'. The benefit greatly outweighed the disadvantage. Hilly Brown, the Canadian short-service officer who at twenty-eight was one of the squadron's most experienced pilots, was sent back to Britain with the modified aircraft and gave a demonstration of aerobatics that persuaded the Air Ministry experts to change their minds. By mid March 1940, all No. 1's Hurricanes had been equipped, and from then on the armour was fitted as standard equipment to RAF fighters, saving many lives.

Halahan's refusal to be baulked was characteristic. He was determined to introduce any innovation that added to the safety and efficiency of his men. Halahan was one of the first to realize that the official range at which fighter aircraft had their eight guns harmonized was misjudged and would significantly reduce their destructive power. Before the war Dowding had decided that concentrating machine-gun fire in a cone 400 yards ahead of a Hurricane or Spitfire was the most effective way of bringing down a big target like a bomber, while keeping his men at the limits of the enemy defensive fire. The decision had been taken in the innocent days when it seemed that bombers were all that Fighter Command were likely to meet. Halahan and his pilots were unconvinced. They doubted that at 400 yards .303 bullets still had the velocity to fly true and penetrate armour, or that the spread would be dense enough to destroy the target, especially if it was a small one like an Me 109. During the squadron's annual month's shooting practice in the spring of 1939, all the guns had therefore been quietly harmonized at 250 yards. The modification meant that pilots had to get in closer. But as events in France were to prove, it made the Hurricanes of 1 Squadron considerably more lethal than those of other squadrons shooting at the official range, and eventually the 250-yard harmonization became standard.

Another innovation was borrowed from the Luftwaffe. British fighters in France had the underside of one wing painted black and the other white, which the pilots felt made them look like flying chequer boards. German aircraft were duck-egg blue, to blend in with the sky and diminish their visibility to attackers lurking underneath. Halahan ordered the squadron machines to be painted the same colour, and this in turn was also adopted by all RAF fighters.

Contrary to his bruiser appearance, Halahan was a thoughtful officer who tried hard to divine the likely nature of the approaching battle and sought to prepare the squadron as best as he could, one evening delivering a lecture on what the war would mean for fighter pilots. He was equally concerned about the well-being of those under his command, introducing rotas to give pilots and airmen regular breaks and arranging diversions and encouraging excursions to make off-duty time as enjoyable as possible. Neuville, a cluster of utilitarian streets relieved by a few rustic half-timbered houses and presided over by a handsome Romanesque church, was welcoming enough. Pilots and airmen were treated with warmth in the houses where they lodged and durable friendships were made. The officers established their mess in the *mairie*. The sergeants set up an English-style pub in a café.

Paulette Regnauld, who was fourteen when the *aviateurs Brittaniques* arrived, remembered them as 'polite and friendly. They mixed in well. There was a certain amount of flirting but they behaved themselves. They were generous and gave us meat and chocolate. At Christmas there was a big party at the *mairie*, where they chased all the pretty girls.'[5] More than sixty years on she still retained some souvenirs. Sitting at the kitchen table in her house in the town square, she produced a postcard from an airman, William Mumford, sent from Uxbridge while on leave in February 1940. A photograph, printed in the dense monochrome of 1940 film, showed Pussy Palmer, Killy Kilmartin and several other pilots standing amiably in front of the church, smiling at the camera. The long shadows cast by the sinking winter sun throw the well-muffled silhouettes of the woman taking the picture and her female companion across the church steps. The pilots are in flying boots and sheepskin jackets. The cold is almost palpable.

Neuville, for all its friendliness, had its limitations. On days off pilots would fly up to Rouvres to meet their friends in 73 Squadron or head off to Nancy, Metz or Bar-le-Duc, where the Hôtel de Metz was their unofficial headquarters and the wife of the owner's son, Madame Jean, welcomed them as if they were family. At Nancy the main attraction was the Roxy, described by Richey as 'low-ceilinged with a dim, religious light. It had a bar at one end and a dance floor at the other. Round the plush-draped walls were crowded tables and comfortable chairs. The bar was invariably surrounded by a throng of British and French air force officers and "ladies of the evening", waiting to be given a drink, a good time and anything else one could afford.'[6] It was a scene that would have stirred memories for Cecil Lewis.

The winter was as cruel in northern France as in Britain. For weeks at a time snow and blanketing cloud made flying impossible. The ground was iron hard, wrecking the tail wheels of the Hurricanes as they taxied out to take-off or touched down after a patrol. The squadron worked hard whenever circumstances allowed. Sightings of enemy aircraft were occasional and usually inconclusive. The pilots found they could not climb quickly enough to reach the high-flying reconnaissance aircraft as they crawled tantalizingly across the sky 20,000 feet overhead. One problem was that their Hurricanes were fitted with early two-bladed wooden propellers. The pitch of the airscrew could not be varied to improve acceleration and achieve the optimum rate of climb the engines were capable of delivering. The problem was solved when the first machine with a three-bladed constant-speed airscrew, which automatically adjusted to the rate of revs to get the best results, was delivered in April 1940. Halahan was the first to fly it, followed by the more experienced pilots, all of whom, the squadron log recorded, 'were greatly pleased by its superior performance'. From then on the old Hurricanes were gradually replaced by the new models, but some pilots were still flying with wooden propellers when the fighting began in earnest.

In March the weather began to improve slightly and patrolling became more intense. Two new pilots arrived at the squadron, Pilot Officer Robert Shaw and Flying Officer Harold Salmon. Shaw, from Bolton, had been one of the first to join the RAFVR and had only been called up to full-time duty at the outbreak of war. Salmon had learned to fly with the RAF in 1933 and was summoned from the reserve in September 1939. Both had done conversion courses to Hurricanes before being posted to France. Halahan was not impressed by their preparations. The record book noted: 'It is observed that new pilots sent out from England are insufficiently trained and [sic] too few hours on type to be familiar with its limitations. They also appear to have had little or no practice on R/T [radio telephony] and to have never used oxygen. It means time taken off from squadron duties to give these pilots the necessary training for active service, and also adds to the precious aircraft hours to allow them to do non-operational flying.' Both men were to remain with the squadron throughout the summer, with Salmon claiming an Me 110 and a probable Me 109. Shaw was less successful. In his brief life as a fighter pilot he shot nothing down. He was himself attacked by a British fighter over the Sussex coast in August and forced to land. On 3 September he failed to return from a patrol and was reported missing, one of the many unremarked young pilots among Fighter Command's dead that year.

The pilots of 73 Squadron had seen more action than those of 1 Squadron. This was due partly to their closer proximity to the frontier, partly to a more aggressive approach that sometimes took pilots scores of miles over the German lines in defiance of standing orders. The most willing to take risks was Flying Officer Edgar 'Cobber' Kain, a twenty-one-year-old New Zealander who had first attracted attention when he entertained the crowds at the 1938 Empire Air Day show with a particularly daring aerobatic display. In November 1939 he destroyed two Dorniers and in

January 1940 won a DFC. Kain was regarded by his peers as a 'split-arse pilot', a term that mixed approval with concern, and his approach bordered on recklessness.

Kain soon became known to British newspaper readers through the efforts of correspondents based at Reims, who, after he had shot down five enemy aircraft by the end of March, proclaimed him the first 'ace' of the war. Halahan disliked this development, as did others further up the RAF chain of command. Halahan preached caution, feeling there was no point in risking precious lives and machines before the real battle started. No. 1 Squadron seldom crossed the frontier. When it did it was at high altitude, turning back in a sweep to draw any German fighters out. Halahan was also strongly against publicizing the acts of single pilots, believing it undermined squadron spirit, and he banned newspaper reporters from the base. The Air Ministry had initially seemed to welcome publicity, sending four experienced journalists to act as press officers to France, but it was soon in conflict with the special correspondents. Despite the eagerness of the hacks to produce patriotic material, officials fretted about security and imposed heavy censorship that resulted in dispatches being slashed and rewritten out of recognition. Air Marshal Sir Arthur Barratt, the commander of the British Air Forces in France, also shared the view that creating 'aces' was bad for the morale of ordinary squadron members. When Barratt forbade interviews with pilots and ordered that all information must be filtered through service press offices, news organizations sulked and finally withdrew their men from France.

But the newspapers had recognized that Fighter Command, whose purpose and character were still known only vaguely to the British public, was a rich potential source of stirring copy and were bent on their myth-making mission. In an aggrieved article complaining about restrictions, the *Daily Express* correspondent, O. D. Gallagher, wrote: 'The young men of the RAF who have not yet spread their wings in wartime need their heroes. They're entitled to them, and whatever the policy-makers may say on this score, they're going to have them.' So it came to pass, but at a time when authority had decided that the propaganda benefits of publicizing fighter pilots overwhelmed all other considerations.[7]

The long-awaited encounter with the Messerschmitts came, finally, at the beginning of March. Cobber Kain had the first success, downing an Me 109 on 2 March over the German lines near Saarbrucken. His aircraft was badly shot up in the fight and he was forced to crash-land near Metz. His attacker was probably Oberleutnant Werner Molders, a veteran of the Spanish Civil War, who was himself in the process of acquiring the status of an ace. Kain's standing, and his at this stage rare first-hand experience of the Luftwaffe's machines, pilots and tactics, persuaded the authorities to bring him back temporarily to Britain to lecture to pilots in training. Christopher Foxley-Norris, by then preparing to join an army cooperation squadron equipped with lethally slow Lysanders, was present when Kain gave a talk on fighter evasion. 'At the end, somebody got up at the back and said, "You've told us how to evade one fighter, sir. What happens if you meet two?" To which the answer was, "Oh, most unlikely. They haven't got many aircraft and they're very short of fuel."' The next time Foxley-Norris saw the questioner he was 'being chased around a church steeple by six 109s'.[8]

The Me 109 was to turn out to be the most feared aeroplane in the Luftwaffe's line-up but that was not how it seemed in the spring of 1940. The attention of everyone in the RAF was equally focussed on by the twin-engined Me 110s, which had been designed with the dual roles of clearing the way for the Luftwaffe bomber fleets and attacking incoming enemy bombing raids. The aircraft's boastful nickname, *Zerstörer* (Destroyer), and its nominal top speed of nearly 350 m.p.h. at 21,500 feet – the same as a Spitfire and slightly faster than a Hurricane – made it the subject of apprehensive fascination. Air Marshal Barratt even offered dinner in Paris to the first pilot to shoot one down.

The distinction fell, collectively, to three No. 1 Squadron pilots, who between them on 29 March destroyed three Me 110s. Johnny Walker, Bill Stratton and Taffy Clowes were ordered up in the early afternoon to patrol over Metz at 25,000 feet. Half an hour after taking off they spotted nine Me 110s cruising unconcernedly in sections of three in line astern, east of the city. Once attacked, according to the squadron record, the German machines 'proved very manoeuvrable, doing half-rolls and diving out, coming up in stall turns'. The ensuing dogfight followed the inexorable physical rules of such engagements, with the advantage shifting from attacker to attacked and back again as they followed each other's tails in a downward spiral that in no time brought the mêlée to a bare 2,000 feet. Walker and Stratton ran out of ammunition and returned to Vassincourt, believing they had crippled one machine, the wreckage of which was later found. Clowes meanwhile had disposed of two. After hearing their accounts, the consensus was that the Me 110s were not as fearsome as their name suggested. The record concluded: 'As a result of this combat it may be stated that the Me 110, although very fast and manoeuvrable for a twin-engined aircraft, can easily be outmanoeuvred by a Hurricane.' The pilots also reported that 'it appeared that the rear gunner was incapable of returning fire whilst [the] Me 110 was in combat because of the steep turns "blacking him out" or making him too uncomfortable to take proper aim.' Barratt kept his promise. Two days later he sent his personal aircraft to whisk the three to Paris for dinner at Maxim's.

On the morning of their success, Paul Richey brought down the squadron's first 109. It was a fine day with high, patchy cloud when he took off with Pussy Palmer and Peter Matthews towards Metz. Noticing puffs of smoke from French anti-aircraft fire hanging in the sky, they went to investigate and saw the pale-blue bellies of two single-engined fighters 1,000 feet overhead. As they climbed to reach them, they were attacked from behind by three other 109s that nobody had noticed. Matthews called a warning over the R/T and Palmer jammed his Hurricane into a sharp turn to the left in what was to become the standard, desperate move to escape a pursuing 109. In doing so he lost control and spun down for 12,000 feet before straightening out. Matthews also dived and turned, and as the G forces drained the blood from his head he blacked out, coming to only at 10,000 feet. Richey continued to climb in a left-hand turn. Watching his tail, he noticed an aircraft moving behind him, but was unsure whether it was friend or foe and waited to see if it opened fire. When it did, he twisted down underneath his nose. 'As I flattened out violently,' he wrote, 'either he or one of the other 109s I had seen above dived on my port side and whipped past just above my cockpit. He was so close that I heard his engine and felt the air wave, and I realized that he must have lost sight of me in the manoeuvre. He pulled up in front of me, stall-turned left and dived steeply in a long, graceful swoop with me on his tail.' The German was faster in the dive than Richey. But when Richey pulled up violently and began climbing steeply, he started to gain on him. When, eventually, he was a few hundred yards distant, he 'let him have it. My gun button was sticking and I wasted ammunition, but he started to stream smoke. The pilot must have been hit because he took no evasive action, merely falling slowly in a vertical spiral. I was very excited and dived on top of him, using my remaining ammunition.'[9]

Many pilots were to feel the same rush of elation at the sight of smoke and flame or the first barely perceptible faltering of control that showed a pilot was hit. The temptation to follow the machine down to its fiery end was overwhelming. It was the same instinct that makes a boxer hover over his dazed opponent as he is counted out on the canvas. A pilot had to learn to suppress this impulse if he was to improve his chances of staying alive. By giving in to it he could lay himself bare to another enemy fighter who, unnoticed, may have fastened on to his tail during the intense seconds of combat. Sure enough, as Richey broke away, he noticed another 109 about 2,000 above him. Instead of running for it, he turned to face him. The German, either through caution or lack of ammunition, fled.

That night there was a celebration, first in the officers' then in the sergeants' mess. Toasts were drunk from a special bottle of rum and a 'victory' card signed. Before the party started, Richey 'went across to the village church opposite the mess to say a prayer for the German pilot I had killed, before I got too boozy. The door was locked, so I knelt on the steps and prayed for him and his family and for Germany.' In fact, as he was to discover later, his opponent had crash-landed near Saarburg and survived.

As the countryside thawed out and the days lengthened, it was clear that the Germans were stirring and the fraught boredom of the phoney war was drawing to an end. Until now Luftwaffe activity had mostly been limited to daily reconnaissance flights, with individual or small groups of Dorniers, Heinkels and Junkers 88s snooping over the Maginot defences and the Ardennes sector of the border between France and Germany. The Messerschmitts had been restricted to patrolling their own side of the frontier, only occasionally venturing into Allied air space. From April the reconnaissance missions were more frequent and grew bolder, probing deeper into France, while the fighters came in large formations of up to forty aircraft wheeling brazenly over Metz and Nancy.

The longer hours of daylight meant longer periods at readiness and the day's patrolling now began at 6.30 a.m. when the first Hurricane slithered out across the clayey mud of the thawed-out airfield and took off towards the German lines. In two consecutive days at the beginning of April, the squadron shot down two Me 110s and two 109s. The tactics they had been taught in training were being revised or jettisoned, and new ones invented, with each new experience. One was the designation of one pilot in a section to act as lookout, criss-crossing the sky to cover all possible approaches and shouting a warning if anything was sighted. The value of the 'weaver', or 'Arse-End Charlie' as he became known, was demonstrated on 2 April when Les Clisby, Flying Officer Lorimer, Killy Kilmartin and Pussy Palmer set off after high-flying twin-engined aircraft. As they approached, Palmer, weaving at the back, noticed Me 109s above, waiting to pounce, and alerted the others in time for them to break off the pursuit and face the attackers, shooting two of them down. Palmer was not so lucky and had to bale out after his reserve petrol tank was struck and set on fire.

In mid April it seemed that the war had finally started when the squadron was moved at a few hours' notice to a new base at Berry-au-Bac, thirty miles north-west of Reims. But after a week, during which the log noted that the 'pilots are all fed up with the lack of activity and the long stand-by hours which seem of no avail', they returned to Vassincourt. The first full day back, 20 April, was the busiest they had so far experienced. In one encounter, Berry and Albonico claimed a 109 each, Hanks downed a Heinkel 111 and Mould a Heinkel 112, the first time the type had been engaged. At the same time, Walker was leading Brown, Drake and Stratton on another patrol which ran into nine 109s. Walker and Brown got one each. Billy Drake opened fire on two as they made off and saw one apparently go out of control. The other he followed to the frontier and watched it crash into a hill. Killy Kilmartin had meanwhile set off in pursuit of a high-flying Ju 88 and caught up with it at 26,000 feet, the limit of its altitude. The pilot dived to shake him off, and Kilmartin's Hurricane had a struggle to get within firing range, but eventually managed to score a hit, forcing the Ju 88 to land. It had been a good day for the squadron, the first in which almost all the pilots had seen action. Halahan noted with satisfaction that 'all the original pilots who were with the squadron when it came to France last September, with one or two exceptions, have had combats with the enemy. It is most commendable that the squadron has worked so well and made it a squadron "show" without any publicized individuality'.

By now it was clear that the main threat from the German side came from the Me 109s. The relative merits and shortcomings of the Hurricane and Spitfire compared to the Messerschmitt was to be an eternal subject of debate among pilots on both sides, who were understandably fascinated by the machines opposing them. Like the British fighters, the Me 109 owed much to the engineering prowess of one man. This was Willy Messerschmitt, whose restless creativity was exercised on a broad range of aircraft from gliders to the first jets. In the Me 109 he attempted to wrap a light airframe around the most powerful engine it would carry. The resulting design problems were as daunting as anything faced by Camm and Mitchell. The thin wings that gave the aircraft its superior performance were inefficient when flying slow, requiring a system of slots on the leading edges to increase lift on take-off and landing. Their fragility placed severe restrictions on the way guns could be mounted. Nor were they strong enough to take the machine's weight, a weakness which meant that the undercarriage had to be supported by the fuselage. This made for a very narrow and unstable wheelbase which was the cause of many crashes on landing. According to one estimate, 5 per cent of all Me 109s manufactured were written off in this way.

The Me 109 was smaller and frailer-looking than both its British opponents. It was shorter and sat lower on the ground. Its wingspan was only 32 feet 4 inches compared with 40 feet for the Hurricane and 36 feet 11 inches for the Spitfire. Its total wing area was 174 square feet, whereas the Hurricane's was 258 square feet and the Spitfire's 242 square feet. It had a top speed of 357 m.p.h., the merest shade higher than the Spitfire and perhaps 30 m.p.h. faster than the Hurricane. It carried two machine-guns mounted one on either side of the upper nose decking, each with 1,000 rounds. Each wing housed a 20 mm cannon and 60 shells.

The pilots of 1 Squadron had a chance to examine the German fighter close up when, early in May, they were summoned to Amiens to examine a machine that had been captured intact. Hilly Brown took the controls and, after a practice, mounted a mock dogfight with a Hurricane flown by Prosser Hanks. From this exhibition, the squadron log noted, 'several facts emerged. The Hurricane is infinitely manoeuvrable at all heights and at ground level is slightly faster. The Me 109, however, is unquestionably faster at operational heights and although appearing tricky to fly and not particularly fond of the ground, possesses many fine features to offset its disadvantages.' The report noted enviously that it had 'an excellent view to the rear' – something the Hurricane definitely did not possess. This sober assessment would turn out to be largely accurate. The aircraft was subsequently flown by Brown to the RAF experimental station at Boscombe Down for further testing.

The air force needed all the information it could get. The phoney war had, mercifully, given Britain the lull it needed to accelerate the manufacture of aircraft and the training of pilots, but it had provided little practical experience of modern air warfare such as the Luftwaffe had gained in Spain and Poland. Unlike 1 Squadron and 73 Squadron, the other four fighter units based in France had had little contact with the enemy. Their job was to support the BEF, which was doing nothing, and the buffer zone of Belgium lay between them and the Germans. Squadrons 85 and 87 were based at Lille–Seclin aerodrome, where they flew sector patrols in their Hurricanes. The two auxiliary squadrons, 607 and 615, which arrived in November still equipped with Gladiators, were in no position to inflict much damage on the Luftwaffe even if they had been called on to do so.

Roland Beamont joined 87 Squadron at Seclin in October after a rare moment of excitement. 'Two days before they'd shot down their first enemy aeroplane. It was a Heinkel 111. I arrived just in time to take part in the celebrations with an Air Ministry photographer out there taking pictures of all the ground crew holding on to various parts of the Heinkel that had been sawn off it with black crosses.' Photographs were also taken of the pilots running to their Hurricanes as if they had just been scrambled, a deception that Beamont was required to join in, even though he had never flown with the squadron. The Heinkel was the first enemy aircraft to fall in France in the Second World War and the pilot who destroyed it, Robert Voase Jeff, a twenty-six-year-old short-service commission officer, was rewarded with the Croix de Guerre by a grateful French government.

The moment soon passed. Beamont discovered that normal activity consisted of 'endless patrols looking for enemy reconnaissance but we very seldom saw them. There was no radar to help. It was just a question of eyeballs.'[10] It was not until January that he had his first brush with the enemy. The squadron had been moved to Le Touquet when appalling winter conditions made it impossible to operate from Seclin. It was a miserable day, with rain and scudding low cloud, and none of the pilots expected to be flying when a call came through from the wing operations room ordering two pilots up on an intercept. Beamont took off with John Cock, one of the Australians who had answered the call for recruits, and they were directed over their radio telephones to climb through the cloud, where they saw a 'small speck' a few miles ahead. Beamont 'didn't really know what it was. I could see it had got two engines. Streaks of grey started to come out of the back of it. It suddenly dawned on me that this was a rear gunner firing tracers . . . miles out of range.' The pair finally reached the German at 19,000 feet, whereupon Beamont blacked out, the victim of inoxia or oxygen starvation, caused by the fact that the tube to his oxygen mask had disconnected. He came to, upside down and diving very fast, in time to roll upright and steer for home.

Nos. 607 and 615 Squadrons had also gained little experience from their months at a succession of bleak fields in the Pas de Calais. No. 615 set off from Croydon to its first French base at Merville. One flight was led by James Sanders, who after leaving Italy aged nineteen in 1935, and securing a short-service commission, had risen to the rank of flight lieutenant and acquired the nickname 'Sandy'. He had recently been transferred to the squadron after a display of high spirits landed him in trouble with Harry Broadhurst, the commander of his old unit, 111 Squadron. One September morning at Northolt, with nothing much going on, Sanders had decided to perform a particularly hazardous trick involving taking off, roaring immediately upwards into a loop, then performing a roll at the top. Unknown to him, a meeting of senior officers was taking place at the time. Such exuberance was out of kilter with the stern mood of the times. He was placed under arrest by Broadhurst, who most of the pilots liked, but whom Sanders thought 'a wonderful pilot but an absolute sod'. Broadhurst took him to see the Air Officer Commanding 11 Group, Air Vice-Marshal Gossage, who was more sympathetic and asked him what he would like to do. Sanders mentioned France. 'He said, right, off you go,' Sanders recalled. 'So I was posted to 615 Squadron, demoted from Hurricanes to Gladiators, which were twin wings, and from a regular squadron to an auxiliary.'[11]

With his departure there was an incident that almost altered the course of the war. Winston Churchill had gone to Croydon to see the squadron off, accompanied by his wife, Clementine. The Gladiators were escorting five transport aircraft loaded with fifty-four airmen and stores, and so had their machine-guns, one on either side of the fuselage and one under each lower wing, cocked and ready. The firing system was notoriously unstable. As Churchill inspected Sanders's machine, Clemmie climbed into the pilot's seat and began asking the functions of various knobs and buttons. Just as Churchill stooped to examine one of the wing-mounted machine-guns, his wife reached for the firing button. Sanders moved rapidly. 'I got her out of the aircraft fast,' he said. 'It suddenly dawned on me what an idiot I'd been.'

For much of the winter 615 Squadron was based at Vitry-en-Artois. Sanders was billeted with other officers in the village in the house of an elderly women who still dressed in black in mourning for the husband she had lost in the previous war. After dinner in the mess, which the officers set up in a local hotel, 'they would arrive back and there would be Margot with a tray with some hot bricks with some cloth wrapped round them. I'd always say, "Non, non Margot, ce n'est pas necessaire," but she'd insist. Then at five o'clock in the morning she'd be there with a *café noir*.' When he returned to see her after the war he learned she had performed the same services for the Germans, for which even-handed hospitality she was branded a collaborator by her neighbours.

The pilots found that interaction with their French counterparts tended to be more social than professional. Sandy Sanders and his comrades 'used to go and have parties at Lille with their squadrons, then we would go to a night-club and they would produce the girls. The French were mad keen on that subject, but all we were interested in was the drinking, having a good party. You might say, "Look at that lovely blonde over there," but that's as far as it went. But the French, one by one, would take the girls away and we'd be left, every one of us, drinking until two or three in the morning, having a wonderful time with the French orderly officer waiting for us to finish our fun and go away.'[12] The squadron's enterprising adjutant had arrived with a suitcase full of French letters, as condoms were known to British servicemen, hoping to sell them to pilots and airmen, but custom was non-existent.

The squadron passed its time training on its obsolete aircraft, carrying out 'affiliation' exercises with bomber squadrons and mounting patrols over the Channel. On 29 December Sanders managed to get within range of a Heinkel 111 flying very high above the sea at 26,000 feet and emptied his ammunition at it without visible result. The squadron was told on 1 January, during a visit by the Under-Secretary of State for Air, Captain H. H. Balfour, that it was likely the unit would be re-equipped with Hurricanes within a fortnight. It was not until 12 April that the first machines started to arrive, and the squadron, like 607 Squadron, had only a few weeks in which to get accustomed to them in conditions of relative calm. The transition was still in progress when the frustrations, apprehensions and scares of the phoney war finally came to an end.

As so often on the eve of a great upheaval, the preceding days passed in an unnatural atmosphere of tranquillity. Denis Wissler arrived in France on 2 May to join 85 Squadron at Sacerat. On 6 May he spent the morning sunbathing, went on patrol for one hour forty-five minutes at lunchtime and spent the rest of the day playing pontoon and Monopoly. The following day he did no flying at all and got 'as sunburned as I have ever been before'. On 8 May, as orderly officer, he was deputed to show a visiting actress, Victoria Hopper, and a concert party over a Hurricane, and in the evening went to the show, which on 'the whole was damn good'. On 9 May he was on patrol again when an excited controller directed them to investigate some enemy aircraft. 'However nothing was seen and we returned home,' he recorded despondently in his diary. 'Nothing else happened during the day apart from some patrols and directly after dinner I went to bed.'

It was the last good rest he would get for some time. The same evening Paul Richey was walking with a French girlfriend in the evening sunshine in a park near Metz when they heard a rumbling in the distance. ' "Les canons," Germaine said. "Nonsense," I tried to reassure her. "It's only practice bombing. There are lots of ranges round here." It was the guns all right, big ones at that: the guns on the Maginot and Siegfried Lines. We walked back towards the town in silence, thinking our own thoughts.'

7

The Battle of France

Although it had been long expected, the arrival of the blitzkrieg on 10 May still came as a shock. The night before, a perfect summer evening, 87 Squadron had received an order putting all pilots on readiness at dawn. 'There was nothing unusual in that,' the squadron diary recorded, 'or in the accompanying warning that the blitzkrieg would start the following day. People had become a little sceptical. It was therefore with no little surprise that we were wakened before dawn by a tremendous anti-aircraft barrage, the drone of many aero engines and a deep thudding sound we had never previously heard. BOMBS!' Shortly afterwards a Dornier raced in low over the small boggy aerodrome at Senon, near Metz, where pilots and ground crews were living in tents in the woods, and machine-gunned some French aircraft parked on the edge of the field.

There were similar rude awakenings at aerodromes all across northern France that Friday morning. In the Pas de Calais 615 Squadron was in the throes of exchanging its Gladiators for Hurricanes. 'A' flight was at Le Touquet when Heinkels arrived at dawn and bombed the airfield, damaging three Hurricanes. The pilots, billeted in a nearby chateau, assumed at first it was a French air exercise. 'B' flight was up the road at Abbeville, also re-equipping. Their base was attacked as well, but to little effect. The duty pilot, Flying Officer Lewin Fredman, gamely took off in a Gladiator to attack a Heinkel at 20,000 feet but failed to connect.

Peter Parrott, a twenty-year-old flying officer with 607 Squadron, was in the mess at Vitry having a cup of tea while waiting for a lorry to take him and two other pilots to the base to stand by. 'We heard the truck pull up, a three-tonner, the usual transport. But instead of waiting with the engine running, the driver ran into the mess, which was an unheard of liberty by an airman . . . He said, "There are German aircraft overhead, sirs!" Then we started to hear the engines so we hurled ourselves into the truck and went up to the airfield. I didn't stop running. I ran into the crew-room and got my kit on still running out to the aeroplane.'[1] As he took off, a stream of Heinkels was moving over the airfield, and he set off to catch them, firing every one of his 2,250 rounds without doing any visible damage. He would fly four more sorties that day to greater effect, shooting down two Heinkels and damaging another two.

During 10 May, the Luftwaffe launched heavy coordinated raids on twenty-two airfields in Holland, Belgium and north-east France, using more than 300 Heinkel and Dornier bombers. On the ground, the terrestrial component of blitzkrieg, the tanks and motorized infantry battalions, sliced through Holland and Belgium's thin defensive membrane. In the air, the balance of forces and the weight of experience was overwhelmingly in the Germans' favour. Their commander, Hermann Goering, had at his disposal 3,500 modern aircraft, many of them crewed by airmen who had seen action in Spain and Poland. The two air fleets – Luftflottes 2 and 3 – could muster 1,062 serviceable twin-engined bombers, 356 ground-attack aircraft (mostly Ju 87 Stuka dive-bombers), 987 Me 109 single-engined fighters and 209 twin-engined Me 110 fighters. The average daily fighter strength that the RAF could pit against this, consisting of approximately forty Hurricanes and twenty Gladiators, was puny in comparison. The air forces of Holland and Belgium were also negligible. The main deterrent to the Luftwaffe in the West was supposed to be the Armée de l'Air. On paper it seemed equipped to put up a robust defence, with an available strength on the eve of battle of 1,145 combat aircraft. The vast majority of these, 518 of them, were single-engined fighters, supplemented by 67 twin-engined fighters. The bomber feet consisted of only 140 machines, and nearly half of these were obsolete.

Despite the obvious imbalance of the force, France should, in theory at least, have been able to inflict significant damage on the invading German bomber fleets, applying a brake to the momentum that was the essential element of blitzkrieg. But the French fighter strength was illusory. Only thirty-six of their machines, the Dewoitines, which could reach 334 m.p.h., had the speed to compete on anything like equal terms with the Me 109s. Most of the fighters were Moranes, which were under-armed and had a sluggish top speed of just over 300 m.p.h. The French early-warning system was primitive. Britain had let France in on the radar secret before the war, but little had been done to develop it, and on 10 May there were only six mobile sets in place, supplied by London. The main work of locating the direction of a raid and ascertaining numbers was done by a corps of observers who called in their sightings over the public phone system. Then there were the pilots. The men of the Armeé de l'Air were brave enough, and worked hard at their aviator *élan*. But many RAF pilots felt that something more than the spirit they showed in the mess and the night-club was required in the air. There was little attempt to coordinate the two forces or share tactical thinking or intelligence. Once the war began, each air force effectively fought on its own.

Given the Luftwaffe's advantages, the first day of the onslaught in northern France was to turn out disappointing and surprisingly painful for them. The dawn raids failed to do serious damage to any of the airfields and the defenders were immediately in the air and hitting back. The pilots of 1 Squadron were active almost constantly from 5 a.m., shooting down one of a group of Dorniers near Longuyon as they raided a railhead and railway station nearby. Later in the morning they brought down another Dornier. Billy Drake, who had been separated while flying with his section near Metz, saw a condensation trail above him and went to investigate, only to find it was a Spitfire on a photographic reconnaissance mission. 'The next thing I saw was a bloody 109 on my tail,' he said. 'When I tried to evade him he suddenly turned up in front of me and I thought, "Christ! I'd better start shooting at him." Suddenly I looked up and there was a bloody great electricity cable in front of me.

He knew the area and he lead me into it!" Drake swooped under the high-tension cable and caught the 109 as it climbed away. 'I gave him a couple of bursts and he went in and that was the end.'

It was the first time he had been in action. Even immediately afterwards he found it hard to recount the incident in any detail. 'It was,' he said later, 'rather like having a motor-car accident. You can't remember what the hell happened.'[2] The opening hours, then the whole of the French campaign, were to pass in a blur for many pilots as one sortie merged into another, day melted into day and perpetual exhaustion tinged the whole experience with the quality of a bad dream.

The fighting on the first day did not finish until 9 p.m., when pilots of 3 Squadron, which had been rushed to France that day along with 79 Squadron, knocked down three Heinkels. They were in action within a few hours of arriving at Merville. No. 3 Squadron had left hurriedly from Kenley after lunch. The few maps available were given to the senior pilots and the rest of the squadron followed their lead. No. 79 Squadron at Biggin Hill was given more notice and had time to arrange for mess kit and civvies to follow on in a transport plane so they would be suitably equipped to enjoy themselves in France. It was not to be. The RAF's retreat on the ground had already begun and all subsequent movement would be backwards. During the day 73 Squadron had been pulled from its forward base at Rouvres to the supposedly more secure airfield at Reims–Champagne. No. 1 Squadron also moved hurriedly in the afternoon, from Vassincourt to Berry-au-Bac north-west of Reims. It was stiflingly hot when they arrived and the air was thick with mayflies. As they waited for the next sortie, a lone Heinkel detached itself from a flotilla overhead and dropped fourteen bombs that rippled across the field, sending the pilots diving for cover. No one in the squadron was hurt. A minute earlier, though, four farmhands had been working the neighbouring field. A shout alerted Paul Richey to what had happened.

We found them among the craters. The old man lay face down, his body twisted grotesquely, one leg shattered and a savage gash across the back of his neck, oozing steadily into the earth. His son lay close by . . .

Against the hedge I found what must have been the remains of the third boy – recognizable only by a few tattered rags, a broken boot and some splinters of bone. The five stricken horses lay bleeding beside the smashed harrows; we shot them later. The air was foul of the reek of high explosive.[3]

The sight of dead civilians was to have a disturbing effect on many of the pilots who served in France, ruffling their careful nonchalance and stirring up feelings of detestation, even hatred for the enemy. That evening Richey flew the last patrol of the day over the aerodrome, noting the effect of the German visitation on the normally dull and tranquil landscape. 'Smoke was rising from several towns and villages: bombed . . . Here and there farmhouses and barns were burning, and the sight of the lazy red flames licking up nauseated me; it was all so thoroughly evil and hellish.'

The last pilots bumped down on the grass airfields of Champagne, Picardie and the Pas de Calais in near darkness. It had been an extraordinary day. Altogether, the fighters of the Advanced Air Striking Force and the Air Component had flown 208 sorties. Between them, they claimed to have definitely shot down fifty-five bombers – Heinkels, Dorniers and Ju 88s – with a further sixteen probable. British losses amounted to seven Hurricanes shot down and eight damaged. Astonishingly, not one pilot was killed, and only three had been wounded.

The Luftwaffe themselves reckoned they had lost thirty-three bombers. Conflicting claims persisted throughout the air battles of the rest of the year. Wishful thinking, the confusion of battle and propaganda considerations inevitably inflated British figures. The Germans also exaggerated their successes and masked the extent of their losses, employing a system that fudged stark realities by assessing the damage to each aircraft in percentage terms. Whatever the discrepancy, it had been a bad début for the Luftwaffe in northern France. The Hurricane pilots fell asleep believing, or at least hoping, that the Germans were less formidable than they had feared. 'Am I browned off,' complained Denis Wissler, who had missed the action, grounded because of his inexperience.

The first day was to turn out to be the best. Things had for once gone more or less according to plan. All the time put into perfecting the Fighting Area Attacks, precisely numbered and laid out in the pre-war training manuals, appeared to have been justified. 'I have never seen squadrons so confident of success, so insensible to fatigue and so appreciative of their own aircraft,' noted the satisfied Officer Commanding the Air Component, Group Captain P. F. Fullard. But it was beginner's luck. The success which even relatively untested squadrons like 607 had enjoyed was due to the crucial fact that the bombers had arrived without any fighter escort in unconscious fulfilment of the Dowding prophesies as to what sort of war his squadrons would have to fight. The Hurricanes had been able to locate their targets with relative ease, simply because there were so many of them. The pilots arriving from England who were accustomed to Fighter Command's by now reasonably sophisticated ground-control system found themselves operating without direction. Relying on reports of sightings from the French observers, interception orders were transmitted from wing headquarters to aerodromes by field telephone. The sketchy information that could be conveyed to the pilots in the air was often unintelligible because of the short range and poor quality of the R/T.

Setting off from Merville mapless into the dusk, Pilot Officer Mike Stephens of 3 Squadron had soon been separated from the rest of his section, and then lost. 'We took off in whatever direction we happened to be pointing, hoping to catch the Heinkels,' he wrote. 'It was hopeless. There was no radar, no fighter control at all. We were wasting effort and hazarding aircraft in the hope of finding our quarry in the gathering darkness.'[4] The official RAF daily report admitted that the fighters 'had much too little in the way of an effective early-warning system'.[5] In the confusion of the subsequent days, that deficiency could only get worse. Nor were the Luftwaffe to make the same mistake again. On the second day, when the bomber fleets returned, they brought the Me 109s and Me 110s with them.

The very limited strength of the France-based squadrons was to be bolstered by several squadrons from 11 Group, including some equipped with Spitfires, flying from bases in south-east England. The fighters of the AASF and AC, however, were overwhelmed by their workload. The Luftwaffe probed deeper and wider behind French lines. German reconnaissance flights roamed over the forward areas, reporting the progress of the French and British land forces moving by prearranged plan to block the anticipated German advance westwards from the Low Countries. At the same time, bombers began systematically tearing up the defenders' lines of communication attacking aerodromes, railheads and bridges.

The squadrons went into action again at first light on the second day, Saturday, 11 May. Reims–Champagne aerodrome was bombed at 5 a.m. by Ju 88s. They were followed by two Dorniers. One of the raiders was brought down when 73 Squadron scrambled a section. The new arrivals from 79 Squadron at Merville also got into action early, shooting down a Heinkel spotted during a dawn patrol. At Berry-au-Bac, 1 Squadron spent the first hours setting up a new dispersal area, having decided the attack the previous day had probably been aimed at a concrete hut where they had first established themselves. The new arrangement consisted of a tent, a telephone to receive orders from 67 Wing headquarters and a trench and dugout to dive into in the inevitable-seeming eventuality of another raid. Now that the battle had really begun, Bull Halahan took his place at the head of his pilots, leading the first action of the day to confront Heinkel bombers, which turned back when they saw the Hurricanes.

The sound of gunfire and bombs rumbled around the airfields of northern France throughout the day, but the pilots had no clear idea of what they were supposed to do. No. 1 Squadron had been reprimanded by wing headquarters at Reims for taking off and chasing bombers on its own initiative. Their job, the pilots were told, was to await orders to escort Allied bombers trying to stem the German attack and to ignore any overflying raiders. Later on, after three large bombs were dropped outside the chateau where the headquarters staff were based, a request came through to mount a patrol in the vicinity.

The French-based squadrons were supported that morning by fighters which took off from bases in southern England on sorties over Holland and Belgium. Twelve Hurricanes from 32 Squadron were sent off from Biggin Hill to support the Dutch air force. They were directed to the aerodrome at Ypenberg, which they were told was in German hands. Pete Brothers led the attack as the CO had only just arrived at the squadron. 'We arrived, and on the ground there were a large number of Ju 52 transport aircraft,' he said later. 'We dived to set them on fire and to my surprise there was nothing to shoot at. They were all burned out in the middle, though the wing-tips and tails were OK. We thought, that's jolly odd. We whizzed around looking for something and found one parked between two hangars so we set that on fire and climbed back up again.' It was not until several months later that the squadron discovered that Dutch forces had recaptured the aerodrome and had blown up the transports on the ground, saving one for escape to Britain only to see it destroyed by their allies.[6]

No. 17 Squadron, based at Martlesham in Suffolk, was ordered in mid afternoon to patrol the Dutch coast. The whole squadron took off in twelve Hurricanes, crossing into Holland just south of The Hague and turning north. It then split up, with the CO, Squadron Leader George Tomlinson, leading 'A' Flight back to circle Rotterdam while 'B' Flight headed on to The Hague. On the way, 'A' Flight was attacked suddenly by sixteen Me 109s, which swooped on them, breaking up the formation into a series of individual combats in what was probably the first mass dogfight of the war. Something of the hectic confusion was conveyed in the officialese of Flying Officer Richard Whittaker's report. 'Eight [came in] for the first attack,' he wrote. 'Afterwards a dogfight developed and I broke away and saw three 109s on the tail of a Hurricane. I did a quarter attack on his port giving a short burst, but had to carry on past him. I then saw another Me 109 and we circled each other feinting for position and I finally got on his tail. I gave him all I had. We had both been flying at very low speeds, trying to turn inside one another. At this point I commenced to stall and lost sight of the enemy aircraft temporarily.' Breaking away, he flew through the smoke shrouding the coast and headed for home. Looking down he saw that 'The Hague as a whole was on fire'. In the same mêlée, Sergeant Charles Pavey found that, when he did a steep turn to the left, a pursuing Me 109 'could not follow me round. I eventually got on to his tail and the enemy aircraft twisted and turned, diving down. I fired intermittently and finally gave him a deflection shot, finishing my ammunition. He then burst into flames, spinning down to the ground, and I followed him down until he struck the ground.'[7]

This was one of three definite 109s claimed by 17 Squadron on the second day, as well as two army reconnaissance machines. But with the first successes came the first losses. Flight Lieutenant Michael Donne was shot down and killed when his Hurricane crashed south-west of Rotterdam. Pilot Officer George Slee also died after being shot down south of Dordrecht. Two others, Pilot Officer Cyril Hulton-Harrop (brother of Montague, killed by his own side in the Barking Creek débâcle) and Sergeant John Luck, managed to bale out after being hit and were taken prisoner. Squadron Leader Tomlinson's Hurricane was badly damaged, but he managed to crash-land and make his way back to Britain. Every one of them had been the victim of an Me 109.

The hazards of peacetime flying had meant that death was never far away, but now the pilots were encountering it in a new and unfamiliar form. Denis Wissler was at Lille–Seclin when the Luftwaffe arrived at noon. 'I came nearest to death today than I have ever been, when two bombs fell about thirty feet away,' he wrote in his diary. 'I was in the ante-room and my God did I run.' A driver was killed in the attack and a cook injured, and a block of sleeping quarters destroyed. That night Peter Parrot's brother Tim was the co-pilot in a Whitley bomber sent on a reconnaissance mission over the German–Belgian border. In the morning Peter Parrot received a signal saying his brother was missing; later he was confirmed dead.

Mortality concentrated minds. That afternoon Paul Richey had been hurrying over to his Hurricane to intercept a big formation of bombers heading for Reims when he ran into an RAF Catholic chaplain he had met previously and liked. 'He asked me if I wanted absolution, puffing alongside me. I confessed briefly. He asked if there were any other Catholics who might want absolution. I said, "Only old Killy in that Hurricane over there – hasn't wanted it for ten years but you can try!" We laughed and I waved him goodbye. But confess Killy did – sitting in his cockpit with the padre standing on the wing beside him.'[8] Richey was shot down an hour or so later, after an extended dogfight between five members of 1 Squadron and fifteen Me 110s. He baled out and landed in a wood, and after being found by some gendarmes was reunited with the squadron the following day. Five days later he was to take to his parachute again.

The shock of the first casualties was offset, to some extent, by the realization that, despite the high speeds and heavy fire-power now employed in aerial warfare, the chances of surviving a combat in which you came off worse were considerably higher than they had been during the First World War. From the outset it was clear that the news that someone was missing was not necessarily a euphemism for their almost certain death. On the morning of the second day Flight Lieutenant Dickie Lee of 85 Squadron had been injured slightly when his Hurricane was hit by flak near Maastricht and he decided to jump. He landed in a field close to where some tanks were parked on a road. He came across a peasant, who assured him the armour was Belgian. Lee borrowed an old coat to cover his uniform and went to investigate. The tanks were German. Lee was taken by the troops for a civilian, but none the less locked up in a barn, from which he soon escaped and made his way back to Lille, arriving two days later. On the same day his squadron companion, Pilot Officer John 'Paddy' Hemingway, was also badly hit by flak, baled out, and returned unharmed to the unit.

By the end of the second day the fighter squadrons could be reasonably satisfied with their own part in the battle. Together they claimed to have destroyed a total of fifty-five enemy aircraft for the loss of thirteen Hurricanes and eight pilots. It was an overestimate. In one case, 1 Squadron reported that it had shot down ten Me 110s over the village of Romilly near Reims when the real number was two. The discrepancy was caused by confusion rather than wilful exaggeration. Air fighting was disorienting and distorted the senses, a fact acknowledged in the squadron's daily report, which observed that 'questioning pilots immediately after combat, it has been found extremely difficult to obtain [precise] information as to what actually happened as most pilots, after aerobatting themselves into a stupor, were still pressing imaginary buttons and pulling plugs [the override boost mechanism to increase power] an hour or so after landing'. Building an accurate picture was further complicated by the inevitable tendency of several pilots to describe the same incident as if it was their unique experience.

The performance of the British fighters was a welcome piece of good news in an overall story of failure. On the first day the general response of the Allied air forces to the German attack had been hesitant and did almost nothing to slow its advance, which proceeded with the speed and energy of a force of nature. The French commander, Gamelin, displayed a paralysing reluctance to provoke the enemy, fearing that if he authorized bombing raids the Germans would respond with a fury his tiny bomber fleet could do nothing to match. Barratt fumed, argued and finally went his own way, dispatching thirty-two Battle bombers against the Germans advancing through Luxemburg. Only nineteen of them came back, the rest having fallen victim to fighters and the German mobile light flak guns. A second attack was ordered and sixteen bombers flew off. This time nine were shot down from the ground or the air and four limped back badly damaged.

The Fairey Battles were disastrously unsuited to the demands of modern aerial warfare. They were slow, clumsy and poorly armed. The fighter pilots were impressed by the cheerfulness and courage of their crews, but even before the fighting began, no one gave much for their chances. On the first day, their vulnerability had been increased by the fact that no fighter escorts were assigned to them. On 11 May they went into action again in another attempt to blunt the thick black arrows already punching out in all directions across the HQ staff maps.

This time they were occasionally assigned fighters to protect them, but the results were still pitiful and the losses heavy. At 09.30 six Hurricanes from 73 Squadron had taken off from Reims–Champagne to protect a group of eight Battles ordered to attack targets in Luxemburg. Seven of the bombers were shot down. The following day, 12 May, five Battles, crewed by volunteers who were only too aware of the odds they were facing, were sent off again, this time with the mission to destroy two bridges spanning the Albert Canal in an attempt to hold up the German army, which had already captured two vital bridges across the Maas, just to the east. Eight Hurricanes from 1 Squadron led by Bull Halahan were ordered to provide cover. On the way to the rendezvous the fighters ran into a swarm of 109s. In the dogfight that followed they claimed to have shot down at least four 109s and two Henschel spotter planes. Halahan's Hurricane was hit badly and he was forced to land. The Battles pressed on to their doom. Two were knocked down by the 109s before reaching the bridges. Two more were brought down by the flak batteries ringing the target. The remaining bomber crash-landed on the way home. Six crew members died in the raid and seven were captured.

The inadequacy of the support the fighters could offer had already been demonstrated the same morning when Hurricanes from 85 and 87 Squadrons were sent to meet up with twenty-four Blenheims, which had also been sent from RAF Wattisham in Suffolk to attack the bridges. On the way to the rendezvous the fighters ran into a succession of enemy formations. In the mêlée that followed, two 87 Squadron pilots were shot down and one of them, Flying Officer Jack Campbell, a Canadian from British Columbia, was killed. The other, Sergeant Jack Howell, managed to bale out, but his parachute only half-opened and he made a high-speed descent. The squadron diary noted that 'although landing extremely heavily he found on recovering consciousness that he was no more than badly bruised and was flying fit within a week'.

The two were probably victims of a section of Me 109s led by Hauptmann Adolf Galland, who was to shoot down more RAF aircraft than any other Luftwaffe pilot operating in the West. In his memoirs he described closing in on the unsuspecting Hurricanes. 'I was not excited, nor did I feel any hunting fever. "Come on! Defend yourself!" I thought as soon as I had one of the eight in my gunsight . . . I gave him my first burst from a range which, considering the situation, was still too great. I was dead on the target, and at last the poor devil noticed what was happening. He rather clumsily avoided action, which brought him into the fire of my companion. The other seven Hurricanes made no effort to come to the aid of their comrade in distress but made off in all directions.'[9] The Blenheims were equally unsuccessful and suffered heavily at the hands of the fighters and the flak. Out of the twenty-four that set out, ten were lost.

It was now clear that there were nowhere near enough Allied bombers to make a difference, nor fighters to mitigate the devastating effects of the Me 109s and the flak batteries. The French bombing raids were as ineffective as the British and their Moranes and Dewoitines no real deterrent to the Messerschmitts. Even if the Allied air forces had been stronger, the resistance they could offer in the air would not have been enough to counter the fact that, on the ground, the battle was being lost.

A handful of reinforcements arrived in the evening of 12 May. Sixteen Hurricanes of 501 Squadron were sent off from Debden and divided themselves between Bapaume and Vitry-en-Artois. This piecemeal offering was unlikely to do anything to quieten the clamour for more aircraft that was coming from the French government and supported by Winston Churchill, who had become prime minister on the day the blitzkrieg began.

Dowding had always regarded the sovereign strategic objective of Fighter Command as the protection of the British Isles. He seems, from the outset, to have doubted France's ability to defend itself. Well-founded pessimism, a cold streak of realism that contrasted with Churchill's sometimes alarmingly romantic approach and a keen appreciation of the paucity of his resources led him to view the sending of any more fighters to the aid of France as an appalling waste. He would oppose every request for further sacrificial offering of pilots and aircraft. But the battle had already created a vacuum, drawing in pilots and machines in a futile effort to stem a German advance that was now flowing westwards with the inexorability of lava.

On 13 May, the first German tanks crossed the Meuse at Sedan, a psychological as well as political frontier. The more intelligent observers who had grasped the nature of blitzkrieg understood that this, most probably, meant the defeat of the Allies was inevitable. Churchill, by his own admission, had failed to appreciate that warfare now moved at what was a lightning pace by the standards of the previous war. Thus, he was relatively unperturbed by the news of a breakthrough, believing that, as on the Western Front a quarter of a century previously, the thrust could at the least be blocked. That day thirty-two more Hurricanes and pilots were ordered off to France to make up the losses. The Luftwaffe was now concentrating on creating havoc in the rear of the French and British armies, smashing road and rail links to prevent the forward movement of men and supplies and wrecking the already fragile communication network. From now on, chaos was to be the *status quo*.

The Allies' ability to manoeuvre was dictated by the activities of the German bombers. While the Heinkels and Dorniers savaged supply lines, the Ju 87 Stukas moved ahead of the advancing Panzers. They had already proved their destructive power in Spain and Poland. The damage they did was as much to morale as to flesh, bone and metal. The mounting shriek of the sirens as they tipped into their dive was a devastating *coup de théâtre* that terrified even the most cool-headed troops. The Allied pilots, though, felt no concern about meeting them. Stukas could only manage a top speed of 238 m.p.h. and when cruising trundled along at just over 200 m.p.h. They were to prove a gratifyingly easy target for British fighters later on. But now, with the Me 109s in almost constant attendance, there were few chances of getting at them.

Despite the dramatic developments, 13 May was a quiet day. There was one raid by seven Battles over Holland, which was mercifully completed with damage to only one aeroplane. The French also sent seven bombers, with a heavy fighter escort, against troop concentrations in the Sedan area and the pontoons the German engineers had thrown across the Meuse. The effect was negligible. Ten Hurricanes were shot down, six of them, including Billy Drake's, by Messerschmitts. He had been on dawn patrol with five other Hurricanes from 1 Squadron at 22,000 feet when he started 'feeling very woozy. I looked down and sure enough I had no oxygen so I said I was going home. Round about 10,000 feet I saw these four [bombers] and it didn't look as if they were being escorted by anybody. Just as I was firing away, I suddenly heard a bloody great thump behind me and a Messerschmitt 110 had obviously got behind and [blown] me out of the sky.'

He felt as if he had been struck hard in the back and the leg and flames were streaming from his engine. 'I tried to get out but I'd forgotten to open the hood and the aeroplane was really brewing up by this time. I released the hood and went onto my back and that probably saved my life because all the flames that were coming into the cockpit went round the fuselage and missed me so I was able to bale out.'

As he floated down he heard the twin engines of the 110 above him, then tracer twinkled past as the Messerschmitt opened fire, apparently at him. He tried to accelerate his rate of descent by tipping air out of the canopy, but the pain in his back was too great for him to lift his arm. The German veered away and he hit the ground only to face another hazard. Drake was wearing an old white flying overall from pre-war days and his hair was very blond. The French peasants who ran to the scene 'thought I was a German. They all had scythes and pitchforks and they were literally coming for me.'[10] His parents' investment in his Swiss education paid off when he yelled in French that he was a British pilot. When he showed them his wings they became effusively friendly and took him to a field dressing station in a school near Rethel that was crowded with casualties, several of whom died while he was being treated. He had two bullets in his leg, and shrapnel and bullets in his back. He was given morphine that did little to dull the agony as the debris was prised out, then moved to the town hospital.

When he did not return the squadron began to worry. Paul Richey had to collect something from Drake's room after lunch 'and saw his meagre possessions spread about . . . a photograph of his mother, a bottle of hair oil, the pyjamas he would need no more. Poor old Billy!'[11] Then a call came through from the hospital that they had an English pilot. Richey went to see him and plans were made to move him to British care. The next day, though, the hospital was evacuated and Drake began a long and painful journey westwards.

That evening eight pilots and Hurricanes from the new batch of reinforcements landed at Reims–Champagne to shore up 73 Squadron.

They were being thrown in at the deep end. None of them had belonged to a squadron before, let alone seen action, having come directly from No. 6 Operational Training Unit. The following day more machines and men, many of them equally inexperienced, were spread around 607, 615 and 3 Squadrons. No. 1 Squadron also received some welcome arrivals when Flying Officer Crusoe and Sergeants Berry, Clowes and Albonico returned from a gunnery training exercise in Britain, making the last leg of the journey on a train that was bombed several times *en route*.

On Tuesday, 14 May, the Allied air forces made their first and last concentrated effort to stem the German advance now pouring through the gaps in the front around Sedan. Every available British bomber was mustered to destroy bridges on the Meuse on either side of Sedan and crush the heads of the columns thrusting into France, and a mixed batch of British and French fighters were ordered to protect them. Altogether eight attacks were launched on crossing points. The first raiders escaped lightly, protected from the flak batteries by the morning mist rising from the confluence of the Meuse and the Chiers. As the hot day wore on, the German gunners perfected their aim and the sky filled with watchful 109s and 110s. When the biggest raid of the day was launched in mid afternoon, the defences were primed. The first wave of twenty-five Battles, accompanied by French Bloch and Morane fighters, arrived at 4 p.m. local time and flew straight into a wall of flak. Then the hovering Messerschmitts descended to pick off the survivors. Eleven of the bombers and six of the fighters were shot down.

The second wave of twenty-three Battles and eight Blenheims was supposed to be guarded by Hurricanes from 1 and 73 Squadron. On their way to the target, however, the fighters were diverted by the sight of a formation of Stukas grouped over La Chesne, south-west of Sedan, where they had been sent to bomb French troops. The Me 109s protecting the bombers were slow to realize the danger. Killy Kilmartin shot down two, while Hilly Brown, Bill Stratton and Taffy Clowes claimed one each before the Messerschmitts intervened – figures that for once were subsequently broadly confirmed by the German reports. In the clash that followed, four 109s were shot down. No. 73 Squadron also ran into Stukas, destroying two and seriously damaging two more. Pressing on to their rendezvous with the bombers, however, they were ambushed by 109s and Sergeants Basil Pyne and George Dibden were shot down and killed. Earlier another 73 pilot, Pilot Officer Valcourt Roe, had also been killed over Namur. These encounters drastically increased the bombers' vulnerability when they arrived over target. Of the twenty-three Battles that set out, only nine returned and five out of the eight Blenheims were lost.

The day saw the heaviest casualties Fighter Command had yet suffered. Fifteen pilots were killed and two so badly wounded that they subsequently died. Twenty-seven Hurricanes were shot down, most of them by Messerschmitts. The dead ranged from beginners like Flying Officer Gerald Cuthbert and Flight Lieutenant John Sullivan, who had arrived the day before, to some of the most seasoned pilots. Among the latter was Les Clisby and Lawrie Lorimer of 1 Squadron, who had set off at breakfast time from Berry-au-Bac with Prosser Hanks and Boy Mould to chase a large formation of Me 110s which had appeared overhead. On first seeing them, their inclination had been to leave them alone, but they were spurred into action by a fitter who urged them to set off in pursuit for the honour of the squadron.

Clisby was last seen going into a dive, the cockpit of his Hurricane belching smoke and flame after having apparently been hit by a cannon shell. No one saw what happened to Lorimer, who also went down. At first they were posted missing. But when there was no news, the other pilots anticipated the worst. Clisby's unquenchable willingness to attack had persuaded Richey that he had 'bought it'. Some time later French troops discovered two burned-out Hurricanes.

Clisby was a month short of his twenty-sixth birthday. The premature worry lines scoring his forehead made him look older. He had a square, heavy jaw, a wiry moustache and downward sloping humorous eyes. He was extrovert, profane, perpetually cheerful and addicted to flying. He had joined the Royal Australian Air Force as a cadet aged twenty-one, and after being awarded a permanent commission he volunteered to go to Britain in 1937, despite the talk of war. He had turned out to be the most effective of the squadron's pilots, destroying at least nine German aircraft in his time in France, and he died not knowing he had just been awarded the DFC. Lorimer had been posted to 1 Squadron from 87 Squadron and had a reputation for being unlucky. This was the third time he had been shot down in five days.

The losses prompted a debate among the pilots about whether they could continue flying and fighting with such intensity. Pilots were carrying out as many as five sorties a day, of one and a half hours each, against forces that always vastly outnumbered them, taking off from often primitive airfields that were subjected to regular bombardment. Despite the danger, the privations and the exhaustion, morale and the will to engage the Germans remained largely intact. On the evening of 14 May, Flying Officer Frank Joyce and Pilot Officer Chris Mackworth of 87 Squadron were sent off on a reconnaissance mission over Louvain. Mackworth's engine would not start, so Joyce went alone. On the way he ran into a large formation of Me 110s and immediately launched a single-handed attack which he sustained until he was wounded in the leg and had to crash-land. He was rescued by some Scottish soldiers and treated at a field hospital, but had to be constantly shifted as the Germans advanced. Gangrene set in and his leg was amputated.

Mackworth had eventually managed to get his aeroplane started and set off on his mission. He also ran into Me 110s while they were strafing a village close to a tented field hospital, attacked them despite their overwhelming numbers and was shot down. He managed to bale out, but his parachute caught fire and when soldiers found him he was dead. His friend Dennis David received a letter later from Mackworth's father 'to tell me that he had heard from one of the doctors at the hospital. They had buried Chris but had no means of marking his grave other than by writing his name on a piece of paper which they put in a beer bottle on top of it.'[12]

Despite the remarkable mental and physical robustness of the British fighter pilots, fear and exhaustion began to take their toll. Richey, who was sustained by a buoyant reservoir of optimism, admitted that by now 'our nerves were getting somewhat frayed and we were jumpy and morose. Few of the boys smiled now – we were no longer the merry band of days gone by.' After his first parachute jump he had already begun 'to feel peculiar. I had a hell of a headache and was jumpy and snappy. Often I dared not speak for fear of bursting into tears.'[13]

There was to be no lessening of pressure on the pilots in the days to come. On 15 May the French government understood that the Battle of France was lost. This realization did not prevent a passionate request for more fighters. Churchill was woken at 7.30 a.m. by a call from the French prime minister, Paul Reynaud, who 'evidently under stress' announced in English: 'We have been defeated,' and informed him the front line at Sedan had been broken. Churchill candidly recorded that, to his mind, shaped as it was by the memory of the previous war, 'the idea of the line being broken, even on a broad front, did not convey . . . the appalling consequences that flowed from it'.[14] When Reynaud went on to beg for ten fighter squadrons, he was prepared to at least consider the plea.

The request was placed on the agenda of that morning's War Cabinet meeting as the second item. Dowding was present and spoke forcefully to bury a proposal Churchill had already backed away from and which had little or no support elsewhere. It was decided that the prime minister inform Reynaud that 'no further fighter squadrons should for the present be sent to France'.

Dowding understood, though, that the reprieve was likely to be only temporary. Sure enough, the following day, 16 May, his superior, Sir Cyril Newall, the Chief of the Air Staff, decided himself that eight flights – the equivalent of four squadrons – should be detached from Fighter Command and sent to France. His initiative followed a conversation with the BAFF commander, Air Marshal Barratt, who had emphasized the terrible fatigue the fighter pilots were now suffering, and additional plans were made for twenty exhausted men to be rotated out for a rest and replaced with experienced pilots from home squadrons.

Churchill, whose attitude towards the expenditure of fighter reserves chopped and changed with the demands of the hour, agreed and the decision was taken at that morning's War Cabinet meeting. It was not to end there. In the afternoon Churchill flew to Paris, where the extent of the catastrophe became apparent to him. He met Reynaud, his minister of national defence, Alain Daladier, and General Gamelin at the Quai d'Orsay with the smoke hanging in the air from piles of documents being burned in the garden in anticipation of the arrival of the Germans. Commanders and politicians radiated defeat and dejection while simultaneously appealing for yet more British aeroplanes.

Churchill's earlier pragmatism was overwhelmed by a romantic desire 'to give the last chance to the French army to rally its bravery and strength'. With an eye on posterity he also calculated that 'it would not be good historically if their request were denied and their ruin resulted'. The telegram containing these thoughts was sent to the Cabinet, which agreed to send six more Hurricane squadrons to France. The practical difficulties of housing them on battered and vulnerable airfields meant that in fact the squadrons – the last remaining Hurricane units not to have contributed to the French campaign – remained based in England. The plan was that each morning three would fly over to a French airfield and operate there until the afternoon, when the other three would relieve them.

The effect was to reduce further what Dowding, in agreement with the Air Ministry, had set as the minimum number of fighters and pilots needed to defend the country. He had already opposed the earlier decision to send eight flights to France in a letter to the Air Council, reminding them 'that the last estimate which they made as to the force necessary to defend this country was fifty-two squadrons, and my strength has now been reduced to the equivalent of thirty-six squadrons'. He closed by demanding that the ministry decide what level of fighter strength was to be left for the defence of the country and to assure him that, when that was reached, 'not a single fighter will be sent across the Channel however urgent and insistent the appeals for help may be'.

All along the front the French were now in panicky retreat and the fighter squadrons were dragged along with them. At dawn on 17 May Halahan and the 1 Squadron pilots received orders to move immediately from Berry-au-Bac to Condé-sur-Marne, between Reims and Paris. Before leaving they destroyed two Hurricanes damaged beyond immediate repair by pushing them into a shell crater and setting them on fire. Many of the fighters lost in France were to go the same way. As the last Hurricane took off, the German bombers arrived, pounding the next-door village of Pontavert, a place of no military significance. The squadron spent only one night in its new home before being ordered to withdrew again, to Anglure, sixty miles to the south-east.

Passing through Reims on the way to Condé, the road party found the city deserted but the roads round about choked with refugees. The Germans were following a deliberate policy of attacking civilian columns to intensify panic, block the roads and further disrupt the Allied communications. Many pilots witnessed the carnage and felt disgust. One day, when Dennis David's aircraft was unserviceable, he went for a walk near the airfield and met a column of Belgian civilians trudging into France.

> The refugees were pushing prams and small handcarts, with a few horse-drawn carts, and there were even fewer cars. Women were carrying their babies, while toddlers staggered along holding their mother's hand or dress. I borrowed an old motor bike from an army unit, and found a scene of desolation which it was impossible to describe. Old men, women and children, grandparents and babes in arms, not to mention dogs and horses, were strewn over the roadside, mostly dead but a few with just a flicker of life remaining. All had been torn to pieces by the bullets from strafing German aircraft, whose aim was to prevent the road being used by the British army, which was hoping to reinforce the British units already fighting the enemy further east. The whole episode utterly sickened me.[15]

Paul Richey, Sammy Salmon and Boy Mould came across a group of refugees passing through Pontavert. They piled up Salmon's Lagonda with bread, bully beef and jam from the stores and distributed them while listening to their stories: 'This child's father had been killed by a strafing Hun; that young woman's small daughter had had her brains ripped out by a bomb splinter.' When they retold the stories later in the mess, there was at first a shocked silence. 'Then a disillusioned Johnny [Walker] almost reluctantly said, "They *are* shits after all." From this moment our concept of a chivalrous foe was dead.'[16] There could be no comfort in the belief that German fighter pilots were above committing such atrocities. The normally languid Peter Matthews was sent one day to pick up a pilot who had crash-landed and 'got mixed up with a terrible bombing and strafing of the roads. It wasn't just the bomber aircraft who were doing the strafing. It was 109s and 110s. That didn't seem to me a fighter pilot's job in life.'[17]

The additional pilots and machines, and the daily squadron excursions from England, did little to curb the Luftwaffe's freedom of action. The new pilots went up to be knocked down in what was becoming a battle of attrition that could end only one way. The newcomers plunged into an atmosphere of disarray, operating with minimal support and the sketchiest of orders. A pilot officer from 'B' Flight of 253 Squadron, who had just turned nineteen, arrived at Vitry on the evening of 16 May to be immediately confronted with a stark picture of what was happening. 'We got out of our Hurricanes and there were two Lysanders [unarmed army cooperation machines] circling. Suddenly two Messerschmitt 109s came and shot them both down, and instead of rushing away or lying down we just stood there gawping at them.' The flight was led by a forty-year-old Canadian, and comprised a sergeant pilot and four pilot officers, the latter 'with no experience at all'. From the beginning to the mercifully swift end all was confusion. 'We didn't know what we were supposed to do. We were stuck in a field. There was another squadron on the other side of the field and if we wanted to know what was going on, someone had to run across to find out . . . they had a telephone, we didn't.'

On 19 May an order was passed to them to take off and climb to a given height. Most of the pilots had early-model Hurricanes with fabric wings, no armour plating, radios with a range of only two miles and wooden two-bladed propellers. The flight commander's machine was fitted with a new variable-pitch propeller, which allowed a faster rate of ascent. 'He was climbing . . . and we were wallowing about below him.

All the instruction we got from him was, "Get the lead out, you bas-tards." We couldn't catch him up. He got shot down before we got anywhere near, and so did the sergeant pilot. Suddenly the air was full of aeroplanes all over the place. I shot at one but whether I hit it or not I don't know. Someone was on my tail so I got out of the way. I found myself completely alone. I didn't even have a map. I didn't know where I was. I thought, well, when we took off the sun was over there, so if I go that way I must be going somewhere near [the base]. I saw an airfield and landed and it was Merville. The first bloke I saw was someone who trained with me.' By the time he reached the base, 'the other three had found it and landed . . . We waited and waited and there was no sign of the flight commander or the sergeant pilot.' Both were dead. The next day the surviving pilots were ordered to fly back to England.[18]

Given the small size of the force, the losses of men and aircraft were brutal and unsustainable. On 16 May, thirteen Hurricanes were lost, five pilots were killed, four wounded and two captured. On 17 May, sixteen Hurricanes were destroyed. No pilot died, but one was taken prisoner. The following day thirty-three Hurricanes were shot down, seven pilots were killed and five taken prisoner. On 19 May, thirty-five Hurricanes were shot down or crash-landed, eight pilots were killed, seven were wounded and three taken prisoner. The following day only twelve Hurricanes were lost and three pilots killed, but by then the battle was winding down and the first units were beginning to evacuate back to England.

The squadron hardest hit was 85, which had seven pilots killed in ten days. On one day alone, 16 May, six of their Hurricanes were shot down, with two pilots killed and three burned or wounded. On 20 May three were killed in an engagement with 109s over Amiens, including the new CO, Michael Peacock, who had been in command only for one day, having taken over from the exhausted Oliver. Two more squadron leaders were to die, Lance Smith of 607 and from 3 Squadron Patsy Gifford, the dashing Edinburgh lawyer who had won a DFC for shooting down the first German raider of the war. At least one officer of glittering promise was among the dead, Flight Lieutenant Ian Soden of 56

Squadron, who had been expected to play an important role in Fighter Command's war. He flew his first sortie in France on Friday, 17 May. The following day he was up at dawn, claiming a Dornier and later an Me 109. By 6 p.m. he was dead, shot down by an Me 110 near Vitry. Some pilots just seemed unlucky. Soden's squadron comrade, Flying Officer Tommy Rose, who survived the Battle of Barking Creek, had been killed a few hours earlier.

The return on these losses could not be justified. The habitual over-claiming gave the impression that the fighters were knocking down at least two Germans for each British plane lost. Churchill even claimed the figure was 'three or four to one'. We know now that in reality the ratio was far less advantagous. After the first two days, before the fighter escorts arrived in force, there were only two days, 17 and 19 May, when the balance rose to two-to-one in the RAF's favour. More worryingly for the future, in the crucial contest between fighters, the Messerschmitt 109s and 110s shot down more Hurricanes than Hurricanes shot down Messerschmitts.

The fighters were engaged in a pointless struggle. That was not, how-ever, how some of the pilots saw it. Looking down from the heavens, ranging the length and breadth of the front, the squadrons should have had a better notion of how the battle was developing than the soldiers on the ground whose vision was restricted to the field in front of them. They also knew from bitter experience the strength and ability of the enemy in the air. Yet, despite the evidence, the pilots were anxious to keep fighting. Their morale seems to have been partly sustained by the message in the score sheet, which, although it may have reflected some-thing like the truth in the case of a squadron like No. 1, was far from an accurate portrayal of the overall picture. 'We were sure we had the measure of the Germans,' Richey wrote. 'Already our victories far exceeded our losses, and the squadron score for a week's fighting stood at around the hundred mark for a deficit of two pilots missing and one wounded. We knew the Huns couldn't keep going indefinitely at that rate, but we also knew we couldn't keep it up much longer without help.'[19] Richey pressed in person for reinforcements, telling a visiting senior officer that sending sections of three or flights of six up to protect bombers was useless and that a minimum of two squadrons was needed to provide proper cover.

But the Luftwaffe was far better equipped for a long haul than the air forces facing them. The squadrons in place since the opening of the blitz-krieg had been in a state of exhaustion almost from the second day. 'I have now had six hours' sleep in forty-eight hours and haven't washed for thirty-six hours,' wrote Denis Wissler two days into the hostilities. 'My God am I tired. And I am up again at 3 a.m. tomorrow.' Pilots dozed off in mid-flight. Wissler's squadron comrade Sergeant Sammy Allard was found asleep in the cockpit after landing one evening and it was decided to leave him there until dawn patrol next day. In the morning he was still unconscious, so he was put in an ambulance and sent to hospital. It was thirty hours before he woke up. The chaos and the influx of retreating French troops meant that beds were scarce. The pilots grabbed the precious chance of oblivion wherever it appeared, dossing down in abandoned houses, in barns alongside refugees, beneath bushes and the wings of their aeroplanes, or simply under the stars. Again and again they remarked how it seemed they had only closed their eyes minutes before they were awoken again. Sometimes it was not far from the truth, with warnings and move orders coming through at all hours, ruining the possibility of a clear stretch of undisturbed repose. Often, when they did lie down, sleep would not come easily, and when it finally descended they would be back in the cockpit, twisting, diving and shooting in a dream-replay of the day's combats. They looked forward to sleep with sensuous yearning, noting the experience as a gourmet records a great meal. 'I took off from Cambrai at about 7.30,' wrote Wissler on 14 May, 'after the best night's sleep I have had since this business started.'

Food, by contrast, seemed unimportant. They kept going on bread, jam and bully beef, and drank in great quantities tea that the ground crews thrust into their hands as they clambered out of their cockpits. On the odd occasions when they were able to find a café that was open or not crowded out, the food tasted of nothing. No. 1 Squadron took over a café at Pleurs, next door to the Anglure airfield. 'We all crowded in and mechanically shoved down bread, eggs and wine,' wrote Richey. 'It might as well have been sawdust.' Women were even further from their minds. When the barmaid tried to flirt with Richey, he found her 'quite pretty in a coquettish way but I could scarcely be bothered to look at a woman these days'.[20]

French dread mounted as the Germans pushed closer. Rumours, many of which turned out to be horribly accurate, swirled through the towns and villages, washing over soldiers and civilians alike, saturating the atmosphere in suspicion. In this humid moral climate the pilots found that their allies could be as dangerous as their enemies. German tactics in Holland, where parachute troops had been dropped in advance of the main attack to wreak havoc behind the lines, made anyone descending from the sky an object of distrust, as Billy Drake had already discovered. Now peasants and soldiers were inclined to attack any parachutist without bothering to establish his identity. Pilot Officer Pat Woods-Scawen of 85 Squadron was shot down in a dogfight with 109s in which he accounted for one Messerschmitt himself. He baled out, to be shot at twice on the way down by French troops. British soldiers could be just as edgy. Squadron Leader John Hill, who was flying his first sortie with 504 Squadron after taking over as commander, was forced to bale out and was blasted with shotgun pellets by a peasant as he approached the ground. Having convinced them he was an English airman, he was then arrested by passing British soldiers, who accused him of being a fifth columnist. When he reached into his pockets to show some identification, they opened fire, forcing him to jump into a ditch. This aroused further suspicions and he was pulled out and beaten unconscious, only being saved by the intervention of a passing French officer who knew him.

Fear of fifth columnists was rampant, apparently with some justification. When Pete Brothers first landed with 32 Squadron to fly for the day from Moorsele in Belgium, they found 615 Squadron, who had by now moved there, 'a bit jumpy, looking over their shoulders the whole time'. That morning a sergeant had failed to turn up at readiness. 'They'd gone to kick him out of bed and they found he was lying on his back with a knife in his chest ... They didn't know if it was a fifth columnist or a refugee come to rob him or what.'[21]

The punishment the German bombers had inflicted on the soldiers and civilians below made them liable to rough justice if they landed behind enemy lines. Bull Halahan came across a crashed Heinkel. He asked some French Senegalese troops what had become of the crew, and was told they had been taken off and shot. Pat Hancock, who had arrived at 1 Squadron at the start of the fighting, was in Sammy Salmon's big Lagonda when they saw a German descending by parachute into a field near Béthienville. 'There was a greeting committee waiting for him,' he said. 'They had been tilling the field and now they wanted to kill him. Sammy said, "We can't have this, Hancock. Bloody French." His car instantly became a tank, through the hedge he went, into the field. We picked up the German. I put my RAF cap on his head and we dispersed the French far and wide.'[22]

By 17 May the Chief of the Air Staff, Air Chief Marshal Sir Cyril Newall, had accepted the hopelessness of the situation. He announced to his peers that he did 'not believe that to throw in a few more squadrons whose loss might vitally weaken the fighter line at home would make the difference between victory and defeat in France'. He concluded that it would be 'criminal' to compromise Britain's air defences further. Churchill agreed and two days later ordered that no more fighter squadrons leave the country whatever the need in France.[23]

What remained of the eight reinforcement flights prepared to withdraw, most of them with only half the aircraft they had arrived with. On 20 May the Air Component squadrons attached to the BEF began to pack up. That evening 87 Squadron set off from Lille to Merville, the thirty-minute journey taking hours because of the blackout and roads clogged with troops and refugees. Roland Beamont described a 'great mass ... all pouring westwards ... pushing perambulators, bicycles loaded up with blankets and pots and pans ... As we tried to get through them in clearly marked RAF vehicles there was a great deal of hostility. I think they felt that here were the British running away.'[24]

Dennis David flew to their new airfield to discover that 'accommodation was nil in the village, and we . . . were thankful to have clean straw to sleep on in a pigsty'. As the morning passed and the traffic outside the airfield was joined by the same retreating Allied troops the squadron had seen at Lille, anxiety grew that they would never get away. All the rumours were bad ones. A young French officer told them 'that Arras had fallen and that the Germans were advancing to the coast. Unbelievable! A battery of 75s stopped at our dispersal point and a harassed *capitaine* told us how Gamelin had been executed by the Paris mob and that the Germans had reached Abbeville [well to the south].'[25] Orders were given for the pilots to carry out strafing attacks on German troops on the road between Cambrai and Arras until troop carriers arrived to evacuate the ground crews, when they would switch to escorting them 'home to England'. These last words, the squadron diary noted, had a profound effect. 'An entirely new atmosphere was noticeable immediately the officers and men read that. A mixed feeling of regret at leaving hospitable France and an unpleasant feeling that should anything happen to the troop carriers or the Hurricanes we should be left very much alone in the world.'

By the following day they were home. Dennis David, who had been shot up in a strafing run, crash-landed but was evacuated in a passenger plane. After months looking down on the plains of northern France he was struck by 'how small and green the fields of Kent looked'. He went home to Surbiton, where his mother sent him to bed. He 'slept without moving for thirty-six hours. She became quite concerned and actually called the doctor, who said I was completely exhausted and should just be left to sleep.'[26] The sister squadron, 85, also made it back. 'I came home last night,' Denis Wissler scrawled in pencil in his diary. 'Bath, bed, booze.'

Bull Halahan decided that his men had now had enough and asked permission for the longest serving pilots to withdraw. The core of the squadron, who had been in France from the first days, left together; including the Bull himself, Johnny Walker, Prosser Hanks, Killy Kilmartin, Bill Stratton, Pussy Palmer, Boy Mould and Frank Soper. Rennie

Albonico, another of the originals, was not with them, having been shot down and taken prisoner on 21 May. Nor was Paul Richey. On the last big day of fighting, 19 May, he had attacked a formation of Heinkels, and after destroying one was caught in return fire. He was hit in the neck by an armour-piercing bullet and temporarily paralysed, only regaining the power in his arms when his Hurricane was 2,000 feet up and locked in a vertical dive. He was found by the French and moved erratically westwards to end up in the American Hospital in the Paris suburb of Neuilly.

Billy Drake also passed through Paris after being collected from hospital in Chartres by an American girlfriend called Helen. Lacking uniform or identity papers, he was again taken for a German at a French roadblock and feared he was going to be shot as a spy until Helen persuaded them to let him go. They went to the Crillon, where she handed over her Buick, its tank miraculously full of petrol, and told him to head for Le Mans, where the British were regrouping. 'The streets were crowded with refugees,' he said, 'and much worse, with soldiers without their rifles, just trudging. They'd had it. It was the most depressing thing I've seen in my life.'[27] At Le Mans there was an emotional reunion with the squadron members who had stayed behind.

Richey, too, eventually joined them after recuperating in Paris, savouring the last days of freedom the city would know for four years. One day, walking down the Champs-Élysées, he came across Cobber Kain sitting at a pavement café with a *Daily Express* journalist, Noel Monks. Kain had chosen to help with the re-forming of 73 Squadron, after those who remained of the surviving pilots returned to England, and was due back himself in a few days. He was young enough to still have acne, but his spirit was frayed. Richey 'noticed that he was nervous and preoccupied and kept breaking matches savagely in one hand while he glowered into the middle distance'.[28]

The following day Kain took off from the squadron base at Echemines, south-west of Paris, and started to perform rolls perilously close to the ground. Among those at the aerodrome was Sergeant Maurice Leng, a twenty-seven-year-old Londoner who was one of the first of the RAFVR pilots to be posted to a fighter unit to replace squadron casualties. 'He'd taken off in . . . the last original surviving Hurricane of 73 Squadron with a fixed-pitch, two-bladed wooden airscrew,' he said later. 'He took off and came across the aerodrome, did a couple of flick rolls and hit the deck. That was it.' The sympathy of the newcomers, who had hardly known him, was muted. 'We all said, "How sad," but we all said, "How stupid."' [29]

The judgement could have served for the whole air campaign. It petered out in a series of withdrawals westwards in ever deepening chaos. Nos. 1 and 73 Squadrons, two of the first four squadrons in, were to be the last out, together with 501, which had been in France since the start of the blitzkrieg, and 242 and 17 Squadrons, which were sent out early in June. No. 1 Squadron was now transformed, with a new commander, Squadron Leader David Pemberton, and an almost entirely new set of pilots. Pat Hancock, one of the replacement pilots, remembered the remaining weeks as 'only retreat, anxiety and lack of knowledge as to what was going on. Communications were almost non-existent. Fighter control, as such, had vanished.' [30] In the first two weeks of June the unit moved four times, in the end taking the initiative to shift itself when it was impossible to contact wing headquarters to obtain orders. They finally left on 17 June. One party departed by ship, boarding two dirty half-loaded colliers at La Rochelle. Another flew from St Nazaire. The squadron had been helping 73 and 242 Squadrons to maintain a continuous patrol over the port to cover the embarkation of the RAF and the remnants of the British army in France. They were unable to prevent the last tragedy of the campaign, the sinking of the *Lancastria*, which went down with the loss of 5,000 lives when a German bomb sailed flukily through an open hatch. Pat Hancock chased after one of the raiders 'for a hell of a way, firing at it but with no success'. Circling over, he saw the victims struggling in the water and threw down his Mae West life-jacket.

No. 17 Squadron was also sent to cover the evacuation, and set up base in tents on the racetrack at Le Mans on 8 June. The same day, Denis Wissler, back with 85 Squadron after a forty-eight-hour leave, was summoned by his commanding officer, Peter Townsend, who had taken over the squadron two weeks before, and told that '17 Squadron had wired and asked for two operational pilots and that he was very sorry but I would have to go, and that at once'. Wissler had only been with 85 Squadron for six weeks, but his first impression on joining was that 'the mob seem damn nice', and he had grown very fond of them. There were only two hours to say goodbye before he left for Kenley. He stopped on the way in London for a solitary, melancholy dinner at the Trocadero, where he 'really got completely plastered and was put to bed by the wing commander'. The same kindly officer woke him up at 3.30 a.m. with some Alka-Seltzer, lent him his bath robe and sent him for a cold shower before he took off.

Wissler left with Count Manfred Czernin, who had been with him in 85 Squadron. Czernin was twenty-seven, born in Berlin, where his Austrian diplomat father was *en poste*. His mother, though, was English, the daughter of Lord Grimthorpe, the polymath who designed Big Ben, and he had been to Oundle public school. There was none the less more than a dash of *Mitteleuropa* in his manner, which made him the object of some teasing. He joined the RAF in 1935 on a short-service commission after a stint farming tobacco in Rhodesia, and served as a bomber pilot before joining the reserve. Unlike Wissler, he had already been in action several times in France and claimed to have shot down four Germans. The pair managed to get lost several times on the way to Le Mans, taking twelve hours over a one-hour journey. The squadron then spent several days patrolling over Rouen and Le Havre, both towns obscured by columns of black smoke coiling up from burning oil tanks. On 12 June Wissler at last had his first taste of fighting when the squadron spotted three Heinkels bombing troopships off Le Havre and attacked. He opened fire on one of the bombers and saw smoke coming from the starboard engine, but modestly did not claim to have shot it down. Czernin, however, fired at another Heinkel in cloud and claimed a 'conclusive casualty'. On a later patrol Wissler had another new and unwelcome experience: coming under heavy ground fire. 'It was most terrifying,' he reported candidly in his diary that evening.

By now the evacuation was almost complete. The squadron returned to Le Mans after a patrol on the morning of Saturday, 12 June, to find the Naafi had gone leaving behind huge quantities of cigarettes and whisky, to which everyone helped themselves. The army had abandoned a batch of Harley-Davidson motor bikes. Pilots and ground staff took the opportunity to ride circuits round the famous track. The same day they moved to Dinard. On 17 June the pilots were at readiness all morning and broke off to eat at a local hotel. Members of a French squadron based at Dinard aerodrome were also there. Peter Dawbarn, a nineteen-year-old pilot officer with 17 Squadron, was among the English pilots who sat down to lunch. There was a radio in a corner of the dining room. When the news came on everyone stopped eating to listen. When the announcement of the capitulation followed there was silence. Then, 'they all burst into tears'.[31]

The newcomers had formed a low opinion of the French. Pilots' attitudes towards their allies differed, depending on when they joined the battle. Many veterans of the phoney war had enjoyed the company of their spirited fellow officers in the neighbouring *escadrilles*, even if they had not found them particularly supportive or even visible during the crucial phase of the Battle of France. No. 1 Squadron had a much-loved Frenchman attached to it as interpreter, Jean 'Moses' Demozay, who was to escape to Britain in an abandoned Bristol Bombay troop carrier and fight bravely and effectively for the RAF and the Free French for the rest of the war. The reinforcement flights and squadrons rarely saw the French. The few recorded encounters were not happy ones. Flight Lieutenant Fred Rosier of 229 Squadron put down at an airfield near Lille, after being nearly shot down in a battle, 'to find the French were there, with brand-new American aeroplanes, fighters, and they were not flying. They were quite friendly, but I was livid . . . They were not participating in the battle at all.'[32]

The French the replacement pilots saw appeared demoralized and apathetic. Peter Dawbarn and the 17 Squadron pilots had come across French fighter pilots on previous trips to Dinard, which they used as a base for patrolling, 'but they never took off as far as I know. We kept taking off, they didn't.' The locals could also seem treacherous. The squadron was convinced that traitors were reporting their movements to the Germans. 'The fifth column is operating here we are sure as Morse code starts every time we take off,' wrote Wissler. The 17 Squadron Hurricanes left from Dinard, fuselages packed with cigarettes and alcohol, and landed at Jersey, where they celebrated their escape in Fighter Boy style with a party. When they left the following day, one Hurricane carried a passenger, a young woman who made the brief journey to freedom with the pilot perched on her lap.[33]

Most of the Hurricanes that went to France never came back. Given the tight margins Fighter Command was working within, the campaign had been ruinously expensive in machines. Of the 452 fighters sent out, only 66 returned when the main force withdrew. Of the missing 386, German fighters and flak accounted for only 208. The rest were abandoned as unserviceable. This was no reflection on the ground crews, who worked continuously while being regularly bombed and strafed, with only a few hours' sleep in tent or field to sustain them before going back on shift. All but intact aeroplanes suffering only light damage had to be set on fire because there were no spares, or the chaotic conditions made repairs impossible. The normally genial tone of No. 1 Squadron diary faltered when it came to describing the waste. 'It has been most noticeable that on a patrol yielding no apparent results as many as two or three aircraft out of six may be struck by shrapnel and on return to aerodrome it has been found necessary to write off all three as u/s, due to lack of proper servicing and maintenance facilities . . . Wastage has so far been in the neighbourhood of thirty-eight, only ten of which have actually crashed. Apparently we in France are the poor relations.'[34]

The pilots of Fighter Command could feel proud of their performance in France. Churchill had claimed that they were 'clawing down two or three' Germans for every British aeroplane lost. It was a vast exaggeration. The Hurricane squadrons reckoned themselves to have definitely shot down 499 bombers and fighters. The true figure was lower but it was at least 299. But with losses of 208 on their own side, it still left the RAF pilots well in the lead. Their success was their own. They were dedicated and aggressive and they made the most of their excellent machines. What they lacked was an effective early-warning system, or any proper control or direction from the ground. The pilots fought using tactics they invented for themselves for objectives that were never explained, if they were ever understood. Given these handicaps, the cost in lives looked relatively low. Altogether fifty-six pilots were killed in the twelve days between 10 and 21 May, and thirty-six wounded, with eighteen taken prisoner. But such losses could not possibly be borne over a long period, and as soon as this battle ended, a new one was beginning.

8

Dunkirk

At Dunkirk some 500,000 British and French soldiers were now penned in, the sea at their backs, awaiting capture or annihilation. The job of finishing them off was given to the bombers and fighters of the Luftwaffe. Goering had proposed the idea. Hitler accepted it, apparently wishing to spare his army for the next stage of the French campaign.

The RAF was given the task of protecting the exhausted lines of soldiers, zig-zagging across the grey North Sea sands waiting to be rescued. This was the heaviest responsibility the air force had yet had to face. The troops were appallingly exposed. Defending them meant not only mounting continuous patrols over Dunkirk port and the beaches on either side. To be effective the fighters would also have to push inland to try to knock down the bombers before they could drop their loads.

Once again, they would be operating at a significant disadvantage in numbers. Despite the losses sustained in the blitzkrieg, the Germans still had 300 bombers and could draw on 550 fighters to protect them. After the depredations of the Battle of France, Air Vice-Marshal Keith Park, whose 11 Group faced Dunkirk, had only 200 fighters at his immediate disposal. The mission, though, had the virtue of clarity and purpose. The pilots knew what they were supposed to do and why they were doing it. The stoicism of the infantrymen as they waited patiently among the bomb bursts was profoundly affecting to the men flying over them, however little this was appreciated on the ground.

The burden of the fighting was to be borne by the squadrons based around London, which would be fully engaged for the first time. Dowding also decided that the time had come to throw his precious Spitfires into the battle. The 11 Group pilots watched the last, painful phase of the BEF's campaign in France with anticipation. To some it seemed to be less of a disaster than an opportunity. 'At Hornchurch,' wrote Brian Kingcome, 'the taste of war at last began to tingle our palates.'[1] 'Operation Dynamo', as the evacuation was code-named, began on the evening of 26 May when a vast flotilla of yachts, pleasure boats, fishing smacks, sailing barges, motor cruisers and dinghies joined more conventional craft in carrying the soldiers back across the Channel.

There had already been some preliminary skirmishing during the previous ten days. The Hornchurch pilots on the evening of 15 May were called to the billiards room of the officers mess for a briefing. There was no briefing room at the base. As Al Deere pointed out, 'there was no need for any; our operations were purely defensive and aircraft were usually launched into the air at a moment's notice, the pilots having only the vaguest idea of what to expect'.[2] Now they were informed that they would be going on the offensive, roaming over the French and Belgian coasts to seek out the Luftwaffe.

When the order came to start patrolling, there was competition among the 54 Squadron pilots as to who would go off first. The honour – for this was how it was seen – went to the twelve most experienced pilots. Al Deere described the excitement, after bumping over the grass at Hornchurch and climbing to 15,000 feet, of crossing the French coast: 'There was a hum in the earphones as the CO's voice crackled over the air, "Hornet squadron, battle formation, battle formation, GO." Symmetrically, like the fingers of an opening hand, the sections spread outwards. As my eyes scanned the empty skies I was conscious of a feeling of exhilaration and tenseness, akin to that experienced before an important sporting event. There was no feeling of fear . . .' When nothing happened, elation soon evaporated. When the squadron returned, the other pilots crowded round to hear about the first real taste of action. Colin Gray, a fellow New Zealander, asked Deere what it had felt like, 'knowing that at any minute a Hun might pop up and take a pot at you?' Deere reported that 'at first I was tingling all over with excitement but when after a time nothing happened I was damn bored'.[3]

It was Johnny Allen, a quiet member of the squadron who stood out because of his strong religious convictions, who scored first, shooting down a Ju 88. Deere's turn came on 23 May. While eating breakfast in the mess that morning, he was called to the phone to speak to his flight commander, Flight Lieutenant James 'Prof' Leathart, so called because he had a degree in electrical engineering. Leathart had just come from a meeting with the station commander, Wing Commander 'Boy' Bouchier, who had learned that the CO of 74 Squadron, Squadron Leader White, had been shot at while patrolling across the Channel and forced down at Calais–Marcq aerodrome. 'Drogo' White was an example of the RAF's fundamentally meritocratic nature. He had started out as a Halton apprentice and been selected for Cranwell, where he won the Sword of Honour. He was regarded as the finest shot in the air force, capable of scoring eighty hits out of a hundred on a towed drogue target, when the average was twenty. None of this had saved him from being shot down on his first sortie, and by a Henschel 126, a relatively slow-moving reconnaissance plane.

Before landing he radioed Johnny Freeborn, who was flying with him, asking him to tell his wife that he was unhurt and would soon be home. This optimistic prediction came true sooner than he could have dared to hope. Bouchier asked Leathart to fly over in a two-seater Miles Master trainer, keep the engine running while White hopped in, then return at sea-level. It sounded to Deere, who with Johnny Allen was asked to fly escort, 'a piece of cake'. They reached Calais without any trouble. Deere sent Allen up to stand guard at 8,000 feet, where Germans might be lurking in the broken cloud. The bright yellow Master landed and taxied over to a hangar, where White was presumed to be waiting. Then Deere heard 'an excited yell from the usually placid Johnny'. Allen had seen a dozen Me 109s heading for the airfield. He attacked, and found himself in the middle of a frantic mêlée, shooting and being shot at.

Deere dropped down to try and alert the Master, which had no R/T, by waggling his wings. As he did so a 109 flashed across his path. He latched on to it and reefed his Spitfire hard over in an attempt to turn inside the Me 109, the crucial manoeuvre in air fighting. If the chasing pilot succeeded in turning tighter, getting inside his opponent, he had the chance to fire a deflection burst, aimed in front for the enemy to fly into. If he failed, the target was always a little ahead, leaving the tracer twinkling harmlessly in his wake. Deere turned inside. He was preparing to fire when Allen's voice again filled his earphones, calling for help. Deere asked Allen to 'hang on while I kill this bastard', and stayed clamped into the turn. Then, 'in a last desperate attempt to avoid my fire, the Hun pilot straightened from his turn and pulled vertically upwards, thus writing his own death warrant. He presented me with a perfect no-deflection shot from dead below and I made no mistake. Smoke began to pour from his engine as the aircraft, now at the top of its climb, heeled slowly over in an uncontrolled stall and plunged vertically into the water's edge from about 3,000 feet.'

Now he went to look for Allen. As he climbed, he was seen by two 109s, which swung round steeply and started after him. Again Deere found that he could comfortably turn inside his pursuers, so that very quickly the roles were reversed and he was chasing them. Deere opened fire on the second 109, causing 'bits to fly off'. Then he and the lead 109 went into an extended dogfight, chasing each other round at high speeds in tighter and tighter circles. Before the end Deere ran out of ammunition, but for reasons he could not later explain he continued the engagement until the German abruptly straightened out and headed east for home. Buzzing with adrenaline, Deere and Allen, whose Spitfire was by now ventilated with bullet holes, did the same. Deere indulged himself with a victory roll over the aerodrome as they came in.

This encounter was the first time a Spitfire had gone up against a Messerschmitt and pilots and ground crew were hungry for details. Deere's account was corroborated by 'Prof' Leathart, who had with White watched the combat from a ditch before they made their escape as soon as the sky was clear. Deere was excited and relieved. It seemed that one of the great questions that the fighter pilots, and those who directed them, had been asking themselves since the start of the war had been settled. Deere believed that as a result of his prolonged fight with the second 109 he had been able to assess practically the relative performance of the two aircraft. The experience of the Hurricanes in France, and the tests carried out on the Me 109 that had fallen into Allied hands, had concluded that the Messerschmitt could out-climb the Spitfire up to 20,000 feet, and always out-dive it, but was less agile at all altitudes. Deere agreed about the dive. The Messerschmitts, unlike the British fighters, had fuel injection, which meant they did not miss a beat at the moment of zero gravity that preceded a rapid descent. That aside, 'the Spitfire was superior in most other fields, and like the Hurricane, vastly more manoeuvrable.'[4] The Spitfire's climbing performance had been significantly improved by the advent of the Rotol constant-speed airscrew.

Later that day there was to be another formative experience for the squadron. That afternoon it took off on cross-Channel patrol and ran into a formation of bombers silhouetted above in the clear sky, heading for Dunkirk. After climbing above, unnoticed, and gaining the maximum tactical advantage, Leathart, who was leading, ordered a No. 5 attack. The four sections of three fanned out into echelon formation, each one tucked into a neat inverted V-shaped 'vic' slanting across the sky in a shallow diagonal, each pilot selecting his target. The flying discipline would have delighted their pre-war instructors. Then a panicked voice on the R/T shouted: 'Christ, Messerschmitts – Break!' The squadron instantly 'split in all directions, all thoughts of blazing enemy bombers momentarily ousted by the desire to survive'.

In the tumbling dogfight that followed, the 54 Squadron pilots claimed to have destroyed eight of the attacking Messerschmitts, but unfortunately no bombers, which were their primary targets. Despite this success, the encounter set off intense discussion of the value of the tactics they had been taught. The criticism was led by George Gribble, a 'very English, very good-looking' twenty-year-old short-service entrant. In Deere's admiring opinion, he 'epitomized the product of the public school; young yet mature, carefree yet serious when the situation required it, and above all possessing a courageous gaity'. Gribble told

Leathart that 'everybody was so damn busy making certain he got into the right position in the formation that we were very nearly all shot down for our pains'. Leathart, who was shortly to take over command, did not argue. He promised that henceforth there would be no more Fighter Area Attacks.[5]

These cross-Channel clashes taught valuable lessons to the 11 Group squadrons. They provided a demonstration of the startling reality of air fighting, but allowed the pilots an opportunity to recover and digest their experiences. Previously no one had known what to expect. During the first days of the Battle of France, 32 Squadron, flying from Biggin Hill, had barely seen the enemy. Michael Crossley noted one day's non-events with typical candour and idiosyncratic punctuation in the squadron diary. 'All set off to France, land at Abbeville, refuel, hear dreadful stories, get very frightened, do a patrol, see nothing, feel better, do another, see nothing, feel much better, return to Biggin Hill, feel grand.'[6]

Mike Crossley was over six feet tall, with jug ears, dark, smiling eyes and a slightly caddish moustache. Between leaving Eton and joining the RAF he had studied aeronautical engineering, worked as an assistant director at Elstree film studios and signed on as an apprentice with De Havilland. He was a natural musician who played the guitar and trumpet brilliantly and had a jokey manner that sometimes appeared to border on the facetious. Crossley, though, could be serious enough when he had to be. Shortly after writing the diary entry he became the first pilot in the squadron to shoot down an Me 109, with a perfect deflection shot, and was to destroy three more in the next four days. Pete Brothers also shot down an Me 109 in the same encounter. In the following week the squadron was in action almost daily, flying offensive patrols and escorting bomber raids, using each sortie to add to its stock of collective and individual knowledge and increase its effectiveness and its members' chances of survival. Its pilots' capacity to learn meant that 32 Squadron remained intact as a fighting force for the next three months and was not withdrawn from the line until the end of August.

Squadron commanders and pilots drew their own conclusions from their experiences and acted on them without waiting to seek approval from above. The nature of the fighting meant that advice or direction from superiors not involved in daily combat carried little authority. To their credit, Dowding and the best of his senior commanders accepted that their own understanding of what was happening could well be inferior to that of even the most junior front-line pilot. They sought their opinions, listened to what they had to say and, when needed, took action.

The new rules of air fighting were being made up with each clash. To succeed, merely to survive, required an adaptability that was found chiefly in the young. In the mayfly span of a fighter pilot's effective life, young meant under twenty-two. The older pilots commanding the squadrons, in whom the parade ground rigidity of the old tactics were strongly ingrained, were for all their experience and flying skills often among the first to go. Roger Bushell, the peacetime barrister who had helped defend Johnny Freeborn and Paddy Byrne and moved up to command 92 Squadron, was shot down on his first day. He would be missed. The squadron was essentially a new creation, having been re-formed only the previous October. Bushell was moved from 601 Auxiliary Squadron to supervise the birth, overseeing training, the switch from Blenheim bombers to Spitfires and infusing the nascent squadron spirit with his personality. He was born in South Africa, moved to England and went to Wellington public school and Brasenose College, Oxford. He was tough, intelligent and warm-hearted, and a good drinker. He was also a sportsman, a superb skier, coaching the British team in the 1936 Winter Olympics. He had a permanently half-hooded eye, the result of a skiing accident, which gave him a truculent look.

Bushell had joined 601 Squadron in the mid 1930s, naturally embracing its credo of taking fun and flying equally seriously, making strong friendships and winning admirers throughout the service. His charm, the squadron chronicler recorded, was 'magnetic and universal'.[7] His forensic talents were at the disposal of all the squadron, fitter and pilot alike. Once he flew himself from London to a distant northern base to defend a ground-crew member, changing out of uniform and into wig and gown to demolish the authorities' case. On the evening of 23 May, 92 Squadron set off on an evening patrol around Dunkirk. Bushell was leading, and when they encountered a formation of Heinkels, heavily protected by Me 109s and 110s, he ordered an attack. Tony Bartley heard him 'swearing on the radio as he plunged into the bomber force' with John Gillies and Paul Klipsch. All three were shot down. Klipsch was killed. Bushell and Gillies were captured. Bushell was last seen standing by his Spitfire, waving his scarf in farewell. He was a troublesome prisoner and was eventually murdered in March 1944 by the Gestapo after being captured in the aftermath of the Great Escape he helped to organize from Stalag Luft 111. He was, Brian Kingcome thought, 'an amazingly great man'.[8] The squadron diary admitted that the losses were 'a very severe blow to us all', and two days later 92 was moved to Duxford to rest and re-equip.

The 19 Squadron commander, Squadron Leader G. D. Stephenson, also went early, on the first day of Operation Dynamo. Once again there were more men than machines, and pilots, with the exception of section leaders, drew lots for who was to go. The twelve Spitfires left at breakfast time and encountered about twenty Stukas over the coast near Calais. They appeared to be unescorted, a circumstance that should have aroused suspicion, but caution vanished as the pilots, most of them going into their first real combat, saw the black crosses and the gull wings crawling unheedingly across the sky and prepared to attack. As they did so, thirty Me 110s came into view. One section, led by Flight Lieutenant G. E. Ball, broke off to engage them. The rest closed in on the Stukas. George Unwin, who had missed out in the draw, heard later what happened from the returning pilots. Stephenson, he said, ordered a Fighting Area Attack No. 1. 'That meant a very slow closing speed in formation "vics" of three, attacking with a very slow overtaking speed so you could get a very good shot at it. That was the idea.'[9] It worked, up to a point. The squadron shot down four, but then the 109s arrived. Pilot Officer 'Watty' Watson was hit by a cannon shell, baled out and disappeared. Stephenson was seen heading inland in a shallow glide, trailing blue smoke. It later turned out he landed safely but was taken prisoner. The squadron claimed five Stukas and two 109s, a reasonable return on their losses, if true. The arithmetic of the squadrons involved at Dunkirk, however, was no more reliable than that of the France-based units. Later they flew another patrol and were again 'bounced' by 109s. Sergeant C. A. Irwin was killed and Pilot Officer Michael Lyne shot in the leg. He nursed his Spitfire back across the Channel and crash-landed on Walmer Beach. This time it seemed that only one 109 had possibly been brought down, and that was unconfirmed.

Stephenson and Irwin were both very experienced men. Irwin was an ex-fitter, typical of the cadre of ground staff who, through ability and ambition, had got airborne and whose professionalism and technical expertise stiffened the pre-war squadrons. Stephenson, like White, had been at Cranwell and was therefore marked out for the RAF's upper reaches. He was regarded as a brilliant pilot and had been an instructor at the Central Flying School. It was a teaching post, but it carried prestige in a service in which skill was of paramount importance. Like the 54 Squadron pilots, 19 Squadron decided after the first day that no matter how flawless the technique, the tactics that Stephenson and his generation epitomized were dead. 'That was the end of going in slow,' Unwin said. 'In fact it was the end of all we knew because we realized we knew nothing. From then on it was get in fast and go out fast. And go close – a hundred yards. Get in close but go in fast and get out fast.'[10]

Some of the younger pilots discovered almost at once that they were good at air fighting. Also that they enjoyed it. 'Prof' Leathart described 'that lovely feeling of the gluey controls and the target being slowly hauled into the sights. Then thumb down on the trigger again and the smooth shuddering of the machine as the eight-gun blast let go.'[11] The best of them were pushed forward to fill the holes in the commanders' ranks. Following the loss of Roger Bushell, Brian Kingcome and Bob Tuck were posted to 92 Squadron as flight commanders. Leathart himself was put in command of 54 to replace Squadron Leader E. A. Douglas-Jones, who had led the squadron on its first offensive patrol on 16 May but had not flown with it since and relinquished command nine days later on grounds of ill-health.

Covering the evacuation meant that pilots were in the air two, three or sometimes even four times a day. Exhaustion set in quickly.

Replacement squadrons arrived at the 11 Group bases to allow the spent units a rest. Some of the new arrivals had seen very little of the war and were slow to appreciate how serious things had become. On 28 May Al Deere returned to Hornchurch after a patrol and noticed that the dispersal areas normally occupied by 65 and 74 Squadrons now had Spitfires with unfamiliar markings. They belonged to 222 Squadron, sent in while 65 and 74 were rotated out for a rest. Later that evening Deere met one of the flight commanders, Douglas Bader, who questioned him closely. Bader, as a pre-war regular and an ex-Cranwell cadet, had become a figure of myth in the RAF by an extraordinary demonstration of will-power, struggling back to serve in a fighter squadron after losing both legs in a flying accident. His biographer wrote that Bader and his pilots were not impressed by their first sight of their Hornchurch comrades and 'gazed, startled, then with mild derision at pilots . . . walking around with pistols tucked in their flying boots and as often as not with beard stubble'. They also noticed that they seemed quiet and preoccupied, but did not consider the significance of this and regarded the guns and the three-day growth as 'line-shooting'.[12]

The accusation of line-shooting could be intended lightly. Jokey boastfulness was an established part of ante-room and saloon bar banter. But it could also be something more grave. It was one thing to shoot a line with no expectation of being taken seriously; another to claim phoney successes or dramatize narrow escapes in an attempt to look heroic. To do so was to break the Fighter Boy code of levity at all times, and with it one of the few social taboos that counted. When Deere read Bader's impressions later, he was not pleased. The Hornchurch pilots' demeanour, he wrote with restraint, 'was no "line-shoot"'.

The experience of the first two days of the evacuation had demonstrated that Fighter Command did not have the resources to mount continuous patrols over the battle area. There were not enough aircraft. Those that were available were limited by the amount of fuel they could carry. Brian Kingcome calculated that the average operational time a Spitfire without overload tanks could spend in the air was between an hour and a quarter and an hour and a half, allowing for five or ten minutes at full throttle (though this could stretch to two hours if the trip was uneventful). It was twenty minutes from Biggin Hill to the French coast. That, theoretically, left the pilots with a good half an hour over the beaches.[13] But, in air fighting, the Merlin engines consumed fuel voraciously, and prudent pilots tried to preserve petrol on the outward journey. Sailor Malan found that 'the only way we could fly to Dunkirk and have enough juice to have a few minutes over the battle area was by coasting and flying at sea-level up from Boulogne'.[14] Even so, the return journey was often fraught with the dread of falling out of the sky.

At first, Park sent patrols off in sixes and twelves – flight and squadron strengths. This ensured that there was a more or less continuous fighter presence in the Dunkirk area from dawn to dusk. But it soon became clear that they did not carry the weight to deter the Luftwaffe bombers and fighters, which always greatly outnumbered the defenders. Fighter Command Headquarters had tried to increase the deterrent effect of the fighters by massing them in 'wings' of two or more squadrons, a tactic which had the drawback of leaving windows in the cover, during which the Germans could bomb unmolested.

On 28 May, 19, 54 and 65 Squadrons were ordered off as a wing from Hornchurch. Al Deere, who had been made up to flight commander, took off, along with 54's eight remaining serviceable Spitfires, on a cold grey morning. It was supposed to be their last sortie before going off for a rest. The formation crossed the coast at Gravelines in rain and mist, when Deere saw a lone Dornier nosing out of a cloud towards the Channel, apparently looking for ships to bomb. He peeled off with his flight to attack. He opened fire at 300 yards, hitting the port engine and setting it on fire. He was about to give another burst when bullets from the bomber's rear gunner struck his engine, hitting the coolant tank. Merlin engines were cooled by a liquid called glycol, which flowed around the block through a vascular skein of metal tubing. Any bullet hitting the nose of the aeroplane was likely to rupture one of these pipes. The glycol drained rapidly away, and the engine seized in a few moments. Deere was enveloped in a fine spray of glycol, which turned to white smoke. He realized he had no hope of making it back to England

and steered landwards, looking for a beach on which to crash-land. The drill was to land wheels up. Wheels down ran the lethal risk of cartwheeling if the undercarriage hit something. He put the Spitfire, Kiwi 1, down on the water's edge, slithering through sand and spray and knocking himself out when his head hit the windscreen. When he came to, he climbed out and found a café, where he was told he had landed at Oost-Dunkerke, half-way between Dunkirk and Ostend. When he looked back, the tide was coming in and sea and sand closed over Kiwi 1 for ever.

A woman in the café bandaged his eye and he set off walking towards Ostend, where, he had been told, he stood the best chance of getting back to England. Deere, like the rest of the pilots, had no idea of the scale of the drama being played out to the south. They had been told they were participating in a planned withdrawal. The refugee traffic was so heavy on the road north that he turned back and decided to take his chances in Dunkirk. Travelling on a borrowed bicycle, he reached the outskirts of the town, where he began to understand the dimensions of the crisis. Seeing three British soldiers in a café, he asked a corporal if he could speak to someone in authority. 'As far as I know,' the corporal replied, 'there isn't anybody in authority at the moment. Me and my mates here are the only members of our company who have got back this far; where the hell the rest of them are and for that matter the rest of the British army, I haven't a clue.' Deere found them a few miles down the road. His outstanding impression was 'one of discipline and control, despite the obvious exhaustion and desperation of the thousands of troops who, arranged in snake-like columns, stretched from the sand dunes to the water's edge'.

A naval officer eventually arranged for him to be taken off in the destroyer HMS *Montrose*. During the long wait, the Luftwaffe was overhead constantly. There was panic when three bombers swept over the beach, bombing and strafing, pursued by a lone Spitfire, which broke off, badly hit, and glided inland. Deere was now in the position of seeing the air battle from the infantryman's point of view. The waiting soldiers felt that the sky had been handed over to the Germans, from where they could bomb and shoot unmolested by the RAF. Trying to board the destroyer, Deere was pushed back by an army major. When Deere explained he was trying to rejoin his squadron, which was operating overhead, he was told: 'For all the good you chaps seem to be doing over here you might as well stay on the ground.'[15] Deere's experience was not unique. A pilot from 17 Squadron, who was forced to bale out, had to fight his way aboard a departing boat after being told it was for the army only. Flying Officer Anthony Linney of 229 Squadron, who also had to abandon his aircraft over Dunkirk on 29 May, arrived in Dover to be abused by soldiers, who almost reduced him to tears.

The charge that the RAF had let the army down was repeated endlessly over the next months, provoking angry words and punch-ups when blue uniform and brown battledress met in pubs. It spread beyond the military, becoming part of the mythology of the early war. Fred Rosier, who had been badly burned while leading a detachment of 229 Squadron in France in May, told how his wife was travelling by train in a compartment with soldiers returning from Dover. 'They were shouting, "Where was the bloody air force?" and so on. [She] turned to one of them and said, "Well, I can tell you where one of them is – in hospital and I'm just about to visit him."'[16]

The accusation hurt the pilots, sometimes angered them, but they tended to understand. The fortitude of the troops impressed them deeply. Looking down on Dunkirk, they saw a scene they would never forget and thanked God they were not part of it. Brian Kingcome from his cockpit saw 'beaches [that] were a shambles, littered with the smoking wreckage of engines and equipment . . . The sands erupted into huge geysers from exploding bombs and shells, while a backdrop to the scene of carnage and destruction was provided by the palls of oily black smoke rising from the burning harbour and houses . . . and hanging high in the still air. And yet there the orderly lines of our troops stood, chaos and Armageddon at their backs, patiently waiting their turn to wade into the sea.'[17] Much of the smoke climbing into the sky came from oil-storage tanks around the town. George Unwin found that 'you didn't need a compass to get to Dunkirk. You took off from Hornchurch . . . and you just flew down the smoke and you were there. Those tanks were still

burning weeks afterwards and it really was desolation, absolute desolation. It was a most incredible sight.'[18]

The pilots knew the effort they were making and the price they were
paying. There were several explanations for the belief they were doing
little or nothing. One was the smoke itself. Some of the action over the
beaches was obscured by the canopy of filth. Another was altitude. Sailor
Malan said afterwards, 'We flew too high to be appreciated by our chaps
and too low for Spits to operate at their best advantage.'[19] Others disagreed. Tony Bartley claimed that orders had originally been given for
the fighters not to venture below 15,000 feet because they would be at
risk from the navy and army anti-aircraft guns, which were considered
capable of dealing with low-flying raiders, and to stay above 20,000 feet,
where they would not be visible from the ground. It was certainly true
that British and French gunners could be a menace and many pilots
reported being shot at by their own side.

Bartley's new commander, Bob Tuck, had little faith in the anti-
aircraft defences and decided to ignore the 20,000 feet instruction. 'We
realized that the dive-bombers were at 15,000 feet . . . Finally we dis-
obeyed orders and we came down and started knocking off the Stukas
. . . Bobby Tuck said, "Let's go down and catch these fellows." '[20]
Another reason for the RAF's apparent absence was that much of the
fighting took place away from the beaches as the fighters tried to intercept the German formations before they could reach the target area. In
the experience of George Unwin, 'Very little fighting took place over the
beaches. What we tried to do was stop these people before they reached
the beaches . . . What fighting did go on, most of it was inland.'[21]

Fighter Command's performance was weakened, once again, by the
absence of a comprehensive warning system, which made it impossible
to predict the approach or strength of the attackers. Hugh Dundas, who
had arrived with 616 Squadron to join the battle, thought that 'probably
half the times we went to Dunkirk, perhaps not quite as much as that,
we didn't actually get engaged at all'. Other squadrons, however, seemed
to be in action every time they went up, which meant that the burden of
strain and risk was unevenly spread. John Nicholas, a flying officer with

65 Squadron who shot down two 109s, remembered being airborne for 'eight hours a day, beginning with being called about three o'clock by one's batman . . . I must have done fifty-six hours in a week, which is more than you'd do in two or three months in peace time.'[22]

Unable to deploy forces at times of maximum necessity, the controllers were forced into the draining and wasteful tactic of constant patrolling. For this there were simply not enough aircraft or machines. 'In ideal circumstances one should have had five or six squadrons there the whole time,' Dundas said later. 'There wasn't anything like the strength to do that from dawn to dusk.'[23] The pilots were convinced none the less that Dunkirk would have had a different outcome without them. As it was, some 338,000 British and French troops were rescued, against the 45,000 that was all that was hoped for when Operation Dynamo was launched. 'So who got them off?' Tony Bartley asked later. 'Fighter Command – let's not kid ourselves.'[24]

By the end of 4 June it was finished. Tim Vigors, who had joined 222 Squadron after leaving Cranwell, went off on the last patrol. 'The town and its surroundings really did now resemble Dante's inferno,' he wrote later. 'All remaining oil stores, fuel supplies and equipment which had not burnt already were now set on fire . . . Vast clouds of flame and smoke billowed into the air.'[25] When pilots from 610 Squadron flew the final sortie of the day, they did not meet a single enemy aircraft. On the beaches they could see the French troops who had missed the last boat to freedom, who waved farewell to them and awaited the arrival of the Germans. The Fighter Command pilots had flown 2,739 sorties. They went gratefully off on short leaves to family or friends, anywhere that gave them a taste of their former lives.

Churchill, searching to find worth in a humiliating episode, glimpsed one shining thing of value in the smoke, waste and ruin and reached out to grasp it. Addressing a House of Commons glowing with relief at the success of the rescue operation, he warned that it would be a mistake to regard Dunkirk as a victory, as wars were 'not won by evacuations.'. He went on, 'But there was a victory inside this deliverance, which should be noted. It was gained by the Royal Air Force.'

In terms of relative losses, this was a bold claim to make. The number of RAF aircraft destroyed was reckoned to be 106, against 390 on the German side, a highly optimistic calculation. German documents found after the war put their Dunkirk-related losses at 132, some of which were shot down by anti-aircraft fire. On the human side of the ledger, fifty-six Fighter Command pilots were killed and six aircrew, the latter gunners on the Boulton Paul Defiants, which made a brief appearance in the battle. Eight pilots were taken prisoner and eleven pilots and one air-gunner were wounded. The figures could not express the whole truth of the situation. There were other crucial elements, concerning experience, leadership and morale, that statistics could not measure.

9

Doing It

Pilots returning from their first proper sortie were inevitably cornered by even greener members of the squadron with the question: 'What was it like?' By now, the middle of June, many of the pilots in Fighter Command had some idea of the answer. They knew to varying degrees the reality of the things they had so often wondered about: what it was to be shot at and to shoot, how it felt to watch friends and enemies die. They had heard the clatter of flying debris against wings and fuselage and been blinded by the oil spray from an exploding aircraft. They knew now the jolt of panic at the yelled warning, the violent, instinctive reaction, the swirling confusion of a dogfight and the strange emptiness and quiet that suddenly followed. These were universal experiences, but the near impossibility of describing combat meant that the stories of the initiated did not help very much. To understand it, to gauge your ability to withstand it, you had to do it.

At Duxford aerodrome at 4 a.m. on 29 May, Tim Vigors was woken with a cup of tea by his batman. He gave his lurcher, Snipe, a farewell hug, telling him he would see him that evening, and was driven out to dispersal. Under arc lights that cut through the pre-dawn murk, ground crews were making last adjustments to the Spitfires. Then the commander of 222 Squadron, Squadron Leader Herbert 'Tubby' Mermagen, who, girth notwithstanding, had performed acrobatics for the King before the war, gave the eleven pilots flying with him that day their instructions. They were to head to Dunkirk in line astern, then patrol in formation, unless told otherwise, and return to Hornchurch. Vigors, like most of the others, had never been in action before.

> I walked over to my aircraft to make sure everything was in order [he wrote later]. My mouth was dry and for the first time in my life I understood the meaning of the expression 'taste of fear'. I suddenly realized that the moment had arrived . . . Within an hour I could be battling for my life, being shot at with real bullets by a man whose one desire in life was to kill me. Up until now it had all somehow been a game, like a Biggles book where the heroes always survived the battles and it was generally only the baddies who got the chop. I was dead scared and knew I had somehow to control this fear and not show it to my fellow pilots.[1]

He flew eastwards, seeing the sun edge above the horizon. Then the towers of smoke over Dunkirk came into view. As they reached the coast one of the weavers flying behind and above warned there were enemy aircraft below. Mermagen led his flight into a diving attack. Vigors was in the other flight, commanded by Douglas Bader, circling overhead. Bader spotted a formation of Me 109s flying 5,000 feet above that appeared not to have seen the Spitfires. They climbed up behind them and were within 1,000 feet when the Messerschmitts realized the danger and turned round to attack. Vigors banked hard to try and cut inside the turn of one German fighter, but was immediately distracted by the alarming sight of glowing white tracer flowing past his port wing-tip. In that moment his first reaction was 'extreme fear which temporarily froze my ability to think. This was quickly replaced by an overwhelming desire for self-preservation.' Fortunately, unlike many pilots, he had done some practice dogfighting which had taught him that, if he tried to climb away, he would present a steady target to his attacker. Counter to his instincts, he went into a second evasive move and 'pushed violently forward and sideways on the stick, which flung my Spitfire into a sudden and violent dive which threw my whole weight with unpleasant strength against my shoulder harness'. It seemed to have worked. The tracer stopped.

He had lost a lot of height in the manoeuvre, and pulling out of the dive he climbed cautiously back up, glancing around constantly, until he was above the mêlée that had developed. Then he dived down into the action, picking out a 109 that was chasing a Spitfire in a circle, and pulled in behind him.

Trying to get him in my sights I pulled hard back on the stick and pressed my right thumb on the firing button in the middle of the spade grip on the top of my control column. My aircraft shuddered and tracers shot out from the front of my wings. I could see them passing harmlessly below him. Keeping my finger on the firing button I hauled back even further on the stick, trying to drag the nose of my own aircraft above him. Gradually the tracer came closer to his tail, but just as I thought I had him, he realized his danger and flicked over on his left side and dived.

Vigors followed, still firing, and optimistically thought afterwards that he might have shot a piece off the 109's tail. He broke off when he again came under attack from behind. This time he forgot his training and pulled into an almost vertical climb, blacking out in the process, and came to in time to see the Messerschmitt diving past. Then, as every pilot was to remark in such circumstances, he found to his amazement 'I couldn't see another aircraft in the sky . . . a moment before the whole sky had been filled with circling and diving aircraft and now there was not one of them to be seen'.

In the calm Vigors looked at his watch and saw he had been flying for an hour and a half. He had been hurling his Spitfire about with the throttle wide open, and was in danger of running out of petrol and crashing into the sea. As he turned for home, his first relieved thought was that he was still alive. Also, his Spitfire appeared undamaged. Apart from just possibly having damaged a 109's tail, he had done nothing apart from distracting the enemy.

His biggest concern was 'how deadly scared I'd been when I first saw those enemy bullets streaming past my wing-tip. I had never known any fear like that before in my life . . . I just fervently hoped I could keep it under control.' Vigors met Bader on landing and gave a suitably stiff-upper-lip account of the engagement. But when he reached dispersal, where the returning 222 Squadron pilots were noisily and excitedly discussing the fight, and saw Hilary Edridge, his best friend in the squadron, neither of them hid their feelings.

> 'Glad to see you in one piece,' I exclaimed. 'How did you do?'
>
> 'Never been more scared in my whole bloody life,' he laughed.
>
> 'That makes two of us,' I replied. 'I was shit scared from the word go.'

The next day Vigors completed his baptism. On the second patrol of the day, 222 Squadron ran into a formation of Heinkels. He latched on to one, but his bullets drifted below it and before he could find another the Messerschmitts arrived. Vigors was chased and pulled sharp right as hard as he could, blacking out but bringing himself up behind the German and finding to his satisfaction that he was turning inside him. They were now on opposite sides of the circle in a classic dogfighting position. Vigors kept reefed tight into the turn, on the edge of unconsciousness because of the terrific G forces, until he almost had the target in his sights. In desperation the German dived for the sea, the tactic Vigors had used the previous day. But by now he was right on top of him and at 200 yards opened fire. 'I saw my bullets ripping into his starboard wing and suddenly he burst into a ball of flame. "Got you, you bastard!" I yelled.' This exultation vanished when he 'felt a tug on my right wing and to my horror I saw holes appearing in the wing-tip'. A 109 darted beneath him and then the sky was clear again. A roll of the controls told him that the Spitfire would get him home.

Examining his feelings on the return journey, he was 'more than happy to have made my first kill' and felt the same satisfaction as when, on his family estate near Clonmel, he had 'pulled down a high-flying pigeon flashing across the evening sky with the wind up his tail.' There was a sombre moment at the thought he had just killed a man. He and his adversary would, he pondered, have 'probably got on well together if we'd met drinking beer in a pub'. The mood did not last long. 'But he was on the wrong side,' he concluded. 'He shouldn't have signed up with that bastard Hitler.' Later he was 'surprised that he did not feel more remorse'. In the space of forty-eight hours, Tim Vigors had tasted many of the common experiences of flying a fighter in combat, short of being shot down, wounded or killed. Fifty hours of training was worth less than one hour of the real thing.

By early summer every squadron in Fighter Command except two had clashed with the Luftwaffe on at least one occasion. At this early stage, operations proceeded in an orderly fashion. Standing at dispersal in the rising light of dawn or the glare of an early summer afternoon, the squadron or flight was given its instructions on the ground by the commander. Then, as the riggers and fitters climbed down off the wings, the pilots hoisted themselves up by placing a right foot in the step set into the left side of the fuselage. They then put their other foot on the wing root and swung over into the narrow cockpit, stowing their parachute in the scooped recess of the steel bucket seat. Next came the nerve-calming routine of strapping in, switching on petrol, starting the engine and checking oxygen and instruments. On the order, they took off methodically and flew in formation until they reached the battle zone. The discipline of keeping position had the same effect as infantry drill, creating a feeling of security, a sense of strength in combination, that almost invariably evaporated as soon as the fighting began.

Everyone, at all times, constantly scoured the sky around them for aircraft. Good eyesight was a life-saver. Exceptional eyesight gave a pilot a considerable advantage, enabling him to see his victim before he himself was seen. Pilots twisted their heads up and down, left and right, continuously. In a regulation-wear collar and tie, necks were soon rubbed raw. It was for that reason that they began wearing the silk scarves which in time became their sartorial symbol.

On the outward journey the squadron, flight or section leader could talk to the other aircraft, and his voice and manner over the R/T was an important element in shaping the mood of the pilots behind him. Confident leaders gave confidence to those they led, and commanders could be forgiven many shortcomings if they had the gift of imparting reassurance. Some, like Deere, Kingcome and Bader, did so with a mixture of humour and profanity, using nicknames, reinforcing the ties of intimacy and affection that bound the best squadrons together. The possibility of giving encouragement and direction disappeared, however, in the explosion of confusion that followed engagement.

With the first sighting of Germans, the first 'Tally ho!', the low hum of anticipation jumped to a sharper pitch. Heads swivelled to the bearing as the pilots searched for the enemy aircraft. They went quickly into the last routine of preparation, dropping the seat to get maximum protection from the engine block in front and the armour plate behind, tightening straps, switching on the reflector sight, checking the range and wing-span indicators and flicking the gun button into the firing position. In the distance, the enemy aircraft seem always to have appeared as alien and malign objects, a different species. They looked like 'flies', 'swarms of bees', 'a milling great mass of little insects', never like birds, though flocks of birds could sometimes be mistaken for Germans by nervous pilots. Getting closer, the sight of the black crosses, edged in white, standing out on wings and fuselages, had a profound effect on pilots looking on them for the first time, striking them as sinister, redolent of death, bringing home with unexpected force the seriousness of what they were engaged in.

Once again, training helped to control feeling and instinct as the fighters responded to the designated attack order and manoeuvred into position. Paul Richey found that, on seeing the enemy, 'all the tension and concentration in my body focused in a wild leap of my heart. It always made me swallow hard a couple of times.' Then it was 'into action, body taught against the straps, teeth clenched, thumb on the gun button, narrowed eyes intent on getting that black-crossed Hun in the sights and holding him there.' He felt his 'pounding heart turn into a block of ice. Not in fear. My brain became coldly clear and I was transformed into a cool, calculating killer.'[2]

Shooting a smallish, nimble object travelling at more than 300 m.p.h., when you are moving at a similar speed while diving, turning and rolling, was extraordinarily hard. The difficulties were multiplied by the heavy G forces that crushed the pilots' heads down on their chests, and turned the blood in their veins to the weight of molten metal. Pilots found that when they finally got within range and opened fire, the bullets did not fly with undeviating, linear cleanliness, but wobbled and wavered. It was no wonder that when they spoke of shooting at an enemy they talked of 'giving it a squirt'. The process was more akin to aiming a hose than firing an arrow. The reflector sight, which replaced the old ring sight, projected a dot of red light on the angled underside of the windscreen. It was bracketed by a set of range bars which could be adjusted to the size of bombers or fighters. Kingcome found, 'It was quite helpful in assessing distances, and the red dot simply indicated the line of flight of your bullets . . . if you lined it up on a static target and were also stationary, you scored a hit. What it regrettably did not tell you was where to aim at a moving target, or how much deflection to allow . . . Such judgements only came from experience combined with instinct.'[3]

The first indication that bullets were striking their target was the sight of bits of debris from the air frame or wings tumbling away, sometimes striking the body of the pursuing fighter. If an engine was hit, oil or glycol might suddenly swamp the pilot's windscreen, obliterating vision. The sight of smoke and fire spurting from an engine marked one sort of end. The other came with the death of the pilot. At such speeds, there was little human contact between the men trying to kill each other. A pilot's head might be glimpsed wedged in the narrow cockpit of a 109, more cramped even than that of a Spitfire, as it flashed past, but it was rarely for long enough to register the features or for a look to be exchanged. The most frequent indication of the connection between shooting and killing was during a rear attack on a Heinkel or Junkers, or, particularly, a Dornier, which at this stage of the war carried less armour than the other bombers. The four barrels poking from the rear turret would suddenly slant upwards, a sign that the gunner had been hit and had fallen forward across the breech of his weapon. Some pilots noticed that, after shooting at an aeroplane without apparent effect, they suddenly sensed an invisible change in the aircraft, a loss of vitality as if the spirit had left it, then saw this instinct confirmed as the machine tipped downwards into a dive that its pilot was no longer in any condition to control.

This was the moment of victory, the 'kill'. Richey maintained that aerial combat was not 'a hot-blooded thrilling affair', but he confessed to 'a savage, primitive exaltation' at the sight of an enemy going down that was 'not very edifying'. The point of a fighter pilot's existence was to shoot down aeroplanes, but when Pete Brothers came to do so, his reaction was 'absolute surprise and astonishment [as] the aircraft went over on its back and some bits fell off and it went screaming down into the ground. I followed it down and saw it crash and thought "amazing".' His next response was alarm. 'I thought, "My God, that's really going to make them cross. They'll be after me." I began whizzing around looking behind me, making sure . . . They were probably going to come and do me for this. Maybe I shouldn't have done it.'[4]

Others felt nothing but pleasure at the sight of their opponent going down. Johnny Freeborn ran across a 109 attacking a Spitfire south of Dunkirk and went in to attack it. The Messerschmitt dipped sharply away, a defensive tactic favoured by the German pilots that exploited the fact that the 109's Mercedes-Benz engine had fuel injection, which allowed a steep dive without loss of power. The Merlin engine did not, which meant it missed several beats at the moment of negative gravity as a Hurricane or Spitfire tipped sharply downwards. The way of overcoming this was to flick the aircraft into a half-roll, then straighten out, throwing fuel into the carburettor. Freeborn went into the manoeuvre and plunged down through thick cumulonimbus, emerging to find the 109 right in front of him. 'He went right down to the ground and I shot the hell out of him. The engine stopped and the propeller was just windmilling.' For once, he was close enough to see his enemy's face. 'He looked bloody terrified. I thought, you German bastard, and I gave him another one. He hit a telegraph pole with the prop and went straight into a farmhouse. The farmer was ploughing outside the house . . . I was very pleased about that.'[5] Sailor Malan, shooting down his first Heinkel 111, found 'the release from tension was terrific, the thrill enormous. I'd been wondering for so long . . . how I'd react in my first show. Now I knew. Everything I had learned had come right. There was hardly time even to feel scared.'[6]

Despite the expectation of being shot at, pilots were often slow to realize they were under attack. Flying was noisy. The throb of a 1,175 horsepower engine blotted out the sound of firing, so frequently the first indication of danger was the sight of tracer, floating towards you, gentle and seemingly innocent, 'like a string of light bulbs'. Kingcome described later how 'tracer comes out at you, apparently very slowly to begin with. You see these lazy, long smoke trails coming at you. They get faster as they reach you, then suddenly whip past your ear at the most amazing speed.'[7]

Being fired on for the first time could have a paralysing effect. George Unwin had had four years of flying experience before meeting a 109 over Dunkirk. 'I saw little sparks coming from the front end of him and I knew he was shooting at me and I did nothing, absolutely nothing. I was just, not petrified, but, I don't know, frozen, for ten or fifteen seconds . . . I just sat there and watched him shoot at me.'[8] The Messerschmitt missed and Unwin lived to apply the lesson he had learned.

Frequently, the bullets came without warning, seemingly out of nowhere, arriving with a sudden heart-jolting shock. Peter Parrott was patrolling in France, unaware of any imminent danger, when he 'heard a couple of almighty bangs on the armour plating behind me', and put his Hurricane into a dive. When he landed he found that only two rounds from the 109 that attacked him had hit. One damaged the radio and another struck one of the fuselage formers. Even so, 'it had sounded as if the whole thing was going to break into pieces, the noise they had made coming in'.[9]

The first indication that the engine had been hit was usually the appearance of oil or glycol streaming back over the windscreen. Unless the damage made the aircraft unflyable, a pilot's first instinct was to stay on board as long as possible in the hope of being able to nurse it back to friendly territory, even if this entailed crossing the suddenly very wide-looking expanse of the English Channel. A crash-landing meant finding the nearest piece of flat ground and gliding in, slipping the aeroplane from side to side to increase wind resistance and reduce the impact speed, keeping the wheels retracted to lessen the chances of them catching in an obstacle and somersaulting. Hitting the ground, bouncing and skidding through the topsoil, the pilot faced a last danger in the form of smashing his head on the thick bulletproof glass of the windscreen.

Peter Parrott, who after surviving France had been posted to 145 Squadron, was in the process of shooting down a Heinkel over the coast-line of the Pas de Calais when he was hit by return fire from the rear gunner, which damaged the radiator and put a hole in the glycol tank. His cockpit was full of water vapour and the only instrument he could see was the oil temperature gauge, which was dangerously high. Wondering how long the coolant would last before the engine seized, he turned towards England, streaming a long trail of vapour. Half-way across the Channel, the rest of the squadron caught him up and Roy Dutton overtook to try and lead him to a safe landing place. 'We crossed the coast at Deal and within inches of crossing . . . the engine stopped . . . I was around three or four thousand feet and looking for somewhere to put the thing down with the wheels up. Manston was too far to the north and Hawkinge was too far on the south side. Behind Deal there are some downs. It was a Sunday evening and a lot of people were out for their evening walk. I picked out these three fields. One was on the upward slope one was slightly curved – the dome so to speak – and then there was the one on the other side which went downhill fairly sharply.' He chose the top of the hill, expecting to bounce along the turf, but instead came to an almost immediate halt, killing two sheep in the process.

Parrott was soaked in glycol – 'sticky, filthy stuff' – but otherwise unharmed. He and his Hurricane were soon surrounded by strollers, then a policeman arrived and Parrott went off to a farmhouse to phone the base at Manston. On the way he met the farmer arriving in a pony and trap. 'The first thing he said was, "Who's going to pay for them sheep then?" In a lordly tone, I said, "The Air Ministry." He grunted, got back in his cart and went off. So I was faced with going down to the farm, facing this angry man again to ask if I could use his telephone. By the time I got there he and his wife were having high tea. There was a large ham on the table. It looked lovely but I wasn't invited.' Parrott called Manston and a car was dispatched together with a guard for the Hurricane. He left the inhospitable couple to their tea and was back in action next day.

The robustness of Hurricanes and, to a lesser extent, Spitfires meant that even quite badly damaged aircraft could be coaxed back to safety. But if the engine caught fire the only choice was to jump. The decision was instantaneous. The sight of smoke and flame curling backwards, wrapping around the Perspex bubble of the canopy, was enough to settle the issue. Like their First World War forebears, all pilots had a particular horror of burning. When they did bale out, it was, almost without exception, the first time they had been on the end of a parachute. There was no place for practice jumps on the pre-war training curriculum and this did not change when the war started. Parachutes had only become standard equipment in 1928, when the extraordinary argument that possession of them would lead to a diminution of fighting spirit was finally dropped. Pilots were taught the drill for leaving their stricken aeroplane. It required sliding back the canopy, releasing your harness then flipping the fighter on to its back so you dropped free. It sounded easy enough in theory, but in the urgency of the moment things conspired to go wrong.

When Fred Rosier's Hurricane was hit and caught fire over northern France, he went into the drill but found the cockpit hood was jammed. He remembered sitting back 'and thinking that that was that. The next thing I was falling, and I suppose instinctively pulled the ripcord. I saw that my trousers were all on fire. I remember the skin leaving my hands as I tried to put the fire out.'[10] Pilot Officer Ronald Brown of 111 Squadron had not even been taught the theory when he was forced to jump from his Hurricane over Abbeville. Ignorant of what to do, he simply pushed the hood back, stood up and was immediately whipped out of the cockpit by the wind, smashing his legs against the tailplane. 'I always remember it was beautifully warm and I wanted to go to sleep. Then something made me say to myself, pull the ripcord you bloody fool. So I pulled it – a sharp jerk. And there I am on my brolly.'[11]

Prosser Hanks, trying to vacate his Hurricane after being hit and catching fire, had the opposite problem. 'I was suddenly drenched in hot glycol. I didn't have my goggles down and the bloody stuff completely blinded me. I didn't know where I was and somehow got into a spin. I could see damn all and the cockpit was getting bloody hot so I undid the straps and opened the hood to get out but I couldn't. Every time I tried I was pressed back. I started to scream then, but stopped screaming and then somehow or other I got out.'[12]

These dramas sometimes happened in view of other squadron members. Seeing comrades die, frequently at very close quarters, was an eternal part of the infantryman's experience. For pilots, the sensations attached to witnessing the death of a comrade seem to have been muffled slightly by a layer of detachment. Searching for his base in northern France after destroying a Me 110, Flight Lieutenant Ian Gleed of 87 Squadron saw a Hurricane flying serenely along and steered to join up with it. 'Just as I am drawing up to formate on this Hurricane, he dips; I catch a fleeting glimpse of flying brick, and seemingly quite slowly, a Hurricane's tail, with the red, white and blue stripes, flies up past my cockpit. I glance behind and see a cloud of dust slowly rising. He must have had some bullets in him to have hit that house. I wonder who it was?'[13]

The victim went to his end encased in a machine, sparing onlookers the horrible details. There was no body to confront. Death usually occurred at some distance from the home base and dealing with the corpse, or what was left of it, was the responsibility of others. Dead bodies, of friend or foe, were strangely absent from the fighter pilots' war. Peter Townsend never saw a corpse in his entire RAF service, first encountering one when as a journalist he covered the Six-Day War in the Middle East in 1967.

On the other hand, the pause between the appearance of smoke and flame and the end left plenty of time to imagine what was happening inside the cockpit. On several occasions, the doomed pilot's R/T was left switched on and his screams, prayers and curses filled the headphones of his companions.

Crashing into the ground or sea at high speed was often referred to with standard Fighter Boy understatement as 'going in'. The blandness of the term served to soften the hard lines of the reality. The lightness of expression used for the darkest subjects had a very serious purpose: to rob fear of its power. Acknowledged, but only occasionally spoken about, fear tainted every hour of a fighter pilot's working day. It was the second enemy. Levels of fear varied. Different pilots felt it with differing intensity in different circumstances. For all but a handful it was a palpable presence that might be banished during the hours of darkness, driven away by the beer and the company of your companions, then fatigue, but was always up and waiting at readiness next morning. Tim Vigors was right. There really was a 'taste of fear'. It was sour and metallic at the same time, and no amount of swallowing or chewing gum could make it go away. Other physical sensations went with it: mild nausea, a feeling of faintness in the head and a slight tingling of the anal sphincter known to pilots as 'ring twitch'.

Unless a pilot could suppress fear, he was useless, and stood a good chance of getting killed very quickly. Hugh Dundas gave a frank account of the unmanning terror that seized him on his first encounter with Germans during the Dunkirk evacuation. As so often, when he saw an Me 109 turning towards him and noted the ripples of grey smoke and flashing lights coming from the nose of the plane, it took him some time to understand what was happening.

'Red blobs arced lazily through the air between us, accelerating dramatically as they approached and streaked close by, across my wing. With sudden, sickening, stupid fear I realized that I was being fired on and I pulled my Spitfire round hard, so that the blood was forced down from my head. The thick curtain of blackout blinded me for a moment and I felt the aircraft juddering on the brink of a stall.' More 109s attacked and the tail-chasing continued, with Dundas wrenching his machine into the tightest and fastest turn he could squeeze from it. He managed one shot ('quite ineffectual') before the Germans moved off. He was left 'close to panic in the bewilderment and hot fear of that first dogfight. Fortunately instinct drove me to keep turning and turning, twisting my neck all the time to look for the enemy behind. Certainly the consideration which was uppermost in my mind was the desire to stay alive.'

Dundas was to find this feeling never went away. 'When it comes to the point, a sincere desire to stay alive is all too likely to get the upper hand. Certainly, that was the impulse which consumed me at that moment that day. And that was the impulse which I had to fight against, to try and try and try again to overcome, during the years which followed.'

Panic descended again later on in the patrol when he found himself alone just north of Dunkirk. Instead of calmly working out his course to reach the Thames estuary and home, he set off blindly in what he thought might be the right direction. In a few minutes he was lost, high over the empty sea, where there was not even a ship to take as a bearing. He found that the 'need to get in touch with the land pressed in on me and drove out all calmness and good sense. I saw that I was flying almost due north and realized that this was wrong, but could not get a hold of myself sufficiently to work things out. I turned back the way I had come, cravenly thinking that I could at the worst crash-land somewhere off Dunkirk and get home in a boat.' Eventually he sighted the coast of France and worked out the simple navigational problem of finding the course for home. As he crossed the estuary at Southend, heading for the little aerodrome at Rochford, he was soaked in sweat, but 'a sense of jubilation had replaced the cravenness of a few minutes earlier'. He felt 'transformed . . . now a debonair young fighter pilot, rising twenty . . . sat in the cockpit which had so recently been occupied by a frightened child.'[14] He taxied over to the dispersal point where the ground crew were waiting to hear his tales of the battle.

Dundas, like Vigors, had been through a rite of passage. The most testing psychological moments in a fighter pilot's career were those that followed the first experience of coming under fire. The overpowering human impulse, having brushed against death, is to run away. The military impulse is to seek cover, but in the absence of clouds that was not an option in the skies. Dundas had been gripped by 'hot fear', Vigors 'scared shitless', yet both chose to stay and fight however inefficiently. By doing so they crossed a threshold and became warriors.

Dogfights rarely lasted more than a few minutes. Their intensity, though, made them exceptionally draining. The fact that exhaustion could set in very quickly was recognized early on at senior levels of Fighter Command, and intelligent decisions were often – though not invariably – made to move squadrons and pilots out of the line for a rest before their efficiency was so diminished that they became easy targets. Deep fatigue could drag depression and moodiness in its wake. Paul Richey, after being forced to bale out on the second day of the air war in France, 'began to feel peculiar' when he got back to the squadron. 'I had a hell of a headache and was jumpy and snappy. Often I dared not speak for fear of bursting into tears.' He was put to bed by the squadron doctor with some sleeping pills but the sound of bombs on the airfield kept him awake. When he did sleep it was only to relive the day's experiences and he found himself 'in my Hurricane rushing head-on at a 110. Just as we were about to collide I woke up with a jerk that nearly threw me out of bed. I was in a cold sweat, my heart banging wildly.' He went off to sleep again, but the nightmare returned and continued to do so at ten-minute intervals all night. 'I shall never forget,' he wrote, 'how I clung to the bed-rail in a dead funk.'[15]

The question he had asked himself as he lay there was how long he would be able to go on. It was clear from the start that there would be no quick victory. The absence of any sense of progress was potentially particularly demoralizing to pilots who were confronting a future which consisted of the endless repetition of a routine that common sense told them was almost certain to finish in death. As early as 16 June Denis Wissler was writing in his diary: 'Oh God I do wish this war would end.' But for him and the rest of Fighter Command, the real war was only just beginning.

10

Before the Storm

During the morning of 4 June, the pilots of 222 Squadron were stood down from further patrolling duties and given the rest of the day off. Tim Vigors heard the good news after returning to Hornchurch from a sortie over the French coast, during the course of which he and Hilary Edridge narrowly escaped being shot down by 109s. Wondering what to do with their free time, Vigors noticed the date. It was speech day at his old school, Eton. He asked Edridge, his constant companion since they joined the squadron together, to go with him to the celebrations.

Driving through the East End they stopped at a pub. Vigors noticed that they were the only people in uniform and customers 'cast glances at us as if we had come down from the moon'. The woman behind the bar remarked: 'You boys aren't half going to have to look after us now. I just hope that there are enough of you.' Edridge mentioned that they had been airborne only a short time before, and shooting at Germans. The other customers did not believe them at first, then tried to buy them drinks.

At Eton, 'the sky was cloudless and the sun shone down on the brightly coloured scene. Pretty girls in picture hats strolled with their blue blazer-clad escorts under the big shady trees which surrounded the cricket grounds. The peaceful murmur of conversation was broken occasionally by subdued clapping as a boundary was struck or a wicket fell. The war was a million miles away. Could this be the same world in which we had battled so few hours ago? Somewhere God had got this day wrong.'[1]

Several pilots had sensed a reluctance among British civilians to accept that what was happening to the rest of Europe could also happen to them. But after Dunkirk and the fall of France the public's complacency, or studied disregard, had faded. Now that it was no longer possible to treat the danger as remote and theoretical, the sense of detachment from the events that characterized the phoney war gave way to defiance, and in some cases alarm.

Official statements designed to reassure seemed as likely to have the opposite effect. On the morning of 18 June, the Ministry of Information issued a leaflet telling the population how to respond to a German invasion. Citizens were ordered to stay at home to avoid the chaos that had gripped Holland, Belgium and France, when hundreds of thousands of refugees blocked the roads, paralysing supply lines and the defenders' ability to manoeuvre. The second instruction stated: 'When you receive an order make sure that it is a true order and not a fake order . . . if you keep your heads you can also tell whether a military officer is really British or only pretending to be so.'[2] The military correspondent of a newspaper circulating in south-east England warned readers to be on the lookout for parachutists, 'mostly young men of the desperado type' whose task was to 'organize local fifth column members and arm them . . . create panic and confusion and spread false news among the civil population'.[3] Such advice made people panicky. A commercial traveller who failed to stop his car in time at a checkpoint near Wrexham, manned by Local Defence Volunteers, was shot dead. Enemy aliens were moved away from coastal areas and innocents were arrested after tip-offs from neighbours on suspicion of being spies.

But the general mood, as disaster piled up on the Continent, was resolute. The bad news brought with it a sense of relief. Somerset Maugham, docking at Liverpool after fleeing France in a crowded refugee ship, recorded that 'in the officials who came on board, in the porters who took our baggage, in the people in the streets, in the waiters at the restaurant, you felt the same spirit of confidence. Fear of invasion? Not a shadow of it. "We'll smash 'em. It'll take time of course, but that's all right. We can hang on."[4] On the morning of 18 June, *The Times* quoted from Wordsworth's sonnet 'November, 1806' when England stood in isolation against Napoleon's army, fresh from victories at Austerlitz and Jena.

> 'Tis well! from this day forwards we shall know
> That in ourselves our safety must be sought;
> That by our own right hands it must be wrought;
> That we must stand unpropped, or be laid low

Other newspapers remembered it was the anniversary of the Battle of Waterloo.

That day Winston Churchill laid the foundations of a new British legend. It had dawned hot and clear, another gorgeous morning in a memorable run of fine weather. The prime minister was due to address the House of Commons in the afternoon after the usual Tuesday-afternoon question time. The Cabinet met at 12.30, but Churchill stayed away so he could work on the text, and was still scribbling changes as he sat in the House on the Treasury benches between Neville Chamberlain and Clement Attlee waiting his turn to speak.

He got to his feet at 3.49 p.m. before a packed House and a public gallery overflowing with ambassadors and VIPs. Despite the grimness of the situation, Churchill started off optimistically, presenting catastrophe as a sort of triumph. He stressed the great achievement of the Dunkirk evacuation, not mentioning the fact that the rescued troops had left most of their heavy equipment behind. He emphasized the obstacles facing a German invasion, starting with the Royal Navy, which 'some people seem to have forgotten' Britain possessed.

With the House settled and primed, he moved to the heart of the speech: 'the great question of the invasion of the air and the impending struggle between the British and German air forces'. Churchill conceded that it was 'a very great pity that we have not got an air force at least equal to that of the most powerful enemy within striking distance of our shores'. But this note of caution died as quickly as it had been struck. Then the old certainty returned, and coursed warmly through the remainder of the speech like vintage Armagnac. In the fighting in France in May and June the RAF, he stated confidently, had 'proved itself far superior in quality both in men and in many types of machine to what we have met so far'. Despite the disadvantages of operating from foreign fields and having lost many aircraft on the ground, the air force 'had still managed to routinely inflict losses of two-and-a-half to one'. In the fighting over Dunkirk, he claimed, 'we undoubtedly beat the German air force, which gave us the mastery locally in the air, and we inflicted losses of three or four to one . . . In the defence of this island the advantages to the defenders will be very great. We hope to improve on the rate of three or four to one that we achieved at Dunkirk.'

Churchill went on to predict victory, and calm any fears about the condition of Fighter Command. 'I am happy to inform the House that our fighter air strength is stronger at the present time, relatively to the Germans, who have suffered terrible losses, than it has ever been and consequently we believe ourselves to possess the capacity to continue the war in the air under better conditions than we have ever experienced before. I look forward confidently to the exploits of our fighter pilots who will have the glory of saving their native land, their island home and all they love from the most deadly of attacks.'

And so the speech surged on towards its famous end:

'What General Weygand called the Battle of France is over. I expect the Battle of Britain is about to begin. Upon this battle depends the survival of Christian civilization. Upon it depends our own British life and the long continuity of our institutions and our Empire. The whole fury and might of the enemy must very soon be turned upon us. Hitler knows he will have to break us in this island or lose the war.

'If we can stand up to him all Europe may be free and the life of the world may move forward into broad, sunlit uplands; but if we fail then the whole world, including the United States, and all we have known and cared for, will sink into the abyss of a new dark age, made more sinister and perhaps more prolonged by the lights of a perverted science. Let us therefore address ourselves to our duty, so bear ourselves that if the British Commonwealth and Empire lasts for a thousand years, men will say "This was their finest hour." '

The Times parliamentary reporter, numb fingers coming to rest at last, recorded 'loud and prolonged cheers'.

That evening Churchill repeated the speech, which was broadcast by the BBC. Some of the pilots at Biggin Hill listened to it in the mess. 'We were standing in the hall drinking beer and our feeling was one of relief,' said Pete Brothers. 'Thank God we were on our own and not saddled with a craven ally.'[5] This sentiment, though he did not know it, was shared by King George VI. Group Captain Grice, the station commander, had the speech typed up and posted around the base. Most of the pilots, though, seem not to have heard it – too absorbed in the process of recovering from the losses of the previous five weeks to hear the prime minister's dramatic definition of the task awaiting them.

Churchill's analysis had, characteristically, been inaccurate in details but correct in essentials. It was true that the fate of Britain now depended on the fighter pilots. It was also true that, henceforth, flying from their own soil and defending their own homeland, they would enjoy significant practical and moral advantages. But the highly favourable ratio of losses he claimed between British and German aircraft in their encounters to date was, as he must have known, an exaggeration. The RAF did not have more fighters than the Luftwaffe. A month later Goering still had at least 760 Me 109s at his disposal against Dowding's 591 Hurricanes and Spitfires. And Fighter Command was, if not exhausted, depleted in men and machines and in serious need of rest, recuperation and reorganization.

Dowding was now engaged in trying to nurse Fighter Command back to strength before its next great trial, patching up battered squadrons, injecting new blood and replacing the lost fighters. Some units which had been particularly hard hit were moved out of the front line. Among them was 92 Squadron, which had lost six pilots, and was posted to Pembrey in Wales, in the 10 Group area, where it spent most of the rest of the summer. After leaving France at the end of May, 87 Squadron moved north to Church Fenton near Leeds to re-form. There, Roland Beamont found only 'the remnants of the squadron': a few of the Hurricanes that had made it out of France and half the original complement of pilots. The ground crews arrived in 'dribs and drabs', having been left to make their way home by ship. Some aircraftmen who had served in France in other squadrons were not to return to Britain before the middle of July. The squadron diary reported that 'during the first fortnight in June, the task of re-forming went steadily ahead . . . not made easier by the fact that practically all equipment, service and personal, had necessarily been abandoned in France'. Another veteran unit of Fighter Command's French adventure, 73 Squadron, which had only seven pilots fit for operations and half its ground crew, and whose remaining Hurricanes were all in need of repair, also moved to Church Fenton. It spent the next months in the relative calm of 12 Group, practising, patrolling and night flying until it was sent back into the middle of the air battle at the beginning of September.

The fighting in France and over Dunkirk cost the lives of 110 pilots. Another forty-seven were wounded and twenty-six taken prisoner. The losses tore holes in the ranks of virtually every squadron. Of the twenty-two units that served in France, only three had not lost pilots through death, injury or capture. The worst casualties had been suffered by 85 Squadron. Out of its normal establishment of eighteen pilots, it had lost, in the space of eleven days, eight killed or missing in action and six wounded. The commanding officer, Michael Peacock was among the dead. Peter Townsend was moved from 43 Squadron to 85 and given the task of rebuilding the unit's strength and identity around the core of the seven surviving pilots.

Dowding's policy was, wherever possible, to take pilots from the most battle-tested units and spread them through the system to provide a core of expertise that would stiffen performance and morale. But there were few to go around. Many of the most experienced pilots were gone. At

Dunkirk alone, Fighter Command lost three squadron commanders killed and one taken prisoner, six flight commanders killed and one taken prisoner, as well as about twelve section leaders, including two senior NCO pilots. Some veterans were in no condition to return to the battle. Paul Richey spent his convalescence as a sector controller, overseeing fighter operations from Middle Wallop in Hampshire. Billy Drake, also recovering from the wounds he sustained in France, was sent on his return as an instructor to the operational training unit at Sutton Bridge in Lincolnshire, where pilots finished their training before being posted to a squadron, and Killy Kilmartin to another at Aston Down.

It was the young and inexperienced who were pushed forward to fill the gaps, including undertrained pilots just emerging from the ranks of the Volunteer Reserve. Peacetime training was lengthy and intense. The *ab initio* phase to teach the rudiments of flying was followed by forty-four weeks of thorough instruction in every aspect of aviation. The final six-week stage, intended to marry the pilot to the machine he would have to fight in, was carried out by operational training units (OTUs). The shortage of new pilots created by the losses of May and early June led to the setting up of three new OTUs, which raced qualified pilots through the conversion programme in two weeks. But shortages were so acute that promising pilots in training were sometimes posted directly from their flying training schools without passing through an OTU, and by the middle of the year the notional length of time in training was often being cut in half to twenty-two weeks.[6]

Charlton Haw had just turned twenty when he arrived at 504 Squadron. He was born in York and left school at fourteen to become an apprentice in a lithographic works. As soon as he was eighteen he had applied to join the RAFVR but failed the medical. He applied again in January 1939 and was accepted. 'I'd always wanted to fly from when I was a small boy,' he said. 'I never wanted to do anything else really. I just didn't think there would be a chance for me. Most of the people who went into short-service commissions at the time had very high educational qualifications. The chances for any normal schoolboy to get in until the RAFVR was formed [were] almost impossible.'[7] Haw was shrewd and assured despite his lack of advanced schooling. He was also a natural pilot, a talent he partially ascribed to the gentle touch he brought to the controls from playing the piano.

In the eight months before the outbreak of war he spent three nights a week in a classroom in Hull learning navigation and flight theory. At weekends, and during a fortnight's holiday from his firm, he went flying at Brough airfield, the test aerodrome for the Blackburn aircraft works, so that by the time the war began he had eighty hours' experience on biplanes. In September he had been called up, but to his disappointment was sent home almost immediately. A month later he was ordered to report to an initial training wing at St Leonards-on-Sea, Sussex. This was based in a seaside hotel requisitioned by the Air Ministry to provide RAFVR personnel with a taste of service discipline. The routine included drilling on the promenade, lectures, formal warnings of the dangers of VD and marathon PT sessions under the supervision of Len Harvey, the famous British boxer. It lasted about a month and was, almost everybody agreed, a waste of time.

In December he moved on to Sealand, in Cheshire, for intermediate and advanced training, and passed out rated above average. In May he was due to be posted to an OTU to convert to Spitfires or Hurricanes. The shortage of pilots meant that just as he was about to leave he received counter orders to join 504 Squadron, which had lost nine of its members – half its strength – killed, wounded or taken prisoner in France. Five other half-trained pilots went from Sealand with him. The squadron was based at Wick in the far north of Scotland, where its duties included convoy protection patrols, interceptions and the defence of the Fleet, anchored in Scapa Flow. Haw found the surviving members friendly and welcoming, and morale 'fantastically good' despite the losses. The process of getting used to Hurricanes started immediately, but progress was hampered by the delay in delivery of new aircraft to replace those lost in France. By the time he had his first fight he had flown a single-engined fighter for only twelve hours. About a month after joining he was over Scapa Flow in a three-man patrol when the leader spotted a Heinkel 111 and dived after it. Haw, in a state of excitement, followed the attack down. Closing in, he noticed 'red-hot chain links' coming towards him. As he broke away a bullet smashed straight through the narrow cockpit and out the other side. 'When I came back they were all slapping me on the back and saying how lucky I was,' he said later, 'and I was lucky. There as no doubt about it.' Having come through this first, crucial, encounter, he was now better equipped to deal with the next one and his chances of survival had significantly improved.

Frank Usmar also had his training cut short. He was on a few days' leave, awaiting a posting to Sutton Bridge when a policeman arrived at his parents' home in West Malling, Kent, where his father was the village postman, and told him he was to report to 41 Squadron at Catterick. Usmar, too, had left school at fourteen and was working as a clerk while studying at evening school to become an accountant. When an RAFVR recruiting office opened in Rochester he applied to join. He learned to fly, was called up in September and did his stint of square-bashing at St Leonards before passing on to No. 6 Flying Training School at Little Rissington. He remembered later that 'when Dunkirk happened we shot through the final stages at a rate of knots'.[8] Waiting at Catterick station for a ride to the base, he was asked by a corporal whether he was there as a replacement for the pilots the squadron had lost at Dunkirk. It was the first time he heard that the unit had taken part in the action. When he arrived he was pleasantly surprised to find three of his friends from Little Rissington had also been posted directly to the squadron: Pilot Officer Gerry Langley, Sergeant Johnny McAdam, another Kent boy, and Pilot Officer Eric Lock. All of them had come from the RAFVR. Only Usmar was to survive the war.

The four had never flown anything faster than a Harvard. A Spitfire was sent down to a nearby bomber station deemed to have a less tricky runway than Catterick for them to practice on. After three satisfactory landings they were considered competent. From then until the end of July they flew with the squadron on its daily routine, which mostly consisted of convoy patrols.

As new pilots were coming in at the bottom of the squadron structures, changes were also taking place at the top. Before the fighting in France began it was possible to command a squadron without necessarily flying with it. This was a legacy of the First World War, when a squadron leader's duties were not restricted to operations but extended to the whole responsibility of supervising a fighting unit. In the Battle of France, commanding officers did fly into battle with their men, particularly as the fighting intensified during the blitzkrieg, but initially squadrons were led by their flight commanders. Now it was obvious that, to provide proper leadership, a commander's place was in the air.

The demise of officers like Squadron Leader Stephenson of 19 Squadron and Drogo White of 74 Squadron also suggested that veteran pre-war officers, despite their seniority and flying skills, were not necessarily best suited to lead. Despite the evidence, appointments of senior pilots who were rich in ability but inexperienced in combat continued to be made over the claims of younger pilots who knew the reality of air fighting. The obvious internal choice to replace Stephenson was Flight Lieutenant Brian 'Sandy' Lane. He was twenty-two years old, and had gone to St Paul's public school. He joined the RAF after losing a dead-end job as a supervisor in an electric-light bulb factory. He was tall and good looking with permanent dark circles under his eyes which gave him a misleading slightly dissolute look. His fellow pilots loved him for his energy and cheerfulness. His leadership qualities were recognized in the decision to give him temporary command after Stephenson was shot down, but Flight Lieutenant Philip Pinkham was chosen as the new squadron leader instead. Pinkham had been with the Meteorological Flight, a sure sign of exceptional flying talent. After taking over, though, he played little part in operations until the beginning of September. The squadron had been chosen to test the claims of cannon over machine guns as a more effective fighter armament, and he was preoccupied with supervising what turned out to be a difficult experiment. Barely had the task been completed than Pinkham was dead, shot down and killed by Me 109s over the Thames estuary in a suicidally misconceived attack. This time Lane was given command.

In some cases, commanders demonstrated as soon as they were tested that they were not up to the job. On 30 May, 609 Squadron was detailed to fly off from Biggin Hill to patrol over the Dunkirk beaches. It was led by Dudley Persse-Joynt, a flight lieutenant, the commander having chosen to fly as an ordinary pilot with green section. On the journey out, green section put down at Manston on the North Foreland and proceeded no further. Stephen Beaumont's diary entry noting this incident was followed by the word, 'why?'[9] After this inauspicious debut, the squadron leader played no further part in operations. He had taken over in January as the Air Ministry's second choice after the first candidate was injured in a car crash. He had previously belonged to another auxiliary squadron, and arrived without having done a conversion course to monoplane fighters. Beaumont noticed early on that he demonstrated no great enthusiasm for flying. One spring afternoon he invited him to join him flying two of the squadron Spitfires. 'The CO showed himself to be competent and held formation steadily, but showed no desire to repeat the performance.'

By the end of June he had been quietly shunted out. Beaumont, a charitable man, wrote many years later that 'no leader of a fighting squadron can ever have had less impact on it. We hardly saw him at all either at the flight dispersals or even in the mess.' He added that he could 'now feel sorry for him rather than blame him ... I can feel some sympathy for him as he must have realized that he was unfitted for his post, but none because he never tried to act to his responsibilities.' Some blamed his lack of leadership for the heavy losses the squadron was to sustain in its disappointing intervention at Dunkirk. Others held the Air Ministry responsible for appointing such an unsuitable officer.

The insouciance of the pre-war days was badly dented by 609's experiences at Dunkirk. Four of the first pilots to join were killed. Persse-Joynt, one of the set of wealthy and well-connected Yorkshire friends at the core of the squadron, failed to return from a patrol on 31 May. John Gilbert, a convivial bachelor known as the 'pink boozer' because of his fresh complexion and taste for beer, disappeared with him. Desmond Ayre, a mining engineer in one of the Peake collieries, crashed to his death after apparently running out of fuel, and Joe Dawson was shot down on 1 June.

It was obvious that the auxiliary ethos of amateurism, albeit of a dedicated kind, and the quasi-familial bonds of place and friendship could not survive the new circumstances for long. On 22 June the squadron got a new commander. George Darley was a great contrast to his hapless predecessor. He was twenty-seven years old, a short-service entrant who had become a regular. Darley had no trouble making the adjustment from peace to war. He already had wide experience, ranging from operations in Aden to controlling duties in Britain and France. He knew the auxiliary system intimately, having been adjutant and flying instructor to two units. He said later that he assumed his appointment arose from his 'awareness of problems peculiar to such squadrons, which were small squadrons of personal friends who had probably grown up together, and in which losses were particularly keenly felt'. On his arrival he found 'the general atmosphere in 609 was depressed, which did not help the younger pilots'. He set about trying to 'restore morale by improving the kill/loss ratio'.[10]

This robust assessment was typical of Darley's approach. Beaumont judged him 'not a man who radiated charm, superficial or not'. Disappointed at their performance and cast down by the loss of friends, the pilots were at first annoyed rather than inspired by Darley's determination to rebuild the squadron spirit and get back into the fighting. Flying Officer Charles Overton remembered that 'initially we couldn't stand the sight of the man'. It was not long, though, before 'our attitude changed to great respect for what he was doing for all of us'.

Darley decided early on that the older pilots would have to go. Beaumont, now over thirty, was 'inwardly relieved' when he heard the news. 'I knew that I was really not suitable as a fighter pilot, let alone a flight commander, but I do not think any of my contemporaries would say I did not try.' The original composition of the squadron had already been altered during the phoney war by the arrival of short-service commission officers and the first of the RAFVR pilots. By the end of the autumn, the core of pre-war members was gone, most of them dead. The same process overtook all the auxiliary squadrons. By the time of the high-summer fighting, death and shared danger had melted most of the pre-war distinctions.

Darley also put his men through a heavy training programme of mock attacks with himself acting the part of the enemy. A lull in the fighting gave the squadrons a chance to practise and to try and apply the lessons of the recent fighting. No attempt was made to pool the hard-won information gathered in combat, let alone to analyse it and use the findings to refine tactics. Intelligence officers restricted themselves to trying to establish the veracity of claims. It was up to squadrons to work out their own approaches. Despite the redundancy of the old system, the temptation was to use it as a starting point in coming up with new solutions. 'We practised a wing formation with the Hurricane squadron yesterday, eighteen machines in formation,' wrote Pilot Officer John Carpenter to his parents from 222 Squadron's base in Kirton-in-Lindsey. 'I have been told that it was quite good from the ground.'

Denis Wissler, back from leave after his stint in France and with 17 Squadron at Debden, applied himself with a particular dedication to training, only too aware of his lack of success and touchingly determined to do well. For a week he spent every day practising formation flying and some new attacks evolved by the squadron, which 'did not work out too well'. But it was still air drill that appeared to matter most. On Friday, 28 June, after two flying sessions in front of an audience of senior officers, he thought his formation flying was 'pretty good but apparently the CO and wing commander thought I was the weak link, though the CO didn't say it was really bad'. Wissler confided to his diary that he was 'a bit browned off at the moment. We were suddenly called to readiness at 9.15 p.m. and weren't released until 10.35 and now we have to get up at 3 a.m. tomorrow.' The pattern was to continue until the end of the month.

The heightened state of alert was in response to the resumption of Luftwaffe activity. From the middle of the month Goering launched regular small raids, mostly at night. The bombs did little serious damage. The main purpose seems to have been to unsettle a population which suddenly found itself in the front line, and to probe the effectiveness of the air defences.

As if on cue, several attacks had been mounted on the warm evening that followed Churchill's great speech. As night fell, groups of German bombers set off across the North Sea, arriving in the early hours of the morning, and scattered bombs haphazardly on towns in eight counties in East Anglia and the north, killing twelve civilians and injuring thirty. Blenheim twin-engined fighters from Wittering in the East Midlands went up to meet them. One was shot down by a Heinkel, which in turn was destroyed by Flight Lieutenant Raymond Duke-Woolley, an ex-Cranwellian from 23 Squadron.

To the south the searchlight batteries around Southend at the mouth of the Thames picked up a formation of bombers. Sailor Malan, with 74 Squadron at Rochford, was in bed. He heard the bombs falling from the direction of Westcliff-on-Sea, where his wife Lynda had just given birth to their first son, Jonathan. Malan stood outside, watching the raid and getting increasingly agitated at the rumble of falling bombs. Normally, night interceptions were considered risky from bases in the area because of the danger from anti-aircraft artillery along the coast and around the Thames estuary. But it was a clear night and the moon was nearly full and Malan was worried. He asked for permission to attack the raiders, which was eventually granted. Shortly after midnight he took off and, climbing to 8,000 feet, found a Heinkel 111 held in the beam of the battery searchlights. Closing in from behind he signalled to the ground that he was in a position to attack, and when the anti-aircraft guns stopped he opened fire. There was only time for a three-second burst before he had to break away to avoid collision. As he pushed his Spitfire into a steep dive, the windscreen was smothered in oil from the stricken bomber, which crashed on to the beach. Turning back, he saw another Heinkel caught in a cone of light above him. He approached it cautiously, opening fire at 200 yards. It caught fire and sank from the sky, landing in a vicarage garden near Chelmsford in an eruption of flame that was seen for miles around.

Finding bombers in the darkness on any but the brightest moonlit nights was a near-impossible task. When it happened it was often as much the result of luck as of skill or science. On the evening of 19 June, Tim Vigors invited a Waaf from the Kirton-in-Lindsey control room to dinner at a restaurant in Lincoln. It was a Saturday night. They set off in his Ford 8, with his lurcher, Snipe, in the back. Dinner was followed by drinks at the King's Head, the RAF pub in the area, where he ran into some bomber pilots and 'got seriously stuck into the beer'. Vigors prided himself on his ability to stop drinking before his capacity to walk or drive became impaired. That night this gift failed him. 'With great care, I steered my way on to the dead-straight road which leads north from Lincoln towards Kirton-in-Lindsey,' he wrote later. 'My blacked-out headlights only showed the road about twenty yards ahead. Mercifully the local council had had the foresight to paint a broken white line down the middle of the road. Fixing this line between my right headlight and the mascot of a racehorse on the front of the bonnet, I proceeded slowly and carefully up the road. I didn't talk much and nor did my companion. I knew I was too drunk to concentrate on anything but driving.'

After dropping off his dinner date he donned a pair of bright-red pyjamas and slid gratefully into bed. Sleep was prevented by an attack of what he called 'bedspin', known to non-aviators as 'the phantom pilots'. While he was struggling to control it, a message was broadcast on the Tannoy in the corridor outside his room, calling for one pilot from 222 Squadron to report immediately to dispersal. Vigors, for reasons he was later hard pressed to explain, decided to volunteer. '"Hell," I said to Snipe. "Anything's better than this. Let's go and see what the flap is." I staggered off the bed, slid into my green silk dressing gown, donned my flying boots and weaved my way back to the car. Snipe followed, looking rather bemused. Even with maximum concentration on the drive to dispersal my path was alarmingly erratic.'

His rigger was waiting for him with a parachute. He urged Vigors to get airborne quickly as a large number of 'Huns' had just crossed the coast. 'My rigger jumped on the wing and handed me my helmet. I pulled it over my head, connected the oxygen and turned it on full blast. Somewhere along the line I had learnt that the best cure for a hangover was a strong dose of oxygen. I hoped fervently that it would have the same effect on bedspin.'

Somehow he got airborne and waited for control to vector him towards the raiders. No orders came. The radio was dead. Desperation dispelled the fog of alcohol. Without instructions from the ground there was no hope of intercepting any enemy aircraft. The obvious thing to do was to land as quickly as possible. He started to turn back the way he had come, maintaining the same speed, hoping this would bring him back to Kirton. Swinging round he saw the silhouette of another aircraft crossing the moon. It had two engines and was clearly one of the returning German bombers. Vigors moved behind and underneath the tail and opened fire. Soon its port engine was belching black smoke and it went into a screaming dive towards the cloud below. He had shot down a Heinkel 111.

Elation at this success was dampened quickly by the realization that he was now miles off course with no means of finding his way home. He decided to descend through the thick cloud, hoping that when he emerged he might spot the runway lights of one of the bomber bases in the area switched on to guide its night-flying aircraft home. At 700 feet, still blanketed in murk, he was on the point of climbing again in order to bale out when he broke through the bottom of the cloud. In front of him, glimmering out of the flat black of Lincolnshire, were the lights of a flarepath. He landed, exhausted and deeply relieved, to find he was at Barkston, a grass field he knew from his Cranwell days. The first person to greet him was one of his old instructors, who took his pyjama-clad protégé off for a drink.[11]

Malan's double success pushed him further into the public eye. Fighter pilots had now moved into the centre of the national consciousness as the importance of their role, underlined by Churchill, was recognized. The men of Fighter Command were engaged in the essential warrior task, defending their loved ones and homes from marauders, and they were doing it over the roofs of those they were protecting. This was enough to make them heroes. The stylish way they did their duty added a further layer of lustre.

The Fighter Boys were extraordinarily good for morale. It was important that they were properly rewarded. In the aftermath of the May and June fighting, the medals began to arrive in quantity. On 27 June, King George VI went to Hornchurch to present a batch to a group of pilots who had emerged from the anonymity of their squadrons and were on the way to becoming national figures. Al Deere, Sailor Malan, Bob Tuck and Johnny Allen all received the Distinguished Flying Cross for gallantry in the face of the enemy. James 'Prof' Leathart was awarded the Distinguished Service Order. The ceremony took place on a warm sunny morning. Afterwards the king took sherry with the pilots in the officers' mess and chatted with them about the relative performances of the Spitfire and the Messerschmitt, a subject on everybody's minds. Deere was particularly proud. 'As a New Zealander, brought up to admire the Mother country and respect the King as her head, it was the honour of a lifetime, an ultimate milestone of my flying ambitions – the Distinguished Flying Cross presented by the king, in the field of action.'[12] Afterwards, on the spur of the moment, the pilots rushed from the mess and lined up along the drive leading to the main gates to salute the royal visitor as he drove off. Underneath the top dressing of irony there was simple, solid patriotism.

Malan, Deere and Tuck were now almost famous, following behind the brief comet trail of glory blazed by Cobber Kain. Kain was not forgotten. He had been on the point of getting married, just before his death, to an actress, Joyce Phillips. His mother and sister Judy were on their way by ship to England for the wedding when the accident happened. A photograph in the *Daily Express* showed the two young women meeting for the first time. The caption reported that 'the two girls talked of Cobber and themselves. They played on the piano "Somewhere in France with You".'

Some pilots had put off thoughts of matrimony to avoid just such melancholy situations. Harold Bird-Wilson had never forgotten what happened after five members of 17 Squadron were shot down on their first patrol over northern France. When the unit withdrew to England, 'the wives of the missing people came daily to the officers' mess and

hung around waiting for information as to the return of their husbands
. . . some of us vowed that we wouldn't marry until things calmed down.'
One of the missing made it home. Another was a prisoner. The other
three were dead.[13]

The war had come at a very inconvenient time for Charles Fenwick.
He was in love with Bunny, a dark-haired girl with smiling eyes whose
good nature shines out from the old photographs. Motoring up to
London from his boring initial training stint at St Leonards once a month
was, he wrote to his mother 'the only thing that makes life bearable . . .
then for a few hours everything is heaven'.[14] They went to shows and
ate at the Strand Palace Grillroom 'very well indeed'. By the end of July
he had made up his mind, and wrote to tell his father.

> Before I joined the war I had little chance of meeting many girls. Since
> then I have had plenty and have made the most of them to see if I was
> as completely in love with Bunny as I had thought. To cut a long story
> short, of all the varied types of girls I have met they one and all either
> bored me to sobs or made me feel slightly sick, particularly if I kissed
> any of them, not through any lack of physical attraction on their part
> but just because I loved somebody else. Now after all this time of 'trial
> and error' I am completely convinced that my love is no passing breeze.
> That being so I will tell you what I would be glad to have your opinion
> on. The desire of both of us is needless to say to get married, the
> question is when.

The answer, of course, was as soon as possible. He asked his father to let
him know 'which side of the balance your vote will go in'. His father
wrote back sympathetically, but argued firmly against matrimony. Fenwick was unhappy, but he submitted. 'Dear Pa,' he wrote a few weeks
later. 'Thanks. You win, you brought me out of a spin and I've come
down to earth all intact although just a bit shaken.'

Women, and wives in particular, complicated things. When Fred Rosier took over 229 Squadron, based at Northolt, later in the year he 'found
that the wives of some of the chaps were living in the vicinity . . . It

wasn't long before I stopped chaps living out. And I said it would be better if their wives moved, because it was affecting, I thought, morale, in that these wives would count the number of aeroplanes leaving and the number of aeroplanes coming back, and were on the telephone to see if Willy was all right. It was far better when we were all living together and in the mess and developing a first-class squadron spirit.'[15]

June drew to an end in an atmosphere charged with anticipation. The countryside was littered with chopped-down trees and derelict cars pushed into fields to block the arrival of the Germans. Overhead, flabby barrage balloons rolled in the warm air. Odd incidents betrayed the tension. At Debden an aircraftman who had never piloted an aeroplane in his life took off in a Hurricane, flew over the airfield and plunged to the ground, killing himself. In the dispersal hut of 72 Squadron at Acklington a sergeant pilot woke up everyone in the dispersal hut, shouting challenges to the German paratroopers he dreamt had just landed.

It was hot, as memorably hot as another summer month in the not very distant past: August 1914. One bright morning a legendary figure from that era descended on the pilots of 72 Squadron at their base at Acklington on the coast of Northumberland. 'We were honoured by the company of "The Father of the Royal Air Force",' the squadron diarist recorded. 'We were all lined up at dispersal standing there in the blistering sun and his very first gesture was to dismiss the parade – suggesting we all squatted down in the shade of the nearby trees. Sitting on the ground, too, he spoke of [the] activities of World War I, associating the duties and responsibilities of the airmen then with those that faced us at present – with the encouraging conclusion that there was no doubt in his mind that we would win through again.'[16]

11

The Channel Battle

A few weeks after Trenchard's visit, three Spitfires from 72 Squadron were ordered off to investigate an unusual aircraft which had appeared near a convoy steaming off Sunderland. It was a Heinkel He 59 biplane, equipped with floats, and was painted white and adorned with red crosses. Undeterred by the innocent-looking markings, Flight Lieutenant Ted Graham led the aircraft into line astern and attacked, spattering the seaplane with 2,500 rounds. It crash-landed close to the beach and its four-man crew was captured by an escorting cruiser. Graham had been right to ignore the red crosses. The aircraft carried cameras and was on a reconnaissance mission.

The little victory of 72 Squadron, though it did not know it, was an indication of the new direction the air war was taking. Trenchard had been wrong on that hot morning when he linked the duties and responsibilities of the First World War airmen with those of the pilots sitting in the shade at his feet. The task facing them was very different from the one carried out by the RFC on the Western Front, and the burden they would have to carry was much greater. The duels over the trench lines in the First World War were an adjunct to the main military effort and decided nothing. Fighter Command was entering a battle that would decide everything.

The German forces had been allowed a short period of relative relaxation after conquering France. It was time now for them to deal with

Britain. The question of how this was to be done had never been clear. Different commanders in different services held strong and conflicting views. Hitler himself had not devoted much time to the subject, having always hoped he could negotiate an agreement with the British government that would leave him free to rule Europe unmolested. When the collapse of France failed to weaken the will to resist, it seemed that Britain would have to be forced into submission.

Hitler announced his intentions in Order No. 16, issued on 16 July, which stated: 'Since England has still not given any sign of being prepared to reach an agreement, despite her militarily hopeless position, I have decided to prepare an operation to invade England and if this becomes necessary, to carry it through. The objective of this operation is to eliminate the English home country as a base for the continuation of the war against Germany and, if this should become unavoidable, to occupy it fully.'

With these words 'Operation Sea Lion' officially came into being. Various invasion plans has been drawn up by the German navy and army since the start of the war. Initial doubts as to the feasibility of the exercise had largely dissolved in the intoxication of victory. Even sceptics like the naval commander Grand Admiral Raeder none the less hoped, as Hitler appeared to, that a combination of blockade and aerial bombardment could, on its own, crack British resistance, removing the necessity for an opposed landing. What the German High Command all agreed upon was that the defeat of Britain, whether through invasion or being battered from the skies, depended on German command of the air. That made the destruction of the Royal Air Force a precondition of success. Hitler spelled it out. A prerequisite of the landing, he wrote in his order, was that 'the English air force must have been beaten down to such an extent morally and in actual fact that it can no longer muster any power of attack worth mentioning against the German crossing'.

The Hitler directive confirmed an operation that had, in fact, already started. The German Armed Forces Supreme Command (the OKW) had anticipated the next stage of the war and had ordered the Luftwaffe to step up operations. By the beginning of July the air force had the use of the entire North Sea coastline from Norway to France from which to spring attacks. The new phase began with an intensified programme of reconnaissance missions, like the one brought to an end by 72 Squadron, probing defences and photographing potential targets. At first these seemed to be no more than a continuation of the harassing missions that had disturbed the sleep of Fighter Command during June.

Then a series of attacks on the convoys, scurrying heavily laden through the Channel to deliver as many cargoes as possible while the going was good, announced the overture to the Luftwaffe's next great symphony of violence. A much earlier Hitler directive issued in November 1939 had envisaged the air force 'waging war against the English economy' once the Anglo-French armies had been disposed of. By bombing convoys, the Luftwaffe was engaging economic targets. But they also hoped to lure Fighter Command into a battle of attrition that would wear it down and weaken it before the opening of the main air attack, which would deliver the fatal blow.

The Luftwaffe operation order of 2 July set two objectives: to close the Channel to British shipping and to clear the air of British fighters. With his usual overconfidence, Goering decided at first that only a limited number of aircraft would be needed. German intelligence, equally inclined to optimism, reckoned it would take between a fortnight and a month to smash the RAF. The job was given to a battle group drawn from Fliegerkorps II, based in the Pas de Calais, and to Fliegerkorps VIII at Le Havre. Oberst (Colonel) Johannes Fink was made Kanalkampf-führer, commander of the air battle over the Channel. He was forty-five years old, sombre, religious and intensely patriotic. He had been one of the five pilots allowed each year to receive flying training under the stringent terms of Versailles. When the order came, he was at the head of a bomber wing, Kampfgeschwader 2, equipped with Dornier 17s, based at Arras some way back from the coast. To this force were added two groups of Stuka dive-bombers and two fighter wings, Jagdgeschwaders 26 and 53. The fighter element was led by Oberst Theo Osterkamp, a First World War veteran who had been shot down by Albert Ball. To close the Channel and grind down the British fighters,

Fink had at his disposal seventy-five twin-engine bombers, sixty or more Ju 87 Stukas and about 200 fighters. Down the coast, Fliegerkorps VIII could provide a similar number of Ju 87s and fighters. The unit was commanded by Wolfram von Richthofen, 'the Stuka general', a cousin of Manfred, who had flown in his unit on the Western Front. Later he had become an energetic advocate of dive-bombing as a battle-winning tactic and put his theories convincingly into practice in Spain, where he was responsible for the Guernica atrocity, Poland, Belgium and France.

Fink set up his headquarters in an old bus on Cap Gris Nez within sight of the White Cliffs of Dover. By the end of the month he had radar, known as Freya, to track ship and aircraft movements and an eavesdropping service which listened in to the radio traffic between RAF sector controllers and fighters. The German air force commanders, pilots and crews were in no doubt about the outcome of the battle ahead of them. Their power, as the chief of operations of Luftflotte 3, Werner Kreipe, wrote later, 'was now at a zenith . . . the pilots were highly skilled . . . Their morale was very high and they were confident of victory.'[1] Standing behind the Channel battlegroup, should it prove insufficient for the job, was the weight of Luftflottes 2 and 3, the Luftwaffe deployment in France. Between them, by the end of July, they had 769 serviceable bombers, 656 Me 109 fighters, 168 Me 110 twin-engined fighters and 316 Ju 87 dive-bombers as well as about 100 reconnaissance aircraft. Many pilots had fought in Spain, Poland and the air battles over France and the Low Countries, and replacements were being turned out of training schools at the rate of 800 a month.

Set against this the RAF could muster only 504 battleworthy Hurricanes and Spitfires, as well as 27 two-man Boulton Paul Defiants. The lack of aircraft was matched by a shortage of pilots. On 1 July, Dowding had 1,069 pilots to fly his aeroplanes. That meant two pilots for each aeroplane. This healthy-looking equation took no account of inevitable losses through death and injury. He cast around for volunteers from other branches of the service and borrowed fifty-two pilots from the Fleet Air Arm. But there were far too few to sustain a war of attrition.

The battle for the Channel, the *Kanalkampf* as the Luftwaffe called it, opened on 3 July. The Luftwaffe moved tentatively at first, sending only fifty aeroplanes that day towards Britain. About a quarter of these were on reconnaissance missions, trying to photograph airfields and ports as part of the intelligence preparations for the main attacks. A small group of Dornier 17s appeared over Manston, a forward airfield perched on an exposed patch of flat land on the North Foreland, and dropped a few bombs before being chased away by the arrival of Spitfires from 54 Squadron. In the north, 603 Squadron destroyed three Ju 88 bombers in separate incidents. The day's total of five enemy aircraft shot down was a poor return for the effort involved. Twenty-eight squadrons had flown more than 120 patrols, a total of 570 individual sorties.

The following day the Luftwaffe launched the first serious attack. The opening raid lasted four minutes. Thirty-three Stukas appeared at break-fast time in the misty sky over Portland on the Dorset coast. They were the best known and the most feared of the German aeroplanes. They were the chief symbol of blitzkrieg, howling down in near vertical dives, releasing their one large and four small bombs on bridges, rail junctions or human beings with terrible accuracy. The first doubts about their vulnerability had been raised at Dunkirk, where British fighters found their lack of speed made them relatively easy to knock down. But they seemed impressive enough on the second day of the *Kanalkampf* as they plunged on ships and installations in the naval base, sinking an anti-aircraft ship and setting a tanker on fire in Weymouth Bay.

By the time fighters arrived from the nearest base, Warmwell, they were long gone. At 2 p.m. the Germans came again. Two groups of Dornier 17s escorted by thirty Me 109s pounced on a nine-ship convoy as it moved through the Straits of Dover. Eight Hurricanes from 79 Squadron were scrambled from Hawkinge, another forward field a few miles south of Manston, but as they engaged the raiders they were bounced by the Messerschmitt escort above and one pilot was shot down over St Margaret's Bay and killed. In addition, small groups of German fighters were given the freedom to roam on 'free hunting' sweeps over the coast, looking for targets of opportunity and daring the British fighters to come up and challenge them. A patrol from 54 Squadron was surprised by one such group of Me 109s which appeared out of cloud, shot up two of the aeroplanes and disappeared, anxious to get back to their French airfields within the fifteen to twenty minutes that was all that their fuel capacity allowed them over target.

Patrolling was wasteful and ultimately unsustainable, given Fighter Command's strictly limited resources. Dowding had not expected to have to protect shipping and had told both the Admiralty and the Air Staff that his fighters could provide only limited help. Radar's usefulness in providing a warning and allowing assets to be deployed more effectively was restricted by the fact that the raiders could form up inland beyond the range of the transmitters. It took less than ten minutes to get across the Channel from the Pas de Calais, but Hurricanes and Spitfires needed a quarter of an hour to climb high enough to attack them effectively. One response was to move the squadrons to forward operating bases so they would be nearer the attackers. But this meant they would have even less time to gain vital altitude.

Dowding had guessed the German thinking correctly. He had to avoid being drawn into an engagement that would leave Fighter Command's pilots exhausted and its aircraft depleted before the main attack was launched. Only token cover was provided for the convoys. Park, the 11 Group commander, ordered his pilots to avoid challenging the German fighters roaming provocatively twenty and thirty miles inland from the Channel. But even with this prudent approach, casualties were unavoidable. On Sunday, 7 July, six fighters were shot down and four pilots killed.

The following day a thick cushion of cloud was piled up over the Channel, providing the Luftwaffe with limitless cover for attacks on shipping. With several convoys scheduled to move through the waters off the south and south-east of England, there were plenty of targets to choose from. A large convoy had set off from the Thames early in the morning and was due to pass Dover after midday. Radar reported intense air activity over Calais and Park ordered up patrols in the area. A section from 610 Squadron at Biggin Hill met the convoy in the early afternoon in time to intercept a group of unescorted Dornier 17s, which it attacked, forcing them to drop their bombs harmlessly in the sea. In the encounter Pilot Officer A. Raven was shot down. He was seen swimming away from his Spitfire, but apparently drowned. Nine Hurricanes from 79 Squadron were sent from Hawkinge to take over. Soon after getting airborne, they were swooped on by Me 109s engaged in a free hunt over the Kent coast. Pilot Officer J. Wood was shot down in flames; he managed to bale out but burnt to death while descending. Flying Officer E. Mitchell crashed to earth behind Dover and was immolated in the subsequent fire, which blazed for an hour. No. 79 Squadron had been in action almost continuously since the Battle of France and its men were exhausted. Three days later they were moved far away from the fighting to Sealand, in Cheshire, to recover.

Despite the fact that serious fighting had barely started, some units were already heavily depleted. On 9 July, 54 Squadron lost two pilots, Pilot Officers Garton and Evershed, bringing the total of casualties to six dead and two injured in ten days. The death of Garton had been particularly distressing. 'Prof' Leathart last heard him over the R/T, screaming that he was on fire and being chased by four Germans. Evershed had been considered a promising pilot and a potential leader.

The losses meant, the squadron diary recorded, that it 'could only muster eight aircraft and thirteen pilots'. Al Deere narrowly escaped being killed on the same day Garton and Evershed died. On his fourth trip of the day he was leading his flight out to sea to investigate a report of enemy air activity and saw a silver seaplane apparently on a reconnaissance mission, escorted by Me 109s. He managed to shoot one of the fighters down and turned towards another. The pilot swung round to face him and the two machines powered head-on towards each other. 'We opened fire together and immediately a hail of lead thudded into my Spitfire. One moment the Messerschmitt was a clearly defined shape, its wingspan nicely enclosed within the circle of my reflector sight, and the next it was on top of me, a terrifying blur which blotted out the sky ahead. Then we hit.'[2]

Deere's engine was on fire and seized up, leaving the airscrew immobile. To his amazement he realized that the blades were bent almost double with the impact of the collision. He yanked at the toggle that released the cockpit hood, but it was stuck fast. His only hope lay in a crash-landing. Half-blinded by smoke, he nursed the aeroplane over land and, before coming to rest on the edge of a cornfield, flopped it down in a great rending of splintering timber from the wooden posts planted in the ground to deter Germans landing. With the strength of desperation, he punched at the Perspex hood until it smashed open and then hauled himself out, sucking in lungfuls of fresh air.

His fists were cut and bleeding, his hair and eyebrows singed and both knees badly bruised from where they had been dashed against the instrument panel when his seat broke free in the collision. Rejoining the squadron at Rochford next day, he was asked if he was fit enough to fly. 'Frankly I had hoped for a day or two off the station, perhaps a quick sortie to London,' he wrote later. 'I was pretty sore and a bit shaken but quite obviously I couldn't be spared.'

Deere's commander, Leathart, admitted that he, too, was exhausted and hoping fervently that they would be taken out of the line before long. The calculation of how much flying a squadron could endure and how many losses it could sustain before its morale buckled and it became ineffective was a fine one, and a peculiar combination of ruthlessness and sensitivity was needed to judge it correctly. The decision, in the case of 54 Squadron, belonged to Dowding and Park, both of whom were trusted by their pilots. Dowding was approaching sixty. He had come to flying late, qualifying as a pilot in 1914 after serving around the fringes of the empire in the artillery. With his feathery moustache and pained demeanour he was an unlikely aviator, but he had a good war with the RFC in France, serving as a squadron leader and ending up a brigadier general. Dowding had a dashing side. Apart from flying, a dangerous and romantic occupation when he took it up, he was a good and brave skiier. In general, though, he seemed grave, careworn and short of friends – 'stuffy' as the universal nickname acknowledged. The loss of his wife after only two years of marriage and the responsibility of bringing up their son, Derek, himself a Fighter Command pilot with 74 Squadron, added another layer of seriousness to a solemn nature. These were not traits normally appreciated by fighter pilots. Then and later, though, his 'Dear Fighter Boys', as he addressed them, felt affection for him, and more importantly assurance. 'Even junior people like myself had enormous confidence in him,' Christopher Foxley-Norris said later. 'He was a father figure. You felt that as long as his hand was on the tiller all was going to be well.'³ Dowding in turn felt a strong paternal bond with his men. Later on, when he turned to spiritualism, he claimed to be in communication with the souls of dead pilots.

The women who worked with Dowding at his headquarters at Bentley Priory could sense warmth behind the stiffness. 'We all admired our Stuffy enormously,' said Elizabeth Quayle, a Waaf operations room plotter. 'We had great loyalty to him. I think you might call it affection. He built up a tremendous *esprit de corps* among us. He was very remote, but if you met him he was always very considerate.'⁴ These qualities did not necessarily recommend him to his senior colleagues and superiors. Dowding's heavily worn sense of duty and touch of lugubriousness – what Trenchard had called his 'dismal Jimmy' side – brought out the bully in some of those above and around him. When his big work was over, he would be disposed of with a bad grace that dismayed the men and women who served under him.

Keith Park was less taut, more approachable, but still someone who glowed with discipline and purpose. He was a New Zealander who had been wounded at Gallipoli, then transferred to the RFC in France, where he shot down twenty Germans. He made a point of showing himself to his men in 11 Group, flying around the bases in his own Hurricane, listening rather than talking. Many seem to have seen the long, lined face, which made him look much older than forty-four, at some time during the summer months of 1940.

Dowding's chronic lack of pilots was alleviated a little by the arrival of foreign airmen now entering the system. Most were Polish pilots, a large number of whom had managed to escape through Romania at the end of 1939 and made their way to France, where they carried on fighting. Altogether 145 of them served in Fighter Command between July and October 1940. Billy Drake, after recovering from his injuries, helped to train them up. He found them, as most did in the RAF, 'very indepen-dent minded. They were all a touch older than we were and a touch more experienced.' They could also 'be a handful . . . they wouldn't take any orders except from their own people'.[5]

Discipline was less strict in the Polish air force, and divisions between ranks less marked. Officers and crews socialized with each other in a way never seen in a British squadron. The reputation for hot-headedness and indifference to air drill was soon established and stuck with them until long after the war. Language difficulties explained some of the Poles' alleged reluctance to follow orders. There were also deeper reasons. Experienced pilots were unhappy with the formation tactics that per-sisted throughout the summer, believing them to be stupid and danger-ous. Contrary to another popular myth, the Poles were not particularly reckless, and their casualty ratios were in line with those of British pilots. It was true, though, that they hated the Germans with an un-Anglo-Saxon vehemence. Some pilots found this aggression admirable. To others it could seem embarrassing, even distasteful. Stories circulated accusing Polish pilots of shooting at Germans as they floated down on parachutes, but there is little hard evidence to show this was a regular practice. The leading historian of the Polish air force in Britain, Adam Zamoyski, does concede that 'it is true that some pilots finished off parachuting Germans by flying directly over them; the slipstream would cause the parachute to cannon and the man would fall to the ground like a stone'.[6]

Given the differences of language, culture and approach, the Poles and the other Continental pilots, Czechs, Belgians and French, fitted surpris-ingly easily into the fabric of the fighter squadrons. British pilots did not try to master the consonant clusters of the Slavic names, simplifying and jollifying them instead, so that Karol Pniak and Boleslaw Wlasnowalski, two of the three Polish pilots who joined 32 Squadron, became 'Cognac' and 'Vodka', and the new soubriquets slotted democratically in alongside the other squadron nicknames. Pete Brothers found the newcomers 'very good value . . . socially everybody mixed in'. However, there was some unease when a German pilot who had been shot down was brought to

Biggin Hill. 'The police captured the chap and stuck him in our guard-room,' he said. 'In the evening we were still at readiness in the dispersal hut and we had him brought over. We had the wing of a 109 propped up against the hut, which [Flying Officer Rupert Smythe] had shot down . . . He'd come back to Biggin Hill with it on the roof of a car. We said to the German, "One of your 109s," but he wasn't going to commit himself. We had a chat to him in dispersal and decided we'd better keep our eyes on the Poles, who were sitting all three together some distance away. We thought, "If we take our eyes off them they'll probably murder him," which I would have done, given the chance in their circumstances, most certainly.' The German, who spoke English, was led away for a drink in the mess. 'He said could he have paper and a pencil. We said, "Why?" He said, "I want to write all your names down because tomorrow the Luftwaffe will blacken the skies, you will have lost and I want to make sure you are all well-treated." He couldn't understand why we fell off our stools laughing.'[7]

Not all foreigners in 32 Squadron were popular. Comte Rudolphe de Hemricourt de Grunne was a twenty-eight-year-old Belgian who had gone to Spain and fought for Franco as a pilot in the civil war alongside the Luftwaffe. He claimed to have shot down fourteen Republican air-craft. He later joined the Belgian air force, and when the country was overrun made his way to Britain. He arrived at Biggin Hill early in August. Brothers considered him to be not a 'Nazi sympathizer so much as a mercenary', but he was regarded as too boastful for the squadron's liking. The 32 Squadron pilots were very impressed when he told them he had flown an Me 109 in Spain and they expected him to have no problems when encountering one from the other side. He managed to shoot one down on his second day in action, but a week later was shot down by another, an event that caused some amusement. De Grunne was to meet his death at the hands of a 109, drowned after a fight over the Channel in May 1942.

Virtually every squadron was enriched by a dash of overseas blood. Of the 2,917 airmen who flew in Fighter Command between 10 July and the end of October 1940, 2,334 were British, 145 were Polish, 126 from

New Zealand, 98 from Canada, 88 from Czechoslovakia, 33 from Australia, 29 from Belgium, 25 from South Africa, 13 from France, 11 from the United States, 10 from Ireland, 3 from Rhodesia and 1 each from Jamaica and Newfoundland. Some pilots liked the mix of nationalities. With him in 92 Squadron Tony Bartley had South Africans, Canadians, Australians and New Zealanders. 'I felt,' he said later, 'that when someone lacked something, the other compensated for it, because of the different part of the world they came from ... We had Czechs and Poles who were very brave and we had a Frenchman ... Together it made an absolutely indestructible team ... Everybody's morale was [compensated] by each others. The whole thing, put together, was undefeatable.'[8] Dowding was less convinced, at least as far as the Poles were concerned. He worried about their numbers diluting squadron identities and from the end of July began making plans for separate Polish squadrons.

Manpower was more of a concern than machines. The appointment of Lord Beaverbrook as Minister of Air Production in May had an almost immediate effect in galvanizing manufacture, and by July the flow of Hurricanes and Spitfires off the production lines was sufficient to keep pace with losses. The fighters had proved their flying ability against the aircraft of the Luftwaffe. But the early summer fighting had increased doubts about the effectiveness of the British fighters' armament of eight machine-guns when compared to the combination of cannon and machine-guns carried by the Me 109.

The Colt-Browning guns in the Hurricanes and Spitfires carried 2,660 rounds in total, enough for fourteen seconds' firing. The bullets were only 7.7 mm in calibre, the same as the ones used by infantrymen, though the introduction of the De Wilde incendiary type had increased their effectiveness. The Me 109 had two wing-mounted Oerlikon cannon and two 7.9 mm machine-guns sited above the engine. There was only enough room in the wings to carry sixty cannon rounds per gun, but they were 20 mm in calibre and usually explosive. The machine-guns each carried 1,000 rounds.

It seemed clear early on that the Me 109 carried the heavier punch. It has been calculated that a three-second burst from an RAF fighter weighed about thirteen pounds. In the same time a Messerschmitt could deliver eighteen pounds.[9] The rate of cannon fire was much slower – only 520 rounds a minute against 1,200 for a machine-gun – but the shells exploded on impact and one or two hits could bring down a metal-skinned Spitfire (though the Hurricane's old-fashioned fuselage construction of struts, formers and fabric made it less vulnerable). This was an advantage in circumstances where a fighter pilot chasing another fighter pilot could expect to have his target in his sights for only a few seconds. To be effective, machine-gun fire needed to smash the engine, set it on fire, shoot off a vital control or kill the pilot. The greater size of the bombers, with their extra structural strength and armour plating, meant that thousands of rounds fired by several fighters might be needed to bring one down. One of the most dispiriting experiences a fighter pilot could have, captured on many a camera-gun sequence, was to catch and hold a bomber in a perfect deflection shot only to watch it cruise blithely through the blizzard of tracer.

The German bombers had steel plates that offered partial protection to their crews and self-sealing fuel and oil tanks with membranes that melted when the metal was pierced, automatically plugging leaks. But the engines were unprotected from the rear, making an attack from astern the fighter's most profitable line of approach. If armour plating was fitted to cover this vulnerable spot, shooting down a bomber would become a very difficult task for a fighter armed only with machine-guns. To penetrate armour and redress the balance, cannon were needed.

This realization produced a flurry of belated activity. Experiments had been going on for at least two years to fit cannon to fighters. Formidable engineering problems were involved. The Hispano guns were potentially excellent weapons, with a high muzzle velocity delivering a powerful and penetrating blow, but the fighters' wings had to be able to absorb the recoil. The armament also needed to be fixed in such a way that the magazines did not create too much drag and impede flying performance. One solution was to fit the guns so they lay on their sides. But this had the effect of slowing the flow of shells to the breech and interfering with the cartridge-ejection system. Also, despite their bulkiness, the magazines held only sixty rounds each, giving the fighter a negligible six seconds of firing time.

These problems were well known. None the less work began on fitting the guns to a new Spitfire type, the Mk IB, with a view to putting them into service. At the end of June the first three were delivered to 19 Squadron at Duxford, which as the most experienced Spitfire squadron in Fighter Command was given the task of trying them out. 'They had to have special wings with this huge blister on top where the magazine fitted,' said George Unwin, who was one of the first to fly them. 'They were absolutely useless. You could only fire [when] absolutely straight and level.' Pilots found that the mildest G forces were enough to make the nose of the bullet dip and jam in the breech when they pressed the firing button. Air-gunnery tests were very disappointing, with guns misfiring constantly. When the more experienced pilots lined up to shoot at a towed aerial target, only one direct hit was scored.

Dowding was under pressure from the government to send 19 Squadron into action as soon as possible to test the new weapons in battle conditions. He resisted deploying it in the 11 Group area, where it was certain to encounter 109s. In the next six weeks, operating mainly out of Fowlmere in the less hazardous air of 12 Group, the squadron had five encounters with German formations. When the cannon shells struck the raiders they did spectacular damage, shooting away propellers and tail-planes and setting engines ablaze. But virtually every aeroplane suffered stoppages on every outing. On 31 August, eleven Spitfires from the squadron went up to intercept a large force of bombers and fighters to the south. In the clash Flying Officer James Coward was shot up, losing a foot, but managed to bale out. Pilot Officer Raymond Aeberhardt, nineteen years old and new to the squadron, was forced down, turned over on landing and was killed. Again many guns had jammed and only two probable Me 110s could be claimed against the losses.

Squadron Leader Philip Pinkham, who had struggled throughout the summer to make the new armament work, had had enough. Strongly backed by his pilots, he petitioned Dowding for the return of their old machine-gun equipped fighters. 'The next day the great man was there and he listened to what we had to say,' George Unwin remembered. 'He had a miserable face. He said, "I won't teach you to suck eggs. You shall have your eight-gun Spitfires back by tomorrow morning." And we did, except that they were all clapped-out Spitfires from an Operational Training Unit, shedding oil all over the windscreen.'[10]

On the morning of 5 September, Pinkham, who had not flown in the operations of the previous weeks, led his men off in these machines with orders to patrol Hornchurch aerodrome at 15,000 feet. On the way, and while still climbing, they saw a mass of forty bombers escorted by the same number of Me 109s above them to the south, approaching the Thames estuary. Before they could reach them another group of RAF fighters attacked the formation, turning it southwards. To the dismay of some of the experienced pilots, Pinkham ordered five Spitfires to follow him up into the bombers while the rest of the squadron took on the escorts.

They were attacking from almost the worst possible position, lacking height and blinded by the glare from the south. 'He flew straight into the sun,' said Unwin later. 'It was a pretty incompetent thing to do.' Pinkham was last seen flying towards a group of Dorniers before apparently falling victim to the Messerschmitts. David Cox, a twenty-year-old sergeant who was flying with him that day, described the decision as 'tactically wrong but morally right . . . The squadron had been told to intercept this formation which was coming in to attack Hornchurch.'[11] What Pinkham should have done, he believed, was to have flown a dog-leg to gain height and bring the squadron in at a speed and position to have taken on both escort and bombers.

Pinkham, though, lacked the tactical experience to see this. He was popular with his men. Cox thought him 'a very fine chap, a real gentleman. He treated a sergeant pilot the same as he would treat an air marshal'. Born in Wembley and educated at Kilburn Grammar School, he joined the RAF on a short-service commission and as a result of his outstanding flying skills had been selected first for the Meteorological Flight and then posted as an instructor. He was twenty-five when he died. Despite his sense of duty and diligence, his lack of combat experience meant he was a poor choice to command a fighter unit.

The cannon problem was eventually overcome by the installation of a belt-feeding system, a solution that had been under consideration from the outset. The decision to persist with an unpromising experiment meant the squadron had been sent into action with guns that were known to be faulty. Thanks to luck and skill, losses had been relatively small, but it had also deprived Fighter Command of the full use of a seasoned unit which could have inflicted much more damage on the Luftwaffe during the middle passage of the summer if it had been armed with its old weapons.

Despite Dowding's reluctance to commit resources in the opening stages, the Germans were now arriving in such numbers that it was impossible to ignore them. Fighter doctrine as laid down by the pre-war planners, based on the premise that bombers would arrive unescorted, had been shown to be utterly unrealistic. Unruffled by this failure, the revived analysis by the senior officers of Fighter Command continued to be based on cheerful hypotheses that bore little relation to what was happening in the skies. Pilots were told that 'whenever possible, fighters should attack enemy bomber formations in equal numbers by astern and quarter attacks at the same level'.[12] At the same time the memorandum was written, fighter squadrons routinely found themselves outnumbered by bombers by five or ten to one. As for the accompanying fighters, the same document suggested that half the flight or squadron should 'draw off their escort and if necessary attack them'.

These instructions were meaningless by the middle of July. On the 13th, six Hurricanes from 56 Squadron led by Flight Lieutenant Jumbo Gracie took off from Manston to protect a convoy coming through the Straits of Dover. Gracie, according to Geoffrey Page, was 'far from being the popular conception of a fighter pilot. He was fat and pasty and had a high-pitched voice, more of a Billy Bunter than a Knight of the Air.' Despite his appearance, he was famously energetic and aggressive. The controller told them twenty bombers on their way to attack the ships had been picked up on the radar, protected by sixty fighters flying above them. Gracie ordered Pilot Officer Taffy Higginson to take his section off to deal with the bombers. He meanwhile led his section, including Page, up into the midst of the fighters where they prepared to do battle at odds of twenty to one. 'I suppose with hindsight I should have been scared stupid,' Page said later. 'But I think I was so busy getting my aircraft ready, making sure the camera gun was switched on and the safety button on the guns was on "fire", generally trimming up the aeroplane for the approaching combat. Then suddenly there was this enormous swarm of aircraft above us and we were climbing up.' When they reached the height of the fighters, they found both Me 109s and Me 110s. The latter reacted to the arrival by going into a waggon-circling manoeuvre, following each other around to give their rear gunners the chance to provide maximum defensive firepower. Page felt his mouth go dry, but still found the Germans' caution when faced by three Hurricanes funny. He 'dived into the circle, firing rather wildly . . then the 109s came down on us'. For the next few minutes he 'registered nothing but flashing wings bearing Iron Crosses, and streaks of tracer'. Then came the phenomenon that never ceased to amaze: the sky was completely empty 'as if the hand of God has wiped the slate clean'.[13]

Page was regarded by his colleagues as an exceptional fighter pilot. The line dividing the merely good from the outstanding was a fine one. Sailor Malan, considering the qualities needed to fly fighter aircraft successfully, reckoned that, unlike among the First World War pilots,

courage, these days, is a minor talent. No man is braver than the next . . . the air raid wardens in Coventry or Plymouth, these men do things under fire which we fighter pilots can only regard with awe. A fighter pilot doesn't have to show that kind of courage. Unreasoning, unintelligent, blind courage is in fact a tremendous handicap to him. He has to be cold when he's fighting. He fights with his head, not his heart. There are three things a first-class fighter pilot must have. First, he must have an aggressive nature. He must think in terms of offence rather than defence. He must at all times be an attacker. It is against the nature of a Spitfire to run away. Second, both his mind and his body must be alert and both must react instinctively to any tactical situation. When you are fighting you have no time to think. Third, he must have good eyes and clean hands and feet. His hands and feet control this plane and they must be sensitive. He can't be ham handed. When your Spitfire is ambling along at 390 miles an hour a too-heavy hand on the rudder will send you in an inadvertent and very embarrassing spin. Your hands, your feet, your mind, your instinct must function as well, whether you're right side up or upside down.[14]

Malan might have added to his list, possession of very good eyesight. He himself was said to have been able to spot 'a fly on the Great Wall of China, at five miles'.[15]

Page was certainly aggressive. Writing to a friend from his days at Cranwell, late in the evening after a night in mess, he confessed: 'I enjoy killing. It fascinates me beyond belief to see my bullets striking home and then to see the Hun blow up before me.' But the sight, he admitted, 'also makes me feel sick. Where are we going and where will it all end? I feel I am selling my soul to the devil.'[16]

Given the disparity in forces it is remarkable that more pilots were not killed in the Channel battle of July. As it was seventy-nine died. The worst losses came on the 19th, the disaster resulting from the failure of machines rather than of men. The Boulton Paul Defiant was a strange conception from the outset. It had no fixed gun that fired forward. Instead, a gunner swivelled around in an electrically powered turret sunk into the fuselage behind the cockpit. The extra weight meant it was slow, managing just over 300 m.p.h. The four Browning guns could generate a reasonable rate of fire, but this only counted if the pilot manoeuvred his partner into a good position. The aeroplane was an anachronism before it ever went into action, reflecting thinking about aerial fighting that had gone out with the First World War. It was the very weirdness of its design that explained the Defiants' brief success. During the Dunkirk campaign, the Germans had at first mistaken them for Hurricanes and, going in from the rear, were unpleasantly surprised when they spat back bullets. On one day, 29 May, 264 Squadron claimed to have shot down thirty-five German aircraft. It was an exaggeration, but there was no doubt that they inflicted significant losses. The Germans soon learned the difference.

On 19 July, the Defiants of 141 Squadron were moved forward to Hawkinge at breakfast time and sent off on patrol. The crews had never been in battle, had only arrived in the south from Scotland a week before and were unaccustomed to 11 Group control procedures. At 2.30 p.m., twelve Defiants were ordered off to patrol just south of Folkestone. Three machines had to be left behind with mechanical trouble. There was no warning from control when, a quarter of an hour later, a swarm of Me 109s from the Richthofen Geschwader crossed the path of the squadron in the air and, identifying them correctly, moved in efficiently for the kill, attacking from below and astern where they were at no risk from the guns. Four Defiants were shot down in the first attack. The gunners, clamped into their claustrophobic turrets, went down with their aeroplanes. One pilot baled out and was picked up wounded from the sea. The remaining Defiants tried to hide in cloud, but one was caught and set on fire. The gunner baled out but was drowned and the pilot was killed on crash-landing. Four made it back, two of them damaged, one beyond repair. Altogether, in the space of less than a quarter of an hour, six machines had been destroyed and ten men killed. The losses would have been even greater if Hurricanes from 111 Squadron had not arrived to scare the Messerschmitts off. Two days later what was left of the Defiant squadron was sent back to Scotland.

Some of the losses of July seemed particularly wasteful. Fighter Command insisted on mounting night interceptions even though the chances of catching anything were tiny. Seven pilots were killed in accidents during the hours of darkness. Most pilots feared flying at night. It was very dangerous and the results were almost never worth the risk. Stephen Beaumont, the most uncomplaining of pilots, was told, one night at Middle Wallop at the end of July, to hold his flight at readiness. He was exhausted, there was no moon and it was pitch-black.

As they settled down at dusk in the dispersal hut they devoutly hoped they would not be required. Half an hour before midnight the operations room ordered one pilot up to investigate an unidentified aircraft near Ringwood. Beaumont thought this was 'stupid, ineffective and potentially dangerous', and said so. He contacted his commander, George Darley, but was told, with some sympathy, that orders were orders. Flying Officer Jarvis Blayney, the son of a Harrogate doctor and one of the pre-war squadron members, was sent up first. He set off with a heavy heart but his engine overheated and then it was Beaumont's turn. He trundled down the runway, swinging his Spitfire from side to side to see the line of the flarepath and managed to take off and climb to 1,000 feet. He cruised overhead, desperate not to lose sight of the dim glow of the lights below, and was greatly relieved to be told to forget the interception and come back and land. He suspected afterwards that Darley 'had been to the Operations Room, expressed his views on the futility of this order and got the controller to recall me'.[17]

July had been unsettling for the pilots, just as the Luftwaffe intended it to be. Kept in the dark about Fighter Command's assessment of the Germans' intentions, the pilots had no idea as to how the battle would develop. Most seem to have shared Brian Kingcome's feeling that what they were engaged in was 'part of a continuing routine, certainly not . . . an isolated historic event . . . merely part of the normal progress of the war, which we assumed would continue unabated until final victory.'[18]

The pilots understood, though, that for the coming weeks and months they were the most important people in Britain. All eyes were on them. Since May the BBC had been broadcasting morale-boosting talks by fighter pilots. On 14 July, Harbourne Stephen of 74 Squadron went on the radio to describe how his squadron, though greatly outnumbered at Dunkirk, had escaped unhurt and knocked down several bombers in the encounter, and recounted Malan's exploit of bringing down the two bombers at night over Essex. The day before, a team from *Life* magazine turned up at Debden to shoot a feature on the fighter pilots who were beginning to be famous across the Atlantic. Denis Wissler was one of those ordered up to provide some formation flying pictures for them. Afterwards the 17 Squadron pilots were called to the mess and posed for a picture. The pilots stand around in frozen, monumental poses. Only one is looking at the camera as the mess steward in a starched white jacket distributes 'half-cans' of beer in silver mugs. The effect is stilted, straining to be epic. One of the subjects is starting to look bored. Denis Wissler, in the centre of the shot, planted squarely in a leather armchair, is scratching his nose, beer in hand as he skims a magazine. Later, the caption reports, 'everyone joined in a harmless battle, hurling the flashbulbs of *Life*'s photographer at one another'. The article did not appear for another year, by which time half the men in the picture were dead.

Were they supermen, the journalists wondered, or the boys next door? Godfrey Winn, a star writer for the *Sunday Express* who visited 54 Squadron on 18 July, decided they were both. The article was called 'Portrait of a Miracle Man'. 'He has captured the imagination of the whole world . . . What is he like as a man?' asked Winn. He went on to provide a composite profile.

> First of all he is a very ordinary fellow. He keeps on stressing that over and over again to you. And if you press him he will assure you that only with the greatest difficulty he reached certificate standard at school and never got his colours as if that had anything to do with it. He roars with laughter at all the references to himself as a knight of the sky and he tells you that the reason why he is a fighter and not a bomber pilot is because they discovered he was better at flying upside down.

Typical pilots laughed a lot, were addicted to music, playing Connie Boswell singing 'Martha' over and over again on the gramophone. They didn't read much, except for thrillers like *No Orchids for Miss Blandish*, a risqué bestseller. They were ordinary, until they stepped outside. 'The moment that he starts to walk towards the flarepath you see the transformation take place before your eyes . . . He becomes impersonal, merciless and completely self-disciplined.'

And, Winn did not need to add, more than a match for the Germans. Unofficial propagandists were already reassuring the public that any imbalance in the odds would be compensated for by the superiority of

British machines and men. The air reporter of the *Daily Express* revealed that the Luftwaffe 'use machines with a life of 50 flying hours. That is as long as they are made to last ... staking all on numbers they don't attempt to train their crews carefully.' O. D. Gallagher in the same paper declared that 'our Spitfire boys enjoy a confidence in themselves that the Luftwaffe pilots cannot have'. He told a recent story of an intelligence officer going over to debrief a pilot who had just returned from a sortie. 'It was some minutes before he could get anything out of the fighter. He sat in his cockpit, eyes bright, grinning, saying: "God they're easy! God they're easy!"' These fantasies provided the pilots with a cynical laugh as they read them in the mess. Only they knew how far they were from the truth.

12

The Hun

The German airmen attacking Britain respected the enemy they were facing and liked to think the feeling was mutual. Contacts between the two air forces in the approach to the war had been frequent, cordial and remarkably open. In October 1938, General Erhard Milch, one of the main architects of the reconstructed German air force, led a senior Luftwaffe delegation to Britain and was given a tour of important installations. His hosts were nothing if not hospitable. When Milch went to Hornchurch, the pilots were told they could answer any questions put to them by the visitors except those concerning defensive tactics, the control of operations and the recently arrived reflector gunsight. Inquiries about the latter were to be turned aside with the reply that it was so new they had not yet learned how to use it.

General Milch chose Bob Tuck's aircraft to clamber on to. He peered into the cockpit, noticed the gunsight and asked how it worked. Tuck prevaricated, as ordered, only to be interrupted by an air vice-marshal accompanying the Germans who offered a detailed demonstration. Tuck said later he had to stifle the urge to ask: 'Sir, why don't we give General Milch one to take home as a souvenir?'[1]

The visit followed several encounters in which each side had tried to intimidate and deter the other by 'revealing' the extent of their preparedness in the air. It was a phoney exercise in which candour was mixed with deception, leaving everyone suspicious and confused. Milch did take away with him a strongly favourable impression of the cadets he met during a trip to Cranwell and told Hitler of their high quality. Afterwards he sent a thank-you gift, two fine, modernistic portraits of Richthofen and the first German 'ace' Oswald Boelcke, which still hang in the college library. With them came a letter expressing the hope that the images 'might encourage the feeling of mutual respect and help to prevent that our two Forces have to fight each other again as they were unfortunately forced to do some twenty years ago'.[2]

But less than three years later they were fighting each other once again, and British pilots who had served in France could feel little respect for men they had seen machine-gunning and bombing refugees. Brian Kingcome's sardonic style wavered when it came to Stukas. It was, he said later, 'a great tragedy in my life' that he had never had a chance to shoot one down. He had conceived 'a special hatred' derived from images of them 'strafing the endless queues of refugees'.[3] For pilots who had not seen such sights in France, the July battles over the Channel were straightforward military encounters which did not strongly engage their emotions. They were shooting, as they often said later, 'at the machine not the man'. This attitude was to harden when the focus of the German attack shifted inland and over the homes of those they loved.

Many German airmen believed that they shared with British pilots an experience and outlook that transcended differences of nationality and the fact that their governments were at war. Some of those who survived were to claim they had no desire to fight Britain, had assumed the war was over with the fall of France and were saddened when told they would now have to try and kill men whom, from a distance, they admired.

Their feeling that they had much in common with their British counterparts was to some extent justified. The pilots facing Britain in 1940 in both fighters and bombers had mostly been attracted to the Luftwaffe, not by ideological reasons, but because they loved flying, or the idea of it. 'Flying brought me a lot of happiness,' Georg Becker, who piloted a Junkers 88, said later. 'I knew I was good at it.' The air offered him an escape from genteel poverty. He was the son of a civil servant who died in a train crash, leaving his wife struggling to bring up four children on a state pension. It was also 'a glamorous thing to do . . . more romantic than being a foot soldier'.[4] For Gerhard Schöpfel, who was to become famous for shooting down four Hurricanes in three minutes in August, flying in the Luftwaffe was 'new and exhilarating'.[5]

Many aspects of the pre-war existence lived by German airmen would have been recognizable to their British counterparts. Off duty, Becker and his comrades 'went to the officers' mess and drank. We had breakfast, lunch and dinner all together. We had the week planned out so we knew when we would be working and we arranged our free time around that. In Brandenburg, we had a boat and would take it out with friends. Some of us had cars. We'd drive to the coast or into Berlin at weekends.'

They called each other by nicknames and enjoyed dogs, cars, sport and jokes. Like the pre-war RAF, they thought of themselves as an élite, semi-detached from the drab, terrestrial world. But this was Germany in the 1930s. At Becker's base they 'had dances where the officers could invite girlfriends but they also had to invite people like the town council and the mayor who we used to call the little Nazis. They had joined in 1933. We used to get them drunk and stick them in a corner and basically ignore them. There were some nice Nazis there too, people who didn't really believe it. We used to stick them in the corner as well.'

German airmen were required to take an oath of personal loyalty which committed them to 'yield unconditional obedience to the Führer of the German Reich and Volk, Adolf Hitler'. So did every other member of the German armed forces. Few of the pilots were active Nazis. That did not mean they were reluctant to fight. As with the expansion of the RAF, the birth of the Luftwaffe offered young, modern-minded German men an opportunity for adventure and an escape from mundane lives. They had not joined the air force necessarily to go to war, but inside its ranks war became simply an extension of duty.

The Luftwaffe had been conceived in subterfuge. Civil aviation in the inter-war years was developed with one eye on military potential. The bombers and fighters of 1940 took their names from men – Claude Dornier, Hugo Junkers, Ernst Heinkel, Willy Messerschmitt – whose companies started out manufacturing commercial aircraft. A state airline, Deutsche Lufthansa, was created in 1926, and its training schools were to provide the Luftwaffe with many of its pilots. The government encouraged youth to be 'air-minded' through gliding clubs which provided a cheap and practical way of teaching the elements of flying and by 1929 had 50,000 members. Some of the preparations were secret. In 1923 Germany negotiated a hidden agreement with Soviet Russia to supply military training at the Lipetsk air base, south-east of Moscow, an arrangement that lasted ten years. By the time the Luftwaffe's existence was officially announced in March 1935, it could rely both on the design teams and factories of the strongest aircraft industry in Europe to provide machines and a large reserve of young air enthusiasts to supply pilots and crews.

Adolf Galland, one of the two most famous of the German pilots of 1940, first took to the air in a glider. The flight lasted only a few seconds and carried him only a few feet above the ground near his home in Westphalia, but it was enough to persuade him he had found his vocation. The family were descended from a Huguenot who had left France in 1742 and become bailiff to the Graf von Westerholt. Successive Gallands had held the post ever since. Adolf's father was a traditionalist, an authoritarian who administered discipline with his fists. His mother was profoundly Catholic, so much so that her devotion was to get her into trouble with the Nazis.

Like some of the most successful Fighter Boys, he learned to handle a gun early, and by the age of six he was shooting hares on the Westerholt estate. At school he was dull. When he read anything, it was war stories, particularly the sagas of Boelcke and Richthofen. At the local glider club, the Gelsenkirchen Luftsportverein, he shone and became the star pupil. Later he would claim that pilots who served a long apprenticeship on gliders 'felt' the air better. In 1932, aged twenty, he was accepted for pilot training at the commercial air school at Brunswick. His talents were recognized and he was summoned to Berlin to ask if he was interested in undergoing secret military training. He spent a few, mostly wasted months training alongside Mussolini's air force. There was a stint as a

Lufthansa pilot flying airliners to Barcelona. Then, at the end of 1933, excited by the prospects opening up in military aviation after the Nazis came to power, he joined the air force. In April 1937 he went back to Spain as a pilot in the fighter section of the Luftwaffe-directed Condor Legion, flying inferior He 51 biplanes. By the time the new Messerschmitt 109s were arriving in sufficient numbers to dominate the air, he was back in Germany in the Air Ministry. It was not until May 1940 and the blitzkrieg that he started to do what he became famous for.

Galland had a complicated and deceptive personality. He seemed, at first glance, to resemble some of the more flamboyant of his RAF counterparts. He liked wine, women and cigars. He appeared good-humoured, gregarious and relaxed in his attitude to discipline and senior officers. All this was true. But Galland also brought a chilly analytical intelligence to the war against the British and was harsh with pilots who failed to reach his standards. He was one of the boys, but also intimate with the big men who ran the war. He was an admirer of Goering until his chief's intolerable behaviour made admiration impossible. He admitted to his biographer that, after leaving his first private meeting with Hitler, 'he felt a mutual respect had been forged . . . for the rest of his life [he] would remember how on that Wednesday afternoon he had been drawn under the intensely focused spell of Hitler's personality'.[6] His high-wattage bonhomie allowed him later to play the part of a professional Good German. He was a prominent guest at post-war fighter-pilot reunions. He and Douglas Bader were photographed together and he enjoyed a sort of friendship with Bob Tuck. Some pilots were never persuaded. In the view of Christopher Foxley-Norris, 'Galland was a shit.'[7]

At the start of July, Galland was still in the shadow of Werner Mölders, who, flying an Me 109, had shot down fourteen aircraft in Spain followed by a further twenty-five during the French campaign. Mölders was tactically intelligent and in Spain developed the system of flying in pairs that was eventually adopted by the RAF. He was introverted and grave-looking, a serious Catholic who passively disliked the Nazis. This did not prevent them loading him with honours and high rank, nor him from accepting. He was the recipient of the first Knight's Cross to go to a fighter pilot and became a general of fighters before he was twenty-nine. Mölders had been shot down early in June by a young French pilot and taken prisoner but released after the armistice was signed between Germany and France. At the end of July he was put in command of the fighter wing, JG51. On Sunday, 28 July, he made his first outing at its head. He shot down one Spitfire from 74 Squadron but was then engaged by Sailor Malan. His Messerschmitt was badly damaged and he received leg wounds that kept him out of action for a month. He was, however, to make his presence felt later on.

He was inspirational and a good teacher. Galland acknowledged that much of his skill was learned from Mölders. Another successful pupil was Helmut Wick, whom Mölders instructed during advanced training and who ended the French campaign with fourteen 'victories', just behind his mentors. Galland, Mölders and Wick shared the same, atavistic approach. When they wrote, they expressed themselves in the same language, drawn from forest and hillside, as that used by Richthofen, whom they regarded as a spiritual forebear (although Mölders saw himself more as Boelcke's successor). Wick declared that 'as long as I can shoot down the enemy, adding to the honour of the Richthofen Geschwader [his fighter unit] and the success of the Fatherland, I am a happy man. I want to fight and die fighting, taking with me as many of the enemy as possible.'[8] A Spitfire from Fighter Command fulfilled one of these wishes by shooting him down and killing him near the Isle of Wight in November. Galland saw his task as being 'to attack, to track, to hunt and to destroy the enemy. Only in this way can the eager and skilful fighter pilot display his ability. Tie him to a narrow and confined task, rob him of his initiative, and you take away from him the best and most valuable qualities he possesses: aggressive spirit, joy of action and the passion of the hunter.'[9]

Such words could never have been spoken or written by a pilot of Fighter Command without provoking bafflement, embarrassment or derision. Then there were the medals. The leading German pilots were encrusted with layers of Ruritarian decoration. They started off as holders of the Knight's Cross, rising through clouds of glory to acquire the

Knight's Cross with Oak Leaves, Knight's Cross with Oak Leaves and Swords, culminating in the highest honour of all, the Knight's Cross with Oak Leaves, Swords and Diamonds. These honours were worn prominently at the neck, and the condition of wanting one but not having one was known as 'throatache'. The RAF had the Distinguished Flying Cross, to which further exploits might add a bar or two, and which was signalled by a scrap of cloth sewn over the left-hand breast pocket of the tunic. Only one Victoria Cross, the highest gallantry award, was won by Fighter Command in 1940. To qualify for consideration for the honour, candidates had to have demonstrated outstanding courage in the face of overwhelming odds. It might have been argued that most pilots in 11 Group in the summer of 1940 were doing this most days.

When the *Kanalkampf* began in earnest, the German pilots were rested, warm with the afterglow of a succession of victories and enjoying the fleshly comforts of a sybaritic country which had come to a fairly rapid accommodation with its occupiers. It was perhaps with some reluctance that they resumed operations. But they went off cheerfully enough and morale remained high as the scope of the campaign widened, deepened and lengthened. Partly by design, partly by force of circumstances, the German air campaign would climb an ascending scale of violence. The bombing attacks on shipping and the free hunts to draw up the British fighters would give way to raids on aerodromes and defence installations, culminating in an all-out air assault. The escalation, in theory, would deliver one of two results. Either Britain would be beaten into submission, making a full-scale invasion unnecessary. Or it would hold out, forcing a landing, in which case much of the preparatory destruction would already have been achieved.

After the war Galland and several other leading veterans of the campaign would claim that they knew from the beginning that the Luftwaffe on its own could not achieve a strategic victory in the air. 'We didn't believe at any time that we could win the battle, to the effect that Britain would surrender,' he said. 'We couldn't force England to surrender by attacking without any operation from the army or navy . . . We were asking that the High Command order the invasion.'[10]

But the army and navy commanders, even the Luftwaffe's own leader, agreed that the invasion could not go ahead until Germany had air supremacy, or at least air superiority. The chances of resolving this conundrum were reduced by Goering's ignorant, impetuous approach. The gap between the airmen's understanding of their own capabilities and their commander's expectations was wide. Goering had latched on to the most optimistic pre-war feasibility study to persuade himself that a war of attrition was winnable and had gone on to assure Hitler that the air force was capable of bringing Britain to negotiations. The pilots and crews learned early that praise was abundant when the going was good, abuse lavish as soon as the momentum faltered. 'At the beginning we had great respect for him,' said Gerhard Schöpfel, 'but later our feelings changed. He began to complain that we were not doing enough, but we needed far more machines and manpower to achieve what he wanted.'[11]

It would not take long for it to become clear that the Luftwaffe was facing a daunting task. But that was not how it seemed at the outset. Many of the men arriving at the airfields of northern France in July believed their superiors' predictions that the campaign would last only a few weeks. The operation was not being mounted from a standing start, but in the flush of several victories won with relative ease.

The German bombers and fighters had suffered steady losses during July – 172 from enemy action and 91 in accidents – but their pilots and crews were confident that when the big push came they would be able to overwhelm the British defences. The fighter squadrons accepted that they were facing the most difficult opponent to date, but were none the less sure they could wipe the Hurricanes and Spitfires from the sky. 'We wanted to make the invasion work and we were sure it would work,' said Schöpfel, who was serving with Galland in Jagdgeschwader 26. 'We believed that we had beaten the English over France and we did not think that here was a force which could defeat Germany. We believed the landing would be possible with our help and that our wings would be able to reach out to London. We thought it would be possible to beat the English in England the way we had beaten them in France.'

The build up of Luftwaffe forces in France was to continue into August, but on the morning of 24 July, before the full wing apparatus was in place, Galland announced that his three squadrons were ready for operations. At 11 a.m. a British convoy nosed out into the Channel from the Medway and a force of eighteen Dornier 17s was sent to bomb it. With them went an escort of forty Me 109s, led by Galland. Spitfires of 54 Squadron at Rochford were ordered up to meet them. At the same time, a further nine Spitfires, of 610 Squadron, took off from Biggin Hill to patrol over Dover and cut off the raiders' retreat. Another six Spitfires, of 65 Squadron, which was operating from Manston, were also sent into the area, and seeing the Messerschmitt escorts were preoccupied with fending off 54 Squadron tried to attack the bombers, but were driven away by fierce and well coordinated fire from their gunners.

No. 54 Squadron was pleased with its showing in its first encounter with Galland's fighters, which went down in the unit's history as the 'Battle of the Thames Estuary'. The squadron diary described it as 'the biggest fight since the second day of Dunkirk and in the face of considerable odds the casualties inflicted on the enemy by the squadron (including three new pilots) can be considered eminently satisfactory and most encouraging'. A claim was made for sixteen Me 109s destroyed; a great exaggeration, as it turned out. The more likely figure was two. One was shot down by Colin Gray; another by Sergeant George Collet, who then ran out of fuel and was forced to land on the beach, writing off his Spitfire.

In the clash the squadron lost one of its best-liked and most prominent members. Johnny Allen was attacked by an Me 109 near Margate. Another pilot saw him putting down in a forced landing with his engine stopped but the aeroplane under perfect control. Then the engine started again and he turned towards Manston, but it cut out a second time. The Spitfire flicked on to its back and went into an uncontrollable spin. Allen crashed to earth near Cliftonville. He was twenty-four-years-old and had been the first member of the squadron to fire a shot in anger almost exactly two months previously. In the meantime he had destroyed seven German aircraft, winning a DFC. The story of how he had been shot down over the Channel during the Dunkirk evacuation, been miraculously picked up by a naval corvette and appeared in the squadron mess later the same evening dressed in naval uniform and carrying a kitbag had been recounted in Winn's article in the *Sunday Express* three days before. The photographs show an open-faced, shyly smiling youth. Deere remembered him as 'quiet and religious . . . out of place' in the boisterous squadron atmosphere, yet an elemental part of the unit. The normally undemonstrative diarist noted that 'the loss . . . will be greatly felt by the squadron'.

Despite this death and the over-optimistic assessment of the damage inflicted on the 109s, the squadron was right to regard the encounter as a moral victory. Its pilots had been considerably outnumbered but had stayed to fight, refusing to be driven off. The over-claiming may have been a result of the fact that, with their fuel warning lights glowing red, many of the German pilots had used their Messerschmitts' superiority in the dive to drop steeply down to sea-level before racing for their home field.

The German pilots returned home to the base at Caffiers to be harangued by Galland, who was dismayed by his men's lack of discipline and apparent unwillingness to engage the Spitfires. This first sortie over England, he told his biographer, had come as an unpleasant surprise. 'The tenacity of the RAF pilots, despite being heavily outnumbered and relatively inexperienced, had been remarkable. It had shocked him to see how inept his own pilots were; and that would have to change. This was no sudden blitzkrieg, bundling a disorganized enemy backwards across indefensible plains; this was the real business of hardened air combat, against an enemy who was going to stand and fight.'[12]

13

Hearth and Home

Early in the summer, as a wave of Germans closed over the Channel ports, Pete Brothers was flying low over Calais when he looked down and saw a cinema belching smoke and flame. In that moment his attitude to the war changed. 'I suddenly thought that the Odeon in Bromley could be next. It came home to me that this was deadly serious.'[1] By the middle of August, bombs were falling every day on placid coastal towns and suburbs where, until then, nothing much had ever happened. This was not the terror bombing that Hitler had reserved the right to order if Britain remained obstinate. It was unintended and accidental, the inevitable consequence of the stepped-up attacks on factories and defence installations prior to the big assault. Civilian casualties were small compared with what was to come. But the sense of violation was great. Bombs tore away walls, opening up homes as if they were dolls' houses, putting all the ordinariness of family life on intimate display. Twenty-five years before, if the wind was in the right direction, the inhabitants of Dover and Folkstone could sometimes just hear the faint rumble of artillery on the Western Front and feel a slight thrill of proximity. Now the sound of gunfire was all around, and for the first time in a thousand years the enemy was visible.

The defenders fought the battles of high summer in view of the people they were defending. Often the pilots were diving and shooting over their childhood homes. Roland Beamont could see his family house in

Chichester every time he took off from Tangmere. John Greenwood, a pilot officer with 253 Squadron, flew head-on into a formation of Ju 88s over Surrey and was horrified when 'they jettisoned their loads which fell between Epsom and Tolworth. My family lived in Tolworth and seeing the bombs exploding I went down to ground level to have a look.'[2] The nearest bomb had been several hundred yards away from his home. When he got back to Kenley he telephoned his mother, who told him she had been sheltering in the cupboard under the stairs during the raid. Peter Devitt of 152 Squadron was flying near Sevenoaks one Sunday evening when he saw Dorniers fleeing from a raid dropping their last bombs on Young's depository, where all his furniture was stored.

In some extraordinary cases, parents watched their sons fighting. On 16 August an intense engagement broke out between a large German formation and Hurricanes from 1 Squadron. One of the British fighters was hit in the fuel tank by a cannon shell and burst into flames. The pilot, Pilot Officer Tim Elkington, managed to bale out and was drifting down into the sea when Sergeant Frederick Berry swooped past him and used the aircraft's slipstream to blow the parachute over land. Elkington landed safely at West Wittering and was whisked away to hospital. The whole event was witnessed by Elkington's mother watching from the balcony of her flat on Hayling Island.[3]

Until August the fighter bases had been insulated from the violence of the war and the comfort and orderliness of mess, living quarters, flower beds, tennis courts and squash courts were undisturbed. The calm was about to be smashed. The mess waiters, batmen, clerks, Waafs, fitters and riggers; the great host of supporters who sustained the men in the sky, were now in as much danger as the pilots themselves. Watching the Germans swarming across in ever-bigger concentrations, many pilots felt a sense of revulsion they had not experienced before. The urbane Brian Considine 'hated them . . . thinking of what they were going to do if they were allowed to do it and what they had already done'.[4] Christopher Foxley-Norris described the sentiment as 'the sort of wave of indignation you get if you find a burglar in your house'.[5] No matter how the feeling was expressed, it gave an edge to the pilots' courage, driving them on to make greater efforts and take bigger risks.

August had opened quietly. Dowding and his senior commanders correctly interpreted the lull as the harbinger of a new and more intense phase. He could view the coming clash with some confidence. Factories were producing more fighters than the Germans were destroying and production targets were being overtaken. On 1 August he had roughly 650 combat-ready aircraft. In contrast to only a month before, he also had an adequate number of pilots. By trying to fight only when strictly necessary, he and Park had kept most of the squadrons relatively fresh. Some, like 54, had done a disproportionate amount of the fighting. But in all only a quarter of the strength of Fighter Command had been on extended duty during July. The problem, as the weeks ahead were to show, was not the quantity of pilots available but the quality. Many of those swelling the ranks had been hurried through training and were still not fully familiar with their machines. The accelerating pace of the battle meant that these novices would be thrown straight into aerial fighting of unprecedented intensity.

Hitler had set the date for the start of the new phase as on or after 5 August. Another directive, expressed in general terms and without naming specific targets, called for the air force to attack 'flying units, their ground installations, and their supply organizations [and] the aircraft industry'. This was in keeping with the imperative to destroy the Royal Air Force before any invasion could begin. In another document he told the three services to be ready to launch *Seelöwe* by 15 September if, by then, a landing had become necessary. Field-Marshal Kesselring, the leader of Luftflotte 2, which covered a line drawn east to west just above Paris, and Field-Marshal Sperrle, commanding Luftflotte 3 below it, differed over the approach. Kesselring favoured a dispersed campaign that would reduce the risk of concentrated, heavy losses. Sperrle backed a short, furious effort, hurling bombers, dive-bombers and fighter bombers en masse to smash the British defences.

Both agreed a sledge-hammer blow should start the assault. The operation was given the Wagnerian code name of *Adlerangriff*, the 'Attack of the Eagles', and *Adlertag* ('Eagle Day') was eventually set for 13 August. The preceding days were filled with dress-rehearsal raids and attempts to knock out radar stations to weaken the defenders' capacity to respond. On the morning of 12 August, Dover radar station was bombed, then a few minutes later those at Rye, Pevensey and the Kentish hamlet of Dunkirk. The damage looked spectacular but was quickly repaired and all stations were back on the air within six hours. The installations were small and well tucked away. The very flimsiness of the criss-cross construction of the transmitter towers made them remarkably resilient to blast. The Luftwaffe was never to achieve its aim of a total blackout of radar, but raids could result in dangerous blind spots in the cover that could last several hours.

While the radar was down, bombers raced in to exploit the advantage, attacking Lympne and Hawkinge airfields on the Kent coast. The decision to target Lympne, which since June had only been used as an emergency satellite field for fighters in trouble, was an early indication that the Luftwaffe's information about the nature and importance of RAF installations might be faulty or incomplete. A few hours later, Manston, sitting vulnerably on the crown of the North Foreland, was strafed by Me 110s closely followed by Dornier 17s dropping 150 high-explosive bombs. The landing ground was pitted with craters and four of the ground staff were killed. Once the smoke cleared and the chalk dust settled, it was seen that the damage was not catastrophic. None of the Spitfires caught on the ground was badly damaged and ground crews laboured to fill in the holes so that the airfield was in action again within twenty-four hours. The raid gave an unpleasant foretaste of what pilots, and particularly the ground staff of Manston, would have to suffer over the next weeks as the aerodrome was hit again and again.

The temporary loss of radar meant that a huge fleet of bombers protected by a fighter escort launched later that morning was already well on its way to its target before it was picked up and a force of forty-eight Hurricanes and ten Spitfires, operating in separate squadrons, sent up to confront it. The bombers were heading for Portsmouth. The bomber force split into two. The first group swung in through a gap in the balloon barrage defending the city and ploughed through a storm of anti-aircraft fire. Bombs hit the Royal Dockyards and the railway station and sank some small ships in the harbour, killing twenty-three people and wounding a hundred. The second group of fifteen Ju 88s turned for the Isle of Wight and dived on the radar station at Ventnor.

The German fighters circled behind and above the bombers, tempting the British fighters to come up. It was an invitation that they were learning to resist. Instead, the Hurricanes of 213 Squadron waited for the first group to emerge from the Portsmouth defences and pounced on them, shooting down the machine of Oberst Johannes Fisser, who was leading the attack. The second group was also set upon by Spitfires from 152 and 609 Squadrons, as it turned for home from Ventnor. Three 609 pilots, Noel Agazarian, James 'Butch' McArthur, who before the war had been a civil aviation pilot, and David Crook had been about to set off from the forward base at Warmwell, Dorset, where they were living under canvas, for London on a twenty-four-hour leave when the order to go to readiness came through. They took off immediately, except for Crook, who was delayed by a faulty radio. He arrived over the Isle of Wight to find 'circling and sweeping all over the sky at least 200 Huns . . . "My God," I said to myself, "what a party!" '[6]

The circling aircraft were the Me 110s on station to protect the bombers. They found themselves in a tactical dilemma. The British squadrons were launching small, successive attacks on the bombers. The escorts faced the choice of coming down in twos and threes to try and chase away the attackers, in which case they would be engaged by other British fighters; or they could descend in a great flock, which meant breaking up the defensive umbrella and creating a free-for-all in which the Spitfires and Hurricanes could get among them relatively unmolested. The raiders had lost ten bombers before their fighters, circling 10,000 feet ahead, could react. When they finally arrived they were punished, and four Me 110s and two Me 109s were destroyed in the space of a few minutes. Agazarian shot down two and Crook one. After landing the British pilots resumed their plan to set off for London, arriving five hours later than intended, and were back in the battle again the following day.

The toll among the defenders had been high, with eleven pilots killed and six wounded. Among the injured was Geoffrey Page. He was sitting on the grass in front of the dispersal tents at Rochford having afternoon tea after a long day of fighting when the field telephone rang and the order was given to take off in squadron strength to meet ninety bandits approaching from the south at 15,000 feet. Only ten aircraft were available. They caught up with the Dorniers as they were heading north past the mouth of the Thames, having dropped their loads. As Page, in the leading section, closed on the nearest Dornier 17, he saw 'all this tracer ammunition coming from the whole formation. They'd singled me out as the target . . . all these things that looked like lethal electric-light bulbs kept flashing by until suddenly there was an enormous bang and the whole aircraft exploded'.

Like most of the pilots Page had never made a parachute descent. The drill was taught in training, however, and now it came to his rescue. Instinctively he released the heavy webbing Sutton harness strapping him to his seat, slid the cockpit hood open and rolled the Spitfire on to its back. He remembered 'popping out of the aircraft like a cork out of a toy gun'. It was not fast enough to save him from the flames. Page was not wearing gloves. His hands, and the area of his face not protected by the oxygen mask, were terribly burned.

Free of the machine, he found himself 'tumbling head over heels through space. I remember seeing my right arm extended and I sort of looked at it. My brain ordered it to bring itself in and pull the metal ring of the rip cord on the parachute, and that was agony because with this cold metal ring and badly burned hand it was like an electric shock.' Somehow he yanked the cord and looked up to see the parachute blossom overhead. A ball-crunching shock between his legs as the harness arrested his descent told him he was safe for the moment, and drifting down he took stock of his situation. 'I noticed quite a funny thing had happened. My left shoe and my trousers had been blown off completely by the explosion. I was just about almost naked from the waist downwards. My legs were slightly burnt and I could hear the fight going on all around.' It was a sound he had never heard before. Engine noise blotted out the noise of fighting.

It took Page ten minutes to drift down into the sea. As the water came up to meet him, he ran through what he was meant to do next. The drill taught him he should twist the release catch on the harness through ninety degrees, then bang it to make it spring open. His roasted hands would not obey. As he settled in the sea the parachute silk and shrouds sank down on top of him 'like an octopus's tentacles. I knew that if I didn't get away from the parachute quickly it would get waterlogged and sink and take me with it.' Desperation numbed the agony and somehow the metal disc flipped open.

The next thing was to inflate his lifejacket, the Mae West that every pilot wore over his tunic. He blew into the rubber tube and was dismayed to see bubbles frothing through the holes where the fabric had been burned through. There was nothing to do but swim for it. Through swelling eyes, he could just see the English coast, and weighed down by his waterlogged uniform and a helmet which his fingers could not unbuckle, he struck out. He remembered that in his jacket pocket was a brandy flask given him by his mother.

'Quite often in the mess over the previous weeks when the bar had closed my fellow pilots had said, "Come on Geoffrey, you've got a flask there, let's have a tot of brandy," but I said, "No, one day I may have an emergency." As I was swimming along I thought that this probably qualified.' There was a further agonizing tussle as he unbuttoned his tunic flap and extracted the flask. He wrenched the cap off with his teeth when 'a dirty big wave came along and knocked it out of my wrists and the whole lot went to the bottom of the Channel'.

Despairingly, he floundered on. He had been in the water half an hour and almost given up hope when he heard the chug of an engine. His descent had been spotted by the coastguards, who sent a launch to search for him. After he persuaded his rescuers, with a stream of obscenities, that he was not a German he was dragged out of the sea and taken back to Margate where the mayor, strangely attired in a top hat, greeted him on the quayside.[7]

Page was very lucky. Fighter pilots on both sides hated the Channel. To the Germans it was the 'shit canal'. To the British it was 'the dirty ditch'. Bomber pilots had a second engine to get them home if the other was shot up or failed. Hurricanes, Spitfires and Me 109s had only one. Putting down on the sea was almost invariably catastrophic. The air intake slung under the fuselages of all three types dug into the water, sending the machine cartwheeling in a curtain of spray before it sank within seconds. Parachuting was barely less hazardous. The further away from land you were, the slimmer your chances of being picked up. British safety equipment was primitive and inferior to that of their enemies. Mae Wests relied for their buoyancy on wads of kapok and a rubber bladder that had to be inflated by mouth. The Germans had rubber dinghies and dye to stain the water to signal their whereabouts to rescuers.

The pilots made great efforts to pinpoint downed comrades. The day before Page was shot down, another 56 Squadron pilot, Sergeant Ronald Baker, was seen parachuting into the sea near a British destroyer. Michael Constable Maxwell recorded in his diary how Flying Officer Percy Weaver '(circled) round keeping him in sight – a most difficult thing to do as the turning circle of the Hurricane is too big and the aircraft is on the verge of spinning all the time. Another tried to get the ships over while I fly overhead watching for any hostile aircraft. It is extremely hard to keep an eye on a Mae West in the water as it is so small.'[8]

When, after an hour, a motor boat finally picked him up, Baker was dead. Many a pilot spent the last minutes of his life savouring the bitter knowledge that he had escaped death in the air only to meet it in the water. Three pilots drowned that day. A week later Park drafted revised orders to his sector controllers, instructing them to send up fighters to engage large formations only over land or within gliding distance of the coast as 'we cannot afford to lose pilots through forced landings in the sea'. Belatedly, a committee was set up at the Air Ministry to establish an RAF air-sea rescue organization with spotter aircraft and launches. But the incompetence of the Air Ministry in failing to put efficient rescue arrangements in place before the fighting began would come to be regarded by the pilots as shameful.

'Eagle Day' began inauspiciously for the Germans. The fine weather of the preceding days faltered. There was cloud over the Channel and a thin drizzle fell patchily on southern England. Goering hesitated. The weather reports predicted the skies would clear in the afternoon. That would still leave time, he decided, to deliver the smashing blow that would begin the final destruction of Fighter Command. The decision to postpone operations was slow in passing down the line. The first scheduled raid of the day was already forming up when it arrived. Sixty Me 110s, led by the *Kanalkampfführer* himself, Colonel Johannes Fink, had taken off early in the morning and climbed to an assembly point where they had been told fighters were waiting to escort them. But instead of slotting in alongside them, 'they kept coming up and diving down in the most peculiar way. I thought this was their way of saying they were ready. So I went on and found to my surprise that the fighters didn't follow . . . I didn't worry much.'[9] The fighters, it seemed, had received the signal changing the orders, but with no radio link between them and the bombers were unable to pass it on.

On reaching the English coast, the formation split, with one group heading for the naval base at Sheerness and the other for Eastchurch aerodrome on the Isle of Sheppey. It was a strange choice of target. Eastchurch was primarily a Coastal Command station, of little importance given the Luftwaffe's current preoccupations. By chance, fighters were present. Dowding had began to shift rested squadrons down from the relative quiet of the north to fill gaps in the front line. At Wittering in the Midlands 266 Squadron had been passing a pleasant summer. On 11 August its members spent the day bathing and boating on the lake next to their dispersal point and were drinking in the mess in the evening when the message came through that they were to prepare to move south at dawn. 'After two months' intense inactivity there was much excitement and speculation,' wrote Dennis Armitage, who had joined the squadron from the RAFVR the previous December. 'I went out to warn the ground staff, the bar was reopened and the news celebrated until about 3 a.m. when we all retired for an hour's shuteye.'[10] A month later, many of those toasting the approach of action were dead.

The squadron was supposed to go to Northolt for the day and return to Wittering in the afternoon. Like so many plans of the time, it had no sooner been made than desperate circumstances rendered it redundant. In the hectic weeks of the summer, squadron leaders would get used to responding to constantly changing orders as Dowding shifted Fighter Command's stance to meet each German feint and lunge. The pilots of 266 ended up spending all day at Northolt before being ordered on to Tangmere, where they arrived in the early evening. The following morning they were told to prepare to fly to Eastchurch the next day, where they were to escort Battles – the sluggish, death-trap bombers that had fared so badly in France – on raids on E-boats in French and Dutch ports. No one had brought a razor or a toothbrush so an aeroplane was dispatched to base to fetch basic kit.

Before they left they were ordered up to patrol over Tangmere, but with strict instructions not to engage the enemy unless absolutely necessary. Twenty minutes later that changed to an order to head south and attack the large bomber formation approaching Portsmouth. It was the first time the squadron had been properly in action. 'Having done so much messing about, waiting, wondering what was going to happen, getting your teeth into something was a great thrill,' Armitage remembered.[11] He shot down one of the three German machines claimed by the squadron. But there was a price to pay. Pilot Officer Dennis Ashton, who the day before had been celebrating the move south, was shot down in flames. He was twenty years old. His body was found a month later by a naval minesweeper and buried at sea.

Armitage finally arrived at Eastchurch that afternoon to find 'an odd place built on a bog with a small, L-shaped, undulating landing ground'. The officers' mess was 'an enormous erection of light girders and plywood. You entered by some steps onto a great verandah running the full length of the ante-room, which was big enough to have housed a dozen full-sized billiard tables.' In the middle was a wide chimney and four cavernous fireplaces. It was rumoured that the building had been designed for use in India but had somehow been misplaced. That evening after supper there was a conference at which the station commander explained the plan. Armitage and the others were told that the planned dawn take-off had now been cancelled because there was no precise intelligence on the whereabouts of the E-boats and that as yet there were no bombs for the Battles. He promised more information at 10 a.m., when everyone had had a good night's rest and enjoyed a late breakfast.

This pleasant prospect was disrupted by the arrival of the Germans led by Fink. The first bomb landed shortly after 7 a.m. Armitage 'awoke to find my bed waltzing about the room, which seemed most unpleasant but was caused by what in reality was a blessing . . . the bogginess of the land. The whole place shook as if we were having a major earthquake, but the bombs . . . buried themselves deeply before exploding, leaving nothing but a little pile of earth.' One bomb struck one of the ground-crew huts, killing sixteen men and injuring several more. Armitage was slightly hurt from a bomb which struck the gutter above the room where he was sleeping and exploded before it hit the ground. The same blast shook the chimney and monumental fireplaces in the mess, where several pilots ducked for shelter as the raid began. They emerged smothered in soot. Another bomb demolished a hangar, exploding the squadron's stock of ammunition, already preloaded in metal trays ready to slip into the guns when the fighters returned to rearm. But only one Spitfire was destroyed and the rest of the fighters, carefully dispersed around the airfield, were untouched. After the engine notes of the departing Germans had faded and the initial relief subsided, the 266 pilots recognized that the squadron had got off lightly. The dead airmen were a tragedy, but the brutal truth was that airmen, even highly skilled riggers and fitters, could be more easily replaced than pilots. Such relative good fortune could not last.

Hurricanes from 151 Squadron at North Weald were sent up to harry the raiders as they headed home. Fink's early unconcern about the lack of fighter protection faded. 'The RAF fighters attacked only singly, but we were a bit scattered, so we simply used the cloud layer. If the fighters were up top we dived down. If they were below we climbed up. But we lost five aircraft . . . I was furious.' After landing 'in this over-excited condition I went straight to the phone, got on to Kesselring and shouted down the line exactly what I thought about it. I asked what . . . the people at HQ thought they were doing to send us out unprotected. Poor old Kesselring was so overwhelmed he was unable to get a word in edgeways. Eventually he said, "All right, all right, I'll come over personally."'

'Eagle Day' may not have started well for the Luftwaffe, but the brightening weather offered a second opportunity. By early afternoon the meteorological reports proved correct. The sky cleared. The order was given for the main attack to begin. It was launched, not directly from across the Channel but from the south-west. A huge mass of aircraft began forming up above the Cherbourg peninsula, made up of 120 twin-engined Ju 88s and nearly 80 Stukas, protected by about 100 Me 109s and 110s. At 3.30 p.m. they began to appear as a thick cluster of blips on radar screens, stretched out across a forty-mile front and coming from the direction of the Channel Islands. The blow seemed to be aimed at the ports and air bases of the West Country, 10 Group's area. Nearly eighty Hurricanes and Spitfires from Exeter, Warmwell in Dorset, Middle Wallop in Hampshire and Tangmere were scrambled to intercept them. This was, by Fighter Command's standards, a very large number of fighters to commit to one action. The momentum of the raiding force carried it through. One group pounded Southampton. Another split off and headed for Middle Wallop, but failing accurately to locate the base dumped its bombs around the village.

10 Group was a quiet sector. Most of the pilots had never seen such an array of enemy aircraft. Kenneth Gundry, who had only arrived at 257 Squadron as a pilot officer ten days before, tried to describe the nature of the experience in a letter to his parents.

We separated as a flight and found ourselves sitting under about eighty Me 110 fighters milling around in a huge circle. Above them were about fifty or more Me 109s. Two of our five got split away by a few stray Jerries buzzing around and then the next thing I knew was a ruddy great earthquake in my A/C [aircraft] and my control column was almost solid. On my left another Hurricane was floating about over a complete network of smoke trails left by cannon shells and incendiary. We had been attacked by another unseen bunch of Me 110s . . . [After] shaking the bleeder off my tail I managed to get some fairly close but ineffective deflection shots into him, but he used his extra speed and dropped clean away, down out of range leaving me with plenty of others to contend with. I joined up with another Hurricane and Jerry just seemed to dissolve. We just couldn't find any at all.[12]

When he landed he found that the tail of his Hurricane was 'shot to hell' and his starboard aileron was splintered in two and hanging off.

Despite its schoolboy language, Gundry's account must have given his parents some feeling of the frenzied struggle going on over their heads and added to their burden of worry. It also reflected the vengeful mood gripping the pilots. Later in the letter he described how 'one poor swine of a Ju 88 was spotted while going back from a raid . . . and about seven of us whooped with joy and dived on him from all directions. His rear gunner put up a marvellous show and was replaced later by the observer, I guess, but he finally went down in a complete inferno of red-hot metal and we could see the column of smoke rising from where it crashed . . . from our 'drome at Tangmere for several hours afterwards.'

The satisfaction of downing a German bomber was enormous. As one Stuka squadron left the Dorset coast for home it ran straight into the guns of 609 Squadron pilots, who shot down six of the dive-bombers, despite the presence of a fighter escort. The attack was led with custom-ary icy professionalism by George Darley, who described later how he 'managed to slip the squadron through the fighters then went right through the Ju 87 formation, taking potshots without throttling back. This enabled the chaps behind to position themselves without having to avoid me.'[13] John Dundas, who claimed one of the victims, wrote in the squadron diary: 'Thirteen Spitfires left Warmwell for a memorable tea-time party over Lyme Bay, and an unlucky day for the species Ju 87.'[14]

'Eagle Day' ended as an anticlimax. It had decided nothing. Fighter Command could feel some satisfaction at its performance. Initial assess-ments put the German losses at sixty-seven with thirteen on the British side. In fact forty-seven Luftwaffe aeroplanes had been destroyed. The human cost had been greatly disproportionate. The Luftwaffe lost eighty-nine pilots and crew killed or taken prisoner, while only three British pilots died. In a war of resources these ratios were comforting.

The Germans were more successful, though, in their new aim of destroying Fighter Command's infrastructure. Despite the early warning and the large numbers of fighters put up to block the raids, the bombers had managed to get through. It was the Luftwaffe's bad judgement that had averted a catastrophe. An afternoon raid devastated the aerodrome at Detling, near Maidstone, killing sixty-seven people, military and civilian, demolishing messes crowded with airmen and flattening hangars. Once again it seemed an unlikely target to choose. It was not a Fighter Command base and its destruction had no effect on the fabric of the defences. None the less it provided a stark demonstration of the havoc that could be wrought if the bombers were directed on to an important target, such as the sector bases which acted as the synapses for the fighter control system.

Luftwaffe activity slackened off on 14 August. A raid was launched at noon that resulted in a swirling dogfight involving 200 aircraft over Dover. Manston was attacked again, and Middle Wallop, this time with more success. A month previously such action would have been memorable. At this frenetic phase of the battle it counted as a lull. Dowding took the opportunity to rotate tired and battered units out of the 11 Group area and bring fresh ones in.

The following day was bright and clear, not what the Luftwaffe's experts had forecast. In the expectation of bad weather, Goering had summoned his commanders to Karinhall, his princely hunting castle near Berlin, for an 'Eagle Day' post-mortem. The intended spectacular assertion of power had flopped, achieving little but losses. It was time to try something different. When reconnaissance flights over Scotland reported clearing skies, Goering decided to press on with another full-scale attack. This time it would be made on two fronts, taking the battle for the first time to the north of England. The forces of Luftflotte 5, based in Denmark and Norway, had taken little part in the fighting so far. Now they were to be brought into play. At the same time virtually every unit of Luftflottes 2 and 3 in France was brought to readiness. The aim was to breach and overwhelm Britain's air defences down the whole eastern and southern flanks of the island on an 800-mile front stretching from Edinburgh to Exeter.

The numbers the Germans were able to muster were greater than anything ever seen in aerial warfare. On the German side were 1,790 bombers and fighters arrayed in a huge, ominously curved crescent. Set against them Dowding had 233 serviceable Spitfires and 351 Hurricanes. The battle opened just after 11.30 when Stukas, strongly protected by an umbrella of fighters, bombed Hawkinge and Lympne on the Kent coast. At Hawkinge they dropped heavy bombs which destroyed a hangar and damaged a barracks block. They also scattered small fragmentation bombs, but the aircraft they were designed to destroy were no longer there, having by chance been ordered off half an hour earlier by the Biggin Hill commander, Group Captain Grice. There was a separate raid by Me 110s on Manston, the third in four days, and two Spitfires belonging to the luckless 266 Squadron, which had moved on there after being bombed out of Eastchurch, were destroyed on the ground. As well as being the target for snap attacks, Manston's position in the Germans' path meant that any enemy aircraft with bombs or ammunition remaining was likely to use the station as an opportunity target before racing home across the Channel. This vulnerability, the base's historian remarked, 'created an atmosphere of danger in which death could come without warning at any time of the day'.[15]

The first force from Luflotte 5 set off from Stavanger on the Norwegian coast in mid-morning. It was made up of seventy-two Heinkel bombers, protected by twenty-one Me 110s. Their targets were aerodromes in north-east England, particularly Dishforth and Usworth. A group of Heinkel seaplanes flew ahead of them, heading for Dundee, hoping to draw away the defending fighters. The ruse worked, and when the aircraft showed up on the radar, squadrons at Acklington, Drem and Catterick were brought to readiness. Once again luck came to the aid of the defenders. As a result of a navigation error, the bombers had been drifting steadily northwards as they crossed the North Sea, so they neared the coast at the point at which the feint attack had successfully lured the

British fighters. When they realized their mistake, they turned quickly southwards, but by now the fighters were in the air and heading towards them. Led by Squadron Leader Ted Graham, 72 Squadron intercepted the raiders twelve miles out to sea over the Farne Islands in Northumberland. 'None of us had ever seen so many aircraft in the sky at one time,' wrote Robert Deacon Elliot, a twenty-six-year-old pilot officer. Faced with so many choices, Graham took time to giving his order. When he tried to speak he was hampered by his chronic stutter. 'By the time he got it out,' Elliot remembered, 'the attack was on. There was a gap between the lines of bombers and the Me 110s coming up in the rear, so in there we went. I do not think they saw us to begin with. When they did, the number of bombs rapidly jettisoned was fantastic. You could see them falling away from the aircraft and dropping into the sea, literally by the hundreds. The formation became a shambles.'[16]

It was, he recorded, 'a terrific scrap'. He saw 'two separate Huns literally disintegrate'. One, a Me 110, had fallen victim to Desmond Sheen, who 'fired at it and it just blew up'. His shot appears to have ignited a long-range tank fitted underneath. He was enveloped in a cloud of black smoke from the explosion, but 'started to climb up again and have another go and a 110 came straight down, head-on at me and I shot at it head-on climbing up, and its port engine went up in flames and it went over my head about ten feet away.'[17] The squadron claimed fourteen destroyed without loss. As usual, the whirling confusion of the engagement made accuracy impossible and the score would later be revised considerably downwards. But there was no doubt that serious physical and moral damage was inflicted on the raiders. A few pressed on courageously. Others scattered their bombs in the Newcastle area before turning out over the daunting expanse of the North Sea. Squadron after squadron came up to hound them on their way. A second large raid, launched from Ålborg in Denmark, was also heavily punished.

The losses suffered by Luftflotte 5 effectively removed it from the battle. It was never again to mount a significant daylight attack from the north on Britain's defences. The Germans had lost 20 per cent of their aircraft, with eighty-one air crew killed or missing. In the north there was little to show for it. Driffield airfield had been hammered, but it was a bomber base and the destruction made no difference to the immediate battle. In the south, the raids did much more damage. The airfield at Martlesham, used as a forward base for squadrons from Debden, was heavily bombed and knocked out for forty-eight hours. Middle Wallop was attacked but escaped lightly. Croydon was the worst hit. The bombs smashed into the terminal buildings, where smart travellers had presented themselves in the inter-war years for flights to the Continent, and destroyed hangars and stores. Some bombs had delayed fuses, exploding hours after the aeroplanes had gone. They killed sixty-eight people and cast a pall of nervous gloom over the base. The destruction was terrible but not catastrophic. Croydon was of secondary importance, unlike Kenley, which had apparently been the real target.

The fifteenth of August became 'Black Thursday' in the folklore of the German air force. It was a tribute to the Luftwaffe's morale that the attacks of 16 August were almost as heavy and were pressed home with the same energy as the day before. But, to the increasing concern of the German commanders, the spirit of the defenders appeared as resilient as ever. If anything, resistance seemed to have taken on a more bitter quality, with the British pilots eager to inflict as much punishment as possible. When a raid came in close to Hornchurch just after noon, the nine Spitfires of 54 Squadron sent up to meet it not only prevented the bombers from reaching the aerodrome, but chased them all the way back to the French coast, shooting down three on the way without loss. For once Al Deere was not with them. He had been forced to abandon his machine the previous day after being shot up on a similar sortie, pursuing an Me 109 all the way back to the Pas de Calais.

The grimness of the defenders' determination was evident in a new tactic, the head-on attack, which began to be adopted by some pilots. It required exceptional sang-froid and was fatal if misjudged. When bombers crossed the Kent coast at Dungeness at noon, 111 Squadron, which had been one of the first units to develop the technique, climbed up to meet them. Among the pilots was Henry Ferriss, who had abandoned his medical studies to take up a short-service commission before the war and had just celebrated his twenty-second birthday. He was one of the most tenacious and experienced pilots in the squadron and had shot down at least nine enemy aircraft. On this day he flew his Hurricane straight towards an approaching Dornier 17 and opened fire. Neither pilot turned away and the two collided and crashed to earth. This event did not dissuade 111 Squadron from continuing with the tactic. Ben Bowring, a Blenheim pilot who answered a call for volunteers for single-seater fighter units, arrived at the squadron a few days afterwards. His motivation was to avenge the death of his best friend, a fellow pilot, George Moore. 'I didn't really think of having any fear at the time,' he said later. 'What had overcome it was the desire to get one's own back for everything that was being done to your friends.'[18] He found the head-on attacks 'nerve-racking' but worth while. The pilots were grimly pleased to notice that, unlike beam or rear attacks, head-on assaults produced an immediate and dramatic effect. 'You could see the front of the aircraft crumple,' Bowring said. He also noticed that the bomber pilots reared up from their seats and stumbled backwards in a futile attempt to escape the stream of bullets.

Sheer weight of numbers meant that the Germans still got through. At 1 p.m. on 16 August it was the turn of Tangmere, most bucolic of Fighter Command's bases, to feel the full force of the German attack. A raid the day before had done some damage before being beaten away by 43 Squadron. This time the Stukas, escorted by Me 109s, gathered in a great buzzing mass over the Isle of Wight. Then, as a signal flare looped down from the lead aircraft, they closed on Tangmere, just across the water, and tipped into their dives. The remaining hangars were flattened, along with the officers' mess, the station workshops, stores, sick quarters and shelters. Six Blenheims belonging to the fledgling Fighter Interception Unit were wrecked. The bombs killed ten of the ground staff and three civilians.

Most of the Hurricanes of 1, 43 and 601 Squadrons were already in the air, but too late to block the attack. They managed to destroy seven dive-bombers as they fled. Two Hurricanes were shot down during the interception. One of these was flown by Billy Fiske, of 601 Squadron.

William Meade Fiske was the son of an international banker from Chicago, an Anglophile who had gone to Cambridge University, married the former wife of the Earl of Warwick, set a record on the Cresta Run and moved in the sporting circles from which 601 Squadron drew its pre-war members. He had volunteered for the RAF two weeks after the outbreak of war and was posted to join his friends in 601 Squadron at Tangmere on 10 July. Fiske was an above-average pilot and a fast learner. He had never flown a Hurricane before making his first flight with the squadron. How he was shot down was never established. He managed to crash-land on the aerodrome and was carried out of the cockpit by an ambulance crew, who reported that he was suffering only from superficial burns on the face and hand. The following day he was visited in hospital by the squadron adjutant who reported that he was 'perky as hell'.[19] But later that day he was dead, apparently having succumbed to shock. Fiske's social standing and American citizenship ensured that his death was extensively reported. The tragedy also had propaganda uses to a government intent on drawing America into the war. Fiske was presented, plausibly enough, as an idealist who had defied the neutrality laws to fight in the cause of humanity. A plaque was placed in St Paul's Cathedral to commemorate 'an American Citizen Who Died That England Might Live'. He was one of eleven pilots from the United States who flew with Fighter Command that summer.

Death was now becoming as familiar to Fighter Command's rear echelon as it was to the pilots. The ground crews were proving themselves as courageous under fire as the men they supported. When a raid warning was sounded at Warmwell, three 609 airmen, Corporal Bob Smith and Leading Aircraftmen Harry Thorley and Ken Wilson, ran out to wind down the thick steel-plated doors on a hangar to protect the Spitfires inside. A bomb smashed through the roof and all three were killed. The pilots using the airfield as a forward base felt particular sympathy for the airmen stuck on the ground under continuous threat of bombardment but unable to defend themselves. John Nicholas of 65 Squadron watched an airman grimly driving a petrol bowser out to a refuelling point during a raid. The driver was decapitated by a salvo from an Me 109 and the bowser went up in flames. Al Deere and the other 54 Squadron pilots were baffled by the insistence on keeping Manston operational, and hated flying from there. Its advanced position was no advantage. It was too far forward to allow a straight climb up to interception height. It was a great relief to pilots and ground crew when, by the end of the month, the airfield was virtually closed down as a fighter base. 'There seemed no tactical advantage in continuing to use an airfield so far forward, especially when it had such a damaging effect on the morale of the pilots and ground crews,' Deere wrote later.[20] The suspicion was that Fighter Command believed that to pull back would have handed a moral victory to the Luftwaffe. If so, it was uncharacteristically stupid and wasteful thinking on Dowding's part.

Civilians, too, had now made their first chilly acquaintance with the meaning of aerial warfare. On 16 August bombs fell on the suburbs of south London. The following day the BBC broadcast an eyewitness account by a young woman, Marjery Wace, who had been in Wimbledon when Dorniers passed overhead. She refused to go to a shelter, instead keeping company with a bedridden old lady. 'The house absolutely shook as if it was made of cardboard,' she told listeners. 'It was horribly alarming while it lasted, and I found myself longing to be in the open. I expect if I had been in the open I should have been longing to be in the house.' After dark she went out to inspect the damage. It was 'a beautiful August night. I could just see a dim outline of a few people sitting in front of their houses . . . as I arrived a stream of people began to enter further up the street . . . they came quietly in groups of three or four. The only sound was from small children crying from sheer weariness as they were carried home by their fathers. And what homes to have to come back to. It was just a small street of small houses, but now the glass had been blown in and the whole insides of the rooms destroyed.' Two things struck Miss Wace as she walked around. One was that 'there was a great deal of truth in the soldiers' attitude to the chances of being hit . . . it's simply a question of luck.' The other was the sight of women patiently cleaning up. 'There's a strange impulse in every housewife to go on sweeping whatever state the world is in,' she observed. 'For quite a number of people explained to me how they had swept up rooms that they agreed no one could possibly live in again.'[21]

The violence was widening and deepening, but the pilots could take comfort in the thought that the Germans, in inflicting it, were paying a high price. On 18 August they at last had their revenge on the Stukas. At about 4 p.m. nearly thirty Ju 87s approached the radar station at Poling on the Sussex coast and prepared to attack. The sun was in their eyes, blinding them to the presence of the Hurricanes of 43 Squadron, who swooped in, to be joined by fighters from four more squadrons. The Stukas were just going into their dive when the attack was launched. In the fight that ensued, sixteen dive-bombers were shot down and two more crashed on the way home. The escorting Me 109s offered little protection. Once the Stukas plunged, it was impossible to keep up with them. They managed to catch up with the British fighters after the damage was done, shooting down four Hurricanes and two Spitfires, but losing eight of their own in the process.

The episode persuaded Luftwaffe commanders to withdraw the Ju 87 from the front-line bombing strength for the remainder of the summer fighting, though a few more sorties were flown. News of the losses stoked Goering's anger at the lack of progress and the elusiveness of the swift victory he had predicted. Once again he called his chief officers to Karinhall to harangue them and issue new directives. Dowding, too, was looking back over ten days of heavy fighting and trying to guess how the battle would develop. Both commanders now knew that the fight would be long and that stamina and morale would decide it.

14

Attrition

Life for the squadrons based in the south was, by the end of August, being lived in a daze of exhaustion, exhilaration and fear. Duty now stretched from dawn to dusk. The day started when the pilots were woken at 4 a.m. and driven out to dispersal, where they ate breakfast in the half-light. Pilots made two, three and four sorties a day, lasting up to an hour each, and on bad days could expect to be in combat on half of them. The weather provided no respite. Of the thirty-seven days from 1 August, twenty-two were 'fine' or 'fair', culminating in a glorious spell at the end of the month when the summer reached its zenith. There were only ten days during which cloud or rain were recorded anywhere. The pilots came to hate the sight of another cornflower-blue morning and yearned for fog and drizzle.

The fatigue was paralysing. Moving to Kenley from the north, Christopher Foxley-Norris was struck by 'how incredibly tired people were. They would go to sleep while you were talking to them.'[1] Al Deere, sitting down at breakfast after a morning flight, noticed that George Gribble 'had dropped off to sleep and with his head nodding lower and lower was gently swaying to and fro in his seat, his bacon and eggs untouched in front of him. As we watched, his face pitched forward into his eggs, much to the amusement of the assembled pilots.'[2] These blackouts could have potentially fatal results. Denys Gillam was one night ordered up to investigate a raid despite the fact that he had been flying all day, and fell off to sleep in the cockpit. 'The next thing I knew the speed was building up and there were lights in front of me and I couldn't make out what it was, and I realized I was upside down diving hard for the ground.'[3]

In the hectic weeks from August to mid September days off were rare. When they came, many pilots simply went to bed. Sleep came down like a coma. Frank Usmar of 41 Squadron woke up, after ten blissful hours unconscious, to learn that a full-scale raid had taken place while he was out. The hours waiting at dispersal appeared to offer the chance of rest. The pilots lounged in Lloyd Loom chairs or deckchairs, reading magazines, playing chess or draughts or cards, occasionally kicking a football or tossing around a cricket ball or dozing in the heat. There was tea to drink, sometimes beer, and a Naafi van would deliver sandwiches. The smell of cut grass and hedgerow flowers mingled with the stink of high-octane fuel, and the drone of insects overlaid the twanging of plates and wires as the Hurricanes and Spitfires baked in the sun.

But the imminence of danger made it impossible to relax. Every pilot had one ear cocked for the jangle of the telephone and the order to scramble. 'Hanging around was the worst part, waiting for the bloody phone to ring,' Robin Appleford, a pilot with 66 Squadron and, at eighteen years old, one of the youngest men flying that summer, said later.[4] For years after the war, the sound of a telephone bell would bring a rush of anxiety. But the call did at least dispel the vapour of unease that clung to the dispersal hut in the hours before action. Appleford found that 'at readiness . . . you were never actually ready when the order came, but as soon as you started running out to the aircraft, once you started the engine, it was all right'. Frank Usmar also hated the sound of the operations phone. He too noted that 'when you were running to your machine, the adrenaline took over . . . Once you got in your aircraft and were roaring away you seemed to have another feeling altogether.'[5]

The apprehension was sharpened by the knowledge of what lay ahead. Some glimpses of the fighting of August and September have come down to us through snatches of cine-film shot by the few camera-guns to be mounted on fighters at the time. Most of the sequences are only seconds long, but they manage to convey something of the confusion and desperation that flooded each high-velocity encounter. They also make it clear how crowded the sky would become when large numbers of aeroplanes clashed inside a few cubic miles of air. In one clip, filmed by Noel Agazarian as he closed on a bomber, the wing of what looks like an Me 110 flashes out of nowhere across the path of his fighter, missing it by a matter of feet, creating a jolt of shock that carries down the years. Despite the shakiness of the images, we can see the essential drama. The cameras were activated when the guns were fired, so the first thing the viewer notices are the white smudges of tracer crawling out towards the hunted aircraft. Often the intended victim seems oblivious, or impervious, ploughing on through the sky while the skein of bullet trails floats harmlessly by. Sometimes the camera records a kill. The fatal moment is instantly recognizable. A piece of debris detaches itself from the enemy machine and goes spinning by, or a gust of flame flares from an engine. A very few sequences last long enough to record the moment of complete destruction when the bomber erupts in a banner of smoke and fire, blotting out the attacker's vision as he swoops through the cloud of debris and burning fuel that is all that is left of his victim.

Official words, particularly the formulas employed by the pilots when, arriving back exhausted after a sortie, they were required by the intelligence officer to fill in an 'F form' combat report, were inadequate to describe the extraordinary drama of what was happening. Even afterwards, the participants often found it hard to find language powerful enough to describe the things they had seen and done.

Tom Gleave, who led 253 Squadron at Kenley, succeeded with a vivid account of an encounter with an enormous force of Me 109s cruising above Maidstone at 17,000 feet. 'Shown up clearly by the sun,' he wrote, 'and stretching fore and aft as far as the eye could see were rows of 109s riding above the haze, each row flying in line astern and well spaced out – all of them heading south south-east. It was a fantastic sight.' Gleave, until now untested in a full-scale battle, was in a section of three Hurricanes. Undeterred by the ludicrously uneven odds, he charged in. Flying into the rows of Messerchmitts, he lined up a target and fired at 175 yards range.

> The thin streaks of yellow tracer flame ran parallel for what appeared to be about seventy-five yards and then bent away to the left in a succession of curves. The hiss of pneumatics, the smell of cordite in the cockpit and the feel of the nose dipping slightly under the recoil all lent excitement to the first real combat in my short-lived career at Kenley. Most of my shot appeared to be going into the engine cowling and cockpit. It was the tracer, fired on a turn, which produced the strange illusion of the shot entering at right angles. The Hun flew straight for a while and then turned gently on to his back. After a short burst of about four seconds I stopped firing and as I did so, I saw sunlit pieces of shattered perspex spiralling aft like a shower of tracer. The Hun slewed slightly while on his back, his nose dropped and he dived beneath out of my sight, going straight down.

Gleave himself came under fire immediately afterwards and discovered he was in the midst of a mass of 109s. 'Tracers passed above and below, curving downwards and giving the impression of flying in a gigantic cage of gilt wire.'[6]

The large numbers of aircraft increased the rawness and intimacy of combat. Dennis Armitage remembered 'the flick of an aircraft's belly as you shot underneath not ten feet below at a relative speed of ten miles a minute'.[7] The fighter pilots were shooting at machines, but at such close quarters it was impossible to ignore the fact that inside them were men. 'It was really quite a shock,' Brian Kingcome said later, 'when suddenly an aeroplane you were firing at would erupt bodies. It brought it home to you . . . that there were actually people in there who you were killing.'[8]

To the novice fighter pilot, the overwhelming feeling when confronted by all this apparent chaos was bewilderment. Non-aviators, when taken through the manoeuvres of a dogfight, are made immediately aware of how extraordinarily disorienting even the most basic moves can be. Sky and earth, left and right, up and down, alternate at intervals of fractions of a second, allowing no time for adjustment. Thought, in fact, has little part in the proceedings. Fighter pilots *in extremis* operate on instinct. Flying a hugely powerful, nimble and sensitive machine is a feat in itself. Flying one in such a way as to bring guns to bear on another fast and manoeuvrable target, while avoiding being shot oneself in the process, is considerably more difficult.

Many of those now sitting at dispersal were attempting to do the second while still having barely mastered the first. The squadrons were better manned than they had been at any time since the spring. Dowding got 53 volunteers from Bomber Command and the Army Co-operation squadrons, and the Fleet Air Arm also contributed. But the high number of pilots 'on state' had still mainly been achieved by compressing training courses and rushing novices into action. It was painful but unavoidable. No amount of practice was sufficient preparation for battles that were unprecedented in size and intensity and whose tactics evolved every day.

Inevitably the untried pilots were often quick to fall. There were at least two cases of pilots being killed on the day they reported to their squadron. Flying Officer Arthur Rose-Price arrived at Kenley on the morning of 2 September to join 501 Squadron and was immediately sent on patrol. In the afternoon he went off on another sortie and was shot down over Dungeness. Pilot Officer Jaroslav Sterbacek turned up at 310 Squadron at Duxford on 31 August. Within a few hours he was over the Thames estuary, attacking Dornier 17s. By the evening he was dead, shot down by Me 109s. Both men were practised pilots. Rose-Price held a short-service commission before the war and had been an instructor. Sterbacek had served with the Czech air force and later with the Armée de l'Air. Neither of them had any real combat experience. As was shown repeatedly, flying skill alone did not guarantee success as a fighter pilot, nor necessarily improved chances of survival.

Terence Lovell Gregg, a New Zealander, who at seventeen was the youngest pilot to receive a flying licence in Australasia, had spent the war as an instructor and on operations room duties when he was given command of 87 Squadron in the second week of July. He was acutely aware of his lack of practical knowledge and allowed his flight commanders to lead the squadron until he felt he was ready. On 15 August an order came to intercept a formation of a hundred Stukas and Messerschmitts. Lovell Gregg felt the time had come to take command in the air. He took off with eight of his pilots, including Roland Beamont, who was surprised to find they were setting course directly for the approaching Germans. 'I just had time to think, "I wonder what sort of tactic he's going to employ. Is he going to turn up-sun and try and dive out of the sun at them or go round to the right and come in behind?"' To his pilots' alarm it became clear he was going to do neither. Instead he 'bored straight into the middle . . . we seemed to be going into the largest formation of aeroplanes you ever saw. Then his voice came on the radio and said: "Target ahead, come on chaps, let's surround them!" Just nine of us.'⁹ Lovell Gregg's Hurricane was soon in flames. He tried to land, crashed into a copse and was killed.

Most of the victims of the fighting of August and September had joined their squadrons before July, and had at least had some time to learn control procedures and get a taste of what was coming before the all-out assault began. But among the dead there were also those who had gone into battle hopelessly unprepared. Many were sergeants who had come through the RAFVR, like Geoffrey Gledhill, who arrived at 6 Operational Training Unit at Sutton Bridge on 6 July for his fighter training. After only four weeks he was posted to 238 Squadron at Middle Wallop. A week later he was shot down and killed.

Pilot Officer Neville Solomon, another RAFVR graduate, was particularly unfitted for action. After basic training he had been taught to fly Blenheim fighter bombers, then abruptly sent on 19 July to join 17 Squadron at Debden. When it became clear he had no Hurricane experience, he was sent back to Sutton Bridge for a conversion course. He was back after twenty days, on 15 August. Three days later, apparently after his first sortie, he was reported missing. He was not around long enough for the squadron diarist to learn to spell his name correctly and is referred to as 'Soloman' in the three sparse mentions he receives.

In 54 Squadron Al Deere received two replacement pilots from New

Zealand who had never previously flown a Spitfire and made just two trips in a Hurricane. There was only time to take them up in a Miles Master trainer, then brief them on the controls of the Spitfire. 'They'd go off for one solo flight and circuit. Then they were into battle . . . These two lasted two trips and they both finished up in Dover hospital. One was pulled out of the Channel. The other landed by parachute.'[10] During the phoney war, pilots would get at least twenty-five hours' experience on a Spitfire before being posted. Some of the longer-serving pilots tried to pass on what knowledge they could. In 87 Squadron, Roland Beamont would 'take our new pilots and put them in the hands of our most experienced pilots and send them off to do dogfight practices . . . The experienced pilot by demonstration would show the junior just how little he knew about it and give him tips as to what he could do to improve his skills, because there were ways you could use your aeroplane to better advantage once you knew it very well. The essence of combat flying was to know your aeroplane's absolute limits so that when you were called upon to use them you could actually get to the limits of the performance without endangering you or the aeroplane.'[11]

For most incoming pilots, though, the learning process was not so gentle. In 616 Squadron, where Denys Gillam was a flight commander, an effort was made 'to give replacement pilots a sporting chance. I always had one as my number two. The trouble was that they had too little experience. The average amount of flying they'd done was about 100 to 120 hours only and their entire attention was focused on the ability to fly the plane rather than to fight. One could get them to the battle reasonably well, but once it was joined they were sitting ducks.'[12] David Cox, a sergeant pilot with 19 Squadron, was taken under the wing of Flying Officer Leonard Haines. 'I can give credit to him for the fact that I stayed alive as long as I did,' he said later. 'He used to say, just keep my tail wheel in front of you and just stick to me. Don't worry about shooting things. If you can follow me, you'll learn to throw a Spitfire about, which I did.'[13]

Others doubted the value of the practice. Bob Doe, who had spent the summer with 234 Squadron in the West Country and destroyed at least five German aircraft, noticed that 'when action happened an experienced pilot would treat his plane purely as a gun platform, which meant that he wouldn't know what was happening to his plane or his number two . . . Although this phase only lasted for a matter of seconds, his poor number two would be concentrating on staying with his leader, who was doing impossible things with his machine, and at the most dangerous time he would not be seeing the enemy around him.'[14]

John Worrall of 32 Squadron rejected three newcomers who arrived without having passed through an Operational Training Unit, considering they would weaken the unit and that sending them into action was tantamount to condemning them to death. Sailor Malan took a tougher view. One of his young pilots was clearly never going to succeed as a fighter pilot. He was, he told his biographer, 'a boy born to be killed. You knew or felt that it was only a question of time before he was picked off.' But Malan felt that 'the cruellest thing in the world would have been to tell him to drop out of the flight, and recommend him for an operational training unit. He had lots of guts. He struggled very hard to be a good pilot. But everything was against him.'[15] Fate took its course. 'We were on patrol one day with this boy flying No. 4 astern. Then suddenly, looking round, he had gone. A Jerry must have sneaked up behind and picked him off.'

The demand for pilots meant standards, inevitably, were relaxed. Candidates who would have been rejected before the war now made it into Fighter Command. Eustace Holden, a twenty-eight-year-old flight commander with 501 Squadron, remembered a new arrival who was 'nice enough, but it was easy for me to see that he shouldn't have been there . . . He thought it was marvellous to be in this front-line squadron, but he wasn't good enough. I could see him being shot up in no time at all.' Holden took him to one side and 'had a few words . . . I said that I wasn't at all sure that he was up to it and I thought it better if he left the squadron. The poor chap was very nearly in tears and it made me feel awful but I still thought that he should go.' Later, the whole squadron took off on an interception. 'This one chap was lagging behind, why I don't know. There were three Messerschmitts up above . . . I kept telling him to come on, come on, catch up. And sure enough one of these chaps came whizzing down and shot him down in the Channel, and he was never seen again. I blamed myself for that.'[16]

Bad weather between 19 and 24 August brought a respite from the grinding routine of daily heavy raids. The pause coincided with another reassessment by Goering of the direction the battle was taking. The impression of overwhelming force created by masses of aircraft moving inexorably in rigid formation towards their targets was misleading. The Luftwaffe was suffering badly. On 15, 16 and 18 August it lost more than fifty aircraft each day and human losses were heavy. Among the casualties were 172 officers, dead, seriously wounded and missing, including 23 of senior rank. The morale of the crews was fraying. The German fighter pilots were at least as tired as their British counterparts. They got little leave or time off. One commander, Oberst Carl Viek, based at Wissant overlooking the Channel, tried to keep his men on the ground in bad weather and send them off for a swim, and forbade those he judged to be closest to cracking up from flying. This attitude earned him a reprimand from his headquarters for 'softness'.

On 19 August Goering summoned his commanders for another conference and another blast of criticism. He blamed the bomber losses on the failure of the fighters to give proper protection, only just stopping short of an outright accusation of cowardice. The charge ignored the by now obvious fact that it was impossible for an Me 109 to keep up with a Stuka once it went into its dive. Also, as he must have known, the fighters were severely restricted in the time they could spend shepherding the bombers by the amount of fuel they could carry. Bomber crews often watched in dismay as the Messerchmitts left them to their fate and turned away to run for home before their petrol gave out.

Goering insisted that the fighters' main task now was the close escort of the bombers. He dismissed the expert view of experienced men like Galland that the most effective way of dealing with the British fighters was free hunts, which by some estimates accounted for the majority of the RAF's losses. The Me 109s would now also have to cover the Me 110s, which had proved themselves vulnerable. Fighters would be protecting fighters. The Stukas, Goering conceded, were fatally unsuited for the job. They would be withdrawn until they could fulfil their proper role of supporting the army when it finally blitzed a path across Britain. The performance would not have been complete without some bloodletting. Several commanders were dismissed, and younger more aggressive officers promoted, among them Galland.

On the same day, Dowding and Park conducted their own analysis. Following the meeting, the sector controllers in 11 Group were issued with new instructions that augmented other orders issued two days previously, designed to close the loopholes in the defence revealed by the preceding ten days of heavy fighting. Between 8 and 16 August, Fighter Command had lost about ninety pilots and another fifty had been wounded, many of them seriously. With the aircraft problem on its way to being solved, pilots were Dowding's most precious resource. The ability to resist depended on suppressing losses to a level that maintained continuity and experience in squadrons, allowing them continuously to regenerate themselves and maintain their effectiveness. It was essential to reduce casualties, impossible to halt them. Dowding and Park resolved that the lives that were going to be lost should be expended in the most effective manner possible.

Preventing pilots from flying over the sea was one way of stemming losses. In addition, orders were again issued to controllers and commanders to stop squadrons taking on German fighters as they swooped in over the coast on free hunts. Park had tried to hold his fighters back from these costly clashes, but the encounters had persisted. It was now emphasized heavily that the overwhelming priority was to knock down the bombers, an approach which, it was hoped, would limit the damage done to the airfields, further injure the Luftwaffe's morale and on the British side slow the attrition of fighters, and more importantly of pilots.

The survival of the fighter bases, particularly the 11 Group sector aerodromes, Northolt, Tangmere, Kenley, Biggin Hill, Hornchurch, North Weald and Debden, had become an overwhelming concern. They were the junction boxes in Fighter Command's control system in the south-east. They housed the sector operations rooms which responded to the information coming in from radar and the Observer Corps and juggled the available resources to meet each threat. Their destruction or serious disruption would paralyse Fighter Command's protective reflexes. The British inferiority in numbers meant survival depended on advance knowledge of the direction and dimensions of German attacks and a command and control structure that made the most efficient use of assets. Without it, the RAF would be fighting blind and weight of numbers would inevitably carry the day.

The key stations had got off lightly in the opening phase of the assault as the Luftwaffe's faulty intelligence and misconceptions directed it to RAF bases which were unconnected with the immediate defensive effort. But the devastation done to Tangmere on 16 August, and the raid on Kenley two days later, which destroyed most of the hangars and forced the evacuation of the sector operations room, suggested the German aim was improving. Park ordered the controllers to ensure that, when the squadrons based around London were in the air fending off mass attacks, 12 Group be asked to provide patrols to protect the sector bases north of the Thames at Debden, North Weald and Hornchurch.

On 24 August, with Goering's admonitions ringing in their ears, the Luftwaffe commanders in France resumed their attack on the RAF in the air, and now increasingly on the ground. The first targets were Hornchurch, North Weald and Manston. Air Vice-Marshal Trafford Leigh-Mallory, the commander of 12 Group, was called on to provide cover in keeping with Park's new directive. Only 19 Squadron turned up at North Weald in time to get in a few shots with their still-malfunctioning cannons before the raiders departed. The rest were guided to their destinations by the columns of smoke and fire rising into the clear afternoon sky. The raids destroyed messes, stores and living quarters and a few aircraft, but barely affected the bases' ability to operate.

The disappointing performance by 12 Group was to mark the start of a feud fought out at the highest levels throughout the rest of the summer, and it opened a debate on tactics that rumbled on into the post-war years. Leigh-Mallory believed that the most effective way to deploy fighters was en masse, grouped together in what came to be known as a 'Big Wing'.

He had tried to assemble such a force over Duxford before sending it to the rescue of the north London stations, but there had been confusion over the order. It took time to put a formation of fifty to sixty aircraft together – at least three-quarters of an hour, even when conditions were ideal. The delay meant that, according to Tom Gleave, speaking later as a distinguished RAF historian, 'of thirty-two Big Wings launched by 12 Group, only seven met the enemy and only once did a Big Wing arrive first at its intended point of interception'.[17] Despite this dismal record and the almost universal scepticism of the pilots, Leigh-Mallory and Douglas Bader, regarded as the author of the idea, persisted in championing the tactic after the war and insisting that a battle-winning innovation had been wilfully neglected.

On the night of 24 August bombs fell on central London for the first time since 1918. Goering had given his commanders the right to choose where they should aim their attacks, reserving for himself the right to order the bombing of Liverpool and London. Hitler did not, at this stage, wish to jeopardize the chance of a political settlement by a massacre of civilians. On the night of 24th/25th a fleet of more than a hundred bombers set off westwards across the Channel to resume their bombardment of Short's aircraft factory at Rochester and the oil storage farm at Thameshaven. Instead of unloading their explosives, however, they flew on, unmolested by night fighters, and dumped their bombs on the department stores of Oxford Street, City offices, the terraced streets of Stepney, Finsbury, Bethnal Green and East Ham. The breach of orders was blamed on an error in navigation. Goering, anticipating a storm of rage when Hitler heard the news, demanded to know who was responsible and threatened the guilty with a transfer to the infantry. The error detonated an explosive chain of events. The following night, eighty-one Wellington and Hampden bombers flew to Berlin and dropped incendiary bombs, most of which landed in open country and allotments, and leaflets. The raid was followed, on Churchill's orders, by others on 28, 30 and 31 August, and would accelerate a dynamic that was to have dire consequences for Londoners in the months ahead.

For the moment, though, the bombing of central London appeared an aberration. The Luftwaffe continued its daylight pounding of the airfields. On 25 August the weight of the attacks shifted to the south and west and attacks were launched on Portland, Weymouth and Warmwell airfield in Dorset. The raid on Warmwell was intercepted by Hurricanes from 17 Squadron and only a handful of bombers got through, hitting two hangars and destroying, with a lucky bomb, the station's telephone and teleprinter cables. On the morning of 26 August the attacks swung back to the 11 Group airfields, with a formation of forty Heinkels and twelve Dorniers making for Biggin Hill. In keeping with the new orders, they were protected by eighty Me 109s and some Me 110s, a ratio of almost two to one. Park sent up seventy Hurricanes and Spitfires and a handful of Defiants to block them, and the raid was eventually turned away without reaching its target. The second wave was aimed at Debden and Hornchurch. This time forty Dorniers were protected by eighty Me 110s and forty 109s. By the time they approached their targets, however, the escorts were running low on fuel. The increasingly apparent vulnerability of the Me 110s meant that the effective strength of the fighter screen was the forty Me 109s, who had the schizophrenic task of fending off attacks on both bombers and their fellow fighters.

The raid began to falter before it reached Debden, with most of the bombers turning south shortly after crossing the Essex coast. Half a dozen Dorniers pressed on unprotected, and dropped bombs that killed three airmen, destroyed buildings and severely damaged an aircraft. The Hornchurch raid was aborted before it reached its target. A third wave was launched in the afternoon against Portsmouth and Southampton, and was also repulsed without significant damage being done to targets. Fifteen bombers had been shot down for no real result. The bomber crews and their commanders complained that they were still not receiving adequate protection, a charge that cannot have been amiably received from the fighter units, which lost fifteen Me 109s and five Me 110s, the former paying the price of trying to protect the latter.

But this was a battle of attrition. Fighter Command's satisfaction at having beaten off the attacks was tempered by the knowledge that victory or defeat would be determined by the ability of Fighter Command to absorb protracted punishment. At its simplest that meant having a steady supply of men and machines to replace losses. But equally important was the quality of morale and the maintenance of squadrons as functioning fighting units.

A day like 26 August could have a devastating effect on the fabric and spirit of a squadron. No. 616 Squadron had arrived at Kenley on 19 August, having spent most of the summer in Leconfield in Yorkshire, and was anxious to get into the action. Hugh Dundas recorded that, 'Joy and jubilation marked our last hours at Leconfield'. Before setting off there was a genial lunch in the mess with plenty to drink. Most of the original auxiliary pilots were still there. Dundas reflected afterwards that 'it never occurred to us that we should not continue together indefinitely'.

They arrived at the new station to a sobering scene. Kenley had been blitzed the day before. Wrecked aircraft and lorries littered the edge of the field and the landing ground was dotted with newly filled craters. The atmosphere in the officers' mess 'was taut and heavily overlaid with weariness. Both the station operations staff and the pilots of 615 Squadron [who were based there] . . . showed signs of strain in their faces and behaviour. The fierce rage of the station commander when a ferry pilot overshot the runway while landing a precious replacement Spitfire was frightening to behold.'

On 26 August, Spitfires of 616 were scrambled and directed to Dover and Dungeness in anticipation of the first raid of the day. They arrived too late to attack the incoming Heinkels, but were quickly set upon by the accompanying Me 109s. George Moberly's aircraft was hit and he baled out. His parachute failed to open and he plunged into the sea to his death. Sergeant Marmaduke Ridley, an ex-apprentice who had joined the squadron early in 1940, was also killed. Teddy St Aubyn, the aristocratic ex-Guards officer and ante-room wit, was shot down and badly burned.

Moberly had learned to fly privately after leaving Ampleforth, the Catholic public school, and had been one of the first two officers to join the squadron. He visited Dundas the day before in hospital at Canterbury, where he was recovering after being shot down. 'He talked to me about personal affairs, about his family and his property,' Dundas wrote. 'He told me that he wanted me to have his personal belongings if he were killed. I had a strong feeling that he had a premonition that he would be.'[18] Moberly's death was particularly painful for Denys Gillam, who counted him as his best friend in the squadron.

Two other pilots, Roy Marples and William Walker, were shot down the same day. Walker, who had been posted to the squadron from the RAFVR, which he joined while a young trainee executive at a brewery, had been woken that morning at 3.30 a.m. by his orderly with a cup of tea. There was a first breakfast at 4 a.m., the usual sombre affair eaten in silence. If pilots were still at dispersal at 8 a.m., a second breakfast – eggs, bacon, sausages, coffee – would be brought out. Walker was to be grateful for his second breakfast that day. He took off with Yellow Section, made up of himself, St Aubyn and Ridley, and was caught when the Me 109s pounced over Dungeness. He decided to bale out, but when he tried to leave found he was still attached to the cockpit by the radio lead fixed to his flying helmet. 'I took off my helmet and fell out. I was still at 20,000 feet and pulled the ripcord. The sky, which moments before had been so full of aircraft, was now without a single plane in view. I had no idea where I was and 10/10th cloud below obscured any view of land. It seemed to take ages to reach the clouds, and eventually on passing through them I was concerned to see that I was over the Channel.' Walker sensibly kicked off his heavy flying boots and watched them spiral down for 'what seemed like ages'. Splashing down and releasing his harness, he looked around, saw land, but did not know whether it was England or France. He noticed the hull of a wrecked boat protruding from the water, swam to it, clambered up and awaited rescue. He was now very cold and very tired. He was, in fact, close to the Kent coast. The wreck he was sitting on was one of many that had come to grief on the Goodwin Sands. After half an hour a fishing boat appeared and he was helped aboard and given tea and whisky.

He was taken into Ramsgate harbour, cheered by a small crowd of civilians, given a packet of ten Player's cigarettes – the Fighter Boys' favourites – and taken to hospital, where his injured leg was examined. He was put to bed under a canopy of electric lights, which it was hoped would thaw his hypothermia. It was eight hours before he warmed up. The hospital had been bombed and the kitchen was out of action. The only food available was two slices of bread and butter. The following day he was put in an ambulance to be taken to the RAF hospital at Halton in Buckinghamshire. On the way they had to pick up an airman from Manston, shell-shocked after the almost constant bombardment. They passed by Kenley so Walker could pick up some kit. He then told the driver to take him to dispersal so he could bid *au revoir* to his comrades. To his dismay, 'hardly any pilots remained. I had not heard of the appalling losses ... nor had I heard of what had happened to the other members of Yellow Section'. The ambulance picked its way across London, taking detours where the roads were closed by bombing. The seventy-mile journey from the coast took almost twelve hours.[19]

Within eight days of arriving at Kenley, 616 Squadron lost five pilots killed or missing, with five others hospitalized. Half of the pilots who had flown down in high spirits from Leconfield were gone. Denys Gillam, who although only a flight commander was effectively leading the squadron, asked for it to be given a week's rest to train up replacement pilots. 'It was very unpopular to suggest that the squadron should be taken out of the line for a short time to give them the chance to recover,' he said later. 'They wouldn't do it and Dowding was very put out by this and kept us there another week. By then we were down to about four pilots.'[20] On 2 September, Gillam was shot down and wounded, and the following day the remaining pilots moved to the relative safety of Coltishall, near Norwich, to re-form.

The blitz on airfields continued on 28 August. By now a pattern had developed in which Luftwaffe attacks came in distinct phases. The first wave arrived over the Kent coast at breakfast time and split up, with one formation heading west and the other turning north towards Rochford. Fighters were sent up, including twelve Defiants, which went in to attack the bombers, oblivious to the Me 109s hiding in the sun. Four Defiants were shot down and three damaged. Five of the crew were killed. One,

Flight Lieutenant Robert Ash, who had given up a risk-free job in the general duties branch at the relatively advanced age of thirty to volunteer for air-crew duty, had baled out but was found dead. There was a strong suspicion that he had been shot while dangling from his parachute. When a second raid approached Rochford later in the day, the remaining crews clamoured to go into action, but this was refused. The inevitable, lethal consequences of deploying Defiants in daylight were at last recognized. Henceforth, they would only fly at night.

The third phase, as shown on the radar, appeared to be another bombing attack aimed at sector airfields, and six groups of fighters were ordered up to intercept. Instead of bombers they found Me 109s and 110s, and the Hurricanes and Spitfires were lured into just the sort of costly and unproductive clash Dowding and Park were so desperate to avoid. Six German machines were shot down, but so, too, were six British fighters and four pilots killed.

Among them was Noel Benson of 603 Squadron. After the war, it was the thought of the novice pilots going unprepared to their deaths that the public found particularly poignant. The fact was that in the fighting of August and September death came evenly, falling on the experienced and the débutant alike. Benson went into battle fully trained, with only some inkling of the nature of what he was confronting but touchingly eager for the fray. He had been to Sedburgh public school before Cranwell, from where he graduated in October 1939. Benson, nicknamed 'Broody' because he got despondent if not flying, finally got his wish for action when the squadron moved to Hornchurch from Turnhouse in Scotland on 27 August. It had been engaged until then in night flying and occasional attempted interceptions of German intruders. Benson's impatience glows through one letter home. 'I am enclosing a photo that a chap took at Montrose,' he wrote. 'I am in the cockpit starting up the engine to go off on a genuine interception. I believe that at the time some trawlers were being attacked but as usual, the enemy went into the low clouds as soon as we appeared.'

Benson was as well prepared as it was possible to be without having experienced full-scale combat. His commanding officer wrote to his father after his death: 'Your son was an excellent pilot with all his wits about him and he was the last of the squadron I had expected to lose.' He lasted just one day. George Prior, an ex-serviceman who had served at Gallipoli, was standing outside his cottage at Leigh Green near Tenterden in Kent on the evening of 28 August, watching seven German aircraft overhead. He later described in a letter how 'a single British plane suddenly dived into them from above, the pilot tackling them single handed. He was hit at once by one of the enemy and I saw smoke pouring from his machine. He then turned and dived towards the ground to about 1,000 feet to save himself, then straightened out.' Prior believed that Benson had deliberately stayed with his aeroplane to steer it away from farm buildings. 'He could certainly have saved himself before his plane got further alight: instead he went on, avoiding the farm etc. and all the houses and the post office and a large Army Service Corps depot . . . he drove on with his machine now ablaze. I saw the flames yards behind it and he had no chance then. He gave his life to save us all at Leigh Green.' He finally crashed a few fields away. By the time Prior reached the spot, 'his machine was a charred mass of metal . . . he met his death in this last act of self-sacrifice'.[21]

Mr Prior wrote his letter at the request of another resident of Leigh Green, Mrs Marguerite Sandys, who campaigned for several months for Benson to be awarded some posthumous medal, but the request was turned down by the Air Ministry. The gratitude of the villagers was an indication of how civilians and airmen were being drawn closer together. Ordinary people were in the war now. Many knew all too well what aerial bombardment was like. On 24 August Portsmouth had been subjected to a four-minute blitz by 250-kilo bombs dropped by Ju 88s, which slipped through a fighter screen and laid waste the naval base as well as the town, killing 107 civilians and injuring 237.

The advent of night-time raids disrupted the lives of millions. Fighter Command issued warnings to local defence authorities of likely raids, classed from yellow, the lowest threat, through purple, to red. Officials erred on the side of caution. The bombers roamed far and wide as they reached out beyond coastal cities to the industrial Midlands and the north. The sleep of everyone in their paths was ruined as people made their way to shelters and the war production effort slowed as factories switched off the electricity until the raiders had left.

Nowhere in the south-east felt entirely safe. Bombers would jettison their loads at random when running for home. Pete Brothers moved his wife away from Biggin Hill to what he thought would be the safety of the small town of Westerham, about five miles away. One late afternoon in August she was preparing for a visit from her husband. 'She was getting ready, sitting in her bedroom with the windows open putting on her lipstick and so on, when someone dropped a bomb and a splinter came in through the open window and smashed her mirror. That got me pretty angry. It could have gone into the back of her head.'[22] Brothers moved her to Lancashire to stay with his parents.

Fighters on free hunts occasionally strafed roads and villages. Joan Lovell Hughes, who was later to marry Christopher Foxley-Norris, was working on a farm at Penshurst in Kent. The excitement of watching the fighting overhead was tempered by the danger from the Luftwaffe. 'The boys, when they'd downed somebody, used to come low over the field, waggling their wings and we would shout, "Well done!" But there were also nasty times when the Germans came over and they would drop their bombs and shoot at anything that moved . . . One night I was cycling alone on my own and a lone raider came along, low, so I flung myself in a hedge and it fired at me and missed . . . They fired at anything that was moving.'[23]

Despite the increasing threat they had posed to the civilian population, crashed German crews could expect decent treatment. Oberleutnant Rudolf Lamberty was forced to crash-land his Dornier 17 near Biggin Hill on 18 August. Climbing out of the flaming wreckage, he saw some 'very excited Home Guard men with shotguns . . . they pointed their guns at me. I was busily engaged in putting out the fire on both my sleeves.' During the confrontation, another raid came in, and everyone threw themselves to the ground while bomb splinters tore the air around them. When the German aircraft had departed, Lamberty and the rest of his crew were led along a road to the entrance to the base. On the way they met some civilians. 'The first question they asked was: "Are you glad it's all over for you?" But we weren't and said so.' Lamberty wanted to get rid of his parachute and offered it to one of the curious civilians, telling him it would make good silk shirts. He asked for help getting his cigarettes as his hands were too badly burned to open his tunic pocket. Someone retrieved them, put a cigarette in his mouth and lit it for him. They were surprised to see the cigarettes were English. Lamberty had bought them in Guernsey a few days previously. He was driven to the base hospital, where he was given a cup of tea with a straw to drink it through. His face was smeared with Tannifax anti-burn cream and he was brought food. Lamberty was unable to eat it as the inside of his mouth was burned. The nurses misunderstood and brought him a different dish to see if that would tempt him. He and another officer were taken to a room for a mild interrogation, but 'they saw we were not capable and left it'.[24] Next day he was transferred to a civilian hospital.

Such courtesy was conditional on the defeated behaving themselves. After a raid on Tangmere in which two airmen were killed, a captured German crew happened to be marched past the bodies. One of the Germans, 601 Squadron's historian recorded, was imprudent enough to laugh. 'A senior RAF officer who was walking to meet them lengthened his stride and punched the German on the nose. That evening the prisoners were given brooms and made to sweep up the bomb debris in the hangars.'[25]

The method of dealing with the German raiders, as they threw themselves repeatedly against Fighter Command's defences, evolved continuously, refined and adjusted by bitter experience. Whatever Park might say about the necessity of concentrating on the bombers, it was impossible to do so effectively without protection. By now a rough division of labour had evolved between Hurricanes and Spitfires. Hurricanes, it was agreed, were slower, but in compensation were sturdier in construction and provided a more stable gun platform. To them fell the job of shooting down bombers. The Spitfires, with their greater speed and manoeuvrability and higher operational altitude, were more suited to fending off the Me 109s and 110s hovering overhead.

The defending fighters were almost invariably greatly outnumbered by those they were attacking. As always, a fighter pilot's tactical position was greatly improved if he was flying higher than the enemy and coming at them from out of the sun. It was a constant complaint by squadrons that they were scrambled too late to climb to an ideal attacking height. Pilots operating from the forward coastal bases were at a particular disadvantage as they had even less time to react before the raiders were overhead or gone. Some commanders used their own initiative and flew inland to gain height before turning back in the direction of the enemy. The first aim of the attacks was to try and split up the disciplined ranks of the bombers. This disrupted the field of covering fire the gunners could provide for each other, churned up the formation into smaller and less defensible groups and separated individual machines from the warmth of the pack, making them much easier to pick off.

'If you could break up the leaders, that was the ideal situation because we knew that they were the pathfinders for the bombing raid,' Harold Bird-Wilson, a Hurricane pilot with 17 Squadron, said later. 'The bomber formations were very good and they [followed] their leader's bombing. The leader dropped his bombs followed by everyone else.' When the protecting fighters saw a Hurricane attack go in, 'they used to come hurling down at us and through us and then back up again . . . "yo-yo" tactics.'[26]

The effectiveness of head-on attacks was now established. Brian Kingcome, who arrived with 92 Squadron at Biggin Hill at the beginning of September from the relative tranquillity of Pembrey in South Wales, discovered that the escorts 'never had time to get to you if you attacked from head on before you had managed to have at least one good solid go at the bombers'.[27] The attacker had a good chance of shooting down the leader, thereby removing the raiders' controlling intelligence as well as unnerving the following pilots. The tactic, though, required tungsten nerves. Its invention was sometimes attributed to Gerry Edge, who had been an auxiliary officer before the war. He flew in May with 605 Squadron over France, where he showed exceptional aggression, shooting down at least six aircraft and damaging many more. Count Czernin of 17

Squadron was another practitioner. He used it not only against bombers but also against Me 110s, as a means of overcoming their habit of forming a defensive circle to enable the rear gunners to put out a retaliatory curtain of fire. The trick was to get in and out with the maximum speed before one or other of the Messerschmitts in the circle broke off to fasten on to the attacker's tail. Czernin's commander Squadron Leader Cedric Williams, tried a head-on attack on an Me 110 on 25 August. His left wing was shot off by the forward fire from the German and he crashed into the sea off the south coast.

The squadrons being fed in to replace exhausted and depleted units had been training hard during their time out of the front line and gaining what experience they could from the interceptions they were called on to make against intruders. But little effort seems to have been made to pass on systematically to the squadrons waiting their turn in the front line the tactical lessons that had so far been drawn from the fighting. On 30 August, 222 Squadron, which had arrived from the north the day before, began operating from Hornchurch. By the end of the day eight Spitfires had been shot down, one pilot killed and three wounded. They had been flying in tight formation and using a weaver to protect their tails, tactics recognized as faulty months before. Individual squadrons did what they could to modify their techniques, trying out flying patterns which allowed more flexibility and a greater field of observation. But in October squadrons were still flying in V-shaped 'vics', in which the leader was supported by two wingmen, each formated closely on him. When Archie Winskill joined 72 Squadron, they 'still hadn't got out of this rather archaic business of flying in tight formations of three, which was ridiculous. It meant . . . keeping in formation and watching your leader rather than flying in the loose two formations which the Germans did which left you completely free to roam the skies.'[28]

The German formation, known as 'finger four' by the RAF pilots who experimented with it and eventually adopted it, was the one developed by Werner Mölders in Spain. The basic unit was the pair: a leader and a wingman who flew roughly two hundred yards behind on the sunward side and slightly below so his partner did not have to look into the glare to see him. The wingman's job was to protect the leader. The formation was known as a *Rotte*. Two *Rotte* made up a *Schwarm*. The tactic was basically protective, and if efficiently applied would give early warning of an attack coming out of the sun. Once battle was joined, however, both sides found that cohesion and control vanished and most of the time pilots had only themselves to rely on.

Since the end of the brief pause lasting from 19 to 24 August, the Luftwaffe had been launching several major raids a day involving hundreds of aircraft. On the first day of the resumed assault, there were six large attacks by a total of at least 500 bombers and fighters lasting from 6 a.m. to 6.45 p.m. After night fell the Germans returned and the residents of southern and western England, South Wales, the Midlands, East Anglia and Yorkshire heard the drone of enemy engines overhead. As well as the raid on London, bombs fell on Liverpool, Sheffield, Bradford, Hull and Middlesbrough and were scattered over areas of Kent, Hampshire, Reading and Oxford.

On the 25th there were no mass attacks until the afternoon, when two were launched by at least 400 aircraft, and once again there was a full programme of night attacks, concentrating on the Midlands. On the 26th there were three main phases directed against the Dover–Folkestone area, then Kent and north of the Thames estuary, then the Portsmouth–Southampton area, involving nearly 500 aircraft, followed by a widespread night bombing. Bad weather on the 27th brought a respite. The following day there were four main raids and a 150-bomber raid on Liverpool by night. The 29th brought a momentary shift of tactics. A huge force of several hundred aircraft appeared on radar screens, building up over the French coast. It turned out to be a ruse. Most of the force were fighters and the small number of bombers were clearly intended as bait to lure up the British fighters, a stratagem which did not succeed.

Given the weight of German numbers and the strains imposed on pilots and controllers alike, it was inevitable that breakthroughs would occur. On 30 August, the Luftwaffe succeeded in pressing home a devastating attack on Biggin Hill. The base had been heavily bombed twelve days before but had remained operational. As one of the key bases in 11 Group's defences, strategically positioned at the gates of London and facing the main direction of the Luftwaffe attack, it was inevitable that further intensive efforts would be made to destroy it.

The first raid came in just before noon, when a group of ninety bombers and an equal number of fighter escorts crossed the Kent coastline and peeled off to attack the London perimeter airfields. Park ordered almost all his fighters into the air and two squadrons were sent down from 12 Group to patrol Kenley and Biggin Hill. A group of Ju 88s nonetheless slipped through and dropped more than thirty bombs, most of which fell in the cornfields around the base and the village next door.

Once again the station's luck seemed to have held. Instead of waiting a few hours to launch the next phase, the Luftwaffe maintained the pressure with successive waves of bombers rolling over the south-east all afternoon. In two hours from 4 p.m., about 400 aircraft swept in over Kent and the Thames estuary, confusing the controllers trying to plot so many courses and direct fighters towards them. At about 6 p.m. a small group of eighteen Ju 88s suddenly appeared, flying very low over Biggin Hill. No warning was given and there was no one overhead to stop them, 79 Squadron being on the ground at the time and 610 Squadron patrolling elsewhere. When the raid swept in, airmen were just leaving the mess after their evening meal. Only sixteen 500-kilo bombs were dropped, but the effect was devastating. One bomb landed directly on a trench crowded with airmen, killing many. One of the four remaining hangars was destroyed, as well as workshops, the armoury, storerooms, the sergeants' mess, the Waaf quarters and airmen's barrack blocks. All gas, electricity and water mains were cut and telephone lines severed. The walls of one shelter caved in under the shock, burying a group of Waafs, all but one of whom were later dug out alive. Altogether thirty-nine ground staff were killed and twenty-six wounded.

The following day 610 Squadron was moved north to Acklington, to be replaced by 72 Squadron. At noon, while the squadron airmen were waiting with their kit to be picked up, the noise of anti-aircraft guns signalled another raid, which left the runways so badly cratered that they were unusable and 79 Squadron, returning from operations over Dover, had to be diverted to Croydon. The ground crews worked themselves to exhaustion during the afternoon, filling in the holes so that when 72 Squadron arrived they were able to land. 'The amazing thing about it,' wrote Robert Deacon Elliot, one of the new pilots flying in, 'was the human factor – no panic, everyone doing their utmost to keep the aircraft in the air. Bomb craters in the airfield being quickly filled in, food being delivered to dispersals to avoid waste of time returning to messes. Land lines installed to run out from ops to squadron dispersals to replace those lost.'[29] The base was to be attacked five times in forty-eight hours, one raid arriving as the station commander, Group Captain Grice, led the burial service for fifty Biggin Hill staff at the small cemetery at the edge of the aerodrome. Despite the effort and the stoicism, the base was no place to leave precious pilots and aeroplanes. The day after it arrived, 72 Squadron shifted a few miles away to Croydon, which, though damaged, was in better shape than Biggin Hill and had the added advantage of the Airport Hotel, where the pilots took their first baths for three days.

The squadron it had replaced, 610, had been pulled out of the line after being at Biggin Hill and Gravesend since July. At the start the unit had twenty pilots 'on state'. Over the two months, nine pilots were killed and six seriously wounded. In addition there were numerous shootings down, crash-landings and balings out. Such figures were high but not unusual. Between 1 July and 6 September, 501 Squadron lost twelve pilots, and 601, squadron of the dashing pre-war auxiliaries, whose insouciant ranks were filled with sportsmen, playboys and adventurers, lost eleven. By the time it was taken out of the line most of its original pilots were gone, dead or posted away. Two of the pre-war members, Carl Raymond Davis and Willie Rhodes-Moorhouse, son of a First World War RFC pilot and winner of a Victoria Cross, were killed on the day before they were due to move to the relative quiet of Exeter. Rhodes-Moorhouse had obtained his pilot's licence aged seventeen at Heston, near Eton, where he went to school, had been engaged at every stage of the war, and was an outstanding pilot who had shot down at least nine bombers and fighters, shared in the destruction of several more and been awarded the DFC. His death was a reminder that skill and experience were no protection against the inevitable shortening of the odds that each combat brought.

Squadrons like 501 and 601 absorbed their losses over a relatively lengthy stay in the line. With others the heart was torn out of the unit in a few nightmarish days. Between 12 and 16 August, 266 Squadron, which had arrived in such good spirits, determined to do well after a summer of relative inactivity in the Midlands, had suffered six pilots killed, including the squadron leader, and two badly wounded. Next it was caught in a bombing raid on Manston on the 17th, the second time the pilots had been battered on the ground since their arrival. There had been twenty-three pilots when they came south. By the end they were down to nine, which meant that every fit man had to go on every trip. Dennis Armitage, wounded in the left leg, walked with a stick and had to be helped into his Spitfire. Fortunately, as he observed, 'there is no place other than bed where full use of the legs is so unimportant as when driving a single-engined aeroplane'.[30] Twelve days after arriving in the south, they were sent back to Wittering to lick their wounds.

Pilots died horribly, riddled with splinters from cannon shells, doused in burning petrol, dragged down into the chilly depths of the Channel by the weight of their parachutes, heavy boots and fur-lined flying jackets. Unless they were killed outright, they had time to recognize they were finished. Often they died in front of their friends, who witnessed the strike of fire, the faltering engine and the long inexorable dive, trailing smoke and flame. On a few occasions, when the R/T was switched to 'on', they heard them die, screaming prayers and curses as they 'went in'. The survivors reacted to the losses in the only way they knew how, with nonchalance and a touch of manufactured, protective heartlessness. There was no open grieving. 'You didn't spend days moping around,' said George Unwin. 'You just said, "Poor old so-and-so's bought it," and that was it.'[31] In 32 Squadron there was a black tradition of inking in devil's horns on the dead man's picture in the squadron group photograph. Pilots in some squadrons put money into a kitty kept behind the bar in the mess so they could be toasted on the evening of their death. There was hardly ever time to attend a funeral. Burial arrangements were often complicated by the absence of a body. The dead men were burned to cinders, or at the bottom of the sea, or still welded, phantom-like, to the controls of their beloved Hurricane or Spitfire buried in mud or sand or water.

Death was 'the chop' and all that was left behind of those who got it were memories and a handful of young man's possessions: cigarette case, cuff links, perhaps a tennis racket or a set of golf clubs. The RAF bureaucracy listed personal effects with poignant precision. Among the effects left behind by Paddy Finucane were: '1 blue leather wallet contg. – 2 snapshots; 2 Religious illustrations, 2 Religious emblems. 1 Black Cat Mascot. 2 silver cigarette cases. 2 cigarette lighters. 3 cabinet photographs (1 with glass broken). 1 Eversharpe pencil.'[32] The melancholy business of sorting out kit was described in a poem by Flight Lieutenant Anthony Richardson:

> The officer in charge
> Made out the inventories, point by point –
> Four shirts, six collars and nine pairs of socks,
> Two uniforms complete, some flying kit,
> Brushes and comb, shaving gear and shoes –
> (He tried a jumper on which didn't fit!)
> There was dirty washing, too, which was a bore,
> Being certain to get lost in the delay.
> A squash racket with two strings gone, and a cap
> That like himself, had seen a better day.
> Then there were letters, beginning 'Darling Dick',
> Photos and snapshots all of the same girl,
> With a pale, eager face and fluffy hair. . .[33]

Frequently there was a car, which would be auctioned at a convenient moment, or driven around until claimed by a relative. Geoffrey Page bought a 1938 Ford convertible that had belonged to Ian Soden, who was killed in France. Soden had acquired it from the estate of another dead pilot. After Page was shot down and badly burned, a fellow 56 Squadron member, Mark Mounsden, wrote to him in hospital asking him what he wanted him to do with it. Page replied that it was his for five pounds. Later he saw the jinxed vehicle being driven through Torquay, where he was recuperating. A badly burned officer was at the wheel.

There was no point in brooding about death. It was too common-place, and in all likelihood soon to be encountered by those who were left behind. 'The death of a friend or enemy,' wrote Page, 'provided food for a few moments of thought, before the next swirling dogfight began to distract the . . . mind from stupid thoughts such as sadness or pity . . . the art was to cheat the Reaper and perhaps blunt his scythe a little.' Events such as being shot down and crash-landing or baling out were almost too commonplace to merit mention. 'Something more spectacular was necessary to draw anything greater than a passing comment.'[34]

Behind the blank exteriors, though, they felt the ache of loss. David Crook was with Peter Drummond-Hay, a 609 Squadron original who had amused his fellow officers with his aspirations to a life of landed leisure, when he was shot down. Returning to their shared room the following day, he saw 'Peter's towel was still in the window where he had thrown it during our hurried dressing eighteen hours before. Now he was lying in the cockpit of his wrecked Spitfire at the bottom of the English Channel . . . I took my things and went to sleep in Gordon's room next door.'[35]

Inside the squadron, the emotional burden of the losses fell most heavily on the leader. It was his melancholy duty to write the letters informing parents that their sons were gone. Dennis Armitage took over 266 Squadron after Squadron Leader Wilkinson was killed and the senior flight commander was shot down and severely burned. At the end of a day's flying from Hornchurch, while the other pilots made off to the pub, he would be left with the paperwork. 'I would get down to the awful job of writing to the parents or wives – not often wives I'm glad to say – of the lads who had not come back . . . I tried hard at first, tearing up several letters before I was satisfied, but I am afraid before the end I had developed a more or less stereotyped letter which needed little more than the name and address adding.'[36]

Some squadron commanders made great efforts to comfort grieving families. No. 603 Squadron had been too occupied with the fighting to send a representative to Noel Benson's funeral, which took place in St Mary's Church in the Bensons' home village of Great Ouseburn, and wreaths from his brother officers and the sergeants' mess were delivered instead. They did, however, invite his father, a Yorkshire doctor, down to Hornchurch for lunch, which was disturbed when the squadron was scrambled. Writing to his brother, Dr Benson described how he had last seen his son only two days before his death when, by a happy chance, the squadron stopped overnight in the neighbourhood on its journey from Scotland to Hornchurch and he had been able to come home for supper. 'You can imagine our joy at the chance of seeing him again, tho' both we and he knew full well what it meant! That "they were flying South".'

Dr Benson's grief was all the more moving for its understatement.

We have no regrets for him. He was happy at school, at Cranwell and with his squadron, on service. He loved every minute he was flying. He was devoted to his home and to his father and mother, loved by all who knew him. He never gave us a moment's anxiety except for his safety and *that* was inseparable from the career he had chosen. I have never known a finer character. If he had been spared he would have achieved eminence in his profession of that I'm certain. Early he has been killed and gladly he has made the supreme sacrifice, but we are left to miss him very, very sorely.[37]

Dr Benson lost only one son. The Woods-Scawen family lost two, on consecutive days. On 1 September, Patrick, a twenty-four-year-old flying officer with 85 Squadron, was shot down in the skies over Kenley, within sight of his old school, the Salesian College, Farnborough. He baled out but his parachute failed to open. The following day his younger brother, Charles, a pilot officer with 43 Squadron, was cornered by Me 109s near

Folkestone and badly shot up. He also baled out, but too low for his parachute to work. He was twenty-two.

The ability of units to absorb deaths and injuries was reinforced by the knowledge that, however heavy their own losses, the German toll in men and machines was greater. The daily official tally put out by the Air Ministry and reported in the press and on the BBC was invariably exaggerated, inflating the number of German aircraft destroyed and minimizing the wastage on the British side. The pilots, who contributed to the inflation by their own understandable habitual overclaiming, believed them, and the figures were an important factor in maintaining morale. But it was essentially true that the balance of destruction lay in the RAF's favour. On only one day in August the 29th, were German and British losses roughly equal.

The Luftwaffe was suffering. The crews had been told regularly by their superiors that Fighter Command was down to its last handful of fighters, yet every day the Spitfires and Hurricanes were still there waiting for them, aggressive and unbowed. They began to wonder how much longer they could go on. Being shot up in a bomber, limping home over the hated sea, was a harrowing business. The Heinkel of Major H. M. Wronsky was hit by anti-aircraft fire near Portsmouth on the night of 31 August/1 September. 'We saw flames right away; the starboard engine was on fire and we thought the whole machine must burn.' They turned back out to sea and smothered the engine with foam from extinguishers, scrabbling for their parachutes that were stacked up against a bulkhead. As they approached the French coast, they saw a British bombing raid in progress near Calais and swung away so as not to be mistaken for a raider. It was clear that they would never make their home base at Villacoublay near Paris. The decision was made to jump, but in their haste they had put their parachutes on upside down and no one could locate their ripcord. By the time the mistake had been sorted out they were too low to bale out.

The ground rose up in front of us – a hill. The machine struck and tore across the top of the hill, ploughing through bushes. We lay there all injured. One man had been so badly cut on the head that he died later. Another man had been hurled right through the perspex of the nose . . . I had a broken nose, broken foot, broken arm. We lay there in the sudden quiet, listening to a hissing noise. We thought it was fire, that trapped and injured as we were, we should be burned to death. But it was only the oxygen bottles. The port engine had been hurled right out of the machine and was lying eighty yards in front.[38]

Day after day the British pilots were inflicting heavy punishment on the raiders. But the Germans continued to come. As August turned into September there appeared no let-up in the grinding, sapping routine. On 31 August the British fighters suffered their heaviest losses so far, with forty aircraft destroyed, nine pilots killed and eighteen badly wounded, half of them burnt. On 1 September Biggin Hill was hit again. The following day there were four major attacks on airfields and aircraft factories. The pattern was maintained until 6 September. Among the 11 Group squadrons absorbing most of the violence, exhaustion was now a permanent condition. 'The Luftwaffe,' wrote Peter Townsend, leading 85 Squadron from Croydon, 'by sheet weight of numbers . . . was wearing us down; we were weary beyond caring, our nerves taughtened to breaking-point.' Townsend was one of the victims of 31 August. The Germans arrived while the pilots were grabbing lunch. 'Their bombs all but hit us as we roared, full-throttle, off the ground. The blast made our engines falter.' For once, Townsend gave way to his emotions. Until then he had 'never felt any particular hatred for the German airmen, only anger. This time, though, I was so blind with fury that I felt things must end badly for me. But I was too weary and too strung-up to care.'[39] His instinct was accurate. His Hurricane was hit and he was forced to jump. That evening doctors at Croydon hospital extracted a heavy-calibre bullet from his foot. A few days later the squadron, after its two senior flight commanders were killed, was taken out of the line.

The most buoyant and resilient personalities were now suffering moments of doubt. In Al Deere's squadron there were only four pilots who had been with him at the start of the summer. His confidence in victory began to falter as he considered the stark reality that he was 'fighting a war with very inexperienced chaps. That could only get worse, progressively worse.'[40] Even Sailor Malan's granite imperturbability could crumble. One night, he told Archie Winskill later, he was overwhelmed by despondency as he sat in his room in Hornchurch and began to cry. Then he dried his tears, persuaded himself they were only a sign of his extreme tiredness, pushed away the images of the day and tried to sleep.[41]

15

Brotherhood

Despite the desperation of the situation, the level of optimism among the pilots had remained remarkably high throughout the summer. Fortitude was a Fighter Boy virtue. In its short life the RAF had established a light-hearted tradition of assuming the worst and mocking misfortune. Underneath the careful insouciance lay a thick seam of resolution. The German attack had uncorked something old and potent. 'It's surprising how fierce one's protective instincts become at the sight of an enemy violating one's homeland,' Brian Kingcome remarked.[1]

Many felt honoured to be fighting, though the conventions of un-seriousness meant that few would have admitted as much at the time. The quality of morale varied from squadron to squadron and base to base depending on how much of the fighting they had had to endure. The strain was greatest in 11 Group. Further out in 10 Group and 12 Group there were longer gaps between engagements and the tension was less acute. 'Nevertheless,' Roland Beamont said afterwards, 'no matter where you were, there was this extraordinary spirit. The squadron pilot was encouraged to believe that there wasn't anything special about the task he had been asked to do – which he had been trained for – and that he was extremely privileged to be in one of the key units in the defence of this country because that was what it was all about . . . the battle for Britain. Without any exhortation at all, the pilots, all the ground staff, all the people concerned were just reminded quietly by the squadron commanders and the flight commanders, whenever it was necessary, that this was the finest job anybody could have in the world and we were extremely privileged to be doing it.'[2]

These softly spoken appeals worked because they were addressed to a fraternity which had already in its short life developed a singular identity and adopted clear values and attitudes. Hectoring, when it was tried, usually had limited results. There were exceptions. Sailor Malan, when he took over 74 Squadron in early August, was regarded as a hard master. 'Sailor was a very tough nut indeed,' said Christopher Foxley-Norris. 'He gave no quarter. If you failed once, you failed.'[3] Tony Bartley remembered Malan explaining how he led his men: 'I kick their arses once a day and I've got a good squadron. Otherwise they'd wind up nothing.'[4] It was in sharp contrast to the approach adopted by another outstanding leader, Al Deere. 'Al was a kindly man,' said Foxley-Morris. 'Extremely tough but prepared to make allowances and concessions.'

Discipline, of a traditional military type, was necessary for much that was done in the air. On the ground it jarred. None of the pilots had joined because they were attracted by convention and the comforts of blind obedience. Relations inside squadrons, more than in any other service units, were based on tolerance and *laissez-faire*. Individualism was respected. At the same time, mutual reliance and the shared dangers inherent in flying tied individuals together. Each unit had a personality and style of its own that its members made an effort to sustain. There was a spirit of collectivity. In the best squadrons there was no room for the self-important. Yet equally, no one was allowed to think themselves insignificant. Doing his rounds of the fighter stations the war artist Cuthbert Orde came to the conclusion that 'a squadron of pilots can be divided into three groups: natural leaders and fighters at the top; then the main body of solid talent containing the germ of leaders of the future, chaps whose qualities will develop with experience; and then I suppose a tail, two or three perhaps, who will never be quite good enough to earn distinction but who nevertheless are pulling their weight for all it may be worth'.

What social distinctions had existed before the start of the summer were eroded by the fighting. The auxiliary squadrons lost their exclusive character as pilots were killed, wounded or posted away. 'Eventually we got pretty well used to everybody,' said Peter Dunning-White, an old Harrovian member of Lloyd's and one of the blades of 601 Squadron before the war. 'It didn't matter what kind of type you were as long as you behaved well.'[5] The new pilots came from everywhere and every class. Death rubbed out the last traces of the line dividing the pre-war short-service officers and the part-timers from the volunteer reserve. The members of 66 Squadron were, according to Hubert Allen, who served in it, 'a truly motley throng, consisting of young men from every walk of life. Regular air force officers, sergeant-pilots who had in peacetime been dockhands, clerks, motor-mechanics; there was even an ex-dirt-track motor-cycle expert with us. Every conceivable type was represented.'

Some of the 'Clickety-Click' personalities were revealed in an unsentimental book which came out in 1942. Ten pilots were asked to write a short chapter about themselves and their war. Three others were killed before they could get started. Of those who did contribute, three were dead before the book was published. The pilots appeared under pseudonyms. 'Bob' was Flying Officer Bobby Oxspring, the son of an RFC veteran, who joined the RAF on a short-service commission in 1938. Allen described him as 'a tallish, good-looking, fair-headed bloke, with a typical schoolboy complexion, liable to blush every now and then . . . he can take his beer like a man, comes from the north and has a typical Yorkshire outlook. A little shy he may appear off-hand at first, but having broken down his barriers of reserve, you would find a loveable, gay, carefree youth of twenty-two years.' 'Bogle' was Flying Officer Crelin Bodie, nineteen, also known as 'Rob', who joined on a short-service commission the month after war broke out. He was 'a strong individualist . . . decidedly unconventional in appearance, usually wearing a uniform which would not pass muster on a ceremonial parade, with a colourful scarf around his neck and a large sheath-knife in his boot. His language is foul but he possesses more character than anyone I can remember.'

Pilot Officer John Kendal – 'Durex' – who had gone through the RAFVR, was 'young and noisy . . . he can imitate every noise conceivable, from an underground train pulling out of a station to the ricocheting of a rifle bullet. Something had to happen before he would shut up. A little of Durex went a long way.' Sergeant Douglas Hunt, 'Duggie', an apprentice at the Bristol Aeroplane Company who joined the RAFVR, had 'a very droll manner and a terrific scheme about a revolution after the war so that the whole of the country can be governed by pilots'. Last on the list was Sergeant William Corbin, known as 'Binder' because he was 'always moaning, usually about leave. He was the image of George Formby except that he was born in Kent and proud of it.'[6]

Corbin was from Maidstone, a builder's son who had gone to a technical school, then trained to be a maths and science teacher. He had joined the RAFVR in April 1939 and arrived at 66 Squadron at Coltishall on 28 August as a sergeant. His first impression was that the officers were all public-school boys, an observation that did not bother him. His academic abilities, he felt, made him their equal. The distinction in status and privilege between men who were doing the same job and taking the same risks would appear unreasonable and unjust in later years. At the time it seemed much less remarkable and most accepted it, illogical though it clearly was. The maintenance of the division between officer and NCO pilots was a hangover from the inter-war years, when the majority of sergeant pilots were ex-apprentices who had been accepted for flying training but might at any stage be required to return to their old trades.

By the late summer just under a third of the pilots flying were sergeants, many of them products of the RAFVR. Their duties were indistinguishable from those of officers. They were there, principally, to fly and fight. The decision whether or not to award a commission to a pilot on completing initial training was based on obscure criteria. One consideration was their leadership potential. The practice seems to have been to commission those who fitted most easily into pre-war conceptions of what constituted an officer and a gentleman. That meant public schoolboys and those who looked as if they belonged to the middle or upper class. Even here the formula was shaky. Don Kingaby, who turned out to be one of the best pilots in Fighter Command, was a vicar's son, and was educated at a public school – King's, Ely – yet was classed as a sergeant when he finished training in the early summer of 1940. Many sergeant pilots shared the same backgrounds as those who had been classified as their superiors.

The nature of the RAF required it to be a meritocracy. Its technical essence made it more egalitarian than the other services. In the RAF, more than in the army or navy, it was possible for an expensively educated son of privilege to be under the command of a man who had emerged from the working class. In 74 Squadron Tony Mould, who went to Mill Hill public school, was a sergeant. His squadron leader, Francis White, started his RAF career as an apprentice fitter. The war accelerated the rationalizing process, but in the summer of 1940 odd gradations remained.

Sergeant and officer pilots went to separate messes and enjoyed different levels of comfort. Away from the front-line stations, in properly appointed bases, officers could still have their own batman or orderly, a privilege which did not extend to the sergeants. Ian Hutchinson was posted from the RAFVR to 222 Squadron in February 1940. At that time, he said later, pilots arriving by that route were 'regarded as the lowest of the low,' particularly by the regular sergeant pilots who had arrived in the squadron from the workshops. 'They treated us differently at first, but when it came to the action then everything disappeared.'

Hutchinson noted that 'as an officer you lived rather better. You had a nicer uniform. [As a sergeant] you had a scratchy uniform, although the scratchiness wore off eventually. Your accommodation was not so grand, although you did get individual or double rooms. You didn't have a batman to wake you up in the morning and make your tea or press your trousers or polish your buttons. You did it yourself. You envied the officers their privileges but nothing more. Nobody felt aggrieved.'[7] Maurice Leng, a sergeant with 73 Squadron, agreed. 'We were very close. There was no officers *versus* sergeants nonsense. Just a marvellous camaraderie.'[8]

Some officers, like Geoffrey Page, found the division stupid. 'I felt it terribly wrong that a man who hasn't got an officer's rank is asked to do exactly the same thing as the officer. You can't climb out of your aeroplane and then say "Cheerio" and you go off to the officers' mess and he goes off to the sergeants' mess. I always thought that it was a very wrong system.'[9] Once at dispersal distinctions usually, but not invariably, disappeared. In 41 Squadron under Squadron Leader Hilary Hood, differences between pilots were minimal. Sergeant Frank Usmar remembered Hood as 'a lovely chap. When you were at dispersal it was nothing for him to say, "Well, if you've got half-a-crown, let's have a game of cards." And we'd play this innocent game and we'd be one big happy family . . . We were sitting there waiting for the telephone to ring and to keep your mind off what's going to happen you play cards and make fun of things.' Hood was killed on 5 September when his Spitfire collided with that of another squadron member, Flying Officer John Webster, while they were attacking bombers over the Thames estuary.

The new squadron leader was less convivial. 'One day the NCOs – that was about half a dozen of us – were sent for to report to the orderly room with our greatcoats on and buttoned up above the throat and buttons polished. We were told by the CO that it was a court martial offence for officers to play cards with the NCOs but they were too much gentlemen to tell us to stay out.' He ordered them to stop. When the sergeants returned to dispersal, the officers asked why they had been summoned. When they heard the story, they glumly accepted the decision. 'So we used to lay on our bed in the corner or in the armchair waiting for the bell to ring to scramble, feeling cheesed off and miserable, and the same thing applied to the officers at the other end of the room, longing to play cards or something, but unable to do it.'[10]

Off the base, where there was no one to object, sergeants and officers often drank together. The social gap between pilots and ground crews was wider, though some pilots reached across it. John Coghlan, a flying officer with 56 Squadron, known as 'Slim', was, according to Corporal Eric Clayton, who maintained his Hurricane, 'a friendly, amusing and unflappable character, overweight and unfit he perspired freely and had a prodigious intake of ale'. Clayton and his fellow airmen would often bump into him with his girlfriend in their favourite Ipswich pubs, 'which resulted in beery and jolly evenings'.[11] The pointlessness of the distinction was evident from the fact that almost every sergeant pilot flying in the summer of 1940 was sooner or later commissioned. Many sergeant pilots went on to high command. Neil Cameron, a bank clerk who joined the RAFVR and was posted to 1 Squadron at the end of September, ended up Marshal of the Royal Air Force.

It was in the air that rank held the least meaning. On the occasions when Flying Officer Ben Bowring was called on to lead 111 Squadron and 'felt he wasn't qualified', he asked Sergeant William Dymond, a regular, to take over instead, while he followed behind.[12] Yet on the ground flying and fighting prowess did not necessarily increase the standing of those who possessed it. An egalitarian spirit and a propensity for knock-about humour and mickey-taking made the establishment of hierarchies of esteem difficult. Pilots admired success but did not subscribe to the notion of 'aces' or show deference to outstanding performers. When an interview with Count Czernin appeared in the London press, in which he spoke freely about his successes, his colleagues in 17 Squadron organized a mock ceremony and awarded him a large cardboard medal. The fact was that most pilots never shot anything down. Fewer than 900 of the 2,330-odd pilots who flew in Fighter Command between July and November claimed victories. There was no shame in that. They knew among themselves that the simple presence of a Hurricane or Spitfire, even if its bullets were not striking home, had a demoralizing effect on the enemy. And they understood very well the courage that was needed simply to maintain yourself in the air.

Brian Kingcome was not a self-effacing man, but he resisted attempts to establish an order of precedence among pilots based on the number of 'kills'. He qualified as one of the most successful pilots of the period. Between 2 June and 13 October he is credited with shooting down at least seven enemy aircraft and damaging many more. The true figure is almost certainly considerably higher as he was careless about recording claims. Kingcome was tall, amused, sceptical, slightly offhand. He had a flattened nose and droopy eye, the result of a pre-war car crash, which did nothing to reduce his attractiveness to women. These were attributes that might make him an object of envy to other men. Yet he was popular and respected. He was convivial and loved a party. He gave credit where it was due. His irritation with attempts to classify him as a hero was genuine. So, too, was a bluntness that could disconcert. 'He didn't suffer fools, there's no doubt about it,' said Sergeant David Cox, who flew with him in 72 Squadron and liked him.[13] He worked hard at insouciance. Geoffrey Wellum, nicknamed 'Boy' because of his youth and innocence, described waiting at dispersal and thinking, in an atmosphere thick with anticipation, that 'only . . . Brian Kingcome, who is reading and sucking a matchstick, looks relaxed. But on second thoughts, when did he last turn a page? I watch quietly and he doesn't.'[14]

The Fighter Boys cultivated ironic modesty. Those who became well known to the public during and after the war were regarded with some reserve. Unlike Kingcome, Bob Stanford Tuck advertised his successes and painted swastikas on the fuselage of his Spitfire marking the number of Germans he had knocked down. This practice, according to Birdy Bird-Wilson, was regarded by the majority as 'a bit of a line shoot'. Douglas Bader, the most famous fighter pilot of the period, aroused mixed feelings in those who fought alongside him. His bombastic nature and tendency to dramatize was in many ways the antithesis of the Fighter Boy ethos. All paid tribute to his courage, aggressive spirit and ability to enthuse those who followed him. There was reticence, though, about his sharp tongue and fondness for the limelight. David Cox regarded him as 'a good leader, there's no doubt about that. I think you could say you admired him. To like him, though, would be a little difficult.' Dennis David, a generous-hearted man, found him, 'very apt to being a bit smart, a bit short'.[15] Christopher Foxley-Norris thought he was 'a show-off', but 'enormously inspirational'.[16] To the ground crews he could be arrogant, bullying and foul-mouthed.[17]

The worst criticism, made all the more damning by its apparent mildness, was that a pilot was 'not entirely genuine'. To be a 'gen man' meant that you knew what you were doing and did it well, honestly and without fuss. Some of those who fell most emphatically into this category were unknown outside the ranks of Fighter Command. Johnny Dewar, who lead 87 Squadron, was at least ten years older than most of his pilots. He was a member of the whisky family and renowned for his hospitality. After graduating from Cranwell, his career had taken him to every corner of the inter-war RAF. He took the squadron over after it was posted to France and fought all through the summer until he was reported missing on 12 September 1940, shortly after being promoted wing commander. His leadership impressed Dennis David, who found him 'full of common ordinary decency'.[18] Roland Beamont, who also served with him, thought 'he might have been a rather paternal type of schoolmaster in his manner, gentle, quiet mannered resolute and totally unflappable. He was all of thirty-two at the time. We thought he was an old man.'[19]

Most of the pilots were between nineteen and twenty-six years old. The extreme circumstances they found themselves in made them more appreciative of father figures than they might have been in peacetime. Among the most popular men in Fighter Command were several station commanders who were admired for their good nature and efficiency in keeping the bases going and the pilots properly looked after. Wing Commander Victor Beamish ran North Weald for the worst part of the summer. Cuthbert Orde, the former RFC pilot turned war artist, described him as 'unique as an individual and probably the best-loved man in Fighter Command'.[20] He was charming and slightly eccentric, roaming the base in mechanic's overalls. He had been the RAF's heavyweight boxing champion in India in the 1930s and had narrowly missed being selected to play rugby for Ireland, where he had been born, in Dunmanway, County Cork, in 1903. While his pilots were standing at the bar with their 'half-cans' in the evening, he would trot around the aerodrome, trying to keep fit. He flew continuously throughout the summer, shooting down about a dozen bombers and fighters and earning the respect of pilots almost half his age. 'I don't think any pilot would dare to do less than his best if Victor was about,' wrote Orde. 'Not because he might get ticked off but because he would feel ashamed.' The ground staff liked him too. To Eric Clayton he was 'a large burly figure with a friendly face and a ready smile ... energetic with a powerful sense of duty; hot-tempered but quick to apologize. He was a pugnacious but warm-hearted Irishman. He was also ready with his praise, altogether a great leader.'[21] Beamish resisted the pull of desk and office to the end and died in the air, shot down over the Channel in 1942.

The personality of Group Captain Richard Grice dominated Biggin Hill. Dick Grice was a veteran of the RFC and had won a DFC in the First World War. He was a comforting presence during the repeated blitzes of the base. Pilots, ground crews and station staff, men and women, were reassured by the sound of his calm voice over the Tannoy warning of an imminent raid then announcing the all-clear, and afterwards the sight of the slim, concerned figure picking his way through the smoke and flame to check on the welfare of his 1,000 charges. He was particularly solicitous towards the female staff, the 200 Waafs who were now indispensable to the functioning of the place, and the women who manned the Naafi. He praised their courage and nourished their morale. When the manageress of the Naafi appeared on the point of collapse through overwork, he overrode her demands to stay at her post and sent her on leave. When she returned she found he had arranged for a pull-over she left behind, embroidered with the names of European capitals she had holidayed in, to have the name of Biggin Hill added.

It was natural that inside each squadron pilots made special friendships or formed little groups who would sit together at dispersal or return to each others' rooms for a last drink after a night in the mess or down at the pub. In 17 Squadron Denis Wissler was particularly close to Birdy Bird-Wilson, and 'Pitters' – Geoffrey Pittman – his favourite companions on trips to bar, cinema or hop. Robin Appleford and Rob Bodie gravitated naturally to each other, both the babies of 66 Squadron, both good-looking. They teamed up for forays into London in an unlicensed, untaxed banger, once piling into a bomb crater as they raced home through the blackout. Like inclined to like. George Unwin formed an alliance with Frank Steere; both were pre-war sergeants and superb pilots. Richard Mitchell and George Johns, West Country boys and ex-Halton apprentices, teamed up together in 229 Squadron. It was also inevitable that there would be outsiders, those who somehow never managed to cross the low threshold that led to acceptance. On 16 October, Wissler noted the departure of two pilots who had been with the squadron for several months, but until then had failed to feature in the dramatis personae of his diary. They were 'both dim types whose posting was expected'.

Fitting in was made easier by the very difficulty of becoming a fighter pilot in the first place. Being posted to a squadron meant that the first and most important test had been passed. The new pilots were joining an élite. Like all élites, it was indulgent towards its own. The social matrix was elastic, stretching to accommodate differences of personality and background. There were common attitudes that were reasonably easy to embrace. Fundamental to the outlook was humour. It was black, broad, coarse or feeble, usually schoolboyish but constant and all-pervasive.

The practical joking and ragging traditions of pre-war days survived and, when the situation allowed, evenings regularly ended with boisterous mess games. 'A wonderful evening terminating at the Schooner,' wrote the unofficial diarist of 73 Squadron of a night in late July. 'The CO, strong as he was, failed to prevent a not unusual ceremony of being debagged.'[22] Ian Hutchinson was playing the piano in the mess one night when a raid came in. He reached for his steel helmet, but another pilot beat him to it. When he placed it on his head, beer cascaded over his shoulders. In 74 Squadron Peter Chesters bombarded his fellow pilots with meteorological balloons filled with water as they ran from the dispersal hut in response to a phoney scramble. The trick only worked once. Later the pilots had their revenge when, while again fooling about on a roof, he managed to get wedged between the walls of a hut and the surrounding blast barrier. His comrades relieved themselves on him before helping him out. Chesters was high-spirited until the end. He was killed when he misjudged his height doing a victory roll over Manston after shooting down an Me 109 the following year.

Mishaps that ended short of death were a subject of hilarity, such as getting shot down by a bomber rather than by one's equal, an Me 109. The joking, as was recognized, served a need. 'One of my greatest recollections of the time was laughter,' Roland Beamont said later. 'Obviously there was a release of tension in seeing the funny side of things. Maybe sometimes the laughter got a little high. Perhaps there was a bit of hysterics in it somewhere . . . We saw things in very sharp outline. If you saw a chum on a parachute, the fact that he landed with a bit of damage was thought of as really rather amusing. The fact that he wasn't killed was extremely satisfactory for all concerned and a cause of merriment.'[23]

The pilots were further bound together by their own argot, a mixture of public-school slang, technical jargon and transatlantic coinages picked up from films and records. The public-school contribution included boyish expressions of enthusiasm as well as boredom (a very British preoccupation). Anything tedious, a broad category, was a 'bind'. Pilots would complain of an uncongenial activity that it 'binds me rigid'. Inevitably, when it came to serious matters, understatement was obligatory. 'Walking out' was parachuting out from a burning aeroplane. Colliding with the ground or sea at several hundred miles an hour was 'going in'. Many a pilot's death was announced with the laconic news that he had 'had it', or 'bought it', or 'gone for a Burton'. The Fighter Boys' enthusiasm for Hollywood movies and American singers and bands provided them with a rich new word-hoard. To the more traditional types, girls were still 'popsies'. But among the racier pilots, young women became 'dames' or 'broads'.

Most pilots were on the look-out for fun, and fun was almost invariably accompanied by alcohol. Fighter Boys were drinkers. Despite the obvious unwisdom of the combination, pilots and alcohol had always gone together. Beer, the tangy sudsy bitter of the county breweries that covered the country, was what they customarily ordered, served in dimpled mugs or pewter tankards, up to eight pints a night. They drank it, when they were not in the mess, in pubs whose nostalgia-wreathed names became as fondly remembered by the pilots as the airfields at which they served: the Red Lion at Whittlesford, the Old Ship at Bosham, the White Horse at Andover, the Golden Cross near Canterbury.

At the height of the summer battles, every effort would be made to get to the pub before closing time no matter how hard the day had been. Pilots at Biggin Hill welcomed the shortening of the days as the summer wore on, as it meant they could reach the brass rail sooner. Often they would be driven there by the station commander. 'Dick Grice had a tannoy speaker mounted on his car and we'd be down at the White Hart and you could hear him coming from a mile away,' said Pete Brothers. '"This is the CO. I want three scotches and two pints of bitter." He'd got a bunch of chaps in the car and and was calling up the bar. You could hear this booming across the countryside.'[24]

The White Hart at Brasted, a pleasant village that straggles along the road from Westerham to Sevenoaks, became the most celebrated of the Fighter Boys pubs. There had been an inn on the site since the seventeenth century. It had steep-pitched tile roofs and thick lintels, large rooms made cosy with beams and fireplaces and stone-flagged floors. The White Hart was not the nearest pub to Biggin Hill, seven miles away across the fields, but it was the most attractive. The bar was presided over by a reserve navy officer, Teddy Preston, and his wife Kath. Among the customers were Moira and Sheila, handsome twins and the daughters of Sir Hector Macneal, a friend of Beaverbrook who lived near by at the Red House. They were, in Brian Kingcome's description, 'tall, elegant, sophisticated and beautiful young women . . . They exuded the indefinable quality that comes from impeccable taste'.[25] Moira, the elder, was married to an air commodore on duty posted to the Middle East. Sheila was the widow of a fighter pilot who had disappeared after being sent on a hopeless mission on a winter night at the start of the war. She was left with a small daughter, Lesley.

Behind the blackout curtains the pilots would banter among themselves and with local customers, flirt with the Macneal twins and, when gently moved on by the local policeman at closing time, look for somewhere else to drink. Tony Bartley recorded the last frantic minutes of a typical session.

'Time gentlemen please,' yelled the barman.
  'Who's for the Red House?' said one of the twins . . . There was a unanimous howl of approval . . . We piled into the station wagon like sardines again, and after a short drive arrived in front of a fine old

red-brick manor house. The twins had gone ahead and were waiting for us at the door. I was shown into the drawing room and had a very large whisky thrust into my hand. Someone put on the radiogram.[26]

After its move to Biggin Hill in September, 92 Squadron ensured there was always somewhere to go by creating its own club in Southwood Manor House, to where the pilots had been moved by Grice, who dispersed the squadrons around surrounding country houses because the incessant bombing made it too dangerous to stay on the base at night. The squadron had a jazz pianist of professional standard in Bob Holland. Other musicians from among the Biggin Hill staff would be drafted in for jam sessions. Writing to a Waaf friend, Holland enthused about their 'wizard billet which is in a fairly large country house we have taken over with a dance floor, piano, drums, double bass and plenty of VR musicians to go with it. We just have a night club here every night. Our drink bill is mounting up to something terrific, but still, what the hell!' Fun was necessary to forget what was happening. The next line in the latter reads: 'Poor old Bill Williams and Drummond were killed this morning. They must move us soon for a rest.'[27]

Pilots pursued fun with the same enthusiasm that they brought to flying. Even at the height of the battles, pilots at the London perimeter bases would manage sorties to the West End. 'There was almost a daily routine at the height of the summer,' remembered Geoffrey Page, who was with 56 Squadron at North Weald. 'We'd land, having been based all day at somewhere like Manston, trying to get on the ground in time . . . to get to the pub. The pubs closed at 10.30, so the rush getting from your aircraft to the local tavern was enormous. We'd make it. The landlady would give us some extra time, then some idiot would suggest we went up to London. We'd bundle into various cars, drive up and stay in a night club until two in the morning. We had to be back on readiness at four. Back we'd come, really not in 100 per cent condition to be doing the job we were doing but happy about it.' They went to the Bag o'Nails in Beak Street or Hatchett's in Piccadilly to bask in the admiration of the young hostesses. These encounters never 'led to anything because you had to get back to the airfield . . . It was just schoolboy enthusiasm and mirth.'[28] Back at North Weald, Page would sober up in the pre-dawn light by walking around the perimeter, acting the part of the keen young officer by pretending to inspect the men guarding the fence.

Some pilots in Al Deere's squadron would dispense with bed altogether after a very late night and simply don their flying jackets and doze on deckchairs in the dew-laden grass at dispersal, waiting for the first scramble of the day. Archie Winskill, based at Hornchurch, would go to Romford with his squadron friends and take the tube to Piccadilly Circus 'to hit the high spots. Often we stayed all night at the Jermyn Street Turkish Baths, which were open all night, and then after a few hours' sleep, went back on the tube to Romford and into the cockpit.'[29] The Antipodeans would meet up at the Tivoli bar close to Australia House and New Zealand House in the Strand. Irving Smith, a New Zealander with 151 Squadron had arranged to meet some friends there one evening but was delayed. His quarters at North Weald had been bombed. He was separated from his kit and had been moved to Stapleford Tawney. He sent a message to the bar saying he would not be coming, but then discovered there was a train that could get him to London by closing time. He arrived to find them holding a wake. 'My message was garbled,' he said later. 'They all thought I'd been shot down and was dead. After that there was a great thrash.'[30]

Away from the metropolis the fun was less sophisticated. No. 87 Squadron, based in Exeter, lived in two hotels but had little contact with the local people. Their main social contacts were with the police and the Royal Marines, who invited them to drinks at headquarters. Internal squadron celebrations could have the quality of a provincial Rugby club piss-up. The unofficial diary of 73 Squadron, based at Church Fenton in Yorkshire, records a dinner held to mark the departure of one of the pilots on 29 August.

Throughout dinner Henry sat miserably, tugging at a large hydrogen balloon tied to his V R collar badge. After he had eaten his fill he was duly escorted to The Ship by the C O and Reggie Lovett [a flight commander], in company with several other members of the sqn. What a night! At 11.30 p.m. he was duly carried out of The Ship screaming loudly for assistance. After several unsuccessful attempts he was inserted into the awaiting vehicle where he peacefully passed out on the floor while being driven back to the mess. On arrival he was carted up to his room where we at last fulfilled our promise and put Henry to bed with his boots on. During the night sundry untoward incidents occurred about which the less said the better! However at 5 o'clock the following morning a certain very soiled-looking figure was seen searching for his teeth with almost frantic energy. They were eventually found in a place where they were very nearly washed away for good, and as a result they spent the rest of the night in strong disinfectant![31]

The authorities took a sympathetic attitude to drink. In July 1940 the Judge Advocate General of the RAF, Foster MacGeagh, pointed out that the Air Force Act had purposely avoided precision over what exactly constituted drunkenness. He drew attention to the observation of his predecessor that it was 'one of those things that it is easier to recognize than to define comprehensively'. He concluded that 'the only safe rule is that no person should be convicted of drunkenness . . . unless the court is satisfied that he was so much under the influence of drink as to be drunk according to the view of ordinary, reasonable men'.[32] In fighter squadrons, that allowed considerable leeway.

Commanders understood the need for release. When his pilots grew more and more fatigued Beamish arranged the rota to try and give everyone one day in four off duty. Sometimes he would accompany them to town, impressing the younger men with the familiarity with which he was greeted by the female habituées of the night clubs. Peter Devitt, commanding 152 Squadron, would send exhausted pilots off to a pub in Swanage to rest for forty-eight hours. Staying in with a cup of cocoa did not guarantee either success or survival. Charlton Haw found that 'throughout the war, people in squadrons who used to go to bed early and not go out and chase a few pints were far more likely to buy it than people who were a little bit on the wild side'.[33]

Laughter and drink edged out thoughts of death. The lowest hour of the day was always the first, sitting at dispersal in silence, smelling the familiar smells of crushed grass, metal, oil and high-octane fuel, waiting for the arrival of the coffee wagon to dispel the beer taste lingering from the night before, nervous sickness stirring in the bowels in anticipation of the first scramble. This was the time when courage was most fragile. Each pilot braced himself to face a day which might bring death or horrible injury. If he survived it was only in order to face the same ordeal the next morning. The ring of the ops telephone was almost welcome. Then, an hour later, they were back on the ground and if everyone had made it home the mood was transformed. It was as if the sun had emerged from behind a cloud. So far, so good. The first, the worst, was over. Having got through it, the pilots' natural optimism persuaded them to hope that the end would not come that day. Clambering out of the cockpits, the relief showed in the shouted banter and the sudden appetite for bacon and eggs swimming in greasy Naafi trays by the dispersal hut. But towards the close of day the foreboding returned. The pilots were strained and tired. Their nerves were on the surface now, exposed by the constant ebb and flow of emotions and sensations: fear, hatred, anger, satisfaction. So many had gone up on the last sortie of the day and not returned. It seemed to be tempting fate. It was without eagerness that they trotted out across the lengthening shadows towards their Hurricanes and Spitfires, and with thankfulness that they bumped down over the grass or concrete and headed for the pub.

The resolution of the pilots, their ability to keep going up day after day, over and over, with each trip shrinking the odds of survival, was sustained by interlocking feelings and convictions. The essential sentiment was loyalty, and it came in several forms. There was loyalty to the country and its inhabitants. Noisy expressions of patriotism were considered bad form in Fighter Command. It took outsiders to see how deep and passionate the attachment was. Tim Vigors had been schooled in England and spent much of his youth there, but considered himself an Irishman to the extent of having a tricolour painted on the nose of his Spitfire. He wrote later that he was 'not possessed of that uncaring patriotism which caused so many young Englishmen ... unselfishly to lay down their lives for their country'. But he believed that had the battles been fought 'over the green fields and purple mountains of Tipperary, in all probability I would have been fired with the same wild, protective feeling for my country which was responsible for the deaths of so many of my brave friends and almost certainly would not be alive ... today'.[34]

Next to this lay loyalty to comrades. The determination not to let down the man next to you is the main ingredient of military courage and the dynamo that drives all wars. 'The strongest feeling was not to disappoint your friends,' said Peter Dunning-White. 'There was no question of not flying. You daren't not take off.'[35] This was particularly true of the leaders. It was impossible to funk it without everyone seeing you turn away. Belonging depended on sharing the risks and the dangers, and also, though it was by no means essential, achieving some success. No matter how fearful they might be, pilots wanted very much to fly and to succeed, even the least experienced. As the attrition of the summer ground on, Ian Hutchinson ended up as the most senior sergeant pilot in his squadron, able to decide for himself whether or not he would fly. 'We were flying from a base near Southend and the scramble call came. One chap came to me and said, "Can't I fly?" I had been flying all the time so I said OK. He went up and he was killed. It was such a shame. He was a lovely chap. I hadn't allowed him to gain enough experience so I blamed myself.'[36]

The pilots were fighting a battle for the survival of Britain. It was only afterwards that the significance of their effort started to become apparent. Most pilots held the silent conviction that they were engaged in a struggle between good and evil. That feeling intensified the longer the war continued. Beyond their allegiance to hearth, home and squadron, a loyalty to humanity drove them on. Brian Kingcome remembered looking at the body of a dead German airman, a member of the crew of a Ju 88 he had helped shoot down near Minehead. 'Gazing at the young man lying in front of me I could not accept that he had been some kind of non-political combatant. He seemed too close to the ideal Aryan mould cherished by Hitler to be a coincidence or accident, and any charitable ... thoughts I might normally have harboured simply remained frozen ... I found myself looking at him with loathing.[37]

Stories circulated of German breaches of the unwritten conventions of aerial war, in particular the cold-blooded shooting of pilots as they dangled defencelessly on the end of parachutes. The pilots of 266 Squadron believed that their commander, Squadron Leader Rodney Wilkinson, had been killed in this way on 16 August. 'He was seen to bale out of his crippled aircraft apparently unhurt but his body was found, so we were told, as full of holes as a sieve,' Dennis Armitage reported. 'This incident stirred up intense hatred of the Germans. Perhaps they had some justification in that a fully trained and experienced pilot was far harder to replace than the machine he was flying, but our "Wilkie" was much loved and the thought that he was shot up while dangling helplessly from a parachute filled us with a vindictive hate that had not been there before.'[38] Other accounts say he died colliding with a Me 109. Squadron Leader Harold Starr of 253 Squadron was certainly machine-gunned to death by a Messerschmitt after he baled out over Eastry in Kent on 31 August. Flight Lieutenant Robert Ash, flying as gunner with a Defiant of 264 Squadron, baled out after being hit on the morning of 28 August. The pilot also jumped and landed with minor injuries, yet Ash was found dead with bullet wounds in his body. Dennis David believed Johnny Dewar had been shot while descending.

There were no accusations that British pilots had ever responded in kind. There were some suspicions, though, that Polish pilots were less fastidious. Peter Matthews was on leave at the beginning of September and went home to Ewell. He was teaching his wife to drive on Epsom Downs when he looked up to see 'Hurricanes shooting down Germans in parachutes. I knew jolly well who they were. They were 303 Squadron boys. Poles. They owned to it.'[39]

As the German attack widened to include civilians, British sensibilities hardened. Pilot Officer Richard Barclay of 249 Squadron reported in his diary how he had led a chase of two Me 109s, one of which tried to crash-land near Manston. 'Just as he was at tree-top height Sergeant X shot at the E/A [enemy aircraft]. It flew straight into some trees and crashed in flames. On returning Butch [Flight Lieutenant Robert Barton] tore a terrific strip off Sergeant X about his unsportsmanship, etc., and we all heartily agreed.' The following day the squadron heard of the bombing of Coventry. Barclay noted: 'We are inclined to think that perhaps Sergeant X's action yesterday wasn't so bad after all.'[40]

Paddy Finucane's detached attitude towards the Germans changed after he visited Southampton to see friends shortly after a blitz. When he returned he was visited by a Polish pilot friend, Boleslaw 'Ski' Drobinski, at his room in the country house near Tangmere where he was billeted. Finucane stood shaving while Drobinski listened. 'It was the longest shave I can remember,' he told Finucane's biographer. 'We talked for about an hour. Speaking slowly to ensure I understood, Paddy said: "Listen, Ski, when this war is over we must make sure there will not be another one. It is a terrible way to settle anything. Until it is, we must shoot down every bloody Jerry from the sky." '[41] For some, the point of the fighting now was to hurt as well as to kill. Sailor Malan told Geoffrey Flavell, a doctor acquaintance, that he changed tactics and now tried to avoid shooting down bombers outright. 'If you shoot them down they don't get back and no one in Germany is a whit the wiser. So I figure the right thing to do is let them get back. With a dead rear gunner, a dead navigator, and the pilot coughing his lungs up as he lands . . . I think if you do that it has a better effect on their morale.'[42]

Killing and maiming were none the less not things to boast about. Most pilots told themselves and the outside world that, when they shot at a German aeroplane, they were aiming at the machine not the man. George Bennions 'was relieved when they baled out'. Another 41 Squadron pilot, Tony Lovell, who was a devout Catholic, 'used to go and see the RC padre and pray for forgiveness . . . He used to get very upset when he'd shot something down, very upset.'[43] Michael Constable Maxwell of 56 Squadron, another fervent Catholic, left behind in his diary an account of the complex evolution of his feelings as he closed in on a Dornier that he had managed to isolate from the fleet.

While attacking the formation I was frightened and excited, but once it had left the others I began to experience the most wonderful and jubilant excitement imaginable. I took a joyful pleasure in the thought that I had made it leave the formation, and all I wanted to do was close in and kill. I had no fear of his bullets, even though a shower of tracer came at me whenever I got within range, and I felt no compunction in shooting something damaged. I just felt a primitive urge to chase and to kill . . .

[But then] suddenly all this changed. I saw that he had had enough and merely wanted to land. The fight was over. He had given in and all he wanted was a safe place to get down. Four humans were in that plane. They were up in the air and in a damaged machine that the pilot was heroically trying to land. This last few minutes [were] the most unpleasant I have experienced in this war. I was safe, they were in danger of death. They crashed and no one got out.

The next day's entry describes an encounter he had with some other pilots with a local lawyer who was friendly with the squadron. 'He is told of the Dornier. "Oh how absolutely splendid of you, I do hope they were all killed!"' Constable Maxwell found this 'the filthiest remark I have ever heard and I was staggered by its bloody sadism . . . it is this loathsome attitude which allows papers to print pictures of wounded Germans. They must be killed and I hope to kill many myself . . . but the act is the unpleasant duty of the executioner which must be done ruthless and merciless [sic] – but it can be done silently.'[44]

No matter how powerful the pilots' motivations might be, they could not dispel the surges of fear that rose and fell with the stresses of the day. Robin Appleford 'got that sort of sick feeling all the time. I think most people if they were honest would confirm this.'[45] Peter Devitt was 'scared bloody stiff most of the time and anybody who says he wasn't frightened . . . was just as frightened as everybody else'.[46] Even Wing Commander Teddy Donaldson, who was notably unsparing of his pilots in 151 Squadron, admitted that the experience of tackling enemy aircraft when hugely outnumbered was 'very, very, frightening'.[47] But the level of fear climbed and fell away. In between the peaks were periods of excitement, even of boredom. No pilot could have operated if gripped by terror.

Few were ever overwhelmed by fear, but for some the struggle was fearful. One pilot in 501 Squadron would pause to vomit as he ran out to his aeroplane. One of George Unwin's sergeant pilots was 'terrified not of the Germans but of the Spitfire. I used to say, look, would you like me to have a word with the CO, and get you on to bombers. "No, no," he said, "that shows I'm a coward." I said, "Be buggered, it doesn't show you're a coward at all if you're prepared to go on bloody bombers." But he wouldn't and eventually he killed himself landing.'[48]

Constant exposure to fear, though, inevitably caused psychological damage. Pete Brothers came across one of his pilots sitting on the grass bathed in sweat and ordered him to report to the medical officer. Later 'the doc appeared and said: "This chap's sick. He's not to fly again. I'm grounding him."' He had been suffering the delusion that he had been shot down in flames, the fate of another squadron member the day before.[49] Fatigue, Birdy Bird-Wilson remembered, 'broke into a chap's mentality in the most peculiar ways. Some really got the jitters . . . others, as I did, had nightmares at night. I used to wake up in the dispersal hut . . . and I was night-flying my Hurricane. This went on for quite a long time.'[50]

Good squadron leaders understood when a man was at the end of his limits and had him posted away for a rest, usually as an instructor at an Operational Training Unit. Peter Down recognized the symptoms in himself. In the middle of September, though he was only a pilot officer, he led the remnants of 56 Squadron out of the line to Boscombe Down. They were given a week's leave, but Down knew that would not be enough. He asked to see Air Vice-Marshal Sir Christopher Quintin Brand, the commander of 10 Group. 'To my surprise he appeared two days later and led me under a tree near our dispersal point away from everybody else and said, "What do you want to see me about?" And I just said I wanted a break . . . I seemed to be doing all the work because of the lack of experience of anybody else. I knew my England without looking at a map and could fly anywhere within reason, whereas the squadron commander at the time didn't have the ability to do so . . . He said, "All right, nice to have spoken to you," and he gave me a pat on the shoulder and left. Three or four days later the signal came through saying I could take myself off as an instructor to Sutton Bridge.'[51]

The training units at Sutton Bridge and Aston Down were staging posts for many strung-out pilots. 'You saw chaps who had really taken shock extremely badly,' said Birdy Bird-Wilson, who instructed in both. 'They'd come into the bar and they'd have a terrible facial twitch or a body twitch and there was nothing you could do to help them except to act back again the same twitch. If they had a facial twitch, while you're drinking your drink, whatever it might be, you did the same back to them. And so they realized they were doing it – it's a very cruel way to be kind . . . It cured chaps in the end, it really did, and they returned to operations thereafter.'[52]

In a small number of cases a pilot's inability to fulfil his duty could not be overlooked and action had to be taken. One pilot came to Donaldson and 'admitted to me that he was a bit terrified and so I said, "Right then, off."' He had already noticed 'too many engine failures. He'd just disappear in the middle of a battle and go home.'[53] Denys Gillam witnessed one pilot who 'went to pieces on the ground, just as he was getting into his aeroplane. The doctor [was] seeing us off. He hit this chap on the chin, hard, knocked him out. He didn't fly again.'[54]

In one case it was the commander himself whose nerve was suspect. In early September Pete Brothers and Bob Tuck were posted to 257 Squadron at Martlesham Heath to replace two flight commanders who had been killed on the same day on the same operation. Brothers discovered that 'morale in the squadron was . . . way down the bottom, naturally. They were a bunch of young chaps, only two of them with pre-war experience. The others were chaps with minimum training. Naturally they were thinking, if these two experienced chaps can be shot down, what sort of chance have we got?'

On the first sortie they flew with the squadron leader, the ground controller ordered them to patrol a line above Maidstone at 20,000 feet. As they did so they saw a large formation of bombers with fighter escorts approaching and alerted the squadron leader. 'He said, "We've been told to patrol the Maidstone line and that's what we'll do until we've been told to do otherwise." So we all pissed off and left him and got stuck in.' Later Brothers worried that perhaps he had made a misjudgement. 'But then this happened a second time, then a third time, and we decided that this chap just wanted to avoid combat at all costs.' A few nights after they arrived, after fortifying themselves with beer, they rang up Keith Park and asked for him to be sacked.[55] The squadron leader was immediately posted away to a training unit. Other pilots deemed to be suffering from 'lack of moral fibre' were put on menial duties like towing drogues.

The pilots' resolution was fortified by the knowledge of the admiration they were held in by everyone in the country. Churchill had acknowledged the nation's debt in a speech on 20 August in the House of Commons, when he expressed the thanks of 'every home in our Island, our Empire, and indeed throughout the world', towards the pilots, who were 'turning the tide of world war by their prowess and devotion. Never in the field of human conflict was so much owed by so many to so few.' This gratitude was already visible to the pilots every time they ventured off base.

Yvonne Agazarian became the most envied girl in her convent school, which had been evacuated to Rugby, when her handsome, adored brother Noel arrived to visit her during a leave. 'The girls were gaga about him,' she said. 'He seemed a wonderful, incredible figure.'[56] Tony Bartley found that after the Churchill speech fighter pilots were 'the epitome of glamour. It was unbelievable. They loved us, and I mean loved. They bought us drinks, appreciated everything.'[57] On trips to London, Robin Appleford and Rob Bodie would wear their flying boots, ensuring a flow of free drinks and the undivided attention of the girls. The practice of wearing the top button undone was now well known. When men in air force blue walked into a pub, eyes would stray to their tunics and the word would go around that there were Fighter Boys in the bar. The pilots were polite to civilians, sometimes actually welcoming the chance to talk about things other than the fighting. Mostly, though, they preferred the warmth and security of their own company.

The great exception to the rule was women. The attitude of the pre-war RAF had been courtly and correct. At Tangmere, the young women Billy Drake met were the sisters of brother officers or the daughters of family friends. They would attend balls at the station, be entertained to drinks in the ladies' room in the mess, and in the summer sail and swim. It was all very proper. 'These were very innocent affairs. You knew the parents. They knew you.' The raffish life of the RFC pilots was alien to the modern young men of Fighter Command. 'There was no bought sex as such. If anybody was oversexed they dealt with the situation but they didn't talk about it.'[58]

For most respectable young men in 1940 the world of sex was remote and mysterious. War would bring it closer, but for many it would remain out of reach. No one knows how many of those who died in the battles of the year went to their deaths without having slept with a woman. The pilots liked to portray themselves as men of the world. Their upbringings, however, had given them little chance to acquire much sophistication in matters of sex. Most of them had passed their adolescence in classrooms and playing fields before entering service life. The majority of RAFVR entrants had been in conservative jobs where there was little opportunity for revelry. The conservative mores of the time swamped their outlooks, ladled on thickly by the heavy hands of their parents. Paddy Finucane wrote home reassuringly to his mother and father from Rochford on 9 August, after a party at a local hospital, 'We had a rattling good time and the nurses were a jolly decent lot and thought the boys in blues [sic] were all heroes. They could not do enough for us. It got rather embarrassing. After a while they all wanted to go for a walk round the grounds. Yours truly played the game and admired the beauty of the evening but not letting myself in for anything.'[59]

Time, everyone knew, was short. Perhaps there was no time at all. It was the classic chat-up line of the military seducer. But it was affection, if possible love, that most pilots seemed to be looking for. Striking up any kind of relationship was difficult in a life of constant geographical shifts, a heavy weight of duty that kept you occupied for all the hours of daylight and which was punctuated by only brief and unpredictable

periods of leave. Keeping in touch by telephone required serious dedication. Three-minute calls were all that wartime restrictions allowed and
they could take hours to be put through. Robin Appleford and Rob Bodie
were lucky. One night at the Tiger's Head in Chislehurst they fell in with
two wealthy civilians who had two young women, Christine and Pamela,
in tow. By the end of the evening the women had switched allegiances
and the four spent several happy weeks together, until the pilots were
posted away.

An RAF uniform, a pilots' wings, could be a passport to sex in the
summer and autumn of 1940. Charles Fenwick went to the aid of a young
woman who was being pestered by an army officer in the bar of a
London hotel. The intervention led to drinks, lunch and a trip to the
cinema. 'As soon as we had settled down to watch a flick I put my arms
around her shoulders . . . then before I can say Jack Robinson, she slips
her hand under my raincoat and into my trousers nearly shooting me
through the roof with surprise.' Fenwick had already lost his virginity to
a thirty-five-year-old woman married to a wealthy industrialist who lived
in the north and left his wife to her own devices. She collected Fenwick
from the Tangmere mess and drove him around the surrounding pubs,
embarrassing him by leaving her Dutch cap on the bar while she rum-
maged in her handbag for cigarettes.[60]

The most obvious source of women was the WAAF. By the middle
of the summer Waafs were to be found on most of the main fighter
bases. The girls of the first war-time intakes were adventurous, reasonably educated by the standards of the time, anxious to show they could
hold their own in a man's world, yet also alive to the possibilities of
romance. Edith Heap, a well-brought-up young woman from Nun Monk-
ton in Yorkshire, arrived at Debden in the autumn of 1940 to work in
the motor transport pool, driving Albion two-and-a-half-ton lorries and
the tractors which laid out the flare paths to guide the pilots in at night.
The women worked hard, their hours were long, and the airmens'
married quarters they lived in three to a billet were cold and damp.
Both the RAF commanders and their own female officers imposed strict
discipline, wary of the consequences of having young men and women

in close proximity, and they did what they could to limit their social lives. The Waafs were only allowed off the base with permission and had to be back by 10.15 p.m.

It was impossible, of course, to keep the Waafs and airmen apart. Edith Heap and her friend Winifred Butler came across the pilots, mostly public-school boys of their own age, as they drove them around the base or ran them to the satellite station at Martlesham Heath. The friends were attractive, funny and independent-minded. Edith had her own car, a baby Jaguar, a classier motor than most pilots could afford, which she sometimes let them borrow for trips to London. The girls were popular and often taken out to dinner at the Red Lion at Duxford or the Rose and Crown at Bishop's Stortford. They had two particular admirers, Jerrard Jefferies, tall, 'quite knockout to look at', with a silver streak in his dark hair, and Richard Whittaker. The relationships never had time to develop. 'Jeff' was posted as flight commander to a Czech unit, 310 Squadron at Duxford. Whittaker was killed over France.

One day Edith met Denis Wissler of 17 Squadron. He was eager, particularly boyish-looking, but perhaps slightly more sophisticated than most. On his first trip to France with 85 Squadron in May, he confided to his diary, he had visited a 'place of doubtful virtue' in Le Havre. But the impression shining from the diary's pages is of an innocent young man, anxious to meet the right girl, fall in love, marry and live happily ever after. His and Edith's first encounter was gauche. He playfully threw some sand at the tractor she was driving and the engine stopped. She offered him the crank handle and ordered him to start it again, which, sheepishly, he did.

Wissler's months at Debden and Tangmere after his return from France were dominated by the desire to succeed as a fighter pilot and the search for a nice girl. His keenness was unquestionable. But he never seemed to be there when the squadron did well. '"A" Flight were over at Martlesham and shot down five machines,' he wrote on 12 July. 'What a party they had.' He, though, was in 'B' flight, which did not get into the action. On the 28th he practised aerial gunnery shooting at a drogue. 'The scores were awful,' he recorded. 'I failed to hit the thing at all.' The following day he had better luck. 'Up at 4.30 and forward to Martlesham Heath. I was with Flight Lieutenant Bayne and Flying Officer Bird-Wilson and after one uneventful patrol we met a Heinkel 111 which was being half-heartedly attacked by Spitfires. We made a head-on attack and then an astern attack, pieces and oil coming out in all directions. The E/ A slowly went down to the water, I thought it was trying to get away low down and made another head-on attack. This time in [it] went into the water.' He was credited with a share in the destruction of the Heinkel.

Many of the diary entries, though, fizz with mild dissatisfaction. On 9 August he broke his wireless transmitter and was fined ten shillings and later, while watching the daily inspection of his Hurricane, got himself covered in oil. He went to bed 'in a damn bad temper . . . everything has gone wrong today'.[61] His days were spent in long periods at readiness, followed by frustrating patrols and interceptions in which little or nothing happened. On the 20th the squadron moved briefly to Tangmere and at last he was deep in the action. On the 25th he was in 'a hell of a scrap' over Portland. He saw two Me 110s he had fired on going down, but the operations record book notes just one 'probable' and only gave him a share. When the squadron learned that it was to return to Debden at the start of September, it was rumoured this would precede a further move out of the firing line to Northern Ireland. 'I hope not,' he wrote.

The squadron stayed in East Anglia. One night his friend Birdy Bird-Wilson asked him to come out to dinner with a girl he knew and her friend. The girl was Winifred Butler. Bird-Wilson was keen on her but was already engaged, an arrangement that was stalled until his situation became less precarious. He thought Denis might take her mind off the loss of Richard Whittaker. The friend was Edith Heap. Both women had by now graduated from driving to the highly responsible work of plotting, shifting the indicators around the map table in the control room to show the progress of the raids and battles. As they drove away from the base for dinner in Bishop's Stortford, Birdy sat in the front with Winifred, and Denis and Edith were in the back. 'We got on like a house on fire and gradually the conversation became two tête-à-têtes,' Edith remembered.[61]

Driving back, they heard a colossal bang, saw flames leaping up from some distant fields and went to investigate. In the excitement, Denis held Edith's hand. They found a stable block ablaze where a departing night raider had jettisoned his bombs. The fire brigade was already there, so they resumed the journey to Debden. 'That seemed to be that,' Edith thought at the time. 'Denis was taking out someone else. It had been a lovely dinner, he had been attentive and fun but not specially interested.' The woman in question he had met not long before at a party in the sergeants' mess. She was, he reported in his diary, 'a sweet little Waaf called Margaret Cameron'. They had 'quite a kissing session after the party was over'.

On the morning of Tuesday, 24 September, 17 Squadron was ordered south to intercept bombers approaching the Thames estuary. Their Hurricanes were still climbing when they saw the formation. As they closed on it, they were surprised to find a gaggle of Spitfires diving towards them, followed closely by a large number of Me 109s. Denis made one attack, broke it off, then climbed to make a second on a group of four Messerschmitts above him. Realizing he was about to stall, he levelled off. 'There was a blinding flash on my port wing and I felt a hell of a blow on my left arm and then blood running down. I went into a hell of a dive and came back to Debden. A cannon shell hit my right wing and a bit of it had hit me just above the elbow and behind.' Somehow he got the Hurricane down, but the shell had blown away most of the port flap and he was unable to stop, slewing off the runway into a pile of stones and cutting his face.

He was taken to Saffron Walden hospital. The following day he had visitors. Edith and Winifred came to see him. He was hungry and the girls went out to buy cakes and sandwiches. The following day he was released and spent the evening at 'a hell of a party in the sergeants' mess'. He also, as he recorded ruefully, 'put up a hell of a black with Margaret [Cameron], as I rather deserted her for two other friends'. On Sunday, before going off on seven days' sick leave, there was another bash in the sergeants' mess. The pilots would arrive after dinner in the mess for the arrival of the band and the dancing would carry on until 10.30 when the Waafs had to leave. Denis was delighted to see his hospital visitor among them. 'Met Edith Heap and fell in love with her at sight,' he wrote before going to bed that night.

When he returned from visiting his parents in London there was yet another party, this time at the 'B' Flight dispersal hut to mark 17 Squadron's imminent move to Martlesham. Edith and Winifred were there, with 'Jeff', who was visiting the base, in attendance. Denis, Edith wrote later, 'just commandeered me. We danced and chatted all evening.' In honour of the occasion the Waafs were allowed to stay until midnight. 'Just as we had to go a rather stormy Jeff arrived in front of me, furious because I had not gone to find him. I told him it was up to him to do that, not me.' Edith felt he was being unreasonable. He had not written while being at Duxford, and anyway had spent most of the evening dancing with Winifred. Edith didn't care. 'I was bowled over. Denis and I arranged to write each day and meet again as soon as our duties allowed it.' Denis was now smitten. 'My God it seems to be the real thing this time,' ran the awestruck entry in his diary. 'She is so sweet and seems to like me as much as I like her.' It was ten days before they saw each other again. Edith managed to arrange a twenty-four-hour pass. They decided to spend the night at Cambridge. 'We couldn't get into the Garden House Hotel,' she recalled. 'Denis came back saying, "We can only have a double room and that's not right, is it?" And I said, "No, it isn't."' They found two rooms at the Red Lion at Trumpington.

During dinner he told her he had something to say to her. They went upstairs to her room. 'He sat on the bed and I leaned against the dressing table. He just said, "Will you marry me?" And I said, "Yes."' Champagne was ordered. They drank it and went to their separate beds. The next day Denis insisted they drive to London to break the news to his family. His parents had moved to Dolphin Square, across the Thames from the Marmite factory which 'Pop' Wissler ran. On the way they stopped off in Cambridge to order an engagement ring. Edith telephoned the base to plead for an extension to her leave, which was granted as long as she was back for duty the following day. Denis rang ahead to Dolphin Square to say he was bringing a friend. When they arrived, Edith 'got ever so apprehensive. I think he did as well. On the way down the corridor to the flat he held my hand. I was in a blue funk by this time.'[62] Denis had said nothing in letters and calls home about Edith and was worried in his diary about keeping them in the dark. 'I don't want to hurt them,' he wrote, 'for I love them so.' There was no cause for concern. 'Denis shot me into the bathroom while he told them the news. I just stood there shaking in my shoes. A yell from the sitting room and I emerged to be hugged and kissed. I belonged to the family from that minute.' There were drinks, then dinner. Despite a bombing raid, everyone 'laughed all through dinner till we ached, completely ignoring all the banging and crashing going on outside'.

Edith took him to Yorkshire to meet her family. Then they spent another forty-eight-hour leave together at Dolphin Square, planning the wedding, set for 4 January, the date of the Wisslers' own anniversary. Denis had been anxious to get married as quickly as possible, and was delighted that she had already applied to leave the WAAF as the regulations demanded. 'Oh my darling it is grand you putting in your discharge now,' he wrote. 'We might speed up getting married a little if you say the word, but it all rests with you, my sweet. I wonder what you bought yourself while you were in Cambridge. I am living for the time I shall find out. Oh darling, I do miss you so, I do so love to be with you. Oh, I need you by me, I love you so, so much.'[63]

Three days after he returned from London, on the morning of 11 November, Denis landed at Martlesham Heath from an uneventful patrol over a convoy. Towards noon the squadron was scrambled again to intercept sixty dive bombers apparently heading for the same ships. Denis was in Blue Section. Edith and Winifred were at work in the control room, which had been moved to Saffron Walden after the summer blitzes of Debden. The 17 Squadron Hurricanes were vectored on to a plot that would bring them into contact with the Germans over Burnham in Essex. Edith tracked the fighters, Winifred the raiders. 'We could hear everything that was going on and all the battle that took place,' Edith said. Over the tannoy came a voice yelling that Blue Four was going down into the sea. 'I knew who that was. It was Denis. I didn't say anything. I just sat there because we had finished our work. They were coming back.' She went off duty but was unable to eat lunch, still forcing herself to hope it wasn't true. She tried to stifle her fears by going to the motor depot to talk to her old colleagues. 'When I got back to Saffron, Bill [her former superior] was waiting for me . . . Yes it was true, he was missing. No parachute.'

The following day she went to break the news to the Wisslers. Pop Wissler's grief was savage and shocking. A little later she was invited to lunch at Martlesham and to pick up Denis's belongings. His body had not been found. He had apparently been shot down by Me 109s while flying into the bombers, after the order to break off the attack had been given. Three days before, while on leave, he made his last diary entry. Once again he had been absent during a day when the squadron had done well. 'Each of the blokes got at least one,' he wrote. 'Total score fifteen destroyed and some probable. Oh God, fancy missing a party like that.'

16

'The Day Had Been a Year'

Saturday, 7 September, like all the preceding days of the month, was sunny, cloudless and hot. It was perfect bombing weather. In the early morning the Germans flew the usual reconnaissance missions to note the damage from the raids of the day and night before. Fighter Command braced itself for the first wave of what was expected to be another series of attacks on the bases. But no bombers came. For six hours the radar screens remained blank. Out at dispersal the pilots wondered at the inactivity, then gratefully took the opportunity to doze in the glowing sunshine. It could not last. Dowding and Park listened to the silence with foreboding. Clearly something ominous was brewing. At 3.54 p.m. the spell was broken. The first report came in that aircraft were forming up over the Pas de Calais. On the cliffs below, Hermann Goering, dressed operatically in a powder-blue uniform clustered over with gold braid, looked up at his aeroplanes. His dissatisfaction with the performance of his commanders and crews had driven him to take personal charge of the last phase of the air attack before the invasion of Britain was launched. The first formation of bombers swept overhead, nursed by an escort of Messerschmitts. It was followed almost immediately by another; then another. In his headquarters, Dowding looked at the counters crowding the table map and guessed that every aircraft the Luftwaffe could muster was heading for Britain's shores.

By the time the last German pilot had taken off, there were nearly

1,000 machines in the air: 350 bombers and more than 600 fighters stacked up in towering ranks. At the bottom were the Dorniers, Heinkels and Junkers cruising in layers that began at 14,000 feet. At the top were the Messerschmitts, ready to plunge on the British fighters, which would have no choice but to accept the challenge and come up to be annihilated. The enemy force moved through the still, warm air across a front twenty miles wide in a tight, throbbing grid, the biggest mass of aeroplanes ever till then to be assembled. Dowding had only one course of action open. At 4.17 p.m., twenty-three minutes after the first radar sighting, he ordered eleven squadrons to scramble. By 4.30 every Hurricane and Spitfire fighter within a seventy-mile radius of London was in the air or awaiting the order to take off.

Pilot Officer Richard Barclay of 249 Squadron was already airborne. He had been patrolling over the Essex coast, looking down at Clacton, Burnham-on-Crouch, Westgate, places he knew from childhood holidays, baking in the haze. When the alert came, he told his parents in a letter home, the squadron 'started to climb hard, turning to get a good look around and there several miles away was a black line in the sky – 35 Hun bombers in close formation – and I gradually began to distinguish about 70–100 other little dots: Hun fighters.' As the squadron turned to attack, he

switched on the electric sight and turned the gun button from 'SAFE' to 'FIRE'. And then things began to happen. We went in at the bombers and as I broke away I saw two dropping back from the formation streaming white smoke from one engine but before I could take stock of the situation the Messerschmitts were on me. I say 'me' rather than us because from this time on I never noticed another Hurricane in the sky until the end of the fight . . . I turned quickly to see if there was anything on my tail and at the same moment two Messerschmitt 109s went past beneath my nose. I turned quickly diving on one and gave him a burst. Nothing happened. Presumably I missed him but the noise of my 8 guns gave me great confidence. I gave the second Me 109 a burst and whoopee! A sudden burst of brilliant flame, a cloud of smoke and a vast piece flew off and down he went, but no time to watch because there's something behind me shooting . . . I turned to the right and saw [an] Me 109 go past with a vicious yellow nose and the large black crosses on the fuselage.'[1]

Barclay dived away from the German fighters, levelling off at 6,000 feet. Ten thousand feet above he could see the bombers beating inexorably on. He climbed up, keeping his distance so as not to be spotted. As he approached, the formation swung towards him and he raced into the leader in a head-on attack, but had to break off when he ran out of ammunition. He thought he had hit an engine. His own had certainly been damaged. Oil obliterated his windscreen. He switched off and glided down over the Thames estuary. Thick coils of black smoke hung over the water from oil-storage tanks blazing from an attack the previous day. There was no chance of making it back to North Weald. He slid the Hurricane into a belly landing on a field five miles from the base. When he got back the squadron had landed, rearmed and refuelled and was setting off again. There was no aeroplane for Barclay and his fighting was over for the day. The squadron had spent much of the summer in the north and had only arrived in Essex a week before. The sights he had seen that afternoon disturbed him. 'The odds today have been unbeliev-able,' he wrote in his diary, 'and we are all really shaken.'

Similar frantic scenes were taking place inside an 800-square-mile block of summer sky as hundreds of aircraft clashed. The cerulean blue over the fields of Kent and Essex was scribbled with the white curlicues of condensation trails and stitched with the glitter of cannon and tracer. Alone, frustrated, awaiting the return of his comrades, Barclay saw three bombers approaching the aerodrome at 16,000 feet. He assumed they 'had come back to finish the job they had started on the 3rd' when 200 bombs had been dropped on North Weald. But the bombers sailed on. They were no longer interested in the airfields of Fighter Command. Their target was London.

The decision to attack had been made inevitable by Churchill's ordering of retaliatory raids on Berlin for the Luftwaffe's mistaken bomb-

ing of the capital on the night of 24/25 August. Hitler was at Berchtesgaden when the RAF Wellingtons and Hampdens arrived over Berlin
early the following morning. They returned two days later, then again
on the 30th and 31st. Hitler went to Berlin and promised in a speech on
4 September: 'If they attack our cities then we will wipe out their cities.'
Earlier General Jodl, Chief of Staff of the OKW, the Armed Forces
Supreme Command, had warned his deputy that Hitler now intended to
strike back 'with concentrated forces when the weather is favourable'.
Considerations of revenge, taken in hot blood, should not have been
allowed to alter the course of the invasion preparations.

The climate of sycophancy pervading Hitler's court and the desire
for self-preservation meant that no one would contradict the Führer.
Goering, anyway, seems to have approved of the plan. The mass raids
could have several beneficial effects. They would continue the campaign
of destruction of Britain's infrastructure. Inevitably, they would draw the
RAF even more tightly into the war of attrition. Fighter Command had
no choice but to defend the capital. It was now becoming obvious to the
Germans that Churchill's government was unlikely to seek negotiations
without further, more violent coercion. A devastating attack such as
those that had traumatized Warsaw and Rotterdam might fatally under-
mine civilian morale and turn the population against its political and
military leaders, forcing them, essentially, to surrender.

Almost every bomber unit in France was thrown into the attack. General Fink, the forty-five-year-old veteran at the head of Kampfgeschwader
2, told his men to make their wills before they took off. So much time
was spent forming up that the fighter escort had run out of petrol by the
time it reached Sevenoaks and had to turn back. The bombers' target
was the Victoria Dock. The huge bend in the Thames at Docklands, the
U-Bogen as the Luftwaffe called it, glinted treacherously in the sunlight,
pointing the way. Despite the lack of an escort, Fink's formation was
relatively untroubled by British fighters on the way in. The order to
scramble had been given too late for many of the squadrons to reach
attacking height by the time the first waves of bombers crossed the coast.
Once over London, though, the Spitfires and Hurricanes began to appear.

'They dived through the bomber formations from a terrific height,' Fink remembered. 'Obviously we had too many machine-guns for them to attack any other way. We had the impression that each fighter had chosen one bomber and was diving to attack it . . . It was a horrible feeling when they came down on you.'[2] But the fleet succeeded in dropping its bombs and got away still holding formation. The fighters inflicted some damage. Fink was the only one of his four-man crew not to be wounded and it was a tribute to the sturdiness of their Dornier 17 that it managed to make it back to the base at Arras.

Oberstleutnant Paul Weitkus was commanding 11 Gruppe of the Geschwader with orders to attack Tower Bridge and the docks. 'We all had sketches of our targets. When we reached [the] Docks there were not many fighters but the guns seemed quite good.' They 'placed the bombs very well and large fires started'. Weitkus had time to take photographs of the burning docks, for his own amusement, with his Leica. By the time they had finished, the sky over London was chaotic. 'You couldn't tell a 109 from a Spitfire in the chaos of diving machines and bursting flak. Whoever saw who first was the victor.'[3]

Coming in to land at Arras, Weitkus swung round and there, 150 miles distant, a great banner of smoke stained the horizon above the stricken city. The sirens had sounded at 4.43 p.m. People were slow to move to the shelters, reluctant to leave the sunshine. The first bombs to ripple across the docks were incendiaries that started blazes that acted as beacons to the bombers that would flow in an almost continuous stream throughout the evening and early morning. The first raid lasted less than half an hour. The all-clear was sounded at 6.15 p.m. The shattered streets were full of rescue workers when the next bombers arrived at 8 p.m., dumping their loads of high explosive into the churning smoke and flame beneath. The docks were hit again, and the Royal Arsenal near by at Woolwich. Bombs landed on Victoria and Charing Cross stations and Battersea power station. Those who had remained in the city centre ran for the steps of the underground stations. Hours passed without the comforting wail of the siren announcing the Germans had gone, the air continuing to get heavier and more foul. People spread out newspapers and tried to sleep. The banter slackened and conversation turned serious. A raid as heavy as this must surely mark the start of the invasion. Even below ground in the shelters they could hear the noise and vibration of the anti-aircraft batteries.

The gunners were unable to identify their targets as it was impossible for the searchlights to penetrate the filth and murk that rolled overhead. The warehouses and stores around the Port of London were stacked with combustible goods which, as the bombs landed, blossomed into flames that ran hungrily from each dry, flammable structure to the next. A Thameside refinery disgorged a torrent of molten sugar that covered the river in burning sheets. A rum store caught fire, the barrels exploded like bombs and the streets ran with blazing spirit. The air was choked with soot, oil, chemicals, burning paint and rubber, bound together into a slimy viscous vapour by the water of hundreds of hoses playing on the inferno as ineffectually as a shower of rain on a volcanic eruption. Firemen were surrounded, cut off, vaporized by the superheated oxygen. Whole areas were abandoned to burn themselves out. This was the hell that the pessimists peering into the future of war in the 1920s and 1930s had predicted, the proof of what would happen when the bomber got through. London was experiencing a firestorm. The fire rose, sucking in huge draughts of cold air at its base that fed its intensity, giving it a demonic life of its own that could only end when there was nothing left to nourish it.

It was the poor quarters, clustered around the Port of London where the work was, that suffered most: Bermondsey, Woolwich, Deptford, Poplar, Wapping. It was easy for the bomb-aimers. They had only to wait for the sight of the big bend in the river, then release their loads. They were almost bound to hit a worthwhile target. If not, the bombs tumbled into the blank, terraced workers' streets, toppling the thin walls, pulverizing the little houses into dust and splinters. That day and night 306 people were killed in London and 1,337 seriously injured. Another 142 died in the suburbs. This was just the beginning. The raids would continue, with one exception caused by bad weather, for seventy-six consecutive nights.

The fighters had been unable to provide any serious protection for the population of London or prevent the German bombers from smashing and disrupting vital installations. Once night fell, the Luftwaffe was free to bomb unmolested and flew hundreds of sorties. The RAF had only two squadrons of Blenheim night fighters at its disposal, one of which, 600 Squadron, had been prevented from taking off by the clouds of smoke blanketing Hornchurch.

Even in the daytime fighters had performed poorly. The order to scramble had been given late. The caution was understandable. Until now the practice had been to hold back until the direction and size of an attack had revealed itself before committing resources, a tactic designed to make the most effective use of Fighter Command's ragged assets. By the time the nature of the first raid of the afternoon of 7 September became clear, the fighters were too late to position themselves to block the air armada or to scatter the formations and dilute their destructive power. They were able to inflict a certain amount of punishment as the first raiders turned for home, usually with their defensive formations intact. But by then the damage was done. The final total for the day was unimpressive. They shot down thirty-eight German bombers and fighters. But in the process they lost twenty-eight machines. More important were the pilots who had been killed.

But to Dowding and Park, standing at Bentley Priory on the western edge of London and watching the fires reflecting off the underside of the smoke *massif* rising over the city, the day offered hope. The Germans appeared to have shifted the focus of violence away from the airfields and defence installations towards the commercial and political target of the capital. But was this a permanent change, or merely a fluctuation? It seemed unlikely that the Luftwaffe would concentrate its effort on London without first having satisfied itself that it had ground down the RAF to the point where it no longer posed an insurmountable obstacle to an invasion.

The destruction of the air force, and in particular Fighter Command, was the starting point for all German planning for a landing. Goering had consulted the two Luftlotte commanders about the attack on London. Sperrle was dubious but easily persuaded. Kesselring was supportive. He assumed that if the southern fighter stations were obliterated, the squadrons would merely be evacuated to bases further north, so the destruction of airfields was not a vital objective. The doctrine prevailing in Goering's headquarters was anyway that the RAF was down to its last handful of men and machines, posing only a minor threat to the bombers. This misapprehension was understandable. Dowding and Park's tactics of using limited numbers of fighters meant the Luftwaffe rarely encountered large defensive forces. The Germans' inclination confronted with a similar situation would have been to have used whatever machines were available en masse. The assumption was that the RAF's resources were draining away and the residual resistance could be swept aside in the fighting over the capital. The timetable for 'Operation Sealion' was pressing. A decision on the announcement of the final preparations was imminent. The barges and boats that were to carry the Wehrmacht across the Channel were clogging the ports. It was time to move on.

It was true that the RAF pilots were weary and apprehensive. The week before the London attack the strain was becoming intolerable. They were under attack in the air and on the ground, flying three or four missions a day before returning to shattered bases where they were always half-listening for the whistle of falling bombs. When Sunday, 8 September, dawned cloudy, the relief among pilots and commanders was profound. 'The weather was bad today, thank goodness, so we had a reasonable rest,' wrote Richard Barclay. 'I think we are all still a bit shaken after yesterday.'[4] It had been a bad day for 249 Squadron. Pilot Officer Robert Fleming had been shot down and managed to bale out, but was severely burned and died of his wounds. Flying Officer Pat Wells was missing, though he was located five days later, burned and in hospital. Two others were wounded. But the pilots were young and recovered quickly. Two days later Barclay was recording his pleasure that he was now 'on state' almost all the time, an improvement on the beginning of the month when a surplus of pilots meant his flying opportunities were limited.

Dowding and Park had placed their faith in a system of rotation, moving squadrons out of the front-line stations of 11 Group when they judged they had had enough and replacing them with units which had benefited from a period in the relative quiet of a base in the north or west. It was the only way to approach an open-ended struggle which would be decided when one side or the other recognized that its losses were unsustainable. There had been times when the temptation had been strong to throw all Fighter Command's resources, dispersed round the country, into one great confrontation with the Luftwaffe. But Dowding had resisted.

Nor was there any question of falling in with the German assumption and withdrawing the main fighter force from its positions in the southeast around London to less vulnerable bases well behind the capital. Whatever the military logic, political considerations, and above all the morale of the civilian population, would not allow it. It was for this reason, it was said, that Dowding had clung to exposed satellite bases like Manston until they were impossible to hold, to the dismay of even such lion-hearted pilots as Al Deere. It was an approach that required strong nerves and a fine appreciation of each unit's stamina and ability to absorb punishment. The system functioned more smoothly if there were occasional gaps in the intensity of the fighting to allow redeployments to be made with a minimum of difficulty. Its existence depended on the bases in the south-east actually being able to operate.

Only two raids were launched during the mainly cloudy daylight hours of 8 September: on the Kent coast and the Thames estuary. The controllers ordered a limited response, which allowed most squadrons a day of partial respite. Pilots flew 65 patrols involving 215 sorties. The previous day there had been 143 patrols involving 817 sorties. In the evening the bombers returned to London in force and pounded the city until dawn. On the 9th there was a flurry of attacks in the late afternoon on the suburban belt south of London, apparently mainly directed at aircraft factories. Once again the damage was limited. The defenders were given good warning and at least twenty-six bombers and fighters were shot down.

Park was now using his squadrons in pairs, throwing them into the formations in concentrated force. The tactic had a demoralizing effect, causing the Luftwaffe commanders to modify their orders. A signal was intercepted from *Gruppe* headquarters directing crews to 'break off task if fighter opposition is too strong'.[5] The decision to combine squadrons was welcomed by advocates of the Big Wing as a tacit admission of the value of the tactic. Several squadrons from Duxford led by Douglas Bader had arrived to take part in the fighting of the 9th. Once again they were slow forming up and were low on petrol by the time they sighted the enemy. They claimed to have destroyed nearly twenty aircraft, but there was little evidence from ground observers or debris to support this. What was certain was that five Hurricanes were lost in the encounter and two pilots killed.

On the 10th poor conditions kept German activity to a minimum. The following day bomber formations managed to penetrate to London in the afternoon and bomb the docks, but when fear of running out of fuel forced the fighter escorts to withdraw they were harried by the British fighters and ten bombers were shot down on the way home. The next two days saw another daytime pause. On Saturday, 14 September, a week after the first big blitz of London, the tempo picked up again with random raids on south London and coastal towns which did little damage to any significant target but killed civilians, nearly fifty of them in the tranquil suburbs of Kingston-upon-Thames and Wimbledon.

It was a different story at night. The raiders returned again and again, but the RAF was not there to meet them. A night fighter, equipped with airborne radar and capable of intercepting intruders, had yet to be perfected. A handful of patrols were dutifully mounted, each of only one or two aircraft. Their presence could only be symbolic. London would have to rely on anti-aircraft artillery, and the number of guns was doubled in the two days following the blitz. The inability of the air force to mount a nocturnal defence was a blessing. It spared the fighters from having to operate on another front, so deepening their exhaustion and accelerating the rate of attrition. The great strategic necessity was the preservation of Fighter Command. Set against that, the bombing of the city was tragic. But in the end it was a lesser tragedy than the destruction of Britain's fighter strength.

Unlike the soldiers on the beaches of Dunkirk, Londoners seemed to accept the RAF's limitations. Tim Vigors shot down an Me 109 on 9 September and was then shot down himself and crash-landed, unhurt, in an allotment plot in Dartford. He salvaged his parachute and was given some tea and whisky by a friendly lady. Unable to make it back to Hornchurch, he arranged to stay with his aunt at her flat in Tite Street and called a girlfriend, Jill, to invite her to dinner. He met her at the Berkeley Hotel and took her on to supper. It was only when it was over that he remembered to call the squadron. His voice was met with relief. His comrades had assumed he was dead. He promised to be back first thing in the morning and resumed enjoying the rest of the evening. They spent an hour dancing at the Four Hundred Club in Leicester Square, then he escorted Jill to the station and the last train home. On the way back to Tite Street, he had a taste of what Londoners were going through. 'Sirens were wailing. Searchlights were lighting the sky over to the East and the thuds of exploding anti-aircraft shells blended ominously with the screech of the sirens. The drone of bombers could be heard above the racket and then the bombs started to rain down. They fell in sticks of three or four and one could judge from the explosions of the first two in each stick where the subsequent ones were going to fall.'[6] Early the following morning, parachute slung over his shoulder, he set off for Fenchurch Street to catch a train to Hornchurch, passing through streets littered with debris and lined with smouldering buildings. No trains were running but there was a bus service. He asked two policemen for directions to the bus stop and they offered to show him the way. 'We walked through the arch onto the road and there was a queue of about a hundred people lined up by the bus stop. As we approached a number of people started looking at us curiously. "There's a bloody Hun!" said one of the leaders.' The crowd surged forward and Vigors realized what was happening. 'The blue/grey colour of my uniform was not dissimilar to that worn by pilots of the Luftwaffe . . . My head was covered by a crop of light blond hair. My parachute, helmet and flying boots made me look like somebody who had just got out of an aircraft. With a policeman on each side of me, they had taken me for a captured German.' The three backed against a wall while the policemen yelled that the pilot was one of their own, but nobody was listening. 'Now there were about forty around us and those at the back of the crowd were pushing forward on the leaders. I was suddenly scared. These wretched people who had seen their homes going up in flames meant business. "Hell," I thought to myself. "What a way for a fighter pilot to get killed: lynched by a bunch of East Enders."' But then those at the front of the mob realized their mistake. 'The ferocious hatred in their eyes turned to horror. "He's RAF," they yelled and started to try and push back the crowd behind them . . . then the reaction set in. I was quickly hoisted on to the shoulders of a few of the front division and carried through the crowd with everybody cheering and trying to clap me on the back.'

Compared to the days of July, the fighting had been hectic. Compared with the relentless activity of the first week of September, the pace had definitely slackened. In the six days before the blitz, Fighter Command flew 4,667 sorties. In the six days after it flew only 2,159. Some squadrons were as occupied as ever, but many in the front line were allowed a brief, longed-for spell of semi-relaxation. The pilots were young, strong and fit, and even a small respite had a powerful restorative effect. More welcome still was the slackening of attacks on the airfields. The Luftwaffe's attention seemed definitely to have shifted. Between 8 and 14 September there were only token raids on RAF bases. The work of repair could go relatively unmolested and unit rotations take place without the fear that newcomers would be arriving and exhausted units leaving in the middle of a raid.

Such was the rate of pilot losses before the blitz began that Dowding had been forced to reconsider the system of rotation. Inexperienced squadrons arriving from the north were suffering heavy casualties in short periods that shattered their cohesion as a unit and forced their early removal from the line. Dowding had reluctantly devised a system to keep seasoned squadrons for longer than he wished at the forefront of the battle, replacing losses with veterans from other squadrons. Units were to be divided into three categories. All those in 11 Group, the most important sector, were classed as category 'A' and were kept up to strength with fully trained pilots, as well as those units in 10 or 12 Group which would be the first to be called in as reinforcements. Squadrons that were fully equipped and up to strength and held as a second-line reserve were 'B' class. 'C' squadrons were those which had suffered the heaviest losses and were to be kept out of the fighting while pilots rested and new ones were trained. Veterans who had survived could, after recuperating, be posted away to replace losses in squadrons in the first two categories.

Dowding had held back a few strong assets. No. 92 Squadron, home of some of the most aggressive and skilful pilots in Fighter Command, had spent most of the summer in Pembrey in South Wales, and was impatient to get properly to grips with the Luftwaffe. On 8 September it arrived in Biggin Hill. Over the next few days, despite the lull, it still lost six aircraft, with two pilots killed and two seriously wounded. Even for a well-rested unit, manned by experienced pilots, the skies over south-east England continued to be a very dangerous place.

The diminished daytime presence of the Luftwaffe was assumed to be an indication that the last touches were being put to the invasion preparations and a landing was imminent. Church bells, the signal that the Germans were coming, had been rung, mistakenly, on 7 September and Local Volunteer Reservists had gamely set off to their roadblocks to stem the German advance. The continental Channel ports were choked with barges and boats and every night the RAF went to bomb them. 'The invasion is expected any moment now,' wrote the politician and diarist Henry 'Chips' Channon on Thursday, 12 September, 'probably some time during the weekend.'[7] In fact Hitler's plans were undergoing another revision. On 14 September, unpersuaded that the preparations were complete, he decided to put off his decision to give the order for the invasion to proceed until 17 September. Before that could happen, though, another great effort was required from the Luftwaffe.

The morning of Sunday, 15 September, was fair in contrast with the thundery, showery and unsettled weather of the preceding days. A warm sun burned off the light haze hanging over the coast. Dowding assumed the change in the climate would mean a busy day and at each sector station a full squadron was kept at readiness from first light. At North Weald Richard Barclay was woken at 4.30 with a cup of tea by an orderly. He was sleeping with the rest of the squadron in the dispersal hut. It was cold and he dressed quickly. He put on an Irvine flying suit over his pyjamas, which acted as insulation against the chill felt at high altitude in the unheated cockpit of his Hurricane, also a sweater, scarf and flying boots, and finally his yellow Mae West. He took down the blackout from the window and saw it was 'a lovely autumn morning with a duck-egg blue sky half covered with high cloud'. He wondered what he would be doing in peacetime: probably preparing to drive over to a relation's estate to shoot partridge and then sit down to a hearty lunch. He reflected that 'now a fine sunny day meant flying, flying, flying and terrific tension all day, gazing endlessly into the burning sun to see what wily Hun was lurking there, a fight or two perhaps, and someone not there to join the drinking in the bar that evening'.[8]

Outside he greeted Airman Barnes and Airman Parish, who were running up the engine of his Hurricane. He climbed into the cockpit and glanced over his instruments, checking that the petrol gauge was showing full and the airscrew set at fine pitch. He made sure that two pairs of gloves were stuffed where he knew where to find them and that his helmet was sitting on the reflector sight, with the oxygen and R/T leads connected up, ready for a fast getaway. He lay down on the grass and 'immediately became unconscious, as if doped'.

In what seemed like only a few moments he was awake again. 'I woke with a terrific start to see everyone pouring out of the hut, putting on Mae Wests, silk gloves . . . I could hear the telephone orderly repeating, "Dover, 20,000 feet, fifty plus bandits approaching from S E."' He ran, still half asleep, to his machine. The crew had already started the engine. They helped him into the cockpit and tightened his straps. He taxied out into position No. 2 in Yellow Section and took off, only full waking up when he switched on his R/T to hear the orders. His mouth 'was like the bottom of a birdcage from last night's party'. It was too early in the morning and he was 'not in the mood'.

The first blips indicating a raid had appeared on the screens of radar stations near Dover at about eleven o'clock. They represented a smallish formation of twenty-seven Dorniers from a base near Paris. Their appearance was passed on immediately to the control room at the Uxbridge headquarters of No. 11 Group, which Winston Churchill, on a whim, had decided to visit that day. The Dorniers had been late arriving at Calais, having had to re-form after scattering while climbing through cloud. When they got there their escorts, three *Gruppen* of twenty 109s each, were waiting for them, circling impatiently and wasting precious fuel. They knew that the extension of the raids to London meant that their already limited time over target was further reduced and they were operating at the outer reaches of their capacity. A further force of twenty-one Me 109s equipped with underslung bombs, protected by a similar escort, was due to overtake them and carry out a nuisance raid that would distract the defenders before the arrival of the main force.

To the controllers, the force of a hundred-plus aircraft now showing represented two possibilities. It might be another major raid aimed at London. It could equally be simply a large group of fighters preparing a free hunt to lure up the British fighters. Park judged, emphatically, that it was the former, and decided to bring all his forces to bear. He immediately ordered two squadrons up from Biggin Hill; then, ten minutes later, nine more squadrons from the airfields around London, eight of them arranged in pairs. He also requested a squadron from 10 Group to cover the south-west approaches to London. Finally, he ordered five squadrons from Duxford, massed in a Big Wing, to take off and be at 20,000 feet by the time they were over Hornchurch. Thirteen minutes after the first scramble order, a second set of orders was issued ordering another ten squadrons to climb to different heights in defensive positions around the capital. By midday, there were fifteen squadrons of Hurricanes, totalling 167 aircraft, and eight squadrons comprising 87 Spitfires in the air.

Park's responses had been developed from nearly two months of intensive decision-making while dealing with daily attacks and refined with the grim experience eight days previously of the first major raid on London. His plan was arranged in three phases. The first bombers would be attacked by Spitfires shortly after they crossed the coast in an attempt to try and break up the formations before they got near the targets. The Messerschmitts would then be expected to come to the rescue. By doing so, though, they would be burning fuel at four times the cruising rate in high-speed chases, further reducing the time they were able to stay with their charges. After the first jarring impact would come a relay of assaults by Hurricane squadrons arriving in pairs from all directions. The last phase would take place in the skies over London, when the remaining squadrons would descend on what it was hoped would by then be a battered and demoralized bomber force and a dwindling fighter escort as, out of ammunition and low on fuel, the Messerchmitts broke off and ran for home.

The advance guard of German fighters crossed the Kent coast just after 11.30 p.m., followed by the Dorniers. The Spitfires of 72 and 92 Squadrons were stationed on their right flank, just to the north and east of Ashford, waiting for them. For once the pilots had the greatly desired advantage of height. The early decision to scramble meant they had reached 20,000 feet. It was freezing up there even at the height of summer, and the cold bit through sheepskin jackets and fur-lined boots and silk gloves. The discomfort was forgotten as the pilots looked down at the Dorniers cruising westwards 9,000 feet below, then looked up to check that the sky was clear of escorts. In fact the German fighters were 3,000 feet underneath. The twenty Spitfires were led by Flight Lieutenant John 'Pancho' Villa of 72 Squadron. He ordered the two squadrons into line astern, then swung his machine over on to one wing and peeled off into a steep dive, followed, in a long chain, by the others. The sight of the British fighters galvanized the Messerschmitts, who turned to meet them. The Spitfires failed to break through to the bombers, although another Spitfire unit, 603 Squadron, which arrived to reinforce, shot down three Me 109s in the space of a few minutes.

But the action had succeeded in drawing some of the German fighters away from the bombers they were supposed to protect. The Dorniers flew on straight into the path of two Hurricane squadrons from Kenley, 501 and 253, who attacked them head-on. Two of the bombers were shot down, a third so badly damaged that it immediately turned for home. Those remaining held their formation, bunching up to maximize their formidable defensive firepower. As they moved westwards another twenty-four Hurricanes from 229 Squadron and the all-Polish unit, 303 Squadron, joined the mêlée. The body of aircraft crawled across the sky towards London. At the bottom were the bombers, plodding stoically on to their targets. Above and around them darted the rival fighters, wheeling, twisting and plunging, scrabbling for an advantage that it was only rarely possible to seize.

The sound of the battle drifted down to the placid fields and villages to a population which, despite the expected invasion, were engaged in the old rituals of a Sunday morning: returning from church or preparing the roast beef for lunch. The action looked far off and unreal. Yet the distant violence would intrude from time to time. Metal and flame would descend out of the azure, bringing with it death. Just after midday a Hurricane detached itself from the turmoil over the village of Staplehurst and dropped, spinning earthwards. The Belgian pilot, George Doutrepont, was dead. The machine roared down, the engine note rising ominously, and smashed into the green-and-cream painted railway station, killing a young ticket clerk and severely wounding the station master, sending flaming debris flying through the village.

The formation butted on. As the first British fighters turned away to rearm and refuel, four more Hurricane squadrons moved in from around the capital to block its path, some engaging the escorts while the rest tried to crash inside the bombers' ranks. Again the Dornier crews held their nerve. By now the Messerschmitt fighter-bombers had overhauled the main body of aeroplanes and reached south London, and were scattering bombs over the Victorian streets of Penge, Dulwich and Norwood.

The main body arrived a few minutes afterwards. By now the German fighters who had shepherded their charges through successive waves of Spitfires and Hurricanes were reaching the end of their reserves of petrol and ammunition and were faced with the choice of crash-landing or running for their lives. As the fuel gauges sank lower and the red warning lights began to glow, they started to swing away. By the time the bombers arrived over their targets, their formations were still intact but the phalanx protecting them had dwindled alarmingly. Through the Plexiglass canopies the bombers could see an unexpected – almost unbelievable – sight. The sky ahead, the air around, was dotted with small shapes that were rapidly getting bigger. Having survived some of the heaviest concentrations of British fighters they had ever encountered, they were now faced with a huge force of yet more Hurricanes and Spitfires, fighters which they had been told by their superiors did not exist.

The anti-aircraft batteries, which had begun to fire as the bombers crossed into the great brick bowl of south London, ceased their barrage for fear of hitting the approaching fighters. The Germans were now in the very unusual position of being significantly outnumbered. Six squadrons, Nos. 17, 41, 66, 73, 257 and 504, were over the city, a stirring sight to the population craning its necks below. More were on their way. A Spitfire squadron, No. 609 from 10 Group, was stationed in the west. And approaching from the north were five squadrons from Duxford, formed in a Big Wing.

The Hurricanes of 504 and 257 Squadrons were the first to engage. Sergeant Ray Holmes followed his leader, Squadron Leader John Sample, who 'more or less took us slap across the centre of the formation. The Dorniers didn't fly particularly tight, which was to their disadvantage. If they had done, they'd have had better fire power to beat off the fighters. But our CO went at them in a quarter attack and more or less went through them and spread them out a bit.'

Holmes discovered again that it was 'surprising how quickly you lose your overall view of a lot of aircraft. We were travelling at 250, 300 m.p.h., and at that sort of speed the air clears very quickly. You make one attack, turn round and come back again and you wonder where everyone's gone. Then, if you're lucky, you see one or two that you can go for, if you've broken them up.'[9] He fastened on to the rear of a bomber and began firing. His windscreen was drenched in flying oil. By the time it had cleared he was on the point of collision and dived steeply to flash underneath its belly. The Dornier had been hit and turned desperately for home. As it struggled out of London, it was attacked again, its second engine failed and it crash-landed in a field near Sevenoaks.

Ray Holmes now turned on a lone bomber and attacked it from head-on. After a few seconds his ammunition was exhausted, but he was determined to hold his course. The left wing of the fighter and the tail wing of the bomber struck with what Holmes later considered was a surprisingly slight shock. Almost immediately the Dornier began to break up, crashing to earth in front of Victoria Station. As it fell, two bombs and a canister filled with incendiary devices tumbled into the gardens of Buckingham Palace. The bombs were not fused but the incendiaries ignited, setting the lawns on fire. Despite the apparent gentleness of the collision, the controls of Holmes's Hurricane were gone. When the nose dipped he baled out. He landed on a block of flats, slithered down the roof and was saved from serious injury when his parachute snagged in the guttering and he found himself suspended a few feet above a dustbin.

With extraordinary determination, the Dorniers had persisted with their bombing run, aimed at the railway viaducts at Battersea. After releasing their bombs, the pilots threw their machines into the tightest turns they could manage and tried to flee the fighters. As they did so, the Hurricanes and Spitfires of the Duxford wing tipped down from 25,000 feet. The confusion was total. The British fighters were getting in each other's way in their determination to get a shot in, and there was a real danger of them shooting each other down. Richard Barclay turned to confront what he thought was an enemy fighter, only to identify it, just in time, as 'one of those confounded Spitfires again'.

As the formation fled, the fighters moved in to pick off stragglers. Rob Bodie attached himself to a crippled bomber limping along with a damaged engine. He raked it with fire and it slipped into a long shallow glide. He watched the gunner bale out, then flew alongside to inspect the damage. The pilot 'sat bolt upright in his seat, and he was either dead or wounded for he didn't even turn his head to look at me, or watch out for a place to land, but stared straight ahead. Suddenly a pair of legs appeared, dangling from the underneath hatch. The other gunner was baling out. He got out as far as his waist, then the legs kicked.' Bodie realized the man was stuck and felt a momentary spasm of pity, then 'thought of the people down below, wives, mothers, kiddies, huddled in their shelters, waiting for the "All Clear".'

But the sight disturbed him. 'The legs still wriggled and thrashed, 2,000 feet above the cool green fields, trapped in a doomed aircraft, gliding down, a dead pilot at the controls. First one boot came off, then the other. He had no socks on, his feet were quite bare; it was very pathetic.' The bomber was down to 1,000 feet. Bodie had an image of the gunner being cut in half when they hit the ground, scraped away like grated cheese. 'In spite of all he stood for, he didn't deserve a death like that. I got my sights squarely on where his body would be, and pressed the button. The legs were still. The machine went on. The pilot *was* dead. He made no attempt to flatten out and land, but went smack into a field and the aeroplane exploded. I saw pieces sail past me as I flew low overhead. I didn't feel particularly jubilant.'[10]

David Cox, who had arrived with 19 Squadron, engaged some of the remaining Me 109s but broke off to attack a fleeing Dornier, which escaped by ducking into a convenient cloud. Keen to shoot something down, he carried on. 'I had plenty of ammunition and flew south a bit. To my right I saw six single aircraft which I thought were Hurricanes. We were always told you shouldn't fly around on your own and you should always try and join up with any friendly aircraft.' The angle he had been approaching from was deceptive. As they approached he realized they were Me 109s. 'Four of them dived away and I saw nothing more of them. Of the others, one climbed behind me and one climbed in front. The one behind attacked and I turned very violently and he just carried straight on . . . but the one who had been above me turned. As he was coming at right angles I fired a ninety-degree deflection shot and he went down and crashed.'[11]

The reluctance of the other Me 109s to engage was an indication of their desperation to get back to their bases. All the remaining raiders were heading for France. A Messerschmitt escort was waiting to shepherd them home. Despite the great concentration of force and the huge expenditure of ammunition, only six of the Dorniers had actually been shot down. The remaining nineteen struggled back some way or another, most of them sieved with bullets, frozen air whistling through the holes in the Plexiglass canopies, their interiors stinking of cordite and petrol, the wounded moaning or unconscious, the dead slumped, still strapped in where the fighters' bullets had caught them. It was not the damage that had been inflicted that was significant. It was the story the survivors had to tell.

The bomber crews were shocked at the strength of the British resistance, their superiors at first disbelieving. While they were being debriefed, another attack was already under way, bigger than the last. This time there were 114 bombers, Heinkels and Dorniers, which had taken off from bases in Holland and northern France to form up over Cap Gris Nez, half-way between Boulogne and Calais, and set course for the pebble promontory of Dungeness, thirty miles across the Channel. They arrived in two waves. In the first were three formations of sixty-eight bombers. The second was smaller, two formations of forty-six bombers. Each formation had an escort of about thirty Me 109s. Another 150 fighters cruised in a loose box around the core of the force, throttling back, swinging from side to side so as to remain just above stalling speed and not outstrip the bombers, with a similar number roaming ahead and on either side to sweep the way clear. Once again the target was London, this time the Royal Victoria and the West India Docks.

The British pilots had landed, spoken to their intelligence officers, briefed the crews on the performance and needs of their machines and flopped down for a few moments' rest while their machines were checked, refuelled and rearmed. Many fell straight to sleep. Richard Barclay and the other 249 pilots 'had a rotten lunch in our dispersal hut sitting on our beds'. The excitement of the morning had not subsided before they were in the air again. At 2 p.m., Park ordered eight squadrons off in pairs to patrol over Sheerness, Chelmsford, Kenley and Hornchurch. Five minutes later he scrambled four more; then a further eight. Reinforcements from 10 and 12 Group were summoned to come to the defence of the capital, including a Big Wing of five squadrons from

Duxford, comprising twenty-seven Hurricanes and twenty Spitfires.

The first clash took place over Romney Marsh. As the Germans crossed over land, the advance guard of twenty-seven fighters from 41, 92 and 222 Squadrons sailed in to the attack. The escorting Messerschmitts broke off to confront them. Pilot Officer Bob Holland, 92 Squadron's brilliant pianist, was shot up from behind. The German pilot watched him slide back the canopy and step out into space. He landed, unhurt, near Staplehurst. Park ordered 303 and 602 Squadrons to scramble. With that, every one of 11 Group's units were now engaged. With outside reinforcements, 276 Hurricanes and Spitfires were facing or approaching the enemy, slightly more than had been in action in the morning. This time, though, the odds were not so favourable. Their task was to stop the bombers, which, if they maintained their formations, were capable of defending themselves strongly. To get to them they had to break through a defensive screen of 450 fighters. With height, the British pilots had the tactical advantage over those providing the close escort. But once they went in to attack they were vulnerable to the German outriders, flying high and wide to swoop as soon as they saw a British fighter commit himself to the dive.

As the German formations breasted the first wave of attacks, they were confronted with the second line of defence, Hurricanes from 213 and 607 Squadrons, who flew straight into them. Pilot Officer Paddy Stephenson of 607 Squadron was unable to avoid a collision, smashing into a Dornier and sending his own and the other machine spinning out of the sky. Tom Cooper-Slipper, a nineteen-year-old pilot officer, after being shot up while closing on another Dornier and realizing he would have to bale out, decided to ram it before jumping. Appalled crews saw him overhaul the bomber and turn into it, knocking it into an uncontrolled dive. Astonishingly, both Stephenson and Cooper-Slipper survived.

The German force was now arranged in three groups approaching London down an air corridor that took it past Maidstone, reaching the widening mouth of the Thames as it flowed past Gravesend, where it would swing left towards Docklands. But before the bombers and fighters reached the targets, they had to fight their way through the third and thickest line of defence, the squadrons now massed before the south-eastern approaches to the city. The bombers cruised on, in bright sunshine one minute, the next tunnelling through the clammy grey of towering stacks of cumulus that reared up from 2,000 feet. Just after 2.30 p.m., ten minutes away from the bombing zone, the British fighters plunged into their third major assault. Bobby Oxspring with 66 Squadron was detailed to watch for fighters while the rest of the squadron tried to get among the centre group of Heinkels. With no threat apparent, he dived towards the action, where he found a bomber which had been chiselled away from the formation and was 'getting a hell of a plastering by four or five Hurricanes and Spits'. He 'gave it a squirt for luck just before he went into cloud. When last I saw him his wheels had come down and he was looking awful sick. My number 3 followed him through the cotton wool . . . along with several of the other fighter boys wasping around. He told me afterwards they succeeded in making [it] crash on a nearby aerodrome.'[12] The Heinkel put down on West Malling, with the fighters still in hot pursuit. It was to be claimed as a 'definite' in numerous individual combat reports.

The presence of the German fighters made such unrestrained behaviour extremely dangerous. Pilot Officer Tom Neil, a friend of Richard Barclay's in 249 Squadron, had just shot down a Dornier and been momentarily mesmerized by the sight of 'spreadeagled arms and legs as two bodies flew past my head, heavy with the bulges that were undeveloped parachutes . . . the crew! Baling out!' Then he was engulfed by Me 109s arriving to take revenge. 'In a frenzy of self-preservation, I pulled and pushed and savagely yanked my aircraft about, firing whenever I caught sight of a wing or a fuselage in my windscreen. They were not sighted bursts, just panic hosings designed to scare rather than kill and directed against aircraft that were often within yards of me . . . a murderous, desperate interlude.'[13]

Such encounters imposed huge physical strains. The crushing G forces endured in steep dives induced blackouts so that in any combat a pilot might be unconscious for several seconds, then come to find he was upside down or screaming towards the ground. At high speeds a fighter's delicate controls became stiff and leaden and it took real strength to shift the stick so that after a fight the pilot's right arm would be throbbing. The layers of warm clothing needed against the intense cold of high altitudes, the oxygen mask that enveloped half the face, became horribly restricting in the intense physical exertion of a dogfight and pilots climbed out of the narrow cockpits soaked in sweat. Almost everyone, even the 'Tubbys' and the 'Jumbos', lost pounds during periods of action.

Despite the vicious attentions of the fighters, the German bombers held their formations and pressed on doggedly through the flowing, incandescent line of tracer and the foul black mushrooms of flak. Now and then a machine would dip earthwards or slip behind, engine coughing, away from the comforting embrace of the pack. But at 2.40 p.m. most of them were still there, approaching London and preparing to go into their bombing runs. The two formations aiming for the Royal Victoria Docks were unable to find the target, which was hidden under a bank of cloud. Just beyond, though, to the north and clearly visible, lay railway lines and a gasworks. They would have to do. The lead bombers tilted towards them. The bomb doors opened and the crews behind watched a ripple of white explosions race across the dingy townscape of West Ham thousands of feet below. The second formation's target, the Surrey Commercial Docks on the south side of the river, was also cloaked in cloud. Three Hurricane squadrons coming in to intercept watched the Dorniers swing into a right turn and head away, scattering bombs as they departed over the suburbs of south-east London.

On the way back they were harassed constantly by fighters and flak. The most vulnerable were the strays, deprived of the reassuring crossfire that a well-maintained formation could put up, reliant on the protection of any Messerschmitts which had noticed their plight and had sufficient petrol remaining to go to their aid, ducking wherever they could into cloud. Some were fortunate enough to meet up with a force of fifty Me 109s that arrived over the middle of Kent to help the bombers home.

As the retreating bombers crossed the beaches of Kent, fringed with barbed wire, scored with trenches and sown with mines in preparation for the invasion, the attacking fighters fell away. Everywhere now the fighters were coming in to land. During the ninety minutes of the action, twenty-eight squadrons had been ordered off and every one of them had been in action. As the pilots reached for mugs of tea and lit up cigarettes, Fighter Command was potentially at its most vulnerable point in the entire summer. For the first time in their handling of the battle, Dowding and Park had thrown all their immediate resources into one fight. A second German raid now, aimed at the airfields, would have caught almost every man and machine in 11 Group and the neighbouring sectors defenceless on the ground. Park had gambled that the thunderclouds which blessedly sprawled over nine tenths of the sky above his main fighter stations would make it very difficult for an accurate attack. The anxious moments passed. One by one the squadrons came back to readiness, waiting for another onslaught that never came.

The combined fighting of the main action of the day, from first sighting to the last bomber trailing over the coast, had lasted less than five hours. In the midday and afternoon engagements the Germans had lost fifty-six aircraft in action and 136 men were either dead or missing. It was the worst day they had suffered so far. The RAF losses had been relatively slight: twenty-nine aircraft, which were easily replaceable, and twelve pilots killed. The pilots could afford to feel a sense of profound satisfaction. Rob Bodie was exhausted when the order came to return to base. 'The day had been a year. I flew to the coast and set course for home. Passing low over fields and villages, rivers and towns, I looked down at labourers working, children at play, beside a red-brick schoolhouse, a bomb crater two streets away; little black heads in the streets turning to white blobs as they heard my engine and looked up. I thought of workers in shops and factories, of stretcher-bearers and ARP wardens. I hoped the 'All Clear' had gone. I was tired. I'd done my best for them.'[14]

17

Autumn Sunset

There were many parties that night as the pilots celebrated the unusual feeling of being in control of their own skies. The next day's newspapers presented 15 September as a great victory for the RAF and one of the most severe defeats the Luftwaffe had yet suffered, and they carried hugely inflated figures of the German losses.

The following morning, rain clouds covered much of south-east England and the bombers stayed away. No one yet felt, though, that the battle was ebbing. There was little sign that the German invasion preparations had been affected by the setback. In the Channel ports the build-up of boats and barges continued, despite a nightly RAF bombardment. Throughout the early autumn, tension remained high. Richard Barclay wrote in his diary on 25 September that 'everyone was rather expecting an invasion to break out at dawn this morning because it was said that the Boche was sweeping the Channel of mines yesterday. Everyone was therefore very much at readiness at 5.50 a.m.' In his squadron there was concern at civilian complacency. On 29 September there was a rare political discussion between the pilots. Among their conclusions were that 'the British people are still fast asleep. They haven't begun to realize the power of our enemies and that they have to give their all, as well as the Forces, to win . . . That the threat of invasion is very real and not a sort of flap or bluff . . . that we need dictatorial methods to fight a dictator . . . that 1 German is nice, 2 Germans are swine.'[1]

The caution seemed justified when, on 18 September, the bombers returned. During the morning there had been several combats at high altitude between German fighters and ninety Hurricanes and Spitfires sent up by Park, who thought the formation showing on the radar screens might indicate a bombing raid. Five Spitfires were shot down, and a pilot killed, a pointless waste of resources. When, later, a small force of bombers heavily escorted by Me 109s appeared over Dover, Park ignored the provocation, and it went on to bomb Chatham and Rochester. When a third, larger force appeared, apparently heading for London, he had to react. At its core were two formations of Junkers 88s flown by inexperienced crews, drafted in to replace the losses. Fourteen squadrons went up to meet them. Geoffrey Edge, the master of the head-on attack, was at Kenley when the order came through, playing a post-lunch game of squash after being released at midday. He managed to assemble six other pilots and they took off hurriedly to be vectored on to a course by the controller that took them into an excellent attacking position. They lay back in the sun, invisible to the bombers and the Me 109s flying closely round them and overhead. Edge ordered his men into a diagonal line, a wingspan apart and two aeroplane lengths between them. He selected the bomber to the left of the leader for himself. They were to try and attack any bomber that had not been hit. The two groups of aircraft were now approaching each other at a closing speed of 180 to 200 yards a second. Edge calculated that would allow five seconds of firing time before he would have to drag back on the stick and roll to the right to avoid collision. He opened fire at 1,000 yards.

'Almost instantly,' he wrote, 'his cockpit starts to disintegrate. His plane swerves towards his leader, crashing into the tail plane. I leave my guns firing on the port side of the formation. The bombers are breaking up and I have moved my aim to my starboard and at this range I just left the guns firing as I aimed at one cockpit after another.' Just before a crash became inevitable, he pulled up, then threw his machine into a steep dive and felt G forces drain the vision from his eyes. As it returned he saw dark shapes flashing past his wings. The Germans were jettisoning their bombs. He had seen no incoming fire from the bombers, who appeared to have been oblivious to the attack until it was too late.[2]

Such encounters could not be endured repeatedly by the Luftwaffe without serious damage to morale. Seventeen aircraft were lost and forty-one men were dead or missing as a result of the day's action. Members of a bomber flight that had lost four of its six aircraft in the raid on London got drunk that evening in memory of their dead comrades and sang a defiant dirge, 'Es blitzen die stahlernen schwingen, Uns hat der Tommy verfehlt' ('The steel wings are flashing, the Tommies have missed us again'). But implicit in the song was the recognition that, despite the assurances of the commanders, the RAF was far from beaten. Each night the bombers were bringing fire and death to London. But the violence seemed to be leading nowhere. Goering assured the crews that their attacks 'at the heart of the British Empire . . . have reduced the British plutocracy to fear and terror. The losses which you have inflicted upon the much vaunted Royal Air Force with your determined fighter combat are irreplaceable.'[3] If the first assertion was true, there was no sign of a British surrender. The second, they knew from harsh experience, to be false.

The pilots and crews were as patriotic as their British counterparts. Their doggedness and determination were testimony to their conviction that they could win. But that assurance was fading. 'At the beginning we weren't particularly taken aback at the resistance,' said Gerhard Schöpfel. 'We thought it wouldn't last. But as it continued we became more and more surprised at how resilient they were and the fact that they didn't back down.'[4]

By the time Goering delivered his morale-boosting address, plans for the invasion had undergone further modification. On 19 September the decision was taken to postpone the issuing of orders for the final preparations once again, this time without setting a new date for the question to be reconsidered. As the other service chiefs pointed out forcefully, the Luftwaffe had failed to deliver the conditions necessary for a successful operation, and was even unable to protect the transports waiting to carry the Wehrmacht to England's shores.

The problems facing 'Sea Lion' were not discernible to British pilots, who felt themselves to be in a limitless conflict. The desperation felt in the squadrons during the end of August and the first week in September had eased, however. Aircraft production was booming and the new Hurricanes and Spitfires were the more powerful Mark II models. By the third week in September, almost every squadron in II Group had a full complement of pilots. Fresh pilots were arriving in the system in quantity, allowing the creation of six new fighter squadrons. Veterans of the fighting of the early part of the summer, who had spent the months from June to September serving as instructors, now rested, were volunteering to return to operations, among them Killy Kilmartin and his old No. 1 Squadron comrade, Billy Drake, who joined fighter squadrons in September and October.

But even with the slight relaxation, the pilots were still suffering. As September wore on the Luftwaffe began altering its tactics. The frequency of daylight bombing raids by large formations fell away, though they continued to be launched intermittently, sometimes with considerable success. On 25 September a fleet of Heinkels devastated the Bristol Aeroplane Co. factory at Filton. The following day the Supermarine works at Woolston, near Southampton, was hit. Production was disrupted, but there was no lasting effect on the supply of machines. On 27 September there was a daytime raid by Ju 88s aimed at London which was beaten back with heavy losses on both sides. Three days later, 100 bombers and 200 fighters launched another attempt to reach London, which again was forced back.

The Luftwaffe was adjusting to the fact that, since 15 September, its circumstances had changed, significantly and for the worse. If it persisted with mass raids in daylight it would face devastating punishment. Instead, Fighter Command was now increasingly having to contend with precision attacks by Me 110s using their speed and their bomb-carrying capacity to hit important targets. At the beginning of October there was a further refinement when each fighter wing was ordered to adapt thirty of its new generation of Me 109s to carry an underslung bomb, thus transforming them into *Jabos* or fighter bombers. The Luftwaffe commanders also took to sending masses of regular Me 109s on high-altitude sweeps over southern England. In his previous, reduced condition,

Dowding would have chosen not to react. Fighters on their own could do little damage except to other fighters. As his forces recovered their strength, however, he decided to confront them in a further assertion of Fighter Command's growing control of British skies.

As the days went by, the pilots flew higher and higher, outbidding each other in the search for altitude and the tactical advantage. Only the Spitfires could get near the Me 109s. Flying at 25,000 and 30,000 feet in an unheated, unpressurized cockpit meant new discomforts. Pilots experienced the illusion that their stomachs were inflating grotesquely. They felt intense pain in their elbows, knees and shoulders caused by tiny bubbles of gas in the blood. The prolonged inhalation of oxygen created a burning sensation when they breathed and the skin around their mouths became raw and tender. Most pilots switched it on at 15,000 feet. Above 20,000 feet it was an absolute necessity. Without it they quickly developed anoxia, or oxygen starvation. It induced feelings of giddiness, nausea, sometimes rapture, then insensibility. A fault in the oxygen supply at great height often meant death. On 10 October two pilots, Sergeant Edward Bayley of 249 Squadron and Sergeant H. Allgood of 253 Squadron died within a few minutes of each other in crashes that were attributed to unconsciousness brought on by oxygen failure.

Leave became more regular, but the hours at readiness were still long and the yearning for rain and cloud that would limit flying was frequently thwarted by the fine weather that annoyingly reappeared just when it seemed that an English autumn had finally set in. The prolonged contact with danger meant that, sooner or later, even the most experienced pilots ran out of skill or luck. Birdy Bird-Wilson was unfortunate to meet Adolf Galland over the Thames estuary on 24 September and was forced to bale out, becoming his fortieth victim. The insouciant spirit cultivated by 92 Squadron was severely tested by a spate of casualties. 'First Norman Hargreaves had gone,' wrote Tony Bartley. 'Then Sergeant Eyles. Gus Edwards was found dead a week after he'd gone missing, in the middle of a forest. Similarly Howard Hill, after three weeks, lodged in the top of a tall tree, decomposing in his cockpit, his hands on the controls and the top of his head blown off by a cannon shell.'[5]

Bartley wrote to his mother on 19 September that, despite the losses, 'the morale of the Fighter Boys is terrific. We will crack the German air force at all costs. This is our greatest and diciest hour but we are proud to have the chance to deal with it.' He made a thoughtful but futile appeal for her not to worry. 'I am safe until my predestined time runs out. I am happy and almost enjoying myself. In these times of danger one gets drawn much closer to one's friends, and a great spiritual feeling of comradeship and love envelops everyone. I can't explain, but everyone seems much better men somehow.'[6]

It seemed to Bartley that the only one unaffected by the searing events was Brian Kingcome, for whom 'the war in the air seemed just an incidental interruption which kept him occupied during the day'. Even Kingcome's composure was disturbed when he was shot down on 15 October, apparently by Spitfires who had either mistaken him for a Messerschmitt or who hit him while attacking a German who was on his tail. He jumped and survived.

But survival meant many things. George Bennions had been patrolling high at 25,000 feet and was about to return to base with the rest of the squadron when he saw a group of Hurricanes being pursued by some Me 109s. He dived towards them and found he was on his own. 'I thought, "I'll just try to attack the rearmost one of the squadron, shoot him down if I can and then get away." It didn't happen like that.'[7] He made one attack and saw his bullets striking the German fighter. Then his machine shuddered with the impact of a cannon shell hitting the right-hand side and exploding inside the cockpit. He found he could not see and felt terrible pain in his right arm and leg. Blinded, he groped at the canopy to push it back one handed as his right arm was useless. So was his right leg. The clarity that seems to have flooded the thinking of many pilots as they faced death came to his rescue. He undid the small hatch on the left of the cockpit, tipped the machine to port and tumbled out. Now the problem was getting the parachute to open. The release cord was on the right of the harness. He reached around with his good hand feeling for it and somehow grasped it, pulled and felt the kick of the harness between his legs as the parachute opened, then blacked out.

He came to in a field, told his rescuers who he was and lapsed into a coma.

He woke up in the Queen Victoria hospital, East Grinstead. While he was unconscious he had undergone preliminary operations performed by the plastic surgeon Sir Archibald McIndoe for severe burns received during his struggle to get out of the cockpit. Bennions was unaware that he was burned. When he tried to open his eyes he thought he was blind. An awful depression descended. 'I felt terribly isolated. I couldn't see. I couldn't hear very well. I couldn't recognize people unless it was somebody very close to me. My wife came down and my mother came down. I felt so deflated, just as though half of my life had been taken and the other half wasn't worth bothering with.' He was told that he had lost the sight of one eye. To save the other, the damaged one would have to be removed. Bennions resisted, knowing this would mean the end of the flying life he loved, but in the end was forced to agree.

He was 'feeling extremely sorry for myself' when he got a message from another patient, a friend who had joined the air force with him from school. He had badly burned legs and asked Bennions to come and see him. Bennions

was on crutches at the time, but I managed to get over there with a hell of a lot of struggle and self-pity. As I opened the door in Ward 3 I saw what I can only describe as the most horrifying thing I have seen in my life. [There] was this chap who had been badly burnt, really badly burnt. His hair was burnt off, his eyebrows were burnt off, his eyelids were burnt off. You could just see his staring eyes. His nose was burnt, there were just two holes in his face. His lips were badly burnt. Then, when I looked down, his hands were burnt. I looked down at his feet also. His feet were burnt. I got through the door on the crutches with a bit of a struggle. This chap started propelling a wheelchair down the ward. Half-way down he picked up a chair with his teeth. Then he brought this chair down the ward, threw it alongside me and said: 'Have a seat, old boy.' I cried. I thought, 'What have I got to complain about?' From then on, everything fell into place.

The man was Sergeant Ralph Carnall of 111 Squadron, who had been shot down on 16 August. He underwent a year of treatment by McIndoe and eventually went back to flying.

For the burns cases, the relief of having escaped death did not survive the first look in the mirror. Lying on the operating table shortly after being shot down, Geoffrey Page caught a glimpse of himself reflected in the overhead lights. He saw 'a hideous mass of swollen, burnt flesh that had once been a face'.[8] Arriving at East Grinstead for reconstruction surgery, he met the other patients, including Richard Hillary, who had been shot down and baled out into the sea on 3 September. 'Standing at the foot of the bed was one of the queerest apparitions I had ever seen. The tall figure was clad in a long loose-fitting dressing gown that trailed to the floor. The head was thrown back so that the owner appeared to be looking along the line of his nose. Where normally two eyes would be, were two large bloody red circles of raw skin. Horizontal slots in each showed that behind, still lay the eyes. A pair of hands wrapped in large lint covers lay folded across his chest. Cigarette smoke curled up from the long holder clenched between the ghoul's teeth. The empty sleeves of the dressing gown hung limply, lending the apparition a sinister air. It evidently had a voice . . . it was condescending in tone. "Ah! Another bloody cripple!" '[9]

The victims were acutely aware of the effect they had on others. Page was taken to the pub by two squadron friends. For a moment he felt he was back in normal life until he overheard the landlord's wife whispering loudly to her husband. 'The poor dears, and them so young and all. Quite turns me stomach.' The barmaid at the Red Lion in Basingstoke, where patients from the hospital at Park Prewett nearby would go for a drink, was by contrast magnificently humane, welcoming burned pilots with a kiss and a greeting: 'My darling, how lovely to see you.'[10] As a Waaf, Edith Heap frequently encountered the ravaged faces, and made sure to always look them, unflinchingly, in the eye. But the sight was desperately upsetting. In 1942 Richard Hillary visited an old comrade, Ron Berry, who had been a sergeant in 603 Squadron with him and was now commanding a fighter squadron. In other circumstances it would have been normal for Hillary to have been introduced to the pilots. 'It was a very difficult decision I had to make,' Berry said later. 'With my young flock I'm afraid I denied him the pleasure of going round the squadron . . . I think one or two of them would have felt it very difficult to stomach.'[11]

As October wore on, the number of daylight bombing raids dwindled but the fighter sweeps persisted, requiring the squadrons to maintain a high level of vigilance. The Hurricane units could do little against them. No. 249 Squadron was still awaiting its Mark II replacements and its aeroplanes were showing their age. Most of them had developed oil leaks that blotted out the windscreens after half an hour in the air. On many patrols the pilots sighted the condensation trails of Messerschmitts high above. They were unable to reach them but lived in fear of them swooping down. On the third trip of the day on 30 September, Richard Barclay noted that 'we had hundreds of 109s above us. We were too high for the Hurricane anyway . . . an awful trip as we were quite helpless, just waiting to be attacked.'

On 12 October the squadron was

up before breakfast, climbing up to 23,000 feet and patrolling all over Kent and south London. We were looking for some 109s which for once were said to be below us. But no luck in the first hour. We were floating about over Dover with 257 Squadron, who were meant to be guarding our tails, below us, when I happened to look back to the left and there was a glistening yellow nose pointed very much in my direction about fifty yards away. I immediately took action to avoid his quarter attack in the shape of a violent turn to the left and lots of bottom rudder. The inevitable result at that height was a flick roll and spin. I got out, had a good look around and saw three 109s 2,000 feet above. I kept a good eye open for the 109s and rejoined the squadron. Unfortunately my No. 2 has not been heard of since this short mêlée.[12]

Nothing had gone right. On the second scramble a wireless fault meant that the pilots were unable to hear the controller and the sortie was abandoned. The replacement pilots arriving at the squadron were proving slow to learn. Barclay complained that 'the new sergeant pilots, of whom we have all too many, didn't take off in their right sections, the resulting chaos taking some time to sort out. We've almost got to train them in formation flying.' The third operation was also 'a farce. As we took off we saw the trails of the Me 109 bombers over London . . . we were scrambled twenty minutes late! As usual this was due to Group's slowness . . . it was ridiculous taking off at all.'

The new tactic of sending off squadrons in pairs that Park had introduced at the beginning of September was proving difficult to operate, as he had known it would be. There were further frustrations as the brother squadrons tried to work out new flying formations to reduce their vulnerability to fighter attack, slowly moving away from the reliance on 'vics' and moving towards the *rotte* system of covering pairs used by the Germans. But the uncharacteristic note of irritability in Barclay's diary had deeper causes. He had arrived at the height of the battle on 1 September. He got his first proper break on 27 October. He was, as he admitted, in need of it. 'I'm glad I've got some leave coming along,' he wrote a few days beforehand. 'I'm getting so intolerant of the shortcomings of the new pilots.' Here and there, between the accounts of beery nights in the mess and at the Thatch in Epping to celebrate a clutch of medal awards, a touch of sadness creeps in. After he heard of the death of his friend Percy Burton he noted: 'I am now the only one left of the five Cranwellians of the squadron.'

Almost everyone had lost a dear friend by now. Tim Vigors spent most of his evenings with Hilary Edridge. Their backgrounds were different. Edridge came from Bath and was interested in music. Vigors was steeped in the horsy traditions of the Anglo-Irish upper class. But, since meeting at the start of the year, they had become inseparable. Almost every night they would drink beer and play darts with the locals in the pubs around the base. Once or twice a week they went to London for dinner and a tour of the nightclubs. On the morning of 30 October, shortly after they had returned from a trip to town, together with Vigors's other constant companion, his lurcher Snipe, they took off together from Hornchurch. They attacked a formation of Dorniers coming in north of Dover and were immediately bounced by Me 109s. A cloud of smoke engulfed a Spitfire on Vigors's right. He knew it must be Edridge. Back at Hornchurch he 'waited in dread. Still no sign of Hilary. All the rest of the squadron were home . . . an hour passed and still no news. I had no appetite for lunch and waited by the telephone at dispersal. At about 2 p.m. the news came through from Group Headquarters. The wreckage of a Spitfire bearing Hilary's markings had been found in a field near Sevenoaks. The pilot was dead.'

Vigors felt something he had never felt before.

A wave of misery swept over me. Up till now I had been able to shrug off the deaths of even my close friends. But this was different. Hilary had been like my brother for the past nine months. We had pooled all our hopes, thoughts and fears and had somehow managed to support each other through the trauma of those times. Now he was gone. I just couldn't get my mind to accept it. I called Snipe and together we walked off down the airfield. I tried to explain what had happened, but he just wagged his tail and didn't seem to understand. Then something occurred which had not happened in years. I started to cry. Snipe realized there was something wrong. I sat down on the grass and he nuzzled up to me. I pulled myself together and suddenly a different emotion took hold of me, an emotion which I had not experienced before in my life. Cold, impossible to control, hatred.[13]

The Fighter Boys had grown up. The days were cooler and darker now. The fabulous summer flickered and died. Lightness of heart was harder to sustain. At Biggin Hill, 92 Squadron fought hard and then drank, joked and flirted at the White Hart or in their improvised nightclub at Southwood Manor. But there was melancholy behind the laughter. At the end of October, Pilot Officer Roy Mottram sent a letter to Bunty Nash, a much-loved Waaf officer known by the squadron from its time at Pembrey, with news of her friends. The old gang were going; dead, wounded or posted away.

92 has a number of strange faces these days [he wrote]. One or two of
them are real good types well up to standard! Bill Watling rejoined us a
couple of days ago and everybody was pleased to meet him again. He
seems little the worse for his experience, but has rather an ersatz
healthy look about his face – the result of his burns – but that will
vanish with time. He is simply itching to be back and wipe off the
'black' as he calls it, and I feel sorry for the next Hun he has in his
sights. Alan is on sick leave at the moment . . . Brian is going on
famously, but the powers that be want to move him to Halton and he
definitely objects in no small manner. X has been having a pretty rotten
time of it and his nerves have been in a pretty shattering state for some
time. He came back today from seven days' leave and I hope he is much
better. He took to the bottle in no small degree and quickly earned the
nom-de-plume 'Boy Drunkard'. That is one of the little things that war
does and is quite beyond the ken of the average layman who fondly
believes the Fighter Boys can stand anything without it showing.[14]

Bill Watling was killed four months later. Mottram survived until the
following August, when he was shot down over France. The Boy
Drunkard sobered up and survived the war.

The strain was continuous, the German attacks relentless. But now
they lacked purpose or meaning. The daylight raids could never change
the course of the war. The nightly blitz caused grief, misery and discomfort, but never the 'mass psychosis and emigration' the Germans
desired. 'Operation Sealion' remained technically alive, but the autumn
gales waiting to sweep the Channel made its implementation unlikely, at
least until the New Year. On 12 October, Field-Marshal Keitel, the head
of the OKW, informed the Wehrmacht that the plan would remain in
effect only as a means of exerting political and military pressure on
Britain, though its execution would remain as a possibility for the spring
or early summer. The great battle faded. Its actual end was never clearly
discernible to the pilots. On 31 October, though, it seemed that some
climacteric had been passed. For the first time since anyone could
remember, neither side lost a man or an aeroplane in battle.

18

Rhubarbs and Circuses

The glorious summer died and autumn faded into winter. Fighter Command changed with the seasons. There were new faces at the top. On 25 November, as soon as it was safe to do so, Dowding was removed and the Deputy Chief of the Air Staff, Sholto Douglas, put in to replace him. At the same time, Keith Park was shifted from 11 Group to make way for Trafford Leigh-Mallory, his old antagonist and a man he detested. The departures were expected, yet the pilots felt unhappy at the speed with which Dowding and Park were sent on their way. They were a distant, unconvivial pair, but their dedication and decency, and the intelligence of their handling of the summer fighting, had won them the admiration, even affection, of those they sent into battle. The official explanation was that they were tired and the circumstances of the war had altered. Dowding went off on a mission to the United States. Park was given a training command. Most in 11 Group felt that the two were the victims of jealousy and intrigue. It seemed to Al Deere that they had 'won the Battle of Britain but lost the battle of words that followed, with the result that they . . . were cast aside in their finest hour'.[1]

It was true, though, that the air war had taken a different turn. From the end of the year, as Luftwaffe daytime activity fell away, Fighter Command increasingly took the offensive. The roles were gradually reversed. Now it was British fighters escorting bombers to strike German targets in northern France, or wheeling provocatively over the Luftwaffe bases, trying to tempt the Messerschmitts up to fight in the RAF's adaptation of Jagdgeschwader free-hunt tactics.

The squadrons had also changed. Many now contained only a handful of the original members who had been there when the serious fighting started. Of the twenty-two pilots who had been with 32 Squadron when it celebrated at the White Hart in Brasted on 15 August, only four, including Michael Crossley, remained at the end of the year. In between, at least a dozen had been posted away. Six had been badly wounded. Another six had been killed. When Al Deere's squadron, 54, was finally moved out of the line, only four of the pilots who first went into battle were left. Its character was modified further when the unit was designated as category 'C'. Its more experienced members were sent off to stiffen front-line units and Deere was given the job of training up novices.

The few were becoming many. The pilot shortage was solved. Young men were pouring out of the operational training units. At the beginning of July there had been forty-four Hurricane and Spitfire squadrons in Fighter Command. By the end of 1940 there were a total of seventy-one squadrons, with a secure supply of ever-improving aircraft. Many of the newcomers, as the months passed, came from abroad. During 1941, 609 Squadron had pilots from Belgium, France, Poland, Canada, the United States, New Zealand and Rhodesia pass through its ranks. The most cosmopolitan squadrons distilled a new spirit from the mix of nationalities and it was noted that they were often the most happy and successful. But it was clear that the old intimacy was cooling.

With the slackening of the crisis, military discipline, eroded by the frantic conditions of the summer, began to be reasserted. No. 92 Squadron was only a year old, but in its brief life it had cultivated an air of separateness and indifference to the rules that had been tolerated or overlooked because of its great success in destroying German aircraft. Its self-absorption had been reinforced during September and October by heavy losses that bound the survivors together, darkened their mood and increased their resentment of outsiders.

During much of the heavy fighting, the squadron had operated without an effective permanent commanding officer. Squadron Leader Phillip Sanders, who had led the squadron from the relative quiet of Pembrey into the heat of Biggin Hill at the beginning of September, set himself on fire lighting a cigarette after returning, soaked in petrol, from a sortie on the 15th. He was succeeded by Robert Lister, a Cranwell graduate and pre-war career officer, who had spent most of the war encased in plaster after a flying accident. Shortly after taking over he was shot down, badly wounded and declared unfit for flying. Instead of choosing a successor from the squadron's veteran pilots, the authorities defied the lessons of the summer and inexplicably went for a relatively elderly and inexperienced outsider, Alan MacLachlan, who had been commissioned into the reserve in 1930. He lasted a week before being shot down and wounded and Brian Kingcome became the de facto squadron commander. The recommendation was finally made that he should take over. Before it could be implemented, Kingcome, too, was out of action, after being wounded and forced to bale out on 15 October.

Eleven days later a new commanding officer arrived at Biggin Hill. Johnny Kent was a Canadian, an outstanding pilot who had gained his licence at sixteen and been an RAF test pilot in the pre-war years. It had been hair-raising work. On 300 occasions he was required to fly into barrage-balloon cables to calculate the damage they did to aircraft and try out devices for cutting through them. He came from a Polish squadron, No. 303, where he had been a flight commander, helping in a short time to turn it into one of the most effective units in Fighter Command.

Kent reached Biggin Hill at tea time, and the mess sergeant pointed out the officers of his new squadron, sitting together at one table. He joined them without telling them who he was. 'My first impressions,' he wrote later, 'were not favourable and their general attitude and lack of manners indicated a lack of control and discipline. I realized I was going to have my hands full.'[2]

Kent was astute enough to understand there were reasons for the pilots' truculence. Despite their impressive performance, they had suffered shocking casualties and were 'disorganized, undisciplined and demoralized'. There was a move to post the squadron north for a rest, which he resisted, arguing that if this was done it would be finished as a fighting force. Instead, he 'begged to be allowed to keep it at Biggin as that would give me the chance I needed to get it into shape – while the stigma of having "had it" could not be attached to it'.

A few days after he took over and was leading the squadron on patrol, they encountered high-flying Me 109s, but several pilots, instead of turning to face them, broke formation and headed for home. It was a case, Kent concluded, of '109-itis'. On landing he threatened to shoot down the pilots himself if there was a repetition. A few weeks later, a weaver failed to break up a formation of German fighters attacking the squadron from the rear. This provoked another tirade. The senior NCOs were summoned and accused of being slipshod and insubordinate. There were some words of praise for the pilots' record in the air, but then he moved on to attack their conceit, indiscipline, drinking habits and clothes. The parties at Southwood House would have to be scaled down and women guests out by 11 p.m. Check shirts, old school ties, suede shoes and pink pyjamas worn under tunics would no longer be tolerated. The theft of aviation petrol to fuel their uninsured, unlicenced cars was to stop.

Kent reckoned later that 'this action made me even more unpopular and I am sure many dire threats were made behind my back, but nothing came of them and gradually it began to dawn on them all that the squadron had become more efficient and that perhaps my tirade had not been delivered simply because I was an unpleasant bastard but because I had done it for their own good'. He appealed to Tony Bartley to help him win the squadron's cooperation. Bartley agreed. Kent's success in the air and willingness to join in the fun at the White Hart hastened the process of reconciliation, and by the time he was posted away six months later to command a training unit, he was held in great affection by most of the pilots.

It was clear, though, that the days of informality were over and the grip of convention was tightening on the Fighter Boys. From the outside it seemed that little had changed. Propagandists continued to present the pilots in the light-hearted image they had created for themselves. Biggin Hill became a centre for media visitors. Sailor Malan, Al Deere and Bob

Tuck became celebrities. The BBC leant heavily on fighter pilots to make broadcasts harking back to the great events of the summer. The scripts were mostly written for them by Ministry of Information apparatchiks, in a Hollywood-tinged style that sounded strange when spoken in the clipped line-by-line delivery the novice broadcasters invariably used. A typical 'talk' was made in December 1940 by James Nicolson of 249 Squadron, describing the action in August in which he won Fighter Command's only Victoria Cross of the war. Speaking in a public-school accent, he described how he chased after his quarry, 'shouting out loud at him when I first saw him, "I'll teach you some manners you Hun!"' The form was to regard broadcasts as a 'line shoot'. Any embarrassment was offset by a fee, from which the Air Ministry insisted on taking its cut.

The old reluctance to promote 'aces' had gone. Certain pilots were pushed towards the newspapers. Paddy Finucane, the good-looking, slightly gauche Irishman who, once the duffer of his training intake, had gone on to become one of Fighter Command's most successful pilots, became a favourite. His crinkly hair, square jaw and faraway look made him a favourite with women readers. Recovering in hospital after accidentally breaking an ankle while jumping over a wall in the blackout in the autumn of 1941, he was inundated with get-well letters. 'I guess you've received tons of fan mail from hero-worshipping dames all over the country,' wrote a land girl who gave her address as 'Amongst the turnips, Wiltshire'. She signed off, 'Boy, don't I wish I'd been a nurse.' Another from 'an admirer', Miss Rose Layton of Heathstan Road, Shepherd's Bush, began: 'Dear Paddy, I read of your accident in the *Daily Herald* and I am very sorry and hope you will get well again soon [as] I know how anxious you must be to get up there again. They can't keep a good man down. Don't think this silly of me Paddy but I would like you to carry or wear this horseshoe I am sending you for luck.'[3]

The zenith of the Fighter Boys' fame coincided with a relative decline in their military importance. Heavy raids by the Luftwaffe in daylight virtually stopped. Instead there were fighter-bomber raids and a continuation of the night offensive. This lasted through the winter, killing 18,000 civilians in the first four months of the new year. Some pilots were diverted to flying night fighters, which slowly became more effective as the radar needed to locate the raiders improved.

Having fought off the Luftwaffe and ensured its own survival, Fighter Command took on a secondary role. From the end of 1940 it served as an adjunct to the British bomber offensive being launched against German targets in northern France. The pilots went from attacking bombers to defending them. They were required to fit into complex tactical arrangements designed to shield Bomber Command aircraft on their way to their targets, to cover them while they did their work and to hold off attackers as they headed home. The missions were called 'Circuses' and could involve a hundred or more fighters, organized into wings, escorting small numbers of bombers. Many pilots realized from the outset that the importance of these operations was slight. They were aimed at appropriate targets: marshalling yards, workshops, refineries and the like. But the number of bombers involved and the loads they delivered meant that the effort was disproportionate to any results. The real purpose was to use the bombers as bait to entice the German fighters into the air with the aim of destroying as many as possible.

As well as the escort duties, the pilots were tasked to fly 'Rhubarbs', low-level attacks against targets of opportunity such as bridges, locomotives, convoys, flak batteries and barges. Sometimes they were ordered off on anti-fighter sweeps, with the hazy instruction from Leigh-Mallory to 'seek and destroy the enemy'. Some of the inspiration for the offensive had come from Trenchard, still a brooding presence. Before taking over Fighter Command, Sholto Douglas had been informed of the old man's view that the time had come to 'lean towards France'[4] with aggressive sallies over the enemy lines like those flown by the RFC above the Western Front.

Both Douglas and Leigh-Mallory had served with the RFC in the First World War and were disposed to listen. Douglas wondered at first whether the likely casualties would justify the results. Leigh-Mallory was persuaded from the outset. Thus began a phase of fighting which killed hundreds of pilots for negligible results. Between November 1940 and the end of 1941, nearly 470 pilots who had survived the Battle of Britain were killed. The campaign got off to a poor start with even the official arithmetic weighing in the Germans' favour. Between January and June 1941, there were 2,700 sorties by fighters, during which fifty-one pilots were lost. Only forty-four German aircraft were claimed destroyed. Inevitably, the real figure was lower, probably about twenty.

The initiative might have fizzled out had it not been for the German attack on the Soviet Union in June. The Circuses and Rhubarbs gained a new ostensible purpose: to force the Luftwaffe to pull back assets from the Eastern Front, or at least to make life in northern France so difficult as to prevent a transfer of the men and aircraft stationed there. The offensive was stepped up. This time the balance seemed more acceptable. Fighter Command claimed to have shot down 731 German aeroplanes while losing 411 itself. The true score was 154 including 51 losses unconnected with British action. 'The combat balance sheet would thus appear to be about four to one in Germany's favour,' judged John Terraine, in his classic history of the RAF in the European war.[5] Nor could the Russians be said to have benefited. The activity persuaded the Luftwaffe to keep a force of fighters in France and the Low Countries. But it consisted at any time of about 260 single-engined aircraft which would have had little effect on the fortunes of the war in the East.

For many veterans of the summer fighting of 1940, flying Circuses and Rhubarbs was more nerve-racking than anything they had experienced during the Battle of Britain. Flying close escort to the bombers meant crawling along at their speed, rocking in the shock waves from the exploding flak and waiting to be pounced on by the German fighters. Now the British pilots were experiencing the same dread that their Luftwaffe counterparts had felt the year previously. To Paddy Finucane, close escort duty was 'murder'. The Rhubarbs were less feared, but were still regarded with apprehension. Al Deere later described them as 'useless and hated'. At best they 'served only as a means of letting off steam in that [they] enabled pilots to fire their guns in anger, more often than not against some unidentified target'. Deere confessed that on the few Rhubarbs in which he was engaged he could not 'truthfully say that the vehicles and the train which I attacked were strictly military targets'.[6]

A graphic account of the experience and the psychological aftermath, written for the psychologists who were by now being used to study aircrew personnel, was given by a pilot who had been shot down and seriously wounded after taking part in fifty sweeps.

On September 17, 1941, after getting separated from the wing during a spot of confusion near Lille, I began returning home alone at 18,000 feet, weaving hard and losing height gradually to keep my speed up. Over St Omer, two Me 109Fs passed 1,000 feet above me and slightly to the left, going the opposite way. I was then at 13,000 feet. I climbed into the sun, intending to beat these two up as soon as I was alone, but I soon ascertained just the opposite and immediately became the centre of a large gaggle, consisting of nine or ten MEs and one Spitfire. I don't remember feeling frightened, only highly interested and thoroughly keyed up . . . I took a lot of evasive action and the Huns did a lot of inaccurate shooting, till it began to look as though I could float about all afternoon without being hit.

Then, as he neared the French coast,

there was a terrific bang inside the cockpit and something feeling like a steam hammer hit me on the back of the head and knocked me for six. I don't think I was ever quite unconscious, or if I was it was only for a few seconds, but complete darkness descended and I hadn't the energy to move a finger. I felt myself fading away, as though going under an anaesthetic. There was nothing left but pitch-darkness and a pain behind my right ear. But a tiny corner of my mind, aloof from everything else, still seemed to be functioning, and I remember thinking detachedly in the dark: 'So, after all it's happened to me too . . . it's come to you who always told yourself there's a way out of every scrape. But there's no way out of this one, buddy, because you are quite blind and you haven't the strength to move a muscle and you are diving down towards the sea with a lot of 109s which are ready to polish you off as soon as you show any signs of revival.

'So there! I wish I could have had a word with the chaps, just to explain how it happened, instead of simply vanishing like so many others. And there are a lot of people I'd like to say goodbye to . . . And you're a clown to be shot down by a bloody Hun anyway. But it's too late for regrets now. It can only be a few seconds now . . . just one almighty holocaust as we hit the sea; then no more fighting, no more fear, no more pain in [the] back of the head. Just peace . . . God, how marvellous!'

At the last second he pulled out of the dive, shook off his pursuers and made a good landing at Hawkinge, despite a terrible head wound and the loss of one and a half pints of blood.

Convalescing in the Palace Hotel, Torquay, he was told that he would not be able to fly for three months.

I pretended to be alarmed but was secretly very glad. For a couple of weeks I slept no more than an hour at a time. When I did there were awful dreams such as being towed around the sky by my foot . . . After I had been on leave for a couple of weeks, I settled down, slept most of the night and ate fairly well. The kindness of my wife and the loveliness of my little boy took things off – made me forget for quite long periods. Then the sleeplessness and the dreams came back and while reading I would suddenly see myself having to bale out of an aircraft. I shivered with fright.'

After a particularly harrowing night he reported his dreams to a doctor. He was referred to a wing commander who reassured him he would not have to go back to flying for several months.

I felt better for a day or two. Then it returned. I began to think perhaps I should have to go on bombers and stick it out for eight or more hours. Rather than that I will go back to my night fighters now where we seldom do more than a 3-hour stretch. Supposing I was petrified with fear and could not fire a gun or read my special equipment instruments,

I should be letting my CO, my squadron, and my country down, and again if I did not go back to my job I am letting them all down and myself by being a coward.[7]

Many of the moral and material advantages the British pilots had enjoyed the previous summer had disappeared. They were no longer flying over friendly fields and beaches within reach of rescuers, but ranging with limited fuel into hostile territory where the Germans' increasingly efficient radar system gave plenty of warning of their approach. It was up to them whether or not they took the bait. Frequently they chose not to and preserved their resources. The enemy then became the light flak guns, which accounted for a large number of casualties. From late September onwards, the German pilots became more aggressive with the arrival into service of the new Focke-Wulf 190s, which, it quickly became clear, had the edge over the improved Spitfire Vs.

The sky over northern France was a very dangerous place. It was the Fighter Boys' turn to experience the desolation of the journey home on drying tanks, the wind thrumming in shrapnel holes and the cold and empty sea below. Baling out unharmed over land during the defence of Britain usually meant an unpleasant shock, rescue with a cup of tea or a shot of whisky, transport back to base and the joyful greetings of friends. Now it signalled the end of the line: imprisonment until the war was over. The apprehension mounted as the French coast approached and the leader's voice crackling over the R/T announced the start of the ordeal with the words: 'Corks in, boys!'

Some were pleased with the opportunity to go onto the attack. Douglas Bader had had a frustrating time during the summer of 1940 and took to the 'sweeps' with impatient energy. In March 1941, he was posted to Tangmere to command a wing of three Spitfire squadrons. With his arrival the pace of activity rose sharply. By mid June his pilots went to France almost every day, except when the weather was bad, flying up to three sweeps. Bader's difficult personality was redeemed by a gift for leadership. The shift from defence to offence might have been expected to weaken morale and motivation, but Bader created in his wing a spirit of cheerful aggression and dedication. Cocky Dundas, a perceptive and humane observer, was seduced by the mercurial, unconventional 'DB'.

'There was a close bond between the three Spitfire units at Tangmere that summer,' he wrote. 'Bader welded the wing into a single unit and we all knew each other well, so that the losses sustained by the other squadrons were almost as painful as our own.' And the losses were heavy. Between 20 June and 10 August, Dundas's squadron, 616, lost twelve pilots, more than half its establishment. Dundas found that, unlike the previous August, when a spate of casualties dented the squadron spirit, 'morale was sky high'.[8]

Dundas found Tangmere in the high summer of 1941 an enchanted place where fear of death heightened the intensity of his joy at living. His memory was of 'sharp contrasts; of the pleasure of being alive and with friends in the gentle Sussex summer evenings; of visits from Diana, when we would dine and dance in Brighton, or sit long on the balcony outside the Old Ship Club at Bosham watching the moon on the water and listening to the tide lapping against the wall beneath us and memories of tearing terror when, at the end of a dogfight, I found myself alone with fifty miles of hostile sky between me and the Channel coast and the hungry 109s curving in to pick off the straggler'.

The era came to an end with Bader's fall. He was shot down in a dogfight with 109s between Boulogne and Le Touquet early in August and taken prisoner. When Dundas returned from leave after Bader's cap-ture, he was dejected at the thought of the endless fighting that lay ahead. 'I knew in my heart that I had little enthusiasm for the prospect,' he wrote later. It took an enormous effort of will to keep going.

There was no disguising the changed nature of the struggle. Dennis Armitage, who arrived at Tangmere later in the summer, felt that it 'wasn't like fighting a battle on your home ground. It seemed to us very pointless . . . it was a political, psychological exercise so that the French could see British aircraft overhead. I didn't enjoy it. I didn't enter into the spirit of it in the same way as I had at the Battle of Britain.'[9] Armitage was shot down on 21 September while trying to keep the formation he was leading on bomber escort duty together. He was hit by an incendiary round, which set his tank and his oxygen supply on fire, but he somehow managed to bale out. The Germans were waiting for him when he landed and 'horribly cocky'. As they stepped forward to arrest him they announced, without apparent irony, that for him the war was over.

And so it was, for Armitage, for Bader and for many others, among them some of the outstanding pilots of the previous summer. Bob Tuck was shot down in January 1942, not by fighters but by flak outside Boulogne during a Rhubarb, and spent the next three years in prison before he escaped and after a dreadful journey reached the Russian lines. Paddy Barthropp had only been back on operations for two days after a six-month spell instructing when he was shot down near St-Omer, baled out and was captured.

At least they were alive. Hundreds who survived the Battle of Britain were to die in Circuses and Rhubarbs. Paddy Finucane lasted until July 1942. Like Tuck he was brought down by ground fire. On the way back from shooting up shipping and a German airfield, the wing he was leading passed over the beach at Pointe du Touquet. Pilot Officer F. Aikman, who was flying as his number two, described how, as they flew over the beach, he saw a small machine-gun post perched on a ridge of sand. 'We were almost on the post before Paddy realized it was there and the soldiers opened up at point blank range.'[10] The radiator of Finucane's Spitfire was hit and he prepared to bale out. He was too low. The engine stopped. He knew what was coming. His last words over the R/T before he hit the sea in a curtain of spray were: 'This is it, chaps.'

Others were killed in the new theatres opening up, in the Mediterranean, North Africa and the Far East. Noel Agazarian volunteered for duty in the Middle East and was shot down in his Spitfire over the Libyan desert in May 1941. The life of the man his family loved as 'Le Roi Soleil' was snuffed out. His sister, Yvonne, was devastated. 'But I didn't cry,' she said later. 'It wasn't done.'[11]

Death seemed very much closer now. The folklore of the mess taught that acceptance was often the precursor to the chop. 'If one once doubted that one was going to survive then the way downhill was pretty quick,' said Denys Gillam.[12] The fatalism was cumulative. After his first tour flying offensive operations, Al Deere was 'always confident that I would come through all right'. On his second one, 'although it was far less hectic, there was always uppermost in my mind the thought that I would be killed'.[13] Pete Brothers, later in the war, 'reached the stage where I thought there was no question of surviving. It was either going to happen today or it was going to happen tomorrow.'[14]

Yet, despite the ever-shortening odds, the compulsion to 'go back on ops' repeatedly dragged men who had demonstrably done their bit away from safe and comfortable desk jobs and instructing posts and back into the realm of danger. Richard Barclay, the earnest Cambridge economics graduate who kept a diary during the late summer of 1940, was shot down at the end of November that year. He was wounded in his legs, ankle and elbows and spent two months in hospital. There was a brief spell as an instructor before he was back in action with 611 Squadron. During a sweep over St-Omer he was attacked by Me 109s and forced to land. He escaped and met up with local resisters, who passed him down the line to the Pyrénées. Once in Spain, he presented himself at the British Embassy and made his way back to Britain via Gibraltar after an eleven-week odyssey. He was given a cushy headquarters job, but was soon agitating to be back in action. At the beginning of July 1942 he was in Egypt commanding 238 Squadron. On the evening of 17 July he was dead, shot down while patrolling in the Alamein area.

Many of those who died and those who expected to die were already embarking on the next phase of their lives. Paddy Finucane had just got engaged before his death to Miss Jean Woolford, a typist at the Ministry of Agriculture. Al Deere's anxiety to get back into the fighting was mixed with tender thoughts about his fiancée, Joan. Richard Barclay, whose diary is interspersed with wistful speculations about how he would be enjoying the perfect autumn days if he was not waiting at dispersal, knew what he was missing. But they went on. 'You didn't stop because you were tired or you didn't like it,' said Denys Gillam afterwards. 'You just kept going.'[15]

By the time the end came the Fighter Boys had long since split up. Those who survived were scattered throughout the now sprawling RAF empire. The others were dead, lying in English country churchyards and sun-baked military cemeteries, buried in estuary mud or North Sea strands or long dissolved in the Channel tides. Of the 2,917 men who fought in Fighter Command the air battles of the summer of 1940, 544 were killed. Another 795 died before the war was over. On 15 August 1945, those who were left were able to believe for the first time that they might live the natural span of a man. Few had any idea of what awaited them as they stepped out into the mysterious world of the normal. But all knew they could never forget what they had left behind.

Epilogue: The Last Note

On 17 September 2000, a chilly Sunday morning tinged with intimations of death and winter, hundreds of guests filed through the west door of Westminster Abbey for a service of thanksgiving to mark the sixtieth anniversary of the Battle of Britain. The rows of hard, narrow chairs were packed with RAF members of all ages and ranks accompanied by their wives, sons and daughters.

After the readings the congregation rose. As the scraping of wood on stone and the coughing died away a towering silence settled over the abbey. Then the Central Band of the Royal Air Force struck up the opening notes of the Battle of Britain March and down the aisle, moving with slow dignity, came eight white-haired men bearing the Roll of Honour inscribed with the names of the airmen who died in the summer of 1940.[1] Pete Brothers lead the procession alongside Christopher Foxley-Norris, with Paddy Barthropp and Tom Neil among those following behind. They were escorted by a phalanx of junior officers, slim and upright, a reminder of the men the survivors had once been. When the service was over, the crowd stood for a while outside, greeting friends, lighting cigarettes, making plans for lunch or preparations for the journey home. A familiar noise cut through the hubbub and all heads tilted upwards. A Spitfire slid out of the low, greyish murk, hung for a few seconds overhead, then disappeared back into the cloud.

At the time about 300 veterans of the fighting were still alive. Two years later the number had fallen to 231. There was a feeling that the service marked the last occasion when the event being commemorated would remain moored to the recent past. Soon death and time would loosen the bonds of memory and it would slip into the realm of history.

The Fighter Boys had already passed into legend. Churchill had created it before the fighting had even properly begun and reinforced it before the outcome was known. The 'Battle of Britain' was his invention. Long before its outcome was decided, the men fighting it had been eulogized as 'The Few'. Despite the power of the rhetoric, the pilots seem to have been only half-aware that they were involved in a historic struggle. It was only when it was over that they began to discern the epic dimensions of the event they had been engaged in.

For most of the pilots the battle had a deep personal significance. For some it was the most important experience of their life, shaping for good or bad everything that came afterwards. For all of them, their participation was a badge of honour that they would wear until they died, arousing an admiration, respect and gratitude that took precedence over all subsequent achievement.

The great question of what to do when it was all over was perhaps harder to confront for the Fighter Boys than for any other serviceman. Staying on in the RAF gave the opportunity to carry on flying and to remain in a familiar world, even if it had become more petty and mundane. Many chose to continue. Dutiful, conscientious Al Deere carried on for another twenty-two years, ending up as commandant of the apprentice school at Halton, and retiring to live nearby until his death in 1995. Christopher Foxley-Norris finished with the rank of air chief marshal and a knighthood. Birdy Bird-Wilson became an air vice-marshal. Dennis David had a long and satisfying career and was air attaché in Prague during the Soviet crushing of the 'Prague Spring' in 1968. Pete Brothers joined the Colonial Service and went to Kenya, but after a few years reapplied to the RAF, commanded a bomber squadron during the Malayan emergency and ended his distinguished service as an air commodore. Billy Drake held a number of staff appointments, retiring as a group captain in 1963 and starting a new life as a restauranteur and property developer in Portugal.

But there would never be another summer of 1940. It was a truth that the routines of peace-time service underlined. Sailor Malan went to staff college for a year, then decided, in the words of his biographer, that 'the air no longer held out anything that would retain his interest and enthusiasm . . . He saw the magnificent combative spirit of the Air Force turn flaccid now the challenge was gone.'[2] He returned to South Africa with his wife and two children to work for the Anglo-American mining heir, Harry Oppenheimer, bought a huge farm and plunged briefly into politics, defending the constitution against Afrikaner extremists. Before he left England he made a last trip to the White Hart to unveil a memorial in the bar parlour, a blackout blind that had been signed in chalk, over the years, by many of the pilots who had passed through the inn door. A replica is there still. Malan died young, aged fifty-two, in 1963, brought down at last by Parkinson's disease. Michael Crossley also ended up in South Africa, where he grew tobacco before his death in 1987. So did Robin Appleford, before moving on to Rhodesia and Kenya, where he worked for a British company for fifteen years before returning to Britain. His friend Rob Bodie was killed in a flying accident in February 1942.

Some found jobs in civil aviation. Paul Richey was European area manager for BP, then took up an offer from his old Fighter Command comrade Max Aitken to work as air correspondent on the family-owned *Daily Express*. He continued to live an adventurous life. He climbed mountains, sailed racing yachts and went deep-sea diving with Jacques Cousteau. To add to the broad row of decorations, there was a medal from the Royal Humane Society, awarded after he dived in to rescue a woman drowning in heavy seas off the Ligurian coast at Portofino. He was working on a definitive history of Anglo-French relations when he died in 1989. Hugh Dundas also joined Beaverbrook Newspapers and moved into television in the 1960s, ending up as chairman of Thames Television. He was knighted in 1987 and died in 1995.

Tim Vigors, after an extraordinary series of narrow escapes, survived the war. In peacetime he pursued the loves of his life, going into the bloodstock industry and breeding some notable champions and founding his own aviation company. Douglas Bader left the RAF in 1946 to work for Shell who awarded him his own aeroplane. The appearance of Paul Brickhill's biography, *Reach for the Sky*, which was turned into a film, established him as a post-war celebrity. He enjoyed his fame and made some good use of it, encouraging disabled people to believe that they could lead, as he had done, not a normal but an exceptional life. He died in September 1982 on his way back from a dinner in honour of Sir Arthur 'Bomber' Harris.

Roland Beamont became a test pilot, then an aviation executive. Tony Bartley also started a peacetime career as a test pilot before following his wife, the actress Deborah Kerr, to Hollywood. He had met her at a film studio in 1941. She was starring in a costume drama. He was doing the flying stunts for *The First of the Few*, which told the story of the Spitfire's inventor, R. J. Mitchell. They married in 1947. Dowding, by now a peer, was among the guests. He alarmed Bartley's father during the service by asking him if he could feel, as he could, the presence of his son's dead comrades. The marriage lasted until 1959, by which time Bartley had launched into a career in television. He died at his home in Ireland in April 2001.

Brian Kingcome found the transition to peacetime service difficult. He tried several times to resign his commission, but was told that, as an ex-Cranwell cadet, he owed it to his country to stay on. In September 1950 he contracted tuberculosis, which he blamed on a bachelor lifestyle of steady drinking, late nights and irregular meals. He spent three years in a sanatorium. On leave, in a bar, deciding what to do next, he ran into an American acquaintance who worked for Twentieth Century-Fox. The man asked Kingcome to be his assistant on the film he was working on. Kingcome resigned his commission the same day. Later he tried to get a management job in industry but was disappointed by what he found. His mistake, he said, was to assume that the ethical standards and codes he had been brought up with at home, at school and in the RAF would apply equally in commercial life. This misapprehension cost him a lot of money.

At one point Paddy Barthropp provided a solution. He had left the RAF in 1958 and used his severance money to set up a Rolls-Royce hire firm. He invited Kingcome to be his partner. Kingcome wrote of Barthropp, that 'underneath a façade of eccentric inanity there lurked one of the kindest, most generous and warm-hearted of men, and everyone sensed it'.[3]

Kingcome's bachelor life came to an end when, with forty approaching, he fell in love with a young woman almost half his age called Lesley. She was the daughter of Sheila, one of the beautiful Macneal twins, and he had known her since she was a child. They had a long, happy marriage, presiding over a successful furniture business until they retired to Devon. Their neighbours there included Killy Kilmartin, who on leaving the RAF in 1958 had started a chicken farm. After fifteen years he had sold it, shifted around Europe for more than a decade and then returned to Devon. With Barthropp, who bought a retreat locally, they formed a convivial trio. Kingcome died in 1994, and Kilmartin in 1998. Cocky Dundas gave an address at Kingcome's funeral. His four chief attributes, he said, were 'courage, determination, a total lack of pomposity or self-importance and an everlasting lightness of heart and touch'.

This approach to life was evident in Kingcome's attitude towards the Battle of Britain. 'Why can't they just talk about B of B pilots?' he once complained in a letter. 'Why does it always have to be heroes? I think it devalues the word and denigrates all those others who were called on to face just as great odds and whose contribution and sacrifices are just as great, but whose exploits hadn't been pushed into the public eye by Churchill's splendid oratory. Dying is what's important, not the time and place you did it.'[4]

It was a typically generous sentiment. By the time it was expressed it was far too late to change things. The event achieved its cinematic apotheosis in 1969. The film *The Battle of Britain* was a serious, almost reverential work. Even after this time, Hollywood was not prepared to tinker with the myth. The technical advisers included Bob Tuck, and on the German side, Adolf Galland. Galland had ended up a much-decorated air force general. He professed to know nothing about Nazi atrocities until learning of them after the war. He was released after a long interrogation and went to Argentina to help train its air force before returning to Germany to start an aviation consultancy. In his autobiography, *The First and the Last*, which appeared in 1953, he presented himself as an amiable, apolitical professional soldier, who brought a touch of chivalry to a nasty business. He was widely accepted as such. He was on good terms with Bader, whom he had treated well after his capture. He was particularly close to Tuck, visiting him at his mushroom farm in Kent and inviting him to his home near Bonn to go boar shooting. Tuck's death in May 1987 affected him strongly. His own, in February 1996, was marked in the British media as the passing of a Good German.

When the war finished many pilots were left with the suspicion that the most exciting and important passage of their existence was over, even though they still had most of their lives left to run. It was equally true for some non-combatants. Edith Heap never forgot Denis Wissler. She married a doctor after the war, but they were divorced after five years. Occasionally, during the intervening sixty years, she is convinced she has felt Denis's presence. 'Once,' she told me, 'I was sitting up in bed, reading, and suddenly there was Denis. He bent down and kissed me. I felt it. It was a lovely warm feeling. Then he smiled at me and faded away.'[5]

Despite their tendency to understatement and self-mockery, it was hard for the pilots to escape the realization that they had been involved in something great. The Battle of Britain, inevitably, underwent historical revision. Doubts have been cast on the seriousness of the German invasion plan and adjustments have been made to the odds that Fighter Command was facing. These re-examinations have done nothing to diminish the pilots' achievement. More than sixty years later it seems as remarkable as ever.

Fighter Command dealt Hitler's forces the first defeat they had suffered since the war began. The battle of attrition that the Luftwaffe was forced to fight had a profound effect on its future efficiency. A Luftwaffe general, Werner Kreipe, later judged that the decision to try and destroy the RAF had marked 'a turning point in the history of the Second World War. The German Air Force . . . was bled almost to death and suffered losses which could never again be made good throughout the course of the war.'[6]

The victory was of colossal importance. 'Our battle was a small one,' wrote Peter Townsend, 'but on its outcome depended the fate of the western world.' It is true that Hitler spent little time on the invasion plan. But according to his assessment of the likely direction of events he did not need to. Either the RAF would be cleared from the skies, opening the way for a landing, or the Luftwaffe would inflict so much damage that the British government would be forced to seek terms. Either outcome would mean the end of effective resistance to the Nazis in Europe and the start of the 'new dark age' that Churchill had foreseen.

The fact that neither came to pass was due to the actions of 3,000 men and their machines and the intelligence of those who controlled them. The balance of forces was not as uneven as the first version of the legend suggested, though there were periodic crises of manpower and aircraft. But the battle was not to be decided by resources alone. It was, in the end, a question of character and morale. The Fighter Boys' thoughts were rarely darkened by the prospect of defeat. 'We knew we had to win,' wrote Townsend, 'but, more than that, we were somehow certain that we could not lose. I think it had something to do with England. Miles up in the sky, we fighter pilots could see more of England than any other of England's defenders had ever seen before. Beneath us stretched our beloved country, with its green hills and valleys, lush pastures and villages, clustering round an ancient church. Yes, it was a help to have England there below.'[7] George Bennions, who was badly burned in the last fighting of the summer and blinded in one eye, believed that his unit, 41 Squadron, battered though it was, 'would have fought on and on until there was nothing left'.[8]

It was a victory of spirit as much as of skill, and the spirit of the Fighter Boys was that of Britain. They came from every class and background and every area. Their values and attitudes were those of the people they were defending. It seemed to the teenage Yvonne Agazarian that her brother Noel and his comrades were sacrificing their lives to defend a way of doing things, 'fighting with a real belief and dying moderately cheerfully'.[9]

They had taken a duty and turned it into a great act, and done so with a grace and style that was almost as significant as the event itself, for it reflected the decency of their cause. The Fighter Boys are almost all gone now. One by one the last of The Few are taking off on the final flight. Their real monument is Europe's enduring peace. But long after the last veteran has departed, they will be remembered. Each September their sons and daughters, grandchildren and great-grandchildren will come to the Abbey to give thanks. Then they will file outside and listen for the pulsing tone of the Spitfire engine, like the note of a grand piano after a bass key has been struck, fading and swelling as if it is trying to tell us something, the most poignant and romantic sound on earth.

Notes and References

Prologue: The White Hart

1 'he had recorded the events of the day': 32 Squadron unofficial diary, quoted in Bob Ogley, *Biggin on the Bump*, Froglets Publications, Westerham, 1990.
2 Mr H. J. Edgerton: quoted in *Daily Mirror*, 16 August 1940.
3 'wrote a war artist': Cuthbert Orde, *Pilots of Fighter Command*, Harrap, London, 1942, p. 10.
4 'would you like to go for a flip?': Charles Fenwick, *Dear Mother*, privately published memoir.

1. Sportsmen and Butchers

1 Gierson: quoted in Nigel Steel and Peter Hart, *Tumult in the Clouds, the British Experience of War in the Air 1914–1918*, Coronet, London, 1998, p. 19.
2 Rabagliati: quoted in ibid., p. 31.
3 Loraine: quoted in Andrew Boyle, *Trenchard*, Collins, London, 1962, p. 95.
4 Lewis: Cecil Lewis, *Sagittarius Rising*, Warner Books, London, 1998, pp. 40–5.
5 'Lewis wrote': ibid., p. 45.
6 Albert Ball: Chaz Bowyer, *Albert Hall VC*, Bridge Books, London, 1994, pp. 32–5.
7 'He had but one idea': ibid., p. 81.
8 'a hero . . . and he looked the part too': ibid., p. 82.
9 'I do so want to leave': ibid., p. 76.
10 'the topping day': ibid., p. 111.
11 'May evening': Lewis, *Sagittarius Rising*, p. 174.
12 'we met Huns': *The Personal Diary of Major Edward 'Mick' Mannock VC*, introduced and annotated by Frederick Oughton, Neville Spearman, London, 1966, pp. 105 and 187.
13 'The Hun crashed': ibid., p. 187.
14 'one general reasoned': Alan Clark, *Aces High*, Cassell, London, 1999, p. 70.
15 'to finish myself': Mannock, *The Personal Diary*, p. 166.

16 'my first flamerino': ibid., p. 168.

17 'All tickets please!': ibid., p. 190.

18 'I don't feel': ibid., p. 198.

19 'saw a flame': ibid., p. 201.

20 'it gave me': Manfred von Richthofen, *The Red Air Fighter*, Greenhill Books, London, 1999, pp. 89 and 96.

21 'honoured the fallen': ibid., p. 94.

22 'The great thing': Peter Kilduff, *The Illustrated Red Baron, The Life and Times of Manfred von Richthofen*, Arms and Armour Press, London, 1999, p. 49.

23 'so you were': Lewis, *Sagittarius Rising*, p. 10.

24 'because he was': John Grider: quoted in Steel and Hart, *Tumult in the Clouds*, p. 293.

25 'Ah! Tu es pilote!': Lewis, *Sagittarius Rising*, p. 75.

26 'In such an atmosphere,' ibid., p. 60.

27 'little black and tan': Mannock, *The Personal Diary*, p. 119.

28 'My system was': Steel and Hart, *Tumult in the Clouds*, p. 310.

29 'So it was over': Lewis, *Sagittarius Rising*, p. 255.

2. Fighters *versus* Bombers

1 'Under Trenchard': H. Montgomery Hyde, *British Air Policy between the Wars 1918–1939*, Heinemann, London, 1976, p. 49.

2 'the prophet Jonah's': ibid., p. 49.

3 'the vital esential': ibid., p. 56.

4 'to really make': ibid., p. 61.

5 'less cause to': Andrew Boyle, Trenchard, Collins, London, 1962, p. 361.

6 'scene of grey corrugated': *Royal Air Force Cadet College Magazine*, September 1920, vol. 1, No. 1.

7 'Nothing that has': ibid.

8 'The first senior': See Tony Mansell, 'Flying Start: Educational and Social Factors in the Recruitment of Pilots of the Royal Air Force in the Interwar Years', *History of Education*, 1997, vol. 26, No. 1, p. 72.

9 'The Cecil Committee': ibid., p. 73.

10 'Air Ministry officials': E. B. Haslam, *The History of RAF Cranwell*, HMSO, London 1982, p. 29.

11 'The curriculum': ibid., p. 28.

12 'Fun was bruising': ibid., p. 27.

13 'In January 1921': *Flight*, 24 December 1924.

14 'The high standard': John James, *The Paladins, a Social History of the RAF up to the Outbreak of World War II*, Macdonald, London, 1990, p. 208.

15 'The policy meant': ibid., p. 113.

16 'It wanted': ibid., p. 142.

17 'Trenchard considered': Boyle, *Trenchard*, p. 519.

18 'The squadron historian noted': Tom Moulson, *The Flying Sword, The Story of 601 Squadron*, Macdonald, London, 1954, p. 22.

19 'before 1939': John Terraine, *The Right of the Line, The Royal Air Force in the European War 1939–1945*, Hodder & Stoughton, London, 1985, p. 50.

20 'As early as': ibid., p. 11.

21 'the only defence': ibid., p. 14.

22 'indicated the obsolescence': ibid., p. 23.

23 'Half an hour later': Paul Gallico, *The Hurricane Story*, Michael Joseph, London, 1959, p. 19.

24 'the sort of bloody silly name': Len Deighton, *Fighter*, Pimlico, London, 1996, p. 77.

25 'Everyone therefore started out the same': Montgomery Hyde, *British Air Policy*, p. 354.

26 'I cannot take the view': ibid., p. 410.

3. 'Free of Boundaries, Free of Gravity, Free of Ties'

1 Drake: interview with author.

2 Brothers: interview with author.

3 'as a special treat': Dennis 'Hurricane' David, *My Autobiography*, Grub Street, London, 2000, p. 11.

4 Sanders: interview with author.

5 Beamont: Imperial War Museum Sound Archive (henceforth referred to as IWM), recording no. 10128.

6 'an RAF biplane': Bob Doe, *Fighter Pilot*, Spellmount, Stapelhurst, 1991, p. 3.

7 'The fact that one was now overhead': Alan Deere, *Nine Lives*, Crécy, Manchester, 1999, p. 15.

8 'there came the drone': Brian Kingcome, *A Willingness to Die*, edited and introduced by Pete Ford, Tempus, Stroud, 1999, p. 8.

9 'were boyishly clear': Geoffrey Page, *Shot Down in Flames*, Grub Street, London, 1999, p. 9.

10 'In one story': Captain W. E. Johns, *Biggles Story Collection*, Red Fox, London, 1999, p. 40.

11 'In another': W. E. Johns, *The Camels are Coming*, Red Fox, London, 1993, p. 97.

12 'the Foreword': Johns, *Biggles Story Collection*, p. 72.

13 Brothers: interview with author.

14 Hancock: interview with author.

15 'Over tea his father': Page, *Shot Down in Flames*, pp. 8–9.

16 Doe: interview with author.

17 'Deere left Auckland': Deere, *Nine Lives*, p. 23.

18 'David had his first lesson': David, *My Autobiography*, p. 12.

19 'and was absolutely thrilled': Johnny Kent, *One of the Few*, Tempus, Stroud, 2000, p. 8.

20 Doe: interview with author.

21 'put the Tiger Moth': Wing Commander H. R. 'Dizzy' Allen, *Battle for Britain*, Corgi, London, 1975, p. 13.

22 'queasy feeling engulfed me': Tim Vigors, unpublished autobiography.

23 'Deere was so impatient': Deere, *Nine Lives*, p. 26.

24 'When the cutters': Patrick Barthropp, *Paddy, the Life and Times of Wing Commander Patrick Barthropp, DFC, AFC*, Howard Baker, London, 1990, p. 29.

25 'To some . . . it seemed': David, *My Autobiography*, p. 25.

26 'Kingcome considered': quoted in Richard C. Smith, *Hornchurch Scramble*, Grub Street, London, 2000, p. 37.

27 'Deere lost his temper': Deere, *Nine Lives*, p. 28.

28 'Kingcome enjoyed': IWM, no. 10152.

29 Brothers: interview with author.

30 Drake: interview with author.

31 Sheen: IWM, no. 12137.

32 Banham: IWM, no. 6799.

33 Nicholas: IWM, no. 12405.

34 'gone were the halcyon days': Peter Townsend, *Time and Chance*, Book Club Associates, London, 1978, p. 95.

35 Doe: interview with author.

36 Sheen: IWM, no. 12137.

37 'Deere . . . spent his first weeks': Deere, *Nine Lives*, p. 33.

38 'a school bully': Barthropp, *Paddy*, p. 20.

39 Gillam: IWM, no. 10049.

40 'Kingcome was to deliver the opinion': Kingcome, *A Willingness to Die*, p. 23.

41 Unwin: interview with author.

42 Brown: IWM, no. 12404.

43 Johns: IWM, no. 11616.

44 Haw: IWM, no. 12028.

45 Berry: IWM, no. 11475.

46 Foster: IWM, no. 12738.

47 Foxley-Norris: interview with author.

48 'Beaumont wrote': S. G. Beaumont, *The Reminiscences of S. G. Beaumont*, privately published, p. 143.

49 Barran: see Frank H. Ziegler, *The Story of 609 Squadron*, Crécy Books, Manchester, 1993, p. 49.

50 'but slow rolls I hated': Hugh Dundas, *Flying Start*, Stanley Paul, London, 1998, pp. 10–12.

51 Foxley-Norris: interview with author.

52 'Hillary was also a poor learner': David Ross, *Richard Hillary*, Grub Street, London, 2000, p. 28.

53 Yvonne Agazarian: interview with author.

4. The Fatal Step

1 Brown: IWM, no. 12404.

2 Beaumont: IWM, no. 10128.

3 Foxley-Norris: IWM, no. 10136.

4 Brown: IWM, no. 12404.

5 'never a plane "so loved" ': Dundas, *Flying Start*, p. 19.

6 Quill: IWM, no. 10687.

7 Unwin: interview with author.

8 Kingcome: IWM, no. 10152.

9 Nicholas: IWM, no. 12405.

10 Considine: IWM, no. 10961.

11 'Kingcome judged': Kingcome, *A Willingness to Die*, p. 64.

12 Drake: interview with author.

13 Deere: IWM, no. 10478.

14 'Half the pilots': Paul Richey, *Fighter Pilot*, Guild Publishing, London, 1990, p. 10.

15 'Deere wrote later': Deere, *Nine Lives*, p. 36.

16 Brothers: IWM, no. 10218.

17 Hall: IWM, no. 10342.

18 'Kingcome recalled': IWM, no. 10152.

19 'Deere wrote afterwards': Deere, *Nine Lives*, p. 36.

20 Winskill: IWM, no. 11537.

21 'Townsend also noticed': Townsend, *Time and Chance*, pp. 99–100.

22 Sanders: interview with author.

23 Hancock: interview with author.

24 'Quill wrote to his mother': letter in Quill family archive.

25 'Bartley decided to visit Germany': Tony Bartley, *Smoke Trails in the Sky*, William Kimber, London, 1984.

26 Bowring: IWM, no. 12173.

27 'Hillary went to compete in Germany': Richard Hillary, *The Last Enemy*, Macmillan, London, 1942, p. 23.

28 'At Cranwell': *Journal of the Royal Air Force College*, spring 1939.

29 Drake: interview with author.

30 Page: IWM, no. 11103.

31 'Hillary was contemptuous': Hillary, *The Last Enemy*, pp. 28–9.

32 'old-fashioned patriotism?': Beaumont, *Reminiscences*, p. 131.

33 Deere: IWM, no. 10478.

34 'spent a lot of time': see Oliver Walker, *Sailor Malan*, Cassell, London, 1953.

35 'wrote an RFC veteran': *Flight*, 18 March 1939.

36 'Kingcome was ordered': Kingcome, p. 61.

37 'Townsend recorded': Townsend, *A Willingness to Die*, p. 99.

38 'Brothers had to appear': interview with author.

39 'Vigors on leave from Cranwell': Vigors, unpublished autobiography, p. 117.

40 'the inevitable, well lubricated games': Dundas, *Flying Start*, p. 12.

41 'what a party': Townsend, *Time and Chance*, p. 102.

42 Haw: IWM, no. 12028.

43 Walker: IWM, no. 10617.

44 'one of the few to be surprised': Fenwick, *Dear Mother*, p. 36.

45 Down: IWM, no. 11449.

46 'Kingcome was struck': quoted in Richard C. Smith, *Hornchurch Scramble*, Grub Street, London, 2000, p. 51.

5. Winter of Uncertainty

1   Freeborn: interview with author.
2   'According to Eric Clayton': Eric Clayton, *What If the Heavens Fall*, RAF Museum, Hendon, ref. 34870.
3   'eighteen years old': in fact he was nineteen.
4   Deere: IWM, no. 10478.
5   'His biographer wrote': Walker, *Sailor Malan*.
6   'Al Deere noted': Deere, *Nine Lives*, p. 41.
7   Quoted in Henry Buckton, *Birth of the Few*, Airlife, Shrewsbury, 1998, p. 89.
8   Maclean: IWM, no. 10788.
9   'Townsend took part': Townsend, *Time and Chance*, pp. 105–6.
10 Bennions: IWM, no. 10296.
11 Paddy Finucane: Pilot Officer B. E. F. Finucane, letters, in IWM, documents archive, ref. 97/43/1.
12 Benson: Pilot Officer Noel Benson, letters in RAF Museum, Hendon, ref. 133331.
13 'told Benson's father later': correspondence and eyewitness account of death of Pilot Officer Benson in IWM, documents archive, ref. 133332.
14 Wissler: diary of Pilot Officer Denis Wissler in IWM, documents archive, ref, 91/41/1.
15 Earp: IWM, no. 11772.

6. Return to the Western Front

1   'wrote Paul Richey': Richey, *Fighter Pilot*, p. 19.
2   'Mould felt bad about his victory': see ibid., p. 24.
3   'Richey noticed': accidental brushes with death, it seemed, could cause more distress to a pilot than encounters with enemies who had set out to kill them. Eric Clayton, a corporal on the 56 Squadron ground staff, was at North Weald in the early spring of 1940 when Flight Lieutenant Ian Soden, a much-admired and highly experienced pilot, landed after practice formation flying with Flying Officer Illingworth and Flying Officer Rose. 'Soden got out of the cockpit looking white, released his parachute and leaned over the tailplane, clearly distressed. As the other pilots approached him, he said: "My God Illingworth! You hit me." Inspection revealed a large dent in the sternpost of the tail fin. Illingworth, a short, cocky fellow, did not seem too perturbed and Rose was slightly amused. What surprised us, though, was Soden's show of distress, for he was a man who displayed little emotion, was rather distant, and, as events proved, very brave' – Clayton, *What If the Heavens Fall*.
4   Matthews: IWM, no. 10451.
5   Paulette Regnauld: interview with author.
6   'the main attraction was the Roxy': Richey, *Fighter Pilot*, p. 29.
7   'Gallagher wrote': in *Daily Express*, 28 November 1939.

8   Foxley-Norris: interview with author.

9   'Richey pulled up violently': Richey, *Fighter Pilot*, p. 46.

10 'Beamont discovered': IWM, no. 10128.

11 Sanders: interview with author.

7. The Battle of France

1   Parrott: IWM, no. 13152.

2   Drake: interview with author.

3   'four farm hands had been working': Richey, *Fighter Pilot*, pp. 69–70.

4   'We took off': quoted in Brian Cull and Bruce Lander with Heinrich Weiss, *Twelve Days in May*, Grub Street, London, 1999, p. 48.

5   'The official RAF daily report admitted': ibid., p. 52.

6   Brothers: interview with author.

7   'Richard Whittaker's report': Public Record Office, diary of 17 Squadron.

8   'Richey had been hurrying': Richey, *Fighter Pilot*, p. 75.

9   'He described': quoted in Cull and Lander with Weiss, *Twelve Days in May*, p. 85.

10 Drake: interview with author.

11 'Richey had to collect something': Richey, *Fighter Pilot*, p. 86.

12 'David received a letter': David, *My Autobiography*, p. 26.

13 'Our nerves': Richey, *Fighter Pilot*, p. 80.

14 'Churchill was woken': see Terraine, *The Right of the Line*, pp. 135–40, for an account of Cabinet discussions.

15 'met a column of Belgian refugees': David, *My Autobiography*, p. 26.

16 'When they retold the stories': Richey, *Fighter Pilot*, p. 90.

17 'Matthews was sent one day': IWM, no. 10451.

18 'A pilot officer from "B" Flight': interview with author.

19 'Richey wrote': Richey, *Fighter Pilot*, p. 108.

20 'No. 1 Squadron took over a café': ibid., p. 112.

21 Brothers: interview with author.

22 Hancock: interview with author.

23 'He concluded that it would be "criminal"': see Terraine, *The Right of the Line*, p. 153.

24 Beamont: IWM, no. 10128.

25 'David flew to their airfield': David, *My Autobiography*, p. 28.

26 'David, who had been shot up': ibid., p. 29.

27 Drake: interview with author.

28 'Richey "noticed"': Richey, *Fighter Pilot*, p. 129.

29 Long: IWM, no. 12217.

30 Hancock: IWM, no. 10119.

31 Dawbarn: interview with author.

32 Rosier: IWM, no. 10157.

33 'one Hurricane carried a passenger': IWM, no. 10093.

34 'No. 1 Squadron diary': quoted in Cull and Lander with Weiss, *Twelve Days in May*, p. 25.

8. Dunkirk

1 'wrote Brian Kingcome': Kingcome, *A Willingness to Die*, p. 74.
2 'As Al Deere pointed out': Deere, *Nine Lives*, p. 46.
3 'Deere reported': ibid., p. 49.
4 'Deere agreed': ibid., p. 55.
5 'Leathart . . . promised': ibid., p. 59.
6 'Crossley noted': quoted in Graham Wallace, *RAF Biggin Hill*, Putnam, London, 1959, p. 116.
7 'the squadron chronicler recorded': Mounson, *The Flying Sword*, p. 51.
8 Kingcome: IWM, no. 10152.
9 Unwin: interview with author.
10 Unwin: interview with author.
11 'Leathart . . . described': quoted in Norman Franks, *Air Battle Dunkirk*, Grub Street, London, 2000, p. 27.
12 'biographer wrote': Paul Brickhill, *Reach for the Sky*, Collins, London, 1954, p. 170.
13 Kingcome: IWM, no. 10152.
14 'Malan found': Walker, *Sailor Malan*, p. 77.
15 'When Deere explained': Deere, *Nine Lives*, p. 70.
16 'Rosier . . . told how his wife': IWM, no. 10157.
17 'Kingcome saw': Kingcome, *A Willingness to Die*, p. 77.
18 Unwin: IWM, no. 11544.
19 'Malan said afterwards': quoted in Walker, *Sailor Malan*, p. 79.
20 Bartley: IWM, no. 11086.
21 Unwin: IWM, no. 11544.
22 Nicholas: IWM, no. 12405.
23 Dundas: IWM, 10159.
24 Bartley: IWM, no. 11086.
25 'Vigors . . . went off on the last patrol': Vigors, unpublished autobiography.

9. Doing It

1 'At Duxford aerodrome': Vigors, unpublished autobiography, contains the whole account.
2 'Richey found': Richey, *Fighter Pilot*, p. 114.
3 'Kingcome found': Kingcome, *A Willingness to Die*, p. 51.
4 Brothers: interview with author.
5 Freeborn: interview with author.
6 'the release from tension': Walker, *Sailor Malan*, p. 74.
7 Kingcome: IWM no. 10152.
8 Unwin: IWM, no. 11544.
9 Parrott: IWM, no. 13152.
10 Rosier: IWM, no. 10157.
11 Brown: IWM, no. 12404.
12 'I was suddenly drenched': quoted in Cull and Lander with Weiss, *Twelve Days in May*, p. 123.

13 'Just as': quoted in ibid., p. 203.

14 'Dundas was to find': Dundas, *Flying Start*, pp. 2–3.

15 'Richey . . . began to feel peculiar': Richey, *Fighter Pilot*, pp. 80–81.

10. Before the Storm

1   'Tim Vigors heard': Vigors, unpublished autobiography.

2   'Ministry of Information instructions': *The Times*, 19 June 1940.

3   'a newspaper circulating in south-east England': *Chichester and Southern Post*, 22 June 1940.

4   'in the officials': quoted in Brian Gardner, *Churchill in His Time*, Methuen, London, 1968, p. 65.

5   Brothers: interview with author.

6   'shortages were so acute': see Fenwick, *Dear Mother*.

7   Haw: IWM, no. 12028.

8   Usmar: IWM, no. 10588.

9   'Beaumont's diary entry': Beaumont, *Reminiscences*.

10 'awareness of problems': Ziegler, *The Story of 609 Squadron*, p. 99.

11 'The first person to greet him:' Vigors, unpublished autobiography.

12 'Deere was particularly proud': Deere, *Nine Lives*, p. 90.

13 Bird-Wilson. IWM, no. 10093.

14 'Fenwick . . . was in love': Fenwick, *Dear Mother*.

15 Rosier: IWM, no. 10157.

16 Unofficial diary of 72 Squadron in RAF Museum, Hendon.

11. The Channel Battle

1   'was now at': quoted in Deere, *Nine Lives*, p. 94.

2   'Deere narrowly escaped': ibid., p. 99.

3   Foxley-Norris: IWM, no. 10136.

4   Quayle: IWM, no. 10609.

5   Drake: interview with author.

6   'The leading historian of the Polish air force in Britain': Adam Zamoyski, *The Forgotten Few*, John Murray, London, 1995, p. 71.

7   Brothers: interview with author.

8   Bartley, IWM, no. 11086.

9   'the Me 109 carried the heavier punch': see Deighton, *Fighter*, p. 77.

10 Unwin: interview with author.

11 Cox: IWM, no. 11510.

12 'Pilots were told': see Anthony Robinson, *RAF Fighter Squadrons in the Battle of Britain*, Brockhampton Press, London, 1999, p. 31.

13 Page: IWM, no. 11103.

14 'courage, these days': quoted in Walker, *Sailor Malan*, p. 101.

15 'was said to have been able to spot': Allen, Battle for Britain, p. 77.

16 'Page . . . confessed': Page, *Shot Down in Flames*, p. 63

17 'Beaumont . . . was told': Beaumont, *Reminiscences*.

18 'Kingcome's feeling': Kingcome, *A Willingness to Die*, p. 99.

12. The Hun

1 'Milch chose Bob Tuck's aircraft': Larry Forester, *Fly for Your Life*, Frederick Muller, London, 1956, p. 59.
2 'Milch . . . sent a thank-you gift': Haslam, *The History of RAF Cranwell*, p. 62.
3 'Kingcome's sardonic style wavered': IWM, no. 10152.
4 Becker: interview with author.
5 Schöpfel: interview with author.
6 'his first private meeting with Hitler': David Baker, *Adolf Galland, the Authorized Biography*, Windrow & Greene, London, 1996, p. 43.
7 Foxley-Norris: interview with author.
8 'as long as I can': Wick quoted in Mike Spick, *Luftwaffe Fighter Aces*, Greenhill Books, 1996, p. 73.
9 'to attach, to track': ibid., p. 128.
10 Galland, IWM, no. 2791
11 Schöpfel: interview with author.
12 'he told his biographer': Baker, *Adolf Galland*, p. 94.

13. Hearth and Home

1 Brothers: interview with author.
2 Greenwood: letter to Dilip Sarkar, in RAF Museum, Hendon archives.
3 Elkington: interview with author.
4 Considine: IWM, no. 10961.
5 Foxley-Norris: IWM, no. 10136.
6 'circling and sweeping': quoted in Ziegler, *The Story of 609 Squadron*, p. 119.
7 Page: IWM, no. 11103.
8 Constable Maxwell: diary of Michael Constable Maxwell, in RAF Museum, Hendon, Research Department.
9 Fink: interview contained in research papers of Alexander McKee (for his book *Strike from the Sky – the Battle of Britain Story*, New English Library, London, 1969), now in RAF Museum, Hendon.
10 'After two months': Dennis Armitage, unpublished memoir.
11 Armitage: interview with author.
12 Gundry: Pilot Officer Kenneth Gundry, letters to parents, RAF Museum, Hendon.
13 'The attack was led': Ziegler, *The Story of 609 Squadron*, p. 122.
14 'John Dundas . . . wrote': ibid., p. 120.
15 'the base's historian': Rocky Stockman, *The History of RAF Manston*, RAF Station Manston, pp. 35–44.
16 'None of us had ever': Group Captain Robert Deacon Elliot, *Unofficial History of 72 Squadron*, RAF Museum, Hendon.
17 Sheen: IWM, no. 12137.
18 Bowring: IWM, no. 12173.

19 Fiske: see David Alan Johnson, *The Battle of Britain*, Combined Publishing, Pennsylvania, 1998, p. 120.
20 'Deere wrote later': Deere, *Nine Lives*, p. 142.
21 Marjery Wace: IWM, no. 2259.

14. Attrition

1   Foxley-Norris: IWM, no. 10136.
2   'Al Deere . . . noticed': Deere, *Nine Lives*, p. 136.
3   Gillam: IWM, no. 10049.
4   Appleford: interview with author.
5   Usmar: IWM, no. 10588.
6   'Shown up clearly': quoted in Francis K. Mason, *Battle over Britain*, Aston Publications, 1990, p. 256.
7   'the flick': Armitage, unpublished memoir.
8   Kingcome: IWM, no. 10152.
9   Beamont: IWM, no. 10128.
10 Deere: IWM, no. 10478.
11 Beamont: IWM, no. 10128.
12 Gillam: IWM, no. 10049.
13 Cox: IWM, no. 11510.
14 'Bob Doe noticed': Doe: *Fighter Pilot*, p. 36.
15 'Malan felt': Walker, *Sailor Malan*, p. 104.
16 Holden: IWM, no. 11198.
17 'Gleave, speaking later': Gleave made his remarks in a paper delivered at a symposium on the Battle of Britain sponsored by the Royal Air Force Historical Society and the Royal Air Force Staff College, Bracknell, on 25 June 1990. It was subsequently published in *The Battle Re-Thought*, edited by Air Commander Henry Probert and Sebastian Cox, Airlife, Shrewsbury, 1991, p. 50.
18 'He talked to me': Dundas, *Flying Start*, pp. 41–2.
19 'Walker, who had been posted': William Walker, private account.
20 Gillam: IWM, no. 10049.
21 Benson: letters of Pilot Officer Noel Benson in RAF Museum, Hendon. See also correspondence relating to the death of Pilot Officer Noel Benson in RAF Museum, Hendon.
22 Brothers: interview with author.
23 Joan Lovell Hughes: interview with author.
24 Lamberty: letter to Alexander McKee in RAF Museum, Hendon.
25 '601 Squadron's historian recorded': Moulson, *The Flying Sword*, p. 89.
26 Bird-Wilson: IWM, no. 10093.
27 Kingcome: IWM, no. 10152.
28 Winskill: IWM, no. 11537.
29 'The amazing thing': Elliot, *Unofficial History of 72 Squadron*.
30 'Armitage, wounded in the left leg': Armitage, unpublished memoir.
31 Unwin: IWM, no. 11544.

32 'The RAF bureaucracy listed personal effects': IWM, Department of Documents, ref. 97/43/1.

33 'described in a poem': Anthony Richardson, 'Because of These', in *Verses of the Royal Air Force*, Hodder & Stoughton, London, 1942.

34 'no point in brooding about death': Page, *Shot Down in Flames*, p. 69.

35 'Peter's towel': Ziegler, *The Story of 609 Squadron*, p. 103, quoting David Crook, *Fighter Pilot*.

36 'left with the paperwork': Armitage, unpublished memoir.

37 'Dr Benson's grief': correspondence relating to the death of Pilot Officer Noel Benson in RAF Museum, Hendon.

38 Wronsky: letter to McKee in RAF Museum, Hendon.

39 'Townsend gave way to his emotions': Townsend, *Time and Chance*, p. 111.

40 'Deere's . . . confidence . . . began to falter': IWM, no. 10478.

41 'he told Archie Winskill': IWM, no. 11537.

15. Brotherhood

1 'Kingcome remarked': Kingcome, *A Willingness to Die*, p. 183.

2 Beamont: IWM, no. 10128.

3 Foxley-Norris: interview with author.

4 'Bartley remembered': Bartley, *Smoke Trails in the Sky*, p. 58.

5 Dunning-White: interview with author.

6 'an unsentimental book': Wing Commander Atholl Forbes DFC and Squadron Leader Hubert Allen DFC (eds.), *Ten Fighter Boys*, Collins, London, 1942, p. 79.

7 Hutchinson: interview with Sophia Coudenhove.

8 Leng: IWM, no. 12217.

9 Page: interview with author.

10 Usmar: IWM, no. 10588.

11 'John Coghlan, a flying officer,': Clayton, *What If the Heavens Fall*, pp. 3–5.

12 Bowring: IWM, no. 12173.

13 Cox: IWM, no. 11510.

14 Wellum: Geoffrey Wellum, *First Light*, Viking, London, 2002.

15 David: interview with author.

16 Foxley-Norris: interview with author.

17 'To the ground crews he could be': see testimony of George Reid, in Dilip Sarkar, *Bader's Tangmere Spitfires*, Patrick Stephens, London, 1966, p. 51.

18 David: interview with author.

19 Beamont: IWM, no. 10128.

20 'Orde describes him as': Orde, *Pilots of Fighter Command*, p. 19.

21 'To Eric Clayton he was: Clayton, *What If the Heavens Fall*, p. 5.

22 'practical joking and ragging traditions': 73 Squadron unofficial diary, IWM, Department of Documents, Box 102.

23 Beamont: IWM, no. 10128.

24 Brothers: interview with author.

25 'in Brian Kingcome's description': Kingcome, *A Willingness to Die*, p. 177.

26 'Tony Bartley recorded': Bartley, *Smoke Trails in the Sky*.
27 Holland: letters to Bunty Nash, RAF Museum, Hendon.
28 Page: IWM, no. 11103.
29 Winskill: IWM, no. 11537.
30 Smith: IWM, no. 11754.
31 'records a dinner held': 73 Squadron unofficial diary.
32 'MacGeagh: Public Record Office, ref. AIR 71.
33 Haw: IWM, no. 12028.
34 'Vigors . . . considered himself an Irishman': Vigors, unpublished autobiography.
35 Dunning-White: interview with author.
36 Hutchinson: interview with Sophia Coudenhove.
37 'Kingcome remembered': Kingcome, *A Willingness to Die*, pp. 86–7.
38 'Armitage reported': Armitage, unpublished memoir.
39 Matthews: IWM, no. 10451.
40 Barclay: RAF Museum, Hendon, Aviation Records Department, ref. B2173.
41 'It was the longest': Doug Stokes: *Paddy Finucane, Fighter Ace*, Kimber, London, p. 43.
42 'Malan told': Walker, *Sailor Malan*, p. 99.
43 Bennions: IWM, no. 10296.
44 Constable Maxwell: Constable Maxwell diary.
45 Appleford: interview with author.
46 Devitt: IWM, no. 10667.
47 Donaldson: IWM, no. 12172.
48 'One of George Unwin's sergeant pilots': interview with author.
49 'Brothers came across': interview with author.
50 Bird-Wilson: IWM, no. 10093.
51 Down: IWM, no. 11449.
52 Bird-Wilson: IWM, no. 10093.
53 Donaldson: IWM, no. 12172.
54 Gillam: IWM. no. 10049.
55 Brothers: interview with author.
56 Yvonne Agazarian: interview with author.
57 Bartley: IWM, no. 11086.
58 Drake: interview with author.
59 'Finucane wrote': IWM, Department of Documents, ref. 97/43/1.
60 'Fenwick went to the aid': Fenwick, *Dear Mother*.
61 Wissler diary: all entries from IWM, Department of Documents, ref. 97/43/1.
62 'Edith "got ever so apprehensive"': interview with author.
63 'he wrote': letter in possession of Edith Kup, née Heap.

16. 'The Day Had Been a Year'

1 'switched on the electric sight': letter of Flying Officer R. G. A. Barclay, RAF Museum, Hendon.
2 'Fink remembered': letter to McKee in RAF Museum, Hendon.

3 'Weitkus: letter to McKee in RAF Museum, Hendon.

4 'wrote Richard Barclay': diary of Flying Officer R. G. A. Barclay in RAF Museum, Hendon.

5 'A signal was intercepted': RAF Battle of Britain Campaign Diary.

6 'a taste of what Londoners were going through': Vigors, unpublished autobiography.

7 Channon: *Chips: the Diaries of Sir Henry Channon*, edited by Robert Rhodes James, Weidenfeld & Nicolson, London, 1993, p. 265.

8 'Barclay was woken at 4.30': Barclay, diary.

9 Holmes: IWM, no. 2807.

10 'sat bolt upright': see Forbes and Allen, *Ten Fighter Boys*, p. 77.

11 Cox: IWM, no. 1150.

12 'getting a hell of a plastering': see Forbes and Allen, *Ten Fighter Boys*, p. 85.

13 'spreadeagled arms and legs': quoted in Dr Alfred Price, *Battle of Britain Day*, Greenhill Books, 1999, p. 86.

14 'The day had been': see Forbes and Allen, *Ten Fighter Boys*, p. 78.

17. Autumn Sunset

1 Barclay: Barclay, diary.

2 Edge: Flight Lieutenant G. Edge, unpublished account, RAF Museum, Hendon.

3 'Goering assured the crews': quoted in Mason, *Battle over Britain*, p. 368.

4 Schöpfel: interview with author.

5 'The insouciant spirit': Bartley, *Smoke Trails in the Sky*, p. 46.

6 'Bartley wrote to his mother': ibid.

7 Bennions: IWM, no. 10296.

8 'Page caught a glimpse of himself': Page, *Shot Down in Flames*, p. 81.

9 'he met the other patients': ibid., p. 98.

10 'The barmaid at the Red Lion': Doe, *Nine Lives*, p. 56.

11 Berry: IWM, no. 11475.

12 'Barclay noted': Barclay, diary.

13 'waited in dread': Vigors, unpublished autobiography.

14 Mottram: letters to Bunty Nash in RAF Museum, Hendon.

18. Rhubarbs and Circuses

1 'It seemed to Al Deere': Deere, *Nine Lives*, p. 172.

2 'Kent reached Biggin Hill': Kent, *One of the Few*, p. 88.

3 Finucane letters: IWM, Archive Department, 97/43/1.

4 'Douglas had been informed': Terraine, *The Right of the Line*, p. 283.

5 'judged John Terraine': ibid., p. 285.

6 'Deere confessed': Deere, *Nine Lives*, p. 211.

7 'A graphic account': Public Record Office, PRO AIR, ref. 149/357.

8 'Dundas, a perceptive and humane observer': Dundas, *Flying Start*, pp. 66-7, 70 and 79.

9 Armitage: IWM, no. 10049.

10 'Aikman described': *The Times*, 18 July 1942.

11 'His sister, Yvonne': interview with author.

12 Gillam: IWM, no. 10049.

13 'Deere was "always confident"': Deere, *Nine Lives*, p. 149.

14 Brothers: interview with author.

15 Gillam: IWM, no. 10049.

Epilogue: The Last Note

1 'Roll of Honour': the roll carries the names of 718 aircrew of Bomber Command and 280 of Coastal Command as well as those of Fighter Command who died during the period.

2 'Malan . . . decided: Walker, *Sailor Malan*.

3 'Kingcome wrote of Barthropp': Kingcome, *A Willingness to Die*, p. 176.

4 'Kingcome's attitude': ibid., p. xi.

5 Edith Heap: interview with author.

6 Kreipe: quoted in Terraine, *The Right of the Line*, p. 219.

7 'wrote Townsend': Townsend, *Time and Chance*, p. 110.

8 Bennions: IWM, no. 10296.

9 Yvonne Agazarian: interview with author.

Index

BOMBER BOYS

PATRICK BISHOP

BOMBER BOYS

Fighting Back 1940–1945

WILLIAM
COLLINS

To Peter, Margaret, Amelia
and Daniel

Contents

List of Illustrations

Mary Mileham. *Courtesy Philip Mileham / Imperial War Museum*

Frank Blackman. *Imperial War Museum*

George Hull. *Courtesy Joan Hatfield*

Joan Kirby. *Courtesy Joan Hatfield*

Frances Dowdeswell. *Courtesy Frances Dowdeswell*

Denholm Elliott and Virginia McKenna, 1954. *Hulton Getty*

Tony Iveson in 1943. *Courtesy Tony Iveson*

Don Charlwood. *Courtesy Crécy Publishing*

Ken Newman. *Courtesy Ken Newman*

Reg Fayers' self-portrait. *Imperial War Museum*

Tony Iveson and some of his crew. *Courtesy Tony Iveson*

Setting off for Hamburg, July 1943. *Imperial War Museum*

Arthur Harris with his wife Jill and daughter Jackie.
Imperial War Museum

Leonard Cheshire. *ww2images.com*

Charles Portal and Ira Eaker. *Imperial War Museum* (H27478)

A B-24 Liberator in a daylight raid. *Ullstein Bild*

A B-17 Flying Fortress drops its bombs. *akg-images*

A Grand Slam bursts on Arnsberg Bridge, March 1945.
From Volume III (plate 23) of *History of the Second World War* by
Sir Charles Webster and Noble Frankland

Cyril March and crew. *Courtesy Cy March*

The Dresden raid. *ww2images.com*

VE Day crowds outside the Saracen's Head.
Courtesy of Lincolnshire Echo

While every effort has been made to trace the owners of copyright material reproduced herein, the publishers will be pleased to rectify any errors or omissions in any reprints and future editions.

Main Bomber Command
stations in the UK

0   10   20   30   40   50

miles

North
Sea

O Group HQ
• Airfield

• Middleton St George
• Croft
• Leeming
• Thirsk   • Wombleton
Skipton-on-   • Topcliffe
Swale
Dishforth •   • Dalton
Linton-on-Ouse •   • Tholthorpe
Allerton O   • East Moor
Marston Moor •   Full Sutton •
Rufforth •   O YORK • Pocklington
Elvington •   • Leconfield
Riccall •   • Melbourne
Breighton •   • Holme-on-Spalding-Moor
Burn •
Snaith •   • North Killingholme
Elsham Wolds
Sandtoft •   • Kirmington
Lindholme •   SCUNTHORPE
Doncaster •   • Finningley   • Grimsby
Bircotes • O   • Blyton   • Binbrook
Bawtry   Sturgate • Hemswell   • Kelstern
Faldingworth •   • Ludford Magna
Worksop •   Ingham •   • Wickenby   • Strubby
Gamston •   Scampton •   • Dunholme Lodge
LINCOLN   • Fiskerton
Ossington •   Wigsley •   Skellingthorpe • Bardney   • Spilsby
Swinderby O   • East Kirkby
Winthorpe •   • Woodhall Spa
Waddington •   Balderton •   • Coningsby
Syerston •   • Fulbeck   Metheringham •
Newton •
Langar   • Bottesford
O Grantham
• Church Broughton
O Eggington
• Tatenhill   • Castle Donington   • Saltby
• Lichfield   Wymeswold •   • Cottesmore
• Woolfox Lodge
North Luffenham •
Nuneaton •   Bruntingthorpe •   Market   Polebrook •
Bramcote •   Bitteswell •   Harborough   • Upwood
Husbands Bosworth •   Desborough •   Warboys •
Honiley •   Harrington •   Alconbury •   Wyton •
Wellesbourne   Molesworth •   • Huntington O
Mountford   Graveley •
• Gaydon   Kimbolton •   • Bourn
• Stratford   • Chipping Warden   Little Staughton •
Edgehill •   Tempsford •
Hinton-in-the-Hedges •   • Silverstone   Bassingbourn •
Croughton •   Turweston   • Cranfield   Steeple Morden •
Barford St John •   Finmere •   • Little Horwood
Enstone •   O Winslow
• Bicester   • Wing
Upper Heyford •   • Westcott   • Cheddington
Weston-on-the-Green •   • Oakley

Carnaby •
Driffield •
• Lissett

• North Creake
• Little Snoring
Sculthorpe •   Foulsham •   • Oulton
Great Massingham •   Swannington •
West Raynham •   • Attlebridge
Swanton Morley •   Bylaugh   Horsham St Faith
Hall O
Downham Market •   Marham •
• Watton
Methwold •   Bodney •
Feltwell •   • East Wretham
Mepal •
• Witchford   • Lakenheath
Waterbeach •   Mildenhall •
• Tuddenham   • Honington
Exning •
O Exning   • Newmarket
Oakington •
CAMBRIDGE   • Chedburgh
Gransden Lodge •   Stradishall •   • Wattisham
Wratting Common •   Woodbridge •
• Ridgewell
Ridgewell •

N
W   E
S

Mount Farm •
Benson •
Hampstead •   High Wycombe
Norris   HQ Bomber Command

LONDON

Main Targets in Europe

| 0 | 100 | 200 | 300 |

miles

Range circles are measured from Lincoln

⊙ ○   Bomb targets

Stockholm •

D E N

Baltic Sea

penhagen

Minsk •

EAST
PRUSSIA

Danzig ⊙

SOVIET
UNION

⦾ Sassnitz
Peenemünde
nemünde ⦾ Swinemünde

⊙ Stettin

R M A N Y

Warsaw •

Berlin ⊙
dam ⊙

POLAND

deburg
Dessau
eipzig   Dresden
⊙   ⊙
na

Chemnitz

Krakow •

Prague •

⊙
Pilsen

C Z E C H O S L O V A K I A

uremberg
Schwandorf
⊙ Regensburg

• Linz   Vienna •   • Bratislava

⊙ Munich
Berchtesgaden

AUSTRIA

• Budapest

HUNGARY

RUMANIA

Bucharest •

• Trieste

Belgrade •

Y U G O S L A V I A

BULGARIA

• Sophia

I T A L Y

Adriatic Sea

Germany

Stalag Luft I — POW camp

– – – – – Siegfried Line

North Sea

DENMARK

Hörnum
Flensburg
Heligoland
Heide
Kiel
Kiel Canal
Brunsbüttel
Stermoor
Lübeck
Wismar
East Friesian Islands
Wilhelmshaven
Schulau
Emden
Bremerhaven
Hamburg/Harburg
Fredebur
Tarmstedt
Wenzendorf
Büchen
Farge
Rotenburg
Hitzacker
Bremen
Hemelingen

N
W E
S

Diepholz
Nienburg
Nienhagen
Aller
Dortmund-Ems Canal
Misburg
Dedenhausen
Amsterdam
Hannover
Dollbergen
Ehmen
HOLLAND
Salzbergen
Osnabrück
Brunswick
Rotterdam
Waal
Ibbenbüren
Salzgitter
Münster
Ems
Biedefeld
Dülmen
Killwinkle
Emmerich
Paderborn
Eindhoven
Rhine-Herne Canal
Hamm
Bernburg
Duisburg
Kamen
Königsborn
Antwerp
Krefeld
Ruhr
Rüthen
Göttingen
BELGIUM
Essen
Düsseldorf
Kassel
Brussels
Louvain
Reisholz
Monheim
Fredeburg
Eschwege
Waterloo
Cologne
Wesseling
GERMANY
Efurt
Weimar
Liège
Aachen
Gotha
Bad Berka
Jen
Bonn
Schmidt
Dulag Luft
Rhine
Neuwied
Wetzlar
Thuringian Forest
ARDENNES
Koblenz
Limburg
Fulda
Lutterade
Moselle
Wiesbaden
Frankfurt
Hanau
Coburg
Schweinfurt
LUXEMBOURG
Mainz
Darmstadt
Bamberg
Bayreuth
Trier
Kreuznach
Würzburg
Pegnitz
Worms
Neunkirchen
Oppau
Mannheim
Erlangen
Verdun
Merchweillen
Ludwigs-hafen
Nuremberg
Metz
Maas
Karlsruhe
600 miles from Foggia
FRANCE
Meuse
Pforzheim
Stuttgart
Strasbourg
Baden-Baden
Danube
Neuburg
Offenburg
Rhine
Breisach
Munich
Freiburg
Freiham

English Channel

0   25   50   75   100

miles

Baltic Sea

Königsberg
Pillau

Stalag Luft I

Rügen

Bay of Pomerania

Danzig

Warnemünde
Rostock

Peenemünde

Allenstein

Swinemünde

Stettin

Poelitz

Vistula

Berlin

Derben

Potsdam

Frankfurt

Posen

POLAND

gdeburg
Froese

Oder

Lübben

itzhendorf
na Leipzig
en Mölbis
itz Rositz

Riesa

Ruhland

Görlitz

Breslau

Meissen

Dresden

Stalag Luft III

Stalag Luft III B

Chemnitz
Schkopau

Freital

Deschowitz
Blechhammer

Malopolska

Brux Roudnice

Bohumin

Oswiecim

Kralupy

Prague

Kolin

Pardubice

Czechowitz

Moravska Ostrava

Bohemian Forest

sburg

Danube

CZECHOSLOVAKIA

Krems

Korneuburg

Linz

Vienna
Schwechat

Floridsdorf

Bratislava

600 miles from Lincoln

The Ruhr Valley

0   10   20   30

miles

Telgte

Ems

Münster

Werse

Hamm

Kamen

Soest

ortmund

MÖHNE DAM

Ruhr

Möhne

Neheim

chwerte   Hüsten

Iserlohn

Ruhr

Brilon

Kassel

Lenne

SORPE DAM

Lüdenscheid

EDER DAM

Eder

GERMANY

Homberg

Morsbach   Siegen

N

W   E

S

Lahn

BERLIN

1:18.000

⊙ *railway stations* ⊙ *overhead and underground railway*
tramway *omnibus*
S.- station of the "Stadtbahn"
F.- station of the "Fernbahn" (long-distance line)
⊕ *post office* ⊞ *theatre* ⚲ *concert hall* ⚓ *monuments*
⊛ *best motor - and bicycle-roads*

Prologue

PERKINS

In the early summer of 1961, sophisticated Londoners were laughing at an entertainment brought to them by four young Oxbridge graduates. *Beyond the Fringe* had been a great hit at the Edinburgh Festival the previous year. Now, night after night, smiling audiences in the capital left the Fortune Theatre feeling they had witnessed something fresh, audacious and above all very funny. The excitement that comes with the anticipation of sudden and unpredictable change was in the May air. The old, hierarchical Britain personified by the prime minister, Harold Macmillan, appeared to be tottering to an end. The shape of the future was hard to make out but it surely belonged to the young, the daring and the irreverent. Alan Bennett, Peter Cook, Jonathan Miller and Dudley Moore were the incarnation of all that.

One of the sketches was called 'Aftermyth of War'. It made fun of legends created during wartime and already planted deep in Britain's consciousness. There was quite a list. It mocked Neville Chamberlain and his 'piece of paper', stoical working-class Londoners and the Blitz spirit and even the Battle of Britain. Then it was the turn of the men who flew in the aeroplanes that bombed Germany.

The sequence opens with Peter Cook, in the uniform of a senior RAF officer, entering to the sound of airmen singing heartily around a piano.

> COOK: Perkins! (Jonathan Miller breaks away from the singing.) Sorry to drag you away from the fun, old boy. War's not going very well, you know.

MILLER: Oh my God!

COOK: . . . war is a psychological thing, Perkins, rather like a game of football. You know how in a game of football ten men often play better than eleven?

MILLER: Yes, sir.

COOK: Perkins, we are asking you to be that one man. I want you to lay down your life, Perkins. We need a futile gesture at this stage. It will raise the whole tone of the war. Get up in a crate, Perkins, pop over to Bremen, take a shufti, don't come back. Goodbye, Perkins. God, I wish I was going too.

MILLER: Goodbye, sir – or is it – *au revoir*?

COOK: *No*, Perkins.

The last lines got one of the biggest laughs of the night. In the stalls, sitting with his wife Margery Baker, Tony Iveson tried to laugh along with the rest. They both worked in the new world of television and were part of the emerging Britain. But not very long before he had been Squadron Leader Tony Iveson DFC of 617 Squadron, and at the front of the bombing war. 'I didn't like it,' he said forty-four years later. 'I remember being upset. I probably wouldn't be now but at the time it seemed unnecessary, in view of how many we lost.'[1]

Of the 125,000 airmen who passed through Bomber Command during the war, about 55,000 were killed. Twenty-one of the dead were called Perkins. The first to die was Flying Officer Reginald Perkins of 54 Squadron who was killed on the night of 14/15 November 1940. He was the pilot of a Hampden which took off from Waddington in Lincolnshire to bomb Berlin. Little is known about his death or those of his three crew mates. Their aircraft is 'believed to have exploded in the air and crashed on the outskirts of Berlin'.[2] The last to die was Flying Officer Robert Perkins of 49 Squadron, the pilot of a Lancaster who was killed with the rest of his crew while bombing the Lutzkendorf oil refinery on the night of 8/9 April 1945, a month before the end of the war in Europe.[3] Nothing at all is known about how they were lost.

As far as I am aware, no Perkins died bombing Bremen, but one might well have done. From 18 May 1940 until the end of the Second World War it was attacked some seventy times. As a result, about 575 aircrew were killed. So too were 3,562 residents.[4] It is this aspect of Bomber Command's war, the death of German civilians, that has preoccupied historians in the years since the *Beyond the Fringe* sketch. All the myths that were the butt of its jokes have since been re-examined and turned out to be remarkably resilient. It is Bomber Command's reputation that has suffered the most. Re-evaluations have found the crews' efforts to be at best misdirected and at worst little better than war crimes.

This last accusation is false and insults truth and justice. Bomber Command, as I have said, attacked Bremen frequently. The first bombs killed thirteen people. They also burned down two warehouses full of furniture confiscated from Jews who had understood what fate awaited them in Germany and fled. Bombers were busy over the city on the night of 17/18 January 1942. Only eight of the eighty-three aircraft dispatched found the target and little damage appears to have been done. The Nazi newspapers in the days following denounced the raiders as 'terror fliers'. As they did so, sixteen Nazi bureaucrats met on 20 January in a villa at Wannsee outside Berlin to co-ordinate the extermination of the entire Jewish population of Europe.

The Nazis were to good as a black hole is to light. The effects of British and American bombing on Germany and the lands the Germans conquered were dreadful and it is right that they should be recorded and remembered. But the Allies' real crime would have been to hold back from using any of the means at their disposal to destroy Hitler and those who sustained his war.

The argument over exactly what Bomber Command achieved will never be settled. One undeniable success, an awkward one to acknowledge nowadays, is that it altered Germany's personality. Saturation bombing may not, as intended, have broken the Germans' spirit. But it helped powerfully to bring about their post-war conversion to peaceful democracy.

History in its current mood has paid limited attention to the ethos and character of the men who fought this most extraordinary war. This book sets out to correct that imbalance. It is for, and about, Perkins. In the process I want also to redress a wrong. There is no national memorial to the men of Bomber Command, no one place where their sacrifice and contribution to victory are properly and thankfully commemorated. I hope that *Bomber Boys* will mark a first step in changing that.

Introduction

After the Whirlwind

No one who saw what Allied bombing did to Germany forgot it. A traveller in an official delegation passing through Berlin two months after the German surrender noted in his diary: 'Berlin . . . is ghastly. I could never have believed how complete the destruction is. We covered [about five miles] and saw less than a dozen undamaged houses and not one in ten was anything more than a burned-out shell.'

Soon afterwards he visited Potsdam, less than twenty miles to the west.'Bert Harris removed the town of Potsdam in half an hour one night in April,' he wrote. 'I have never seen anything so complete . . . the usual procession of handcarts, prams etc. and the same slab-faced people as in Berlin.'

The sight, he felt, was the finest possible lesson to the Germans of the folly of initiating wars. Yet he 'came away feeling very sorry for these people and when I eventually said so I found all the others felt just the same.'[1]

The man who wrote these words had played a central part in creating the scenes he witnessed. He was Marshal of the Royal Air Force Sir Charles Portal, who as Chief of the Air Staff had overseen the bombing campaign. 'Bert Harris' was his subordinate, Air Marshal Sir Arthur Harris, the head of Bomber Command who had put Allied strategic theories into devastating practice.

A little afterwards, a veteran pilot who had taken part in many of the raids flew over some of the areas he had bombed. 'It was a fine clear day and we flew at 4,000 feet,' wrote Peter Johnson, 'a good height for an overall view and we saw as we passed something of what had happened to, amongst others, Hamburg, Lübeck, Hanover, the Ruhr towns, Cologne, Aachen and Düsseldorf and so south

Potsdam, 1945.

to Stuttgart, Nuremberg and Munich . . . the general devastation was almost unbelievable. In town after town hardly a building seemed to be intact, hardly a house seemed to be habitable. All that showed from the air were rows and rows of empty boxes, walls enclosing nothing . . . the whole area was, for the time being at least, dead, dead, dead.'

Johnson could not help wondering 'whether this truly dreadful sight represented a degree of overkill, whether such destruction had really been necessary to stop the production of arms for the Nazis in the greatest industrial complex in Europe.' He reassured himself with the thought that even when the Ruhr was encircled by Allied forces the German people 'were still obeying Hitler's frenzied calls for resistance to the last man'.[2]

The debris was to hang around accusingly for years. In March 1949 the American diplomat George Kennan returned to Hamburg where he had served in pre-war days. He visited the large residential districts east of the Alster. 'Here was sweeping devastation, down to the ground, mile after mile,' he wrote. 'It had all been done in three days and nights in 1943, my host told me. Seventy-five thousand persons had perished in the process. Even now, after the lapse of six years, over three thousand bodies were estimated to be buried there in the rubble.'*

These sights demanded reflection, and justification or judgement. The natural response of most of those who planned or carried out the attacks was the same as Portal's. The Germans, unquestionably, had started it. They had, as Harris predicted in a much-repeated proverb, sown the wind and reaped the whirlwind. Kennan, however, felt differently. For the first time since the war ended, he wrote, 'I felt an unshakeable conviction that no momentary military advantage – even if such could be calculated to exist – could have justified this stupendous, careless destruction of civilian life and of material values, built up laboriously by human hands over the course of centuries for purposes having nothing to do with this war. Least of all could it be justified by the screaming non-sequitur, "They did it to us."'[3]

The debate over the morality of all-out aerial bombardment had been under way long before the strategic air campaign began and would rumble through the post-war years to the present day. But the first reaction of those who gazed across the haunted mounds of rubble that were all that remained of scores of German city centres was simple awe at the destruction that had been wrought. The onlookers thought they knew what a blitzed town looked like. The results of what bombs did were on display in many of Britain's major cities. But none of them looked like this.

During the war Bomber Command had been a priceless asset to government propaganda, as a symbol of Britain's resolve and its willingness and ability to take the war to the enemy. Its actions were thoroughly publicized and its pilots and crewmen ranked as heroes. It fought a continuous campaign from the first day of the war to the last, interrupted only by the weather. The enormous effort and the great sacrifice of life this entailed were honoured and the destruction done to the enemy was presented as a vital element

* The actual number of victims of the raids carried out on Hamburg between 27–30 July 1943 was closer to 40,000 dead.

in the victory. In peacetime, the wrecked towns and the grave pits filled with the bones of civilians became an embarrassment and the Bomber Boys faded from the official legend. On the afternoon of 13 May 1945 Churchill broadcast his Victory in Europe speech. There was praise for everyone who had contributed to the war effort. But apart from an allusion to the damage done to Berlin, the main activities of the bomber crews were barely mentioned. There were campaign medals for those who had fought in Asia, the Middle East and Europe. There was to be no specific award for the men who had set about dismantling Hitler's empire from the air.

The public memory of the air war was selective. People seemed inclined to consign the bombing campaign and those who had fought it to the past. The pilots of Fighter Command, however, had a special place in the post-war consciousness. Scores of books were written by them and about them. Men like Douglas Bader, Bob Stanford Tuck and 'Sailor' Malan were celebrities. They were The Few and the battle that they fought was relatively short, roughly four months from the beginning of July to the end of October 1940. The men who crewed the bombers were The Many and their struggle went on and on. Of the 125,000 who passed through the fire, only Guy Gibson and Leonard Cheshire won any lasting fame. Gibson had led the Dams Raid of May 1943, a feat of dash and daring, quite unlike the demolition work which Bomber Command conducted every night. Cheshire was known not so much for damaging people as for healing them, in the homes he set up after the war.

Nobody, it seemed, wanted victory to be tarnished by reminders of the methods that were used to obtain it. Harris had a simple explanation for the ambivalence. 'The bomber drops things on people and people don't like things being dropped on them,' he remarked after the war. 'And the fighter shoots at the bomber who drops things. Therefore he is popular whereas the bomber is unpopular. It's as easy as that.'[4]

There was much in what he said. In the United States, which was never touched by aerial bombardment, there was no such uneasiness and the crews of the Liberators and Flying Fortresses were honoured alongside the rest of America's fighting men and their deeds praised in films like *Twelve O'Clock High*. The official assertion that Americans were engaged in precise bombing, rather than the area bombing practised by the British, was widely accepted, even though the distinction often meant little to the people underneath.

The strategic air campaign fought by the RAF and the USAAF was a terrible novelty. For the first time, aeroplanes were used in huge numbers against large population areas to smash an enemy's capacity to make war by destroying its industry and demoralizing its civilians.

The German Blitz of British cities over the winter of 1940–41 provided the campaign's initial justification. Bomber Command's subsequent *raison d'être* was that it was the main means of exerting direct offensive pressure on Germany, within its own territory. At first the crews flew smallish aeroplanes carrying negligible bomb loads and were guided by primitive navigational aids. In the month of February 1942 when Harris took over his men dropped 1,001 tons of bombs. Better aircraft, new technology, cleverer tactics, Harris's ruthless style and – above all – the courage and skill of the crews, turned the air force into the most potent proof of Britain's will to win. In the month of March 1945, with Allied troops closing on Berlin, they dropped 67,637 tons and the Americans 65,962. By the end, the hurt the Luftwaffe had done to Britain had been repaid over and over. German air attacks against the British Isles, including those by V weapons late in the war, killed just over 60,000. Estimates of the deaths caused by Allied bombing of Germany range between 305,000 and 600,000. The cities touched by the Blitz were scarred but not devastated. In 1945 Germany's seventy biggest towns and cities were in ruins and one in five dwelling places destroyed.[5]

This disproportionality caused very little anxiety at the time. Germany had struck first and deserved the retribution the RAF was meting out. What concern might have been felt at the suffering of German civilians faded in the knowledge of the price the Bomber Boys were paying to deliver this vengeance. It was impossible to hide the losses and the government did not try.

This was a home-front war and civilians along the outbound and inbound routes to the Continent were present at the opening and closing scenes of the action. During the war years the RAF in Britain grew into the most visible of the services. In the bomber station-cluttered east and north there seemed almost as many airmen and -women as there were civilians. 'By the time I got there Lincoln had turned blue,' remembered Reg Payne, a wireless operator who was based at Skellingthorpe just outside the city.[6]

Bomber Command grew and grew as the volunteers arrived in numbers that never slackened even during the darkest hours of its campaign. Behind each man flying, there were many more keeping them in the air. There were fitters and riggers and armourers maintaining the huge aeroplanes. There were WAAFs who drove the crews to their hangars and staffed the operations rooms when ops were on. There were the women who served them their dinner before they took off and, with luck, their breakfast when they returned home. RAF men met and mingled with local women in dance-halls and pubs, flirting with them, sometimes sleeping with them, often marrying them. Homesick young men were adopted by families and would slip away for an afternoon in front of a coal fire in a front parlour that reminded them of the family life they had left behind.

The many Britons who had seen the RAF going into action, droning overhead on their way to and from Germany and France and Italy, relished the sight. They learned of what they did there from the newspapers and BBC radio for whom Bomber Command's actitivies provided the main source of good news for much of the war. The tone of the reports was exultant. 'The Vengeance Begins!' was the strapline on the *Daily Express* front-page story of Monday 1 June 1942 announcing the first thousand-bomber raid on Cologne. The sky over the city was 'as busy as Piccadilly Circus'. One bomber passed over every six seconds and 3,000 tons of bombs were dropped in ninety minutes*. It was particularly pleasing to report that the official communiqué from Berlin admitted that 'great damage' had been done. 'Germans squeal "havoc, misery"'' was the headline on the story of how the Nazis had reacted to the raid.

The RAF had saved the country from invasion by winning the

---

* The real figure was 1,455 tons.

Battle of Britain. It had failed, it was true, to prevent the Blitz. But now, night after night it was carrying the war to the Reich, paying the Germans back in kind and contributing mightily to the downfall of Hitler and the Nazis.

That was how it was seen by British civilians as they read accounts of devastating attacks on previously obscure towns such as Essen, Duisburg and Gelsenkirchen and great cities like Hamburg and Cologne and, above all, Berlin. This was how it was presented by Harris, a natural propagandist, who strove to create the impression that with each raid the road to victory and peace was one step shorter. This was what was believed by the majority of the men who were flying the aeroplanes. They tended to be bolder and more imaginative than the rest of their contemporaries. Flying was dangerous but they preferred its perils and the relative informality of RAF life to the drudgery of existence as a soldier. In letters and diaries they reveal a high degree of idealism and optimism and a strong sense that they were fighting not only to destroy a present evil but also to lay the foundations of a future good.

In a letter to the father of his friend Andrew 'Paddy' Wilson, who was killed during a raid on Düsseldorf in June 1943, Sergeant John Lobban, the sole survivor of the crew, wrote: 'They died for the greatest of causes, the freedom of the peace-loving nations and I only wish that fate could have let us play a greater part in bringing the war to a close.' It had been their first operation.[7]

Such idealism is found mainly in the young. Many of the Bomber Boys were barely out of their teens, though the almost constant strain they lived with made them seem older. They were called Dougie and Ron and Ken and Reg and Bill. They came from the middle reaches of society and were strongly marked by their time. In their short lives they had felt the numb emotional pain left by the last war and sensed the mounting dread among their elders as the next one approached. They knew what poverty was and had witnessed the cruelties of interwar capitalism. If there was a dominant political outlook among the crews it was a mildly sceptical socialism and belief in social justice. But overlying it always was a profound sense of duty. None of them set out to destroy German cities and few cared to reflect too closely on the effects of their bombs. But like the rest of their generation, they possessed a patriotism and respect for authority that had barely been dented by their knowledge of the First World War. It was easier for them to do what they did because they tended to believe what they were told about the purpose and progress of their struggle. It was an outstanding peculiarity of the strange new conflict they were engaged in that there was no real measure of gain. Armies could gauge success by the amount of ground taken or the number of enemy killed or captured. Navies could do so by the quantity of enemy tonnage sunk. But how did you judge the achievements of a bombing campaign?

The authorities continually proclaimed the effectiveness of Bomber Command's actions. Early communiqués created an illusion of extraordinary efficiency, of bombs slanting down on strictly military targets with scientific precision. This optimistic view was based largely on the reports of the pilots dropping the ordnance, an unreliable measure as it was to turn out. It was only after two years of war, when a report based on an analysis of aerial photographs revealed the hopeless inaccuracy of most bombing, that tactics and equipment improved and the gap between reality and propaganda began to close. By the end of the war Bomber Command could obliterate any target it wished to and did so, sometimes flattening towns whose military importance was minuscule. But the value of such destruction was always open to question and afterwards there was disagreement over what it was that Bomber Command had achieved.

Harris lived another forty years after the last bomb was dropped. Right until his death he fought to persuade the world that his Command's contribution to victory had been decisive. His arguments were based not so much on the data provided by the American and British official surveys of damage conducted after the war, but more on the word of Hitler's munitions minister, the silky and self-interested Albert Speer. The surveys themselves failed to settle the arguments that raged throughout the war over how bomber power should be applied and started a new round of controversy.

The questions of how much material harm bombing did to the German war effort, and whether the energy and sacrifices involved were worth it, have never been fully answered and never will be.

It was even more difficult to determine the psychological effect of bombing. Bombs were spiritual as much as physical weapons. Air strategists had been arguing since aeroplanes were invented that the *moral* power of bombing was as great as anything it did to factories or homes, perhaps much greater. By destroying the will of workers to work, air attacks could do as much effective damage as they did when they smashed up a steelworks or assembly line.

This convenient belief grew as it became clear that pre-war assumptions about bombing accuracy were absurdly optimistic. The first bombs were aimed at small targets and hit nothing. Better then to aim at a large target and hit something – anything – for in a built-up area no bomb would be wasted. Even if a bomb missed the factory it was aimed at, the chances were it would hit the home of someone who was employed there. It might kill him and his family. Death or fear of death would keep him away from work. If enough bombs were dropped, so the theory ran, workers might eventually turn against their rulers and force them to stop fighting.

Even before the war the evidence available from the German and Italian bombardments of Madrid and Barcelona suggested that this was not necessarily so. Britain's own experience of the Blitz pointed to a more startling conclusion: that aerial bombardment could actually toughen resolve and deepen resistance. For much of the war, there was a prevailing belief that Germany would crack if only it was hit hard and often enough. The RAF's pre-war professional judgement that in a totalitarian state, coercion trumped public opinion, was soon forgotten in the desperation to achieve results.

The lack of any accurate understanding of what the campaign was achieving was characteristic of the oddly disconnected way in which the war was waged. Even those dropping the bombs felt they were engaged in a surreal exercise. Looking down from a Lancaster or Halifax at Essen or Berlin from 20,000 feet you saw nothing that connected you to the earth you knew, only a diabolical *son et lumière* of smoke and fire. 'I would try to tell myself . . . that this was a city,' wrote Don Charlwood, an Australian navigator with 103 Squadron. 'A place with the familiar sights of civilization. But the thought would carry little conviction. A German city was always this, this hellish picture of flame, gunfire and searchlights, an unreal picture because we could not hear it or feel its breath. Sometimes when the smoke rolled back and we saw streets and buildings I felt startled. Perhaps if we had seen the white, upturned faces of people, as over England we sometimes did, our hearts would have rebelled.'[8]

Harris liked to call the successive phases of the air war 'battles'. There was a Battle of Hamburg, a Battle of the Ruhr, a Battle of Berlin. But they were not battles as most people understood the word. There was not one enemy, waiting and visible, but many. The crews were constantly at the mercy of the weather and mechanical failure. On the approach routes and over the targets they faced searchlights, flak and night-fighters. There was no relaxation on the way home. The last minutes were sometimes as dangerous as the time over target as the skies above the base filled with aircraft, many of them sieved with flak and cannon holes, clinging to the air with their last few gallons of petrol, praying for the signal to touch down.

Flying in bombers was an extraordinarily dangerous activity. Harris, with his usual harsh honesty, asked people to bear in mind that 'these crews, shining youth on the threshold of life, lived under circumstances of intolerable strain. They were in fact – and they knew it – faced with the virtual certainty of death, probably in one of its least pleasant forms.'[9]

Altogether 55,573 Bomber Command aircrew – British, Canadian, Australian, New Zealanders and others – were killed. That is out of a total of 125,000 who served. Another 8,403 were wounded and 9,838 taken prisoner. In simple terms that means 44.4 per cent of those who flew, died. The real picture was rather grimmer. Many of those included in the overall aircrew figure were still training when the war ended and never saw action. According to one study, the true figure is closer to 65 per cent. The chances of death then, were appallingly high, far higher than those facing soldiers and sailors. The life expectancy of an airman was considerably shorter even than that of a junior infantry officer on the Western Front in

1916.[10] To Peter Johnson who swapped a cushy instruction post for operational flying, the enterprise sometimes seemed like the Charge of the Light Brigade, over and over again.

It was no wonder that crews discussed obsessively the odds on their survival and tried to discern some pattern in the tapestry of death. It was very confusing. Some 'sprog' crews fresh from a training unit got the 'chop' first time out. But so did veterans on their last but one trip of their thirty-operation tour. Good pilots died inexplicably and poor ones blundered through. It was all down to luck and Lady Luck, capricious tart that she was, had to be wooed and cosseted constantly. The modern young men in the bombers were as superstitious as mediaeval peasants. Final preparations would be thrown into chaos if someone lost his lucky silk stocking or remembered he had forgotten a pre-operation ritual. They also developed a mediaeval fatalism. Flying was 'dicing' and death was 'the reaper'.

But despite death's towering presence, it could still seem curiously remote. It was a common experience to see an aeroplane just like your own, ahead of you in the bomber stream, suddenly explode as flak ignited hundreds of gallons of petrol and thousands of pounds of explosive. It was not unusual to watch as a night-fighter nosed upwards beneath the pregnant belly of an unsuspecting neighbour and with one squirt of its vertically-directed guns sent it screaming down.

After witnessing these dreadful sights, crews were often struck by the complexity and selfishness of their feelings. 'Suddenly,' wrote Harry Yates, a Lancaster pilot, 'ahead of us in the stream a vic of three kites was consumed in a prodigious burst of flame which immediately erupted outwards under the force of the secondary explosion. The leader had been hit in the bomb bay, the others were too close. No one could have survived, I knew. There was no point in looking for parachutes. I flew on straight and level, Tubby standing beside me, both of us dumbstruck by the appallingly unfair swiftness and violence of it all. But there was still that deeply-drawn breath of relief that somebody else, and not oneself, had run out of luck. And hard on the heels of *that* was a pang of guilt. One grieved for whoever was in the kites and wondered if friends might not be coming home . . .'[11]

For all the danger, operations involved little that could be described as exciting or could later be interpreted as glamorous. There were stretches of tedium. For wireless operators and bomb-aimers there was little to do for much of the time. Only the navigator and the pilot were kept permanently occupied and there was not much fun in flying bombers. Piloting a Lancaster was nothing like skidding across the skies in a Spitfire. It was a task rather than a pleasure, requiring endless tiny adjustments and constant vigilance. Guy Gibson, the leader of the Dams Raid, compared bomber pilots to bus-drivers.

There was a complete absence of comfort. The rear gunner, stuck at the 'arse end' of a Lancaster, froze. The wireless operator, stuck next to the port inner engine, often roasted. Everyone was swaddled in multiple layers of clothing surmounted by parachute harness and Mae West lifejacket. It was hard work moving around the cramped, equipment-stacked interior, where every edge was sharp and threatened injury.

On the ground life was far removed from the ease of the RAF's pre-war existence and there were few of the comforts or entertainments available to the fighter pilots of 1940 when they touched down at the end of the day. Writing to his wife from his first squadron, Flying Officer Reg Fayers was anxious to dispel any idea that the organization he had joined resembled 'Max Aitken's RAF'. Aitken, Lord Beaverbrook's son, had fought in the Battle of Britain and was a model of style and sophistication. 'You are fastidious and sweetsmelling cleanliness,' Fayers declared. 'You are gentle, you are comfort . . . the RAF is opposite in all respects.'[12]

The defining sound of Bomber Command life was not the cheerful blare of the mess gramophone but the patter of rain on a Nissen hut roof. The pervading smell was not the whiff of expensive scent but the reek of coke from a smoky stove. Opening the doors of their quarters the crews looked out not at the green, upholstered Sussex hills or the fertile fields of the Weald but the vast skies and watery steppes of Lincolnshire.

Fighter pilots went to the pub by car. Bomber Boys travelled by bike or bus. They drank flat, weak beer in drab pubs and dance-halls where they competed for the favours of young women war-workers. Sex was in the air but when it took place it was often urgent and utilitarian. What they really wanted was love and it flared up often, as fierce and incandescent as the pyrotechnics that marked the targets they bombed. Sometimes it was just as ephemeral.

But once on 'ops', the world of lovers, friends and families beyond the base dwindled and faded, to be replaced by a different reality. The future stretched no further than the next few hours. Life was reversed. Night became day and day became night, the time when the crews went to work. Then, to each crew member the only people who mattered were those around him. There were only seven people in existence and the universe had shrunk to the size of a bomber plane.

1

Learning the Hard Way

On the morning of Sunday 3 September 1939, at bases all over Britain, ground and air crews stood by for the announcement that after many false alarms they were finally to be launched into battle. At Scampton, 'Sunny Scampton' as it was wryly nicknamed on account of the usually dismal Lincolnshire weather, the men of 'A' Flight, 89 Squadron, were smoking and chatting in the flight commander's office while they waited for the prime minister to speak on the radio. At 11 a.m. the talking stopped and the room filled with the low, apprehensive voice of Neville Chamberlain telling them that, as of that moment, a state of war existed between Britain and Germany.

Until then, the flight commander, Anthony Bridgman, had been a study in unconcern. Now he took his feet from his desk, exhaled a slow stream of cigarette smoke and spoke, 'quietly and rather strangely' according to one who was present, to his men. 'Well boys, this is it,' he said. 'You had better all pop out and test your aeroplanes . . . there will probably be a job for you to do.'

There was. In the early afternoon they were called to the lecture room where the squadron's CO, Leonard Snaith, a distinguished pilot whose gentle manner set him apart from the boisterous, public-school ethos of the pre-war RAF, announced 'we are off on a raid'. The targets were German pocket battleships, believed to be lying in Wilhelmshaven harbour, the great heart-shaped North Sea inlet. Their orders were to bomb them. If the ships could not be found, they were allowed to attack an ammunition depot on the land. The six crews detailed to the task were warned that 'on no account' were they to hit civilian establishments, either houses or dockyards, and that 'serious repercussions' would follow if they did so.

They surged to the crew room to climb into their kit and wait for a lorry to take them to the aircraft. They were flying in Hampdens, up-to-date, twin-engined monoplane medium bombers with a good range and a respectable bomb-carrying capacity. They had a bulbous but narrow front fuselage, only three feet wide, and a slender tail that gave them an odd, insect look. It was cramped for the four men inside, but the speed and handling made up for it.

Before they could leave, news came through that the initial take-off time of 15.30 had been put back. The men lay outside on the grass, smoking and thinking about what lay ahead. Another message arrived saying there had been a further delay, provoking a chorus of swearing. By now everyone's nerves were fizzing. One pilot, despite a reputation for cockiness, found his 'hands were shaking so much that I could not hold them still. All the time we wanted to rush off to the lavatory. Most of us went four times an hour.'

At last the time came to board the lorry and just after 6 p.m. the engines rumbled into life and the Hampdens bumped down the runway. For all their training, few of the pilots had ever taken off with a full bomb load before. The aircraft felt very heavy with the 2,000 pounds of extra weight but they lumbered into the air without mishap and set course over the soaring towers of Lincoln cathedral, over the broad fields and glinting fens and rivers of Lincolnshire, and out across the corrugated eternity of the North Sea for Germany.

As they approached Wilhelmshaven, the weather went from poor to atrocious. The gap between the grey waves and the wet cloud narrowed from 300 to 100 feet. Gun flashes could be seen through the murk but there was no telling where they came from.

Eventually, Squadron Leader Snaith's aircraft swung away to the left. The appalling conditions and the impossibility of knowing precisely where they were had persuaded him there was no point in carrying on. The initial disappointment of one pilot gave way to the realization that Snaith was right. 'For all we knew,' he wrote, 'we were miles off our course. The gun flashes ahead might have been the Dutch Islands or they might have been Heligoland.'

They dumped their bombs into the sea and headed for home. By the time they crossed the coast at Boston it was dark. Most of the

Pilot and co-pilot at the controls of a Wellington.

crews had little experience of night flying and one got hopelessly lost. Luckily, the moon picked up a landmark canal and they followed it back to Scampton, landing tired, and rather disillusioned, at 10.30 p.m. 'What an abortive show!' wrote the captain of the errant aircraft. 'What a complete mess-up! For all the danger we went through it couldn't be called a raid, but nevertheless we went through all the feelings.'[1]

But at least everyone had got back alive. If Bomber Command's first offensive operation was a disappointment, the second was a disaster. On 4 September more attacks were launched against German warships off Wilhelmshaven and further north, at Brunsbüttel, in the mouth of the Kiel Canal. A force of fourteen Wellingtons and fifteen Blenheims set off. The weather was dreadful. Ten aircraft failed to find the target. The Blenheims managed to reach the pocket battleship *Admiral Scheer* and the cruiser *Emden* at Wilhelmshaven. They even landed three bombs on the *Scheer*. The bombs failed to explode. The *Emden* was damaged when a stricken bomber crashed on to it. But five of the attacking aircraft were destroyed, most by flak from the fleet's anti-aircraft guns.

Some of the Wellingtons claimed to have located targets to bomb at Brunsbüttel but if they did they caused them little harm. Four aircraft were shot down by German fighters. A gross navigational error meant that two bombs were dropped on the Danish town of Esbjerg, 110 miles to the north, killing two innocents. The day's efforts had achieved nothing and resulted in the loss of nearly a quarter of the aircraft dispatched.

These initial efforts displayed many of the myriad weaknesses of Bomber Command as it set out to justify the extraordinary claims that had been made in its name in the years between the wars. The operations were based on sketchy intelligence and preceded by only the most perfunctory of briefings. The aircraft were the best the RAF could offer but the navigation equipment available to guide them to their targets was primitive, and some of the bombs they dropped were duds. The training the crews had received, long and arduous though it had been, had still not properly prepared them for the job. And the tactics they were following were clearly suspect, given the losses that had been sustained.

On the other hand, the episode did provide a demonstration of the potential of Bomber Command's underlying strength. The crews had shown a powerful 'press on' spirit, with fatal results in the case of most of those trapped in the seven aircraft that went down. Despite the paltry results, nothing could be inferred about the quality of the airmen. The man whose memoirs provide the basis for the account of the first raid, the pilot of the Hampden who got lost, was the twenty-year-old Guy Gibson, who three and a half years later was to lead the triumphant Dams Raid. At the time, though, these first operations served mainly to expose the RAF's weakness and to reveal the huge gap between what a bomber force was supposed to do and what it could in fact achieve.

In their short life, bombers had gained an awesome reputation for potential destructiveness. The prospect of unrestricted air warfare tinged the mood of the interwar world with quiet dread. It cast the same shadow of fear and uncertainty over life as the thought of nuclear holocaust did in the post-war years. The sense of doom was fed by a tide of alarming articles and books.

A novel, *1944*, published in 1926 was typical of the genre. The fact that its author, the Earl of Halsbury, had served on the Air Staff's Directorate of Flying Operations in the First World War appeared to lend particular weight to its arguments. The tale was told in the brusque, conventional prose of contemporary thrillers, but the message was revolutionary. Its hero, Sir John Blundell MP, is regarded by his colleagues as a crackpot for his insistence that another world war is inevitable. The next conflict, he believes, will bring about 'the total obliteration of civilization not more nor less. Total obliteration, phutt, like a candle.'

He warns anyone who will listen that in 'not more than twenty years' fleets of bombers will be roaming the skies of Europe, dropping poison gas. The country's air defences will prove useless. The government will be paralysed. Lacking leadership or a militaristic tradition to maintain discipline, people will turn on each other. When the first raid occurs, Sir John's son Dick is sitting down to dinner at the Ritz with his girlfriend Sylvie. 'Above the night noises of a great town could be heard the faint but unmistakeable hum of aeroplanes. Presently they became louder and there was an uncomfortable hush throughout the restaurant. To Dick . . . the noise seemed to be coming from everywhere. Trained to appreciate such things, he knew there must be an immense number of machines. Somewhere to the south came the sound of a futile anti-aircraft battery . . . like a swarm of locusts a mass of aeroplanes was just discernible, lit up by the searchlights, as yet mere specks in the sky. More anti-aircraft guns were heard coming into action, somewhere down the river. Bursting shells winked like fireflies in a tropical forest . . . the raiders were through and over London . . . they had easily broken through the carefully-prepared but utterly inadequate defence that met them.'[2]

Dick and Sylvie manage to escape the capital. On their way westwards they see anarchy and cruelty everywhere. A band of proletarian refugees from Plymouth turn cannibal, preying on stragglers who stray near their Dartmoor hideout. Almost everyone behaves badly. In a country mansion, upper-class loafers meet death in a last orgy of drink and drugs. At one point the pair run into a crowd of scavengers. '[It] was not made up of the English [Dick] had known. They were a new race, a hard, grim, cruel race, changed completely by days of want, total lack of discipline and above all by the complete dissolution of the bonds which knitted their civilization into a kindly, altruistic society.'

Halsbury was serious. He claimed his assertions were based on current scientific fact.[3] Official projections of what unrestricted air war might mean were scarcely less alarming than his lordship's imaginings. They took as their starting point the results of German air raids on Britain in the Great War, which started with Zeppelin attacks in January 1915 and continued with raids by Gotha and Giant bombers. Altogether, they killed 1,413 people and injured 3,407. The great majority of the casualties were civilians. From this data it was calculated there would be fifty casualties for every ton of bombs dropped. In 1937 the Committee of Imperial Defence, which brought together the country's most senior airmen, soldiers, sailors and bureaucrats, was informed by its experts that the Germans had the means to maintain an all-out air assault on Britain for sixty days. This would result in the deaths of up to 600,000 people and serious injury to 1.2 million.

A year later the Ministry of Health estimated that between 1 million and 2.8 million hospital beds would be needed to deal with casualties. The huge numbers of dead would have to be interred in mass graves. In April 1939 a million burial forms were sent out to local councils.

Like Halsbury, the government also assumed that the public's nerve would fail. The scattered bombing of the previous war had produced flickers of panic and despondency. Concentrated attacks were expected to trigger widespread hysteria. A report to the Committee of Imperial Defence in 1931 proposed throwing a police cordon around London to prevent a mass exodus and discussions began in 1937 to recruit 20,000 reserve constables to keep order in the capital. It was thought that the first duty of the army, should Germany attack, was to 'maintain confidence, law and order among our civil population before attempting to fulfil any other role'. In the spring of 1939 the War Office warned army commanders of the sort of work their men might be expected to carry out. In one scenario, 'crowds without food have taken refuge in the open land in the suburbs. Civil authorities have organized soup kitchens which are being rushed by hungry people. Troops are required to restore order and organize queues.'

It was suggested that psychiatric casualties might outstrip physical casualties by three to one. In 1938 a committee was formed of senior psychiatrists from the London teaching hospitals and clinics to plan wartime mental health requirements. Its report to the Health Ministry proposed a network of centres providing immediate treatment in the bombed areas, outpatient clinics and roving teams of adult and child counsellors.

These dire predictions were a reflection of a fear that gripped everyone. 'We had entered a period,' Churchill wrote later, 'when the weapon which had played a considerable part in the previous war had become obsessive in men's minds. Ministers had to imagine the most frightful scenes of ruin and slaughter in London if we quarrelled with the German dictator.'4

Much of the alarm had been generated by the man who was regarded by both politicians and the public as the country's greatest authority on air war. Hugh Trenchard had risen to be head of the Royal Air Force during the First World War. He was known as 'Boom' to his colleagues, a reference to his foghorn voice. They regarded him and his utterances with what now seems like extraordinary reverence. 'What a character he is!' declared Sir John Slessor, one of his many disciples and a wartime bomber group commander. 'The enormous lanky figure; the absent-minded manner, shot with sudden flashes of shrewd and humorous insight; the illegible handwriting; the inarticulate speech – always a lap or two behind his racing brain; his wonderful capacity for getting people's names mixed up. Boom was a constant source of joy to those who were lucky enough to serve under him.'[5]

Lord Trenchard, as he became, was forceful and confident and contemptuous of ideas that were not his own. He had been head of the first separate bombing force, created in 1918 to repay the Germans for having bombed England. He had started out, though, as a doubter, sceptical of what aircraft could achieve on their own. His conversion to the value of strategic bombing, when it came, was absolute. Through the Twenties and Thirties he became the foremost advocate of using aeroplanes to smash the enemy into submission on their own territory. He was to exercise a powerful influence over RAF and government policy right into the early years of the war, with dogmatic assertions which were seldom backed up by data.

An early and often-repeated dictum was that 'the moral effect of bombing industrial towns may be great, even if the material effect is, in fact, small.' Later he refined this into the doctrine that 'the moral effect of bombing stands undoubtedly to the material effect in a proportion of 20 to 1', an observation that had no basis in measurable fact. After the slaughter of 1914–18, the prospect of any war, let alone one that promised annihilation of civilians from the air, was horrifying to governments and populations alike. In the pre-Hitler years there were several international attempts to outlaw the bomber: at Washington in 1922, The Hague in 1923 and Geneva in 1932. They all ended in failure, undermined by pessimism, cynicism and the impossibility of uninventing the machine that defined the century.

Britain had been at the forefront of attempts to ban the bomber and had held back from spending on the development and production of bomber aircraft in the hope that they would not be needed. The rapid rearmament of Nazi Germany after Hitler's victory in 1933 forced the abandonment of this policy and the start of a scramble for military parity.

The hope was that a sizeable bomber fleet might deter a German attack. If not, it would provide the means, and given Britain's geographical position and dearth of soldiers, the *sole* means of striking back if Germany dared to attempt an aerial 'knock-out blow' at the start of hostilities.

By the end of the First World War, Britain was already committed to a policy of strategic bombing. The main work of the air force between 1914 and 1918 had been tactical: to support the army, flying reconnaissance missions, spotting the fall of artillery shells and attacking German soldiers in the field. Later, bigger aeroplanes and heavier bomb loads raised the possibility that the air force could play a strategic role in defeating the enemy, by attacking the factories and foundries and power plants that turned the engines of modern industrial war.

The possession of a long-range bombing fleet suited British needs. A Continental power like Nazi Germany saw aeroplanes largely as an adjunct to its land forces who would carry out the main work of conquest. This was reflected in its choice of versatile, medium-sized aircraft which could blaze a trail of destruction to clear the path for its advancing armies, as well as carrying out conventional bombing.

Britain's case was very different. It had no plans to invade anyone and saw air power chiefly as a means of defence – but a defence founded on aggression. Trenchard had stimulated the offensive spirit among his pilots on the Western Front, rarely flinching from the losses that that policy inevitably entailed.

Some in the RAF argued that Germany could be defeated by bombing alone. That was always an extreme view. However everyone, including the chiefs of the other services, agreed that the air force had a major role to play in destroying Germany's war industry, demoralizing its population, and preparing the ground for the army to finish the job.

This was the essence of strategic bombing, and in the interwar years it was the RAF's ability to wage a strategic bombing campaign that provided the chief justification for its existence. Everything was geared to attack, with only minor consideration given to the defensive role of aircraft. Bombers outnumbered fighters by about two to one through the period. There was a brief, fortuitous diversion from this path in 1937 when the Air Staff was forced to accept the argument of Sir Thomas Inskip, brought in as Minister for the Co-ordination of Defence, that Britain needed a strengthened fighter force to ward off the immediate threat from the German air force. But the RAF's resultant triumph in the summer of 1940, when the Battle of Britain swirled in the sky over southern England, did nothing to subvert the doctrinal orthodoxy that it was attacks that won wars.

Despite this preoccupation, the RAF started the war with a bomber fleet that was totally inadequate to carry out its own stated aims. The machines of the early Thirties were ungainly and saddled with uninspiring names. The Boulton Paul Overstrand, the Fairey Hendon and the Handley Page Harrow did not sound likely to strike fear into the enemy. They were stop-gaps, filling the ranks until the arrival of the new generation of aircraft. The programme to re-equip with giant, four-engined aircraft, which eventually produced the Stirling, Halifax and Lancaster, was launched in 1936, but it took until 1942 for them to start arriving on the squadrons. Bomber Command's heaviest bombers at the start of the war were two-engined Wellingtons, Hampdens and Whitleys, which were reasonably advanced for the time but plainly insufficient for the task that the air force had set itself.

The RAF's blueprint for waging war was contained in the Western Air Plans, first drawn up in 1936. They rested on the belief that bombers could find and destroy the factories, oil installations, roads and railways that were the object of a strategic force's attentions. This was to turn out to be a hugely mistaken assumption.

The plans supposed that Germany would start the war either by attacking Belgium and France or by launching an all-out bombing campaign on Britain. In the first case, Bomber Command was to attempt to slow down the advance of the German army by striking its supply lines. In the second, it was to reduce the power of the Luftwaffe assault by attacking aerodromes and other aviation targets. At the same time, the Air Staff who directed the command's efforts were also eager to disrupt the enemy's supply of oil. The dream of bringing the German military to a halt by starving it of fuel would persist to the last days of the war.

In the event the Germans took their time digesting their prey before raising their eyes hungrily westwards. Britain did little to provoke them. Until the invasion of Norway in April 1940, the RAF confined itself to intermittent raids on shipping and leaflet-dropping sorties over Germany and the conquered territories. This was partly a reflection of the scrupulousness that was Britain's official policy. Thirty months before the start of the war Prime Minister Neville Chamberlain announced to the House of Commons that Britain would only bomb purely military objectives and take every measure to avoid civilian casualties. A few days after it began, the RAF's Director of Plans, Air Commodore Sir John Slessor, promised that 'indiscriminate attack on civilian populations as such will never form part of our policy'.

But the caution was also a reflection of reality. The air force was weak and inadequately equipped and in no position to risk its men and machines unnecessarily. The phoney war period provided Bomber Command with a desperately needed space in which to measure its capabilities and build up its strength. The propaganda leaflet drops, which look faintly ludicrous to modern eyes, may have done little to subvert the Nazi regime but they served another useful purpose. They provided crews with crucial experience of night flying over enemy territory, at very little cost.

Night flying, it was to turn out, was a vital skill. The first lesson the RAF learned when tested by wartime conditions was a painful one. The prevailing wisdom was that bombers, if they held to a tight formation, could defend themselves in daylight from attack by German fighters. So great was the faith in this belief that only five of the thirty-three operational squadrons had received any training in flying in the dark.

The theory was thrown into doubt from the beginning. German fighters, directed by radar, savaged the bombers sent off on shipping searches over the North Sea. In two attacks on 14 and 18 December, half of the thirty-four Wellingtons dispatched were destroyed. The myth of the self-defending daylight bombing formation lingered on until the spring when it was demolished by another punishing encounter with reality. Following the German invasion of Norway and Denmark in early April 1940, Bomber Command was ordered to disrupt the advance. On 12 April, nine Hampdens and Wellingtons out of a force of sixty were shot down by fighters while trying to bomb shipping in the Stavanger area. It was the last appearance of the two types in daylight operations. Henceforth bombing at night-time would become the norm for these aircraft and the heavier ones that succeeded them.

Britain held back from launching attacks near population centres for as long as it could. With the German invasion of the Low Countries on 10 May 1940 and the Battle of France that followed, restraint was gradually abandoned. Everyone knew that sooner or later civilians would be killed. The only question was how many. In the early months of the war the Germans had been as anxious as the British not to take innocent lives, fearing it would provoke a retaliation that would make the negotiated settlement that Hitler desired more difficult. But it had happened nonetheless.

At dusk on 16 March 1940, at the hour the locals call the 'grimling', a 27-year-old Orkney Islands farmer called James Isbister heard the sound of aircraft. He left his wife and three-month-old son and went to his cottage door to look. Silhouetted against the northern sky were the broad wings and slender bodies of a fleet of four Heinkel bombers. They seemed to be heading for Scapa Flow, a sheet of sheltered sea, surrounded by low hills, where warships of the British fleet were anchored. As the aircraft closed on the fleet other shapes appeared in the sky. A cluster of small, dartlike machines hovered above the bombers before swooping down among them. What looked like blue electric sparks glittered from under their wings and stitched across the sky. The RAF had arrived. The German formation that had looked so sure of itself held firm for a moment, then wavered and broke. The bombers lunged in all directions, desperate to shed their loads and head for home. One came directly towards Mr Isbister. It flew very low, near enough for him to have been able to notice the camouflage of the fuselage, grey-green like the scales of a pike, and its pale belly and glass snout. On the underside, where the wings met the body, were two cross-hatched panels. They swung open and dark shapes tumbled out. The bombs fell in a stick, sending up fountains of dirt. The shrapnel left a pretty starburst shape in the turf. James Isbister was caught in the blast and earned the sad distinction of becoming the first civilian to be killed by Germans in the British Isles in the Second World War. The following day the people from round about went to survey the damage. Among them was the poet George Mackay Brown. 'We felt then a quickening of the blood, a wonderment and excitement touched by fear,' he remembered. 'The war was real right enough and it had come to us.'[6]

When the German army began its great surge westwards, the RAF at last moved to put its war plans into action. Bomber Command had been engaged from the beginning in trying to stem the flow of armour as it flooded into Belgium, Holland and France, bombing bridges and communications and suffering terrible punishment from mobile flak batteries and fighters in the process.

Initially raids were restricted to targets west of the Rhine. On the night of 11/12 May, an attack was launched on Mönchengladbach, the first on a German town. The thirty-seven aircraft that took part were aiming for road and rail junctions but bombs fell among houses and blocks of flats. They killed three Germans: Carl Lichtschlag, sixty-two, Erika Müllers, twenty-two, and a two-year-old girl called Ingeborg Schley. The dead also included a British citizen. Ella Ida Clegg had been born fifty-three years before to a British father who left Oldham to work as a factory foreman in the Rhineland. Nothing else is known about her. She was listed in official records simply as a 'volunteer'.[7] She will be remembered only as one of the first batch of civilians to die in the air war in Germany. These first corpses had names, but that did not last long. Such tragedies soon became commonplace as aerial war dragged ordinary people on to the battlefield and names gave way to numbers.

Four days later Bomber Command visited for the first time a target to which it would return over and over again in the years ahead. Nearly a hundred aircraft set off to attack sixteen different oil and rail targets in the Ruhr, the smoky, densely-populated agglomeration of steel and coal cities clustered along the Rhine river system, which was the heart of Germany's war industry.

It was a puny raid by the standards of what was to come, but it was later counted by Bomber Command's official historians as the first action of the strategic air campaign. The targets included factories in Dortmund, Sterkrade, Castrop-Rauxel and Cologne. One bomb, aimed at the IG-Werk at Dormagen, landed on a farm and killed Franz Romeike, a dairyman. Local rumour had it that he had switched on a light on his way to the lavatory and attracted the attention of a bomb-aimer. The story revealed an exaggerated notion of the accuracy of bombing, but an entirely realistic understanding of how randomly death could arrive in an air raid.

By attacking industry and communications, Bomber Command was fulfilling its *raison d'être* but the events of the rest of the summer meant it was deflected from concentrating on this activitity. In July, having swallowed France, Germany turned its attention to Britain, launching the Luftwaffe across the Channel in an attempt to clear the skies for a possible invasion. Bomber Command was ordered to weaken the enemy's air strength at its source by destroying aluminium plants, airframe factories and stores. It was also tasked with attacking airfields and sinking the barges appearing in the North Sea waterways to carry the invasion troops. On top of all this, it was expected to continue hitting oil, communications and industrial targets when it could.

The weight of Bomber Command's duties meant there was no concentration of effort and the effects of their bombing, apart from on troop transports, were negligible. Nonetheless, throughout the summer the Air Ministry showered its commander-in-chief, Sir Charles Portal, with directives. Portal was a realist and a sceptic, whose perfect manners and quiet demeanour hid a mind that was as cool and hard as marble. It was he, as much as anyone, who led Bomber Command away from its pursuit of a precision that was, initially at least, unattainable, and towards a policy of annihilation. Portal queried, in his courteous but firm fashion, the wisdom of attacking the German aircraft industry. Many of the targets were sited in remote areas. He pointed out that 'the very high percentage of bombs which inevitably miss the actual target will hit nothing else of importance and do no damage and the minimum amount of dislocation and disturbance will be caused by the operations as a whole.' He also advocated that when initial targets could not be reached because of bad weather, aircraft should be free to dump bombs on alternatives, thus increasing 'the moral effect of our operations by the alarm and disturbance created over the wider area'.

With these observations, which caused some surprise and concern at the ministry, Portal opened the way to a crucial shift in bombing policy. In his view, any damage was better than none and undermining *morale*, the moral effect in the language of the day, was a very important and desirable product of aerial bombardment. The Air Staff felt the need to sound a cautionary note. It felt that 'moral effect, although an extremely important subsidiary result of air bombardment, cannot in itself be decisive'.[8] For the time being, at least, it maintained its faith in what it believed were selective, precise attacks.

Portal was being indiscreet in advocating so frankly the spreading of panic. But he was stating a belief that had been accepted inside the air force from the earliest days. Despite undertaking that the RAF would not attack the civilian population as such, it was understood that any attack on land-based strategic targets would result in civilians dying. Trenchard's independent force had killed 746 innocent Germans in the 242 raids it mounted in the six months of its existence.

Few moral contortions were necessary to justify certain civilian deaths. Many took the view that the factory worker manufacturing shells was as lawful a target as the artilleryman firing them. The killing of women and children naturally caused revulsion. But at the same time it was widely accepted that all bloodshed, or the threat of it, had beneficial results in lowering enemy spirits and undermining the will to sustain the war effort. This was no more than a reflection of Trenchard's dictum that the moral effect of bombing was twenty times that of the material effect. The question was, as the Air Ministry reply made clear, whether the issue of morale could be decisive. And if it could, should morale itself be a primary target of strategic bombing?

The first reports filtering out of Germany suggested that this might be the case. Germans had been led to believe that they would be largely untroubled by air attack, and very well protected if any should occur. The thin evidence available, from neutral journalists and diplomats and a handful of spies, spoke of shock and dismay among ordinary citizens that the war had entered their towns.

Meagre though this testimony was, it reinforced the conviction in some quarters that German nerves were weaker than those of the British. This was Trenchard's belief. It was not Churchill's, who in October 1917, when calls for revenge for the German air raids were at their loudest, had dismissed the idea that a response in kind could produce a German surrender. 'Nothing that we have learned of the capacity of the German population to endure suffering justifies us in assuming that they could be cowed into submission by such methods,' he wrote.[9]

Even if the Germans' pluck was suspect, it was questionable whether this would produce any immediate advantage for Britain and its allies. An influential subcommittee reporting to the Chiefs of Staff had pointed out with some understatement three years before the outbreak of war that 'a military dictatorship is likely to be less susceptible to popular outcry than a democratic government'.[10] This was only common sense, but it was to be very often forgotten or ignored.

The Battle of Britain and the Blitz provided the great test of British morale. In the first two months of the air war, 1,333 people were killed as German bombs missed their targets or were scattered at random when the raiders headed for home. On the night of 24 August the first bombs fell on central London and a fortnight later it experienced its first heavy bombardment. That month 6,954 civilians were killed all over Britain, and a further 6,334 in October. This was death on a hideously larger scale than had been endured in the previous war.

In the capital, the bombs were ostensibly aimed at docks, railways and other locations with an arguable military or war-industrial value. In practice they landed everywhere. They fell on Westminster Abbey, St Paul's Cathedral, Kensington Palace, Lambeth Palace and Buckingham Palace, twice. They hit hospitals and theatres, the London Zoo and Madame Tussaud's. They crashed down on rich and poor alike, the brick terraces of the East End and the stucco squares of Kensington and Mayfair. But the great sprawl of London meant that the violence lacked concentration. As one part of the city was 'getting it bad' another was having a relatively quiet night. The capital adjusted quickly to death from the air. The damage was spectacular but had minimal effect on the war effort. There was little sign of the collapse of morale feared by the authorities, even though the Blitz was to continue, night after night, until the following spring.

Churchill had reacted to the first London raid by ordering an attack on Berlin. It went ahead on the night of 25 August. The city was covered with thick cloud making aiming virtually impossible. The incendiary bombs that did fall within the city limits did little damage, mostly landing harmlessly in open country. There were three further raids on Berlin in the next few days. The prime minister wanted to spread the attacks throughout Germany but faced resistance from the Air Staff who continued to argue for narrow and selective targeting.

But as the German bombardment persisted, such a detached view became untenable. As a concession to the new mood, on 21 September the Air Staff directed Portal to continue the assault on Berlin. The bombers should aim for 'legitimate' targets such as railways and the like. But the object was also to cause 'the greatest possible disturbance and dislocation both to the industrial activities and to the civil population generally in the area'.[11]

To Portal, the directive did not go nearly far enough. Ten days before he had offered a new policy to the staff, based on direct retaliation. He suggested twenty German towns should be warned by radio broadcast that each attack on a British town would be repaid by a heavy, indiscriminate attack by Bomber Command on one of their number. Alternatively, a town like Essen, the home of the arms manufacturer Krupp, which could be regarded in its entirety as a military target, could be subjected to overwhelming bombardment. Another approach was to select a military target, presumably a barracks or suchlike, for an all-out assault in 'the knowledge that the normal spread of such a heavy attack would inevitably cause a high degree of devastation to the town.'[12]

Portal's views, combined with those of the prime minister, forced the Air Staff planners to think again. They had stuck to their view in the belief that precision bombing was attainable and producing desirable results. They regarded the inevitable civilian deaths as incidental to the main aim of destroying strategic targets, not an end in themselves.

Portal's position was strengthened by a German decision to raise the stakes in the air war. On the night of 14 November, a force of 449 aircraft was sent to Coventry in the Midlands. The air raid killed 554 people and seriously injured 865, almost all of them civilians. Its political impact, though, was to prove far greater than the physical damage inflicted. What happened in Coventry would shape the direction of the air war.

2

Coventrated

Coventry was an obvious and, by the standards that Britain had set itself, a legitimate target for aerial attack. Its mediaeval core and fine cathedral and churches did not alter the fact that it was an important centre of war industry, crammed with aircraft and motor-car factories and machine-tool and instrument works.

The people who worked in Coventry liked the place. Many had come from elsewhere to man the production lines and were pleasantly surprised to find themselves in a city of manageable size and that nowhere was far from open country. Rearmament had made it prosperous. By 1940 its population had grown to nearly 240,000, double what it had been thirty years before.

Even with the influx of outsiders, civic pride was strong. 'People were self-disciplined and proudly self-reliant,' wrote Dennis Field, a Coventry schoolboy at the time of the raid who went on to join Bomber Command. There was a marked communal loyalty summed up in the signature tune of the city's favourite entertainer, Sydney James, who appeared every week at the Rialto. As he played the organ, the audience would sing along.

> Looking at life and wearing a smile
> Helping a lame dog over a stile
> Don't mind the rain
> Forget your umbrella
> Or lend it, for once, to the other fella
> Making the best of all that you find
> Leaving your cares and your worries behind
> Laughing at your troubles and your trials and your strife
> Yes, that is the best way of looking at life . . .[1]

An air of complacency seems to have hung over the pleasant streets of Coventry in the early part of the war. Its politics were Labour, a consequence of the strong trade-union movement rooted in the factories. Coventry people made weapons but many were opposed to their use. Pacifism and the disarmament movement were strong. In Coventry, as elsewhere, a strange mood of insouciance, verging on fatalism, was noticeable as the violence grew nearer. When, in the spring of 1939, the authorities offered Anderson bomb shelters at a price of five pounds (free for the lower-paid) there were few takers. Those who accepted had their legs pulled for being 'windy'.

In June 1940, when the first bombs dropped on Ansty aerodrome just outside the city, they were seen as a novelty. People set out in cars and on bicycles to gawp at the craters. The thrill soon wore off. Between 18 August and the end of October Coventry was attacked seventeen times, killing 176. As the casualty list lengthened, people started leaving the city at night, 'trekking' to the safety of the surrounding countryside. The better off went by car, the less affluent by bus. The very poorest piled bedding on to prams and walked out, sleeping under bridges.

By the time of the big raid people had grown accustomed to the howl of the sirens and the nuisance of shifting down to the basement or heading to the nearest public shelter. For the workers of the fire service and Air Raid Precautions, the attacks provided good practice. They had seen mutilated bodies and knew what an air raid felt like.

Despite the acknowledged threat, Coventry's defences were weak, with only thirty-six anti-aircraft guns protecting the city. There were searchlights and fifty-six reassuring-looking barrage balloons wallowed over the city, but they were not much of a deterrent on the fatal night. RAF night-fighters found tracking intruders in the dark an almost impossible task and their success rate was to remain pitifully low until enough aircraft were fitted with radar.

A shelter-building programme had been accelerated as the raids continued and there was room inside them for most of the population but many of them were damp and cheaply built. The council's emergency committee kept an informal log of what was being said in bus queues and pubs. The state of the shelters, the feebleness of the anti-aircraft defences and the absence of British fighters were consistent themes of complaint.[2]

Coventry's transformation from an obscure Midlands city to an international symbol of civilian suffering and the inhumanity of modern war started at dusk on Thursday 14 November when crews of the Luftwaffe Pathfinder Force Kampfgruppe 100 boarded Heinkel 111s and took off from a base at Vannes, north of Saint-Nazaire. Coventry was one of three targets that night. The others were Wolverhampton and Birmingham.

The moon began to rise over Coventry at 5.18 p.m. Everyone would later recall its extraordinary brightness. It gleamed on the cobbles of the old city and the lead roof of the cathedral. The sight made people nervous. The citizens had come to fear a bomber's moon. At 7.10 p.m. the sirens sounded. This was early for a raid to be announced and the apprehension deepened. Ten minutes later the Germans were overhead and the bombardment began. It started with small incendiaries. They made a curious swishing noise as they fell. By now people had learned how to deal with them, picking them up with a long-handled shovel and dropping them into a bucket of water or sand.

But they came down in huge numbers and the emergency services and volunteer firewatchers were soon overwhelmed. At 9.31 p.m. the first high explosive (HE) bombs hit the ground. A firewatcher's log recorded at 9.40 p.m.: 'Cathedral blazing fiercely. HEs all around the city centre.' The sirens had sent women and children hurrying out into the blacked-out streets to seek the public shelters, or down into their basements or back-garden Andersons. 'When the sirens sounded I was doing homework in our front room,' Dennis Field remembered. 'The continual drone of engines and falling bombs made it quickly obvious that the raid was unusually heavy and Mum and I soon decided to go to next-door's shelter where we had an open invitation when things looked sticky. It was cold and we took extra coats ... the bombs rained down ... many times we crouched down expecting the worst ... occasionally there were colossal bangs and blasts which blew open the door. I wanted to go out and see what was happening and to help if I could but demurred to Mum's pleadings and restricted myself to occasional peers outside. The sky seemed aglow with the brightest huge conflagration lighting the sky in the direction of the city centre.'

After the initial fire-raising attack lit up the city the main force of bombers converged on it in three streams, crossing the English coast at Lincolnshire, Portland and Dungeness. The raid had been planned in considerable detail. Each of the eight bomber units involved had been assigned an objective. Their targets included the Alvis aero-engine factory, the Standard Motor Company, the British Piston Ring Company, the Daimler works and the Hill Street Gasworks. The greatest destruction was done to the Daimler factory to the north of the city centre, which produced among other things rotating gun turrets. The site was struck by up to 150 HE bombs and 3,000 incendiaries. The Alvis factory was bombed flat. Altogether twenty-seven war production factories including twelve engaged in making aeroplanes were hit.

The raid reached a climax around midnight. A survivor remembered 'a night of unforgettable horror – the scream of falling bombs – the shattering explosions – the showers of incendiaries, literally thousands, and then . . . perhaps the most horrifying sight of all – the sudden fires leaping up, their flames, fanned by the wind, rapidly spreading and enveloping all within reach.'[3] The smell of the burning city reached up to the bombers. A crewman, Hans Fruehauf, who had taken part in the first London raids, looked down on the lake of fire and wondered what he was doing. 'The usual cheers that greeted a direct hit stuck in our throats. The crew just gazed down at the flames in silence. Was this really a military target, we all asked ourselves?'[4] A 'Front Reporter' for the German propaganda service was a passenger in one of the aircraft. He had no doubts of the legitimacy of what he witnessed. 'We could see enormous fires raging, some white and brilliant, others dark red. Then came the high spot of the raid, the dropping of the bombs . . . a tremor went through the machine as the bombs dropped . . . our bombs had hit their mark; the fires extended . . . it is the nerve centre of the British armament industry which had been hit, and I am proud that I witnessed this.'[5]

The anti-aircraft guns soon ran out of ammunition and there was no sign of RAF night-fighters so the Germans were free to bomb as they pleased, swooping in low to improve accuracy. As mains were shattered and hydrants buried under rubble, the firemen's hoses ran dry. Crews drafted in from outside watched impotently as Coventry burned. The fire was fiercest in the old city centre. John Shelton who owned a stables in Little Park Street described the din of 'falling walls, girders, pillars, machinery crashing four storeys, the droning of the planes as they let go their bombs and the rattling of shrapnel on corrugated sheeting'. It seemed to him that no one caught in the open could possibly have survived.[6]

The fire created weird effects. In Broadgate, in the heart of the city, the smell of roasting meat from burning butcher shops mingled with the scent of fine Havanas from the tobacconists, Salmon and Gluckstein. Inside the shelters, the air was thick with plaster and brick dust shaken loose by the pounding, and the stench of filth from the primitive or non-existent latrines. The overwhelming feeling was of powerlessness. It was better to be outside doing something. The ARP and Auxiliary Fire Service workers, the ambu-lancemen, doctors and nurses found they were too busy to be afraid. The urge to not let oneself down, to be seen to be coping and doing one's best was a strong antidote to fear or at least a help in suppressing it. 'Everyone was working as a member of a team,' said a student nurse at Gulson Road Hospital which was inundated with casualties after the Coventry and Warwickshire Hospital suffered heavy damage. 'Even the consultants who were normally treated like little gods and who to us poor nurses never seemed to be in the best of moods became human.' During her training she had dreaded having to assist at an amputation and had arranged to be off duty when such operations were scheduled. 'The blitz on Coventry changed all that for me. I didn't have time to be squeamish.'[7]

Despite the ferocity of the attack, rescue workers struggled on. Instead of reducing the value of life, the scale of the slaughter seemed to increase it. Every death averted, every existence saved, was a small victory. The hope of preserving a life drove the rescue teams to extraordinary lengths of selflessness. Les Coleman, an air-raid warden, heard a baby crying from beneath the rubble of a demolished house. He and his mates scrabbled for hours at the pile of bricks, fearful of using picks and shovels in case they hurt the child. Overhead the Luftwaffe were busy and the bombs fell steadily. They only stopped digging when the crying faded to silence.[8]

The all-clear sounded at 6.16 a.m., eleven hours after the first warning. Few heard it. Most of the electricity cables that powered the sirens were cut. Gradually people crept from the shelters into a drizzly morning and a changed world. The first thing they did was to look for their houses. Dennis Field found his, 'like most around, with windows out and roof damaged and clearly uninhabitable.' At least it was still standing. Whole streets had disappeared and landmarks vanished. The town seemed to have dissolved. The survivors walked through mounds of smoking debris flickering with flame, around craters big enough to swallow a bus. The most shocking sight was the cathedral. It lay open to the sky. The roof and the pillars had collapsed and everything inside the nave had burned to ash, piled up within the sagging external walls. All that remained was the spire and tower.

Coventry had been hit by 503 tons of high explosive, 56 tons of incendiaries and 127 parachute mines. The city was like others which had expanded during the Industrial Revolution. The workers' houses were huddled along the flanks of the factories they worked in. It was inevitable that the German bombs, no matter how well aimed, would hit them. Altogether 42,904 homes were destroyed or damaged, 56 per cent of the housing in the city. The number of dead was put at 554. Another 863 were seriously injured.

This was the most concentrated attack of the Blitz to date. To Britain and its allies it seemed that the Germans had set a new standard in ruthlessness. Those who took part in the raid believed they were engaged in a respectable act of war. At the pre-operation briefing, crews were told by their commander that Coventry was 'one of the chief armament centres of the enemy air force and has also factories which are important for the production of motor vehicles and armoured cars.' If the raid succeeded, he said, 'we shall have dealt another heavy blow to Herr Churchill's war production'.[9]

The raid was indeed a great success. Eight hours after it ended, German radio listeners were told that bombers had 'inflicted an extraordinarily heavy blow on the enemy' and that Coventry had been 'completely wiped out'. In the broadcast a notorious word was heard for the first time. What the bombers had done was to *koventrieren*, to Coventrate, the city.[10]

Until now civilian spirits had held up well in air attacks. Coventry provided a new and sterner test of morale. The raids on London so far had been heavy but scattered. The attacks on places like Liverpool and Southampton had been limited and of much shorter duration. The violence against Coventry seemed more focused and therefore potentially more traumatic than anyone else had experienced. It was here that the question of whether Britain could take it might be answered.

The first evidence was troubling. As people struggled to recover, a feeling of numb hopelessness appears to have set in. By now there were reporters around to record the city's mood. Hilde Marchant, a thoughtful and courageous *Daily Express* correspondent who had witnessed the war in Spain, arrived while fires still burned and buildings toppled. She came across a dazed-looking group standing helplessly in the street, 'occasionally asking when bread was coming into the city. There was no clamour, just sullen resentment at the inconvenience. They had patience because they were too weary to be angry.' Outside the Council House, the municipal headquarters, she saw a long queue. 'Men without collars and still in their carpet slippers. Women in woollen dressing gowns and slippers just as they had come from the shelter . . . asking for food and money.'

When an aeroplane appeared overhead there was a wild scramble and women hauled their children to the nearest shelter. The aircraft shifted in the sky to reveal RAF roundels, but it was some time before anyone was persuaded to come out. Some people had never left the shelters after the all-clear. Peering into one, Marchant saw two adults and two children 'with greenish faces, so still that they looked dead'.

The Morning After.

A team from the pioneering social study group Mass Observation, veterans of bomb attacks on London and elsewhere, arrived in Coventry on Friday afternoon less than a dozen hours after the raid finished. Their report claimed the attack had caused 'unprecedented dislocation and depression', compared with what they had seen before. 'There were more open signs of hysteria, terror, neurosis observed than during the whole of the previous two months together in all areas,' it said. 'Women were seen to cry, to scream, to tremble all over, to faint in the street, to attack a fireman and so on. The overwhelmingly dominant feeling on Friday was the feeling of utter helplessness. The tremendous impact of the previous night had left people practically speechless in many cases. And it made them feel impotent. *There was no role for the civilian. Ordinary people had no idea what they should do* (original emphasis).'[11]

The lack of organization or direction was unsurprising given the power of the attack. The mayor and his officials, the men who ran the city's services, had all suffered the same experience as everyone else. An individual report by a Mass Observation representative suggested that Coventry's relative smallness meant the 'shock effect of the bombing was much greater than in London . . . everybody knew somebody who was killed or missing . . . everybody knew plenty of people who had been rendered temporarily or permanently homeless. And these subjects occupied literally 90 per cent of all conversation heard throughout Friday afternoon and evening. Even in Stepney at the beginning of the Blitz there was not nearly so much obsession with damage and disaster.'

This was to be expected and no indication of despair. But the observer also noted that people seemed anxious to leave Coventry behind, reporting that 'the dislocation is so total in the town that people easily feel that *the town itself is killed* (original emphasis).'[12]

This was the reaction that the authorities had feared, opening the way to anarchy. It was particularly disastrous if it happened in Coventry. If the city descended into chaos and flight, who would man the war factories when they were rebuilt, as they would have to be if the struggle was to continue?

Senior government figures rushed in to test the mood themselves. The Home Secretary Herbert Morrison, the Minister of Health Aneurin Bevan and the Minister of Aircraft Production Lord Beaverbrook converged on Coventry. The city officials who met them were angry. They demanded to know why there had been no night-fighters to protect them and so few guns. Morrison wrote later that he found 'an almost total lack of will or desire to get the town moving again' and detected an 'air of defeatism'. This was desperately unfair. The men in front of him were still in shock from an experience that was unknown to the men from London. The chief fire officer, who showed up covered in grime from the smoke, fell asleep at the table.

Lord Beaverbrook, the Canadian-born press baron and crony of the prime minister, seemed particularly unsympathetic. Instead of offering any apology for the absence of fighters he made a florid speech, reminding the officials of their duty to get Coventry working again. This was the brutal truth. Coventry was essential to the war effort and the resumption of production was given precedence over easing the plight of survivors. The first major decision was to set up an organization under the chairmanship of a powerful local car manufacturer, William Rootes, to oversee the restoration of gas, water, electricity and transport so that the war factories could function again.

Apprehension rather than defiance was the prevailing sentiment in Coventry's shattered streets on the morning after the Blitz. There was no reason to doubt that the Germans would be back again that night and no expectation that anyone would be able to stop them. The story went round that they had deliberately left the cathedral spire intact to provide an aiming point for the next bombardment.

As the short day wore on the city emptied. It reminded Hilde Marchant of what she had seen in Spain and Finland. 'Yet this was worse . . . these people moved against a background of suburban villas, had English faces . . . they were our own kind.' Both sides of the road were filled with 'lorries, cars, handcarts and perambulators . . . the lorries were packed with women and children sitting on suitcases or bundles of bedding . . . the most pathetic of all were those who just leaned against the railings at the roadside, too exhausted to move, their luggage in heaps around them and a fretful tired child crying without temper or anger . . .' Those with relations round about were hoping they would have room to take them in. Those without were looking for cheap or free lodging with strangers and often they found it. Church halls and Scout huts opened up to supplement the existing emergency centres. Some gave up looking and slept under hedges or against walls.

But over the following days, people began to drift back. Many spent the day in town then trekked back to the country in the evening. There was no real choice but to return. Coventry was where their lives were. There, they joined a significant number who had stayed put, either because their duties demanded it or out of a refusal to be driven out. The pride involved in having endured quickly asserted itself. Tom Harrisson, one of the founders of Mass Observation, arrived on Friday afternoon and found the city in low spirits. 'It would be an insult to the people of Coventry to ballyhoo them and exaggerate their spirit,' he said in a talk broadcast after the BBC *Nine O'Clock News* the following night. The most common remark he had heard from people as they first surveyed the mess of their city was 'poor old Coventry'. But by Saturday, he found the mood had changed. 'I was out in the streets again before daylight. It was a mild clear morning and the first thing I heard was a man whistling. Soon people began crowding through the town but today they were talking, even joking about it. Instead of the despair I heard them say "we'll recover – life will go on, we can get used to it." People still felt pretty helpless but no longer hopeless. The frightened and nervous ones had already left. Those left behind were beginning to feel tough – just as the people of London had felt tough before them.'

A week later a visitor noticed a card in the window of a half-wrecked baby-clothes shop.[13]

BUSINESS AS USUAL

KEEP SMILING

There will always be an ENGLAND

It was the spirit of Sydney James, the Rialto troubadour.

The story of what had happened in Coventry was played down in the BBC's first big news broadcast of the day at 8 a.m. By 1 p.m. it was being given unusually full treatment. For the first time, the Ministry of Information allowed a blitzed city other than London to be mentioned by name. This was gratifying for those who endured the raid but the official version of what had happened differed sharply from what they had experienced. According to the BBC 'the enemy was heavily engaged by intensive anti-aircraft, which kept them at a great height and hindered accurate bombing of industrial targets.' It did admit heavy casualties – a figure of a thousand was given – and that many buildings had been destroyed and damaged. The attack, it emphasized, was an 'indiscriminate bombardment of the whole city'. This account was repeated in the following day's newspapers. T. S. Steele of the *Daily Telegraph* described the operation as a 'terror raid'. He accused the Germans of seeking 'to reproduce the Spanish tragedy of Guernica on a larger scale', a reference to the Condor Legion's destruction of the Basque capital in 1937.

Steele repeated the line that a fierce anti-aircraft barrage had kept the raiders five miles above the city. 'There was not even a pretence at an attempt to select military targets,' he wrote. 'For ten hours raider after raider flew over at an immense height and dumped bombs haphazard (*sic*) at the rate of nearly one a minute on the town. The result is that factories which are legitimate military targets have escaped comparatively lightly. The brunt of the destruction has fallen on shopping centres and residential areas – hotels, offices, banks, churches and – no Nazi raid is complete without this – hospitals.'

Much of the information contained in the reports came from a Ministry of Home Security communiqué. Faced with the magnitude of the raid, the government had chosen to play the story up. The wisdom of publicizing the attack was questioned at the War Cabinet meeting on Monday 19 November. The Secretary of State for War, Anthony Eden, had listened to Harrisson's Saturday night talk on the BBC and felt it had 'been a most depressing broadcast'. The prime minister disagreed. The effect of the publicity had been considerable in the United States and in Germany he said.

American correspondents indeed covered the raid in detail and seized on the city's ordeal as a symbol of British steadfastness and Nazi barbarity. The Germans responded by claiming that 223 had been killed by the RAF during a raid on Hamburg carried out the night after the Coventry attack (the true number was in fact twenty-six who died when bombs hit the Blohm and Voss shipyard). The assumption was that transatlantic indignation at what had been done to Coventry had stung Germany into insisting that its civilians were also suffering. To one watching American, it seemed clear what was coming next. Raymond Daniell of the *New York Times* told his readers that people in Britain now found it difficult to escape a feeling that a 'war of extermination is beginning. Each bomb that falls intensifies hatred and stimulates the demand for retaliation in kind.'

The note of the all-clear siren had barely faded before calls for retribution began. When King George visited the city less than two days afterwards a man in the crowd called out to him: 'God bless you. Give them what they gave to us! We can take it.'[14] The intelligence reports reaching the city's emergency services during the raids that preceded the big attack suggested that people had thought bombing attacks would be worse than they in fact were. As a result, 'more people than hitherto now feel that indiscriminate bombing of Berlin would be an unwise policy.'[15]

That attitude had now changed. Hilde Marchant had been one of the first to report the calls for revenge. She had issued one of her own. 'The Nazis added one more word to the English language – "Coventrated",' she wrote. 'Let us add one more – "Berliminated".' Her observations had been contradicted by Harrisson in a throwaway remark at the end of his broadcast. 'I see some reporters stressing the fact that Coventry is clamouring for reprisals,' he said. 'That wasn't borne out by my own observations . . . it only makes Coventry realize that this sort of thing doesn't end the war and only makes it more bitter.'

This judgement was not supported by the findings of his own teams. A fortnight after the raid they asked people in the streets of the city what they would like the government to do. 'Knock bloody hell out of them,' said a forty-five-year old man, described as middle class. 'For every one he gives us, we ought to give him twenty,' said a sixty-year-old working-class male. Another, youngish man replied. 'We're fighting gangsters, so we've got to be gangsters ourselves. We've been gentlemen too long.'[16]

Whatever gentlemanly attitudes lingered among those making Britain's war decisions were about to disappear for the duration of the war. It was a month before the government moved to avenge Coventry. The attack took place on the night of the 16/17 December and the target was Mannheim, an industrial town that straddles the Rhine in south central Germany. There were 134 aircraft on the raid, the biggest force to be used so far. At first sight there is nothing in the operations book or subsequent intelligence reports to suggest that the purpose of the raid was any different to many that had preceded it. The order was to attack the industrial centre of the town and the primary targets were the Mannheim Motorenwerke and naval armaments factories. The clue to the special nature of the raid lay in the bombs that the aircraft were carrying. There were a few 1,000-pound bombs and many more 500- and 250-pounders, packed with high explosive and designed to knock down walls and collapse roofs. But by far the largest number of bombs were incendiaries, weighing only four pounds each but capable when dropped in sufficient numbers, as Coventry knew all too well, of setting a city ablaze.

The raid was led by eight Wellingtons which carried nothing but incendiaries in their bomb bays, flown by the most experienced crews available. The aircraft that followed them were to use the light of the fires they started as their aiming point and in the words of Sir Richard Peirse, who succeeded Portal as commander-in-chief of Bomber Command, 'to concentrate the maximum amount of damage in the centre of the town.' It was a perfect moonlit night over Mannheim and the returning crews thought they had done well. More than half the aircraft claimed to have hit the town. Some reported later that when they flew away at 3.30 a.m., the target area was a 'mass of fires'.

In fact the raid was only a partial success. The first Wellington 'fire-raisers' failed to accurately identify the centre of the city and many incendiaries fell in the suburbs which were then bombed by the following aircraft. Other bombs fell on Ludwigshafen on the western bank of the Rhine. The city authorities reported 240 buildings destroyed or damaged by incendiaries and 236 by high explosive. They included thirteen shops, a railway station, a railway office, one school and two hospitals. The total casualty list was thirty-four dead, eighty-one injured and 1,266 bombed out of their homes. Of the dead eighteen were women, two were children, thirteen were male civilians and one was a soldier.

The Cabinet had given their approval for the plan three days before. If they had hoped for destruction to match that done to Coventry the reconnaissance photographs told another story. It was a disappointment and the exercise was not repeated for some time. But it was the shape of things to come.

3

'To Fly and Fight'

Bomber Command was poorly equipped to face the challenges of this new and vulnerable phase of its existence. In one respect, though, it was extraordinarily rich. The quality and quantity of men available to it were the best Britain and its overseas Dominions could provide. The Bomber Boys were all volunteers and the supply of aircrew candidates never slackened, even when losses were at their most daunting.

They were an extraordinarily varied bunch. Most were British. There was a sprinkling from the diaspora of the defeated nations, Poles, Czechs, Norwegians, French and Belgians, wanting their revenge on Germany. They were outnumbered by large numbers of Canadians, Australians, New Zealanders and South Africans, the 'colonials' as they were mockingly but affectionately called, whose lands were not directly threatened by Nazism but who, driven by a sense of adventure or fellow-feeling for their British cousins, none-theless offered themselves for what it was soon understood were among the most dangerous jobs in warfare.

For imaginative boys growing up in the 1930s, the prospect of going to war in an aeroplane carried an appeal that the older services could never match. Aviation was only a generation old and flying glowed with glamour and modernity. In the years before the war Peter Johnson, languishing in a hated job as a breakfast-cereal sales-man, looked at this world and longed to join it. 'I read aviation magazines,' he wrote, 'watched the activities at an RAF aerodrome from behind a hedge and even once penetrated into a flying club on the pretext of finding out the cost of learning to fly. That, needless to say, was well out of my income bracket but the contact with the world of flight, the romantic instructors in their ex-RFC leather coats, the hard, pretty girls with their long cigarette holders, the rich young men boasting about their adventures, fitted perfectly with my picture of a dream world to which, if I joined the Air Force, I could find a key.'[1]

By the time the great wartime expansion began, the RAF's aura of chic had faded. There was little that was dashing about Bomber Command. The new aircraft were big, blunt and utilitarian and the men who flew in them were unmistakably sons of the modern age.

The pre-war professionals were, on the whole, skilled and conscientious fliers, but they masked their seriousness behind a show of pseudo-aristocratic insouciance. The new boys were much less sophisticated. They came from all backgrounds and classes, and the prevailing ethos was democratic and popular. In their writings, in their work and play, they seem sterner, more earnest and more grown-up. The white flying-suited paladins of the RAF of the 1920s and early 1930s had joined to fly rather than to fight. The newcomers had signed up to do both.

On the outbreak of war, young men flocked to join the air force. In the initial rush, the recruiting staff were sometimes overwhelmed. Edward Johnson, who went on to fly as a bomb-aimer on the Dams Raid, was working for J. Lyons, the bakers, in Leeds when war broke out. 'I tried very hard to join up but in the initial stages they kept sending me back because they had nowhere to send people that were volunteering . . . it was a case of calling regularly to see if they'd made up their minds they were going to let us join.'[2]

As an eighteen-year old trainee surveyor, Arthur Taylor joined the Territorial Army before the war and was called up on the day war was declared. Within a few months he was bored and responded eagerly to an official circular announcing the RAF was looking for volunteers. So too did many of his companions. 'About twenty-two applied immediately,' he wrote. 'Understandably our colonel took a poor view of this and pointed out that few of us were bright enough to be accepted. The number of applications then dropped dramatically to fifteen.'[3]

In the month of September 1939, the Aviation Candidates Board at Cardington near Bedford interviewed 671 young men. The recruiting officers were delighted at the quality of the applicants. The board could afford to be choosy. Of the 671 who presented themselves, 102, or 15.2 per cent, were rejected.

The surplus of suitable manpower persisted throughout the war. In the first quarter of 1944, when Bomber Command was suffering terrible losses during the Battle of Berlin, the board still felt able to turn away 22.5 per cent of the volunteers who applied. The great majority of applicants had not waited for an official summons before stepping forward. A much smaller proportion had chosen the RAF after being called up. There were also a number seeking a transfer from the army. The general standard of education of the army candidates tended to be lower than that of the pure volunteers, the board's head, Group Captain Vere Bettington, observed, and a higher percentage of rejections was to be expected. RAF personnel working on the ground also responded well to appeals to 'get operational'.

At first, candidates were required to hold the School Certificate, the multi-subject examination taken by sixteen-year-olds before going on to higher education, but by August 1940 this proviso had been dropped. Nor was leaving school before the age of sixteen considered a bar. The initial test included intelligence, mathematics and general knowledge papers. But Bettington never rejected an applicant on educational grounds alone. 'A candidate's desire to fly and fight,' he declared, is 'of primary importance.'⁴

The old RAF's sensitivity about its *arriviste* origins had given it a tendency to snobbery. This was dissolved in the flood of men from modest and poor homes taking up the flying duties that had formerly been the preserve of the sons of the military, clerical, medical and colonial middle classes. Harry Yates, who left school at fourteen and worked as a junior clerk in the offices of a printing company in the south Midlands, wondered as he waited for a reply from the RAF whether his lack of education would disqualify him. 'Could it be,' he wrote, 'that, in reality, becoming one of these pilot types required a university education or even an old school tie? Was it the preserve of the sons of the well-to-do? But this, as I was to discover, was far from true. Terrible thing though it was, the war brought opportunity. The great British class system counted for surprisingly little. I saw nothing of it in all my RAF days.'[5]

The impulse to fly had been stimulated in many applicants by an early encounter with aeroplanes. Brian Frow went to the 1932 Hendon Air Show with a friend from his south-London prep school. 'I was spellbound,' he remembered. 'A hostile fort was bombed with live missiles; balloons forming life-sized animals were chased by big game hunters in fighter aircraft and eventually shot down.' In the school holidays he cycled to Croydon aerodrome with an aircraft recognition book in his satchel, identifying and recording every-thing that flew. The fact that his eldest brother, Herbert, had been killed in action flying in the First World War did not dent his enthusiasm. Herbert's loss was commemorated by a shrine in the family home made out of the wooden propeller of his doomed aircraft.[6]

Ken Newman, another south-London boy, also made regular pil-grimages to Croydon, which was only a mile or so from his home. 'As a boy, and like so many others of my generation, I had been fascinated by aeroplanes,' he recalled. 'They were seldom seen in the sky and caused open-mouthed surprise when they were ... I used to go and watch, from the roof of the airport hotel next to the terminal and flight control building.' Sometimes an hour or more would pass between the arrivals of the Imperial Airways and KLM airliners 'but every take-off and landing was exciting, particu-larly when the aeroplanes came close to the hotel building.'[7]

In opting for the RAF, volunteers were exercising a choice, and choices were rare in wartime. By doing so, they avoided being drafted into a less congenial branch of the services, and in 1939, there was no more unattractive option than the army.

The young men arriving at the recruiting centres had been born during, or just after, the end of the First World War. They had heard tales of the Western Front from their fathers and male relations. Dennis Field, the Coventry boy who had witnessed the Blitz from his back-garden shelter, had an uncle who had been in the trenches. 'His pugnacity and bitterness were apparent even to a youngster,' he wrote. 'My friend's father was a signaller in France and only reluctantly talked of the moonscape devastation, or mud, barbed wire, shell holes, bodies and rats and lice and drownings in mud and filth. My youthful picture was overwhelmingly one of revulsion.'[8]

In the streets, the sight of men who had lost limbs, the wheezing and hacking of gas-damaged lungs, told young men what they could expect. Aeroplanes were intrinsically dangerous, everyone knew that. But they were also exciting. And death in an aeroplane seemed quicker and cleaner in comparison with what they would face on land.

Jim Berry, who became a Pathfinder pilot, used to look with fascination and a tremor of fear at a German bayonet which his father had brought back from the trenches. '[He] used to tell us stories about the first war and it sounded horrific to me,' he said. 'The mud and the mess. It was something we looked at with a fair amount of horror as children. I thought that's not for me at any price. If I had been made to go I would have had to go but I thought, well, I'm going to volunteer so I volunteered and (went for) aircrew.'[9]

The RAF, as Group Captain Bettington said, was looking for people who were eager not only to fly but to fight. The First World War had generated a hatred of conflict and yearning for peace that was evident in the great popularity of the pacifist movement. Yet the hope amongst the young that they would not be called on to take part in another great war seldom hardened into a determination not to do so. Charles Patterson, born in 1920 and brought up in middle-class comfort by his mother and sister after his parents separated, found that his early childhood 'was overshadowed by the terrible First World War and the appalling suffering and sacrifices which were implanted in me not just by my mother but by all the grown-ups with whom I came into contact.' It was 'something so appalling that it just could not be ever allowed to happen again, because if it did, it would be virtually the end of the world.'

He felt, nevertheless, that 'if another war came I would inevitably have to join up as soon as it began, to try and fight. It was very firmly implanted in my mind that the greatest sacrifices in the first war had been endured by the ordinary Tommy. What I believed and was taught was that if these young, working-class boys could show such courage it made it absolutely imperative on me to not let them down, or at least make an effort to live up to what they had done should another war come.'

As the war approached Patterson considered his choices. It was quite simple really. 'I could never have stood up to the rigours of fighting on land and in dust and heat and dirt and so on. That simply would have been quite beyond me.' He knew something about flying from his brother-in-law, an RAF pilot who had taken him up in a Gypsy Moth when he was ten. Like many others he had seen *Dawn Patrol*, a remarkably bleak and unidealized story of First World War aviators which nonetheless pushed many adolescent boys into the arms of the RAF. '[It] had a tremendous influence on me. It struck me that although the casualties were very heavy it was much the most exciting and wonderful way to go to war.'[10]

The decision to fight was made easier by the seeming inevitability of the conflict. The Germans had left Britain with no choice. To the older airmen, this came as no surprise. Peter Johnson, who was nearly five when the first war broke out and whose naval officer father was killed in 1914, felt that 'mass hatred . . . was inoculated into my generation against the Germans'.[11] He was at least ten years older than most of his comrades in Bomber Command. The writings and recollections of the younger men do not reveal much evidence of instinctive loathing for the Hun.

A surprising number of them had some direct or indirect contact with events in Germany. When he was about fourteen, Ken Newman made friends with a German boy called Erich Strauss who had come from Stuttgart to visit his grandmother. 'It was during one of our walks around Mitcham Common that he told me he and his family were Jewish and that the Jews in Germany were being given a very hard time by the Nazis,' he wrote. 'I was not quite sure whether he was telling the truth or was exaggerating to impress me.' In 1938 he visited Germany with a school party, travelling by boat and train to Cologne then sailing up the Rhine to Mainz, staying in youth hostels along the way. 'In every one were parties of Hitler Youth who marched about in military-style uniforms, and every morning and evening attended a flag raising or lowering ceremony with arms raised and shouts of "Heil Hitler!"' Even so, they seemed friendly enough to the English visitors. Every young person he met 'repeated again and again that the last thing they wanted was another war with Britain and France.' [12]

Informal attempts had been made to forge friendly links with Germany in the years between the wars through school trips and exchanges. Sometimes they were too successful. In the spring of 1936 thirteen-year-old Ken Goodchild went on a visit with some schoolmates from No. 6 Central School in Morden, Surrey. They were in the Rhineland when the Germany army marched in, and visited Cologne, which he was to pass through seven years later as a prisoner. On their return their families were surprised to see they were wearing swastika lapel badges. In 1937 Ken went again and was present in Düsseldorf when Hitler arrived to open an exhibition. The Führer exchanged some friendly words with the master accompanying the boys and patted some of them on the head. Goodchild was perhaps the only Bomber Command airman to have stared the enemy leader in the face.[13]

In the same year, Leonard Cheshire, a restless, rather wayward eighteen-year-old, who had just left Stowe public school, went to stay with a German family in Potsdam before he went up to Oxford. The head of the household was a retired admiral called Ludwig von Reuter. He was not a supporter of the Nazis but shared some of their opinions, telling Cheshire that 95 per cent of humanity were worthless and war was a valuable means of keeping them down. Cheshire went on to become one of the most dedicated and ruthless pilots in Bomber Command.[14]

Before the war it was still possible to differentiate between Nazis and 'decent' Germans. 'How I loathed the Nazis,' wrote Guy Gibson. 'How could the common people of Germany allow such a world-conquering crowd of gangsters to get into power and stay in power? Ruthless and swaggering, domineering brutality, that was their creed.' His anger was directed with almost equal vigour against British politicians, the 'rotten Governments, the Yes men and the appeasers' as well as those who voted for them.

Leonard Cheshire (*left*) and opponent, Germany, August 1936.

Gibson blamed the older generation for allowing another war to happen. But he was also concerned about the willingness of his contemporaries to fight it. On 1 September 1939, having been called back from leave to rejoin his squadron, he passed through Oxford with his friend Freddy Bilbey who had been studying biology there. After a lengthy session in a pub they went to have dinner. 'It was fairly late and we were pretty hungry, and fed like kings with some excellent 1928 burgundy, but what a rotten crowd to be seen at that place – drunken, long-haired, pansy-looking youths, mixed with foppish women. They so disgusted me that I asked Freddy if they were undergraduates . . . "Good Lord, no!" he said. "They are the types who try to look like undergraduates." [15]

Gibson's doubts about some 'varsity men may have stemmed from the Oxford Union debate of a few years before in which the motion that the house would not fight for King and Country had been carried. The event had been treated as if it was a genuine barometer of young, privileged opinion. It turned out to be utterly misleading.

Robert Kee, a handsome, rather bohemian history undergraduate, might possibly have attracted a suspicious glare from Gibson had he encountered him in an Oxford pub. But Kee was as contemptuous as Gibson was of the appeasers and as eager to get to grips with the Nazis. 'At the time of Munich all of us at Oxford hated what was going on,' he said. 'We all thought [the politicians] were doing exactly what the Nazis wanted them to.' He was in France with his tutor A. J. P. Taylor when war was declared and rushed back to sign up for the RAF. [16]

Whatever subtleties of feeling might have existed towards the Germans in 1939 faded with the end of the phoney war, and they became, simply, the enemy. Soon they were all too visible, in the skies over Britain. The Battle of Britain provided the most effective recruiting sergeant the RAF could have hoped for. Michael Beetham was a seventeen-year-old schoolboy in the summer of 1940. At the start of the holidays he went to stay with his father, a company commander with the York and Lancaster Regiment then based on the hills just outside Portsmouth at Hillsea barracks. 'It was a lovely summer and the Battle of Britain was just beginning with the German bombers bombing Portsmouth naval base,' he said. 'God, it was spectacular. We went outside and saw the bombers going in and the Hurricanes and Spitfires diving in and having a go at them. I said to my father, that's what I want to do. He obviously wanted me to join the army. I couldn't put my name down until I was eighteen but I did it as soon as I could. I joined the air force to be a pilot. I'd never flown in my life but I wanted to do what those chaps were doing.' [17] At the same time Edward Hearn, a young estate manager, was watching dogfights in the skies over his home in

Folkestone, Kent. 'I thought at that time that if I've got to go to war then I'll go in an aircraft.' He decided to keep his decision from his parents in order not to add to their burden of worry. All his siblings were in the process of joining up. He signed on in Maidstone. 'When I got back my mother said why aren't you at work? I told her, and she said well, I suppose it had to happen sooner or later.' Eddie ended up serving as bombing leader alongside Michael Beetham in 50 Squadron.

Bruce Lewis was standing with his friends outside the tuck shop during mid-morning break at Dauntsey's School in Wiltshire when 'we heard the grinding growl of unsynchronized German aero-engines . . . the Battle of Britain was at its height and schoolboys knew all about these technical matters. The twin-engine Luftwaffe bomber flew low over the school, and then, thrill of thrills, came the shapely little Spitfire in hot pursuit, the distinctive whistle from its Merlin engine sounding almost like the wind itself.' Later they heard the bomber had been shot down. Amazingly, the victorious fighter pilot was an old boy of the school, Eric Marrs, who destroyed six German aircraft before being killed the following year.

At that moment Lewis jilted the Royal Navy, his first preference, and chose the RAF. It was two years before he could join up. He had a talent for drama and got a job as a radio actor with the BBC. His father, a professor who had been badly wounded at the Somme, wanted him to go to university which would gain him exemption from war service for three years. To Bruce, 'such an existence would have been impossible – to sit studying in complete safety while others of my age were dying for their country was not on.' [18]

The start of the Blitz reinforced the realization that the air was now a crucial battlefield as well as the belief that it was in the sky that the war would be decided. Bill Farquharson, who had been raised in Malaya where his father was in the colonial service and was awaiting call-up, was serving with Air Raid Precautions in Birmingham when he was ordered to rush to Coventry to help out after the raid. The experience made him 'angry and yet dead scared'. He felt no particular desire for revenge. He had already made up his mind to go into the air force and the experience 'confirmed the fact that I preferred to be up [in the air] rather than down there'.[19]

Len Sumpter, a Corby steelworker and former Grenadier who had been recalled to the colours at the start of the war, was training recruits at the Guards Caterham depot when it was hit by German bombs. 'We took a real hammering,' he said. 'A lot of people were killed there.' When advertisements appeared calling for volunteers for aircrew he applied, impelled by the thought of 'a little bit of excitement' and 'a bit of personal anger'.[20]

Britain's vulnerability was brought home to Ken Newman when in August 1940, a month after his eighteenth birthday, he watched Croydon airport being attacked by waves of German bombers. When the Blitz began he made his way each day from his home in Norbury to the City where he worked in the accounts department of a mortgage company. One Sunday night in October, the sirens sounded and he hurried his parents to their air-raid shelter. He was 'just closing the door when I heard bombs screaming down towards us. There was no mistaking they were about to hit us or fall very close indeed and I must admit that I was very frightened and thought our end had come. Crump went the first bomb, quite near . . . accompanied by the sound of splintering wood, smashing glass and falling masonry . . .' So it went on. When quietness returned he opened the shelter door. The air was swirling with brick dust and the house was gone. There was 'no sleep for us at all that night. My mother was weeping in a corner of the shelter, partly over the loss of her much-loved home and also in relief that we had survived.' Later, when asked for his reasons for wanting to join the RAF he told the chairman of the selection board that he was 'keen to become a bomber pilot in order to have my revenge'.[21]

Those who had already joined up were glad they had done so when they heard the news from home. Doug Mourton, a wallpaper salesman before the war, was undergoing his RAF training at Abingdon when on 17 September his mother wrote to him from south London. 'Things are very uncomfortable here at present but we are getting used to it . . . they don't give us five minutes' peace. [Aunt] Beat's house was bombed and they have come to live with us. There [are] fourteen of us living in the cellar . . .'[22]

The recruits went off to war in a spirit of optimism. Joining up dispelled the feeling of impotence that aerial bombardment generated and the air force provided the most immediate means of hitting back. There were some restless spirits who welcomed the excitement and openings that war has always offered.

When the storm finally broke Leonard Cheshire was leading what would seem to many an enviable existence, studying law, none too diligently, at Oxford. He was easily bored and game for challenges, which had led him to join the University Air Squadron. His log book recording his flights paused at the end of August 1939. Under the heading WAR he wrote: 'a heaven-sent release . . . a magic carpet on which to soar above the commonplace round of everyday life.'[23]

By the end of 1940 every Briton was faced with an unavoidable truth. There could be no accommodation with the Nazis. If Britain was to remain Britain it would have to fight and after the fall of France the RAF was the only force in the world that was directly attacking the Germans on their own ground.

Thousands of miles away, across oceans and hemispheres, this conviction was felt almost as deeply as it was at home. Imperial attitudes and arrangements were changing. Colonies had become Dominions and were taking their first steps to independence. Yet the cultural and emotional fabric of the empire was still densely woven and strong. At the start of the war, the official instinct of Canada, South Africa, Australia, New Zealand and Rhodesia was to rally to Britain, even though their interests were, for the time being at least, unthreatened by Hitler's foreseeable ambitions. They immediately offered their young men to bolster the ranks of the RAF.

Altogether 130,000 men from the Dominions served as airmen in the RAF, almost 40 per cent. One in four of the Bomber Command aircrews was from overseas and 15,661 lost their lives. Of those, 9,887 were from Canada. Canada's cultural ties with Britain were less established than those of other Dominions. Volunteers tended to think of themselves as answering a call to fight for their own country, rather than going to the aid of a faraway mother nation. Ralph Wood came out of church in Woodstock, New Brunswick, on the morning of Sunday 11 September to find newsboys hawking special editions of the local newspaper, the *Telegraph-Journal*, announcing that Canada was at war with Germany. As he walked back to the home of the parents of his girlfriend Phyllis he confronted the choices before him.

> I knew I had fear of being labelled [a] coward or yellow if I didn't volunteer my services to my country. I knew also that I had fear of losing my life if I did volunteer. There was no contest. All that remained was to choose the service I would join. The Navy? No way! I'd probably be seasick before we left the harbour, let alone battling those thirty-foot waves at sea . . . The Army? Well according to stories of World War I, which was the only reference we had to go by, this meant mud, trenches, lice, bayonets, etc. This was definitely not my cup of tea. Air Force? This was more appealing as it presented a picture of your home base in a civilized part of the country accompanied by real beds with sheets, fairly good food, local pubs with their accompanying social life with periodic leaves to the larger centres and cities. The hour of decision was at hand but it didn't take me an hour to decide on the Royal Canadian Air Force. Being a fatalist, I was pretty sure my number would come up, and in the air it would be swift and definite.[24]

Wood was volunteering out of a sense of duty to Canada and it seems that, at first, he expected to be doing his fighting at home. If the discovery that he was to be sent to England caused him or his comrades any concern there is no mention of it in his frank and cheerful memoir.

Australians and New Zealanders seem to have had a more developed feeling of kinship with Britain and a stronger sense of a shared destiny. Don Charlwood was proud of his English ancestry. His great-grandfather had been a bookseller in Norwich until 1850, when he transferred the business to Melbourne. As soon as Charlwood was able, he volunteered for the Royal Australian Air Force, in the knowledge that it meant crossing the world to go to the rescue of a country he had never visited.

Like Charles Patterson he felt that his generation 'never really emerged from the shadow of the shadow of the First World War . . . the rise of Nazism was a lengthening of the same shadow over our youth. When this threat was faced by Britain in 1939, the response in Australia was not only that we, too, must face Nazism, but that we must stand by the threatened "Homeland".'[25]

The Dominion airmen sometimes appeared to feel an attachment to the British Empire that was stronger than that of the British themselves. One of Bomber Command's great leaders, Air Vice-Marshal Sir Don Bennett, raised in the Great Dividing Range town of Toowoomba in Queensland, spoke of the 'true British, of . . . Australia, of Canada, New Zealand, South Africa, Rhodesia and the Old Country itself.'[26]

By the end of 1940, then, the push of the war and the pull of the air was driving tens of thousands of young men towards Bomber Command. They were rich, middling and poor and they came from every corner of Britain and its empire. They were the best of their generation and they were heading for one of the worst tasks of the war.

4

Crewing Up

The process by which these disparate and largely unskilled young men were moulded into effective members of a bomber crew was one of the great achievements of the wartime RAF. It was thorough, on the whole efficient, and surprisingly imaginative, qualities which seemed quite out of keeping with the prevailing pre-war service ethos of myopia and conservatism. Noble Frankland, who had joined the University Air Squadron on going up to Oxford in 1941 and went on to join Bomber Command and co-write the official history of its war, reckoned that by the end of operational training 'most crews [had] a reasonable basis upon which to test their fortunes and their courage.'[1] The instruction period certainly lasted long enough. Ken Newman, who volunteered in May 1941 and was selected for pilot training, did not fly his first operational mission until the spring of 1944. A gap of about two and a half years between joining up and going into battle became the norm.

The strategic air campaign was, essentially, made up as it went along. Circumstances changed rapidly in the early days and it was some time before a regularized training programme evolved. With the coming of the four-engined heavies, the Stirlings, Lancasters and Halifaxes, the system settled down to produce a continuous stream of competent and well-prepared airmen.

The long journey to an operational squadron began with a visit to the RAF local recruiting station. Applicants were given a medical, an academic test and a brief interview after which the most obviously unsuitable were weeded out. Volunteers were applying simply to join the RAF and had no idea in which branch of the service they would end up. In the early stages, many dreamed of becoming fighter pilots. But by the end of 1940 Fighter Command's hour had passed. The air war now belonged to Bomber Command and it was there that most volunteers would be sent. Even while the Battle of Britain was at its height, Churchill told the Cabinet and the Chiefs of Staff that 'the fighters are our salvation, but the bombers alone provide the means of victory.'

Official propaganda emphasized their vital role. The first successful film of the war, *Target for Tonight*, which came out in July 1941, was a drama-documentary which used no actors, only RAF personnel who played themselves. It followed the crew of a Wellington, F for Freddie, preparing and executing a typical raid on a typical target in Germany, piloted by Charles 'Percy' Pickard, a blond, impassive, pipe-smoking paradigm of the pre-war RAF. The flying scenes, although spliced with authentic footage, look amateurish and unreal now and the airmen act their parts with a touching diligence but an almost total absence of technique. It was nonetheless a wild commercial success and was seen by audiences all around the free world.

Recruiting posters portrayed the crews as gallant and spirited, the natural successors to the Fighter Boys. Noble Frankland needed little convincing that Bomber Command was the place to be. 'I thought that the defence of Great Britain was over and the next step was to smash the Germans up. I was quite keen to take part in smashing up the Germans, which I think was a fairly common sort of instinct, but I actually had an opportunity to do it.'[2]

As the war progressed, it became clear that bombing was drudge work, tedious and repetitive, and with the added disadvantage of being highly dangerous. Some volunteers who were chosen to fly were dismayed when they heard what it was that they would be flying. Dennis Field had done his initial instruction on single-engined Harvards and was looking forward to going on to fighters. As he moved to the next stage of his training 'a special parade was called and the CO announced that the whole course would be trained for multi-engined aircraft and, we inferred, four-engined bombers. I felt totally deflated at the news. The very little I knew about them gave the impression that I should become a glorified bus-driver.'[3]

For Harry Yates, the ex-clerk who had worried that he was too humble for the RAF, distaste for the grim, mechanical nature of the work over-rode appeals to duty. In early 1943, after a spell serving as an instructor, he decided that he wanted to go to the front line of the air war. 'My expectations were quite specific and they were high: night fighting in Mosquitoes or Beaufighters or, failing that, ground-strafing in Beaufighters. Flying a bomber didn't figure anywhere. Indeed the whole point was to avoid it.' The RAF's priorities dictated otherwise and he was sent to Bomber Command.[4]

At the beginning of the war Bomber Command's most pressing need was for pilots. As aircraft grew in size and complexity, its requirements became much broader. The bombers in service in the early period contained an assortment of crews. The Whitley and the Wellington carried five men, including two pilots. The cramped and narrow body of the Hampden held four and had room for only one pilot. All types had an observer who acted as both navigator and bomb-aimer as well as a wireless operator and one or two gunners. The observer role was eventually split into the separate categories of navigator and bomb-aimer.

In August 1940 the first of the new generation of bombers began to appear, starting with the Stirling and followed by the Halifax and then the Lancaster, which by the end of the war was flown by 75 per cent of Bomber Command squadrons. It had been decided late in 1941 that a second pilot was superfluous. He rarely gained any flying experience and was little more than a passenger. Second pilots were dropped and replaced by flight engineers, highly trained technicians who monitored the running of the aircraft during flight. This was an important decision. Pilot training took longer and cost more than the other aircrew roles. With only a single pilot needed, more aircraft could be put in the air. If the practice of using two pilots had persisted, the great raids of 1942 that announced the opening of the main offensive would not have been possible.

By spring of 1942 there were six aircrew jobs for which volunteers could be considered: pilot, navigator, engineer, bomb-aimer, wireless operator and air gunner, of which there were two. After the initial vetting stage candidates were sent to an Aircrew Selection Centre. On the first day they faced a fairly demanding set of academic tests which were marked on the spot and the failures sent home. The following morning there was a rigorous medical. To pass 'Aircrew A1' required a higher level of fitness than was demanded by the other services. Next came an interview, typically by a panel of three senior officers. Dennis Steiner, a confectioner's son from Wimbledon, who passed through the Oxford selection centre in August 1941, found it 'more of a friendly chat than an interview. I knew that I had been accepted when it was remarked that I would like flying. As I left the room one called out "good luck lad".'[5] Successful candidates were sworn in, issued with their RAF number and then, anti-climactically, told to go home and wait to be summoned. This period of 'deferred service' could last many months.

Eventually they were called to an Air Crew Reception Centre where basic training began. The newcomers marched, saluted, went on endless runs and listened to hair-raising lectures from the medical officer. These, wrote James Hampton, who was the youngest of three brothers who volunteered for aircrew and the only one to survive, warned the new arrivals, virgins almost to a man, about 'some of the shocking and terrifying diseases that abounded and of which they had previously been unaware. These diseases had certain things in common. They could not be caught from lavatory seats and they invariably ended with General Paralysis of the Insane followed shortly by death.'[6] Venereal diseases were a service obsession. At his training centre in Babbacombe near Torquay, Brian Frow's sheltered, middle-class innocence was shaken by lectures given at 'great length, complete with slides lurid enough to frighten even the bravest from casual intercourse for life.'[7]

The RAF was adapting as fast as it could, but no one had told the pre-war regular NCOs who served as drill instructors and were not about to change their rough old ways. Cyril March, who went down the pit straight from his school in Durham, was told after a wait of more than a year to report to the reception centre at Lord's Cricket Ground in London. The NCOs 'let us know in no uncertain manner that we were now in the RAF. They had one thing in common. They were fatherless to a man. There was the sergeant who told me to get my hair cut twice in one day, the sergeant who said he would cure our stiff arms after various inoculations [then] gave us a scrubbing brush, a bucket and a long flight of stairs to scrub down.'⁸

Institutionalized, low-level sadism was not uncommon. Bruce Lewis, who volunteered on his eighteenth birthday, early in 1942, regretted that 'a fine service like the Royal Air Force should have tolerated such an unworthy reception camp' like the one he passed through at Padgate near Warrington. 'Enthusiastic young volunteers entered this gateway to their new career only to be cursed at, degraded and insulted by the low-quality types on the permanent staff.' He felt 'well prepared for all this bullying nonsense having tasted the rigours of life in public school. But some of those lads were away from home for the first time. I used to feel sorry for the ones I heard sobbing in our hut at night.'⁹

After a month, cadets moved on to one of the Initial Training Wings (ITWs) which had been set up in universities and requisitioned resort hotels, where they spent six to eight weeks. There was classroom instruction in airmanship, meteorology, mathematics, Morse code and aircraft recognition. Drill and PT accounted for four hours a day of a six-day week. The courses were tough and the standards high. An 80 per cent success rate was needed to pass.

There was leave at the end of the course and a chance for the cadets to return home to show off their uniforms. Cyril March had spent the worst part of a bitter winter at Bridlington, billeted in the attic of a run-down boarding house. He set off, 'not being sorry to leave frozen "Brid" and feeling very grand in our new uniforms with the distinctive white Air Crew Cadet flash in our hats. I got off the train in Durham to be surrounded by my young brothers and all their mates, all wanting to carry my gear. When we got on the bus to go up home they wouldn't let me pay; I felt like a conquering hero instead of a comparative sprog.'

By the end of the ITW course the cadets had been sifted into the categories, 'trades' in RAF parlance, in which they would fight their war. The path to an operational squadron now diverged as trainees proceeded to specialist flying, engineering, navigation, bombing, gunnery and wireless schools. There was some room for further adjustments. Pilots 'washed out' in the testing conditions of ever more advanced training were often re-assigned as navigators or bomb-aimers. But most would stay in the occupation to which they had been assigned until the end.

The British climate made it one of the worst places in the world to train airmen. In another act of surprising foresight, the Air Ministry had come to an agreement with the Dominions to make use of the blue skies they possessed in abundance. The result was the Empire Air Training Scheme which began operating in April 1940. At its peak in 1943 there were 333 training schools outside the UK, ninety-two of them in Canada with most of the rest in Australia, South Africa, Rhodesia and India. There were five in the United States. Over the war years they turned out more than 300,000 aircrew for all branches of the RAF.

To leave wartime Britain for North America was to move from monochrome to Technicolor. The transformation began on the boat, often one of the great passenger liners that in peacetime had plied the transatlantic route. Dennis Steiner sailed from Gourock on the Clyde to America on the *Queen Elizabeth* to continue his training. As Ireland slipped away he sat down for his first meal. 'We had pork chops and snow-white bread. We hadn't realized how grey our wartime bread had become.' The film stars Merle Oberon, Edward G. Robinson and Douglas Fairbanks who were sailing back to the United States added an extra touch of glamour. The liner docked at New York where the cadets boarded a train for a twenty-seven hour journey to the main receiving centre at Moncton in New Brunswick, Canada.

Dennis Field arrived in Canada in May 1942 to carry on his flying training. 'The lights, lack of civic restrictions, unrationed goods and food, hospitality of the folk of the small town suddenly flooded with servicemen and the novelty of our new surroundings was appreciated,' he wrote. At cafés and drugstores they wolfed down 'huge T-bone steaks covered with two eggs sunny side up and chips, followed by hefty helpings of real strawberry flan and ice cream.'

Those coming the other way found England welcoming and even sophisticated compared with puritanical provincial Canada. Ralph Wood, now trained as a navigator, arrived at the Uxbridge receiving depot in the spring of 1941. He was on his way to the Operational

Training Unit (OTU) at Abingdon, Berkshire, before joining 102 Squadron, a Royal Canadian Air Force unit. 'It was here that we were introduced to English food, English pubs and English girls – in that order,' he wrote. 'The pubs were happy new experiences for Canadians used to the dingy taverns of home where one was made to feel uncomfortable, if not immoral . . . the food was plain, palatable and rationed. The girls were friendly and good company . . .'[10]

Training was fun, by and large, whether at home or abroad. It was a time of instant friendships and hard, satisfying work relieved by horseplay, laughter and mild excess. Young men who in peacetime would have been rigidly separated by class and circumstances were thrown together and found that they got along fine. Henry Hughes, who was one of eleven children of a poor but happy family in Bolton, Lancashire, was waiting for a Morse test while training in Blackpool when 'suddenly an airman at our table started to sing "A Nightingale Sang in Berkeley Square" in a really posh Noël Coward-type voice.'[11] The singer was Denholm Elliott who went on to become one of Britain's best-loved post-war actors. Elliott was at RADA when the war began and had volunteered for the RAF on his eighteenth birthday. He found service life 'rather exciting. I was mixing for the first time with many different types of men from different strata of society and I found that I was [getting] on really quite well with them. I had been living in a fairly monastic world since the age of nine, in prep and public schools and had never till now seriously rubbed shoulders with such a spectrum of different classes of people. I hardly realized that they existed. I found myself making great mates with all sorts of people I would probably never have met had it not been for joining up to meet the national crisis.'[12]

Discipline was more flexible now. It needed to be. The trainees were individually-minded and, if not for the war, would have been unlikely to have chosen a service career. They were some of the most adventurous spirits of their generation and tended to chafe at unnecessary restrictions and unearned authority. That did not mean they lacked discipline. Rules, they knew, could be broken. But orders had to be obeyed.

Once the trainees arrived at their specialist schools, flying became part of their daily existence, and so inevitably, did death. There was no system which could take the danger out of learning how to operate a bomber. Walking back to Abingdon after a night in the Red Lion pub, Ralph Wood and his fellow-Canadians watched a Whitley which was practising take-offs and landings crash into the commanding officer's house killing all the crew. It could happen to anybody. Sergeants McClachlan and Iremonger shared a billet with Dennis Field during advanced flying training at South Cerney. They were a worldly pair who seemed to exude confidence. One morning they failed to turn up after night-flying training. They had been killed colliding with each other. When Brian Frow and seven other trainees arrived at the OTU at Cottesmore, they were told by the chief instructor that he had a 'little job' for them before they started. 'This was to act as escort officers at the mass funeral in Cottesmore village for five students who had crashed on the airfield during the week before. We subsequently learned that there had been four fatal crashes in the previous week.' By the end of the war 8,090 Bomber Command personnel had perished in training accidents, roughly one seventh of all who died, and 4,203 were wounded. The suspicion that many of these deaths had been avoidable created some anger and resentment.

At the end of specialist training everyone was promoted. The majority, about two thirds, became sergeants. The rest were commissioned as pilot officers. The criteria used to award commissions were vague. The logic that leaders were automatically officers was not always followed. The captain of a bomber was the pilot, and it seemed sensible that the captain should hold the senior rank. But it was not unusual for a sergeant pilot to be outranked by his navigator or bomb-aimer. Operating a heavy bomber involved shared responsibility and intense mutual dependence. The anomalies and injustices of drawing distinctions of status, as well as pay and conditions, between men who fought and died inside the same claustrophobic metal tube grated particularly on the Canadians who were providing so many men.

The matter surfaced in May 1942 at an air training conference in

Ottawa. It seemed to the Royal Canadian Air Force that there was 'no justification for the commissioning of some individuals whilst others are required to perform exactly the same duties but in NCO rank.' The Canadians pointed out the inequities of pay, transportation and travel allowances. Dividing crews into commissioned and non-commissioned officers meant, in theory at least, the end of socializing on an equal footing. Sergeants would go to the sergeants' mess, officers to the better-appointed officers' mess. They argued that it could only be bad for team spirit if 'the crew, as an entity is not able to live and fraternize, the one with the other, during leisure and off-duty hours.' A radical solution was proposed. Everyone flying in a bomber should be an officer.

The RAF avoided answering the Canadians' detailed points, but did try to define the qualities that made an officer. Commissions were granted, 'in recognition of character, intelligence (as distinct from academic qualifications), and capacity to lead, command and set a worthy example. Many aircrews (*sic*), although quite capable of performing their duties adequately, have no officer qualities.' The debate fizzled out.

Despite the relative absence of awkwardness about class in the RAF, there was plenty of evidence to suggest that being educated at a public school was no handicap when it came to obtaining a commission. Arriving at Brize Norton Flying Training School in April 1941 Brian Frow and his fellow-trainees were addressed by the chief ground instructor, a squadron leader aged about fifty, with First World War medals on his chest. After a welcoming speech he told his charges he was going to select flight commanders and deputies from among the cadets who would act as leaders and principal contacts between students and staff.

'We were all sitting in the hall and he started. "Stand up all of those who were in the OTC (Officer Training Corps) at a public school." About twenty stood up. "Any of you who failed to pass Cert A, sit down." This left some ten standing. "Sit down those who failed to reach the rank of corporal." Two more sat down. "Failed to reach sergeant." Three more sat down. (He) then said, "You five airmen report to my office for interview."'

When Frow arrived, 'The first question was "Do you have any close relations who were commissioned in the Royal Air Force?" I had two brothers, and when I said that one was a squadron leader . . . that was sufficient.' He was 'amused and somewhat embarrassed by this method of selecting the cadet flight commanders and their deputies . . . By a process of elimination, he had dismissed all cadets who had not attended public school, who had not been in the OTC, who had failed to pass Cert A and who had no close relations commissioned into the RAF.' Frow was duly appointed commander of 'A' Flight.

At the same time as they were graded by rank, the cadets earned the right to wear the brevet appropriate to their aircrew category. To outsiders there seemed something unformed about the single wing and circle insignia. It prompted an article by Godfrey Winn, a star writer of the day. 'Don't ask the man with one wing when he will finish his training and get the other half of his wings,' he advised. 'Don't ask him anything. Just shake his hand and offer him a drink.'

Aircrew members were proud of their trades. Many had started out hoping to be pilots. Few of those who were reassigned resented for long the new roles they had been allotted. It was the crew that mattered more than one's individual part in it.

Flying a big bomber was entirely different from flying a Spitfire or a Hurricane. It was the difference, it was sometimes said, between a sports car and a lorry. A four-engined bomber was an immensely complex machine, whose systems needed constant checking. It was a responsibility rather than a pleasure. Tony Iveson who flew Lancasters with 617 Squadron believed that bomber pilots needed 'a steady personality, and you could tell that from what you heard about how they behaved off duty . . . I was a natural bomber pilot. I was patient. I liked precise flying.'[13]

Fighter pilots wrote about flying in the language of love and passion. There are no descriptions in letters and memoirs of the joy of flying a Halifax or a Lancaster. In fighter squadrons it was considered disrespectful to refer to your aircraft as anything other than an aeroplane. Bomber Boys called theirs 'kites'. Operational flying over Germany could mean trips of seven, eight, nine hours. These journeys involved high drama at take-off and landing and intense fear over the target area. But between these peaks of feeling there were long passages of boredom and fatigue, especially on the journey home, even though the danger was far from over.

Crews were organic entities and the prevailing atmosphere was egalitarian. Nonetheless, there was no doubt that it was the pilot who ultimately was in charge. He was responsible for the lives of the other six members of the crew, to the extent that if the aircraft was irretrievably damaged or on fire and about to explode he was expected to stay at the controls until the others had baled out.

The pilot, together with the navigator and the bomb-aimer, were essential for a bomber to be be able to bomb. It was extremely desirable to have a flight engineer, wireless operator and mid-upper and rear gunners. But a sortie could succeed without them.

The pilot's concern was to reach the target. The navigator's job was to find it. Don Charlwood, a navigator himself, felt that 'as a group [they] tended more to seriousness than the men they flew with'.[14] The job, and the training it required, were demanding and exhausting. Noble Frankland, like many navigators, had started off wanting to be a pilot but failed to make the grade. Despite his high intelligence he found the course at his elementary navigation school 'academically the most difficult thing I had ever tackled'. Astronavigation required an ability to think in three dimensions, 'a very, very difficult concept for somebody who is not mathematically gifted or trained'.[15] In the early days navigators had no radio aids to guide them to targets. Even with the advent of Gee, Oboe and H2S, which used radio and radar pulses to direct aircraft on to targets, the navigator's job was the most mentally testing of aircrew tasks, requiring constant alertness at every stage of the journey.

Once the navigator had guided the aircraft to the target area the bomb-aimer took over. As the aircraft went into its bombing run, he became the most important person aboard. He lay face-down in the Perspex nose, exposing the length of his body to the flak bursting all around. Pressing his face to the lens of the complicated bomb-sight, he called course corrections to the pilot as they went into the

Plotting a course.

final run, ordered the bomb doors open and, when he was satisfied, pressed the button that sent the bombs tumbling into the night. In those final moments, every man aboard was clenched in expectation, pleading with him to finish the job and let them head for home. Good bomb-aimers possessed an almost inhuman sangfroid which allowed them to divorce all feelings for their own safety and that of the crew from the necessity of getting their bombs on the target, or the colour-coded pyrotechnic markers dropped by the leading aircraft to highlight the aiming point. On his debut trip with 49 Squadron to Hagen, in the eastern Ruhr, Donald Falgate, who had defied his parents' wishes to join up, was 'determined I was going to get my bombs slap-bang on the target and there was no way I was going to release them if I couldn't get the markers in the bombsight.'

The pilot tried to weave to avoid the bursting flak as they went in, toppling the gyroscope that kept the bombsight level, making it impossible for Falgate to aim accurately. He ordered the bomb doors closed and insisted on going round again. 'I won't repeat what was said over the intercom by various crew members,' he said when telling the story later. It was only on the third run that Falgate was satisfied and pressed the bomb release. 'I was unpopular, very unpopular,' he recalled many years afterwards.[16]

The complexities of four-engined bombers created a need for an extra crew member to assist the pilot. Many flight engineers were ex-groundcrew airmen who already had mechanical skills. Their training included a spell at an aircraft factory producing the type of bomber they would fly in to ensure that they were fluent in all the systems of the huge new machines. In a Lancaster they sat next to, and slightly behind the captain. Their duties included monitoring the panels of dials and warning lights, one for each engine, which were situated on the side of the fuselage out of the pilot's line of sight. This left him to concentrate on his flying instruments. Their most important responsibility was nursing the fuel levels to ensure there was enough petrol to get home. Engineers received elementary flying training and could theoretically fly the aircraft in an emergency. In practice, if the pilot was dead or too badly hurt to function, the engineer was likely to be in a similar condition.

The wireless operator had, according to Bruce Lewis, who served as one, 'a lonely existence, mentally isolated from other members of the crew for long periods of time while he strained to listen through the static in his headphones for faint but vital signals.' These told him the aircraft's position which he passed on to the navigator. He also manned the radar monitor which warned of the approach of night-fighters.

The gunners had what appeared to be the worst job of all. They lived in metal and Perspex turrets that poked out of the top and the back of the aircraft, washed by whistling winds that could freeze them to their guns. They carried the huge responsibility of defending their mates, constantly scanning the night for flak and fighters. Yet the long hours of staring into darkness meant it was all too easy to lose concentration, even fall asleep. If a night-fighter was spotted a decision that could mean the difference between life or death had to be made. You had seen him, but had he seen you? There was one sure way of ensuring he had, which was to pour glowing tracer fire in his direction. If you got it wrong, your end was particularly lurid. Everyone had a story of seeing the rear gunner being hosed out of a shot-up bomber that had hobbled back to base.

Yet some chose the job. It was the quickest way to an operational squadron with the actual gunnery course taking only six weeks. The training, though, was thorough. By the end, many could manipulate the turrets so well they could trace their names on a board with a pencil wedged in a gun barrel. Cyril March had seen an RAF recruiting poster in the window of Stanton's furniture store in his native Durham appealing for Tail End Charlies and 'decided there and then that I would become an air gunner, none of the other trades appealing to me.' For all the privations and dangers of the job it was possible to get used to it or even enjoy it. 'In the end you learned to love it, strangely to say,' said Peter Twinn, who had abandoned a safe job in a reserved occupation to join up. 'You were the king of your own castle, right back there on your own. You never spoke to anybody unless the pilot gave you orders, so there you were sixty feet from the rest of the crew, all together at the front of the aircraft. They could see each other, they were near each other and they had that bond of being together. But the rear gunner, no, he was right out on a limb, down the other end looking the other way. Many of the raids lasted seven, eight, eight and a half hours . . . you never left your turret at all. It was lonely but you got used to it. And you were there for the crew's protection and they were a lovely crew.'[17]

After finishing their specialist training pilots, navigators and bomb-aimers had a further spell at an advanced school before finally arriving at an OTU. Wireless operators and gunners went there directly.

At the OTUs the British came together with their Australian and New Zealand counterparts from the Empire schools (the Canadians formed their own, separate group of squadrons). It was here that one of the most crucial processes in the training programme took place, the welding of individuals into crews. For each member, the crew would from now on be the centre of his existence. Life beyond the base, the world of parents and family and home, drifted to the margins of their thoughts. The six men you would share your bomber with were now the most important people in the world.

The process of selection was called 'crewing up'. In devising it the RAF departed from its strictly utilitarian selection and training methods and took an enormous leap of faith. Instead of attempting a scientific approach to gauge compatibility they put their trust entirely in the magic of human chemistry. The crews selected themselves. The procedure was simple. The requisite numbers of each aircrew category were put together in a large room and told to team up. Jack Currie, who reached his OTU at the end of 1942, 'hadn't realized that the crewing-up procedure would be so haphazard, so unorganized. I'd imagined that the process would be just as impersonal as most others that we went through in the RAF. I thought I would just see an order on the noticeboard detailing who was crewed with whom. But what happened was quite different. When we had all paraded in the hangar and the roll had been called, the chief ground instructor got up on a dais. He wished us good morning . . . and said: "Right chaps, sort yourselves out."'

Currie stood among the other sergeant pilots and, trying not to stare at anyone in particular, looked around him. 'There were bomb-aimers, navigators, wireless operators and gunners and I needed one of each to form my crew. I didn't know any of them; up to now my air force would have been peopled by pilots. This was a crowd of strangers. I had a sudden recollection of standing in a surburban dance-hall, wondering which girl I should approach. I remembered that it wasn't always the prettiest or the smartest girl who made the best companion for the evening. Anyway, this wasn't the same as choosing a dancing partner, it was more like picking out a sweetheart or a wife, for better or for worse.'

Like most pilots, the first thing Currie looked for was a navigator. He saw a knot of them standing together. But how was he to pick one?

> I couldn't assess what his aptitude with a map and dividers might be from his face, or his skill with a sextant from the size of his feet. I noticed that a wiry little Austra-

lian was looking at me anxiously. He took a few steps forward, eyes puckered in a diffident smile and spoke: 'Looking for a good navigator?' I walked to meet him. He was an officer. I looked down into his eyes, and received an impression of honesty, intelligence and nervousness. He said:

'You needn't worry. I did all right on the course!'

I held out my hand. 'Jack Currie.'

'I'm Jim Cassidy. Have you got a bomb-aimer? I know a real good one. He comes from Brisbane, like me. I'll fetch him over.'

The bomb-aimer had a gunner in tow and while we were sizing each other up, we were joined by a tall wireless-operator, who introduced himself in a gentle Northumbrian accent and suggested that it was time for a cup of tea. As we walked to the canteen, I realized that I hadn't made a single conscious choice.[18]

At some OTUs new arrivals were given up to a fortnight to team up. Harry Yates, having got over his disappointment at not being posted to a fighter squadron, arrived at Westcott with the ambition to 'skipper a well-drilled crew, the best on the squadron, every man handpicked, utterly professional at his job and dedicated to the team.' He started his search in the officers' mess where he found himself at the bar next to Pilot Officer Bill Birnie, a stocky New Zealander navigator who 'seemed to be the sort of tough-minded chap who knew the score'. During the evening's socializing he noticed a young pilot officer wearing a wireless operator's badge. For a wireless operator to be commissioned so early in his career suggested exceptional ability. So Rob Bailey, 'tall, slim and blessed with the dark, aquiline looks that women tend to admire', was in.

The following day the 220 men of the intake assembled in a hangar to finish off the process. They were mostly formed into twos and threes now and there was 'a lot of movement and noise', as they scrambled to complete their teams. Bill Birnie disappeared into the crowd and returned 'with a bronze-skinned giant in tow. This was Flight Sergeant Inia Maaka, the first Maori I'd ever met and I knew the bomb-aimer for me.' Mac, as he immediately became known, 'was a stranger to the inner tensions and vanities that make liars of the rest of us'. He had wanted to fight the war as a pilot and had won a place at elementary flying school but had not been selected to advance and been reassigned to bombing school. 'He clearly loved the job,' Yates recorded, 'there wasn't a hint of second best.' It was Mac who found the gunners: Geoff Fallowfield, an extrovert eighteen-year-old Londoner and Norrie Close, a taciturn Yorkshireman, who was a month younger still. 'So there they were,' Yates marvelled later, 'my crew: a straight and level Kiwi, a ladykiller; a Maori warrior; and two lads as different as chalk from cheese.'[19]

Such assorted crews were the norm. The mysterious chemistry that had brought them together was durable. Many crews forged bonds of affection and respect that, if they came through the war, lasted until the grave. It was rare for an Englishman to have met a Canadian or an Australian, yet when crewing up they seemed drawn to each other, confirming the wisdom of the process. Group Captain Hamish Mahaddie, who was tasked with finding talent for the Path-finder Force, which was formed to lead the main bomber force to the target, believed that 'the best crews were a mixture'.[20]

The system was not perfect. At Bruntingthorpe OTU Cyril March teamed up with an Australian skipper, navigator and wireless operator. The rest of the crew were English. 'We did our job and had one or two good thrashes but we were never all together and to my mind we didn't gel.' Their first training trip was a fighter affiliation exercise in which the pilot was expected to throw the Wellington around the sky to shake off the 'attacker'. After a row with the navigator, he appeared to lose control and ordered the crew to crash positions. The bomber landed but overshot the runway coming to a halt in the grass. The next trip took place in clear sunshine but the captain still managed to lose his way. March 'felt so bloody helpless. I was doing my job, telling them when we were passing over airfields and such. I couldn't help thinking [what] if this were Germany on a black night with duff winds etcetera – Christ!' Word of the crew's failings reached the station authorities. It was split up and its members redistributed. This time March was lucky. The first of his new comrades was Ken Ford, a Londoner, who with the rest of the crew, became his lifelong friends.

> Ken took me to meet my new skipper, a tousle-haired fair Aussie with steady blue eyes and a friendly grin. 'I'm Neville Emery,' he said, 'Bug to my mates.' I had noticed he had been eyeing me up and down and asked him why. 'Oh nothing mate,' he said laughing. 'Kenny was telling me that you were an old married man.' I was just twenty-one. I met Des Gee the Aussie wireless operator, again blond and blue-eyed; then Ray Brooker, a dark Englishman from Cambridge, the bomb-aimer with a ready smile. Then I met Terry Sayles, a Yorkshireman from Doncaster, the navigator. I told him my name was Cyril. 'Hi Cy,' he said and that was my name thenceforth. Des got me a bed in their Nissen hut and helped me move my gear in. That night they weren't flying and they said, 'Coming down the village for a jar?' 'Sure,' I said.
> 'Where's your bike, Cy?' Terry asked. 'Bike!' I replied, 'I haven't got one.' He got one, I don't know where and I didn't ask. Off we went in formation. I knew I was in a crew at long last.

They came back in high spirits, yelling 'Bring out your dead' as they wobbled on their bikes over rickety planks bridging the Leicestershire ditches. Cyril was happy and content. 'I knew then that with these lads we would survive, no doubt about it.'

This, in the end, was what the airmen were searching for as they milled around the hangars looking for kindred spirits. An efficient air, a friendly manner were all very well. But in the end, the most attractive quality anyone could possess was to seem lucky.

Inevitably, when the mating ritual finished, a gaggle of wallflowers remained. 'At the end of the day there were some odd bods left around who . . . had no choice but to take the leftovers,' said Tom Wingham, who flew with 102 Squadron. '[You] had a feeling that they weren't going to make it and inevitably they didn't. They didn't have that same sort of "gel". I suppose you could say they had the smell of death about them and it was not funny.'[21]

The men that would lead them through the final stage of training and into the daunting world of 'ops' seemed old, even though many were only in their mid-twenties. These were the veterans, 'tour-expired' survivors of thirty operations or more. 'It was our first close contact with people who had completed operations, surviving against unlikely odds,' wrote Dennis Field. 'Gongs were common, almost part of the dress, and worn without flamboyance. Although we were keen to hear and learn all we could, in off-duty hours they stayed detached and there was little line-shooting in our presence. We realized that within a few months we should all meet some ultimate experience.'

Instructing posts were the reward for survival. Not that such jobs were free of risk. Half of the flying done at OTUs was at night. The darkness, and the sometimes clapped-out machines which were used for training meant that deadly accidents were routine. After agreeing to fly with one captain, Dennis Steiner was approached by two other pilots whom he had to turn down. Subsequently, one flew into the ground for no discoverable reason, killing himself and all his crew. The other developed engine trouble during a flight and ordered the crew to bale out. 'Their luck ran out soon after when at night a practice bomb from another aircraft fell on them and they crashed,' he wrote. 'None of the crew survived. The line between surviving or not was becoming very thin.'

It seemed to Ken Newman that at least some of the accidents were due to criminal recklessness rather than the demands of war. In February 1944 he went to a Heavy Conversion Unit for a month's training. This was where crews familiarized themselves with the types that they would be flying on operations. Newman was learning his way around the Halifax. 'The aircraft were old, poorly maintained and in the most part barely airworthy. But it was constantly drilled into us that complaints would not be entertained and if we refused to fly because we thought a Halifax was not airworthy, or for a reason that the staff decided was trivial, we would be treated as LMF [Lacking in Moral Fibre, the RAF bureaucratic euphemism for the accusation of cowardice].' This was very much the view of the chief flying instructor who Newman held responsible for the death of one of his best friends and all his crew.

He had met Alec, 'a tall, likeable chap' while training in South Africa and caught up with him at RAF Lindholme where the HCU was based. One night he was detailed for a high-level cross-country flight, even though the weather forecast had warned of heavy cloud and severe icing conditions. To reduce the risk, it was essential to fly at maximum altitude. 'Alec took off and after a while found that his aircraft would not climb above 15,000 feet. Consequently he returned to RAF Lindholme. Wing Commander X heard about this and ordered Alec to continue the exercise, refusing to believe that the aircraft could not reach a safe height and accused him of being LMF. Intimidated, Alec and his crew went off. The following day we heard that his aircraft had crashed into a Scottish mountain and all were dead.' The instructor was to die in an accident a few months later.[22]

The road to the operational squadrons was long and expensive. It cost on average £10,000 to train each crew member, the equivalent, according to one indicator, of about £850,000 in today's money. This was a lot to pay to get each Bomber Boy into battle. It did not, however, mean that when they got there, their lives would be worth very much.

5

Dying in the Dark

Bomber Command lost 4,823 men and 2,331 aircraft on operations in the first two years of the war. There was very little to show for it. In that time it dropped only 35,194 tons of bombs. That was two thousand tons *less* than it dropped in the single month of May, 1944. Despite the great effort, the resulting destruction was often small and the casualties inflicted were minimal. A typical night's work was that of 29/30 August 1941. More than 140 aircraft were sent to attack railways and harbours in Frankfurt. They reached their target successfully and began bombing. They managed to do some damage to a gasworks, a barrel warehouse and a few houses and to kill eight people. In the course of the operation one Hampden was lost without trace. Another crashed in France killing all on board. A Halifax crew baled out over England after running out of fuel but two men died in the process, one after his parachute got caught in the tailplane. A Whitley was forced to ditch off the Essex coast. All in all, the operation resulted in the loss of sixteen lives – two for every German killed – and seven aircraft. Despite the sacrifice, the attack barely bothered the Frankfurt authorities who nonchalantly recorded the raid as 'light and scattered bombing'.

The perils of each trip mounted as the German fighter and flak defences adapted and improved. In March 1941, Doug Mourton arrived at 102 Squadron to fly as a wireless operator on Whitleys. One night his crew were detailed to attack Hamburg. Initially, it seemed 'a comparatively easy trip'. They took off in bright moonlight and as the target approached Mourton could see another Whitley flying a parallel course. 'Suddenly it exploded. What had been an aircraft a few seconds before, was now a mass of debris, flying through the air. It had apparently been hit by an anti-aircraft shell, most likely in its bomb bay . . .' He learned later that the pilot had been Alec Elliot, his best friend on the squadron with whom he had passed many nights in the pub and played innumerable games of crib while waiting in the crew room.[1]

After enduring such experiences the crews were reluctant to believe that their efforts were being wasted. To be able to carry on it was necessary to persuade oneself that the risks were worth it. From the air it was impossible to know whether or not a raid had succeeded. The sight of big fires burning below was taken as a measure of success. But they could not know what these blazes were. The Germans soon suspected that the attacking aircraft had often only the haziest idea of their whereabouts. They developed a system of decoy fires which they hoped the arriving aircraft would mistake for the target. It worked very well. Many a crew returned home satisfied they had carried out their mission after bombing empty countryside.

A different sort of deception was being perpetrated on the home front. Government propaganda painted a picture of continuous success. A broadcast by Flight Lieutenant J. C. Mackintosh, a bomb-aimer in a Hampden, made night bombing sound like a cool, precise science. His script started with the bold assertion that 'when the war began we were well-trained in finding targets in the dark and were therefore never compelled to bomb indiscriminately through the clouds.' He went on to describe a recent attack on an oil refinery. At first, the crew thought it a tricky target. But the fact that it was sited near a bend on a river which would provide a useful navigational reference caused them to decide that 'perhaps, after all, it would not be such a difficult job to find.' As they entered the target area they located the river but after three runs through anti-aircraft fire had still not spotted the objective. Mackintosh gamely called on the skipper to go round once more. Then, 'there it was. The dim outline of an oil refinery wonderfully camouflaged. It was getting more and more into the centre of the sights. I pressed the button and my stick of bombs went hurtling towards Germany's precious oil. The rear gunner watched the bombs burst and in a very few seconds those thousands of tons of valuable oil had become hundreds of feet of black and acrid smoke.'[2]

Whitley.

This was strategic bombing as dreamt of by the Air Ministry planners. But it was rare indeed that events followed Mackintosh's script. A more typical experience was that of Eric Woods, who had joined the RAF before the war as a reservist and qualified as a navigator before being sent to 144 Squadron. His first operation was on the night of 9/10 October 1940 and the target was the Krupp factory in Essen, one of the first of many that would be launched against this citadel of German military industry. At the briefing the crews were told they could expect only scattered cloud over the target. But 'from the outset it was obvious that the Met people had got it wrong as a solid mass of cloud was clearly visible below and as we progressed eastwards we saw that the cloud was becoming denser ahead. We pressed on but two ominous developments took place: a film of ice appeared on the windscreen and an opaque mass of rime ice began to spread out along the leading edge of each wing.' His Hampden's twin engines started to run rough as ice found its way into the fuel inlet system. 'There was a hurried conference since it was pretty obvious that the target was unlikely to be identifiable, so the decision was taken to fly on and see what happened when we reached our ETA (Estimated Time of Arrival). In the event at that time we were still in dense cloud, the whole mass being lit up by searchlights sweeping below, with frequent bright flashes which could have been anti-aircraft fire or bomb bursts, I certainly knew not what.' With no sight of the ground and dreadful weather conditions a decision was made not to bomb but to seek some alternative target on the way home. As they headed homewards 'the cloud began to break up to the west, quite the opposite to what the weatherman had said . . . we did in fact fly along the Scheldt estuary and as we passed over the port of Flushing the navigator let go with our total load and I clearly saw bomb bursts though I wasn't sure precisely where they landed.'[3] Only three of the aircraft that set out reached their target.

The basic problem remained navigation. There was no accurate means of directing the bombers to faraway targets and none would arrive until March 1942. In the meantime, navigators relied on dead reckoning and the main instrumental aid was the sextant. This was still the pioneer age of bombing. 'The aircraft were without heating and the cold was appalling,' wrote Doug Mourton later. 'The crews flew clothed in layers of silk, wool and leather and yet they were still bitterly cold. Vital systems jammed, wings iced up for lack of adequate de-icing gear [and] guns froze . . .' The navigator gave his pilot a course on take-off and then, if he was lucky and the skies were clear, looked out for landmarks to check if they were on track. When visiting Germany they left England's shores over Flamborough Head then scoured the sea below for the Friesian Islands off the Dutch coast, where German night-fighters lurked, straining to get at the raiders. If the conditions were right, the navigator might use his sextant to obtain a fix from the stars, but only if the pilot was willing to fly straight and level long enough. The crews were given a weather forecast before leaving, but they were notoriously unreliable. Predicted winds failed to blow and unpredicted ones drove the bombers hopelessly off course. It was no wonder that German targets were sometimes unaware that they had been the subject of an attempted attack.

The gap between what was expected of the RAF and what it could in fact deliver was enormous. The man whose task it was to narrow it was Charles Portal, appointed to the top air force post of Chief of the Air Staff (CAS) in October 1940 at the young age of forty-seven. The promotion came after a brief, six-month stint as the Commander-in-Chief of Bomber Command. He was to stay in his post for the rest of the war. Portal was short and stocky, with a lean, creased face, hooded eyes and a large, hooked nose which gave him the look of one of the falcons he had reared when a schoolboy at Winchester. He was at Christ Church, Oxford, when the war broke out in 1914, and immediately suspended his studies to go to France as a motorcyclist with the Royal Engineers. In 1915 he joined the Royal Flying Corps and finished the war as a lieuten-ant-colonel. His intellectual gifts and boundless capacity for work ensured that his subsequent climb was sure and fast. His character and demeanour contrasted sharply with that of Arthur Harris. He hid his feelings behind a mask of scrupulous courtesy and expressed himself quietly and subtly. Whereas Harris was capable of rough bonhomie, Portal never unbent. Those around him noticed that beyond his family he had no close friends, gently repelling company when he dined at the Travellers' Club at the end of his long working day.

Portal's part in the policy of attacking whole cities, 'area bombing' in the bureaucratic euphemism of the day, is little known or remembered nowadays, while Harris's name will be linked to it for ever. But his enthusiasm for the project was, at the outset at least, just as great as that of his subordinate and he was prepared to express himself forcefully in support of it even when Churchill's faith faltered.

As head of Bomber Command at the start of the Blitz he sympa-thized with the public desire for revenge and had joined Churchill in urging reprisals on a reluctant Air Staff. On arriving at the top, he stressed the need to destroy the resolve of the German people by smashing their towns and cities. The rhythms of Bomber Com-mand's activities would vary from time to time as it was diverted to deal with various threats and crises. But, until the run-up to D-Day, this was to be the central theme of the air war.

In successive directives Portal continued to point his men towards industrial and military targets. But great emphasis was given to the will-sapping potential that he claimed would result. On 30 October

1940, as London prepared to endure its 53rd night of continuous bombardment, he wrote to Sir Richard Peirse who had replaced him as C-in-C, Bomber Command, that

> the time seems particularly opportune to make a definite attempt with our offensive to affect the morale of the German people when they can no longer expect an early victory and are faced with the near approach of winter and the certainty of a long war ... if bombing is to have its full moral effect, it must on occasions produce heavy material destruction. Widespread light attacks are more likely to produce contempt for bombing than fear of it. I am therefore directed to say that as an alternative to attacks designed for material destruction against our primary objectives, it is desired that regular concentrated attacks shall be made on objectives in large towns and centres of industry with the prime aim of causing heavy material destruction, which will demonstrate to the enemy the power and severity of air bombardment and the hardship and dislocation that will result from it.

Berlin was put first on the list for Bomber Command's attentions. If it was clouded over, other towns in central and western Germany were to be considered. Aircraft industry and oil targets might also be selected, as long as they were 'suitably placed in the centres of the towns or populated districts'. The directive envisaged sending greater numbers of aircraft, carrying a mix of bombs. The first to arrive would drop incendiaries to set the target area ablaze. The following force would then 'focus their attacks to a large extent on the fires with a view to preventing the fire-fighting services dealing with them and giving the fires every opportunity to spread.'[4] This amounted to an explicit announcement that the strategic aim now was to achieve blanket destruction, disruption and death.

In reality, Bomber Command lacked the resources to carry out such an apocalyptic plan. Even if it had the aircraft and equipment, it would never be able to mount a concentrated and relentless campaign while it was subject to the apparently insatiable calls on its services from the War Cabinet, navy and army.

On top of the strategic targets, oil and now cities, Bomber Command was supposed to support the navy by laying mines at sea. In March 1941 another great responsibility was loaded on to its shoulders. German submarines and bombers were wreaking terrible damage on the transatlantic convoys carrying the cargoes that kept Britain alive and threatening to sever Britain's vital ocean links with America. Churchill ordered Portal to concentrate on attacking the yards that built the U-boats and the pens where they sheltered, as well as the factories and bases which produced and housed the maritime bombers. Bomber Command did its best against these targets, and the great German warships *Gneisenau* and *Scharnhorst* in their haven at Brest, but the effects were limited. Its aircraft were withdrawn after four months and it was left to Coastal Command and the Royal Navy, aided by improvements in technology and resources, to turn the Battle of the Atlantic Britain's way.

The diversion deflected Peirse from his intention to use the improved conditions of spring to systematically pursue oil targets. The 'oil plan' had many powerful supporters inside the Air Staff and among civilian specialist strategic advisers. They saw the destruction of synthetic oil plants, which transformed Germany's rich coal reserves into liquid fuels and lubricants, as a quick way of bringing the enemy to its knees. The plan would swing in and out of favour throughout the war. But the prescription was easier than the practice. Despite the claims of official propaganda, when oil targets were attacked, the results were often miserable. The plants were sited away from the big towns and were hard to find and even harder to destroy or damage. If the bombers missed them, as they usually did, their bombs hit nothing but fields and forests. The new practice of using high-flying Spitfires for photo reconnaissance the morning after a raid allowed an operation's success to be assessed scientifically rather than relying on the visual reports and blurry night-time images submitted by the crews from onboard cameras. In the absence of hard evidence, optimism about the progress of the campaign had remained high in the upper reaches of the RAF.

The daylight pictures showed it to be misplaced. No assumptions could be made about bombing accuracy. The truth, according to Sir John Slessor, who had taken over 5 Group of Bomber Command in May 1941, was that the crews were 'failing to find and hit any but the most obvious targets on the clearest moonlight nights'.[5]

It became clear to Portal that, as things stood, the only target that Bomber Command could be guaranteed to find was a largish town. The attacks on London, Coventry, Southampton, Plymouth and elsewhere had provided more than enough justification for retaliating in kind. Britain had suffered an unprecedented loss of innocent life. By the time the Blitz petered out in May 1941, more than 41,000 civilians had been killed and 137,000 injured. Such a policy, Portal now believed, was not simply *faute de mieux*, but a logical and desirable course of action.

The new, or rather resumed, thinking was spelled out in another Portal directive to Bomber Command dated 9 July 1941. It stated that a comprehensive review of Germany's political, economic and military situation disclosed that one of 'the weakest points in his armour' lay in the morale of the civilian population. It called for 'heavy, concentrated and continuous area attacks of large working-class and industrial areas in carefully selected towns'. At the end of August the formula was extended to smaller towns so that they too could experience 'the direct effect of our offensive'.[6]

This marked another important step in the shift from scrupulousness to ruthlessness. Before the war the British government had assured the world it had no intention of bombing civilians. Now the RAF had been nudged on to a heading which made the mass killing of civilians inevitable. The faith that was put in the belief that this would produce beneficial results by undermining the Germans' will to fight on was puzzling. Nothing that had happened in the war to date supported Trenchard's dictum that the moral effect of bombing was twenty times greater than the material effect. If anything, the experience of Coventry, London and other blitzed towns like Plymouth and Liverpool, suggested the opposite. Yet in the absence of any immediate alternative, what was an ill-founded opinion began to take on the solidity of an iron law of war.

Trenchard was an old man now but he was still regarded with reverence by the military establishment and his views were treated with respect. In May 1941 he sent a memorandum on the current state of the air war to the Chiefs of Staff. He reduced the complexities of the problems facing the RAF to one simple proposition. It was, he reiterated, all a question of national morale and who could stand their losses best. There was no doubt about the answer. For Trenchard, the 'outstanding fact' of the current situation was 'the ingrained morale of the British nation which is nowhere more strongly manifest than in its ability to stand up to losses and its power to bear the whole strain of war and its casualties.' History had proved 'that we have always been able to stand our casualties better than other Nations.' As for the enemy, 'all the evidence of the last war and of this, shows that the German nation is peculiarly susceptible to air bombing. While the A.R.P. services are probably organized with typical German efficiency, their total disregard to the well-being of the population tends to a dislocation of ordinary life which has its inevitable reaction on civilian morale. The ordinary people are neither allowed, nor offer, to play their part in rescue or restoration work; virtually imprisoned in their shelters or within the bombed area, they remain passive and easy prey to hysteria and panic without anything to mitigate the inevitable confusion and chaos. There is no joking in the German shelters as in ours, nor the bond which unites the public with A.R.P. and Military services here of all working together in a common cause to defeat the attacks of the enemy.' This, he concluded 'is their weak point compared with ourselves and it is at this weak point that we should strike and strike again.' Such a policy would mean 'fairly heavy casualties' for those doing the bombing, but Trenchard had faith in their toughness. In his judgement, 'the pilots in the last war stood it, and the pilots in this war are even better and, I feel, would welcome a policy of this description.'[7]

Where Trenchard got his information from was a mystery. At least one pilot had a very different appreciation of the morale question. In the early winter of 1942 when Bomber Command was beginning to bring the war to the German people Guy Gibson was still unconvinced that domestic morale would collapse. 'We are dealing with the mass pyschology of a nation and a bad nation at that,' he told Charles Martin, the adjutant of 106 Squadron. 'It is run, organized and controlled by Gestapo and SS Police . . . the fact still remains that if they were to give in they would have everything to lose and nothing to gain. I think myself they will fight to the end.' Gibson had little time for 'people who go around talking so much bull about the crack appearing and once the crack has appeared the foundation will weaken etc., etc.'[8]

Most people who were running the war agreed with Trenchard. It would have seemed defeatist to say otherwise. Identifying morale as the main target also provided some hope of progress at a time when there was little to show that Bomber Command was achieving anything. Any scrap of evidence was seized on as proof of the wisdom of this course. In September 1941 the American correspondent William Shirer who knew Nazi Germany well, wrote a piece in the *Daily Telegraph* saying that attacking war industries was not enough. 'What [the RAF] must do is to keep the German people in their damp, cold cellars at night, prevent them from sleeping and wear down their nerves. Those nerves are already very thin after seven years of belt-tightening Nazi mobilization for total war. The British should do this every night.' The cutting was reverently placed in an Air Ministry file. The Ministry of Information maintained its own survey. It had concluded as early as December 1940 that 'the Germans, for all their present confidence and cockiness will not stand a quarter of the bombing that the British have shown they can take.'

In the middle of 1941 support for the bombing offensive was sustained by faith rather than evidence, but the absence of a rational foundation for belief meant only that the flame of conviction burned all the brighter. It was not only Portal and the Air Staff who believed. The heads of the navy and the army became fervent converts. At the end of July 1941 they had produced a statement on general British strategy in which they declared their support for Bomber Command's mission and admitted they were relying on an all-out attack by the RAF to create the conditions for a land invasion and victory. Inter-service jealousy over resources, hitherto a genetic condition, was forgotten as the air force was offered everything it wanted.

They approved the building of heavy bombers as a first priority 'for only the heavy bomber can produce the conditions under which other offensive force can be employed.' They endorsed the view that the focus of attack should be 'on civilian morale with the intensity and continuity which are essential if a final breakdown is to be produced.' If the plan was pursued 'on a vast scale, the whole structure upon which the German forces are based, the economic system, the machinery for production and destruction, the morale of the nation will be destroyed.' This was just the 'bull about the crack appearing' that Gibson had found so unconvincing.

Soon afterwards an attempt was made to translate what were instinctive suppositions into hard formulae. In September 1941 the Directorate of Bomber Operations at the Air Ministry began working on a new plan. In an important departure from previous practice it was based not on what Bomber Command might do, but on what the Luftwaffe had already done. By analysing the damage caused by German air attacks on London, Coventry, and other English towns, the planners came up with a yardstick of what was needed to mount an all-out offensive on German towns.

They used an 'index of activity' to gauge the effects of bombing on a town's ability to function. Coventry, it was reckoned, had suffered a 63 per cent reduction in its index of activity the morning after the raid. The calculation included not just physical destruction but also psychological damage; fear and demoralization. It had taken Coventry thirty-five days to recover. Four or five follow-up attacks on the same scale, it was reckoned, would have crippled the city's ability to operate. A sixth raid would have put it 'beyond all hope of recovery'.

Using the same encouraging extrapolations that were always employed with such calculations, it concluded that if 4,000 bombers were directed against forty-three towns with populations of 100,000 or more, Germany would be finished. At the time, the average daily availability of bombers was just over 500. Portal approved the plan and passed it on to the prime minister promising 'decisive results' in six months if he was given the aircraft required.

But Churchill's initial enthusiasm was faltering. A minute study of reconnaissance photographs ordered by Churchill's scientific adviser Lord Cherwell had revealed in undeniable detail the blindness of the bombing effort. The work was carried out by D. R. Butt, a civil servant with the Cabinet secretariat. His job was to analyse photographs taken on one hundred night attacks during June and July 1941. The results, published in August 1941, were dismaying. The essential finding was that of those crews claiming to have attacked a target in Germany, only one in four got within five miles of it. Over the Ruhr the proportion was one in ten. The statistics related only to aircraft recorded as attacking the target. One third of the crews failed to get within five miles of it.

These figures, if true, were shocking and at Bomber Command, Sir Richard Peirse and his senior officers tried to dispute them. Churchill, however, had been persuaded. He was in no mood then, to give a positive reception to another plan based on the unverifiable. His view was summed up in a pessimistic minute of 27 September that contradicted everything he had previously said as prime minister on the subject of bombing. 'It is very disputable whether bombing by itself will be a decisive factor in the present war. On the contrary, all that we have learnt since the war shows that its effects, both physical and moral, are greatly exaggerated.'

These words caused great anxiety to Portal and his men. Churchill appeared to be saying that he had no confidence in their approach to the air war. Portal took several days thinking about his response. His reply, when it came, was robust. He told the prime minister that it was too soon to come to such a definite conclusion as a serious bombing campaign had yet to begin. It was difficult to believe that any country could withstand indefinitely the scale of attack contemplated in the new plan. German air raids in the previous year caused death or serious injury to 93,000 British civilians. This result had been achieved with a small fraction of the bomb load Bomber Command hoped to employ in 1943. He repeated what had now become an article of faith. 'The consensus of informed opinion,' he declared, 'is that German morale is much more vulnerable to bombing than our own.'

Portal was calling Churchill's bluff. The prime minister's doubts had come very late in the day. The whole bomber programme, aircraft production, aircrew training and technical developments were based on the understanding articulated by the Chiefs of Staff back on 31 July that bombing on an unprecedented scale was the weapon Britain had to depend on to bring victory. He pointed out that if Churchill had 'ceased to believe in the efficacy of the bomber as a war-winning weapon' then a new plan would have to be produced. This would mean a complete reshaping of the RAF's main effort and remove it from the battlefield for many months to come. Britain would be denied its only means of waging war on the enemy's own territory.

Churchill had no real choice but to back down and he did so, but not before sounding a sour cautionary note. 'I deprecate,' he wrote on 7 October, 'placing unbounded confidence in this means of attack and still more in expressing that confidence in terms of arithmetic.' In the end, he concluded, 'the only plan is to persevere'.

This period marked the lowest point in Bomber Command's war, a demoralizing period of costly experimentation. In its short life, aerial warfare had gained enormous importance in the minds of politicians, soldiers and the public. But no one yet understood exactly what it was for. Defending the failures of the early years Slessor reminded a post-war audience that '*this was the first air war* (his emphasis.) . . . we had embarked upon it, not only with totally inadequate weapons and woefully incomplete intelligence about our enemy but with vitually no experience whatever to guide us.'[9] Operations had never achieved a consistent tempo as the emphasis shifted from target to target and even, as the Battle of the Atlantic broke out, from land to sea with squadrons being transferred temporarily or permanently to Coastal Command. Throughout the year preconceived expansion plans had to give way to the constant diversion of aircraft and crew to other theatres.

During 1941, 1,341 aircraft were lost on operations, meaning that the average first-line strength had been destroyed roughly two and a half times over. These great sacrifices failed to make any significant impression on Germany. The ports of Hamburg, Kiel and Bremen had suffered some damage, but the Ruhr, the heart of Germany's war industry, remained almost completely intact. Bomber Command's main achievement had been to give heart to the Blitz-battered British people. As it did so, its own morale was beginning to fray. In 106 Squadron, where Michael Wood was piloting a Hampden, 'there was a story going around that the accounts related by one of our crews were suspect and did not tie up with the accounts of the target area put forward by the rest of the squadron. The CO became suspicious and arranged to plot the course of the aircraft in question. From the information gathered, it transpired that the aircraft was flying up and down the North Sea dropping their bombs in the drink and, after the necessary time lapse, flying back to base.' Wood never verified the story. But the fact that it was doing the rounds was indicative of the low mood.

One pilot from 144 Squadron was court-martialled for a similar-sounding incident. Sergeant W, a married man with two young children who had been a grocer in civilian life before joining the RAF in 1938, was accused of 'failing to use his utmost exertions' to carry out orders. He had been detailed to attack Frankfurt on the night of 22/23 July 1941. On his return, he reported that the mission had been successful. A few days later, the navigator on the trip informed a senior officer that they had never reached Germany at all. The pilot maintained that the navigator, who had been borrowed for the operation, was incompetent and had failed to provide the correct headings to reach the target, resulting in them flying around the North Sea for nearly seven hours. The navigator maintained that the skipper was 'windy' and had never intended to carry out the attack. Sergeant W was backed up by three other members of his crew. He was an experienced pilot who had spent seven months on the squadron and whose conduct had until then satisfied his CO. Had he reported the failure to complete the mission it was unlikely that matters would have developed as drastically as they did. As it was, he told the court-martial, 'after landing and thinking back over the trip, I decided to say nothing about getting lost. In consequence the personal experience report was made out as for a successful trip.' The worst interpretation was put on his actions. He was found guilty and sentenced to be reduced to the ranks, imprisoned with hard labour for two years and discharged with ignominy from the service. The sentence was cut to six months on appeal.[10]

For all the institutional belief in British resilience, no one in authority was going to tell anyone, civilian or airman, how little the campaign was really achieving. 'Fortunately,' wrote Slessor, ' I think the crews were for the most part sustained by the belief that they were hitting the enemy harder than they actually were.'[11]

The futility of the effort was starkly revealed on the night of 7/8 November. The weather forecast was abysmal, with thick cloud, storms, ice and hail predicted. Sir Richard Peirse nonetheless ordered 392 aircraft, a record number, into attacks on Berlin, Cologne and Mannheim, as well as smaller operations against Boulogne and Ostend. The weather was particularly atrocious along the North Sea routes leading to Berlin. Of the 169 bombers sent to Berlin, less than half got anywhere near it. Those that did, barely scratched the city. The official survey reported damage to one industrial building, two railway premises, a gasometer, two administrative buildings, thirty houses (fourteen of which were destroyed), sixteen garden sheds and one farm building. Eleven people were killed and fourteen injured. Bomber Command however lost twenty-one aircraft, 12.4 per cent of those dispatched. Eighty-eight airmen died; eight for every German killed by their bombs. All together thirty-seven aircraft were lost, 9.7 per cent of the force. This loss was double what had been suffered in any previous night operation. Peirse had gone ahead despite protests, notably from Slessor who had been allowed to withdraw his 5 Group aircraft from the force and send them instead to Cologne. His refusal to cancel the operation seems to have been driven by a desperate desire to achieve results when faith in his leadership was dwindling. It was a gamble rather than a calculated risk and it was taken with the lives of men whose fate he held in trust.

Some of those taking part in the raid had sensed disaster from the beginning. Sergeant John Dobson, only nineteen years old but already one of 218 Squadron's most experienced pilots, was woken at 6 a.m. on the morning of 7 November, an unusually early hour that suggested that a daylight operation was planned. Half-asleep, crotchety, some of them mildly hungover, the squadron slouched to the briefing room. Dobson sat down and his crew grouped themselves on the chairs around him. There was 'no greeting, just a plain and dismal silence'. He pulled out his cigarettes from his pyjama pocket and 'exercised the Skipper's prerogative of offering each crew member a fag. A sharp, grating sound, puff, puff, puff and then silence once more. The whole room was silent and pent up with a fierce concentration. No celluloid sallies here, no carefree chatter which film-struck spinsters associate with an operational briefing . . . we were all in the bluest of blue funks so that no one dare speak for fear of voicing with his eyes or gruffness his innermost, uppermost fear of the unknown. More especially today it was felt, because of the unusual hour, which [preyed] heavily on the superstition of fliers.'

Wing Commander Kirkpatrick climbed the three steps to the dais. He was a pre-war regular and his crews liked and trusted him, 'just the man for any job which would get this damned war over quicker,' in Dobson's view. The order of the day that he read out was unlike any other the audience had previously heard. Instead of being given a routine railway junction or gasworks to aim at, the squadron's mission was directed against a factory twenty miles south-east of Berlin which was believed to be researching experimental weapons. The target was to be be completely demolished 'at all costs'. Should the bombs fail they were to strafe the factory at low level. The success of the mission, he stressed, would obviate great loss of life in the future.

The 'met' reports were read out which predicted three storm fronts and blanket cloud over the continent, though this might clear to eight-tenths cover by the time the aircraft arrived giving the captain the option of bombing through the holes in the murk or risking flying below it. The wing commander then went on to confirm what Dobson's gut had told him. The heavy bomb load meant that it would be touch and go whether there was enough fuel to get them back. The squadron sat 'entranced and dumb-founded as the words ate like acid into their brain, numbing all senses but that awful emptiness of fear in the stomach.' They spent the rest of the morning trying to lose themselves in 'doing those hundred and one . . . things to keep the mind from death.' The music on the mess gramophone did nothing to lighten the gloom. Even the liveliest tunes were simply a reminder of a world they might never return to.

At lunch Dobson could not bear to eat. He slipped away early to look over his Wellington, K-Kate. It was raining heavily but he 'did not pause to collect a greatcoat, feeling somehow that it was superfluous and not in keeping with the dread feeling all around . . .' But the weather provided a spurt of hope. 'I gazed upwards at the lowering clouds whilst the increasing rain stung my pupils and made tiny, salty tears run into my face and aggravated the soreness of my cheeks where I had shaved. Could it be . . . that ops were scrubbed?'

He ran back to the mess where he met his crew who told him that ops were still very much on. They were coming to the end of their tour and shared his fear of what lay ahead. Speaking on behalf of the rest, the navigator informed Dobson they had decided 'we are certainly not going to chuck our lives away on this damned death but no glory stunt.'

Dobson went to tell the CO, who came straight to the point. Was Dobson going to join the mutiny? He replied, 'not without certain trepidation, "no sir." To see the relief shining in his eyes . . . was gratitude enough but he rose and patted my shoulder gently, almost fatherly, and said, "Thank you, Dobson."'

He was allotted a new crew and learned to his dismay that they were 'sprogs' straight out of training and virgins when it came to operational flying. He was further alarmed by the discovery that the man flying as 'second dickey' or assistant pilot, was an Australian. The prevailing superstition had it that Australians were prone to disaster on their first show.

Dinner was even more depressing than lunch. When they reached the aircraft 'the rain was falling in an ever-increasing tempo, drumming like bullets on the fuselage.' Dobson's misgivings were well-founded. Before they had even crossed the English coast they came under fire from a German intruder. He dived into cloud to escape, emerging in time to see the sky in front twinkling with red stars as the first coastal flak batteries opened up. Dead ahead there was a huge sheet of flame as a bomber exploded. Then it was their turn. Dobson threw the Wellington this way and that 'but more flak concentrated on us until it seemed as though the whole sky was a mass of flaming, eye-scarring bursts. And the smell like the smell of death itself; cloying, foetid, lingering in . . . nostrils wide with fear.' A heavy burst plunged the Wellington into a downward spiral. 'Completely out of control isn't fun at any time but in a welter of up-coming flak our predicament was terrible. The crew were in a frenzy, yelling and screaming over the intercom.' They levelled out at 3,200 feet but were now pinned against the sky by searchlights. Dobson felt 'the intensity of the beam on one's face simply sapped the strength from one . . . the eyes burned like all the fires of hell as I strove to penetrate the terrific vista of light.'

Eventually they left the searchlight batteries behind. They crossed the Dutch border and set course for their objective. Long before they reached Berlin they could see the flak barrage glowing above it. Their target was to the south. As they turned away, two night-fighters bore in on them from ahead and below, riddling the fuselage with tracer. Dobson, a former Hurricane pilot, threw the Wellington into a violent turn, a manoeuvre which had the lucky effect of bringing one attacking Messerschmitt into the front gunner's sights, just as he was climbing away. 'Bits began to fly from the fighter as the murderous hail of bullets from the two Brownings, so ably wielded, bit into his fabric, his engines and his tanks . . . the last we saw of him he was spinning down in a death dive and no pilot got out.' The other fighter was shaken off in the turn.

They went on. Dobson had to drop through a thick layer of clouds, 'so solid, so absolutely like a new earth that one wanted to step out on them and walk,' to have any chance of finding the target. By the time the Wellington emerged only 2,000 feet were showing on the altimeter. Ahead they could see parachute flares, and artillery flashes lit up the target area. Bert Faltham, the navigator-cum-bomb-aimer now took charge. As he led them in the flak increased in intensity until 'the sky around and ahead was a vast, twinkling maelstrom of light.' At last Faltham called out, 'Bombs gone Skip!' and the Wellington's 3,500-pound load fell away. Dobson climbed, taking 'what seemed like a leaden century' to reach 18,000 feet where he levelled off.

About an hour and a half from home Dobson allowed himself to start thinking that they might just make it. Then the sky ahead reddened with a flak barrage which flared up and died away before he could identify its location. Suddenly there was 'a terrific crack, like a whip going hard against naked flesh, whilst a gale roared through the hole the flak had created . . . a nucleus of bursts held us in their thrall, smashing into the fuselage at every point, tearing huge gaps . . .' For the next forty-five minutes Dobson fought to keep the aircraft steady but it started to slide into what seemed like a final descent. He gave the order to bale out. 'One by one the crew filed past my seat and dropped through the opening at my feet. When the last one . . . had vanished I trimmed Kate, tail heavy, so that in a few moments her nose would come up and she would spin in to her complete destruction. Then, still holding the stick, I slid from my seat and as the aircraft swayed slowly backwards I fell forward through the hole in the manner approved. The time was 05.00 . . . Height 1,500 feet.'[12]

Such was the end of K-Kate, one of thirty-seven aircraft lost that night. Peirse's determination to restore his and his command's reputation had brought disaster. Two months later he was removed. The Berlin calamity prompted the War Cabinet to put an end to big raids for the rest of the winter to preserve lives and aircraft and allow the new policy to take shape. In the coming months only limited operations with small numbers of aircraft were sanctioned. It was to be another fourteen months before Berlin was attacked again.

6

Enter 'Butch'

Though it might not have appeared so to despondent crews that winter, Bomber Command's overall prospects were slowly improving. The Bomber Boys rarely caught a glimpse of the big picture. But during the second half of 1941 the wider war had taken on a new and encouraging direction. The German invasion of Russia in June had transformed the Soviet Union from an enemy to an ally. With the entry of the United States into the conflict after the 7 December attack on Pearl Harbor, all the riches of America were unlocked for use in the fight against the Nazis.

The pause in major operations ordered after the Berlin disaster gave an exhausted, depleted and dispirited force the chance to catch its breath and gather its strength. Over the months that followed the recent volunteers started to arrive in force at their operational squadrons. The first of the new generation of four-engined heavies, the Stirlings and Halifaxes, began to replace their two-engined predecessors. On Christmas Eve, 1941, the first of the Lancasters landed at RAF Waddington in Lincolnshire. Soon its blunt, menacing lines would be seen everywhere. Some of the new aircraft carried desperately-needed new electronic navigation aids. By the time Harris took over Bomber Command at the end of February 1942 the force was approaching a position where it could start applying the policies on which those running the war were now agreed.

Shortly before his arrival there was an event which gave heart to the battered squadrons. One day in early March 1942, Peter Johnson visited a bomber station in Nottinghamshire to have lunch with the base commander. Entering the mess he found a group of young officers in the middle of a raucous party. His host explained they were celebrating a 'wizard prang' the night before. 'Come and look at the photos,' he said. 'They're the best ever. Teach those bloody Frogs to play along with the Boche.'

Johnson examined the pictures taken during the raid and agreed they were 'remarkable indeed'. They showed the Renault works on an island in the Seine just outside Paris, overlaid by a mass of explosions, flares and fires. It looked as if 'the factory was a complete write-off and that it would hardly be worth the enemy's while to try to recover significant production from the chaos.'

A shout of 'NEWS' cut through the triumphant hubbub. The 'din of laughter and talk was followed by a chorus of "Ssssshh, ssssshh." Tankards in hand, everyone gathered round the radiogram . . . "I bet we're on first," said someone. "Unless they've murdered ole Hitler!" The cool tones of the BBC announcer gave this, the most outstanding success of Bomber Command in two and a half years, pride of place.' Johnson was reluctant to drag the CO away from the party and excused himself, pleading an appointment with a visitor from the staff. Ignoring shouts of 'Fuck the staff!' and 'Teach them to fly!' he departed. He drove away deep in thought. 'What I had seen was, I realized, something of a "one-off" born of the exceptional success of the night's operation. But I was very conscious that the camaraderie, the sense of being an exclusive band of brothers, in this, the first wartime bomber squadron I had known was something quite apart from the rest of the service.' He applied immediately to leave his post commanding the Ossington Advanced Flying Training School and get on to operations.[1]

The Renault factory at Billancourt had been chosen by the Air Staff on the direction of the War Cabinet. It was turning out an estimated 18,000 lorries a year, most of which went to the German military. This was thought to justify the risk of French civilian casualties. The attack went ahead on the night of 3 March 1942. The results, for the time, were devastating. The operation involved 235 aircraft, the greatest number so far sent on a raid, which arrived in three waves. The attack was opened by a vanguard of the most experienced crews who dropped large numbers of pyrotechnic markers. This was the first, full-scale attempt to use flares to identify targets which the main force could then use to aim at. The bombers went in very low at between 1,000 and 4,000 feet to increase accuracy and minimize the danger to locals. The works were only lightly defended by anti-aircraft guns. A record tonnage of bombs went down and the damage they did was considerable. About 40 per cent of the buildings were destroyed and production was halted for four weeks at a loss of nearly 2,300 trucks.

The precautions against spilling French blood, however, had little effect. Blocks of flats housing the workers were clustered around the factory and 367 people were killed. This was twice as many as had died in any RAF raid on a German city so far. This did not detract from the feeling that the Renault attack was a great success. Heavy damage had been done to a precise target with minimal losses. Only one Wellington failed to return.

But the episode was, as Johnson had realized, far from the normal run of Bomber Command operations. There was no cloud below 10,000 feet and almost full moonlight. Most importantly, all the crews had enjoyed a practically flak-free outing which enabled them to make low-level attacks. These conditions made a reasonable degree of precision possible. This was never going to be the case in Germany and it was in Germany that the big battles would have to be fought.

The man now leading the offensive had an ideal service background for the job. Arthur Harris had joined the Royal Flying Corps in 1915 and flown on the Western Front before being given command of a home defence squadron where he acquired a reputation as a pioneer of night flying. Between the wars he served in Iraq, helping keep rebellious tribes in line by bombarding them from the air. He knew how Whitehall worked from stints at the Air Ministry, notably as director of plans in the crucial mid-thirties period. He also understood and got on with Americans, having served as head of the RAF delegation in Washington during 1941.

It was Harris who bore the brunt of post-war revulsion at the destruction of Germany. But no matter how enthusiastically and unswervingly he may have pursued the policy, the idea of pulverizing cities had not originated with him. As he pointed out in his memoirs: 'There is a widespread impression that I not only invented the policy of area bombing but also insisted on carrying it out in the face of a natural reluctance to kill women and children that was felt by everyone else. The facts are otherwise. Such decisions are not in any case made by Commanders-in-Chief in the field, but by the ministries, the Chiefs of Staff Committee and by the War Cabinet. The decision to attack large industrial areas was taken long before I became Commander-in-Chief.'[2]

The first directive from the CAS to greet Harris had indeed confirmed the direction that had been set. 'The primary object of your operations,' it said, 'should now be focused on the morale of the enemy civil population and in particular, on the industrial workers.' Portal was concerned that perhaps the meaning of his orders was not clear enough. He wrote to Air Vice-Marshal Bottomley who had drafted the directive: 'I suppose it is clear that the aiming points are to be the built-up areas, *not*, for instance, the dockyards or aircraft factories . . . this must be made clear if it is not already understood.' He need not have worried. Harris knew very well what was expected of him.

It was Harris's bad luck to look and sound like a bully whose determination to win took little account of the lives of German civilians or indeed his own men. He was broad, short-sighted and bad-tempered and wore a small, bristling moustache which added to the impression of porcine belligerence. He was easily angered by anything he perceived to be criticism and seemed to relish using the most wounding language in crushing it. He seldom saw any validity in views that did not chime with his own. In the words of the official historians, he had 'a tendency to confuse advice with interference, criticism with sabotage and evidence with propaganda.'

Harris spent his early years seeking his fortune in Rhodesia, a part of the world he loved, and the crack of an invisible sjambok could often be heard in his dealings with his subordinates. The accuracy of this impression appeared to be confirmed by the nickname bestowed on him by his men. The public might know him as 'Bomber' Harris, his peers as 'Bert' but to the crews he was 'Butch', short for 'butcher', in reference to his willingess to spend their lives. Very few of them had a chance to form an opinion based on direct knowledge. Jack Currie and his companions at Wickenby 'never met our Commander-in-Chief, never saw him, never heard his voice . . . he was in fact distanced from us by such far echelons of rank and station, that he was a figure more of imagination than reality. Uninhibited by any bounds of truth, we were able to ascribe to him any characteristic that our spirits needed. It pleased us to think of him as utterly callous, indifferent to suffering, and unconcerned about our fate.' There was, he thought, 'a paradoxical comfort in serving such a dread commander: no grievance, no complaint, no criticism could possibly affect him . . . we chose to believe that Harris lived in utter luxury at Claridge's, and that with his morning beverage a servant brought him a jewelled dart, which he casually cast at a wall map of Europe above his dressing table. He would then take up the silver scrambler telephone and call High Wycombe. "This is the Commander-in-Chief. The target for tonight is . . ."'³

As a pilot in 617 Squadron, Tony Iveson felt that the gap that separated him from his chief served to reinforce Harris's authority. He was 'a colossus, up there running the show, like Zeus from Olympus.' He accepted, as most airmen did, the explanation for his decision not to tour bases. 'If he'd gone to one station he would have had to go to them all and if he was coming they'd be painting stones and parading and all this lark and taking them away from their proper job.'⁴ This was a deferential age and service life inculcated a reflex respect for seniority. 'At twenty-two years of age, Harris to me was a God,' said Jim Berry, another pilot. 'We used to refer to him in all sorts of ways, but there was an underlying respect for Harris [that] everybody had, I think.'⁵

On the occasions when he did drop in on the crews he had a galvanizing effect. Reg Fayers was one of the minority who saw and heard him in person. Harris visited Holme-on-Spalding-Moor on 15 September 1943 to talk to 76 Squadron. It was at a time when it was suffering from a worrying incidence of 'early returns', the term used for when crews arrived back having failed to bomb. After a forceful speech he asked the crowd for their questions. Fayers, an independent-minded man inclined to scepticism, wrote to his wife that he felt 'privileged, really, to hear . . . the boss of the whole show. I even asked him a question. I've always been for his ideas . . . his faith in the efficacy of our bombing is terrific and catching altho' I'd already caught it. I still think [Bomber Command is] winning this war more certainly than anything else. I pray God I may see peace in six months.'[6] The following day Harris went to Elsham Wolds where the crews greeted him with sustained cheering.

Harris understood the value of a touch of menace. But he also knew it was wise to show a softer side from time to time and he could be charming and even gentle with his favourites, such as the *beaux idéals* of Bomber Command, Cheshire and Gibson. Leonard Cheshire described being summoned shortly after he had been awarded his VC. 'He sent for me . . . I thought I'd done something wrong . . . he was very nice and fatherly and very friendly and I liked him very much.'[7]

Harris arrived at Bomber Command at a good time. From March 1942, aircraft began to be fitted with a new navigation system called *Gee*. With *Gee*, the great problem that dogged Bomber Command's efforts and limited and defined its activities started to be solved. It worked on a system of radio pulses. Three stations strung out over 200 miles transmitted radio signals which were picked up by a *Gee* box on board the aircraft. Measuring the time difference between the pulses provided co-ordinates which were displayed on a cathode ray tube in the navigator's cabin. A competent 'nav' could get a fix which, within a few minutes, gave the aircraft's position to an accuracy of between half a mile and five miles. There were drawbacks. Because of the curvature of the earth, the range of *Gee* was limited to 350 miles. The Germans soon learned how to jam it, making it unreliable once over the Dutch coast. But *Gee* set the bombers on a true course on the outward journey and was a great help in bringing them home to base on their return.

Gee was later joined by *Oboe*, which came into service on 20 December 1942. It also operated on transmissions from ground stations in England but was more accurate. It was claimed that at its best it could hold an aircraft to within sixty-five feet of its position. *Oboe* got its name from the musical pulse it emitted which was audible to the pilot. Variations from the course were marked by variations in the pulse. As the target approached, a second signal was heard, a series of dashes followed by a series of dots. When the dots stopped, the bomb-aimer pressed his button. The big advantage of *Oboe* was that it allowed targets to be marked and bombed even in cloudy conditions. Initially, however, the *Oboe* ground stations could communicate with only a limited number of aircraft.

These aids were supplemented in January 1943 by *H2S*, a radar device which was carried on board and did not rely on external signals. A transmitter in the aircraft's belly reflected a picture of the ground below on to a TV screen in the navigator's cabin. The blips of light that appeared could be difficult to interpret, especially over big cities.

These were great improvements, but they did not mean that Bomber Command was now capable of bombing precisely. What the new technology did was to get aircraft to the target area, rather than pinpoint the target to be hit.

The new aeroplanes, though, were the best any commander could wish for. The faithful but outmoded aircraft of the first, disappointing years of the air war, were disappearing to be replaced by four-engined machines, far bigger than anything that had been seen before.

The first to appear was the Short Stirling which went into service in August 1940. It was eighty-seven feet long and stood very tall, slanting upwards sharply so that the cockpit was nearly twenty-three feet above the tarmac. But the Stirling was also slow, with a maximum speed of 260 mph and its unimpressive 740-mile range and 19,000-feet altitude limit meant it was the poor relation of the bomber fleet. The Avro Manchester made an appearance at the end of 1940 but its underdeveloped Vulture engines made it lethally unreliable and it was soon phased out.

The crews felt happiest in a Halifax or Lancaster. The Handley Page Halifax began operating in March 1941. It suffered from severe initial design faults but eventually evolved into a fine and trust-worthy aircraft. To the Canadian Ralph Wood, who switched from Whitleys in May 1942, the 'Hallybag' was a 'beautiful four-engined bird'. It had three gun turrets, front, mid-upper and rear. It could cruise at 280 mph and carry a bomb load of 8,000 pounds or three and a half tons. It took seven to fly a Halifax; a pilot, navigator, flight engineer, bomb-aimer who was also front gunner, wireless operator, mid-upper gunner and tail gunner.

Wood inhabited the 'dinky little navigator's compartment [which] was below and in front of the pilot's cockpit. You went down a few steps and entered a small section with a navigator's table down one side, ahead and below the pilot's feet.' Wood doubled as the bomb-aimer/front gunner. A curtain in the nose hid 'the even smaller compartment where I would huddle with my Mark Fourteen bombsight . . . when we got reasonably close to the target.' The gun he was supposed to operate when needed was a Vickers gas-operated .303 machine gun, which was mounted on a swivel and stuck out through the Perspex nose, high above the bombsight. They were 'popguns' in the eyes of the crews, a poor defence against an attacking night-fighter armed with cannons and, Wood had been warned, notorious for jamming. 'All you had to do was look at it the wrong way and it would plug up on you.'[8]

The Avro Lancaster was a masterpiece of military aviation design. It was capable of carrying great loads of up to 14,000 pounds. Later special aircraft were adapted to deliver the monstrous 22,000-pound Grand Slam bombs. Despite its phenomenal lifting power it was fast and manoeuvrable. It could reach nearly 290 mph and was nimble enough to corkscrew out of trouble when under attack from a night-fighter, though the technique was far from infallible. It was reliable and safe, with the lowest accident rate of the bombers. Tony Iveson had already notched up about 1,800 hours flying time in many different types when he first flew one. 'The Lanc was a lovely aircraft,' he remembered. 'It was splendid, day or night.' Ken Newman 'liked the Lancaster from the first moment that I climbed aboard.' The cockpit layout 'was much more sensible than that of the Halifax' with everything within easy reach. It was only in an emergency that the main design fault became apparent. The thick spar that lay across the fuselage supporting the wings was very difficult to negotiate when moving forward and aft and was a significant impediment in emergencies.

The heavies conveyed a feeling of strength and menace that inspired confidence in those who were to fly them. To the trainee bomber crews seeing them for the first time they looked huge and threatening. Noble Frankland thought them 'incredibly sinister and powerful', an impression that was deepened by their glistening black surfaces. They were huge, bigger than anything the Germans had, and as impressive as the American Liberators and Fortresses that would soon appear. The Halifax was seventy feet long and had a wing span of 104 feet, long enough for forty men to line up on in group photographs. They were as fast as the Americans and they carried heavier bomb loads. No one looking at them could doubt that they meant business.

Harris's first major change in operational procedures was to end the practice of splitting up the force and sending it to bomb two or three targets over a protracted period. His study of the German air attacks on Britain convinced him that the Luftwaffe had squandered a great opportunity by not focusing its attacks. The principle now was concentration. Henceforth the pattern was to dispatch as many aircraft as could be mustered against one target. Attack times were shortened which increased the chances of collisions but reduced the time in which the flak gunners had the bombers in their sights. They were aiming for saturation, swamping the defences and over-whelming the emergency services by sheer weight of violence. The method of destruction favoured by Harris was fire. Incendiaries were at least as important as high explosive. It was easier to burn down a city than to blow it up. The purpose of bombs was to rip off roofs and knock down walls, choking the streets with mounds of brick and stone and timber that would cripple the movement of firemen and rescue workers. Then the four-pound incendiaries would float down into the shattered buildings and start blazes that would feed on the winds whipped up by the blasts. The aim was, he said, to start 'so many fires at the same time that no fire-fighting services, however efficiently and quickly they were reinforced by the fire brigades of other towns, could get them under control.'[9]

The first major demonstrations of the new technique came with attacks on Lübeck and Rostock. Lübeck, as Harris admitted, was not a vital target, although it housed a a medium-sized port and a U-boat building yard. It was chosen because it was relatively simple to find and, given the part-wooden construction of many of the houses, 'easier than most cities to set on fire'. The raid was launched on the night of 28 March, and the aiming point was the centre of the *Altstadt*, the old quarter where the streets were narrow and crooked and the buildings were highly flammable. A separate attack was mounted on a machine-tool works. Two thirds of the 300 tons of bombs that were dropped were incendiaries. As well as the small magnesium incendiaries, the load included a thirty-pound bomb designed to fling benzol and rubber in a ten-yard radius from the point of impact. In mounting the attack Harris was testing a theory. The main object 'was to learn to what extent a first wave of aircraft could guide a second wave to the aiming point by starting a conflagration.' He ordered 'a half an hour interval between the two waves in order to allow the fires to get a good hold before the second wave arrived.'[10]

The fact that Bomber Command was now engaged unapologetically in area bombing was acknowledged by a change of terminology so that it now gauged success in terms of acres destroyed. Analysis of reconnaissance photographs suggested that 190 acres of Lübeck had been devastated, or 30 per cent of the town's built-up area. Most appeared to have been consumed by fire. This reckoning was an overestimate but not a wild one. The German survey counted 3,401 buildings destroyed or seriously damaged. Of those, all but 331 were houses and flats. The attack destroyed a factory which made oxygen equipment for U-boats. But it also ruined the Marienkirche, a church of great religious and architectural importance. Up to 320 people were killed, the heaviest death toll in a raid on Germany so far, but still far short of the 1,500 who had been killed in London on the night of 10 May 1941. The weakness of the town's defences meant Bomber Command's losses were relatively light, twelve aircraft out of the 234 sent out, most of which appear to have been knocked down *en route*. Harris was delighted with the

The shape of things to come: Lübeck, March 1942.

results. He had, he wrote later, 'conclusively proved that even the small force I had then could destroy the greater part of a town of secondary importance.'[11]

A month later four raids were aimed in quick succession at Rostock, culminating on the night of 26/27 April. Rostock was a town much like Lübeck, on the water and with a combustible old centre. Incendiaries made up most of the bomb load. All together, by Bomber Command's calculations, the attacks destroyed 60 per cent of the main town area. Again the crew losses had been low. About 200 Germans were killed, a figure that would have been considerably higher if many had not fled after the first raids. A Heinkel factory on the southern edge of town was singled out for special attention by separate forces, including Guy Gibson's 106 Squadron. This double-thrust combining an attempted high-explosive precision attack, Billancourt-style, with a general area attack with incendiaries was to become common practice.

The main weight of the raids, though, fell on the town itself. Josef Goebbels tried to salvage what propaganda advantage he could from the devastation by describing the action as a *Terrorangriff*, a terror attack. The term would stick and those who were carrying them out soon became *Terrorflieger* or terror flyers. Germans suffering these attacks or hearing about them agreed. But far away in California, one German had no doubts about the brutal justice of the raids. 'I think of Coventry, and I have no objection to the lesson that everything must be paid for,' said Thomas Mann, the great novelist and son of Lübeck in a radio broadcast. 'Did Germany believe that she would never have to pay for the atrocities that her leap into barbarism seemed to allow?'[12] Harris calculated that the two attacks had devastated 780 acres. He reckoned that Bomber Command had now 'about squared our account with Germany'.[13] By that he meant that it had inflicted as much destruction and death on Germany as the Luftwaffe had on Britain. German bombing had wrecked about 400 acres of London and 100 acres of Coventry, apart from the damage done to other blitzed cities.[14]

The Lübeck and Rostock raids had been relatively small. By the end of May, Harris was ready for his first spectacular. He knew the value of publicity and the prestige it could bring to him and his command. He wanted to demonstrate to the world the growing power of the bombing fleet. He set out to mount an operation that would impress his superiors, attract the admiration of the Americans and Russians who were now Britain's allies, bring cheer to British civilians, and frighten Germany. The logic of concentration suggested that the more bombers that could be dispatched on one mission the better. The figure of one thousand carried a certain poetic potency.

He took the idea to Churchill and Portal who gave enthusiastic approval and the planning began. Harris had only a little over 400 fully operational aircraft and crews at his immediate disposal and struggled to reach the magic number. Many machines and men came from operational training and conversion units.

This was essentially a huge and risky experiment which if it succeeded would set the pattern for the future. To handle the huge number of aircraft, it was decided they would fly in a 'bomber stream'. This, theoretically, would bring important defensive and offensive advantages. Every aircraft would follow the same route at staggered times, flying in different air corridors to reduce the risk of collisions. Thus, it was hoped, the vulnerability of the fleet to the German night-fighters who were growing increasingly active, operating in defensive boxes on the main approach routes, would be limited. It would also reduce the time over target and exposure to the defending flak batteries. At the same time, the bomber stream would deliver a continuous torrent of bombs that would overwhelm the defences and cause maximum disruption and terror creating the best conditions for apocalyptic conflagrations.

The first 'thousand' raid took place on the clear, moonlit Saturday night of the 30/31 May 1942 . The target was Cologne, Germany's third largest city. It had been subjected to many raids, most recently in March when, in the first successful *Gee*-led raid, 135 aircraft had attacked the city doing considerable damage and killing sixty-two people. Now seven times that number were launched against it. Harris's message to the departing crews left no doubt about the significance of the operation. 'The force of which you form a part tonight is at least twice the size and has at least four times the carrying capacity of the largest air force ever before concentrated on one objective,' he declared. 'You have an opportunity therefore to strike a blow at the enemy which will resound, not only throughout Germany, but throughout the world.' All together, 1,047 aircraft took part in the raid including seventy-three of the new Lancasters. They carried 1,455 tons of bombs of which two thirds were incendiaries. The aim was to set Cologne ablaze. The city's configuration with broad streets and modern buildings meant that fires did not take hold with the same hungry energy as they did in the old Hanseatic towns. The damage was still impressive. According to local records 3,330 buildings were destroyed, 2,090 seriously damaged and 7,420 lightly damaged, almost all by fire. The flames were indiscriminate. The conflagration devoured 13,010 homes, mostly apartments, and seriously damaged 6,360 more. Nine hospitals, seventeen churches, sixteen schools and four university buildings as well as numerous other premises that could not be considered military or industrial targets were burnt or blasted down. Ralph Wood, looking down from his Halifax, saw what seemed to be the 'red hot embers of a huge bonfire'. The German records list damage being done to seventeen water mains, five gas mains, thirty-two electricity cables and twelve main telephone routes. The only military building mentioned is a flak installation.

The death toll established a new record. At least 469 people were killed. Of these 411 were civilians and 58 military, most of whom had been manning flak batteries. The RAF traumatized Cologne in the same way that some eighteen months before the Luftwaffe had traumatized Coventry. Some 45,000 people had been 'bombed out'. As in Coventry, many fled the city, about a fifth of the 700,000 population according to local estimates. As in Coventry, the raid created a symbol of destruction and suffering in the form of a ruined cathedral.

Brian Frow was now a pilot with 408 Squadron which was charged with dropping parachute flares to light up the target for the main force. 'At briefing we were told that the aiming point for 5 Group was the square in front of Cologne Cathedral,' he wrote. This was 'a bow to realism; it was well known that in area attacks against cities at night, the bomb pattern followed the design of a triangle, with the apex at the aiming point, widening and falling back along the inbound track of the raid.' After the first bombs landed the aiming point was covered by dust and smoke, making accurate aiming impossible. There was also a tendency for anxious crews to release their bombs early. By taking the cathedral as a landmark the bomb load would fall into the densest part of the city where the maximum destruction would be achieved. Afterwards, Konrad Adenauer who had been the anti-Nazi mayor of the city, wrote that 'there was no gas, no water, no electric current and no means of transport. The bridges across the Rhine had been destroyed. There were mountains of rubble in the streets. Everywhere there were gigantic areas of debris from bombed and shelled buildings. With its razed churches, many of them almost a thousand years old, its bombed-out cathedral, with the ruins of once beautiful bridges sticking up out of the Rhine, and the vast expanses of derelict houses, Cologne was a ghost city.' The damage was light compared with what was to come. It was, in Frow's words, merely 'a foretaste of what was to befall the Hun'.[15]

These attacks met with noisy approval from the British press and public. Even George Orwell's tender conscience was untroubled by what was going on. The Germans, he warned, in a radio broadcast a few days after the raid, deserved no quarter. 'In 1940, when the Germans were bombing Britain, they did not expect retaliation on a very heavy scale,' he said. '[They] were not afraid to boast in their propaganda about the slaughter of civilians which they were bringing about and the terror which their raids aroused. Now, when the tables are turned, they are beginning to cry out against the whole business of aerial bombing, which they declare to be both cruel and useless. The people of this country are not revengeful, but they remember what happened to themselves two years ago, and they remember how the Germans talked when they thought themselves safe from retaliation.'

It was not until the following spring that mammoth raids became routine. Bomber Command was still growing and simply did not have the strength to maintain a tempo of heavy attacks. Cologne, was, in the opinion of Hamish Mahaddie, then a pilot with 7 Squadron who was to go on to be a leading figure in the foundation of the Pathfinder Force, something of a 'con trick', whose main purpose was to establish the feasibility of such an exercise and by extension the value of the strategic bombing campaign.[16] If so, the ruse worked. Cologne and the raids that preceded it went a long way to silencing the doubters and establishing strategic bombing solidly at the heart of Allied war planning.

The successes of the first phase of the Harris era were, however, relative. *Gee* had improved navigation but not transformed it. The bomber fleets still had difficulty finding the target. The arrival of the Pathfinders brought a further, important improvement. The Pathfinder Force was not a Harris invention and he opposed it with all the considerable vigour he could muster against ideas which were not his own. The principle was that to aid accuracy an elite unit formed from the best crews would fly ahead of the main force and illuminate aiming points with target-marking bombs for the following aircraft to aim at.

The concept had been raised inside the Air Ministry at the end of 1941 before Harris took over and was promoted by a powerful Air Staff lobby. It was led by Group Captain Syd Bufton, the director of bomber operations at the Air Ministry. He had commanded 10 Squadron early in the war and pioneered a technique of using his best crews to locate targets with flares. The Australian Don Bennett, who was to command the force, remembered Harris fighting 'tooth and nail to try and stop it'. He 'argued that the best crews were too valuable and that putting them out in front to lead the rest . . . would also expose them to greater risk. The losses amongst your best crews would be so high that it would be prohibitive. In other words you'd lead all the force with a good bunch of people in front but not for long because the leaders would be shot down and lost.' Bennett's solution to this problem was to surround the half a dozen or so Pathfinder Force (PFF) crews with a phalanx of 'supporters' to help bear the brunt of the flak. The system worked and PFF losses were no worse and in fact slighly better than those of the main force. The other objection, a valid one as Bennett admitted, was that skimming off outstanding leaders would weaken squadrons as well as denting their morale. 'Naturally they all looked to their squadron commander and to have their squadron commander whisked away down to headquarters Pathfinder Force . . . may have been a great honour to the person concerned but it was a tremendous loss to the squadron.'[17]

Harris's opposition was supported by all his group commanders. But it was clear to Portal that despite the recent technological improvements and successes, Bomber Command's efficiency was still severely limited and anything that offered the hope of improvement should be tried. He backed the Air Staff view and Harris was ordered to drop his objections and form the new force. He did not concede quietly. He insisted that instead of selecting the best crews, the PFF would be made up of four ordinary squadrons, one from each night bomber group. Portal, knowing when to cede ground, agreed.

The Pathfinder argument shone a light on the battle of ideas about how the strategic air campaign should be fought. Those who backed the PFF regarded area bombing as a temporary measure which could be dropped once improved technology and expertise allowed the RAF to perfect the technique of precise attack. Those who opposed believed city-battering was an end in itself which, if pursued hard enough, was the surest path to hastening victory. It was a debate that was to continue until the end.

At this point, Portal was firmly on the side of obliteration. The entry of America into the war had greatly increased the potential assets available to conduct a massive strategic bomber campaign. The first American aircraft and crews arrived in Britain at the beginning of 1942 and in August began their initial, tentative sorties, bombing rail yards, not in Germany but in France. American bombing doctrine was very different from that of the RAF. The United States Army Air Force believed firmly in the achievability of precise bombing on carefully chosen military and industrial targets. To maximize accuracy, they were organized chiefly to bomb in daylight.

These factors were to complicate the evolution of a harmonized Anglo-American approach. For a time, though, it seemed to Portal that it would soon be possible to muster giant air armadas against the Reich. In the autumn of 1942, he told the Chiefs of Staff that if the bomber force could be greatly expanded to between 4,000 and 6,000 aircraft, devastating results could be achieved. Scientific analysis of the impact of bombs on Britain had produced some plausible-seeming projections of the effects on Germany of an all-out campaign. Portal claimed that if 50,000 tons of bombs could be delivered each month in 1943, rising to 90,000 tons by the end of 1944, the effects would be catastrophic for Germany. Twenty-five million Germans would be made homeless, 900,000 would be killed and one million seriously injured. By the middle of 1944 these tonnages were indeed being achieved, and with far fewer aircraft than had been thought necessary. The results were less catastrophic than predicted. But there was no doubt that Portal regarded such imagined destruction would speed victory.

There was to be no question of Bomber Command suspending

its activities until ideal force levels had been achieved. In between the peaks of its campaign there was almost continuous activity as crews dropped mines in the sea and carried out minor raids on secondary targets. These activities could be as dangerous as any other, as Denholm Elliott, the young RADA hopeful turned wireless operator, found out on the night of 23/24 September 1942.

He had recently arrived at 76 Squadron and on his third operation was ordered off with the rest of his crew in their Halifax, K-King, to bomb the submarine base at Sylt, a spit of land poking into the North Sea. The trip, he remembered, got off to a bad start. 'As we were walking out to the plane the engineer who had been servicing it said "What are you?" I said, "I'm wireless op for K for King." He said, "Oh dear, oh dear," and I asked "Why?" "Well [he replied] the last wireless operator for K for King got a cannon shell up his backside." That didn't encourage me too much.' Elliott did not improve morale by telling his crewmates that he had had a dream the previous night in which they were shot down.

They came in low over the target at 1,000 feet. 'This was the first time I was actually encountering anti-aircraft fire and it really was a most unpleasant sensation,' – he remembered. 'A shell bursting beneath you lifts the plane about fifty feet upwards in the air. You certainly find instant religion.'

Then Elliott felt 'the most enormous explosion . . . the port outer engine was on fire . . . all the lights went out. I was fumbling desperately to find the wire clippers to send a distress signal on the automatic SOS but the plane was going down and there just wasn't time. I just jumped out of my seat which was at the very front of the plane and tore to the middle of the aircraft, as it was going down, and got into the ditching position with your feet up against the central spar and your hands behind your neck to take the shock.' As he passed the navigator, who was also taking up crash stations, 'he sort of grinned in a sickly way . . . that was the last time I saw him.'

Elliott's skipper, Squadron Leader Barnard, managed to put K-King down on the North Sea with the smallest of bumps. But water immediately flooded into the fuselage as they fought to get the escape hatch open. 'I'm afraid I was very ungentlemanly,' Elliott confessed. 'I was scrambling over everybody else to get out. As far I was concerned there was no question of a polite "after you, my dear Charles . . ."'

Five of the crew managed to struggle out. Floating in the moonlight, buoyed up by his lifejacket, rescue seemed very far away and Elliott assumed he was doomed. He found himself thinking of his friends in the squadron whom he would never see again. But his hopes rose when he saw they were only about a mile from land. The aircraft was still afloat. The survivors clambered on top but it was clear that K-King would soon sink. The inflatable dinghy which was supposed to be released in emergencies had failed to emerge. Somebody volunteered to slither back inside and pull the switch. The dinghy shot to the surface. They pulled themselves on to it one by one. A debate began about what to do next. There was a suggestion they try to paddle to neutral Sweden, a mere 300 miles away. It was Elliott who talked them out of it and proposed firing off the distress flare and heading for shore. The signal fizzed into the night sky and not long afterwards a tug pulled up alongside and took them aboard. On dry land they were met by 'a picture postcard Nazi officer with a monocle and a long cigarette holder' who announced that for them the war was over.[18]

It would be some time before Bomber Command could bring its full weight to bear on Germany. During the winter it was diverted to bombing industrial targets in northern Italy. Early in 1943 it was called in again to attack the French ports of Lorient, Saint-Nazaire, Brest and La Pallice from where German submarines were once again threatening the Atlantic sea lanes. Lorient was hit eight times between mid-January and mid-February. By the end the town was ruined and deserted and many of its civilian inhabitants were dead. The U-boats and their crews, however, were virtually unharmed. The Germans had been left alone since the raids of 1941 and had used the time to build pens encased in thick concrete which conventional bombs were unable to penetrate.

The attacks shifted to Saint-Nazaire. On 28 February 427 aircraft bombed the port destroying two thirds of the town and killing twenty-eight inhabitants. Having seen what had happened to

Lorient, most of the population had fled. The almost total lack of positive results led to the cancellation of further operations, sparing Brest and La Pallice.

By the spring of 1943 the elements for an all-out attack on German cities were at last in place. In February 1943, Harris had more than 600 heavy bombers available to him and the numbers were growing. On the grand strategic front, the war was swinging the Allies' way. At Stalingrad, the German army was on the verge of defeat and surrender. Between 14 and 26 January 1943 Churchill and Roosevelt, along with the combined British and American Chiefs of Staff, met in the weak sunshine of Casablanca, to seek agreement on how their campaign should proceed and what part the RAF and the United States Army Air Force (USAAF) should play in it.

The role of Bomber Command was spelled out in what became known as the Casablanca directive. Harris was told: 'Your primary object will be the progressive destruction of the German military industrial and economic system, and the undermining of the morale of the German people to a point where their armed resistance is fatally weakened.'

Harris thus had the highest official approval to proceed with a campaign of all-out destruction. He chose to devote the rest of the spring and summer to hurling Bomber Command's greatly expanded destructive power against the Ruhr. Between March and the end of July, Bomber Command launched forty-three major operations, two thirds of which were aimed at the area. The RAF used the geographical designation 'Ruhr' loosely. It took in not only the Ruhr area itself but the whole industrial conglomeration along the Rhine and the Lippe. It was one of the great productive regions of the world, providing Germany with most of its coal and almost half its electricity. It was ugly even in peacetime, overhung with a perpetual haze, a de-natured monochrome sprawl of mills and factories churning out iron, steel and chemicals to feed the ravenous Moloch that Hitler had called to life. This was the heart of Germany's might. The aim of the Battle of the Ruhr was to stop it beating.

The Ruhr had been attacked many times before but with little effect. The innacuracy of navigation techniques, the perpetual blanket of smog and the strength of the defences combined to protect it. The crews, with their habitual dark humour, called it 'Happy Valley'. The news, at briefing, that it was the target for that night, provoked groans of dismay. But at least the journey was short, usually less than a six-hour round-trip, which reduced exposure to flak, fighters and bad weather.

The Battle of the Ruhr was an exhausting and bloody slog, in which night after night, large forces of up to 800 aircraft pitched themselves against the heaviest flak defences in Germany and the most experienced and best-equipped units of the Luftwaffe to deliver ever greater weights of bombs. The levels of killing and destruction soared. The same cities were attacked over and over again until, after studying the reconnaissance photographs that he pasted into 'blue books' for the enlightenment of important guests, Harris was satisfied. Essen, in the very centre of the Ruhr and the home of the Krupp steel works, was bombed five times. The raids killed nearly a thousand people, destroyed about 5,000 homes and damaged Krupp's, but not so badly as to seriously reduce production. The actions cost Bomber Command ninety-five aircraft.

In the midst of this grim catalogue of demolition and loss, one operation stands out. The Dams Raid of 16/17 May gave a much more positive demonstration of Bomber Command's abilities and the technological advances that had been made since the beginning of the war. It was carried out by 617 Squadron which had been formed in March from selected crews under the leadership of Wing Commander Guy Gibson, by now the pre-eminent operational leader in Bomber Command. The main targets were the Möhne, Eder and Sorpe dams. They were to be attacked with bouncing bombs designed by Barnes Wallis, the scientist who had invented the geodetic construction technique used in the Wellington.

The dams had been selected for attack by the Air Ministry before the war. They were a prime example of the sort of targets a strategic bombing force should be going after. The Möhne dam, south-east of Dortmund, held back nearly 140 million tons of water and was the main source of supply to the Ruhr valley, twenty miles away, as well as a provider of hydro-electric power. The even larger Eder reservoir south-east of Kassel supplied the water for an important canal which linked the Ruhr to Berlin. A successful attack on these targets could do severe damage to the German war economy.

The crews were the cream of 5 Group. For six weeks they trained intensively under Gibson's critical eye, practising the low-level approaches which were necessary to release the bombs at the right height. Harold 'Hobby' Hobday, a trainee insurance worker in pre-war life, had just completed twenty-six operations with 50 Squadron as a navigator and was preparing to go off on an advanced navigation course when his skipper Flight Lieutenant Les Knight was approached by Gibson and asked if he was willing to join 617. Knight agreed, leaving Hobday with a dilemma. He decided to ditch the course and stick with his mates. 'I didn't want to let my crew down,' he remembered later, 'and I was quite keen on bombing. I loved the life . . . I liked the idea of the crew staying as one integral part of the set-up. I wouldn't have liked the thought that another navigator would have taken my place in my own crew.'

At 617 Squadron's base at 'Sunny Scampton' he met Gibson and quickly formed an impression of a man who although friendly 'would not stand any nonsense'. If anyone drank before flying 'he'd be down on them like a ton of bricks . . . one chap had a pint of beer before he was going on training and he was severely reprimanded.' Gibson delivered his rockets personally and with withering effect. 'He'd do it in front of the squadron and, of course, that made you feel about two inches high.'

Day and night the crews skimmed Scottish lochs and Welsh lakes at fifty to a hundred feet with no idea what they were preparing for. The first thought was they were to be sent against the battleship *Tirpitz,* a menace to shipping and the subject of numerous unsuccessful attacks. They also practised synchronizing the beams of two searchlights fitted to their Lancasters so that they harmonized at one spot, sixty feet above the ground, at exactly the right height at which the bombs should be released.

On Saturday 15 May, the day before the raid, pilots and navigators were finally told the target. The following morning all 133 crew of the nineteen aircraft that would take part gathered in the huge airmen's dining room to be briefed. The first to speak was Ralph Cochrane, the 5 Group commander. 'Bomber Command,' he told them, 'has been delivering the bludgeon blow on Hitler. You have been selected to give the rapier thrust which will shorten the war if it is successful.' Then Gibson outlined the plan before handing over to Barnes Wallis. He struck Hobday as 'a very kindly man, obviously very dedicated, frightfully clever ... but a fatherly type ... we thought he was a marvellous man. Everybody did.'

Wallis described how his bomb, if delivered correctly, would hit the water and skip along before exploding just below the parapet of the dam. Models of the dams were unveiled and studied. Hobday recalled a hum of animated chatter after the briefing closed. The crews 'were confident. There was no doubt about that. [This] was a marvellous thing to be on. It was so different from any bombing we'd ever done before and much more exciting. We thought it was a great effort.'

The squadron began taking off just before 9.30 p.m. One aircraft had to return after it struck the surface of the sea and lost its bomb. Another was so badly damaged by flak that it abandoned the mission. A further five were shot down or crashed before they reached the target. That left twelve. Hobday's crew had a trouble-free flight until they reached the Möhne dam where they held off while Gibson and four other aircraft launched their attacks through a blizzard of light flak. On the fifth attempt the dam wall crumbled.

Gibson now led four other crews on to the Eder. The dam was in a deep valley and surrounded by wooded hills. The Germans regarded the daunting terrain as sufficient protection and had not bothered with flak batteries. The first attack was made by Flight Lieutenant David Shannon's crew. Lying in the belly was Len Sumpter, a former guardsman who had switched services and become a bomb-aimer after seeing his comrades die in a Luftwaffe air raid. He was unhappy with the approach and told Shannon to go round again.

Gibson ordered Squadron Leader Henry Maudslay, a highly experienced pilot and the holder of the DFC, to go next. His bomb left the aircraft late and struck the parapet, exploding as the Lancaster passed overhead. Hobday 'saw the bomb go up in a huge flash . . . Gibson called the pilot and there was a very faint reply, very faint indeed . . . it was obviously someone who was in a great deal of trouble.' Maudslay struggled to keep the aircraft flying for another forty minutes before it was brought down by flak near Emmerich. There were no survivors.

Shannon's aircraft went in for another run and this time Sumpter was satisfied with the height, distance and speed. The bomb bounced twice and sank at the dam wall before exploding, sending a tower of water climbing 1,000 feet into the night sky. A small breach was seen in the dam but Gibson had to be sure.

At last it was the turn of Knight's crew. They attacked at 1.52 a.m. with the moon on the starboard beam lighting up the lake. After an initial dummy run they went round again, this time in earnest. Hobday 'wasn't tense. I was excited. It was a great thrill.' The only distraction was another pilot who came over the VHF radio offering tips on how to succeed. He was brusquely cut off. Gibson, who was flying alongside, watched the bomb bounce three times, hit the dam and explode. This time 'the thing broke . . . we watched the water billowing down the ravine from the dam . . . I could see cars going along and being overtaken by this wall of water . . . It really was fantastic, a sight I shall never forget.'

They headed for home and 'a very nice reception'. After debriefing and many celebratory drinks Hobday fell off to sleep in an armchair in the mess. The only unhappy man at Scampton was the inventor of the weapon who had made possible the success. Hobday thought Barnes Wallis 'looked shattered, because so many planes were missing. We were used to it of course, although it was rather more than average.'[19]

In fact eight out of the nineteen aircraft dispatched had been lost and fifty-three crew members killed. The raid had been an enormous success, though it failed to fulfil the more extravagent hopes of the planners. Two great dams had been destroyed. The breaching of the Möhne caused widespread flooding and disruption of railways, roads and canals and reduced the water and electricity supply to the

Ruhr. The destruction of the Eder dam caused considerable damage to waterways in the Kassel area. Houses were wrecked, bridges swept away and 1,294 people drowned, 493 of whom were foreign workers and prisoners of war. This was a new record. At least as important was the propaganda success that resulted. The Dambusters legend was created. Their feats showed Bomber Command as it preferred to be seen, wielders, in Cochrane's words, of the rapier rather than the bludgeon.

But it was with the bludgeon that it did most of its work. An operation that took place on the night of 13/14 May was far more typical of Bomber Boys' efforts at this time. Just after midnight on 14 May 1943, Arthur Taylor, who was now a bomb-aimer with 218 Squadron, took off with the rest of his crew from Downham Market in their Stirling, I-Ink, to attack Bochum in the dead centre of the Ruhr. He was setting off with more than his usual share of anxieties. Arthur had begun to lose confidence in his skipper, Bill, whom he suspected of being 'windy'. They were carrying an all-incendiary load. Arthur was 'determined to get there at all costs, with or without Bill.'

It was a beautiful moonlit night and he found his way quite easily until sometime before the target area, 'the *Gee* went u/s (unserviceable)' and they found themselves separated from the bomber stream and alone over Düsseldorf. 'Being the only kite there, they gave us all they'd got,' he wrote. 'Bill panicked and circled about in a frantic endeavour to get out, losing height all the time. Before we left Düsseldorf we were at 6,000 feet, picked up by immense cones of thirty to forty searchlights at a time, and a sitting target for light, medium and heavy flak.' It was at this point that Bill gave the order to bale out. Taylor replied that 'if we did we would never reach the ground in one piece. Bill then said, "You bloody well fly it then" and I ran up the steps and grabbed the second pilot's controls. I steered a straight course and in a few minutes we had left Düsseldorf behind.'

Bill recovered his composure and took over again. The respite did not last long. To get to Bochum they passed over the southern outskirts of Essen where 'for several minutes we were fired at continuously. There was a clap like thunder when flak hit the aircraft and a strong smell of cordite.' At last they arrived at the target. 'The place was ablaze. Immense fires covered the ground reflected red on a great pall of smoke that hung above the town.' They launched their bombs into the inferno and turned homewards.

A check on the intercom revealed that Jock the rear gunner was in desperate trouble. Arthur went back to help. He found he 'had obeyed the order to bale out but had pulled the ripcord too early and his parachute had partly opened, jamming him in the hatch. He had received the full blast of the explosions and was in a dazed condition when I pulled him back into the kite.'

Arthur struggled back along the fuselage, clambering laboriously over the centre spar and into the cockpit. 'I sat next to Bill to quieten him down and in case he was hit . . . I had to hold the throttles all the way as I-Ink was shaking badly.' Between them, they nursed the aircraft back, crossing the Dutch coast at the Zuyder Zee, and arrived over Downham Market in the half-light of dawn and with only a few gallons of petrol to spare.

This was not the end of the drama. The radio was wrecked, so they decided to land without permission. 'Just as I thought everything was OK I looked at Bill to find that he had let go of the controls and had both hands over his eyes. The kite swerved suddenly to port and the next thing I knew we had pranged into the control tower.' Arthur headed for the escape hatch but the way was blocked by Paddy, the flight engineer, who was wielding an axe, trying to hack his way through the fuselage. 'I remember tapping him on the back and asking him if he had tried the hatch . . . with that everyone tore hell for leather out of the kite.'

The starboard wing of the aircraft had ploughed through the briefing room demolishing much of it but mercifully only injuring a few of the people inside. But I-Ink had also careered into a lorry bringing back crews from the raid, cutting it in half and killing Sergeants Denzey and Lancaster.

The kite had had it. The turret of Len, the mid-upper gunner, was sieved with shrapnel, a splinter of which had grazed his nose on the way through. The Perspex astrodome observation point which bulged from the top of the fuselage had been whipped away by blast while Paddy had been looking through it.

They traipsed off to see the medical officer. Jock was sent to the sick bay with a deep cut to his head. The doctor gave Arthur and the rest 'two little yellow pills each which all but knocked me out before we reached the billet'.[20]

Shortly afterwards the crew announced they were sacking Bill. The crew was split up and Arthur was posted to a new station.

Bochum had been a costly operation. All together sixteen aircraft had been lost, killing sixty-four airmen. Another twenty-one were taken prisoner. So it was to go on all through the summer. Between the start of the campaign in early March to the end of July, when the battle was suspended after Harris chose to switch the attack to Berlin, Bomber Command lost just over a thousand aircraft. But it had also dropped more than 57,000 tons of bombs, often with devastating effects. On the ground, after three and a half years of the air war, the apocalyptic fate that Bomber Command's leaders had promised German cities was becoming a reality.

7

The Feast of St Peter and St Paul

In Germany's big towns the people watched the havoc and waited their turn. During the spring and summer of 1943 civilian casualties rose steadily. In an attack on Essen on the night of 5/6 March, 482 died. A few weeks later, on the night of 20/21 April, the Baltic city of Stettin was bombed and 586 were killed. Three weeks afterwards 693 died in Dortmund. A new record was set on the night of 29/30 May when 710 aircraft attacked Wuppertal in the heart of the Ruhr. They were aiming for the Barmen district, one half of the long, narrow town. The Pathfinder marking was deadly accurate and the bulk of the main force's bomb load tumbled into the narrow old streets. The fire that followed swallowed 80 per cent of the buildings. Some 3,400 people were killed, five times more than in any previous area raid.

Cologne had the unwanted distinction of having been the target of the first thousand-bomber raid, in May 1942. In that attack 469 people were killed. A year on, such a death toll had become commonplace. There had been several subsequent raids on the city, none of which came near to matching the trauma of that night. That was to change in the early hours of 29 June, a day which the fervently Catholic inhabitants celebrated as the feast of St Peter and St Paul.

Catholicism contributed greatly to Cologne's strong and idiosyncratic identity. Of the pre-war population of 770,000, around 600,000 were of the faith. It was a northern city but with a southern outlook and way of doing things. It prided itself on its open-mindedness and humour, displayed in the annual carnival, the biggest and most celebrated in Germany, a theatre of the absurd in which an elaborate procession of floats mocked the authorities.

Enthusiasm for Hitler was muted in Cologne. In the Reichstag elections of 5 March 1933, the Nazis gained 33.1 per cent of the votes, considerably less than in other parts of Germany. They fared better in the local elections, winning 39.6 per cent. By forming a coalition with two other right-wing parties, this was enough to give them control of the city council. The existing mayor, Konrad Adenauer of the Catholic *Zentrum* party, who had vigorously opposed the Nazis and snubbed Hitler by refusing to receive him at the local airport, was deposed. Dr Günther Riesen was installed as the Nazi mayor.

So began the Nazification of Cologne. It proceeded as in the rest of the country, propelled by the enthusiasm of the true believers, and the opportunism or passivity of the rest. With Nazi rule came a gradual degradation of trust. Dr Hans Volmer watched the moral corrosion set in among the 600 staff of the Cologne employment exchange where he started work in 1936. 'It was a conglomerate of the diligent and the indolent,' he wrote, '[the] oppressors and the oppressed, of those who were or wanted to be National Socialists and others who weren't or didn't want to be. Officials, SA and SS people busily kept each other under surveillance . . . the greater part of the employees were very anxious about possible measures being taken against them on account of the political attitudes. An incredible mistrust was spreading. The slogan was "not a word too many . . ."'[1]

Much of such anti-Nazi feeling as existed was caused by the regime's treatment of the Church. Anti-Catholic measures began in the 1930s but slackened after Hitler proscribed any further action against Catholics or Protestants to avoid unrest. The local party seized on the emergency created by the thousand-bomber raid to resume its campaign of persecution, however. The celebration of religious public holidays was banned and the Gestapo took over all confessional kindergartens and orphanages. The greatest uproar was caused by the seizure of eighteen convents and monasteries in the archbishopric of Cologne, an episode known as the *Klostersturm*. Nuns were turned out of their convents overnight and set to work in munitions factories. The theological college was also closed down.

Resistance to the moves was determined and courageous. The Church was led by Cardinal Joseph Frings. His predecessor, Cardinal Schulte, suffered a heart attack during a bombing raid on 10 March 1941 and died shortly afterwards. Unlike Schulte, who had tried to find compromises with the Nazis, Frings was tough, humane and charismatic. He was a popular figure in the air-raid shelter in the hospital at Cologne-Hohenlind. 'The Cardinal would borrow our Karl May books [German children's literature] to take his mind off things and to forget the fear,' remembered Gerhard Uhlenbruck, a teenager who went on to become a professor of medicine. 'I was fascinated by [his] extraordinary composure and his fine sense of humour.'[2]

He was leading a dedicated flock. Despite the repression of Catholic youth organizations, Cologne cathedral would be packed with young people on great Church holidays. 'On the feast of Christ the King, to disturb the service, the Hitler Youth would sometimes march round the outside of the cathedral playing drums and trumpets,' said Albert Roth who was sixteen in 1942. 'The older ones amongst us would go outside and a fight with the Hitler Youth would ensue.'[3] Although religious youth organizations were banned, the teaching of the faith was still allowed in classrooms. Some priests used religious instruction periods to preach against the regime. 'Often these sessions were used to take a critical stand against the political situation,' wrote Wilhelm Becker. 'I remember our chaplain, Otto Köhler saying that Hitler was the Antichrist . . .'[4]

But as much as the Church protested against its own persecution, it did almost nothing to protect the Jewish or Roma and Sinti gypsy people of Cologne. Many Jews had fled by the time the war began but in 1940 there were still 6,044 registered in the city. The campaign of oppression, humiliation and dispossession began almost immediately the Nazis arrived in power. Within a month of the takeover, stormtroopers forced their way into the regional court in Reichensperger Platz. They dragged out Jewish judges and lawyers in the middle of proceedings, placed signs declaring 'I am a Jew' around their necks and paraded them around town on dustcarts.[5] At the end of September 1938, all remaining Jewish lawyers and doctors in Cologne lost their right to practise. Jews were not allowed to leave their buildings after 8 p.m. and were only permitted to shop in certain stores. They became exiles in their own city. In the wake of the law prohibiting Jews and non-Jews from sharing dwelling space, certain buildings were designated as 'Jew houses' into which the outcasts were crammed. Erna Schoenenberg, who was deported to Theresienstadt concentration camp in 1942 and murdered in Auschwitz in 1944, wrote to her brother Julius who had escaped to Shanghai: 'The married couple Steiner live in our former dining room, and our former sitting room accommodates the two Levys. The two of us live in your former bedroom and the store room.'[6]

As Bomber Command's attacks took their toll, Jewish homes were seized to shelter those who had been bombed out and Jewish property was systematically stolen. The first deportation to the death camps took place on 21 October 1941. Jews were permitted to take fifty kilograms of luggage each. They were told to chalk a number on each suitcase so it could be reclaimed when they reached their unknown destination in the east. In fact all the baggage was immediately taken to the customs administration where it was auctioned off to the citizens of Cologne.

After the thousand-bomber raid the city authorities set up a special department to offer seized Jewish goods to the homeless. Regular auctions were held to dispose of heaters, vacuum cleaners, cooker hobs, cooking utensils, irons, hair dryers, gramophones and records, opera glasses, cameras, sofas, cupboards, beds, lamps, chairs, crockery, clocks, sewing machines, picture frames, mirrors, curtain rods and more. They were offered to Cologne's citizens as 'non-Aryan property' and thousands of people flocked to the sales.

For the Nazis it was an easy way of deflecting the grumbling and resentment that had come in the wake of the bombing. The legalized looting also had the effect of widening the circle of those who benefited from the persecution of the Jews.

There was another deportation on 30 November 1941, and a further spate after the thousand-bomber raid. Of the 6,000 Jews living in Cologne in August 1941, only half remained at the end of the year.

The deportations were carried out openly. The Jews left from the Cologne-Deutz station, jeered on their way by the SS and the SA who sang insulting, anti-Semitic songs. Crowds of curious citizens stood by. The Swiss consul in the city, Franz-Rudolf von Weiss, reported to Berne that he had heard people complaining about the 'bad taste' of the spectacle. But there was no protest on any scale from the public or the Church.[7]

Individual, courageous acts of help towards the Jews are hard to quantify. There were, however, some. A schoolgirl, Anne Winnen, recalled how 'once a week, my mother would prepare a parcel for them in our butcher's shop. In the evening, when it was dark, she would let them in by the back door. One noticed how one by one they stayed away. We knew exactly what was happening but what could one do individually? Everybody was afraid.'[8]

The people of Cologne had begun the war in a mood of light-hearted stoicism similar to that displayed in Coventry before the big raid. At a midsummer night's party in 1940 the programme included a firework display 'courtesy of Tommy and Flak, London and Cologne'.

By the night of 28 June 1943, all such levity had long disappeared. Cologne was the nearest big German city to the British bomber bases. It was in the first trench of the very front line of the air war. Already it had been bombed fifty-eight times with varying degrees of intensity. The previous raid had come only twelve days before but a large part of the force had been recalled because of bad weather and thick cloud over the target. About a hundred aircraft struggled on to the city, destroying 400 houses and badly damaging a chemical works.

Apart from the attacks, the inhabitants also had to contend with the disruption and nervous wear and tear caused by the frequent blare of public air-raid warnings which sounded whenever there were Allied aircraft in the vicinity. So far there had been twenty-seven that June. The signal sent everyone trudging to the air-raid shelters. The noise of the sirens induced resignation rather than panic. By now, the population had become well used to life underground.

Public bunkers were built from reinforced concrete and were

relatively robust but access to them was controlled and party not-
ables and their families got first call on the space. Most of the
population had to make do with the cellars of their own homes or
apartment blocks. Few regarded them as secure refuges. 'We sit in
the cellars, defenceless, almost every night,' wrote one Cologne
resident. 'I have reinforced the ceiling so that it will withstand the
rubble above, but ceilings are no protection against even medium-
sized bombs. It is a terrible feeling when the engines drone above
us and when we hear the whine of the falling bombs.' They learned
to identify the progress of the raid from the sounds outside. 'First
there was the rattle of incendiaries . . . then blow by blow, the heavy,
heavy impacts. As our cellar was not deep, we were crouching on
mattresses on the floor by the opening. Everyone had a wet cloth
over their head, a gas mask and matches. When the heavy bombs
fell, we pressed the cloth to our face and kept our ears and nose
shut with our fingers because of the blast.'[9]

Each cellar was connected to its neighbour by a hole in the wall,
knocked through so that people could move from one to the other
if the shelter collapsed. The feeling of insecurity was well founded.
Of the 20,000 people killed by air raids in Cologne during the
war, three out of five died inside shelters, asphyxiated by carbon
monoxide as fire devoured the oyxgen in the air, crushed by falling
brick, stone and timber, scalded by bursting hot-water pipes or
battered by blast. Nonetheless, public shelters were always packed,
so that the authorities imposed restrictions on who had the right
to enter. Jews, gypsies and foreign slave labourers were naturally
excluded on the grounds of their *Untermenschen* status. But such was
the overcrowding in the bunkers of the Rhineland in the summer of
1943 that the bar had to be extended. Able-bodied men between the
ages of sixteen and sixty and 'uniform wearers' were only allowed in
at the highest level of alert when a raid was imminent.

The rules in the public bunkers were enforced by wardens recruited from the local party. In the private shelters a member of the
house community was in charge. As well as their policing duties,
they were expected to fight fires, removing the incendiaries that
crashed through roofs and into attics before a blaze could take hold.

Public bunker wardens seemed to relish their power. There were numerous stories of their bullying, arrogance and eagerness to punish those under their charge for the most trivial infractions.

For all the drawbacks, it seemed better to be in the shelters than outside them. In bad periods people went to them and stayed put. Bunker life was vile.'Just a few days in the bunker are making people dulled, coarse and indifferent,' wrote a male ambulance worker. 'Initially they are overwrought, then they become grumpy and monosyllabic. They steal things, show no respect for women and children. Any sense of order and cleanliness disappears. People who were formerly well-groomed don't wash or comb their hair for days. Men don't shave. They neglect their clothes. They come [to see me] dirty and stinking. They don't use the lavatories in the bunkers any more but find some dark corner.'

The women, it appeared, were as bad. 'Mothers are neglecting their children . . . About 70 per cent of bunker inmates have the so-called "bunker disease" [scabies] and there is no water, hardly any heating, no opportunities to delouse. I am horrified when I see children, ill with scarlet fever or diphtheria and wrapped in blankets.' From his own observations and the reports of his fellow medical workers it seemed that everyone had lost their dignity and humanity. 'Decent people become like animals after losing house and home, dwelling like cave men in the bunker night and day to escape with nothing but their lives.'[10]

On the night of the great raid, the people of Cologne could feel reasonably confident as they went to bed that they would still be alive in the morning. The sky was overcast which would make life difficult for the *Oboe*-equipped Mosquitoes leading the Pathfinder crews. They would have to drop their target indicators so they lit up above the cloud, a less accurate method than if they ignited on the ground. In fact the cloud cover offered no protection at all.

All together 608 aircraft – Lancasters, Halifaxes, Wellingtons, Stirlings and Mosquitoes – took part in the raid. The Mosquitoes arrived over the target at around 1 a.m. By the time the bombers had departed they had dropped 162,038 incendiaries and 1,084 high explosive bombs, a ratio that increased the chances of creating an inferno. The sixteen heavy flak batteries around the city, supported by the light and medium flak guns on the east bank of the Rhine put up a strong defence but were eventually overwhelmed.

Heinz Pettenberg, a forty-three-year-old journalist, married with three young children, recorded in his diary that the alarm announcing imminent attack sounded at 1.12 a.m. 'Suddenly they are there,' he wrote. 'Engine noise, flak. We had just taken the children into the cellar and had brought the suitcases down and suddenly the raid is in full swing. The air is trembling with the thunder of the four-engined bombers . . . It's 1.30 a.m. and the following fifty-five minutes are an eternity.'[11]

The Pettenbergs lived in the relative safety of the suburb of Lindenthal. In the centre of town, Albert Beckers and his family were cowering in their cellar shelter directly beneath the bombardment. He too noticed the way 'the aircraft engines made the air vibrate. We were like rabbits in a warren. I was worried about the water pipes. What would happen if they burst and we would all be drowned? The air shook with detonations. Stuck in the cellar we hadn't felt the hail of incendiaries but above us everything was ablaze. Now came the second wave, the explosives. You cannot imagine what it is like to cower in a hole when the air quakes, the eardrums burst from the blast, the light goes out, oxygen runs out and dust and mortar crumble from the ceiling.'

As the cellar roof sagged they scrambled through the breach in the wall to the neighbouring shelter. In the midst of the terror there was a moment of grotesque comedy. 'A corpulent woman got stuck and we had to push and pull to get her through. She wailed, and some people were laughing, even in this potentially fatal situation. I prayed loudly, repeatedly. The "Our Father".'

It was clear that if they stayed underground they would be entombed. But at street level they faced incineration. The Beckers family made their choice. They struggled up the cellar steps and outside into the Waidmarkt, a square in the old town overlooked by the church of St Georg. It was a 'dreadful spectacle. Showers of sparks filled the air. Large and small pieces of burning wood floated through the air and landed on clothes and hair.' The fire was eating oxygen. They found a restaurant, crammed with refugees from the flames. Someone found some beer and people were gulping it down to slake their parched throats. A dog was whimpering with fear. It seemed to Beckers that this was no better than what they had escaped from. They set off again, finally staggering into the concrete public bunker on Georgsplatz, 'half blind and poisoned by smoke. It was completely full and wounded were being carried in all the time.' They stayed there until dawn. Then, with the all-clear sounded, they stepped out to look for another refuge, passing on the way 'the shrunken, charred corpses piled in a heap by the tower of St Georg.'[12]

In the panic and the chaos, children were easily separated from their parents. Hans Sester, a fourteen-year-old schoolboy, followed his mother and father, younger brother and sister after they smelled phosphorus smoke from incendiaries seeping into their cellar and ran outside. In the street 'it seemed that the tarmac had caught fire and melted from the phosphorus. Across the street a part of the old orphanage was ablaze and it seemed as if the high wind would whip up the flames even further.' There was a howling in the air, like a hurricane. It was, he learned later, the sound of the blaze devouring the oxygen.

His father, a postman, led them away, carrying his two-year-old daughter, Karin. Stumbling through the smoke they came across a group praying loudly, imploring Jesus to show them compassion. After a few dozen yards Hans became separated from the rest of the family. He was in a street called the Perlengraben, site of the old orphanage. He 'fled down some dark stairs into the air-raid shelter of the orphanage where I was given a drink of water and was able to press a wet hankerchief to my smarting eyes.' The next morning he went out to look for his family and found his six-year-old brother, who had also got lost but had been rescued by a woman. They comforted each other and after fruitlessly looking for their parents on the corpse-strewn Perlengraben, set out across the smoking rubble in the direction of the outlying district of Weiden where their aunt lived. Hans was still blinded by smoke. His little brother led him by the hand.

They waited at Weiden for the rest of the family to show up but they waited in vain. They were all dead. Their mother's body had been found in a wing of the orphanage. Her time of death was given as 2 a.m. The bodies of their father and sister were never identified. Sester never saw his mother's 'charred remains, thank God'.[13] An adolescent schoolgirl, fifteen-year-old Gertrud L, was not so fortunate. She was one of a number of girls asked by the authorities to record their experiences in essays written in the autumn after the raid. She too became separated from her family during the attack and spent the following day searching hopelessly. The next day she tried again. 'A man told me me that my mother and my sister were dead. I could not believe it. Then the man showed me where my mother lay. She was lying on her front, one hand holding her hair. Beside her there were others, headless, charred.' Her sister, whom she had last seen with her mother and who had an infant son, was not there. 'Another man told me that as they lifted my sister out, her child was drawing its last breath. They tried to revive him with oxygen but it was to no avail.' Gertrud tied a piece of paper with her mother's name to the body but it came loose when she was carted away. She was buried as an 'unknown'.[14]

The raid ended at 2.45 a.m. It had lasted ninety-five minutes. A few hours afterwards, Heinz Pettenberg, the journalist, left the safety of the suburbs to survey the damage. Walking in, he passed large numbers of rescue workers drafted in from outside. He soon realized that 'something terrible had happened'. He was 'walking through a destroyed city'. The fires were still burning and the heat was unbearable. Everything he knew and loved in his home town seemed to have been destroyed. His newspaper's office had disappeared. 'At the Bollwerk lie the collapsed ruins of the ancient inn "Zum Krützchen", where we spent so many happy hours . . . there is not one house left on the Heumarkt and the house of my grandparents, Rheingasse 5, has gone . . . on the Waidmarkt, the irreplaceable St Georg in ruins. The Blaubach – rubble, the Postrasse, the Waisenhausgasse, rubble, rubble. One can hardly see anything. The smoke, poisonous, blue-black, drags through the streets . . . from time to time people with swollen eyes appear amidst the clouds of smoke, gasping refugees, holding a few saved possessions. The swollen cadaver of a dead horse lies on the street, and then – a picture of horror – corpses, twisted, barely covered up.' Remembering the thousand-bomber raid of a year before he asked himself, 'What was the thirty-first of May . . . compared with this! I will never forget this terrible walk.'[15]

The city records show nearly 6,500 buildings were destroyed. Of these, 6,368 were houses and apartment buildings, underneath which the population was cowering. A further 3,515 suffered heavy damage. Two hospitals, seventeen churches, twenty-four schools, two theatres, eight cinemas, seven post and telegraph offices, one railway station, six banks and ten hotels were also swept away. The list also includes twenty unspecified 'official buildings,' four 'military installations' and forty-three 'industrial installations'.[16] Given the great breadth of the violence done to Cologne it is hard to see them as anything other than incidental targets. The Gestapo headquarters, in the Appellhofplatz in the middle of town, by some malign miracle, remained intact. The back yard was equipped with a gallows where towards the end of the war civilians and many slave labourers were hanged for petty offences like stealing a cooking pot. The death toll from the bombing established another record. This time 4,377 were killed, nearly ten times more than in the 'thousand' raid, and probably another 10,000 wounded.

Harris was relentless. The people of Cologne were still numb with shock when bombers appeared again. Four days later another major operation was mounted against the industrial areas on the east bank of the Rhine. Some twenty factories were hit along with the homes of the workers who laboured in them. More than 580 were killed and 70,000 bombed out. There was a further attack on 8/9 July in which another 502 civilians died.

As a result of these three raids in a little over a week, 350,000 lost their homes. Some were rehoused in the few inhabitable buildings remaining in Cologne. Many more were evacuated or fled the city and the surrounding area under their own steam. The exodus was desperate and chaotic. Evacuees who had fled to the surrounding countryside had to return to the city to get a train that would take them to safety. 'In Opladen [a small town north of Cologne] the train stops,' a male traveller, Herr Roemer, recorded in his diary entry for 6 July 1943. 'The journey is to continue in buses and after a long wait they finally arrive. Hundreds of people storm [the first] vehicle. Squashed children and women scream, men curse. Everyone is laden down with luggage and boxes. Many are carrying bedding. A few soldiers are sitting on the roof. We drive for an hour to Cologne. Here are thousands of people at the station, on the platform. Next to me is a heavily pregnant woman with two children and luggage. She is weeping bitterly. A train arrives. There is a surging back and forth. The train is overloaded. The platform is still packed with people bickering. The transport police remove some people from the running boards and the locomotive.' When the train reached Bonn a fight broke out in Roemer's compartment. On the wall of another he noticed 'a chalk drawing. A gallows from which hangs a swastika. Everybody sees it but nobody wipes it away.'[17] Many of those who fled the city did not return until the war was over. In 1940 it was the home of 770,00 people. By March 1945, the population was 40,000.

The authorities paid close attention to the mood of the city. The material gleaned by the army of informants who cocked their ears to conversations in streets, shops and workplaces was disquieting. A survey by the SS security service, the *Sicherheitsdienst* (SD), delivered nine days after the attack, reported widespread defeatism and bitterness and cynicism towards the regime.

In the immediate aftermath the Hitler salute was rarely seen. The leaflets that the RAF had showered by the million on Germany finally had a readership. People picked them from the rubble, read them and discussed their contents with their family, friends and workmates, disregarding the dire penalties that could result if they were caught.

Caution was fraying. Suffering made people bold. The authorities were amazed by the lack of circumspection. The strength of the attack was a profound shock to a nation that had been told that the enemy was weak and victory was inevitable. 'Many people are under the impression that [the enemy], in the future development of the war, are actually much stronger and will overcome us,' ran one passage of the report. 'They [think] the outcome of the war is in doubt and people are nervous and feel weighed down by this.' The fear showed in the sour, unfunny jokes: Hitler's favourite singer Zarah Leander has been summoned to Berlin. She is going to sing her most famous hit for the Führer – 'I Know One Day A Miracle Will Come'.

But the Nazis could take some comfort from the fact that the raid had created anger as well as despondency. The attack on Cologne cathedral had provoked particular indignation and vengeful feelings. The fact that the thirteenth-century Gothic masterpiece had only been damaged rather than destroyed made little difference. For many a devout *Kölner*, the sight of the smoke-blackened spires provoked rage. 'This is the worst thing they have done yet,' a labourer was quoted as saying in the SS report. 'I don't know much about culture but I want to smash the heads of the English for this.' It was just the sentiment on the lips of people in Coventry nearly three years previously when their cathedral had been blitzed.

For others, the damage done to this great symbol of faith seemed like a portent. It was a sign that 'God had turned his face away from the Germans' or a punishment for the destruction of the temples of the Jews.

The fear caused by the St Peter and St Paul raid rippled outwards across Germany. The refugees who fled Cologne to all corners of the Reich took their stories with them. The SD reports from Franconia, far away in the south, spoke of a 'panic-like fear of the Anglo-American air war and its expected consequences'. They noted 'growing nervousness and anxiety at the fact that the enemy seem to have the upper hand in the air and at our own powerlessness'. The utterances of the Party high-ups were given little credence. People preferred to get their news now from Swiss radio rather than official broadcasts. Around Stuttgart, morale was said to be 'under pressure'. Overflights by Allied aircraft increased the sense of dread amongst those below and the feeling that it would be their turn next.[18]

The raids, then, seemed to be having the desired effect. Factories were being flattened and vast acreages of housing reduced to blackened rubble. The long rows of coffins laid out for the official mass burial ceremonies left no one in the Ruhr in any doubt that the war had arrived on their doorstep and they were as exposed to death as their husbands, brothers and fathers on the Eastern Front. People were frightened. More than 28,000 fled Aachen after a raid in mid-July that killed only 294 people. Seven weeks later most of them had failed to return.

As the Battle of the Ruhr progressed the area's defences inevitably improved making operations increasingly dangerous. By the end of May, Harris had 800 aircraft at his immediate disposal, four fifths of which were four-engined bombers. Germany was full of attractive targets. Concentrating on the Ruhr meant that much of the rest of urban Germany was having a quiet time. To preserve his resources and to maintain the principle that all Germany should feel the lash of the bomber offensive, it was necessary to move on.

Hamburg was an obvious target for another spectacular. It had been chosen for the first 'thousand' raid until the weather forecast ruled it out. It was the second-biggest city in Germany with a population of 1.8 million and the country's most important port. Ships were built there including U-boats. Despite all this, and the fact that it was reasonably easy to identify due to its proximity to the Baltic coast, it had so far got off lightly. It had been attacked ninety-eight times by Bomber Command since the beginning of the war but with little serious effect.

At the end of July the Battle of the Ruhr was over and the Battle of Hamburg was about to begin. The plan envisaged four major raids over ten nights in which 10,000 tons of bombs were to be dropped. The first came on the night of 24/25 July. Practice had intensified the concentration of aircraft in the target area and reduced their time in the danger zone so that on this night the 728 aircraft which reached Hamburg were able to drop 2,284 tons of bombs in fifty minutes. Defences were baffled by the use for the first time of *Window*, bundles of aluminium foil which were dumped out of special chutes cut in the bombers' fuselages and which, for a time at least, baffled the radar operators who could not decide whether or not the blips they made on their screens represented aircraft.

The city was well beyond the range of *Oboe*. This may have reduced the accuracy of the bombardment. By now there was a well-established tendency for the bombing to 'creep back' as crews dropped their loads into the first fires and smoke they saw, spreading the zone of destruction backwards from the target. On this raid it was six miles long. The central and north-western districts of the city suffered badly and 1,200 people were killed.

The following day there were more aeroplanes over the smoking city. These were the B-17 Flying Fortresses of the American Eighth Air Force making their first appearance in support of an RAF operation. The huge plumes of smoke hanging in the air made it impossible for them to identify the industrial targets they had been ordered to destroy. They returned the following day but then withdrew from the battle, leaving it to the Lancasters, Halifaxes, Stirlings and Wellingtons.

The second raid followed seventy-two hours after the first. The Pathfinders' marking was slightly off the city-centre aiming-point but the bombing was tightly concentrated and the 2,326 bombs dropped fell within a small radius.

The bomb load was made up of 50 per cent incendiaries, less than normal, but the effect it created was extraordinary. The night was hot and dry and the fires that sprang up charged through the working-class areas of Hammerbrook, Hamm and Borgfeld, devouring everything combustible. The exhausted fire services could do nothing to slow them and the blazes only began subsiding when there was nothing left for them to consume.

The death toll dwarfed anything yet achieved by Bomber Command. Some 40,000 people died, most of them asphyxiated by carbon dioxide after the fire leached all the oxygen from the air, sucking it from the shelters. The two following raids on 29/30 July and 2/3 August killed only 387. Almost everyone else had fled.

This was by far the most terrible blow suffered by German civilians since the beginning of the war. In his report on the catastrophe, the police president of Hamburg abandoned bureaucratic prose and admitted his difficulty in finding words to describe what had happened. 'Speech is impotent to portray the measure of the horror,' he wrote. Each night of attack was followed by 'a day which

Aftermath of a firestorm. Hamburg, July 1943.

displayed the horror in the dim and unreal light of a sky hidden in smoke ... the streets were covered with hundreds of corpses. Mothers with their children, youths, old men, burnt, charred, untouched and clothed, naked with a waxen pallor like dummies in a shop window they lay in every posture, quiet and peaceful or cramped, the death struggle shown in the expression on their faces.' The picture inside the shelters was 'even more horrible in its effect, as it showed in many cases the final distracted struggle against a merciless fate. Although in some places shelterers sat quietly, peacefully and untouched as if sleeping in their chairs, killed without pain or realization by carbon monoxide poisoning, in other shelters the position of remains of bones and skulls showed how the occupants had fought to escape from their buried prison.'

In the minds of the authorities, at least, the victims of the raids were martyrs. 'Posterity,' wrote the police chief, 'can only bow its head in honour of the fate of these innocents, sacrificed by the murderous lust of a sadistic enemy.' If the British had hoped to create chaos and despair they had not succeeded as 'the conduct of the population, which at no time and nowhere showed panic or even signs of panic . . . was worthy of the magnitude of the disaster.' Instead there was 'an irresistible will to rebuild'.[19] German civilians suffered terribly in the summer of 1943. The RAF had achieved a scale of destruction that far surpassed anything that been seen in the history of aerial warfare. But whether or not the population was approaching a state of paralysing moral collapse was impossible to tell and the question was not about to be settled.

8

The Reasons Why

In the course of their tours, airmen seldom talked about the value of bombing or the morality of what they were engaged in. If they had doubts, they tended to keep them to themselves. They were fighting a sharply focused war. They had a public obligation to carry out the duty they had volunteered for. They had a duty to themselves to survive. These realities created a cast of mind that could make them seem impervious to all other considerations.

A few hours before his first mission, an apprehensive Peter Johnson joined a large crowd in the briefing room. They were addressed by a WAAF intelligence officer, 'a formidable lady who minced no words'. The target, yet again, was the Krupp works in Essen.

'Yes, they've been damaged,' she shouted over the chorus of groans and expletives. 'But make no mistake, they're still turning out guns and shells aimed at you.' She predicted that the defences would be stronger than ever, giving details of the known searchlight and flak dispositions. '"They're going to give you HELL," she spat. "See that you give it them back!"' She sat down 'visibly affected by her own vehemence'.

Johnson found this performance distasteful coming from a non-combatant but he was impressed by the dangers she had so forcefully described. Looking around at the others he was surprised to see that they seemed 'almost totally untouched by what they had heard'. Many had their eyes closed. Their concerns were simply 'the details of route and navigation, which colour of target indicator they were to bomb and what they could do to make sure they arrived on time and got home safely.' He concluded that 'while the fierce lady was probably convinced that she was striking a significant blow in the great struggle, for the bulk of her audience she was whistling in the wind.'[1]

The face the Bomber Boys showed to the world was sardonic and displays of patriotic enthusiasm were considered *infra dig*. It was an ethos that did not encourage self-regard. The contrast with the Americans was marked. One Sunday night in the autumn of 1944 Ken Newman and his comrades sat down to watch a film in the anteroom of the officers' mess at Little Staughton. A few USAAF officers were also present. The movie celebrated the fictional feats of a band of American aviators who volunteer to fly B17s in Europe. 'All the RAF officers present were nearly doubled up with laughter at this rubbishy Hollywood propaganda,' he wrote. 'But when the lights were put on the faces of the USAAF aircrew were a picture – it was all too clear that they had taken the film completely seriously and identified themselves with the actors. They were visibly moved and tears were streaming from their eyes; ours too but for a very different reason.'[2]

Their studied coolness did not mean that the crews did not think about what they were doing. The reserve masked a solid belief in the virtue of the cause. With a very few exceptions, the men of Bomber Command accepted that Germany had wantonly provoked a war then prosecuted it with a ruthlessness and fanaticism that justified almost any amount of retaliation in kind. By the end of 1943, German civilian casualties far outstripped those that the Luft-waffe had inflicted so far on Britain, but any notion of proportion-ality had long disappeared.

It was one of Hitler's great negative achievements that he suc-ceeded in hardening the hearts of men to whom violence was unnatural and repellent. The sense that what they were doing was essential pervaded Bomber Command. Like many others, Michael Scott, a navigator with 110 Squadron, recoiled at the idea of killing yet he had volunteered for the RAF knowing that he was putting himself in exceptional danger. He was a sensitive, music-loving intellectual who taught at Cheam, where the children of the elite were prepared for the best public schools. He wrote short stories and thought of himself as an anarchist. He was sceptical about

Britain's motivations, believing that the desire to 'retain our spoils from foreign conquests' outweighed the commitment to freedom. The spectre of a Nazi-ruled world dispelled his doubts. He set out his reasons for joining up in a letter to his father, to be opened in the event of his death.

'Dear Daddy,' he wrote. 'You know how I hated the idea of war and that hate will remain with me for ever. What has kept me going is the spiritual force to be derived from music, its reflections of my own feelings and the power it has to uplift the soul above earthly things . . . now I am off to the source of music and can fulfil all the vague longings of my soul in becoming part of the fountain whence all good comes. I have no belief in a personal God but I *do* believe most strongly in a spiritual force which was the source of our being and which will be our ultimate goal. If there is anything worth fighting for it is the right to follow our own paths to this goal and to prevent our children from having their souls sterilized by Nazi doctrines . . . And so I have been fighting.' Scott was killed during a daylight minelaying trip near Texel on 24 May 1941.[3]

Not many of those taking part talked or wrote like Scott. Even though they might have shared his conviction that they were engaged in a fundamental struggle between good and evil, they were unlikely to express such sentiments in public. In the pubs and the canteens the conversation was more likely to be about girls and beer than death and war. It was part of an RAF culture of studied light-heartedness. Reg Fayers lamented the lack of discussion about the aims of the campaign. 'I feel we should all be alight . . . with a flame to inspire us on this crusade to save whatever-it-is. But nobody is.'[4]

Even Fayers did not claim to know precisely what it was they were fighting for. If anything, it was a desire to maintain a way of life that the Nazis were dedicated to destroying. 'I'm fighting so that in the future people will have the chance to live as happily as we did all together before the war without interference,' wrote Eric Rawlings, a twenty-one-year-old from north London, to his parents before his death in 1942. 'Where young 'uns like myself could make the most of the marvellous opportunities which you gave me for twenty years and for which I know you made many, many sacrifices. God bless you all and may everything turn out right in the end.'5

Everyone knew what they were fighting against. The memory of the Blitz persisted as a bitter inspiration long after the German assault had faded out at the end of May 1941. Roy MacDonald, a mid-upper gunner with the PFF, was doing his basic training at Uxbridge when the attacks began. 'One night I got caught up in it and had to sleep down on Piccadilly platform. The raid was tremendous. Then . . . I was posted up to West Kirby just in time for the Blitz on Merseyside and so I saw plenty of what they were doing to us . . . the idea was that if we could keep on doing it back they would pack up or finish the war . . . I'd no conscience about what we were doing, none at all. I don't think anybody did. It had to be done. That was the way we looked at it anyway.'6

After the invasion of the Soviet Union in June 1941 the Luftwaffe was able to mount only occasional raids against Britain. These, together with the V1 and V2 rocket attacks of 1944 and 1945, did little damage to the war effort or morale, but they kept the spirit of revenge sharp and bright. Sergeant Bernard Dye, an air gunner with 622 Squadron, lost his best friend in a German raid in April 1942. 'Nick was my best pal,' he wrote afterwards.

> We were brought up together and played together. We joined youth organizations and had some good fun. He was liked by all. It was a bright and sunny morning . . . my pal was on his way to work. He probably was whistling or humming a tune to himself. He was always happy in life. Then it happened, out of the clear blue sky [came] the Nazi bombers . . . then came the whistle of bombs, red-hot shrapnel was flung far and wide, people fell to the ground and got up no more. My pal Nick was hit in the back, he died some six hours later a lingering death. Nick was a good pal the best you could get. I cannot realize he is gone. When I'm sitting behind my guns I will remember Nick. Nick couldn't hit back, he

was helpless. But I will hit the Huns, hit hard too. I will
get my revenge for my dear Pal Nick who was buried
today.[7]

For George Hull and his crew the violence they were inflicting on
Germany was meant personally. Writing to brown-eyed, brown-
haired Joan Kirby on 16 February 1944 after returning from Berlin
he told her that they always dedicated their 'cookie', the biggest
bomb in a normal load, 'to someone or something. There was the
first on Berlin, reprisals for John [Joan's brother killed in a bomber
training accident], with an extra on Frankfurt for both John and his
Dad. There have been cookies from the people of Australia, the
people of Manchester the people of London etc. But tonight's effort
was dedicated to all the brown-eyed brunettes we know (don't ask
me for all their names!).'

Ten days later he was on his way to Schweinfurt when the route
took him over London while a raid was in progress. It made him
'burn with rage . . . I thought of your folks and mine underneath it
all and I would not have turned back if we had caught fire.' Hull's
decency caused him to reflect on the 'ultimate futility of all this
slaughter'. But such thoughts were stifled easily by his hatred of the
German regime. 'I never lose sight of the fact that if our feelings
rule our judgement we might suffer terrible consequences. Think of
it. Nazis in Britain, desecrating our land, destroying those beautiful
things that you and I hold dear, fouling our women in brothels,
wholesale slaughter – perhaps your dad shot for not obeying an
order or my mother forced to billet German officers while suffering
insults. It's true. Can you see the Nazis sparing Britain, the country
above all which held out against them and turned the tables?'

He was writing having just landed and was suffering from a 'post
ops headache'. He felt 'washed out completely and as usual fed up
to the back teeth.' But glowing through the fog of weariness there
is a burning determination to carry on. 'Of course I hate the job but
idealism is not enough. I am fighting for the people I love and the
boys who have already paid the full price. To give in to matters on
ideological grounds is to let them all down.'[8]

The campaign could, in one sense, be regarded as a continuous act of retribution for those who had died, on the ground and in the air. The survivors felt a strong impulse to avenge dead comrades. By striking back they were exacting a price for their loss and investing it with value and meaning. 'There was [this] feeling that those who were left would carry on,' said Jim Berry, a Pathfinder pilot.[9] One bomber from 467 Squadron was named 'Jock's Revenge' after a flight engineer who had been killed while flying in her. As he dropped his bombs on Duisburg on his first mission, Ken Newman thought of his 'brother-in-law Victor and his now fatherless son'. Victor had been killed in a Halifax over Magdeburg, leaving behind a wife who was five months pregnant.[10]

Berlin's heavy defences and great distance away made it an unpopular target. But there was some satisfaction in knowing that they were bringing the war to the Führer's front door. 'There was something special about attacking the Big City,' wrote Peter Johnson. 'The feelings were partly . . . fuelled by the picture of Hitler himself, cowering there below in his bunker.'[11]

But it was not Hitler who was suffering. Looking down from his rear gunner's turret at the towns and villages of Lincolnshire as he headed off to bomb Böhlen, Cy March could not help comparing the tiny figures in the streets below to those he was going to attack. 'We took off . . . vowing to do as much damage to Germany as we could. We set course to the East and I noticed that over this [part of the] country the blackout wasn't so good, doors opening etc. I got to wondering about the people below us, going for a pint, meeting a bird for the flicks, and the people we were going to. Probably doing the same, but in for a nasty shock.'[12]

By the end of 1942 no one was in any doubt about the effect the bombs were having. It was not hard to imagine how the victims felt. Tom Wingham, a navigator with 102 Squadron, remembered looking down on his first trip to the Ruhr. 'It was quite a ghastly sight to see the amount of flame and explosions . . . I made up my mind that if ever I had to bale out over the target, I wouldn't. I would rather go down with the aircraft because I was sure that if you landed in that, the populace would tear you to bits.'[13]

Some commanders, like Harry Yates's New Zealander CO Jack Leslie, seemed to revel in the damage they were doing. 'I want you to really burn this place,' he told 75 Squadron before an operation on the Lens marshalling yards in the summer of 1944, signing off with: 'See you in the smoke.' These last five words, Yates remembered, 'were to become very familiar to us. Some of Jack Leslie's more gung-ho briefings could be strong meat. Exhortations to blast this and burn that and descriptions of the enemy as vermin or bastards left no doubt about the CO's fighting spirit or the commitment he required from his men.'[14]

Some crews appreciated the bloodthirsty approach. Doug Mourton of 102 Squadron remembered that 'the first time we were given a civilian target to bomb I must say that the majority of the aircrew there raised a cheer because I suppose so many of them had come from towns that [had suffered]. Many of them probably had relations that had been killed in the indiscriminate German bombing and they were very pleased to be doing the same thing.'

Mourton did not share this attitude. As his tour progressed he grew increasingly uneasy about what he was doing. At one point he thought of refusing to fly 'because I hadn't volunteered to incinerate women and children.' He was persuaded to carry on by the argument that 'this type of bombing . . . would make the war end quicker and . . . more lives would be saved than sacrificed.'[15] Willie Lewis was also tempted to revolt when on 29 May 1943 he learned that the target for the night was Wuppertal, thirty miles south of Essen. The briefing officer did not disguise the fact that it was crammed with refugees from the Battle of the Ruhr. According to his account he informed his skipper John Maze that he had 'a good mind not to come'.

He told him that 'up to now, I've kidded myself that I was fighting a man's war risking my neck killing men and being shot at in return but what the hell do they call this? It's deliberate murder of the sort that we've called the Jerries names for for the last three years.' He felt strongly the 'confounded hypocrisy' of the situation. 'There's that Air Marshal type talking on the radio telling everyone what brutes the Germans are and how we wouldn't dream of doing anything like it ourselves and yet we arrange a trip like this.' Maze, with his usual pragmatism, replied that by refusing to go he would be 'branded as yellow, that's all' and declared to be lacking in moral fibre. Lewis bowed to his skipper's worldly logic, blustering that he would 'never pretend that we are nice clean little boys doing a respectable job from now on. We are only mean bastards taking orders from a bunch of hypocrites.'[16] Lewis's premonitions about Wuppertal were well founded. The town was only lightly defended. The PFF marking was excellent and the incendiaries that whistled down on the flares sparked a minor firestorm which burned down 80 per cent of the built-up area. About 3,800 people were killed, almost all of them civilians.

Lewis's finer feelings were eclipsed by the horrors of the trip. At one point T-Tommy was coned by searchlights but managed to wriggle free. Another Halifax half a mile in front was not so lucky. Watching the flak bursting around the doomed aircraft as a fighter hosed it with cannon fire Lewis felt a guilty thrill of relief that they had escaped, then foolish as he remembered that only that morning he had 'been feeling sorry for the Germans'.[17]

As he had pointed out, it was sometimes difficult to overlook the similarities between the crimes with which the Germans were constantly charged and some of Bomber Command's activities. Charles Patterson, now flying a Mosquito for the RAF Film Unit, was tasked with taking cine pictures of the immediate aftermath of a daylight raid on a steelworks at Denain in northern France. At his group commander's suggestion he also dropped some bombs of his own. There were different delays on the fuses from half an hour to twenty-four hours. 'If a German had done it to us,' he said later, 'we would have said [it was] frightfully caddish and wicked and unsporting. But when we did it to the Germans it was considered rather clever and imaginative.'[18]

The demands of operational life did not encourage reflection. Johnny Jones, a rear gunner with 467 Squadron, found his conscience stirring as he bombed Munich on the night of 7/8 January 1945. 'It must have been hell on earth for the poor devils down below,' he wrote in his dairy. 'Mass murder. Whole families wiped out no doubt. I could not help but think when the bombs left the a/c [aircraft] what a terrible thing I am doing. It must be *wrong*.' Five weeks later he took part in the great raid on Dresden. On this occasion his diary records only that the 'damage done must have been colossal'.[19]

Sitting in a prisoner of war camp with almost nothing to do, protracted contemplation came more easily. Geoffrey Willatt, taken prisoner after being shot down on his way to Mannheim on the night of 5/6 September 1943, ended up in Stalag-Luft 3 near Bremen. In the spring of 1944 he noted in his diary the deteriorating behaviour of one of his friends. 'Suddenly George seems much worse and I hadn't realized how bad he was till one day he took me to a secluded place and burst into tears! It appears, or at least he says, that at the beginning of the war he nearly turned conscientious objector and now worries about all the women and children he's killed ... he began by being vague and preoccupied, then was unable to concentrate on anything, had a short period of religion which did him no good at all and then a period of self-persecution (cold showers, running round the circuit till exhausted etc.).'

Willatt diagnosed an acute case of 'barbed wire psychosis' and asked him why the deaths he had caused weighed on his mind 'when there are thousands of other aircrew prisoners who don't worry. I tell him he must live a useful life after the war but his mind won't now function enough to argue it all.'

Despite the well-intentioned interventions of the other prisoners in his hut George's mental condition continued to deteriorate. 'No one dare look at him because it gives him a hunted feeling & yet everyone is being too kind to him – an embarrassing feeling for him I know and no help.' He spent a few days in the camp hospital but seemed even worse on his return. 'He walked up and down the room five steps each way for half an hour with his head in his hands. We take it in turns to follow him when he goes out – so afraid that he'll jump over the wire and get shot.' Eventually George was taken away to the German mental hospital at Lamsdorf with two other prisoners.

Willatt's recipe for staying sane was exercise and the suppression of barren reflection. 'I haven't yet heard of a person going "round the bend" who took part regularly in games,' he noted after George was taken away. As for guilt, it was pointless debating the rights and wrongs until the war was over.[20]

Peter Johnson was in a persistent anguish of doubt about what he was doing. He was born in 1909, joined the RAF in 1930 and lived through the fear and moral confusion that accompanied the rise of the dictators. He had struggled against the anti-German feeling that gripped Britain in the pre-war years, an attitude that survived even the invasion of Poland, but not the attack on the Low Countries. After that he 'hated Hitler and hated the Germans who loved him'.

Nonetheless the first 'thousand' raids made him uneasy. They seemed to have more in common with the Blitz than the precision attacks like the raid on the Renault works at Billancourt, the event that had inspired him to volunteer for ops. A book of drawings by a Polish refugee, Joseph Bato, tugged at his conscience. They were simple, understated sketches of London districts just after the Germans had visited. One showed a terraced house whose front had been torn away, 'exposing to the street the shattered remains of the quiet, decent life that went on in [it].'

Writing to his girlfriend Shelagh in the summer of 1943 Johnson voiced his hesitation in language that revealed the depth of his doubt.

> Of course the Royal Air Force aims for military objectives, but ... I swear to you my sweet, that nothing that ever happened in London in any way approached what I saw in Dortmund ... no German pilot ever looked down on London and saw the obscene red mass of flames that was Dortmund last month or Hamburg last week. And this is only the beginning, for nothing can stop us now. Nothing but the end of the war can stop the destruction of practically every city in Germany, destruction that will make Bato's drawings look like the record of a peevish child bored with its bricks.

On one occasion Johnson let his feelings slip in public. Shortly after taking over 49 Squadron in April 1943 he was summoned to 5 Group headquarters near Grantham to look after a VIP guest. The visitor was Sir Kingsley Wood, the chancellor of the exchequer, who had served as secretary of state for air before the war. Johnson's job was to take him through each step of a raid. Wood was to stay at the base until the aircraft had returned and the crews were debriefed. During the evening he was shown some reconnaissance photographs taken after an attack on Düsseldorf a few weeks previously. The chancellor, a cheerful, Pickwickian figure, seemed very satisfied with what he saw. Johnson had viewed a few post-ops photos but nothing like these. 'Seen through the stereoscopic glass the detail was staggeringly clear, showing just rows and rows of apparently empty boxes which had been houses. They had no roofs or content. This had been a crowded residential area, long streets of terraced houses in an orderly right-angled arrangement, covering virtually the whole of the six-inch square photograph. There were one or two open spaces but the chief impression was just those rows and rows of empty shells, a huge dead area where once thousands of human beings had lived.'

Johnson heard himself saying: 'God! The Germans will never forgive us for this.' In an instant the chancellor's cheery demeanour vanished. '"What do you mean, forgive *us?*" he snapped. "Let me tell you, it's we who'll have to forgive the Germans and what's more I hope we don't do it too quickly."'[21]

Wood was only saying what most people felt. That did not mean that there was no controversy about the morality of the bombing campaign. There were politicians and churchmen who shared Johnson's moral discomfort. It was one of Harris's rough virtues that he never tried to disguise the aims or consequences of his strategy. The government, however, consistently avoided admitting the full truth about its policy and persistently refused to acknowledge that one of the main purposes of much of Bomber Command's actions was the destruction of cities themselves. The critics of area bombing were led by Richard Stokes, the loquacious Labour MP for Ipswich. Stokes had no faith in strategic bombing, arguing that the war effort would be better spent in building more ships and fighters, nor in the view that sustained bombing could crush Germany's spirit. As early as May 1942, he told the Commons: 'I have been through practically every raid in London and to most of the places that have been badly blitzed and I do not believe for a single moment that you are ever going to destroy the morale of the people by bombing from the air.' The idea that Germany could be brought down by bombing, he concluded 'is absolutely puerile'.[22]

But the core of his objections to the strategic air campaign bombing was ethical. The bombing of Cologne was not only 'strategic lunacy' but 'morally wrong as no real effort was made to limit the targets to military objectives ... women and little children are women and little children to me, wherever they live.' A further immorality, Stokes, argued was that the architects of the campaign were asking good men to do dreadful things. 'It fills me with absolute nausea,' he said 'to think of the filthy task that many of our young men are being invited to carry out.'[23]

Stokes tried repeatedly to get the government to admit what was going on. On 31 March 1943 he asked the secretary of state for air whether 'on any occasion instructions had been given to British airmen to engage in area bombing rather than limit their attention to purely military targets.' Sir Archibald Sinclair replied that 'the targets of Bomber Command are always military, but night bombing of objectives necessarily involves bombing the area in which they are situated.'[24] When he repeated the question in a slightly different form on 1 December, asking him whether 'the policy of limiting objectives of Bomber Command to targets of military importance has or has not been changed to the bombing of towns and wide areas in which military targets are situated' he was referred to the previous statement.

Concerns about the campaign were also felt at the opposite end of the political spectrum. In November 1943 the Marquess of Salisbury, a Tory grandee, wrote privately to Sinclair in a troubled frame of mind. He was full of praise for the bravery of the bomber crews but was worried by Harris's assertion that the campaign would go on 'until the heart of Nazi Germany ceases to beat'. Salisbury wanted reassurance that this did not give the lie to the government's repeated assertions that only military and industrial targets were being bombed. The letter asserted that 'there is a great deal of evidence that makes some of us afraid that we are losing moral superiority to the Germans . . . of course the Germans began it, but we do not take the devil as our example.' Three days later Sinclair responded. 'Our aim [he wrote] is the progressive dislocation of the German military, industrial and economic system. I have never pretended that it is possible to pursue this aim without inflicting terrible casualties on the civilian population of Germany. But neither I, nor any responsible spokesman on behalf of the government, has ever gloated over the destruction of German homes.' This smooth reply made no mention of the several directives issued to Bomber Command in which the destruction of the morale of the German people was identified as a central objective.[25]

There were dissenting voices from the established Church. The most serious critic was George Bell, the Bishop of Chichester, who on 9 February 1944 used his secular pulpit in the House of Lords to dissect government policy. Bell was a veteran anti-Nazi and no pacifist. He accepted that in attacking military and industrial targets the killing of civilians was inevitable. However, he told his fellow-peers, there had to be a fair balance between the means employed and the purpose achieved. 'To obliterate a whole town because certain portions contain military and industrial establishments is to reject the balance,' he said. Despite the official sophistry, Bell understood what was going on, even if others did not.

'I doubt whether it is sufficiently realized,' he said, 'that it is no longer definite military and industrial objectives which are the aim of the bombers but the whole town, area by area, is plotted carefully out. This area is singled out and plastered on one night; that area is singled out and plastered on another night . . . how can there be discrimination in such matters when civilians, monuments, military objectives and industrial objectives all together form the target?'[26]

Stokes accepted that his was an unpopular view in parliament but insisted that he spoke for a substantial minority outside it. On

27 May 1943 he asked Deputy Prime Minister Clement Attlee if he was aware that 'a growing volume of opinion in this country considers indiscriminate bombing of civilian centres is both morally wrong and strategic lunacy?' This prompted the Labour member for Doncaster, Evelyn Walkden, to disagree. He declared that whatever Stokes might think 'the rest of the country admire the RAF.' Attlee observed that Walkden 'probably more accurately represents the views of [the people] than the hon. member for Ipswich [Stokes].'[27]

If by that he meant that the great majority of people were squarely behind the campaign he was right. Speaking in support of Bell in the Lords debate Lord Lang of Lambeth, who had recently retired as archbishop of Canterbury, deplored the idea that anyone should 'gloat' over the unfortunate necessity of destroying military objectives and their surrounding neighbourhoods, or regard it as 'worthy of almost jubilant congratulations'. However he seemed to see 'a good many signs of the spread of this particular mood . . . amongst some of our people.' He had recently received a 'fairly full correspondence where the language in which this mood is expressed is to me shocking.' The letters were not from cranks and fanatics but from 'apparently, sane and sober citizens. This is the kind of thing – "Let them have it, they did it to us, let us do it to them tenfold, pay them back in their own coin," and all the language with which we are all too familiar.'[28]

Whatever the misgivings of some clerics and brave mavericks like Stokes, most British people felt no guilt about laying Germany waste. They were not inclined to draw a distinction between Germany and the Nazi state. Their attitude was reflected in a parable written by J. B. Priestley which appeared early in the war and was widely and approvingly circulated. 'In the middle of a great civilized continent,' it began, 'far from the sea which brings a breath of the outer world to freshen men's minds, secret people dwell. Ever and ever again they become crazed with a spell of hero worship. A leader arises among them who tells them they are greater than the other peoples of the world.' The secret people of Germany 'are worse than fools in their folly. When the madness comes upon them, out leaps a primitive, barbarian, beast-like instinct. They kill without pity, rejoicing in blood.' It ended with a very un-British exhortation. 'The Hun is at the gate. He will slaughter the women and the children . . . out then and kill . . . the extermination of the wild animal is the plain business of Europe's citizens.'[29]

As the most visible participants in the war against the Germans, the bomber crews had the overwhelming approval of those they were fighting for. It was essential in sustaining their morale. To ordinary people they were bathed in the same heroic light as the fighter pilots of the Battle of Britain who had gone before them and there were few ethical hesitations about the work they were doing. They were regarded as the finest of their generation, noble and self-sacrificing, who were dying in the defence of everything that mattered. 'Andrew will always be remembered by all who knew him as the one of the best of our young men,' wrote the Rev. T. G. Eakins to the parents of Sergeant A. J. N. Wilson, killed on the night of 11/12 June 1943 over Holland, after only two previous trips. 'He was a man of vision and high ideals . . . with a very great love of his home, his parents, his sisters and brother and all the things worthwhile in life. His love of these was so great that he was prepared to sacrifice even himself in order that they might be kept safe.'

Another letter of condolence from Dorothy Courtney Roberts, a family friend, recorded her pride that she 'knew him first as a boy at home and then as a Royal Air Force pilot – manly and with high ideals. That is how I shall always think of him . . . God grant that we shall never forget the sacrifice that he with so many others made for us and our country.'[30]

A waiting father's anxiety and pre-emptive grief could be numbed a little by the thought that if his boy had been killed he had died in a great cause. Writing in February 1945 to Squadron Leader the Rev. George Martin, the Pathfinder Group chaplain who tirelessly corresponded in detail with every grieving mother, father, wife, sibling and sweetheart, Mr Seymour Legge still did not know whether his son was dead or alive. He was prepared for the worst. 'We feel that the country would lose as well as ourselves if this should be the last we ever hear from him,' he wrote. 'He had no need to enter the RAF as he was in a reserved occupation. But after the loss of his wife in the 1940 air raids, he felt he could delay no longer. He is one of those who make this land of ours worth preserving.'[31] His son, Flying Officer K. C. S. Legge, disappeared without trace while on a Mosquito sortie to Berlin.

The RAF had from the beginning been well aware of the propaganda value of its operations. The RAF Film Unit had a staff of cameramen who went along on selected raids and provided dramatic pictures for the newsreels. Newspapers and the BBC covered Bomber Command's work in reverential detail and romanticized those who flew in it. Even the left-wing *New Statesman* magazine presented the crews as 'Glamour Boys', a title previously bestowed on the pilots of Fighter Command whose virtue had been unquestionable. Newspaper and radio correspondents sometimes accompanied the crews on raids taking the same risks and dying the same deaths. On the night of 2/3 December 1943, J. M. B. Grieg of the *Daily Mail* and Norman Stockton of the *Sydney Sun* were killed in separate aircraft with 460 Squadron on a raid on Berlin.

The BBC took a more detached approach than the newspapers, and correspondents were urged to report the bombing campaign in a 'scientific' way. The corporation took its time getting one of its men aboard a bomber. The first to accompany a crew on a Bomber Command raid was Richard Dimbleby, who went with Guy Gibson in a 106 Squadron attack on Berlin on the night of 16/17 January 1943. The capital had not been bombed for more than a year. Despite the BBC's strictures, Dimbleby's broadcast left no doubt about his admiration for the Bomber Boys and the justice of their fight. They took off from Syerston just after 4.30 p.m. 'It was a big show as heavy bomber ops go,' he reported later. 'It was also quite a long raid as the Wing Commander who took me [Gibson] stayed over Berlin for half an hour. The flak was hot but it has been hotter. For me it was a pretty hair-raising experience and I was glad when it was over though I wouldn't have missed it for the world. But we must all remember that these men do it as a regular routine job.'

The journey out was relatively uneventful. But they 'knew well enough when [they] were approaching Berlin'.

There was a complete ring of powerful searchlights, waving and crossing. Though it seemed to me that when many of our bombers were over the city, many of our lights were doused. There was also intense flak. First of all they didn't seem to be aiming at us. It was bursting away to starboard and away to port in thick yellow clusters and dark, smoky puffs. As we turned in for our first run across the city it closed right around us. For a moment it seemed impossible that we could miss it. And one burst lifted us in the air as if a giant hand had pushed up the belly of the machine. But we flew on, and just then another Lancaster dropped a load of incendiaries. And where a moment before there had been a dark patch of the city, a dazzling silver pattern spread itself. A rectangle of brilliant lights, hundreds, thousands of them, winking and gleaming and lighting the outlines of the city around them. As though this unloading had been the signal, score after score of fire bombs went down and all over the dark face of the German capital these great incandescent flowerbeds spread themselves. It was a fascinating sight. As I watched and tried to photograph the flares with a cine camera, I saw the pinpoints merge and the white glare turning to a dull, ugly red as the fires of bricks and mortars and wood spread from the chemical flares. We flew over the city three times for more than half an hour while the guns sought us out and failed to hit us. At last our bomb-aimer sighted his objective below, and for one unpleasant minute we flew steady and straight. Then he pressed the button and the biggest bomb of the evening, our three-and-a-half-tonner, fell away and down. I didn't see it burst but I know what a giant bomb does and I couldn't help wondering whether anywhere in the area of its devastation, such a man as Hitler, Goering or Himmler or Goebbels might be cowering in a shelter. It was engrossing to realize that the Nazi leaders and their ministries were only a few thousand feet from us. And that this shimmering mass of flares and bombs and gun flashes was their stronghold.

In this way Dimbleby linked the attack directly to the possible harm it might do to the certified villains of the war. Few of his listeners could have failed to visualize its likely consequences for ordinary Germans. But nor would they have doubted his support for the 'six brave, cool and exceedingly skillful men' he flew with and the righteousness of Bomber Command's campaign. Dimbleby went on to make another nineteen trips, a remarkable feat of courage by a non-combatant.

'Perhaps I am shooting a line for them,' he finished up, 'but I think that somebody ought to. They and their magnificent Lancasters, and all the others like them, are taking the war right into Germany. They have been attacking, giving their lives in attack since the first day of the war ... "Per Ardua ad Astra" is the RAF motto and perhaps I can translate it as "through hardship to the stars". I understand the hardship now. And I'm proud to have seen the stars with them.'[32]

The crews made a good impression on normally sceptical outsiders. Martha Gellhorn, a stern opponent of the glamorization or sentimentalization of war, softened when she came to write her piece for *Collier's* after a week with the crews in November 1943. The Bomber Boys touched her well-hidden maternal side. The pilot of one crew she interviewed just before they took off was 'twenty-one and tall and thin, with a face far too sensitive for this business'. The others were 'polite and kind and far away. Talk was nonsense now. Every man went tight and concentrated into himself, waiting and ready for the job ahead, and the seven of them who were going together made a solid unit, and anyone who had not done what they did and would never go where they were going could not understand and had no right to intrude.' She stayed up to await their return and watched the survivors setting off for breakfast 'with mussed hair and weary faces, dirty sweaters under their flying suits, sleep-bright eyes, making humble comradely little jokes, and eating their saved-up chocolate bars.'[33]

Martha Gellhorn.

Gellhorn, a sophisticated and sceptical American, saw the crews in much the same way as they were viewed by the British public. Their gentle image was a total contrast to the grim task they had been set to do. They were waging a war of aggression, but there was little in their demeanour to show it. Portrayals of them emphasized their passivity, tolerance and innate good nature.

This was nothing more than the truth, judging by an RAF internal recording captured during a raid on Essen in April 1943. The names of the men and the identity of their squadron are not known. The three dominant voices aboard T-Tommy reveal a typical medley of backgrounds and accents. The bomb-aimer sounds what used to be called 'educated'. The navigator speaks in rich Yorkshire. The pilot's genial tones are harder to place but, at a guess, he is from suburban London. The flight engineer, who says only a few words, could be from anywhere. The matter-of-factness everyone displays seems astounding and also rather humbling to modern ears attuned to a risk-free world.

It begins just after they drop their bombs and turn to flee the target area.

> BOMB-AIMER: Bombs gone.
> PILOT: OK.
> NAVIGATOR: Have the bombs gone?
> PILOT: Yes.
> (In the background can be heard the *thump* of flak, which intensifies and slackens throughout the recording. There is also the harsh ebb and flow of oxygenated breathing.)
> NAVIGATOR: OK. Well, I can read my watch in the searchlight. That's 21.54. The idea is to steer oh-two-zero.
> PILOT: Oh-two-zero, OK.
> NAVIGATOR: Flak directly beneath us. And searchlights underneath us too.
> PILOT: Come on T for Tommy. Get cracking.
> NAVIGATOR: Watch your height.
> PILOT: I'm watching everything... How many searchlights would you call that?
> NAVIGATOR: Too many, I reckon.
> PILOT: Couple of thousand.
> NAVIGATOR: Yeah, searching for us... bastards.
> PILOT (as a searchlight fixes them): Oh hell...
> BOMB-AIMER: Certainly illuminates things, don't it?
> PILOT (breathing heavily): Sure does. (Pause.) I could do with a pint.

BOMB-AIMER: They're firing at us now.

PILOT (mildly interested): Are they?

(There is a big explosion.)

PILOT: That's close.

NAVIGATOR: Well, it's coming close, I can feel it.

PILOT: Yes, I can see it.

BOMB-AIMER: Round to port the heading is, skipper.

PILOT: OK.

BOMB-AIMER: If we press on a bit this way we might get out.

PILOT: Yeah.

(There is a *thump thump thump* from passing flak shells.)

PILOT: You could light your fag on any of those.

(The thumping intensifies.)

UNIDENTIFIED VOICE: Wow, that was a bit close.

NAVIGATOR (matter-of-factly): I think we've been hit, personally.

PILOT: [We'll] lose a bit of height.

NAVIGATOR: That was close.

PILOT: Yeah.

BOMB-AIMER: Searchlights looking for us now. We're pressing on more or less on course.

PILOT: Righty ho.

NAVIGATOR: We'd better press on north until we're clear of this issue.

PILOT: Yes, that's what I'm doing.

(*Thump thump.*)

BOMB-AIMER: Hallo skipper. We've been holed in the front here. There's oil leaking out of the front turret but it's nothing to worry about.

PILOT: OK. . . (To the flight engineer) Could you glance over the temperatures of the engines?

FLIGHT ENGINEER: Could I what?

PILOT: Glance over the temperatures. . . Were we smack on the target today?

BOMB-AIMER: I don't think so. Searchlight on you.

NAVIGATOR: It seemed to be all right to me.

BOMB-AIMER: There's a few searchlights ahead, about a hundred.

NAVIGATOR: It all goes to show, there's only one way to attack this place and that's through cloud.

PILOT: Yeah.

NAVIGATOR: By God, I've never seen anything like this before.

BOMB-AIMER: Neither have I.

PILOT: Four thousand-pounder just gone off, good show.

NAVIGATOR: That's not bad at all.

(The thumping intensifies.)

PILOT: Yes, it's not a bad prang.[34]

The world of Bomber Command was brought to the stage by Terence Rattigan, who left his career as a playwright at the start of the war to join the RAF as a wireless operator/air gunner. *Flare Path* was first performed in London in August 1942 a few months after the first 'thousand' raids. The action takes place in the residents' lounge of the Falcon Hotel in the fictional Lincolnshire town of Milchester, where wives stay to be near their men at the neighbouring bomber base. The play centres on Pat, an actress before the war, and her husband Flight Lieutenant Teddy Graham whom she married in haste during a week-long leave. She is visited by Peter Kyle, a British film star and former lover. Kyle wants her back. She is greatly tempted. Her feelings are tested when Teddy is sent off on a last-minute mission. During the long hours of waiting Pat realizes where her duty lies and in the morning tells Kyle she will not be leaving with him. 'I used to think that our private happiness was something far too important to be affected by outside things, like the war or marriage vows,' she says. 'It may be just my bad luck, but I'm in that battle, and I can't . . . desert.'

The man she is standing by is a refreshing contrast to the Holly-wood sophisticate, Kyle. He is gauche, innocent and friendly and totally lacking in pretension, full of Gellhorn's 'humble jokes'. He feels strong affection for his rear gunner Sergeant David 'Dusty'

Miller, a former London bus conductor, and the feeling is returned. But Teddy is more complicated than he seems. After returning from the raid he breaks down, stricken by 'plain bloody funk'. He blurts out to his wife his fear of being grounded for Lack of Moral Fibre which he describes as 'the official phrase for – no guts'. This was probably the first public admission that such a designation existed. The play was also frank about losses. One of the bombers crashes on take-off while the wives are watching from the hotel and the BBC reports a heavy toll on the radio news.[35]

There was no attempt to censor *Flare Path*. The Air Ministry thoroughly approved of its message and when it opened at the Apollo Theatre most of the RAF's top brass were there. The play was ultimately concerned with sacrifice and sacrifice was the positive side of loss, for it suggested that the dying was worth it. This was the theme of Noël Coward, who was proving himself a master at arousing and distilling the nation's sentiments, in a poem that generated a powerful emotional charge. There is no mention of the Germans. The emphasis instead is on the selflessness of the crews, droning overhead as the rest of Britain lies abed.

> Lie in the dark and listen
> It's clear tonight so they're flying high,
> Hundreds of them, thousands perhaps,
> Riding the icy, moonlit sky.
> Men, machinery, bombs and maps,
> Altimeters and guns and charts,
> Coffee, sandwiches, fleece-lined boots
> Bones and muscles and minds and hearts
> English saplings with English roots
> Deep in the earth they've left below,
> Lie in the dark and let them go,
> Lie in the dark and listen . . .

Jack Currie found it 'succinct and stylish but . . . slightly blush-making.' He spoke for many when he recorded later that 'largely unmoved by exhortation, praise or condemnation, I satisfied what need I had for motivation by the companionship of the men from far-off lands around me, and the sight of the cathedral and the wide, green fields.'[36]

Most of the effort to explain Bomber Command to the outside world had little effect on what those within it were thinking or doing. It was as Currie said. The horizons of their universe rarely stretched beyond the crew and the aircraft and the next operation. If they needed an overarching belief to sustain them it was the thought that every successful attack brought victory, and above all peace, a little closer. That gave point to the terrible work they were doing. 'Did you notice what your husband did to Hannover by any chance?' Reg Fayers asked his wife after a major raid on 8/9 October 1943. 'War's end is much nearer 'cos of Bomber Command.'

9

The Battle

Harris liked to present the campaign as a series of 'battles'. It was a commonplace word to describe a strange and completely novel form of fighting. The crews were often struck by the oddness of the war they were waging. They attacked, at night, an enemy they could not see. Their targets were not soldiers or fellow-aviators but buildings, and inevitably, those who lived in them. The engagements were brief and fought far away. There was nothing connecting them to the battlefield. It was a war they visited, then left.

'Life on the squadron was seldom far from fantasy,' wrote Don Charlwood. 'We might, at eight, be in a chair beside a fire, but at ten in an empty world above a floor of cloud. Or at eight, walking in Barnetby with a girl whose nearness denied all possibility of sudden death at twelve.'[1]

Roy MacDonald, a mid-upper gunner with the Pathfinder Force, found it 'a Jekyll and Hyde experience'. After finishing an operation 'it was funny, if you weren't on the night following, to be able to just ride your bike among the fields and think, well it's not many hours since we were in another completely different world, and just thinking once or twice about friends who hadn't come back. It was . . . schizophrenic.'[2]

Even in battle it was possible to feel disengaged. Reg Fayers, the gentle 78 Squadron navigator who had questioned Harris when he visited Holme-on-Spalding-Moor, described the sensation in a letter written to his wife Phyllis in the summer of 1943. 'Lately in letters I've mentioned that I've flown by night and that I've been tired by day, but I haven't said that I can now claim battle honours – Krefeld, Mülheim, Gelsenkirchen, Wuppertal and Cologne. I suppose I've been fighting in the Battle of the Ruhr. But it hasn't felt like that.'

Like many he was surprised at the emotional distance he felt from those he was bombing. 'It's aloof and impersonal, this air war. One has no time to think of [the] hell happening below to a set of people who are the same as you except that their thinking has gone a bit haywire. It's a fair assumption that when Tom [the bomb-aimer] dropped our bombs the other night, women and boys and girls were killed and cathedrals damaged. It must have been so. Were it more personal, I should be more regretting I suppose. But I sit up there with my charts and my pencils and I don't see a thing. I never look out. In five raids all I've seen is a cone of searchlights up by Amsterdam.'[3]

Fayers was shut away in his 'office', curtained off from the sights of the battlefield. As a pilot, Peter Johnson had no choice but to see what was happening but he too found there was something unreal about the spectacle. 'The defences which threatened us were visible enough, the twinkling of innumerable shells exploding in the barrage, the probing fingers of the searchlights, the constant threat from fighters against whom we had little defence. All these we knew but we were not really fighting against them, we were simply trying to evade them. And our own part in the fighting was quickly over. In the glare of searchlights, with the occasional winking of anti-aircraft shells, the occasional thud when one came close and left its vile smell, what we had to do was search for coloured lights dropped by our own people, aim our bombs at them and get away.' The use of target indicators meant that it was easy to forget that the bombs were falling on people and buildings. 'The crux of our every operation,' he wrote, 'lay in the few minutes when the bomb-aimer kept the clear, beautiful colour of a target indicator in his sights, gave his directions and ultimately loosed our load at a firework . . .'[4]

Mounting a raid was a complex business requiring enormous thought, skill and effort. The many variables made each one different. However by the middle of 1943 a routine had been established. Each morning the crews of each squadron woke with no knowledge of what the night would bring. The big decisions were taken far away at Harris's headquarters at High Wycombe, west of London, then passed on to the commanders of the formations that would carry out the attacks.

By now there were seven front-line groups. Number 1 was equipped entirely with Lancasters and operated from South Yorkshire and North Lincolnshire. The light bombers of Number 2 Group were removed from Bomber Command in May 1943 and attached to the American Second Tactical Air Force in preparation for D-Day; 3 Group had Lancasters and was based in Cambridgeshire and Huntingdonshire. The airfields housing 4 Group, equipped with Halifaxes, were in the North and East Ridings of Yorkshire; 5 Group had a mixture of Lancasters and twin-engined Mosquitoes, the sleek, fast beauties of the air war, used for target-marking as well as for precision attacks. It was centred on South Lincolnshire and Nottinghamshire. Airmen of the Royal Canadian Air Force (RCAF) made up the personnel of 6 Group, which operated out of the North Riding and County Durham. The Pathfinder Force was designated as 8 Group and flew Lancasters and Mosquitoes from airfields around Ely in the Cambridge fens. The last group, 100, was sited in north Norfolk and used American Liberators and Flying Fortresses to fly radio and electronic countermeasure missions to jam the German radar during operations.

Crews would hear after breakfast from their flight commanders whether they would be operating that night. If not, an empty day lay ahead. Their job was unlike any other military occupation. Frank Blackman, an Englishman who flew with 429 Canadian Bomber Squadron, explained to his girlfriend Mary that 'aircrew are not like anybody else in the services. They are qualified to fly and damn-all else.'[5] NCOs and junior officers had no men to lead and no other duties but their operational ones. Free days were welcome if they followed a heavy period of raids. But the necessity of completing thirty trips in order to finish a tour and escape from front-line duties meant most were anxious to hurry on and get it over with. Don Charlwood was stationed at Elsham Wolds in the exposed north-west of Lincolnshire when freezing fog shut the airfield down. 'The fog remains,' he wrote in his diary, 'the intense cold and stillness remain; the sun has gone for ever. No ops now for ten days. This is not as pleasant as it sounds. Thirty ops must be done and until they are done the pressure is on. These long gaps give one too much time to think.' There was much to think about. At the time of writing he and his crew had 'still seen no one reach thirty'.[6] In winter, cancellations were routine. Very often they came at the last minute, as commanders hung on waiting for the weather to improve.

Invariably, this deflated crew spirits. An RAF report into operational stress written in August 1942 spoke of 'the disastrous effects upon morale of repeated cancellation of sorties, especially when late in the day.' One of the squadron commanders consulted 'said that "last-minute scrubbing" was the most demoralizing factor with which he had to contend in managing an operational squadron.' He would 'much rather send his squadron on a raid even with 10/10 cloud over the target than subject them to the disappointment, frustration and demoralization of last-minute cancellation due to weather conditions . . .' Frustration was more likely to be generated by a desire to get an ordeal over with than a yearning to have a crack at the enemy. But it was real and damaging enough. A station medical officer quoted in the report told of a freshman who was 'scrubbed seventeen times before he got his first trip. He only lasted three trips after this, and then said he had had it.'[7]

If ops were on, the destination was first revealed to those that most needed to know – the station, squadron and flight commanders and flying control officer. Most of the airmen had to wait until the afternoon to find out where they were going. In the meantime they checked the serviceability of their aircraft, perhaps taking it for a test flight, and passed the time afterwards reading, trying to get some sleep or writing letters. The target was first revealed to the pilots and navigators at a preliminary afternoon briefing. There were specialist briefings for wireless operators and bomb-aimers. Then there was a general gathering for all taking part.

Freshman crews, virgins on their first missions, might feel a thrill of anticipation, even pleasure as they prepared for the evening's events, happy in the thought that all their training was finally going to be put to use. The usual sensation, though, was a low buzz of dread that could only be dispelled by action. Don Charlwood, on hearing that he was about to embark on his first trip, felt an odd mixture of excitement and fear. 'The mood about us changed to something elating but strangely unpleasant, as though suddenly we had been stripped to spiritual nakedness. Half-laughingly men [went off] to write last letters.'[8]

Bomber Command's rapid professional evolution meant that by 1944 preparations were exceptionally thorough. The main briefing took place a few hours before take-off. The 120 or so squadron members taking part in a typical raid filed into the briefing room, usually a utilitarian hut, after being checked at the door by an RAF Police NCO, and sat down in the rows of chairs or forms, each crew clustering around its skipper. Within a few minutes a haze of cigarette and pipe smoke hung in the rafters. They came to attention as the station and squadron commanders strode in and mounted a low dais where a map was propped on a stand, hidden by a blackout curtain. With the announcement 'Gentlemen, your target for tonight is . . .' the CO whipped away the cover and revealed their destination. An ominous red tape on the chart marked the route from base to target. The least welcome objectives were the Ruhr – 'Happy Valley' – and the 'Big City' as Harris called Berlin. Roy MacDonald hated the thought of the Ruhr. 'When they shut the door and pulled the curtain away from the board to show you where you were going I used to die. My heart used to leap out of my chest.'[9]

Bad news was often met by yelled expletives and cat-calls, and sometimes with mournful humour. 'With a deft flick of the wrist, the CO uncovered the wall map behind him,' wrote Harry Yates. '"Gentlemen," he began as always. "The target for tonight is . . . Kiel." As always the gentlemen responded with groans . . . but one bright spark shouted out, "Sir, can we be excused. I promised to meet my girlfriend at eight o'clock."' It was a well-worn joke, but founded in truth. Many an airman had a date he would not turn up to, that or any other night.[10]

The squadron leader then handed over to the senior intelligence officer (SIO) who assessed the importance of the target and explained why it was to be attacked. He, sometimes she, as it was not unusual for WAAF officers to hold intelligence posts, gave details of previous raids and explained why it had been chosen. The SIO also revealed what was known about flak and searchlight positions which were marked on the map with red and green celuloid overlays. Any 'spy' rash enough to use the first person plural when describing the operation ahead was instantly met with shouts of 'What do you mean "we"?'

The squadrons had specialist leaders for each aircrew role who now gave their own briefings. The navigators were taken again over the route and given the turning points. Frequent diversions were commonplace to keep the German defences guessing about the intended target. The wireless operators were reminded of the frequencies of the night. The bombing leader detailed the payloads and the ratio of high explosive to incendiaries and explained the timing and phasing of the attack and colours of the target indicators and aiming point markers. The meteorological officer then gave details of wind speeds, cloud conditions and the weather likely to be encountered over the target.

The RAF had started the war with poor quality bombs that were more metal than charge and that frequently failed to go off. In the spring of 1941 they began to be replaced by a new series of High Capacity (HC) blast bombs, led by the 4,000-pound 'cookie', a fat, green-painted cylinder which appeared to have no aerodynamic qualities whatsoever. They were supplemented with Medium Capacity (MC) bombs which came in sizes of 500, 1,000 and 4,000 pounds. These were mixed with incendiaries. The most common was the hexagonal 4-pound version of which Bomber Command dropped nearly eighty million. As the war progressed, the recipe for the bomb mix changed. In 1940, incendiaries made up only about 5 per cent of the load. During the Battles of the Ruhr and, later, Berlin, the proportion was closer to 66 per cent. The blast bombs blew buildings apart. The incendiaries set fire to the debris. It was this devastating cocktail that caused the Hamburg firestorm and those that followed it.

The CO wound up the meeting with some words of encouragement. In some squadrons, it was the practice for the padre to say a prayer before the final preparations began.

'The target for tonight is . . .' 57 Squadron learn their destination, 30 March 1944.

As the room emptied, the medical officer stood at the door doling out benzedrine 'wakey-wakey' pills to those who wanted them. The crews then headed to the mess for their pre-operational meal. Usually it was bacon and eggs, a treat in a land where rationing had made the mundane exotic. There were a few slack hours before the propellers started to turn. The crews were now sealed off from the world outside. Phone calls to wives or girlfriends were forbidden. Even for someone as practised as Guy Gibson, this was a time of intense anxiety. 'Most people will agree with me when I say that the worst part of any bombing raid is the start,' he wrote. 'I hate the feeling of standing around in the crew rooms, waiting to get into the vans that will take you out to your aircraft. It's a horrible business. Your stomach feels as though it wants to hit your backbone. You can't stand still. You laugh at small jokes, loudly, stupidly. You smoke far too many cigarettes, usually only halfway through, then throw them away. Sometimes you feel sick and want to go to the lavatory. The smallest incidents annoy you and you flare up at the slightest provocation . . . all this because you're frightened, scared stiff . . . I have always felt bad until the door of the aircraft clangs shut; until the wireless-op says "Intercom OK," and the engines burst into life. Then it's all right. Just another job.'[11]

About ninety minutes before take-off they went to the crew room to change. Bomber Command uniform was never standardized. You chose from a haphazard variety of kit, including on occasion the odd civvy item, the gear that made you comfortable. Dennis Steiner wore 'thick woollen long johns and vest, thick knee-length stockings, shirt and electrically heated jacket. This had leads which went down inside your trouser legs to heated slippers. There were also heated gloves which clipped on to the sleeves of the jacket but I rarely wore those. On top of this went a rollneck pullover and a battledress uniform. I had sewn a fur collar on to the jacket. It didn't do much for the warmth but was soft and comfortable. Flying boots were thick sheepskin and I wore three pairs of gloves, first silk, then chamois and finally woollen. I did have a pair of leather gauntlets but they were clumsy and after one was sucked out of [a] chute I never bothered to replace them.'[12]

They wore a whistle on their collars to summon help if they went down in the sea and dog tags stamped with their name and service number. The material used was virtually indestructible and could withstand even the fiercest fire. Steiner also wore a silver medallion with an engraving of two bluebirds and the encouraging message *je reviendrai*, given to him by a girlfriend. Such talismans were central to individual survival routines. Panic could ensue if someone reached the aircraft to find he had left behind the lucky charm that he believed his life depended on. 'Luck and a Lancaster were our daily bread,' wrote Jack Yates. 'We loved the one and couldn't expect to live without a large slice of the other. We all carried a keepsake, a sign of our trust worn around the neck or pocketed next to the heart. It could be the ubiquitous rabbit's foot or a rosary, letter, St Christopher, coin, photograph, playing card . . .'[13]

As a Lancaster skipper Jim Berry was occasionally irritated when he was given a strange aircraft and found its interior festooned with the jujus of the previous occupants. 'Very often there would be rabbits' feet and little things hanging up. I would never have them. I used to say take them down I don't want them. [The crew] said, well they might be good luck. I would say, they might be good luck for somebody [else] but I don't want them . . . it was quite grotesque sometimes, there were so many bits hanging about.' Nonetheless, during the later part of his remarkable stint of sixty-four operations he kept a lucky farthing, given to him by his batwoman, in the finger of his flying glove.[14]

Swathed in multiple layers of clothing airmen waddled rather than walked. The bulk was necessary. It was cold up there, even with the electrically-heated linings that became standard issue by the middle of the war. The aircraft had some hot-air heating but it tended to be erratically distributed. According to Ralph Wood, a navigator, 'a Hallybag was always a deep-freeze proposition, even at the best of times. There were supposed to be pipes giving off heat throughout the aircraft but this was a laugh.'[15] In the Lancaster, however, the heating duct outlet was next to the wireless operator so he and the navigator tended to roast, while in the cockpit the pilot, engineer and bomb-aimer froze. Whatever the aircraft it was the gunners, stuck in the back, who felt the cold the most.

Finally, they struggled into Mae West lifejackets and parachute harnesses. They picked up their parachutes on the way out of the locker room together with a thermos flask of coffee, boiled sweets, chewing gum, and a bar of Fry's Vanilla Chocolate Cream. They were also issued with escape kits in case they were brought down in enemy territory, containing maps of France and Germany printed on scarves and handkerchiefs, phrase sheets, local money and compasses concealed in pens and buttons. The kits contained passport photographs for use in forged documents. They were unlikely to have been very convincing. Base photographers tended to set their subjects in the same rigid pose, cutting them off at the neck to hide their tunics. As a last precaution they left behind anything that might identify their unit or its location. 'We were required to empty our pockets and were given two numbered and differently coloured pouches for the contents,' Ken Newman remembered. 'The contents of one of these would be sent to our next of kin if we did not return but the contents of the others would not . . . some married aircrew had clandestine girlfriends and naturally did not want their photographs or letters to be sent to their wives.'[16] The procedure inspired a poem by the RAF poet, John Pudney.

> Empty your pockets, Tom, Dick and Harry
> Strip your identity; leave it behind.
> Lawyer, garage-hand, grocer, don't tarry
> With your own country, your own kind
>
> Leave all your letters. Suburb and township,
> Green fen and grocery, slip way and bay,
> Hot spring and prairie, smoke-stack and coal tip,
> Leave in our keeping while you're away.
>
> Tom, Dick and Harry, plain names and numbers,
> Pilot, observer and gunner depart.
> Their personal litter only encumbers
> Somebody's head, somebody's heart.[17]

Then it was time to board the lorries that ferried them to the aircraft. At dispersal, the pilot and the flight engineer went over the aircraft with the groundcrew for a final check. There was a pause for a last cigarette, perhaps a piss against the tail wheel for good luck. The remaining minutes on the ground were solemn and unsettling. One summer night in 1943 Willie Lewis, a flight engineer who was to survive fifty-two operations, was waiting to board his bomber for his first trip to Germany. They were going to Essen. 'The dispersal was far remote from the aerodrome,' he wrote, 'set with its back against a wood, in which the final rustlings of the birds could be heard as they settled themselves down to sleep. The leaves crackled in the quiet air and the darkness which was rapidly settling about them had a close warmth, earthy and comforting . . . the realization that there were simple creatures in the undergrowth and trees close at hand, going about their peaceful, age-enduring existence unaffected by, and unaware of war was strangely moving.'[18] It was a relief to climb the ladder and struggle down the fuselage to their positions.

The ignition whined, the propeller blades made a few jerky revolutions then blurred into invisibility as the engines caught. One by one, the pilots edged the aircraft forward, anxious not to stray from the narrow tarmac strip that led to the runway and bog down in the soft ground. The night air throbbed with the confident roar of a hundred aero engines. The lead bomber swung into the runway and as the light on the controller's van flashed green, rolled down the track. When it was only halfway into its run, the next was already on its way. Despite the immense force the Merlin and Hercules engines that powered the Lancasters and Halifaxes could generate, each take-off seemed a struggle. The bombers were often laden with well over their recommended all-up weight and they clambered rather than soared into the air. There was a last little ritual. At the side of the runway, whatever the weather, a small knot of ground-crew and WAAFs waved farewell.

On occasions it was possible to enjoy the sensation of flight and, at the right time of the year, the beauty of the darkening sky. Taking off on a long trip to Milan in August 1943 Lewis and his crew climbed through a thick layer of cloud at 10,000 feet and set course towards the setting sun. As flight engineer, he sat up front with the pilot and could see everything. 'The great sea of cloud underneath turned golden,' he wrote. 'Then it became a huge flood of scarlet which made way for crimson and mauve as the light faded, [then] funereal violet for the last few moments before darkness leapt upon the world. A pallid moon which had occupied one unobtrusive corner of the heavens simultaneously glowed with increased density until from a faded orb it became the dominating feature of the sky.'

The surrounding bombers were slowly swallowed by the dusk so that all that was left was the dim glow of their navigating lights. Aboard their Halifax, T-Tommy, Lewis and his mates sat in silence, listening to the rasp of their breath through their oxygen masks. As they flew south, the cloud disappeared and by the time they crossed the coast the weather was perfectly clear. They were now in enemy territory. The navigating lights were switched off.

'The night sky was beautiful. The splendour of the full moon high above was reflected in a mist over the sea. [We] were suspended in a vast blue dome. The light was so bright that T-Tommy shone silver in it, the roundels on her wings standing out as clear as if it were day . . . ahead lay a completely empty sky.' After twenty trips the crew were now accustomed to the rhythms of the journey. They had 'fallen into the familiar routine. The powerful mechanism of the aircraft had overborne [our] individuality and welded [it] into the machine.' Through their masks they breathed 'the fresh tang from the oxygen tubes and the smells of rubber and oil. A constant flow of hot air gushed into the cockpit . . . warming the forward positions. Outside the barrier of glass in the cold crispness of the atmosphere the exhaust manifold shone against the outlines of the engines. The wingtips swayed gently up and down amongst the stars. The gun turrets turned slowly from side to side, and the face of the mid-upper gunner stared out grimly, his body hunched over his weapons.'[19]

Cy March, the ex-miner now serving as a rear gunner with 467 Squadron, admitted later that when staring out into darkness 'as black as a sheep's bum, I [experienced] something I daren't tell anyone for years in case they thought I was bomb-happy. I could hear the most beautiful singing and music in my earphones . . . none of the crew said anything so I knew it was only me who could hear it. I heard this on many of our trips and could never explain it, but I wasn't complaining for it was really beautiful, barmy or not.'[20]

Over the sea there was no more time for dreaming. The gunners fired a few bursts to test their guns. As sea gave way to land the navigator called out 'enemy coast ahead'. Dennis Field had his 'usual physical reaction' when he heard the words and 'after a bit of a struggle in the confined cockpit . . . managed to relieve myself into my can' which an obliging member of the crew then emptied down a flare chute.[21] Crossing the coast the crews got their first sight of the dangers that awaited them. The shores of the Low Countries and France were fringed with flak batteries and flak ships. Routes were chosen to avoid the main concentrations, but intelligence never kept pace completely with the enemy's ever-shifting dispositions.

By now the Germans were watching, tracking the incoming fleet on their radar system. The crews began the simple but effective counter-measure, shovelling out bundles of *Window*, which created at least temporary confusion on German radar screens.

The defenders would know an attack was coming from the increased radio activity that preceded every big operation as wireless operators checked their equipment. The German radar early-warning system stretched in a thick band from Denmark down the North Sea coast before sweeping south to block an approach from the west across France. It was named after its creator, General Josef Kammhuber. The Kammhuber Line was made up of seventy-four 'boxes' each containing one *Freya* and two *Würzburg* radars. As the radar picked up the incoming aircraft the information was trans-mitted to a night-fighter control room where controllers directed the defensive battle. They followed the situation on a large screen, assisted by *Luftwaffehelferinnen*, the German equivalent of WAAFs, who shone narrow points of light on the screen depicting the pos-itions of friendly and hostile aircraft.

Once the attack began, German night-fighters took off and circled a radio beacon to await orders. Their positions were picked up by radar and beamed on to the screen as a blue light. The incoming bombers were marked with a red light. The controller's aim was to set the fighter on a course where he could see a bomber or track it down with the *Lichtenstein* short-range radar with which each air-craft was fitted. By the middle of 1943 Germany had about 400 night-fighters, armed with 20 mm or 30 mm cannon. Some were equipped with upward firing *Schräge Musik* cannons. These allowed the fighter to creep up on the bomber from below where it was invisible to the crew and fire a burst into its explosive-packed belly. Along the route the controllers sought to insert twin-engined fighters into the bomber stream.

As the bombers flowed onwards, the eyes of all the crews sifted the darkness for enemy aircraft. But on long trips, fatigue and boredom blunted concentration and attacks usually came without warning. Donald Falgate was peering out of the bomb-aimer's nosecone on the approach to Magdeburg when he saw tracer floating towards him. 'He was on to us before we saw him,' he remembered. 'He made the first attack from the rear and from above which was unusual. He'd obviously come on us quite by mistake. If it was a radar interception they usually picked you up from below.' There was a brief first burst of fire and the fighter, a Ju 88, veered away. The pilot just had time to check that no one was hurt when the German came in for a second attempt. He was too near to focus his guns and the shots went harmlessly by. As he closed in from astern for a third attempt the rear gunner yelled a warning and the captain finally took evasive action. '[He] screamed out: "Corkscrew! Port! Go!"'

The corkscrew was the bombers' only real defence against fighters. It was a testament to the strength and aerodynamic qualities of the heavies that they could be thrown about the sky with a violence that, if they were lucky, could shake off their smaller, nimbler pursuers long enough to escape into the darkness beyond the fighter's limited onboard radar range. The manoeuvre required the pilot to shove the aircraft down into a diving turn until it was screaming through the air at 300 mph. Then he jerked it upwards to climb in the opposite direction. Done properly, it meant the fighter could not hold his quarry in his sights long enough to get in a good burst. It was enough to see off Falgate's pursuer. 'We managed to evade him and get into cloud . . . but it was a very scary time . . . It wasn't until we got back to base that we found bullet holes in the fuselage and two huge holes in the mid-upper turret where the shells had gone through. The poor mid-upper gunner nearly froze to death.'[22]

Leutnant Norbert Pietrek who was based at Florennes in southern Belgium on one of the main routes to the Ruhr gave an account of a night action from the perspective of the hunter. On the evening of 16 April 1943, a warning came in that a double force of British bombers was in the air. They were heading for Mannheim and the Skoda armaments factory at Pilsen.

Pietrek and his Messerschmitt 110 were scrambled to patrol in a box codenamed 'Tomcat'. Before he arrived he was told over the radio beacon by his controller that he had a *Kurier* for him, the Luftwaffe codeword for a heavy bomber. Turning on the course he was given he saw a 'Lancaster, 200 metres to my right and somewhat higher . . . I therefore push the throttles through the gate to catch up with him and then, as I have learned during training, position myself exactly underneath it, adjust my speed to that of the bomber, pull up, and then fire a long burst through a wing between the engines and its fuel tanks.' The move was thwarted when the Lancaster went into a steep dive. Pietrek gave chase. Before he could open fire, however, the bomber flew into a hillside and exploded. It was the first aircraft he had destroyed and he enjoyed the experience. 'Really,' he recalled later, 'it is quite a splendid matter to chase one big *Viermot* [four-engined bomber] into the ground without firing a single bullet.'

His blood up, he was eager to strike again. He headed back towards the beacon, cursing the RAF jamming that was blocking his link with the controller and spoiling his chances of further 'trade' that night. Then, while circling the beacon, he spotted what he described as a 'barn door', a large, easy target in the shape of what appeared to be a passing Stirling. He fired off a few rounds which passed in front of the bomber and alerted the crew to the attack. 'A wild twisting and turning begins,' he recalled later. 'Much too close for comfort, green lines of tracer from the Tommy's tail turret swish past me. We climb and turn, a steep spiral to the left, pull up, the same manoeuvre to the right, up again, and so it goes on and on. Never could I have imagined that one could carry out such wild manoeuvres with a giant [aircraft] like this . . .'

In the frantic exchange of fire Pietrek managed to hit the starboard outer engine. It appeared to ignite but the flames then died down only to flare and gutter again and again. Pietrek thought, 'That pilot must be a madman! He still flies eastward despite one dead engine . . . and is obviously determined to press on and discard his load of bombs on a German city . . . 'Well my dear boy, there is no way that you will pull that off!'

He continued the chase as the bomber sank ever lower. In the back of the Messerschmitt his wireless operator, Otto, slaved to fill the ammunition pans to keep his cannons firing. The stream of tracer from the bomber's mid-upper gunner kept him at bay. Eventually, though, he was able to 'creep up on him from beneath, pull up and level out swiftly and . . . fire a burst exactly over the top of the fuselage. A ball of fire and the turret has disappeared. That's what you get when you cause me so much trouble!'

He put the last, fatal touches to the encounter with a burst that set the port outer engine on fire, only breaking off when he ran out of ammunition. The bomber was by then doomed. Pietrek lined up alongside and watched it slide to earth. He found it a 'strangely beautiful sight, the big black bird . . . well comrade, your fate is sealed. That will be clear to you chaps inside that wounded bird too.'[23]

Sometimes high-flying aircraft dropped flares to help the night-fighters see their targets. The feeling of exposure was appalling. Cy March was well on his way to Böhlen when 'suddenly a string of flares lit up above us, lightening the sky into daylight . . . they continued until there was a double row for miles on our track. We knew fighters were dropping them, but where were they, behind, above or below the flares? Our eyes must have been like saucers looking for them. It was like walking down a well-lit road in the nude.' They were saved by a signal aborting the mission and dived away for the cover of darkness and home.[24] The sky was full of nasty surprises. Some crews reported seeing mysterious bursts of flame. The authorities explained them away as 'scarecrows', designed to frighten crews, though the likelihood is that they were exploding aircraft.

Despite the weight of the German defences it was to possible to reach the target area without encountering fighters. Some gunners completed a tour without ever seeing a German aircraft or firing their guns in anger. It was just as well. The turrets were fitted with Browning .303s which took rifle-calibre bullets and had a short range. They became even less effective after the Luftwaffe improved the armour on its fighters. They offered very little protection to the bombers and perhaps their main value was as a psychological deterrent.

In these unequal circumstances, if a gunner spotted a fighter he was wise to hold his fire. During his tour as a rear gunner Peter Twinn 'never fired a shot because if you did then that immediately gave your position away to other fighters who were in the area who couldn't see you and they would come straight in, pinpoint you and that was it. More often than not if you did open fire it was the last thing you did.'[25]

The first sign that the fighters had found a victim was often a small fire in the blackness ahead, followed by a huge explosion as the bomb load went up. It was an experience that produced conflicting emotions. There was horror, pity, but above all thankfulness that it had happened to someone else.

The fighters posed an intermittent threat all the way out and all the way back and shot down more bombers than did the flak batteries defending the towns. In the last three months of 1943, fighters caused the loss of 250 aircraft whereas flak was responsible for downing only ninety-four.[26] Nonetheless, it was during the twenty or so minutes over the target that the crews felt in the greatest peril.

By the middle of 1943 most area raids ran to a standard pattern. During the raid on Duisburg on the night of 12 May, 238 Lancasters, 142 Halifaxes, 112 Wellingtons and 70 Stirlings took part, led by 10 Mosquitoes of the PFF. They approached the target at staggered heights and intervals. The bottom layer of the stream flew at 15,000 feet, the middle at 18,000 and the top at 20,000–22,000 feet. Each level was two minutes behind the other. On the outward and inward journeys the middle of the bomber stream felt a safe place to be and the turbulence caused by the surrounding aircraft was reassuring. Above the objective the proximity of your comrades became a menace. At Duisburg, all 572 aircraft flew over the target in about twenty-five minutes. Those at the lowest level faced the greatest danger, not only from flak but also from the bombs falling from above. Initially there had been fears that such concentration would lead inevitably to collisions. In practice, the discipline of the pilots meant that mid-air crashes were surprisingly rare.

Arrival in the target area was signalled by searchlights probing the sky, followed by the blossoming of anti-aircraft fire. It was a daunting sight. On the approach to Hamburg and Berlin, it seemed to Doug Mourton that 'the anti-aircraft was so concentrated that from fifty miles away it looked impossible to get through it'.[27] The switch from the cold comfort of the dark to the obscene brightness of the battlefield was shocking. Peter Johnson, approaching Essen on his first operation, noted how alone his aircraft felt, 'suspended in a black vacuum', with nothing to be seen except the yellow flares dropped by the Pathfinders to show where to turn on to the target. But then 'instead of the pitch darkness there was suddenly a mass of searchlights, slowly, methodically scanning the sky over a huge area. At the same time streams of tracer, some white, some coloured, followed the searchlight beams at quite low heights . . . lastly, at levels from well above our height to four or five thousand feet below came a dazzling display of twinkling stars, the Ruhr barrage of heavy ack-ack. There seemed to be hundreds of bursts almost simultaneously. You were quite unconscious of the invisible but lethal load of shrapnel each burst vomited into the sky.'[28]

Doug Mourton, on his first trip to Cologne, could see the flak all too clearly, 'pieces of luminous metal . . . not only luminous but looking as if they were on fire' that thudded into the side of the aircraft.[29] The once empty-seeming sky was suddenly full of horrifying sights. As the Pathfinder pilot Jim Berry began his bombing run over Kiel one night 'the sky got quite a glow on. I felt that we were on fire because I could see this red glow everywhere. I looked around and everything was bathed in this red glow but no one said anything.' Then he noticed the cause of the strange effect. 'Just above and to the starboard side was a Lancaster . . . It was ablaze from end to end. It was a terrible sight and it was not very far away. He was slightly higher than we were and I thought if he falls my way I will have time to get away.' Eventually 'it just fell away to the starboard side and away from me so that was fine. But it was an awful thing to see. I didn't see anybody get out.'[30]

In these last, climactic moments Don Charlwood was sometimes struck by the madness of what he was doing. As he flew, crouched at his navigator's station, into a blizzard of flak above Bremen he 'looked at the commonplace things on my desk – pencils, a scribbling block, a pear ripened in the Staffordshire sun – and suddenly I thought of them as wonderfully sane, inanimate though they were.'[31]

The point of the searchlights was to dazzle the pilot and bomb-aimer and light up the bomber for the flak batteries. Once the radar-guided master searchlight, tinted an unearthly blue, picked up an aircraft it was joined by others so that the intruder was caught in a cone of dazzling light and became the object of the attentions of every gun within range. The effect was hideously disorientating and unnerving for the crews. To Roy MacDonald it was like 'a thousand flashlights going off at the same time. It was blinding.'[32]

Once 'coned' the only way out was to corkscrew. Peter Johnson's first experience of it was over Stettin. 'The near-blindness induced by eight or ten of these very high-powered beams coming from every side produced the frightening sensation of being caged by light. No matter how you struggled the dazzling beams would hold you and you lost all sense of movement. It was as if you were motionless in the sky, shells exploding all around you, waiting for the one which would destroy you, knowing that every fighter in the area had marked you for his prey.'

Johnson warned the crew to stand by to corkscrew. But it seemed the searchlights 'were locked on to us like a vice and, pull and push the control column as I would, taking us into the steepest dives and climbs I dared risk, they clung to us as if they were glued to our shape. The rear gunner warned of an aircraft following us but I was already doing the most violent manoeuvres of which I and the aircraft were capable. Then suddenly one of the searchlights left us and then another and another . . . somehow their co-ordination had been upset though three or four still held us.' Sweating, and with his aching arms, forearms and wrists, he ' kept the throttles at maximum and, miraculously, they lost us. Still close, the beams kept brushing over our wings, probing, probing until suddenly, they went out all together. It was a queer sensation to be back in the merciful dark.'[33]

The bomber stream followed the Pathfinder crews whose job was to illuminate the target area with flares, then to drop brilliantly coloured red, green and yellow target indicators (TIs) on the aiming point. The task of the main force was to place their bombs on whichever colour marker they had been allocated by the master bombers, who began to operate from August 1943. The job of the master bomber was extraordinarily dangerous, even by Bomber Command's extreme standards. They circled the bombing zone, observing the fall of the bombs, all the while issuing instructions and corrections to the crews by radio telephone.

Whatever the terrors of the initial approach, nothing matched the dread-filled minutes of the bombing run. To deliver their loads pilots had to fly straight and level allowing the aimer to line up his sight on the marker he had been allocated burning below. The finale was signalled by a blast of freezing air which flooded the fuselage as the bomb doors opened. For the next minutes the bomb-aimer took control, lying face-down in the nose and calling adjustments to the course of the final approach to the skipper over the intercom. The captain, in turn, was taking direction from the master bomber. This was the 'tinny voice' in Willie Lewis's taut description of the climax of T-Tommy's trip to Gelsenkirchen on the night of 9 July 1943.

> In the nose . . . Joe is lying stretched over his bombsight the illuminated cross of which is in line with the town coming up. He is speaking.
>
> Joe (quietly): 'Bomb doors open, skipper.'
>
> John: 'Bomb doors open.' (He pulls a lever on his left. There is a jerk and the aircraft settles down again.) 'I'll put on the radio telephone.' (He presses a switch on the panel and a tinny voice comes over the intercom.)
>
> Voice: 'Come right in, chaps. It's not a bit dangerous. Bomb on the red flare.'
>
> Joe (Cutting across the voice.): 'Left, left, skipper.'
>
> John: 'Left, left.'
>
> (The aircraft jerks slightly to port. The illuminated cross on the bombsight lines up towards a flare halfway down.)
>
> Joe: 'Left, left.'
>
> John: 'Left, left.'
>
> (The aircraft moves again and the flare starts coming down the line towards the centre of the cross. Joe's thumb tenses on the button.)

Voice: 'There's a very good line in yellow just gone down. Bomb on the yellow.'

John: 'Can you see that yellow, Joe?'

Joe: 'Yes, skipper. Straighten up. I think I can manage it.' . . . (Crashing as ack-ack explodes around them, rocking the aircraft violently.)

Joe: 'Right, right, skipper.'

John: 'Right, right.'

Rammy (rear gunner): 'You'll have to get moving full kick as soon as the bombs are gone, skipper. It's getting bloody hot back here. The flak's very close.'

John: 'Shut up.'

Joe: (Presses the button and the aircraft leaps into the air as the load leaves.) 'Bombs gone'.[34]

To be a master bomber required tungsten nerves and supernatural composure. One master bomber who was hit while over the target calmly broadcast that he was on fire and going down. He wished the main force crews good luck before disappearing from the air waves. Their detached interventions were not always appreciated, coming as they did when every member of every crew was straining to get in and out in the fastest possible time. Jack Currie was in one of 300 Lancasters, flying in a concentrated wave over the centre of Berlin on 3 September 1943. As it approached the target, 'the PFF marker flares began to blossom on the ground. On the radio the circling master bomber passed instructions to the attackers. On the whole his words were cool and helpful, but he fell from grace with one slightly patronizing remark, which invited a harsh response and got it.

'"Come on in main force, the searchlights won't bite you!" Few were the transmit buttons left unpressed, few were the bomber captains who did not reply: "F . . . off!"'[35]

As the cookie fell away the bombers performed a great leap upward that sent relief and hope surging through the hearts of the crew. There was still one task left. Harris had insisted on the need for a photograph to be taken over the area where the bombs were supposed to have landed. The six-photograph sequence took another thirty seconds, moments, wrote Willie Lewis, of 'stark, fierce terror'.

With the last click of the camera the job was finally done but several hours of mortal danger still lay ahead. As they left the target area and its umbrella of flak the night-fighters were waiting for a second bite at their quarry. Flying Officer Geoffrey Willatt, a bomb-aimer with 106 Squadron, had only two more trips to complete his tour when on the night of 5/6 September 1943 he was sent to bomb Mannheim.

'At last I said "bombs gone" and the aircraft bounced up as the cookie went,' he wrote in his diary a few weeks later. 'A further period straight and level while the photo is taken and then we turned off. The air seemed full of aircraft and quite near a squirt of cannon fire streamed through the air like a string of sausages and we drift through puffs of smoke from nearby bursts of flak. A Halifax with one wing on fire charged past our nose losing height in a shallow dive.' His skipper, Pilot Officer 'Robbie' Robertson, put the bomber into a corkscrew before levelling out. It was then that the fighter struck. 'The most startling thing about it was the noise. Normally you can hear nothing above the roar of the engines, not even flak unless splinters hit the aircraft, or bombs dropping. This then was a metallic, ripping, shattering, clicking sound repeated three or four times at split-second intervals. The nearest simile I can think of is the noise made by two billiard balls cracked together but magnified a thousand times and loud enough to make my head sing.'

The din made him duck, a reflex that saved his life. He looked up to see 'a foot wide hole in the instrument panel behind and above my head and another in the side of the nose, a few inches above my head as I'd crouched down.'

The engines were still roaring but the nose was dropping and the aircraft seemed to be sliding down the sky. Willatt knelt on the step and peered into the pilot's compartment. What he saw appalled him. 'The seat was empty . . . this was shock enough in itself but then I could see a tangled mass of people lying in a static heap at the side of the pilot's seat and inextricably entangled with the controls. They were all hit and probably dead.' The pilot had been killed instantly by a cannon shell to the head. The flight engineer was mortally wounded. Willatt 'tried to call up on the intercom – it was dead – and it was impossible to climb back over the bodies to speak to anyone.' The aircraft was now well on fire with the port inner engine and wing ablaze and flames licking down the fuselage. He decided there was 'no alternative but to go through the hole.'

He clipped on his parachute, removed his helmet, pulled away the hatch and lowered himself into space, one hand clamped to his rip-cord handle. Almost immediately he felt 'a sickening jerk on my groin as the chute opened. I don't remember pulling the cord. I was practically unconscious from lack of oxygen . . . there was a horrible tearing, burning feeling between my legs where the harness pulled and my fur collar was clapped tightly over my face and ears. Both my boots were tugged off by the wind and my feet were freezing cold.'

Even in this extreme of pain he noticed that 'the target was still burning nicely, bombs thumping, flak cracking and searchlights waving about.' He was suddenly aware of his immense good fortune. 'What a good thing I wasn't dangling in the air in the middle of it!' As he drifted down the intricate parachute drill drummed into him during training kept running through his mind: 'twist if necessary by crossing straps so as to face downwind with knees slightly bent but braced and arm across the face to protect it. Land lightly on the toes and bend the knees.'

Nothing like this happened. The ground came up five minutes sooner than he expected and, with his legs held rigid, he landed with a thump on his heels. Despite following the escape procedure to the letter he was picked up a few hours later. He was lucky, as his captors let him know. He was led to the wreckage of his aircraft. One of the soldiers pointed to a 'grim lump under a tarpaulin' and pronounced the names of the dead men lying under it: 'Robertson, Shadbolt, Hodder, Green.' The rest had fallen elsewhere. Group Captain F. S. Hodder was the station commander at Syerston where the squadron was based. Official policy discouraged officers from flying operationally but he had dutifully gone along for the trip to show solidarity with his men.

Relief at having escaped from a doomed aircraft was quickly overtaken by anxiety of what would happen on the ground. Fear of the reception he would get was very much on Geoffrey Willatt's mind when after his short spell of freedom he emerged from a haystack and came face to face with a farmer. 'There were farm people dotted round the fields in all directions and I was definitely caught,' he wrote in his diary. 'I don't like men with pitchforks, even if they do look scared so I timidly said "RAF" and tried not to look like a Terror-Bomber.' In fact he was treated with politeness by the soldier and policeman who arrested him. When he arrived at a Luftwaffe barracks 'an officer in shiny boots and another in a monocle received me most courteously. I was parked on a bed . . . with some soup, potatoes, sauerkraut and a jug of coffee with sugar . . . some typists giggled and asked me if I was married . . .'[36]

Such amiable treatment was by no means the rule. Passing through Aachen on his way to a PoW camp after being shot down over France, Flight Sergeant Gerry Hobbs of 617 Squadron found himself next to a troop train. The soldiers spotted him and he was 'subjected to a lot of abuse and catcalls. I didn't need to know German to understand their feelings and gestures as they were probably heading for the front.' At Cologne, an elderly lady belaboured another British prisoner with an umbrella.[37]

Some of the prisoners passing through a war-battered Germany on their way to captivity had known it in peacetime. Fate took Ken Goodchild back to Cologne, which he had visited as a schoolboy, after being shot down over Holland in May 1943. He arrived with four other prisoners by train from Brussels and was 'taken off the train by four guards.' When they asked why they needed so many 'they said they had to protect us from the civilians, otherwise they'd lynch us.'

After the war it was reckoned that possibly 350 Allied airmen who survived being shot down were subsequently murdered by Germans on the ground.[38] Civilians who took part likely knew that they had nothing to fear from the authorities. Official policy was to allow them to have their way. In August 1943, Heinrich Himmler had declared that it was 'not the business of the police to get mixed up in altercations between the population and "terror fliers"' who had baled out. As the war progressed and the bombing worsened officials seemed to positively encourage lynchings. In February 1945, Gauleiter Hoffman of South Westphalia directed that surviving aircrew were 'not to be spared from the outrage of the public. I expect the police to demonstrate that they are not the protectors of these gangsters and anyone who ignores this order will have to answer to me.' Indeed, helping survivors was a crime, and several kind-hearted souls suffered for doing so. In the autumn of 1943, two men from Dorsten in the Ruhr were sent to a labour camp for giving coffee and bread to two Allied airmen.

After the war, though, the perpetrators of lynchings sometimes had to face the victors' justice. In one case, six men were put in front of a military court on charges of the ill-treatment and killing of an unknown British sergeant pilot who baled out with his crew during a raid on Bochum, in the Ruhr, on 24 March 1945. He landed in a field watched by a crowd who rushed towards him. The airman was wounded and feebly raised his arms to surrender. Franz Brening, who later served as a prosecution witness, tried to help him by removing his parachute and laying him on the ground. The mob were having none of it and began punching and kicking the victim. One of them, Stefan Weiss, seized a rifle from a German soldier standing passively by and tried to shoot the airman but the gun jammed. Another, Friedrich Fischer, sent a young boy off to fetch a hammer. He then, according to the court records, 'struck the airman a violent blow on the back of his head resulting in the breaking of his skull.' Fischer was heard afterwards 'to boast of what he had done.'

Fischer was sentenced to death. He admitted the crime but blamed 'incitement by the mass' in his appeal. He also asked the court to bear in mind the suffering he had endured as a result of Allied bombing. Weiss cited 'Goebbels propaganda' and 'daily bomber attacks.' Neither was successful as a defence. Fischer was hanged. Weiss was sentenced to twenty years' imprisonment but was released after six.[39]

Ken Goodchild and his comrades made it safely into captivity. Their experience, though, had demonstrated the folly of imagining that the danger in the air diminished the nearer you got to home. They had just been starting to believe they might make it back alive when night-fighters attacked over Holland. It was the end of a nightmarish trip. A flak shell had ripped through their Halifax ten minutes from the target but miraculously failed to explode. A second burst blew off the front turret flooding the aircraft with freezing air and wounding the navigator. Showing amazing resolution they carried on, completed the bombing run and headed homewards.

Without a functioning navigator they were unable to judge the correct course and wandered away from the comfort of the returning bomber stream. They were easy meat for the Junkers 88 and Focke-Wulf 190 which swooped just as the coastline came into view. The starboard wing was soon ablaze and dripping great gouts of flaming petrol from the tanks. The nose went down into a shallow dive and no amount of wrestling with the controls could pull it up. Goodchild

> went to the centre of the aircraft and discovered that the whole middle part of the aeroplane was one ball of flame so there was nothing we could do to get out of the back. The skipper gave the order to abandon the aircraft so the engineer and myself got hold of the wounded navigator and brought him forward to the front escape hatch [and] opened it. There was a safety device there which if you had a wounded member of crew who couldn't operate his parachute then you attached the line to his ripcord, threw him out and that line pulled the ripcord for him. At the same time the bombardier went immediately after him so that he would land somewhere close by and be able to render assistance. The engineer was the next to go and he sat on the edge of the escape hatch. I went back into my cabin to blow up all the radio equipment, destroy all the code lists and [when I came] back the engineer

was still sitting there so I booted him in the backside and out he went. I later discovered that the reason he hadn't gone earlier was simply because he was tied to the aeroplane by his oxygen pipe and by his intercom wire. It all got caught up and when he actually jumped I nearly throttled him.[40]

All the crew, including the wounded navigator Chic Henderson, survived the jump.

Once over the North Sea it felt like the worst was over. To glimpse the lightening sky at the end of a long, rough trip was like slowly waking up from a nightmare. Returning from a raid on Koblenz during which they had survived an attack by night-fighters Harry Yates was finally given the course for Mepal, the crew's home station. 'That precipitated a gradual change of mood. We descended through light cloud and levelled at 6,000 feet. Visibility was good. Moonlight played on the English Channel. We began to feel more relaxed. No, we began to feel good. This had been another demanding raid, a night of the hunter. But we had not been snared . . .'[41]

Jack Currie knew he was not supposed to smoke but 'on the long ride home over the North Sea the temptation was usually too strong for me.' When they had descended below 10,000 feet and oxygen masks were no longer needed he would 'loosen my straps, engage the automatic pilot, sit back and really enjoy that cigarette. At those moments, cruising home on half-power with the darkness, while the dawn began to touch the sky behind my left shoulder with a few bright strokes of gold, the crew cocooned in warm leather and fur, lulled by the gently throbbing metal, the terrors of the night would soon disperse.'[42] In some crews, the wireless operator ignored regulations and tuned the radio to a music station.

There was one more peril to be overcome before the wheels kissed the tarmac. Getting down was harder than getting up. Pilots had to wait for a landing order before they could touch down and the weight of numbers meant that they were sometimes forced to fly circuits until their turn came. Landing and take-off are the most dangerous times in flying. The returning aircraft were often shot up, their controls and surfaces battered by flak and shell and their skippers numb with exhaustion. Severely damaged aircraft were diverted to emergency airfields in Kent, Suffolk and Yorkshire with extended and broadened runways.

The operation ended where it had begun, in the briefing room. Intelligence officers doggedly probed the exhausted survivors of the night about what they had done and what they had seen, eager for any detail that could build their picture of the strength and disposition of the defences. Then, weary and subdued, the crews left to hand in their parachutes, drink a cup of tea and eat a plate of bacon and eggs before crashing into bed, trying to push from their minds the thought that the following night they might have to do it all over again.

10

'A Select Gang of Blokes'

Even by the standards of wartime, when sacrifice becomes the norm, the bombing campaign required extraordinary commitment to sustain it. The motivations that drove bomber crews were complicated but there were certain shared attitudes that bound them together. The most essential was the mixture of devotion, affection and trust that crew members felt for each other.

Serving in a bomber was an intimate experience. As Doug Mourton pointed out, when flying 'each one was directly or indirectly dependent on the other for his survival. There was mutual trust and reliance. This promoted fondness, affection and respect.' Mourton found that 'friendships thus forged, had a depth and unique quality that never existed with friendships before, and for me never after.' There was also a deep personal relationship between aircrew and ground crews. They were 'as one, winning and losing together'.[1]

Bomber Command was staffed with men who in peacetime would have been unlikely to choose a service career, and had no strong feelings of institutional loyalty to the air force. Reg Fayers, a fastidious man who was repelled by the rough side of service life, admitted that after two and a half years in uniform 'on the whole I've disliked the RAF. I doubt I could name six things I've positively liked.' Top of the list were his crew, 'a select gang of blokes, Ken Porter, Joe, Tony, Mac, Ken Brewster, Red and Lofty, than whom I'll never meet better. For those, I wouldn't have missed it.'[2]

The crewing-up technique recognized brilliantly the importance of human chemistry. Crews got together because, instinctively, they felt each other to be competent or lucky. But there was also an element of subliminal mutual attraction. Despite the almost invariable disparities in background and geography, crews tended to like each other. Going to war in a big aeroplane required intense interdependency. Men who functioned competently together in desperate circumstances formed strong bonds of liking and respect. The crew took the place of the family, a little universe whose dynamics were more important and absorbing than those of the world outside. Bomber squadrons were large, with up to 200 operational airmen backed up by hundreds more ground staff, and therefore rather impersonal. The sense of unit identity was much less pronounced than it was in Fighter Command. Its members tended to come together only at briefings and debriefings. Len Sumpter, the guardsman turned 57 Squadron bomb-aimer, found 'you didn't get friendly with other crews. You said "good morning" to them and this and that. But you never really got intimate with them . . . you were your own little band of seven and that was it.'

Sumpter's crew was a typical mix of class and nationality. His pilot was an Australian, David Shannon, who was only twenty years old and looked it yet was already recognized as a superb pilot. The navigator was a Canadian, Danny Walker, the quietest member of the crew. They nicknamed the skinny wireless operator Brian Goodale 'Concave' because when he was working 'he was always bending forward . . . his head was forward and his feet were forward and his bottom was sticking out.' Jack Buckley, the rear gunner, liked a drink and drove racing cars. Bob Henderson, the flight engineer, was a 'tall, staid Scotsman' who only occasionally joined his comrades on their sprees in Lincoln. The front gunner was Brian Jagger whose grandfather had been a portait-painter who had royalty among his clients. All flew with 617 in the Dams Raid of May 1943.

They 'all got on very well together . . . and I think that applied throughout the whole squadron. All the crews were the same I think which was caused by being thrown together so much. You just had to get on with people. You couldn't afford to be indifferent.'[3]

Loyalty to your crew could create conflicts of emotional interest. Cy March should have felt pleased when he was granted fourteen days' sick leave after breaking his finger. It would mean a delirious fortnight with his wife Ellen, whom he had only just married. 'I knew I should have been over the moon but I wasn't, for we knew we were to be posted to 467 RAAF Squadron very shortly.' He went off to the canteen where he knew the 'boys' would be. They congratulated him on his good luck. But March told them miserably: 'I'm worried I'll lose you rotten lot if I go.' The skipper, Neville 'Bug' Emery told him: 'Go home, enjoy yourself, give Ellen our love and don't worry. We will wait for you; we aren't going to break a new bod in.'[4]

The break-up of a happy crew felt as traumatic as the sundering of a happy family. Ken Newman was dismayed to be told that, for reasons that were never explained, his crew were to be split up after only a few operations together. He was 'shocked and upset by this disclosure'. When he complained to a senior officer 'he dismissed my protests out of hand ... with tears in my eyes I went outside his office and told the other members of my crew who were waiting there.' They were equally unhappy and demanded an immediate interview with the officer. 'This was granted and they all pleaded with him to be allowed to stay together with me as their pilot. He was unmoved and just snapped at them too that a decision had been made and would not be reversed whatever they said.'

Such insensitivity appears to have been rare. Newman learned later that the orders came from his former squadron commander with whom he had fallen out, though 'for what reason we deserved this form of punishment I could not ... imagine.' The good companions were packed off to other squadrons as 'spares'. The parting was painful. 'I was losing great friends ... who I had lived with, flown with on training and on operations and had trusted implicitly for the previous nine months.' Newman set off for his new posting 'with a heavy heart and feeling utterly miserable and lonely'.[5]

Of course not all crews were as harmonious. Willie Lewis arrived at his squadron in April 1943 pleased that after all his long training as a flight engineer he was about to put his hard work to use. 'The future held no frightening menace, only the justification for everything which had taken place till then. The sun could not have shone more brightly that day nor the birds in the hedgerow have sung more sweetly.' His captain was John Maze, at twenty the youngest of the crew. 'The skipper and I immediately made friends. I had left school at fourteen. The skipper went to university. But on the squadron I was never made to feel inferior for a moment.' He was less enthusiastic about two other crew members. Ron, the mid-upper gunner, was an ex-car salesman who had already done a tour in the Middle East and been commissioned as a pilot officer. Lewis resented his haughty manner. 'He wore his uniform with dignity and enjoyed being an officer. He mixed little with the crew and they had the unpleasant feeling that he was trying to patronize them.'

Joe, the bomb-aimer, was thirty-six, by far the oldest in the crew. Before the war he had been a policeman in South London, 'running in bookmakers' touts and prostitutes'. He 'regarded all the members of the crew with good-natured contempt. The skipper because he was a boy of twenty who had a cultured voice, a father who was an artist and had been to a university. Dave [the navigator] because he "was only an errand boy" – he had served in a shop in civilian life. Jock [the wireless operator] went about with Dave so he was just as useless.' He despised 'Rammy' the garrulous Yorkshire-born rear gunner 'because, well, he was just Rammy'.

Joe had done some flying and navigation training and was free with his advice to both pilot and navigator. Maze, despite his youth had the authority to keep him in his place. But for all Joe's irritating ways, Willie and the rest of the crew felt there was something comforting about him. He had a self-assurance 'which made him good to fly with. Looking at him the crew felt that they were safe, for anybody who loved himself so wholeheartedly must survive and surely could not come to any harm.' Their hunch turned out to be justified. Later on when they were faced with emergencies he was 'to prove as capable and resourceful as he was exasperating'.[6]

The crucial element in crew cohesion was confidence. If one member lost the trust of his fellows, everyone's morale withered. The system recognized this and in special circumstances agreed to the removal of the weak link. Bill Farquharson lost a propeller in mid-flight when piloting a Wellington during training. The crew were forced to bale out and he crashlanded. Bad luck pursued him to his squadron, 115, where 'we had the odd mishap, engine failures and hydraulics failures.' Farquharson's crew were all sergeants. He was an officer. In the sergeants' mess they came across a pilot whose crew had been borrowed by the wing commander. 'They chummed up with him and decided that they would like to fly with him. They came to me and that was that. They put it very nicely. It wasn't that they thought I was a poor pilot or anything like that. They reckoned I was a pretty good pilot to have got them out of [difficult] situations. But they thought I was an unlucky one . . . that happened to lots of chaps.'

When the situation was explained to the squadron commander, Wing Commander A. G. S. 'Pluto' Cousens, he agreed that Farquharson would have to find another crew. 'I was very disappointed indeed [but] Cousens spoke to me and said these things happen, and perhaps for the best, because if the crew is a little dithery it spreads. Perhaps they want to argue with you – "shouldn't you do it this way or that way." And you've no time for arguments. You've got to act.'[7]

If the crew was like a family then the aeroplane was the family home. They were given pet names and there was consternation if the personal 'kite' was unavailable. 'If you had any faults on the plane of course you had to wait until they were fixed, or borrow another one,' said Len Sumpter. 'And we didn't like borrowing planes because you got used to your own plane. It was like when you . . . walk into your own house. If you go into another house, a stranger's house, you've got the feeling that you're not right. But you could always tell when you were in your own plane. I don't know why I'm sure. Whether it was the sound of it, the smell of it or what.'[8]

There was also luck to consider. Don Charlwood always felt happiest in B-Beer, even when it was playing up. During a raid on Essen in January 1943 there was trouble with the port outer engine. The following day the crew was ordered back to Essen again. They learned that though B-Beer had been repaired they were flying in L-London. B-Beer had been given to Sergeant B. E. Atwood, a Canadian pilot who had been attached to the squadron for one night. This, as far as the crew was concerned, was unacceptable and the skipper, Geoff Maddern, went to protest to the CO. 'The Wingco,'

Charlwood believed, 'had intended giving us the better of the two aircraft but to us, L-London was unthinkable.' They had endured two bad experiences in aircraft code-named L. It was an unlucky letter. The CO granted their request. Atwood got L-London and they flew in B-Beer. But that night the port outer engine failed again, catching fire just after take-off. They dropped their bombs into the North Sea and headed back to Elsham. On landing, Charlwood went to see his girlfriend. When he returned to the crew room he found Geoff 'sitting moodily by the fire' talking to the flight engineer, Doug Richards. 'As I came in he glanced up. "Atwood has gone. [he said] L failed to return."

'We were silent for several seconds, then Doug said something we had forgotten in our moment of self-recrimination.

'"I think it might have gone the same way with them if they had taken B. They wouldn't have been prepared for that port outer. We were."

'Geoff was poking the fire. "I suppose that's the way it goes," he said.'[9]

The decision to maintain distinctions between commissioned and non-commissioned ranks within crews meant that they lived different lives when not in the air. Facilities were better for officers than NCOs though sometimes the differences were slight. Sergeants slept up to ten to a Nissen hut whereas officers' quarters offered a higher degree of comfort. Reg Fayers was delighted with the improvement in his accommodation after he was commissioned as a pilot officer. 'I'm sharing with a pilot called Wright who should soon be leaving,' he wrote to Phyllis. 'The room has at least the elements of comfort, including a chest of drawers, a fireplace conspicuously *sans feu*, a table, chairs, and wow, two mirrors.' The habit of dressing for dinner seemed 'a pleasant thing to do'. Even small privileges like the right to wear a soft, Van Heusen officer's collar rather than the stiff, chafing NCO variety were much appreciated.[10]

The quality of life depended on the quality of the station and amenities differed considerably. Fayers was at Holme-on-Spalding-Moor which had opened in 1941 and had been built to reasonably exacting pre-war standards. Dennis Field was based at Tuddenham, in Suffolk, one of the 'pre-fab' bases thrown up hastily in 1943. Promotion meant 'merely a change of Nissen huts . . . there were slightly fewer occupants and occasionally a WAAF swept and cleaned out.' The service in the mess was virtually the same. The main difference he noted, was a sombre one: 'when a crew did not come back, there might be one, or at most two empty beds next morning instead of six or seven.'[11]

The change in status could be unsettling. When Doug Mourton was made a pilot officer he went to Burberry's in London to be fitted with two barathea uniforms and a Crombie overcoat and went on fifteen days' leave 'feeling rather proud, especially as I walked along and acknowledged the salutes of the airmen and soldiers.' But when he returned to duty, he found he 'did not like living in the officers' mess which was so different to the sergeants' mess which I had been living in for several years. The atmosphere was different. I knew no one and felt out of it.'[12]

On base officers had to be formally invited into the sergeants' mess. Away from the station it was easy to mix even though official policy frowned on it. Good skippers took little notice of the rule. 'Officers weren't encouraged to go out at nights with the other ranks,' Reg Payne remembered. 'It was taboo. [But] we did have get-togethers.' Michael Beetham, his captain, organized private dinners for his crew and their wives and girlfriends at the Saracen's Head, the Lincoln hostelry where, during the war years, aircrew drank, flirted and relaxed. 'We had a room upstairs, a room with service. There was a fire in winter time. You rang the bell, the waiter would come to the door and you'd give him your order and he'd go downstairs [then] bring your drinks up.'[13]

As promotion was fairly rapid with many NCOs being commissioned after a reasonable period on operations the social divisions did not seem as irksome or unfair as they might have appeared to outsiders. There were occasions, though, when the distinction rankled. When the King and Queen visited Scampton on 27 May 1943, just after the Dams Raid, Len Sumpter, then still an NCO, was annoyed that they went straight to the officers' mess for lunch. 'All the photographs were taken with the officers in front of the officers' mess. But the flight sergeants and the sergeants didn't see a sign of the King and Queen. They didn't come near our mess. And yet there were more NCOs on the raid than there were officers.'[14]

When it came to medals it did seem that an officer's courage was more likely to be recognized than that of an NCO. The majority of aircrew, more than 70 per cent, were not commissioned. Yet the Distinguished Flying Medal (DFM), for acts of valour, courage and devotion to duty performed by an NCO, was awarded far less frequently than the Distinguished Flying Cross (DFC), which was given to officers. DFMs accounted for less than a quarter of the combined total of almost 27,000 DFMs and DFCs relating to the war.

The men of Bomber Command were among the boldest and most individualistic of their generation. They had been propelled towards the RAF by a sense of adventure as well as duty. It was unsurprising that the rigorous professionalism they showed in the air was not always reflected in their conduct on the ground, so that to some of the more unbending older officers they sometimes appeared more like civilians in uniform than proper servicemen. The pre-war culture of conformism and respect for authority meant that British volunteers were in the end reasonably adaptable to authority, if more apt than their peers in other services to question it. The men from the Dominions came from a less stratified world where rank was not automatically deferred to and discipline was founded on respect. Ken Newman was returning to Wickenby from an operation against oil storage depots in the Bordeaux area in August 1944 when he was ordered to divert to a faraway airfield in Scotland, as the base was about to be blanketed in low cloud. He thought it better to land at Sturgate in Lincolnshire which was much closer to home. This decision got him into trouble when he got back to Wickenby. He was told that as a result of his disobedience the trip might not count towards the crew's total of operations. When he passed this on his men, the Canadians in the crew 'were very angry indeed. This in their eyes was a prime example of the stupidity of senior RAF officers and of the "bullshit" that they had been warned about before arriving in the UK, and which they regarded as intolerable.' They threatened to telephone the Canadian High Commission in London. The authorities relented and let the operation stand.[15]

Everyone, no matter where they came from, was only too aware of the exceptional risks they were taking. They were disinclined to put up with displays of arrogance or attempts to impose mindless pre-war discipline. Flight Sergeant George Hull, a cultured Londoner who emerges from his many letters to his friend Joan Kirby as notably decent and dedicated, had to endure a dressing-down from the station commander at Coningsby after two WAAFs were reported for returning to their quarters after midnight in breach of the rules. Hull and some fellow NCOs had been seen chatting innocently to them earlier in the evening. The group captain accused them of 'disgraceful conduct', and doubled the offence by referring to them as 'errand boys and chimney sweeps'.

'Well feeling ran rather high I can tell you [Hull wrote]. As for the "Errand Boy" remarks, that is the statement of an out-and-out snob . . . Such [are] the antics of the brasshats in the RAF.' The crew retaliated by chalking 'Errand Boys' on the side of their Lancaster when they set off for Berlin the following day. The CO later apologized.[16]

Attempts to get crews to smarten up seemed ludicrous given the dangers they were facing. Cy March once got a 'rollicking' from a senior officer for the offence of allowing his air gunner brevet to come loose. 'He told me to go away and come back tidied up. I went away, put on my best blue, bulled up to death and went back. "That's much better," he said, "go away and keep smart." I could see us saluting before taking evasive action and asking permission to shoot.'[17]

The crews were facing nightly death, engaged in an open-ended struggle the point of which was often hard to discern. Persuading them to carry on doing so required subtle and intelligent leadership. Guy Gibson exemplified one approach to the problem. He was short, with rubbery good looks and a loud, confident manner that hid occasional deep depressions and agonies of self-doubt. He had the power to enthuse and inspire, and was sent by the government to give pep talks to war-workers and on morale-boosting missions to the United States.

Nonetheless many of the aircrew who encountered Gibson felt some ambivalence towards him. He had not been overly-popular among his colleagues in the pre-war RAF who found him boastful and bumptious, and later, after he had proved he had much to be boastful about, some still found his energy, flamboyance and unhesitating opinions off-putting.

He could, as Harold Hobday who flew with him on 617 Squadron noted, be 'the life and soul of the party' at squadron piss-ups, at least with fellow-officers. He also had a fine understanding of the dynamics of crew relationships. 'There was a bit of a rivalry between navigators and pilots. He came up to me and he said "You're a navigator, aren't you? I'll swap jackets with you." So we swapped jackets in the mess. It was rather a nice touch, because it made everybody feel how friendly he was.'[18]

It was his other side that Len Sumpter, who flew with him on the Dams Raid, saw. He only met him once to speak to. 'That's when he tore a strip off me,' he later remembered. Two days before the attack Sumpter took part in a dummy run at Reculver beach but released his bombs too early. 'He had me in the next morning and told me off about it.' There were no hard feelings. His Grenadier background made him appreciate discipline. Nonetheless he felt the faint chill of hauteur when he saw him around. 'He certainly wasn't a mixer down on the floor as far as we were concerned, the NCOs . . . Gibson had just a little bit of side.'

Cheshire however 'had no side or anything. He was one of the best. He wasn't blustering. Some people tell you to do something and you've got to do [it] that way . . . he'd put it in such a way, nicely, that you'd do it without being told to do it. He had a manner with him, softly spoken, quiet, never lost his temper, always smiling. And always joking too. He could be a little sarcastic sometimes but in a nice way . . . he was the best chap I met . . . as far as squadron commanders were concerned.'[19]

Cheshire struck everybody who came across him as remarkable in every way; exceptionally tough, brave and good. He possessed a warmth and humanity that touched all who were fortunate enough to serve with him. When Tony Iveson went to report to him on his first day at 617 Squadron he was greeted with an enthusiasm 'that made you feel he had been waiting to see you all day.'[20] He worked very hard at winning trust and affection and made sure he learned everybody's name, from the crews to the cooks. A story was told of how a wireless operator who had just arrived at Linton where Cheshire was commanding 76 Squadron felt an arm around his shoulder as he was boarding a truck to head out to dispersal. 'Good luck, Wilson,' said the CO, to the pleasant amazement of the newcomer who never imagined he would know his name.

He was without any trace of the snobbery that afflicted some senior officers and was as friendly towards the ground crews as he was with his airmen. Cheshire's manner masked a determination that was as strong as anybody's in Bomber Command. He was every bit as ruthless as Harris and shared his view that the more Germans that were killed the sooner the war would end. The government were quick to spot his potential. Like Gibson he wrote a book and gave morale-boosting lectures in war factories.

Cheshire's outstanding qualities made him a daunting act to follow. Many a commander fell short of the ideal he represented. On their way to 76 Squadron in the summer of 1943 Willie Lewis asked his skipper what sort of outfit they were joining. According to Lewis's thinly fictionalized account, Maze replied that it had 'quite a reputation. It was Cheshire's until about two weeks ago and you know what a fine type he is.' If they were expecting similiarly inspirational leadership they were in for a disappointment. His replacement

> stared at them across the table with cold, hard eyes. They were just another crew to him and not an attractive one. A tall, thin pilot with a stoop, an officer gunner and a group of shabby-looking NCOs . . . how long would they last, he asked himself? Not very long! Even the smart crews disappeared in no time. Just the same it was his job to welcome them.

'How long have you flown on Halifaxes?' he asked. His thin, black moustache, set in a white face, made the question appear [like] a sneer.

'Forty-four hours sir,' replied John.

'Hmm. Hardly enough to learn how to land it properly. You fellows are sent on here only half-trained and we have to do our best to make you operational quickly. It's not good enough . . .'

He sighed wearily and glanced towards the side wall where a score of photographs showed the existing crews . . .

'I'm not going to disguise from you that we are losing crews steadily so there won't be much time to give you training flights. You'll get one crosscountry and that's all.'

After telling Maze that he would fly two trips as 'second dicky' with an experienced pilot he dismissed them. Jock, the wireless operator, thought him a 'damn unfriendly type' who 'made me feel as welcome as a leper'. Joe the bomb-aimer remarked that he did not 'look to me as if he would like anybody'. Jock disagreed. 'Oh, he likes himself all right. You can see that.'[21]

The best squadron commanders were those who conveyed an understanding of what their men were going through. On his first day at his conversion unit Don Charlwood reported to 'a pale boyish squadron leader who wore the ribbons of the DSO and DFC over his battledress pocket. Of his words I remember very little but his dark, staring eyes I have never forgotten. I felt that they had looked on the worst: and on looking beyond it, had found serenity. They gazed from an impassive face with a challengingly upthrust chin and firm mouth.' This was David Holford who won the DFC at eighteen and the DSO at twenty-one. He was now only twenty-two but had already completed sixty operations. His men loved him. A year later when Halford was in charge of a Heavy Conversion Unit at Lindholme, Charlwood heard a flight sergeant say that if Halford decided to return for a third tour half the base would follow him. He did eventually go back on operations and was killed in 1943 while landing in fog. In Charlwood's valuable judgement 'he was the personification of all that was best in the RAF.'[22]

Squadron leaders were not required to fly on every operation. But it was essential if they were to maintain their authority to go on some, and they were expected to accompany their men two or three times a month. The crews were contemptuous of those who put themselves down for relatively easy trips to France and Italy and grateful to COs who volunteered to share the dangers of Berlin or the Ruhr. Ken Newman had a particular admiration for his CO at 12 Squadron, Wing Commander John Nelson. He was 'a thick-set New Zealander in his thirties who was liked and respected by every-one. He led the squadron from the front and was often in trouble with the Air Officer Commanding No 1 Group for taking part in too many operational sorties . . . But John Nelson headed the oper-ational order whenever the target was a tough or interesting one. Moreover he seemed indefatigable, as he was always present at briefings and in the debriefing room when the squadron's aircraft returned . . . whatever time of day or night . . .'[23]

Displays of reckless courage were by no means appreciated, how-ever. One night Doug Mourton found himself flying with Squadron Leader Burnett who had just arrived on the squadron but had already established a reputation as a 'press-on type'. The target was Hamburg. It was, Mourton wrote later, 'one of the most nerve-racking flights I had taken part in. The anti-aircraft that night was particularly heavy and on the run up to the target we were caught in about twelve search lights. It was so bright it was impossible to see. If Stevens [an earlier skipper] had been the pilot he would have shouted to the bomb-aimer, "Drop those bloody bombs and let's piss off home," but Squadron Leader Burnett was made of different stuff.' He put the aircraft into a steep dive and jinked and weaved his way out of the searchlights' glare. Then to Mourton's dismay he announced they were going in again. 'The majority of aircraft had now left and once again the searchlights came on us and the anti-aircraft began noisily banging all around us. Somehow we got out of it, but it was only purely by luck, and eventually we left the target area and returned home.'[24]

Many of the Bomber Boys were young, green and away from home for the first time. If they were lucky there was someone on the base who took a fatherly interest in their feelings and concerns. Brian Frow found such a figure when he was posted to 61 Squadron at North Luffenham. Flight Lieutenant 'Cape' Capel was the squadron adjutant and a veteran of the First World War. He was was 'a tower of strength to me personally. He seemed to be aware of matters which were not obvious, and able to advise without being patronizing.' When he discovered that while Frow could pilot a four-engined bomber he could not drive the Hillman runabout allotted to each flight he saved him any loss of face by giving him a few lessons. He then took him for a test drive to a local pub where they spent a pleasant evening talking about everything but the RAF. 'This display of support, so essential to a newly commissioned, very inexperienced skipper was a tremendous boost and had a vital but subtle effect on my development as a Bomber Boy,' he wrote. 'It certainly helped me to face the terrible events that I was about to witness and experience.'[25]

In the air it was on the shoulders of the skipper that the burden of maintaining morale weighed the heaviest. Confidence was the great sustaining quality and Willie Lewis's skipper John Maze had it in abundance. Pilot Officer John Maze was really Etienne Maze. He was the son of Paul Maze, a French painter who became an unlikely but firm friend of Arthur Harris. He seemed unshakeable, cool to the point of numbness. It seemed at times, alarmingly, as if life meant little to him. But there was also an earthiness there and a love of comfort that reassured. Soon after he met Lewis he told him his father had a beautiful young mistress. 'His eyes glowed and he obviously would have loved to go to bed with her.' Maze found the long journeys to and from the target tedious. Hanging around in the air above the base waiting to get down was particularly tiresome. Even though the bombers were free of their loads on the return leg, it still took longer than the outward trip, partly because they were flying into the prevailing westerly wind, partly because they flew slower than their maximum speed to help crippled aircraft keep within the relative safety of the bomber stream. As one of a hundred blips on the German radar screens there was a reasonable chance of slipping through the defences whereas a lone smudge was naked and exposed.

Maze knew this. However he 'was twenty years old, a healthy, youthful animal with all a young man's indifference to such an explanation . . . Let the lame dogs look after themselves as *we* shall if the time comes to do so. Meanwhile *we* live, *our* "kite" is not knocked about and *we* are bored.' Lewis believed that Maze was 'born impatient' and seized by the conviction that 'there was too much fuss in the world. He was prepared to go to any lengths to ensure bombing correctly, but the moment that was over he was desperately anxious to get home in the shortest possible time from a feeling of utter boredom and the knowledge that they had done the job well.'

For the first three operations he followed the flight plan dutifully but on the fourth flew back faster than instructed and was the first bomber to reach the base. After that, T-Tommy was almost invariably the first to touch down. He was in an equal hurry to get into the air. He received regular dressings-down from the squadron commander for breaking the speed limit set on the journey to the runway.

Maze was fun. The ground crews adored him and he held his own at parties. On his twenty-first birthday he took the crew to a pub, 'got hopelessly drunk, broke one of the cues of the billiard table and went on singing a filthy [song] from his schooldays.' He might be little older than a schoolboy, but Lewis recognized that 'there was nothing soft about him.' He seemed to disdain fear. 'Look here, Joe, I'm sick to death of you getting frightened all the time,' he once snapped at the bomb-aimer. 'It's like having an old woman sitting next to me.' When Joe replied that he was 'not frightened, just a bit apprehensive,' he was told: 'Well *don't be*.'[26]

Pilots could feel a responsibility for their crews that transcended their own safety and survival instincts. There were several well-attested cases when skippers had kept a stricken aircraft flying long enough for the others to bale out, even though they knew they would die doing so. Flying Officer Leslie Manser was captain of a

Manser VC.

Manchester during the Cologne 'thousand' raid when it was hit by flak and caught fire. Both pilot and crew could have baled out safely but Manser insisted on trying to get his aircraft and his men home. When it became clear that this was impossible he ordered the others to bale out. The official citation for his Victoria Cross described how 'a sergeant handed him a parachute but he waved it away, telling [him] to jump at once as he could only hold the aircraft steady for a few seconds more.' As the crew floated safely to earth they saw the Manchester 'still carrying their gallant captain, plunge to earth and burst into flames.' They landed in Holland and five of them managed to evade the Germans and make their way back home.

Perhaps even more extraordinary was the fortitude shown by Flight Sergeant Rawdon Middleton, an Australian Stirling pilot during a raid on the Fiat works at Turin in November 1942. He pressed his attack through a storm of flak and delivered his bombs but was hit by shrapnel which tore out his right eye and ripped away his nose. Despite being barely able to see, or to speak without great pain and loss of blood, he managed to nurse the damaged bomber over the Alps. There was a discussion as to whether they should jump. Middleton, according to his citation, 'expressed the intention of trying to make the English coast so that his crew could leave the aircraft by parachute,' even though he knew that owing 'to his wounds and diminishing strength . . . by then he would have little or no chance of saving himself.' When they crossed the English coast there was only five minutes' worth of petrol left. He ordered the crew to jump. Five of the crew left the aircraft safely while two chose to stay on and help their skipper. The bomber crashed into the sea killing all aboard. Middleton too received the VC. The awards were made easier because there were witnesses alive to tell their remarkable tales. There were surely many other stories of amazing bravery and devotion which will remain buried with the dead.

The crew took some of its character from its skipper. But the joint identity was always stronger than the individual. No one in the chain of command was more motivating or inspiring than the collective spirit of seven men engaged in the enterprise of dealing death and trying to cheat it. The crew was where it began and where it ended. Writing to Joan from his dreary base in a mood of self-pity George Hull told her 'Thank God for the crew . . . a fierce bond has sprung up between us . . . we sleep together, we shower together and, yes, we even arrange to occupy adjacent bogs and sing each other into a state of satisfaction.'[27]

It was the crew that dissolved despair and doubt. Don Charlwood had 'little belief in the rectitude of our war or any other war,' when he arrived on his squadron. 'Nor could I believe that more good than evil would arise from our mass bombing.' Yet after a few operations he realized his attitude had altered. 'On the squadron one could not for long admit cynicism, or pessimism, even in the face of the worst. Whatever my frame of mind had been when we had come to Elsham, I realized that now it had changed. Then I had been alone; now I had become one with a crew and a squadron. To demean them was impossible.'[28]

11

The Big City

After almost four years of war Bomber Command had failed to do any critical damage to Berlin. If one of the main objectives of the strategic air campaign was to destroy German morale then the Big City was the best place to attack. Berlin was protected by its distance from the bomber bases, and by its very size which enabled it to absorb much punishment. It sprawled over more than eighty square miles and the townscape was interspersed with lakes, waterways, parks and woods. The centre was designed for victory parades. Broad boulevards led into spacious squares. There were statues everywhere. As the saying went, even the birdshit was marble. There was no *Altmarkt*, no wooden-built mediaeval quarter for Harris to burn down.

Despite these drawbacks, he yearned to attack Berlin. He was convinced that an all-out assault on the heart of Nazidom would bring the war to an end. He had used the short summer nights of 1943 to batter the Ruhr. As the hours of darkness lengthened, he intended to exploit the cover they provided to switch the assault to the capital.

Harris's mission of destroying German cities had been endorsed at the start of the year at the Casablanca conference, when the British and the Americans met to co-ordinate their approach to a war which was now going their way. There, Bomber Command had been told its primary object was the 'progressive destruction of the German military, industrial and economic system, and the undermining of the morale of the German people to a point where their armed resistance is fatally weakened.'

Berlin had been mentioned specifically as a suitable objective for night attack. A few weeks after the conference ended, a directive from the Air Ministry to Harris drew attention to the recent Soviet

199

success at Stalingrad, where, on the last day of January, the bitter siege had ended in German defeat and abject surrender. It passed on the view of the War Cabinet that 'it is most desirable . . . that we should rub in the Russian victory by further attacks on Berlin as soon as conditions are favourable.'[1] This was probably Churchill talking. In 1942 he had sent several impatient memos demanding to know when the dismantling of Berlin would begin.

All this suited Harris very well. It was in line with previous directives which had given him the latitude to develop the technique of area bombing so that attacks were becoming steadily more devastating, and to his mind, more effective. There was nothing to suggest that he would be expected to pay more attention to the doctrines of the Americans who were by now increasingly active in the air war, albeit in a different role to that adopted by Britain. The Americans attacked by day and maintained their faith in precision operations. The British bombed by night, hitting what they could.

Harris was not against precise attacks on specific targets. The Dams Raid was the proof of that and Bomber Command carried out many other less celebrated but no less effective missions like it. But he believed they were only a subordinate part of the main strategy of bombing Germany's major cities flat.

His composure was to be badly disturbed by new orders which superseded the Casablanca directive. The Pointblank directive, issued early in June, threatened to alter the course of Bomber Command's war dramatically.

It reflected a harsh new reality in the air war, and the Americans were feeling its impact painfully. The Eighth Air Force had begun flying from England in August 1942. At first it confined its operations to France. The USAAF believed that to be sure of hitting the target it was necessary to bomb in daylight. It was confident that the firepower that its Fortresses and Liberators could bring to bear when grouped in disciplined formations would provide enough protection to make day-time bombing viable without the protection of escorting fighters.

The Americans' experience in France seemed to justify this confidence. When they started operating in Germany, bombing

Wilhelmshaven on 27 January 1943, the results were similarly encouraging. Out of ninety-one bombers sent, only three were lost. It soon became clear that these figures were freakishly low. As operations continued, losses climbed. In May they rose to 6.4 per cent of all attacking aircraft, a level that could not be sustained. Many were victims of flak. But the main threat came from the German fighter force which grew steadily stronger throughout the year.

As the peril increased in the months after Casablanca, the commander of the Eighth Air Force, Brigadier-General Ira C. Eaker, made a plan to deal with it. He proposed a combined American-British bombing offensive to crush the reviving German air force and win air superiority for the Allies.

Pointblank framed the means of achieving this crucial goal. It reasserted the American belief in precision bombing by concentrating effort on selected targets which if attacked effectively would have a devastating effect on German military operations. To achieve success it was essential to first sweep the German fighters from the skies. This was stated in the first draft of the directive, issued on 3 June, with a clarity that left no room for misunderstanding. It ordered the American and British forces 'to seek the destruction of enemy fighters in the air and on the ground'. That meant attacking factories that made airframes, engines and ball-bearings, repair facilities, component stores and anything else that kept the Luftwaffe flying.

The approach made clear sense. By establishing air superiority, the job of the Allied air forces would become much easier and safer and their efforts more efficient. It was the obvious lesson to be learned from the defeat of the German air force in the Battle of Britain. One of the reasons the Luftwaffe lost was that they switched the force of their attacks away from airfields and aviation factories and on to towns, giving the RAF a lifesaving respite.

Harris did not see it that way. He regarded the Eaker approach as desirable but unattainable and therefore a waste of effort and resources. His response was to mount a slogging, bureaucratic rearguard action of the type he excelled at. In doing so, he had the passive backing of Portal, even though Portal had been party to the drafting of Pointblank. He nonetheless allowed his subordinate to interpret the new orders in a way which contradicted their intention. Portal's indulgent attitude was in part a bow to reality. Harris enjoyed close relations with Churchill and made use of the proximity of Bomber Command's headquarters at High Wycombe to the prime minister's country retreat at Chequers to visit him at least once a week. A head-on confrontation would do no one any good. Bomber Command continued to pursue its mission along the lines laid down at Casablanca and the work of destroying the German air force fell largely on the shoulders of the Americans.

Harris laid out his plans for Berlin in a minute to Churchill on 3 November 1943. They were bold, even by his extravagant standards. Whatever he thought of American methods he was eager to have their aircraft in on the attack. With their help, he declared, 'we can wreck Berlin from end to end ... it will cost between us 400–500 aircraft. It will cost Germany the war.'[2] The Americans were sceptical, as Harris must have known they would be. He was later to use their negative response to dodge the blame for what was to be recognized by everyone but himself as a dreadful defeat.

Harris's confidence had been bolstered by the successes of Bomber Command's summer campaign culminating in the raids of July and August that destroyed Hamburg and spelled out what 'undermining the morale of the German people' would mean in practice. The Hamburg raids showed what the RAF was now capable of. Two thirds of the population, about 1,200,000 people, were evacuated from the city or left under their own steam, leaving the rubble to a core of heroic defenders. The unsurpassed horror of what happened was beyond the control of even the Nazi propaganda apparatus. Bomber Command had managed to frighten Germany. Adolf Galland, the Battle of Britain Luftwaffe pilot who at the time was inspector of fighters at the German air ministry, wrote later that a 'wave of terror radiated from the suffering city and spread through Germany ... In every large town people said "what happened to Hamburg yesterday can happen to us tomorrow" ... After Hamburg in the wide circle of the political and military command could be heard the words: "The war is lost."'[3]

The Nazi leadership was now seriously concerned about how much punishment the population would be able to absorb. Hitler's munitions minister Albert Speer said at his post-war interrogation that 'we were of the opinion that a rapid repetition of this type of attack upon another six German towns would inevitably cripple the will to sustain armament manufacture and war production.' He reported to the Führer his opinion that 'a continuation of these attacks might bring about a rapid end to the war.'[4] But as Speer learned, it was unwise to underestimate the resilience of civilian morale. The majority of workers who fled Hamburg returned soon after. It was calculated later that less than two months of production had been lost.

Gains in the bombing war tended to be temporary. An important element in the Hamburg raids had been the use of *Window* which gave the attackers a strong initial advantage over the German defences. But the brief history of military aviation showed that new developments were quickly neutralized by counter-measures. The rule was to be proved again.

Under the existing system, the Germans' first line of defence had been the curtain of night-fighters based at aerodromes back from the North Sea and Channel coasts. As the incoming bombers passed through the radar 'boxes' of the Kammhuber line, they were picked up on the German radar screens. Ground controllers would then direct individual fighter areas on to their quarry.

'[He] would tell you,' said Peter Spoden, a German night-fighter pilot, '"We have a target for you five miles ahead . . . turn left now, a little bit more to the left. Higher, higher, speed up. Four miles, three miles, two miles. And if the ground controller was clever he brought the target up above you so that you were in the dark below and you [could] see the British bomber as a kind of silhouette. The first [thing] you saw were the eight flames from the exhaust from the four engines. Then you were closing in . . .' The arrangements were strictly localized and the night-fighter squadrons were manned by veteran *Experten* who appreciated the decorations and promotions arising from their relatively easy victories.

The method, though, had its limitations. The men flying the

Me110 night-fighters.

Messerschmitt 109s and 110s felt just the same determination to defend their homes and families as had their RAF counterparts during the Battle of Britain. Peter Spoden was an eighteen-year-old student at Hamburg University when the RAF bombed his home town of Essen in 1940. Like many young Germans he had learned to fly gliders at the air schools originally set up by the Nazis to circumvent restrictions on military activity. After the raid he joined the Luftwaffe with the specific intention of becoming a night-fighter pilot. He shared the frustration of the younger pilots at the limitations imposed by the system. He was flying in a box named 'Orion' over Rügen Island when the great Hamburg raid went in. 'I could see Hamburg. I could see the immense fire and I also could see closer to me two or three four-engined planes like moths against the cloud . . . I told my controller, "please let me go" but he did not have any radar reception there . . . I asked him again, "I can see them, I can see them." I was an eager young pilot and I had not had any great success at the time.'[5] Permission was refused. For Spoden and his peers, the arrival of *Window* inadvertently created just the freedom of action they sought.

The confusion it had sown was alarming, but temporary. The

Germans responded quickly and cleverly. The controllers learned to follow the cloud of *Window* as it formed on their screens and deduce from that the direction and likely objective of the bomber stream. As the raid developed, fighters were summoned from all over to harass the raiders as they converged on the target. Over the city the fighters would use whatever light was available from the search-lights, fires and marker flares to locate their quarry as they flew straight and level on the last crucial minutes of the bombing run. It was dangerous work. The flak batteries were supposed to keep their fire below a certain height but such instructions could be forgotten in the heat of battle. They harried and struck at the intruders all the way back, with gratifying effectiveness.

The efficiency of the German defences was further improved by the arrival of new aircraft. By early 1944, Junker 88s had mostly replaced Messerschmitt 110s as the standard aircraft of the night-fighter force. Their ability to find their targets was greatly improved by onboard radar and their killing capacity increased by a new armament which arrived in the summer of 1943. These were cannons, known as *Schräge Musik,* which were angled to fire upwards and slightly forward. The tactic was to slink up below the victim and fire a burst into its belly, heavy with high explosive and incen-diaries. The resulting explosion could prove fatal to attacker and quarry alike.

The strengthened German fighter force was therefore as much a danger to the British as it was to the Americans. Once they came within range of a fighter there was little a bomber could do to defend itself. A fully-laden Lancaster could only manage an airspeed of 180 knots on the way out and 210 on the return. Their .303 machine guns were not a serious weapon. The only defence was the corkscrew and that was only intermittently effective against a smaller and more nimble opponent. As Noble Frankland knew from bitter experience, once located, the odds were heavily against the bombers. The truth was that 'outpaced, outmanoeuvred and out-gunned by the German night-fighters and in a generally highly inflammable and explosive condition, these black monsters pre-sented an ideal target to any fighter pilot who could find them, and it was the night-fighters which caused the overwhelming majority of the losses sustained by Bomber Command in the Battle of Berlin.' At this stage of the war the figure stood at about 70 per cent.[6]

Despite the enormous dangers and difficulties involved, Bomber Command entered the battle in an optimistic mood. Hamburg had impressed everybody. Even Harris's critics in the Air Ministry gave their firm support. The mood was buoyed up by two other cheering developments. On 17 August the Americans carried out their first deep penetration operation in Germany. True to their doctrine of precision targeting they sent out 376 B-17 Flying Fortresses against ball-bearing factories in Schweinfurt and the Messerschmitt works at Regensburg. They lost sixty aircraft but inflicted serious damage on both objectives. That evening Bomber Command carried out a precision raid of its own. Nearly 600 bombers set off in the moon-light to blast the German research and rocket production base at Peenemünde on the Baltic coast. The operation set back the programme by several months.

In this positive atmosphere the decision was taken to mount some preliminary raids before the main effort. The first phase opened with three attacks in late August and early September. The results were sobering. The bombs missed the city centre, little serious damage was done and losses were heavy. On the first raid, in which 727 aircraft took part, nearly 8 per cent of the heavy-bomber force was lost, the heaviest toll in one night so far in the war. Most of them were Halifaxes and Stirlings. On the third raid, only the better-performing Lancasters were sent. Even so, out of the 316 despatched, 22 were lost, a rate of 7 per cent.

There was a respite until winter and darkness set in. Given the poor results of the initial attacks, Harris also wanted to wait until the new type of *H2S* onboard radar arrived. The battle proper began on the night of 18/19 November and was to continue until 31 March 1944. There were sixteen major attacks on Berlin, as well as an equal number of heavy raids on other German cities designed to unbalance the defences and keep the controllers uncertain as to the objective that night.

The Battle of Berlin was the harshest test to which Bomber Command had yet been subjected. The target was far away and was reached by flying long hours through freezing and treacherous skies. Harris wrote afterwards that 'the whole battle was fought in appalling weather and in conditions resembling those of no other campaign in the history of warfare. Scarcely a single crew caught a single glimpse of the objective they were attacking ... thousands upon thousands of tons of bombs were aimed at the Pathfinders' pyrotechnic skymarkers and fell through unbroken cloud which concealed everything below it except the confused glare of fires.'[7]

The brevity of the tactical advantage bestowed by *Window* was apparent in the first few days of the campaign in the weight of losses sustained by the Stirlings and Halifaxes, now the most elderly machines in Bomber Command's line-up. Stirlings were handicapped by their inability to reach the same altitude as the others and were forced to occupy the bottom layer of the bomber stream. This was the most vulnerable position and they suffered accordingly. Between August and the third week in November 109 Stirlings were destroyed, a loss rate of 6.4 per cent. At this point, the decision was taken to drop them from the front-line force. They never took part in operations in Germany again and their squadrons were given less dangerous work until they could be re-equipped with Lancasters.

The Halifaxes moved into the hazardous spot vacated by the Stirlings and suffered an even worse fate. In the eleven weeks from mid-December 1943 to mid-February 1944 nearly 10 per cent of all Halifax sorties to Germany ended in disaster. In January 1944, the worst month of the battle, the Canadian 434 Squadron lost 24.2 per cent of the aircraft it sent to Berlin, 102 Squadron lost 18.7 per cent and 76 Squadron 16.7 per cent. These losses were unbearable and once again Harris was forced on to the defensive. After another painful night over Leipzig on 19/20 February he withdrew a further ten squadrons.

The Battle of Berlin had a shape and chronology that made it easier to follow than Harris's previous 'battles'. In it, he pitted the aircraft available against what he took to be weakened German defenders in an effort to deal a crushing blow to the enemy's heart.

It was a battle of attrition that, as was clear long before the finish, would only end one way.

Harris started out with 700 four-engined bombers, a larger force of heavy aircraft than he had yet had at his disposal. They were capable of carrying bomb loads of 1,500 tons on each raid, quantities that if the targets were correctly marked, would result in the systematic wrecking of the city, district by district. As always, there were grave problems in finding exactly where to drop the bombs. Berlin was 250 miles beyond the range of *Oboe*. It was up to those Pathfinder marker aircraft that were equipped with *H2S* to spot the target. Berlin's vast spread made it difficult to pick out individual features on the blotchy picture painted by the electronic echo. The image was further confused by the lakes, canals and rivers of that watery city.

The Battle of Berlin required new levels of fortitude and endurance from the Bomber Command crews. To sustain their morale they had to believe that they were making progress. Many of those taking part were new to the game. Reg Payne and his crew had arrived at Skellingthorpe to join 50 Squadron just after the battle began. Skipper Michael Beetham and the rest of the crew gathered for the main briefing on the afternoon of 22 November 1943. The last squadron raid had been against the railway line linking France to Italy at Modane, which was widely regarded as a 'piece of cake'. Payne was hoping for a return trip, a nice gentle way of easing into ops. He was to be disappointed. When the CO strode in, 'he drew the curtain straight back and said your target for tonight is Berlin ... on the map there was this red line going up over the Baltic somewhere, towards Denmark and down ... it was a bit of a shaker really ... the crews were aghast. They all went "oooh." They knew it was going to be an eight-hour trip.'8

To add to their burden, Harris had ordered that each Lancaster should carry 2,000 pounds of extra bombs. Getting airborne with the standard load was nerve-racking enough. As freshmen, Beetham's crew were spared the extra cargo.

Sixteen of the squadron's twenty-two crews were on that night. It was a big operation with 764 aircraft; 469 Lancasters, 234 Halifaxes,

50 Stirlings and 11 Mosquitoes. It was the largest force sent to Germany yet. Payne sat in his little wireless-operator's den, curtained off from the rest of the crew. As they rumbled down to the runway he looked out at the port inner engine and felt nervous. He could see 'the flames coming off the exhaust . . . after we were given the green light the pilot released the brakes and the engines went full bore so you thought they were almost out of control.' The sight of the two-foot-long flames licking over the top of the wings caused him to remember that 'there were two thousand gallons of petrol in those wings as well as the five tons of bombs on board.' It only needed one engine to malfunction for the take-off to fail. On short runways the pilots would instruct the engineer to remove the gate on the throttle to push up the revs a dangerous little bit higher. The engines could only stand five minutes of it before they overheated and seized up. Sitting powerless at his little desk Payne felt 'that the take-off was more frightening than anything else.'

As a new crew, they were at the back of the bomber stream. The idea was that by the time they got to Berlin the target would be ablaze and easily recognizable. They circled Lincoln cathedral then headed north and east. Payne checked his onboard radar and picked up occasional test broadcasts from base. Close to Denmark they saw a few searchlights and some desultory flak rise from the shores of Sweden. As Germany approached, Payne started shoving bundles of *Window*, lying in the gangway next to him, up to the nose where the bomb-aimer pushed them through a chute.

Nobody troubled them until they approached Berlin. The weather was terrible and many of the night-fighters were grounded. Then, ahead, he could see 'the searchlights in the distance and the glow underneath the clouds. I realized that this was the real thing when the gunners said an aircraft had just been shot down behind us.' Each sighting of a blazing bomber was noted by the navigator in his log to report to the intelligence officer when, or if, he returned.

The mayhem was building outside but inside Beetham's Lancaster there was a weird calm. 'There was no real excitement at all,' Payne remembered, 'it was all very well controlled.' Berlin was covered with cloud. They had been ordered to bomb on the green and red markers, which hung over the murk. The bomb-aimer, Les Bartlett, coaxed Beetham on to the right line. The bomb doors opened. Payne felt the blast of freezing air, a welcome antidote to the heat from the engines. Beneath his feet he could feel the grind and jangle of the shackle holding the cookie as the bomb left its moorings, and the aircraft leapt upwards. For a few more agonizing seconds the Lancaster ploughed on straight and level until the camera flash signalled the end of the immediate ordeal.

They swung away and into the flak. Payne switched out his light and climbed into the astrodome. 'It was about ten-tenths cloud and the searchlights never really got through. All they did was make the clouds glow. They showed the Lancasters up. You could see them going over the top of it like black fish . . . the flak was coming right through the clouds. You could smell it as well. Some of the fumes would get into the aircraft especially on the bomb run when the bomb doors were open.'

On this, his first trip, he felt 'excitement more than anything'. Casualties were light. Bad weather kept the night-fighters on the ground. Only twenty-six aircraft were lost, 3.4 per cent of the force. Despite the appalling visibility, the results were good. The devastation stretched from the centre west across the smart residential areas of Tiergarten and Charlottenburg and out to the suburb of Spandau. Several firestorms were ignited and a huge pillar of smoke towered nearly 19,000 feet the following day. About 2,000 died in the attack and 175,000 were bombed out of their homes. Thousands of soldiers were brought in to calm the chaos.

On the afternoon after the raid, Marie 'Missie' Vassiltchikov was leaving her office in the information department of the ministry of foreign affairs when the hall porter told her another air raid was imminent. She was twenty-six years old, an exiled Russian aristocrat who had been tossed by the fortunes of war into the cauldron of Berlin. There, she had made friends with a small, upper-class group of dedicated anti-Nazis. 'I took to the stairs two at a time to warn those of my colleagues who lived far away to stay put as they might otherwise be caught in the open,' she wrote in her diary. Just after she arrived at the flat where she lived with her father, the flak opened up. It was 'immediately very violent.' Her papa, who scraped a living teaching languages, 'emerged with his pupils and we all hurried down to the half-basement behind the kitchen, where we usually sit out air raids. We had hardly got there when we heard the first approaching planes. They flew very low and the barking of the flak was suddenly drowned by a very different sound – that of exploding bombs, first far away and then closer and closer, until it semed as if they were falling literally on top of us. At every crash the house shook. The air pressure was dreadful and the noise deafening. For the first time I understood what the expression *Bombenteppich* [bomb carpet] means.'

At one point there was a shower of broken glass and all three doors of the basement flew into the room, torn off their hinges. 'We pressed them back into place and leant against them to try and keep them shut.' Missie jumped to her feet at every crash. Her father, however, 'imperturbable as always, remained seated . . . the crashes followed one another so closely and were so earsplitting that at the worst moments I stood behind him, holding on to his shoulders by way of self-protection. What a family bouillabaisse we would have made!'

Before the all-clear sounded they were warned to get out of the house by a passing naval officer. The wind had risen and there was a danger of firestorms. They left the basement and 'sure enough, the sky on three sides was blood-red.'[9]

The fires passed the Vassiltchikovs by but the raid claimed the lives of 1,500 people that night. The attack was a new and appalling experience for Berliners. One of Missie's colleagues in the foreign ministry, Hans-Georg von Studnitz, arrived with his wife in the city after a few days away with friends in Pomerania just after the raid finished. The population, he wrote in his diary, had 'lived through an indescribable experience and survived what seemed like the end of the world.'

Their train stopped in the suburbs. They set out to try and reach home by foot but were forced to give up. 'The air was so polluted with the smell of burning and with the fumes of escaping gas, the darkness was so impenetrable and the torrents of rain so fierce that our strength began to fail us. Our progress was further barred by uprooted trees, broken telegraph poles, torn high-tension cables, craters, mounds of rubble and broken glass. All the time the wind kept on tearing window-frames, slates and gutters from the destroyed buildings and hurling them into the street.'

And this was only on the outskirts. When, the following morning, they finally reached the city centre by underground and emerged at Alexanderplatz, the bombers had long gone but Berlin was still a 'burning hell. . . all around the destroyed station in the Alexanderplatz the great warehouses were burning fiercely. Further towards the city stood the Royal Palace, the former residence of the Hohenzollerns, in the middle of a tornado of fire and smoke . . . we crossed the Spree into the burning banking quarter. The Zeughaus, the university, the Hedwigskirche and the National Library had all been reduced to ashes . . . the Tiergarten looked like some forest battle scene from the First World War.'[10]

At the edge of the Tiergarten stood a huge flak tower and reinforced concrete shelter which could hold up to 18,000 people. Even those inside could feel the ferocity of the attack. The tower received a direct hit and, according to Konrad Warner, 'the massive building was shaken to its foundations. The light went out and suddenly there was a deadly silence.' When he finally emerged after the all-clear, his coat was set on fire by the blizzard of sparks.[11]

The two consecutive attacks had created far less devastation than had been done to Hamburg. It was, however, to turn out to be the high point of the campaign. Bomber Command went back fourteen more times before the end of the Battle of Berlin but with nothing like the same success.

The poor results came at a high price. On the last trip of the month, on 26/27 November, twenty-eight Lancasters were destroyed and fourteen more crashed on landing. On 2/3 December the German controllers identified Berlin as the target in sufficient time for the area to be swarming when the bomber stream arrived. This time, a total of forty bombers were lost.

The American journalist Ed Murrow, famous for his broadcasts from Britain during the Blitz, accompanied 619 Squadron commander

'Jock' Abercromby on the trip. He described the experience in a powerful piece of reportage which went out on his *This is London* programme. It was an eventful night for Murrow who did not hide the intense fear he felt over the target. He told his audience that 'the thirty miles to the bombing run was the longest flight I have ever made. Dead on time . . . the bomb-aimer reported "target indicators going down". At the same moment the sky ahead was lit up by bright yellow flares. Off to starboard another kite went down in flames. The flares were sprouting all over the sky – reds and greens and yellows and we were flying straight for the fireworks.' The bomber he was in, D-Dog, 'seemed to be standing still, the four propellers thrashing the air but we didn't seem to be closing in.' Then, without warning 'D-Dog was filled with an unhealthy white light. I was standing just behind Jock and could see the seams of the wings. His quiet Scots voice beat into my ears: "Steady lads, we've been coned." His slender body lifted half out of the seat as he jammed the control column forwards and to the left. We were going down. Jock was wearing woollen gloves with the fingers cut off. I could see his fingernails turn white as he gripped the wheel. And then I was on my knees, flat on the deck, for he had whipped the Dog back into a slashing turn. The knees should have been strong enough to support me, but they weren't, and the stomach seemed in some danger of letting me down too . . .' As the bomber flipped over Murrow glimpsed what was happening on the ground. 'The cookies . . . were bursting below like great sunflowers gone mad . . . I looked down and the white fires had turned red; they were beginning to merge and spread just like butter does on a hot plate.'

Berlin, he said later, 'was a kind of orchestrated hell – a terrible symphony of light and flame. It isn't a pleasant form of warfare.' The men he flew with spoke 'of it as a job.' Before he left Woodhall Spa he looked into the briefing room where 'the tapes were stretched out on the big map all the way to Berlin and back again. A young pilot with old eyes said to me "I see we're working again tonight."'

And so the labour went on, dangerous, dispiriting and without

any obvious signs of progress. The authorities were eager to emphasize the importance of the work and the value of the sacrifices. The
anonymous editor of the 115 Squadron news-sheet stressed that
Berlin would be the target 'until the place is wiped out. It is the
HQ of nearly everything that matters in Germany – Armaments,
Engineering, Foodstuffs, Administration. Berlin is the "London of
Germany". Until Berlin is Hamburged Jerry's mainspring is wound
up.'[12] Freeman Dyson, a civilian scientist at Bomber Command
headquarters, wrote afterwards that 'the boys in the Lancasters were
told that this Battle of Berlin was one of the decisive battles of the
war and that they were winning it. I did not know how many of
them believed what they were told. I knew only that what they were
told was untrue.' Dyson, who worked in the Operational Research
Centre, had studied the bomb patterns from photographs which
showed they were being scattered over an enormous area. It was true
that Berlin contained a great variety of war industries and administrative centres. 'But Bomber Command was not attempting to find and
attack these objectives individually. We merely showered incendiary
bombs over the city in as concentrated a fashion as possible, with a
small fraction of high-explosive bombs to discourage the fire-
fighters. Against blanket attacks the defence could afford to be selective, with fire-fighters giving priority to dousing fires in factories and
leaving houses to burn.' He concluded that with bomber losses
rising sharply there was 'no chance that continuing the offensive in
such a style could have any decisive effect on the war.'[13]

Dyson's prescriptions were unrealistic. Everyone wanted precision. But the technology could not deliver it. The Harris approach
relied on weight of numbers. But as the battle progressed it was
clear those numbers were dwindling alarmingly. On the thirteenth
trip, during the night of 28/29 January 1944, forty-six aircraft were
lost, 6.8 per cent of the force of 677 aircraft that had been sent out.
On 30/31 January Harris launched his last attempt on Berlin. The
German controllers failed to intercept the stream on the way in but
the fighters eventually caught up, hounding the bombers throughout the return flight. One Halifax and thirty-two Lancasters were
shot down.

Bomber Command was bleeding, but there was little to show for its sacrifices. It was inflicting pain on Berlin, but with nothing like the intensity needed to produce any serious collapse of morale. Many of the bombs were wasted. The sprawling city could soak up a huge amount of violence. Reports showed that for all the damage done to the built-up areas and though the centre of Berlin was effectively flattened, many of the bombs so painfully and expensively delivered were falling into open country.

The level of dread felt by the crews when they heard they were going to Berlin mounted. Michael Beetham's crew found themselves back in the Big City the night following their debut. On their return they found that their Lancaster's flaps were not working and were forced to divert to the emergency landing strip at Wittering. Two nights later they were ordered to Berlin again. On the way back they were told Skellingthorpe was fogged in and they were to land at Pocklington. That too was covered in low cloud so they switched to its satellite, Melbourne. At least three aircraft were lost trying to land there that morning. One ran out of fuel and crashed into a farmhouse, killing five of the crew and a widow and a forty-year-old female lodger who were living there. Another ran off the runway and got bogged down, to be hit by another bomber as it landed. All survived. Beetham got his team down but as they were being driven by a WAAF back to the base they heard over her radio two crews who were trying to land being told to head their aircraft out to sea and bale out.

The odds against the crew surviving seemed infinitesimal. 'We were beginning to think that's only four operations and we've got thirty to do,' Reg Payne, the wireless operator, remembered. So it continued. On 3 December on a trip to Leipzig they were badly shot up by a Ju 88. On 29 December, on their way yet again to Berlin, a thirty-pound incendiary bomb dropped from an aircraft above crashed through their wing. Luckily the fuel tank was already empty.[14]

Yet even these experiences did not match the night of 30/31 March 1944. The target was Nuremberg, one of the alternative destinations chosen to keep the German controllers wondering whether or not Berlin was the target. Bright moonlight was forecast. Such conditions offered great advantages to the defender and it was expected that the operation would be cancelled. But a weather update predicting high cloud along the route and clear conditions over the target persuaded Harris to press ahead. There was further confusion when a Mosquito from the Met Flight returned from a reconnaissance trip to report that the reverse was likely. There would be no sheltering cloud on the way, but plenty over Nuremberg itself. Despite this up-to-date intelligence the order to stand down never came, and 795 aircraft were dispatched. The Germans were not fooled by diversionary raids and fighters were waiting along the route, picking up the stream as it reached the Belgian border. They followed it through the moonlight all the way to Nuremberg and back again. Altogether ninety-five bombers were lost, nearly 12 per cent of the force. Hardly any damage was done to the city. The wind forecast was wrong and upset navigational calculations so that 120 bombers attacked Schweinfurt, fifty miles to the north-west of the intended target, though again to little effect.

Looking out of the astrodome, Reg Payne could see 'aircraft being shot down all around us . . . we could even see the aircraft registration letters it was so clear.' They were painfully aware they were leaving condensation trails in the clear night sky and dived to lose them but it was no good. 'The fighters had a field day.'

The Nuremberg catastrophe was the last disaster in a losing battle. The losses could not continue. Nuremberg marked the end of the Battle of Berlin. Harris maintained to the last that if the Americans had joined in, his claim that the war could be finished by bombing alone would have been vindicated. But it was clear even to him that to continue under the prevailing conditions would mean disaster. The night-fighters controlled the sky. Between November 1943 and March 1944 1,047 British bombers were destroyed. During that period the number of aircraft available for operations varied from about 800 to just below 1,000. That meant that the German air defences disposed of the entire bomber strength available at the start of the battle. The bombers, which never had the ability to defend themselves, were losing even the capacity to evade. In the words of Noble Frankland, 'the tactical conditions of daylight had invaded the night.'[15]

Harris admitted defeat in early April. The battle had cost twice the number of aircraft he had told Churchill it might be necessary to lose as the acceptable price of victory. The sacrifice had not 'cost Germany the war'. He laid out the harsh lesson he had learned in a letter to the Air Staff. He wrote: 'the cost of attacking targets in Berlin under weather conditions which gave good prospects of accurate and concentrated bombing is too high to be incurred with any frequency.'

Belatedly, he turned his attention to some of the technical faults that had contributed to the heavy losses. The bombers' chances would improve, he said, if the gunners were better armed. He also pointed out that visibility from the turrets was abysmal. Even if improvements were made overnight this was unlikely to redress the imbalance significantly. It would have to wait for the advent of the protection that long-range fighter escorts could provide before the mortal threat of the Luftwaffe's night-fighters receded.

Long before Harris's change of heart, some of the crews had started to lose faith. This was reflected in the increased rate of 'early returns' when aircraft turned back because of real or imagined technical difficulties. Out of sixty-six sorties flown by 115 Squadron in the first three weeks of December, eleven crews turned back without reaching the target area. This compared with the figures for May during the Battle of the Ruhr, when there were only two aborted missions. The tendency was particularly marked in squadrons equipped with Halifaxes which had shown themselves to be specially vulnerable to night-fighters. The decision to load yet more bombs on the Lancasters, slowing them down and making them less manoeuvrable, thereby depriving their pilots of their main defensive advantage, also produced displays of indiscipline. Some captains took to dropping part of their bomb load in the North Sea on the way out to give themselves a better chance of evasion. The lengthening tail of the creepback over the bombing area was another sign that nerves were fraying.

But the great majority of the crews never wavered and persisted with their duty, even though there was little sign that their efforts were worth it. There were, however, limits to courage, as the men leading the campaign were obliged to remember.

12

The Chop

Fear of the chop loomed over everyone. Even the outwardly nerveless like the Australian Dambuster veteran Dave Shannon felt its shadow. He and Leonard Cheshire were about to board their aircraft one evening, Germany-bound, when Cheshire remarked on the wonderful sunset. 'I don't give a fuck about that,' said Shannon. 'I want to see the sunrise.' The great question was the extent to which that dread could be controlled. Bomber crews had an intimate relationship with death, which stalked their careers from the first months of training. Non-combat crashes accounted for 15 per cent of overall fatalities. The pointlessness of these losses made them stick in the mind. Reg Payne remembered how, having survived the worst of the Battle of Berlin, he was sent on a fighter affiliation exercise over Yorkshire. A Canadian pilot was flying alongside his skipper, Michael Beetham, and two extra gunners joined the crew. When the fighter made its mock attack the Canadian put the bomber into a screaming corkscrew. As they dived at 300 mph the port outer engine caught fire. Beetham ordered the crew to jump.

There were ten men aboard. Beetham, the Canadian and the navigator slipped easily through the front hatch. At the back of the aircraft, though, there was chaos. Payne struggled rearwards from his wireless operator's desk to find five men huddled around the side exit. The bomb-aimer had already jumped but the others clung to the fuselage, each urging the other to go first. Don, the flight engineer, was already doomed. As it was only a training exercise he had not bothered to bring his parachute. The others were paralysed with fear. Their last position had been over the Humber estuary. It was February. Spread below them was a thick, grey blanket of cloud with no way of knowing if sea or land lay underneath. Finally Jock

Higgins, the mid-upper gunner, lunged for the door 'but instead of going out like you should do rolling up in a ball with your back to the slipstream so as to miss the tail, he stepped out and hit it.' For a moment it seemed that the tailplane would slice him in half then his parachute opened and 'flipped him off as quick as lightning like flicking a fly.'

Payne went next. As he plunged through the cloud he tugged frantically at his rip-cord with no result, before realizing that he was pulling the wrong handle. He looked up to see one of the stricken bomber's blazing wings 'coming down like a leaf'. Fred Ball the rear gunner, with whom Payne had endured so much, and the two extra gunners, 'didn't get out . . . they just didn't [manage] to do it.'[1]

Crashes such as this were especially bruising to morale. Lives had been spent for nothing. The mortality rate at OTUs, which were often equipped with clapped-out and underserviced aircraft, was particularly high. In the six months Doug Mourton spent as an instructor at Wellesbourne, fifteen aircraft and crews were lost. 'An OTU should be a safe enough place,' he wrote, 'but actually we were flying with dodgy crews in dodgy aircraft . . . Wellington 1Cs which were very old and obscure.'[2]

Training accidents often provided the crews with their first sight of a dead body. Corpses were curiously absent from the war the crews were waging. Guy Gibson's nerves were rattled by the sight of a Wellington which crashed-landed one snowy night and burst into flames. The following morning Gibson and his friend Dave Humphries went to look at the wreckage. 'As we got closer we could smell that unpleasant smell of burnt aircraft, but when we got really close we could see quite clearly the pilot sitting still at his controls, burnt to a frazzle, with his goggles gently swaying in the wind hanging from one hand. Without a word we began to retreat and were back in our operations hut within a few minutes.'[3]

In the air, death was often instantaneous. A cannon shell or a lump of molten flak would hit the bomb bay and the aircraft and those inside it were blown to pieces. There were also times when individual members were killed in a fighter or flak attack while others survived. The swing of the scythe was impressively arbitrary.

Reg Fayers described in a frank letter to his wife the death of a young sergeant pilot called Wittlesea, 'a nice kid with bags of enthusiasm,' who was flying second dickey. They were on their way back from Nuremberg. Fayers was visiting the Elsan toilet when they ran into flak. H-Honkytonk 'was thrown around the sky and me with it, until Steve got her out of this nasty stuff which had been our worst yet.' A large chunk of shrapnel hit the port outer engine which promptly caught fire. 'At the same minute, Witt said: "I think I've been hit, skip. I think I'm going to pass out." . . . By the time we were out of the flak, Lew found Witt to be unconscious – no more than five minutes at most. It took several more minutes for Lew and Phil to get Witt back to the rest position and find the wound and treat him. Anyway I think Witt was already dead. He died very soon anyway, and there was so much blood about he must have died from the loss of it, and the shock of course.'

The crew were too preoccupied with nursing the damaged aircraft home through an area thick with night-fighters to brood much on the death. Fayers recorded his surprise when informed that Witt was dead: 'I wrote in the log "second dickey died." It was nothing more than that.' They eventually landed safely at Ford, an emergency aerodrome on the Sussex coast. The following day they went to examine 'Honkytonk' and discovered that 'the piece of flak fragment that killed poor old Witt was no more than an inch and a half across. It came thru the nose of the kite by Tom's right hip, up thru two pieces of metal, right thru my seat – upon which I was not sitting by the grace of god.' Fayers' trip to the Elsan had probably saved his life. Wittlesea had been correspondingly unlucky. The shrapnel had hit an important artery in his thigh and he bled to death. As Fayers reflected, 'I don't think there's more than a breath of wind or a feather's weight between life and death.'[4]

The spirit of death was everywhere. The crews accorded it an awed, mediaeval respect. To them, death was The Reaper and they sensed when one of their number had been brushed by his bony fingers. Brian Frow's writings do not show him to be a fanciful man but he recorded how, when waiting on long winter nights in the ante-room for ops to begin, he came to recognize 'the chop look'.

Tail End Charlie.

It was a very real feature and whether it was true or not we believed it. Some aircrew would spend time playing snooker, cards or reading. A few just sat and pretended to doze; but sometimes their faces lost colour and they would nervously flex their muscles. If approached they would talk in raised voices and they invariably missed the 'aircrew supper' of eggs, bacon and beans. They could be seen visiting the [lavatories] too often and a few would sit outside the telephone call box trying to get through to their friends or relations, but forgetting that all 'off station' calls were banned during alerts, and that the phones were cut off. These were some of the symptoms of the 'chop look'. We believed that anyone who had it was aware that he was near to death; he seemed to have been informed by some extraterrestrial power, be it God or intuition.

Frow noticed it in his friend 'Shack' Shackleton, who like him was nineteen years old. 'He had gone through training with aplomb and was a popular and lively figure. One night . . . we had received a postponement of take-off and were sitting around in the mess, waiting. I saw to my horror that Shack had the dreaded symptoms, but I was unable to comfort him. By now we had completed four successful operations without serious incidents so Shack had no specific reason to be suffering from nerves.' At eight o'clock operations were scrubbed and Frow and his friend relaxed. Two days later Shackleton was assigned to an attack on the *Scharnhorst* in Brest docks and failed to return.[5]

Everyone had a similar story. Don Charlwood remembered 'a particularly coarse but good-natured Australian' known to everyone as 'Bull' approaching him as he prepared to set off for Turin. A trip to Italy was generally regarded as a 'piece of cake' given the anti-air gunners' reluctance to stay at their posts during raids. Crews marked each mission over Germany or France by painting a bomb on the nose of their aircraft. Italy merited only an ice-cream cone.

'Listen son [Bull said], you're not going tonight. If anything happens to me, could you get my personal belongings home to my mother?'

I looked with astonishment at his ruddy face, taken unawares by the sudden change in him.

'I suppose the Air Force would do it, but you know the way it is.'

I stammered, 'They say the target's easy – '

'I know all about that son, but I've got an idea. Anyway, you'd do that for me?'

'Of course.'

But that Turin could claim 'Bull' I refused to believe.

Charlwood woke the next day to see a van removing 'Bull's' belongings from the hut opposite.[6]

Not all premonitions turned out to be accurate. Cy March remembered how 'before going on a particular operation, I felt all day long that this was to be my last trip. All aircrew have had that feeling I suppose. We turned on to the runway for take-off and there, in a field was a dead tree, with a dirty great black crow sitting on one of its branches, just like a horror film. My blood turned to ice. We got the "green" and off we went. It was one of the easiest ops we ever did.'[7]

The knowledge of your own fragile mortality was all-pervading. Edwin Thomas displayed a touching emotional reticence in the many letters he wrote to his mother throughout his brief RAF career. He was anxious not to upset her by revealing the dangers of his job but occasionally even he could not keep death out of the picture. 'My dear mother,' he wrote on 24 September 1942 from RAF Harwell. 'I have arrived safely at this huge camp and am settling down in the sergeants' mess . . . when I first arrived in the dormitory I pointed to an empty bed and said "is this anyone's?" "No," came the answer. "He's missing."' Three weeks later he described running into a friend whom he had met during training. 'He and I shared a room and it is very interesting to hear news of the boys I knew – most of whom appear to have gone for a burton.' Just before Christmas he asked if she remembered him mentioning 'my old friend Wee Baxter from Blackpool. He was killed in a night crash last Tuesday, poor old chap. Only last week we were talking about prangs and he said "I shall be all right, I have a good pilot." They say that only the good die young . . .'

It was not long before he joined their number. He arrived finally at 78 Squadron at Linton-on-Ouse at the end of March 1943, two and a half years after joining up. At last all his training was going to be put to use. 'Our crew are to do our first op tonight,' he wrote. 'Do not worry because this squadron has a fine reputation and loses few kites. We have been waiting the last few days for this job and all feel very bucked and excited (note the steady hand).' This was one of the last raids of Bomber Command's spring diversion to the Atlantic ports and it went off smoothly. 'The whole business was little different from an ordinary crosscountry night flight . . . we arrived there nine minutes ahead of the bombing time so we had to circle it until we could bomb. The flak was said to have been light by the veterans but there was sufficient to keep us weaving and turning.'

Thomas knew very well that a trip to France was not the same as a trip to the Ruhr. Nonetheless, it was an enormous relief to have finally been tested in battle, no matter how gently, and his letter to his mother of 8 April was cautious but optimistic, talking about a possible twelve days' leave in four or five weeks' time. 'This will suit our purpose admirably because Pat, the rear gunner, will be twenty-one in May and is going to have a GRAND PARTY. I have never in all my two-and-a-half years in the RAF had so much time to spare. I inspect the wireless equipment of our kite in the morning and sign as having done so and if no ops, I buzz off to York in the afternoon with the crew.'

Thomas loved dancing and claimed to have worn out his shoes in the dance-halls of York. He asked his mother to send a pair from home, 'as soon, soon, soon as you can. I don't want to be deprived of my favourite enjoyment. I will reward your kindness by saving some more sweets and a tin of orange juice.' It was his last letter. Thomas's Halifax, K-Kathleen, disappeared on the night of 16/17 April while attacking the Skoda works at Pilsen.[8]

Empty beds had the same gloomy effect as the empty chairs at breakfast in the messes of the Royal Flying Corps on the Western Front. The RAF's administrators were keen to remove evidence of losses as quickly as possible. Sergeants were issued with a haversack to carry their wash kit which hung on numbered hooks at the mess. Reg Payne remembered how 'they would put up a notice in the mess saying will all members remove their [haversacks] from the pegs from 11 o'clock until 1 o'clock.' He passed by the mess just after the deadline had expired to see 'them throwing all the ones that were left into a wheelbarrow. They [belonged to] the ones who'd gone missing.'[9]

The loss of friends was confirmed by the doleful letters FTR – Failed To Return – chalked up on the crew blackboard. The rules of survival meant that grief had to be curtailed. 'The first time I lost a good pal, one I'd trained with, I felt very, very sad,' Roy MacDonald remembered. 'I went out into York determined to get absolutely blotto. I can't remember how much I drank but I remained horribly, stone-cold sober. But after that you just said, "well that's tough," and forgot them.'[10]

Surviving meant overcoming odds that, it was all too apparent, were stacked toweringly against you. From the beginning it was clear that the crews would have to be given some hope that they were, nonetheless, beatable. The Air Ministry worked on devising a limit on the amount a crew would have to fly before being switched to non-operational duties. Initially the line was drawn at 200 hours, which, it was thought, would allow a 50–50 chance of survival. There was an obvious objection to this yardstick. Because of the difference in flying speeds, those manning twin-engined bombers would only have to do thirty trips to reach the limit whereas those in the heavies would have to do forty. In August 1942 Harris's office made an interim ruling that crews would have to complete thirty operations before they were 'tour expired' and eligible to move on to a six-month stint instructing at a training school. This became official policy on 1 May 1943. Anyone who completed a first tour was not expected to do more than twenty on a second. Pathfinder Force crews were set a single continuous tour of forty-five sorties.[11]

It was the squadron commander who decided what constituted a completed sortie. Their interpretation of the rules could vary from a degree of sympathy that in some eyes approached laxity to a rigidity that bordered on the inhuman. By the middle of the war most COs were veterans who had completed a tour themselves and their attitudes were conditioned by their own reactions and behaviour. The keenest commanders were likely to regard any failure as an indication of slackness or loss of nerve.

Early returns, 'boomerangs' in RAF parlance, when a crew turned back because of a fault in the aircraft, were rigorously investigated. Pilots who had experienced genuine mechanical failures prayed for the trouble to be identified in order to avoid the suspicion that they were shirking, and to have another precious operation to count towards their thirty.

The establishment of a limit on operations showed an awareness in the upper reaches of the RAF of the weight that the crews were being asked to carry. But their concern stemmed from practical as much as humanitarian considerations. If the best and keenest airmen were allowed to continue until they were killed it would rob the organization of experienced, and perhaps inspirational, leaders. The point of nursing men through a first tour was so they could do a second, or even, some argued, a third. 'Those men who return for their second tour are immensely valuable,' a squadron commander told investigators from the RAF's Flying Personnel Research Committee. 'They are experienced, well-trained and teach the others. They usually come back as officers making valuable Flight Commanders or seconds in command.' Even so there was a limit to what anyone could do and it was the responsibility of senior officers to impose it. Otherwise a good man was likely to feel bound by duty to push himself on until he was broken or dead.

'Percy' Pickard, the seemingly imperturbable, pipe-smoking star of *Target for Tonight*, survived seventy bombing trips and numerous missions dropping agents into France before being given command of 140 Wing. This was made up of three Mosquito squadrons and was tasked with low-level bombing in daylight. It was an unfortunate appointment. Night bombing was very different from precision daylight raiding and Pickard was, it appeared to those around him, worn out. Charles Patterson who flew with him, regarded him as a 'splendid character. But it was quite plain to me that he should never have been allowed to go on. He was a nervous wreck . . . he was obsessed with getting on operations . . . but his brain was really too tired to really sit down and tackle the detail . . . it was quite obvious that he should have been rested, no matter how much he wanted to go on.' Pickard's wing was in 2 Group which was commanded by Basil Embry, who liked taking risks himself and did not mind ignoring the rule book. He had been shot down over Dunkirk in 1940 and captured, but escaped and made his way back to England via Spain and Gibraltar to fight again. As an Air Vice-Marshal he was considered too great a security risk be allowed back on operations. He nonetheless continued to take part in attacks flying under the pseudonym 'Wing Commander Smith'. He could hardly refuse Pickard's entreaties to get back into action. Patterson thought it a stupid and wrong decision. 'A man who'd made a staggeringly splendid contribution to the war was denied his future . . . Embry ought to have recognized that after [so many] trips on light bombers there was no basis on which to start off a completely new career on low-level daylight bombing.'[12] Pickard's fame was such that senior French Resistance figures asked for him to lead a special operation in early 1944 to breach the walls of Amiens jail where dozens of their members were held awaiting execution. Operation *Jericho* was a success and 258 prisoners escaped. Pickard's Mosquito was shot down leaving the target and he and his navigator Bill Broadley were killed.

Later in the year the most illustrious name in Bomber Command kept what had seemed like an inevitable rendezvous with violent death. Guy Gibson had become a 'professional hero' as a result of the Dams Raid, in the words of his biographer Richard Morris. He was adopted by the prime minister and went with him to Canada in the late summer of 1944. There he embarked on an exhausting programme of speeches, dinners and press conferences, playing up the strong comradeship between Canadian and British aircrews and trying to persuade America in general of the value of the strategic air campaign. On returning to Britain, with Churchill's support, he sought and won the nomination for the Conservative seat of Macclesfield in Cheshire.

But these were diversions. During 1944 he became increasingly restless with his safe, largely desk-bound new job and strained to get back on operations. Eventually his wish was granted. On

19 September, he made his debut as a bombing controller, directing a raid on the twin towns of Mönchengladbach and Rheydt, on the German-Dutch border. Gibson was flying a Mosquito, an aircraft with which he was unfamiliar. The marking was erratic and the bombing confused. After leaving the target area his aircraft ploughed into a polder near the Dutch town of Steenbergen. The Mosquito exploded in flames. He and his navigator, Squadron Leader James Warwick, were incinerated. Gibson was twenty-six. In common with several of the legendary airmen of the First World War, whose complexity and charisma he shares, his end was mysterious. The cause of the crash was never discovered.

As well as accepting that there should be a restriction on the length of a tour, those at the top also understood that there was a limit to the losses that the organization could endure. This calculation was not a simple matter of manpower and resources. It was a question of effectiveness. If the campaign was to be pursued with the maximum aggression, what percentage of wastage could be sustained without a drastic fall in efficiency and morale? The proportion of aircraft missing from 1940 to the end of 1944 fluctuated from 1.8 per cent to 4.4 per cent of sorties dispatched. But during periods of intense activity such as the Battle of Berlin, losses could climb much higher. In January 1944, 11.4 per cent of the Halifaxes from 4 Group sent to Germany failed to return, a disaster that had resulted in them being withdrawn from operations against German targets.

Bomber Command planners concluded that 'the higher the loss rate the lower the level of experience and the lower the operational effectiveness.' In other words, fewer veterans and more freshmen meant poorer results. Poor results and high losses were damaging to morale. It was efficiency rather than spirit, though, that was the main concern. A paper from the office of the director of bomber operations concluded that a strategic bomber force would become relatively ineffective if it suffered operational losses in the region of 7 per cent over a period of three months' intensive operations, and that its operational effectiveness might become unacceptably low if losses of 5 per cent were sustained over this period.[13] The definition of ineffectiveness was never spelled out. It appeared to mean a degree of carelessness, recklessness and absence of judgement that meant that the crews were more of a danger to themselves than they were to the enemy.

During the first period of Harris's command, from the end of February to the end of May 1942, the overall rate stood at 3.7 per cent. During the Battle of the Ruhr period it climbed to 4.3 per cent. But these were the figures for all operations and all units. Against specific targets and among individual units, levels could be much higher. The losses of aircraft attacking Berlin during the battle reached 6.3 per cent. Five squadrons, 75, 434, 620, 214 and 623 suffered appalling rates of between 15 and 20 per cent.

On these sort of percentages, the chances of survival were pitifully small.

It was officially calculated that with a loss rate of 8 per cent, only eight out of a hundred crews would finish a tour. The figure dropped to less than three crews if the figure rose to 11.4 per cent. Whatever the statistics the cold reality was that in 1942 less than half of all heavy bomber crews would survive their first tour and one in five would make it through a second. In 1943, only one in six could expect to survive one tour, and one in forty a second.[14] The question of odds obsessed the crews and was the subject of endless debate. Optimists argued that the risk remained the same for each trip. Pessimists claimed that the laws of probability determined that it increased with every flight. Experience taught that some targets were less hazardous than others. The statistics bore this out. Bombing Germany was around four times more dangerous than bombing France.[15] Yet, as the death of 'Bull' over Turin had demonstrated to Don Charlwood, there was no such thing as a safe destination.

Nor, it seemed, did the skill of the captain and the expertise of the crew seem to make much difference. In January 1944 Dr Freeman Dyson at the operational research section at Bomber Command HQ made a statistical study of survival factors. An earlier report had confirmed the official doctrine that a crew's chances of living increased with experience. 'Unfortunately,' Dyson wrote later, 'when I repeated the study with better statistics and more recent data, I found that things had changed.' His conclusion was 'unambiguous'. The decrease of loss rate that came with growing experience, which had existed in 1942, was no longer present in 1944. There were many individual cases of experienced crews nursing home badly-damaged bombers that novice crews would have been unable to fly. But they 'did not alter the fact that the total effect of all the skill and dedication of the experienced crews was statistically undetectable. Experienced and inexperienced crews were mown down as impartially as the boys who walked into the German machine gun nests at the Battle of the Somme in 1916.'[16]

There were technical improvements which might have increased the survival rate. But no one in the upper reaches of Bomber Command seems to have paid them much attention. The provision of parachutes and the extensive escaping drill that was taught during training promoted the hope that even if you were shot down there was a realistic chance of surviving relatively unharmed. The truth was that the likelihood of emerging alive from a doomed aircraft was less than one in four. Of the 4,319 men aboard the 607 heavy bombers shot down attacking Berlin in the Battle, only 992 (22.9 per cent) survived. The odds altered depending on what aeroplane you were in. Lancasters, despite their reputation for general flying safety and reliability, were nonetheless difficult to escape from. The number of men surviving from a seven-man crew averaged 1.3 compared with 1.8 for a Stirling and 2.45 for a Halifax. The Hally enjoyed several features that increased crew safety. The escape hatches were easily accessible. The wireless operator and the navigator were in the nose of the aircraft, close to the forward escape hatch. In the Lancaster and Stirling they and the upper gunner were in the mid-section and had to claw their way along the fuselage past bulky equipment battling the dynamic forces of a plummeting machine to get out. To get to the rear door, they had to negotiate the main wing spar which ran across the body of the aircraft. This was difficult enough in normal clothing. Fully dressed and burdened with Mae West and parachute harness it was virtually impossible.[17]

For the first years of the war pilots received some measure of protection from the steel plates fitted behind their seats. Later, as loads increased, they were sometimes removed, apparently to improve lifting capacity. Ken Newman 'never saw bomber pilots so angry before or since', after the move was announced in the summer of 1944.[18] Little was done to investigate the merits of flak jackets, such as those issued to American airmen. The survival rates of the Americans were significantly better than those of Bomber Command.

Dyson and his colleagues at the operational research centre thought hard about reducing casualties and came up with what they thought was a promising proposal. It was clear that the bombers' .303 machine guns offered little or no protection from night-fighters. Why not rip out the two main gun turrets and their associated hydraulic machinery? This would lighten the aircraft's weight and improve aerodynamic performance, add fifty miles per hour to its speed, and increase its manoeuvrability. Even if this did not significantly reduce aircraft losses it would definitely save lives, as gunners would no longer be needed. The proposal was passed up the line. The process of bureaucratic filtration, however, 'eliminated our sharper criticisms and our more radical suggestions . . . the gun turrets remained in the bombers, and the gunners continued to die uselessly until the end of the war.'[19]

After the German defences, the biggest enemy facing Bomber Command was the weather. The determination of Harris and his commanders to maintain a high tempo of aggression meant that operations often went ahead when to the eyes of the crews the conditions were unacceptably dangerous. The quality of weather forecasting was also extremely variable resulting in situations like that on the night of 16/17 December 1943 when twenty-nine Lancasters were lost and 148 men were killed trying to land in thick fog on returning from Berlin. To Ken Newman, who was finishing his training at 1656 Heavy Conversion Unit, Lindholme at the time, it seemed that 'the fog should have been forecast and the attack aborted. We all strongly suspected that the weather forecasters had been ignored or over-ruled by the top brass. The atmosphere was such that we who were waiting in the wings for our turn to operate against Germany rapidly came to the conclusion that the

Commander-in-Chief and his staff at Bomber Command – and Churchill come to that – regarded us in much the same light as the dyed-in-the-wool generals of the First World War regarded their soldiers – in a word, expendable.'[20]

Yet for all the towering dangers of fog, flak and night-fighters, there was no discernible pattern to the way that death made its choices: Newman himself marvelled at how he had completed a full tour of thirty operations including eighteen to Germany and several others against heavily defended objectives and had 'returned with my Lancaster undamaged with not even a scratch on the paint.'[21]

The crews recognized the unpredictability of it all in the name they gave to what they did. 'We nearly "diced" last night,' Reg Fayers wrote to his wife on 7 October 1943. 'It always happens the same night we come back from leave, but fortunately it was scrubbed.' Two weeks later, looking forward to a promised leave he predicted that 'we shall almost certainly "dice" again before then, and I'd rather we did. Too long between ops can be bad, and anyway we want to get them finished.'[22]

The temporal horizon extended no further than the next trip. 'Useless business, this, thinking about the future,' Guy Gibson wrote, and he was right.[23] 'It was pretty obvious that a lot of us were never going to return,' said Bill Farquharson. 'I was going to do all I could to stay alive but the chances were against me and I realized this.'

A Canadian in his squadron, 115, went as far as to keep a book on who would not be returning. 'He used to say, "Do you know Bill, you're on the chop list tonight?" and I'd say, "Oh am I? Jolly good Bob. What are the odds?" . . . anyway, chaps complained about it and he had to stop it. He [replied] that there was nothing wrong with it. We know some of us are not going to return. It was his way of overcoming [his] anxiety about not returning.'

Some men ticked off each trip in their diaries or in their heads as one step closer to safety. Farquharson preferred not to think about it. 'I really tried not to count. You can't help it though – another one off. You had to treat every trip in exactly the same way, no matter how easy you might think it might be . . . you didn't let up on anything as far as I was concerned and neither did the crew.'[24]

Everyone shared the warm but illogical conviction that whatever might happen to the others, they were going to beat the odds. Whatever Dyson's research might say, there was great comfort to be had in exercising a rigorous professionalism so that death if it came was due to fate rather than inefficiency. Harry Yates believed that a rough pattern developed in the way a tour progressed. 'A tour was a construct of three aspects,' he wrote, 'each distinct, each characterized by a potentially lethal weakness. In the beginning, of course, was naivety. A few hours flying together at OTU and Finishing School barely qualified as preparation for the real thing. From the moment a sprog crew arrived on station it had to learn – before the lesson was driven home by the enemy. There was plenty of help at hand. The path to survival was well-trodden even though not everyone reached its end.'

The dozen or so ops in the middle of the tour, he thought 'tended to coincide with the assumption that this learning period was over. The log book was filling up. The enemy and Lady Luck had done their worst. One was not blasé about being shot at but had reached a certain, internal accommodation with it. Instead of operating at maximum vigilance throughout, there might . . . perhaps . . . occasionally be a tendency to cut corners or relax a little. But *might* and *occasionally* were enough. Even that was complacency and it invited the Reaper along for the ride.' Towards journey's end aircrew had survived and surmounted these hazards. They were secure in the knowledge of their own expertise. 'But then came the even more insidious danger of staleness. It was all too easy to weary of the sheer repetition of operational life. The months of Battle Orders and Briefings were bound to pall, along with the pills to keep you wide-eyed or to knock you out; the ops scrubbed on the tarmac and others re-ordered because of scattered bombing; and always, the pals known but briefly and who, in the relentless drive to mount the next op, somehow went unmourned.'

Of these three killers, he believed, 'the cruellest was naivety, but the most undeserved was this business of going stale like old bread.'[25]

Before the thirty-trip limit came in some commanders had already noted the tendency of crews to get sloppy when they thought they saw safety beckoning. One wing commander reported that 'if ever I hear a man say "this is my last trip" either I don't send him on the trip or I tell him he has another dozen to do, then send him twice more and unexpectedly take him off.'[26]

The confidence that mounted with the accumulation of operations was never robust enough to displace fear. Indeed as the end of the trip approached it was common to feel a gathering anxiety that at the last moment the prize of life would be snatched away. There were many stories of crews going missing on their last but one mission. Fear is unsustainable for protracted periods. It waxes and wanes, not always in direct proportion to the current level of peril. Everyone felt it. Most extraordinarily, almost everyone managed to control it. The first thing to do was to acknowledge its existence. David Stafford-Clark, one of the few trained psychologists to work as a medical officer on a bomber station, observed that it was acceptable to show fear. '[Men] could say "I'm scared shitless" and that was fine.'[27] This frankness was echoed in one of the songs that raised the roof of mess and pub in many an eastern county town, sung to the tune of 'The Long and the Short and the Tall'.

> They say there's a Lancaster leaving the Ruhr
> Bound for old Blighty's shore
> Heavily laden with terrified men
> All lying prone on the floor . . .

The most powerful antidote to terror was the greater anxiety of losing control in front of one's colleagues. The Mosquito pilot Charles Patterson listened with mounting alarm as his commanding officer briefed him on a mission that appeared to have only the slimmest chance of success. He and his navigator were to fly alone over Magdeburg and return via Berlin and Rostock to obtain an up-to-date weather report in advance of a major raid that evening. The aircraft would be pushing its range to the limit. As there were no other daylight operations scheduled, that day his lonely Mosquito presented the sole target on offer to the entire might of the Luftwaffe.

'To show how bad it was . . . the squadron commander said he was sorry that he'd had to send me on this. But it had to be done. Somebody had to do it. And he looked at me and said with a twinkle in his eye "and you're not married you, see. Which is a factor we have to take into account."'

As he crossed the Suffolk coast climbing to reach his operational height of 25,000 feet he 'began not to feel myself, and then this feeling got worse . . . I thought this is awful . . . it had crossed my mind [something] which I couldn't control, was taking me over.' He considered turning back but was immediately struck by an even more unpleasant sensation. 'The thing that came to my mind was that if I went back I would have to say to Eddie [the CO] when I landed, and he said "why have you come back?" – I would have to say, ". . . because I don't feel well . . ." I suddenly saw in my mind clear as daylight . . . him standing in front of me while I said it. And the thought of that was so appalling that I just kept going on climbing.' The feeling of nausea turned out not to be panic at all but anoxia caused by a disconnected oxygen pipe. Patterson reflected later that 'the interesting thing was that such was the force of Eddie's influence over his pilots and his crews that it was purely the thought of him that made me keep going, even when I was running out of oxygen at 25,000 feet.'[28]

Nor did anyone want to be thought of as having let down those who kept them in the air. That meant the entire base. 'Aircrew were regarded on the station as pretty special,' said Michael Beetham. 'When you went off on operations masses of people would be down at the end of runway cheering and waving you on your way. Your ground crew would get round and make sure that everything was right on the aeroplane and be really looking after you to see that everything was perfect . . . How could you chicken out really? . . . that was a driving force. You were being made something special. It's something you had to live up to and you feared letting them down more than you feared the German defences. I regarded it that way and I found it very uplifting.'[29]

Ultimately, though, it was the respect of the crew that mattered most. In David Stafford-Clark's experience a crew member might decide halfway through the tour that he was going to 'go LMF'. Then 'the crew would say stop talking rubbish. We're all going to finish this together. And then the end of the story is that they all do finish together but maybe they only finish together because on the next trip they're shot down. But leaving the crew meant letting the side down. Somebody else has to come in. It is very, very disruptive and traumatic. It happened very, very rarely.' It did, however, happen.[30]

13

Crack Up

One day early in 1945 the crews of 150 Squadron were ordered to the parade ground of their base at Hemswell and told to form three sides of a square. As they stood to attention a sergeant was marched into their midst by the station warrant officer. The sergeant had been found guilty by a court-martial of avoiding his duty. His punishment was a period of detention and reduction to the ranks. According to Dennis Steiner who was there 'the Adjutant read the sentence and when he got to the words "reduced to the rank of aircraftman" the SWO who was standing a pace behind the sergeant, took a took a pace forward and ripped off his sergeant's chevrons which had already been unpicked and lightly tacked on. At the end of the sentencing, he was made to double off the square, no doubt to a period of misery.' It was, Steiner, thought, 'a most humiliating performance for everyone'.

The prisoner's story was pitiful. At the end of his limits of endurance, he had tried to get extra leave by telephoning the squadron office from a public telephone by the main entrance of the base, pretending to be his wife's doctor and warning that she was seriously ill. The sergeant was immediately given leave but on returning tried the subterfuge again. Suspicions were roused and he was watched and caught making another fake call.[1]

Jack Currie witnessed a similar ceremony at Wickenby after two Canadian gunners were found guilty of desertion, having failed to turn up at a pre-op briefing. 'The runaways eventually returned to face the inevitable court-martial, and it was ordained, perhaps *pour encourager les autres,* that the sentence be pronounced before us all.' On a cool, grey morning the full complement of the base was mustered by flights and squadrons on the parade ground. 'The

Station Commander made his entrance, wearing his peaked cap with the "scrambled egg" instead of the usual faded forage cap . . . the drama of the day began.' The miscreants were marched on to the parade ground from the left flank. In a formal, toneless voice, the adjutant read out the charges and the sentence of the court.

'The ensign,' wrote Currie, 'stirred limply on the staff. At the rear of No. 3 Squadron there was a quickly stilled disturbance as a fainting aircraftman was led away. As silence fell again, the Station Commander marched to one of the offenders and, with sure, quick movements, ripped the chevrons from each sleeve and the brevet from the breast. The gunner was a tall, aquiline fellow who might have stepped from a page of Longfellow's *Hiawatha*. He stood erect and motionless, staring straight ahead. The grey-blue sleeve showed darker where the tapes had been. The other gunner stood with shoulders bowed, and would not raise his eyes. He flinched at the Station Commander's touch. It was a dreadful moment.'[2]

Such ceremonial degradations were unforgettable and intended to be so. Yet courts-martial were used only rarely to maintain discipline. They were messy and time-consuming. By the time the proceedings began, witnesses had often been posted away or were dead. Usually they were fellow-airmen who detested the idea of ratting on a comrade.

It was, anyway, impossible to put on trial every member of Bomber Command who displayed signs of weakness. The existing martial law contained in the Air Force Act was much too heavy an instrument to deal with problems which, as the RAF had been forced to recognize from the earliest days, were inherent to combat aviation.

In the First World War both the Royal Flying Corps and the Royal Naval Air Service had accepted that pilots could break down under the stresses of their work. Rest homes were set up in the stylish Channel resort of Le Touquet where officers could recover after being ordered there by the squadron medical officer. There was a consensus among early researchers, some of whom had direct experience of the air war, that psychological pressures were as powerful as physical strain. When a man broke down, as he invariably would if he kept on long enough, it was a normal reaction to an abnormal situation. Fear, and its consequences, were the natural response to the unique rigours of aerial combat.

By the start of the next war, this commonsensical analysis had given way to a new view, expressed by men fluent in the theories of modern psychology. This maintained that character was the most important factor in how an individual coped with the mental buffeting of war. For all the modernity of those who framed it, it was a regressive perspective but it came to dominate the RAF's approach to psychological casualties. It was laid out in an Air Ministry pamphlet circulated among medical officers just before the start of the war. It restated the opinion that stress was cumulative and that 'everyone has a breaking point'. However it tended to blame character defects, rather than the accumulation of fear, for psychological collapse.[3]

'Morale [it read] is of the greatest importance both in the maintenance of efficiency and in the prevention of breakdown. It depends largely upon the individual's possession of those controlling forces which inhibit the free expression of the primitive instinctive tendencies. It is based upon the sentiments acquired during education and training. Its essence is the ability to live up to an ideal, to face dangers and difficulties with confidence and tenacity of purpose, and to be able to sacrifice personal interests and safety in the course of duty.'[4] In other words, good morale would overcome the base desire to run away. It could be inculcated by the right upbringing and reinforced by service discipline and values. But essentially it was a matter of character. Strong characters displayed patriotism, tenacity, and self-sacrifice. The weak were vacillating, undependable and ineffective.

In a well-organized selection and training programme such types should have been identified and discarded long before they reached a squadron. The RAF training programmes by the middle of the war were indeed thorough and efficient. Nonetheless, some men deemed unsatisfactory still got through. The question was how to deal with them.

Despite the reversion to Victorian notions of the paramountcy of character, the system had some elasticity. It acknowledged the omnipresence of fear and was subtle enough to perceive that orders were carried out with varying degrees of enthusiasm. From early in the war the RAF tried to devise a method for deciding who was unable to fly because of a genuine psychological condition, and who was simply unwilling. The next step was to form a plan for patching up the former and getting rid of the latter.

Most of the work on aviation psychology was done by two men, civilian specialists who had joined the RAF medical service in 1939. They were Charles Symonds, who became the senior consultant in neuropsychiatry and rose to the rank of Air Vice-Marshal, and a younger practioner, Denis Williams. In a key report, which appeared in August 1942, Symonds and Williams set out the findings of their investigation of psychological disorders in flying personnel of Bomber Command.[5] Much of the evidence contained in it came from questionnaires and interviews with station and squadron commanders and medical officers.

They started off by making a disinction between flying stress and the effects that arose from it. The former was defined as 'the load of mental and physical strain imposed upon a man by flying under war conditions'. The effects varied depending on 'the weight of the load, and the mental and physical stamina of the individual'. When the load grew too heavy to carry, the strain could be manifested in signs of 'fatigue, anxiety, or inefficiency' and in any number of other ways.

Commanders and medical officers were instructed to keep their charges under constant observation. It was a complicated task. The guidelines for spotting signs of deterioration and the variety of recorded symptoms were highly detailed and sometimes contradictory. Following the official advice also required a reasonably close knowledge of the personality of the man in question for any alteration in his manner to be noticed. Bomber squadrons contained up to 200 airmen. They were subdivided into crews, often hermetically sealed social subdivisions. There was the further barrier created by commissioned and non-commissioned rank. It was hard for commanders to know all of their men well, though the best of them, and the more conscientious medical officers, tried.

The symptoms fell into four categories: changes in appearance, talk and behaviour, loss of keenness for flying duties, loss of efficiency and alcoholic excess. Strain changed people in different ways. One general rule seemed to be that sufferers began to behave in a manner that was in complete contrast to their normal conduct. 'A quiet man will become sociable and garrulous,' observed one medical officer, 'and a normal man quiet, solitary and moody.' In others, their usual demeanour became sharply exaggerated. 'The change in behaviour has no particular direction,' a station commander reported. 'They are apt to be a bit more extreme in their behaviour one way or the other.'

Essentially, any behaviour that appeared out of the ordinary, and life in a bomber squadron allowed considerable latitude, was a ground for concern. The signs ranged from 'making weak remarks around the mess and roaring with laughter at them' to 'becoming irritable, sarcastic, truculent and out for trouble.' In contrast, 'unusual quietness, with a desire for solitude' was equally worrying, especially if the subject had previously been a good mixer. 'He ceases to be one of the party. He may remain in it without interest, or keep drifting away, starting a game of shove-halfpenny, but soon losing interest in even that. He breaks off a conversation and . . . later becomes unoccupied and lacks all initiative.' They tended to sit around in armchairs, staring blankly ahead or dozing. They looked 'tired and haggard, pale, worried, tense and nervy or miserable and depressed'. Undue reference to the events that had wrought these changes also signalled danger. 'He talks about the people who have been shot down in the searchlights. In discussion in the mess he enlarges on the casualties and in his mind leans toward the dangers rather than concentrating on the job in hand.'

This sad condition of loneliness and anxiety was characterized by a station commander as a 'state of alarm'. With it often came an increased consumption of cigarettes and alchohol. Most of the crew members smoked and drank. Getting drunk was a natural and recognized antidote to the strain of the job as well as the most common means of celebrating survival. It took some doing to stand out.

These were the off-duty symptoms. During operations there were other generally agreed portents of trouble. Investigators put them under the heading of 'loss of keenness' and they started at the pre-op briefing. It was noted that 'a keen man will react to the announcement of a "heavily defended target for tonight" with immediate professional interest, but if he is suffering from stress he will show his lack of keenness by immediate preoccupation with the defences.' He might start asking 'unnecessary questions' about the sortie or appear half-hearted in the mess. On the other hand there were others who 'overcompensate and appear wildly enthusiastic, emphasizing their keenness too forcibly'.

It was in the air that the trouble became fatal. There it became categorized as 'loss of efficiency'. This state produced 'foolish errors of judgement, or gross carelessness, leading to bad landings or crashes.' Over enemy territory 'carelessness or recklessness may lead to catastrophe.' This observation, as the report admitted, had to be theoretical as the deadly consquences of the mistake meant that no one was likely to be alive to bear witness to what had actually happened.

If an aircraft suffered repeated damage but made it home it was taken as evidence that the pilot's judgement was going. 'He forces himself to go in regardless of risks because he is afraid that his nerve is getting shaky.' In the case of a navigator, he may 'make silly mistakes . . . gives wrong fixes or sets the wrong course . . . he may go to pieces over the target.'

On the other hand, returning without a scratch might also be evidence of shattered nerves. Early returns were regarded as one of the surest indications of the state of morale both in individuals and squadrons. Even in the best-maintained aircraft it was inevitable that once in a while a crew would be forced to abort its mission because of mechanical failure. However the fault had to be serious and real if the captain were to avoid arousing official attention. Commanders were on the lookout for defects which were 'trivial or imaginary' including 'minor engine troubles, such as a fall in revs or oil pressure, turret trouble, or difficulty with the intercom.' The decision to turn back was the captain's and it was on him alone that the responsibility for doing so fell. 'Once they occur they tend to be repeated, a different reason being found each time.'

Different commanders took different approaches to the problem. Some ordered a full, potentially humiliating investigation if an aircraft returned twice without reaching the target. It was the practice of one to check the trouble himself if a fault was reported before take-off. If he found all was well but the pilot was still reluctant to fly, he would stand him down for further investigation and ask a spare pilot and his men to take over. Another went around each crew before take-off to ascertain they were happy with the condition of their aircraft, thereby making a 'boomerang' all the harder to justify.

Failing to reach the target without good reason was an extreme example of 'inefficiency'. Over the target it could manifest itself in other, equally undesirable ways. The investigators recognized that shredded nerves might result in recklessness. But they could also lead to excessive caution which diminished the crew's contribution to the raid. Some pilots would drop their bombs hopelessly high, while the so-called 'fringe merchants' would scatter their cargoes before they reached the aiming point.

Such nervousness emanated from fear of death. But those suffering it seemed to die as frequently than those who did not. There was no accurate way of telling. Dead men could not speak. But it seemed logical to one medical officer that 'if . . . carelessness, recklessness and loss of judgement result from excessive stress, there must surely be an abnormally high casualty rate in the aircrews who, through one member, have become inefficient.' Symonds and Williams also judged that shattered nerves increased the likelihood of death, particularly among those who never gave any formal indication, oblique or direct, that they were suffering. This 'sort never report sick. They show their signs and symptoms in the mess, but they keep on flying and in the end write themselves off, because they have become inefficient through loss of judgement.'

The other 'sort' were those who felt their spirit weakening, though they were unwilling initially to acknowledge this directly in front of authority. According to one MO they 'report sick with some trivial complaint which has no real physical basis. After a talk if you ask them why they have come to sick quarters they will say that they are afraid or that they panic in the air.'

Sinusitis, visual defects, airsickness, even boils were employed to avoid flying. It was only when the condition had been cured or discounted that the patient admitted his fear. It was then up to him to choose whether to return to flying or cry off with all the dire consequences that entailed. The report found 'the result of the decision is usually unsatisfactory.' Those that went on soon cracked. Those who gave up were lost to the effort for ever as surely as if they had been killed.

A larger category did report sick but refused to admit they felt any psychological strain, even though examination suggested this was the root cause. Base doctors noted a higher incidence of such cases if a big operation was in the offing, even among 'very good men'. The most common symptoms were discomfort, nausea, mild dyspepsia and diarrhoea. These, it was felt, were literally 'a visceral response to impending danger'. Some medical officers told their patients frankly that their illness was a product of fear. This, in many cases, at least initially, had the effect of reinforcing resolution.

It was unusual for these men to assert that they could not carry on with operations. 'They all exaggerate the point that they don't want to come off flying. But later, if they are kept on, they may say they do not think it fair to the rest of the crew that they should carry on, because they are afraid that they may let them down.'

Commanders and medical officers were more impressed with those who openly admitted their fear or revealed that their nerve had gone. By doing so they had demonstrated strength of character and consequently the chances of returning them to operations were better. 'The man who comes up complaining of inability to carry on is the honest type,' one respondent said. 'There is more chance of getting him back to flying than the others.'

The medical officers making these observations were, by peacetime standards, little qualified to do so although they did receive some psychiatric training on joining the service. Psychiatric and psychological studies were underdeveloped in Britain at the start of the war. Although the military had recognized that psychiatry could

A sight to inspire fear. A flak battery opens up as an attack goes in.

not be ignored in maintaining morale, the tendency in some quarters was to regard its terminology as jargon that described existing conditions which could more easily be diagnosed by observation and commonsense. In the experience of David Stafford-Clark, one of the few medical officers who had specialized psychiatric knowledge, 'psychiatry was regarded in those days as an extremely cranky operation.'

MOs were expected to know the men they were treating. When ops were on they sat in on the briefing, waved the crews off and were waiting for those who returned when they arrived for the post-attack interrogation. They were encouraged to mix with the crews off duty in mess and pub. The aim was to 'think squadron and live squadron every minute of the day,' but not in such a way that made them appear to be snooping.[6] Separate messes created an obstacle for the conscientious MO and several suggested that the system should be scrapped in favour of an aircrew club that all could attend. To get round the problem, one squadron medical officer arranged for crews to come to the sick bay for ultra-violet treatment, during which he would strike up conversations aimed at winning their confidence and learning their concerns. Another organized 'informal talks on oxygen, equipment and quasi-medical affairs, ostensibly for education, actually for observation and personal contact.'

Medical personnel were also expected to go on the occasional operational trip. Stafford-Clark did so regularly. 'I decided that once in a while, the person that they would turn to when their morale was shaky should participate in what they were doing . . . I found it absolutely terrifying [but] one of them was kind enough to say "it was a great comfort to have you with us, Doc." '[7] The station medical officer at Wyton, Wing Commander MacGowan, was at forty an old man by RAF standards. He nonetheless took part in many operations, including several to Berlin. He told Freeman Dyson that 'the crews loved to have him go along with them. It was well known in the squadron that the plane with the Doc on board always came home safely . . . at first I thought he must be crazy. Why should an elderly doctor with a full-time staff job risk his life repeatedly on these desperately dangerous missions? Afterwards I understood. It was the only way he could show these boys for whose bodies and souls he was responsible that he really cared for them.'[8]

The quality of medical officers varied considerably. There were those like Stafford-Clark who understood that dispensing reassurance, understanding and sympathy was at least as important as doling out sleeping pills and amphetamines or acting as a military GP. Then there were the likes of Jack Currie's MO at Wickenby who was approached in the ante-room during a drunken sing-song by a Canadian crew member whose nerve had long gone. He was 'shaking horribly in every limb; his head spasmodically jerked sideways and, every few seconds, his left eye and the corner of his mouth twitched. He placed a trembling hand on the doctor's arm and croaked: "I'll fly, Doc. Tell them I'm fit to fly. I was pretty bad this morning, but I'm OK now." The MO, raising a tankard, glanced at him.

'"Yes, you look all right to me."

'"Gee, thanks, Doc." [The Canadian] staggered away, alternately grimacing and twitching, and the choir, refreshed, struck up again . . .'[9]

The RAF went to considerable trouble to establish whether there was a medical explanation for a man's inability to carry out his duties. Nonetheless, it also maintained that there were airmen whose failure to perform was due to weakness of character rather than any illness. The bureaucratic formula referred to them as those 'whose conduct may cause them to forfeit the confidence of their Commanding Officers in their determination and reliability in the face of danger.' There were two categories: 'the man who is maintaining a show of carrying out his duties,' and, more worryingly, the 'man who has not only lost the confidence of his Commanding Officer in his courage and resolution but makes no secret of his condition and lets it be known that he does not intend to carry out dangerous duties.'

The ministry letter dealing with what it was clear even at the time of writing in April 1940 would be a persistent problem, acknowledged that such men might be suffering from a genuine medical condition. It made a soothing reference to the possibility that with encouragement and tactful handling they might once again become useful squadron members. But, it went on, in a passage that was to resonate throughout the rest of the war, 'it must however be recognized that there will be a residuum of cases where there is no physical disability, no justification for the granting of a rest from operational employment and, in fact, nothing wrong except a lack of moral fibre.'[10]

LMF was born. Essentially it was a device to punish an offence which fell outside the conventional military crimes of cowardice or desertion. The designation was controversial from the outset. The RAF's chief medical consultants, including Symonds, objected to the terminology, though his suggestion that it should be replaced with the phrase 'lack of courage' hardly seemed more scientific.

Making the judgement was extremely difficult. Symonds himself admitted that there was no clear line between an 'anxiety neurosis' and a normal emotional reaction to stress. He nevertheless concluded that 'in the interests of morale, a line must always be drawn.'[11] The process was thorough and complicated. Cases came to light in several ways. A squadron commander might notice a lack of determination and reliability in one of his men. Alternatively a man might report to him that he was unwilling or unable to carry on his flying duties. In both cases the suspect would be referred initially to the medical officer. Often it was the medical officer himself who learnt of an impending problem when someone reported sick with real or imagined ailments that prevented him from flying. It was then up to him to determine whether or not there was any physical or nervous reason to explain the subject's condition. If the MO felt unwilling to pass judgement the patient was passed on to a specialist, consultant or one of the twelve Not Yet Diagnosed (Neuropsychiatry) centres set up by the RAF early in the war.

The guidelines struggled to be fair. They emphasized that it was 'highly important . . . to eliminate any possibility of medical disability before a member of an aircrew is placed in [the LMF] category.' A medical diagnosis made life simpler for all concerned and some MOs were willing to oblige in order to spare a man the ignominy of being thought a coward. Subjects found to have physical or nervous problems were treated on the station, sent on leave, admitted to hospital or passed on for a more specialized examination. The vast majority of those who were removed from flying duties were stated to be suffering from 'neurosis' rather than cowardice. The proportion was roughly eight to one. Between February 1942 and the end of the war, 8,402 RAF aircrew were thus diagnosed, a third of whom were from Bomber Command. In the same period there were 1,029 cases of LMF.[12]

Medical officers were not qualified to categorize a man as LMF. Nonetheless the initial diagnosis could be crucial. A man who was found fit for flying duties was automatically open to the charge of LMF. If inadequate medical cause, or no cause at all was found, the matter returned to the hands of the CO who, after interviewing the individual and consulting his record, decided whether or not he was lacking in moral fibre. His report was then passed up the line to the Air Ministry. The punishment for LMF was shame. Officers and NCOs alike were remustered as Aircraftman Second Class, the lowest RAF rank. They lost their entitlement to wear the aircrew brevets they had laboured so hard to win. They were segregated from their fellow airmen and quarantined in Aircrew Disposal Units.[13]

The LMF procedure was designed as a deterrent. Wing Commander Jimmy Lawson, who was closely involved with its administration, admitted in an internal review that 'the intention was to make the chances of a withdrawal, without legitimate reason, as near impossible as could be . . . if withdrawal had been an easy matter without penalty, this would have undermined the confidence and determination of some of those who continued their duties loyally and effectively.'[14]

Official guidelines put great emphasis on the need to act quickly. LMF was considered to be contagious by RAF bureaucrats and squadron commanders alike. Cheshire was brisk and unemotional about LMF. 'I was ruthless with "moral fibre cases",' he said later. 'I had to be. We were airmen not psychiatrists. Of course we had concern for any individual whose internal tensions meant that he could no longer go on; but there was the worry that one really frightened man could affect others around him.'[15] Peter Johnson's technique with LMF cases was to 'try to shuffle them as rapidly as possible off the station via the "trick cyclist" . . . who could produce some medical grounds. It wasn't the pleasantest of tasks. You always remembered that these men were volunteers who had failed, not conscripts who had revolted.'[16]

Breaking down was felt as an enormous personal failure by those to whom it happened. It was a tragedy as powerful as any encountered in the life of the crews and they recognized it as such. Jack Currie remembered at the beginning of the Battle of Berlin coming across a newly-arrived sergeant pilot who was 'a casualty neither of flak or fighters, but of an enemy within himself. He came back early from the mission . . . and gave as a reason the fact that he was feeling ill. Next night he took off again, but was back over Wickenby twenty minutes later. Again he said that he had felt ill in the air. I had seen the crew together in the locker-room clustered protectively around their white-faced pilot. They may have thought that some of us would vilify him, but no one except officialdom did that. We knew what was wrong: the so-called lack of moral fibre, and most of us had felt that at times.' But most did not succumb. In the battle of fears, the greater terror of letting down your comrades almost always prevailed. Currie felt only sympathy. 'Goodness knows what hell the wretched pilot lived through – the fear of showing cowardice is the strongest fear of all in most young men.' All the years of training, all the hazards that marked the journey to an operational squadron, counted for nothing. The pilot 'soon . . . disappeared, posted to some dread unit especially established to deal with such unhappy cases.'[17]

One 115 Squadron pilot spotted the signs of collapse in his wireless operator even though their tour was well advanced and the end in sight. 'When we were in the air he started to speak out of turn. He said "I'm not very happy with this wireless set, sir . . ." I said don't worry about it. He said you shouldn't go on without a working wireless. I said well I am . . . he kept this up and I said I want you to forget about it, I'm the skipper of this aircraft. We're going to complete this trip. But by this time he'd already got the rest of the crew a bit concerned . . . I told them all to shut up and I said to this other chap if I have another word from you I'll have you arrested when we land . . . it was all quiet after that. We got back and we landed and we had a good trip.' The pilot had the wireless checked. There was nothing wrong with it but he did not report the matter. 'I had a word with him and he admitted that he was wrong. I said to him you need a rest. I spoke to the squadron commander and they sent him off for a rest and he came back again later [and completed his tour]'.[18]

Despite the official reluctance to identify *prima facie* cases of LMF there were some circumstances that made action inevitable. A blank refusal to fly could not be overlooked. Flight Sergeant X appears to have made his aversion to operational work very clear long before he was posted to 103 Squadron at Elsham Wolds in the summer of 1942. After a short while he wrote to his commanding officer stating that 'owing to complete lack of confidence, I ask to be relieved of aircrew duties and be reverted to ground duties.' He had, he explained, volunteered as a pilot [in July 1940] but had been selected instead as an air gunner. During flying he suffered from catarrh and eye trouble and had injured his back in the gym. He had asked to be remustered and had hopes of being commissioned to serve as a trainer on the Link flight simulator. He was surprised when he heard he was being posted to 103 Squadron. In addition to his medical complaints he was 'a married man with three children [which] adds to my dread while in the air.' He would, he concluded 'rather be doing ground duties with complete confidence than flying in mortal fear.'

It seems strange that someone so clearly lacking enthusiasm should ever have reached an operational squadron. His commanding officer wasted little sympathy when submitting his recommendation. 'I consider [wrote J. F. H. du Boulay] that this NCO has been drawing aircrew pay without earning it since enlistment and that he is a coward with no qualifications for a commission in any trade, or NCO's rank. As a Flight Sergeant his example is deplorable and I request that he may be removed from this Squadron immediately. I strongly recommend that he be deprived of his Air Gunner's badge, reduced to the ranks and made to refund part of the pay which he has received without earning it since his enlistment.'[19]

This was an open and shut case. Sergeant X appeared to belong to that group of men identified by David Stafford-Clark who had passed the point where they cared what anyone thought of them. That of Sergeant Y, a wireless operator with 150 Squadron, which occurred at the same time, was more complex. He too, the official correspondence reported, announced that 'he has completely lost confidence in himself and no longer wishes to continue operational flying.' Searching for reasons to explain his loss of nerve his commanding officer reported that he had crashed-landed when his air-craft ran out of fuel returning from his first op but no one had been injured. That had been to Lille, a relatively easy target. Since then he had been to Essen four times and carried out one mining trip. In his report Wing Commander E. J. Carter, the 150 Squadron CO, remarked that 'at no time has Y been subjected to any particularly bad experience.' Yet Essen in the summer of 1942 was one of the most dangerous destinations. Y had carried out four operations in eight days at the beginning of June. They were all launched between 4.35 and 6.35 in the evening. Given the summer light they might as well have been carried out in broad daylight.[20]

He would seem to have suffered a classic reaction. The crews themselves had noticed that pessimism and optimism came in cycles. The same appeared to be true of fear. Symonds and Williams reckoned there were three critical periods in a tour and the first six ops were the toughest. Their reporters observed that 'between the third and sixth trip there is a great likelihood of "waverers" reporting that they cannot go on with their duty. There was striking agreement in the story. "In the first few trips he sees what he is up against, in the next he makes an effort, but by the sixth he has thrown his hand in." He usually manages the first three. He is invariably an unsuitable individual and the outlook is usually hopeless.' Another critical period came around the twelfth to fourteenth operation, when the dangers of the business were appallingly clear but the end of the tour stretched dismayingly into the distance. In such cases men 'with explanation and encouragement control their fear, and nearly all go back to complete their tour.' Some who had endured a particularly hard run tended to flag when there were only five or six trips left to go and the finishing line was in sight. These, the specialists recommended, if rested, would go back to fulfil their duty. The same was true of those who had been shaken up by a particularly nasty experience such as a bad crash or a forced landing in the sea.[21]

The need to deal with nervous cases was recognized by the crews. As Harry Yates pointed out, 'no crew could afford to have one of their number snap on board and plunge everything into hysteria and chaos.' But despite all the official thought that went into the subject, manifest in the dense thickets of procedure, there was still a widespread belief among those doing the fighting that the system was insensitive and sometimes unjust. They knew better than anyone the difference between a coward and a man who had reached the limits of his courage. They also resented the calculated humiliation of men who, whatever their failings, had volunteered to serve at the axe-edge of the war.

An instructor who served with Doug Mourton at the OTU at Wellesbourne refused to fly with a partly-trained crew when Harris drafted in OTU personnel to make up the numbers for the Cologne 'thousand' raid. He reasoned that having survived one tour 'he did not want to get killed with a crew who were not very proficient.' When Mourton returned from the operation his friend had disappeared.

> He had been found guilty of LMF ... the punishment would have been that he would be stripped of his sergeant's stripes and crown and sent to another station. The marks where his sergeant's stripes had been removed would be perfectly obvious and everybody would know what had happened to him. Besides this he would have been given no trade and as a consequence would be given all the tasks of an air force station, such as washing up, cleaning out latrines etc. It was quite a severe punishment for somebody who, just on one occasion, had refused to fly. And he would have been quite happy to have been posted to an operational squadron as part of an experienced crew.[22]

No one seemed to know what happened to LMF cases after they disappeared from sight. Where to put them was a continuing problem for the authorities. Initially they were sent to the RAF depot at Uxbridge but their proximity to airmen in training was thought to be bad for morale. Later they were posted to the Combined Aircrew Reselection Centre at Eastchurch in Kent where the same objection was encountered. There was a further move to the Aircrew Disposal Unit at Chessington in Surrey. There they were isolated from other airmen and treated humanely. The regime was intended to improve their self-esteem, restore their confidence and rebuild their belief in the war effort through 'motivational' lectures with titles like 'What Shall We Do With Germany?' and patriotic films. Under the benign eye of the commander, Squadron Leader R. I. Barker, they visited cathedrals and zoos and attended a weekly dance in the drill hall.

When Chessington was taken over by Balloon Command there was a final move to Keresley Grange near Coventry, where on 8 May 1945, the inmates trooped to the local church for a service of thanksgiving for victory in Europe.

The war was barely over before the term LMF became an embarrasment to the RAF and it was dropped in 1945. The numbers of people accused of it have never been firmly established. A scholarly recent study of the subject has calculated that an average of 200 cases of LMF were identified each year in Bomber Command.[23] Given the stresses of their occupation the figure seems very small. It can be seen, from one side, as an indication of the stigmatizing power of the charge of cowardice. More importantly it is a tribute to the remarkable steadfastness of the vast majority of those who flew with Bomber Command.

14

Home Front

When the crews touched down at the end of a mission they were returning to a monochrome world of flat fields, dank huts, drab food and weak beer. The memoirs of the pilots of the Battle of Britain are suffused with the sunshine of the summer of 1940. In the letters and diaries of the Bomber Boys it seems to be always cold and dark, no matter what the season. Life on bomber bases was often dismal and primitive, far removed from the elegance and comfort enjoyed by the pre-war RAF. A lucky few were installed in well-equipped stations that had been built to the highest specifications in the nineteen-thirties. The majority lived in the cheap, temporary constructions thrown up all over East Anglia, Lincolnshire and Yorkshire as the campaign got under way. The pre-war bases looked like giant architect's maquettes with their neat brick rows, hedges and flower beds. In wartime even a permanent base like Wyton in Huntingdonshire (now Cambridgeshire) was transformed, as a civilian visitor noted, into an ugly sprawl of 'endless puddles, barracks, warehouses full of bombs [and the] rusting wreckage of damaged equipment not worth repairing.'[1]

The RAF spent lavishly on maintaining its front-line aircraft. It was miserly when it came to the welfare of its front-line troops. They were housed ten to a Nissen hut, thirty-six feet long by sixteen feet wide corrugated iron humps which had no insulation. The only heat came from a coke-burning stove and in the bitter winters of the war years they became an icy purgatory. The men slept on iron bedsteads under rough blankets, whose meagre warmth had to be supplemented by the addition of a greatcoat when the temperature dropped. They washed in distant ablution blocks reached along muddy pathways in water that was seldom more than tepid. These privations did not extend to the 'penguins', the non-flying base adminstration staff who often lived in greater comfort than the crews they were supposed to look after.

Bad conditions caused resentment and chipped away at morale. Shortly after arriving at his Heavy Conversion Unit at Wigsley near Newark in Nottinghamshire in the autumn of 1943 George Hull sent a gloomy letter to his friend Joan Kirby. 'I seem to have fallen decidedly into the soup or what have you in being posted to this station,' he wrote. 'Even the name is obnoxious. Wigsley, ugh! Pigsley would be more appropriate yet I doubt whether any pig would care to be associated with it. The camp is dispersed beyond reason. If I never had a bike I doubt if I could cope with the endless route marches that would otherwise be necessary. Messing is terrible, both for food and room to eat it. Normally we queue for half an hour before we can even sit, waiting for it. Washing facilities are confined to a few dozen filthy bowls and two sets of showers an inch deep in mud and water.

Hull and his companions tried to alleviate the misery by heading to the nearest pub each evening and returning 'three parts cut'. At Wigsley, Hull's disillusionment with the RAF touched bottom. 'Don't for a moment . . . imagine that I want to be associated with the above nonsense' he wrote, a reference to the RAF crest at the top of the headed notepaper, which he had scored through with four angry lines.

Holme-on-Spalding-Moor, which sat on the plain between the River Humber and the city of York, was notoriously uncomfortable. James Hampton, who served with 76 Squadron, declared that 'on no other Royal Air Force station, before or after, did I ever encounter such intolerable living conditions.' On arriving at his Nissen hut in August 1944 he found it completely empty of furniture. Previous inhabitants had fed it all to the stove when the coke ran out. The only fittings were shelves, provided to store personal possessions, which the authorities had sensibly decided to have made out of asbestos. One wash house had to do for 400 aircrew, who queued up for the sixteen tin bowls and a few showers.[2]

But stoicism and resignation were Bomber Boy virtues. The men grumbled, but at least they were alive. With that in mind, they could put up with almost anything. Dennis Field found Tuddenham, in Suffolk, with its widely-dispersed sites and intermittently heated water, no different from any other pre-fab station he had been on. But it was 'Utopia compared with the jungle, desert, Italian mud or Arctic Sea.'[3] Newly installed at Holme, Sergeant Reg Fayers described his new quarters to his wife. The wash house was 'tastefully decorated in yellow, brown and rust with a discarded thrush's nest stuck up on one of the pipes . . . so I washed in clean soft water – why does cold water seem so much more clean? – and sang my bloomin' head off . . . then in my boudoir wear – wellingtons, pyjama trousers, tunic dressing gown of tender RAF blue with a navigator's badge rampant and oil stains magnificent I paraded into my study to write good morning to my wife.'

Fayers's 'study' was a corner of his Nissen hut, which, he reported, 'is just about the nearest we airmen get to "home" . . . Out of [the] roaring night and with ground mists at dawn garlanding the morning and welcoming our return we come tiredly and competently down to egg and bacon and this – a bed . . . faithfully waiting in the corner of a corrugated tunnel, MY bed because my two kitbags stand by it, my three-year-old slippers proudly inscribed FAYERS on the left and 963752 on the right, stand under it and my tunic hangs from . . . one nail.' It was 'a place to sleep . . . a place for dreams; that's my home darling.'[4]

Fayers was a romantic. There was another way of looking at things. Don Charlwood remembered the lowering experience of returning to Elsham after a mid-winter leave and opening the hut door to be met by 'the smell of last night's fire, of dirty clothes and unwashed bodies . . . gunners were asleep in shirts that appeared to have been welded to their bodies by the dirt of weeks.'[5]

Communal living shrank the boundaries of privacy. It was only rarely that a man could be alone. Frank Blackman, who described himself in a letter to his girlfriend Mary Mileham as 'somewhat lacking in the boisterous aspects of manliness', sometimes found the public nature of air force life intolerable. On 8 July 1943 he settled down in his room at East Moor in Yorkshire to write to her but was almost immediately interrupted. Even though he was an officer, he shared a room with three Canadians. 'The first has just come in and as usual when he has had a few beers is so talkative that he keeps on without stopping for more than a yes or no to keep him company. As I write now he is giving me a dissertation on flak, fighter belts, searchlights and relative losses of aircraft etc. . . . I've no doubt that unless I'm rude to him which I fear I shall be very shortly he will finish up on navigation – which is his final subject when all else fails. By the time he quietens down the other two will be in and then goodbye to all peace. They've been in to York and one at least will be tight.' The disturbance did not necessarily end when sleep descended. One of Blackman's roommates had been 'having nightmares and has kept us in fits of laughter after the preliminary shock of being woken up at about 3 a.m. [by him] hollering his head off.'[6]

A room of one's own, even one so basic as that allotted to Ken Newman at Lindholme after he received his commission, was the peak of gracious living. It was 'simply but adequately furnished, with a built-in wardrobe and a basin with hot and cold water. Better still there was a WAAF batwoman to make the bed and clean the room as well as polish my shoes and buttons. It felt like heaven in comparison with the sergeants' barrack room and particularly the Nissen huts that I had been living in . . .'[7]

As front-line warriors the crews might have reasonably thought they were entitled to the best food available. Their diet, though, was little better than that endured by civilians. They counted themselves lucky to sit down to bacon and eggs before they took off and again when they landed. Additional luxuries were rare. When not flying they lived on Spam and dried eggs, sausages and lumps of nameless fish. They filled the gaps with bread, smeared thinly with margarine and fishpaste or jam. To supplement the shortages of fresh produce there were plates of vitamin capsules to which the airmen were expected to help themselves.

To guarantee a share of this sparse fare you had to arrive early. Breakfast in the sergeants' mess at Holme started at 7.30. By 7.45

the meagre supplies of cereal and milk had run out. Tempers were short at the start of the day. The aircrew sergeants were allocated an area that was far too small for their numbers and they often had to wait until a table became free followed by a further delay until a harassed waitress was able to serve them. The permanent staff sergeants had a separate dining room which, the crews noted with bitterness, was rarely more than half full.

The Canadians were appalled at what they were expected to eat in British messes. At Abingdon, Ralph Wood had his first encounter with brussels sprouts, 'a kind of minature cabbage, eaten boiled. At our mess the cook must have boiled them and reboiled them until they emerged a sickly green gob . . . Small wonder that we looked forward to a snack in the village where we had the big choice of Welsh rarebit . . . beans on toast, or fishpaste on toast.'[8]

Letters home throb with a sensual yearning for peacetime food. The occasional parcels of treats sent by family and friends were received with rapture. 'Darling,' wrote Reg Fayers to Phyllis, 'I'm eating myself to death in a lovely orgy of pears, grapes and apples.' Bernard Dye felt it worth recording in his diary on 9 January 1944 the simple entry: 'received two oranges and two lemons'.[9] Doug Mourton befriended a worker at a farm near his Driffield base who supplied him with buckets of chitterlings, a doubtful mix of pig liver and stomach lining, which he would never have touched in peacetime. Mourton was extremely resourceful at scrounging. The British crews were envious of the lavish food parcels, packed with luxuries like tinned cheese and butter, received by the Canadian crews. He and his friend Jock noticed that when a new consignment arrived a list of recipients was pinned up at the local post office. 'Jock and I would look down this list and when the names corresponded with people who had been killed we went [in] and claimed the food parcels. We would then cycle back . . . and excitedly open the parcels, which contained tinned meat, chocolates and other items that were very hard to come by, indeed non-existent in England . . .'[10]

Even in the depths of wartime, luxury was available if you could pay for it. George Hull's friend Joan Kirby who was serving with the

WRNS at the HMS *Cabbala* shore base in Lancashire reported to her family that she had 'been having some nice food lately. Not at Cabbala I hasten to add but at the Midland in Manchester on Sunday, namely hors d'oeuvres, lobster, cream sauce etc. brandy trifle and cream, coffee and drinks.' Her host at the hotel was a 'Yankee named Bob. He's a really nice chap for a change and as long as we keep on being hungry at the same time and he's still got some money he suits me.' Such largesse was way beyond the pocket of a British airman. Bomber Boys were more likely to experience the sort of dates that Dennis Field took his future wife Betty on in Cambridge, where she was studying at Homerton College. On fine evenings they would spend pleasant hours wandering along the Backs. But 'on cold, wet and dark nights it meant joining a queue in the hopeful expectation of seeing a film. It did not matter what was on because it would be warm and dry inside. Alternatively, after a long wait we might get a couple of seats in a café and make beans on toast and a cup of tea last as long as possible. The only other possibility was to shelter under a dripping tree in the park and admire the view in the blackout. The glow of cigarettes, the nearest equivalent to a brazier, from neighbouring elms showed that we were not alone in our predicament.'[11] It was unsurprising that the Yanks stirred envy and hostility in the breasts of their British counterparts.

Among the bleak, utilitarian infrastructure of Bomber Command there were a few outposts of graciousness. After the horrors of Wigsley, the operational station of Coningsby was a sybaritic dream to George Hull. 'We've struck oil at last,' he announced to Joan. 'Coningsby the Beautiful, Coningsby the Comfortable.' The Nissen hut days were over. He was 'lording it in a double bedroom which contains a deal table and radiator' with a fellow-crew member, Jack Green. Suddenly Bomber Command life was not so bad. 'The food is eatable (so far),' he wrote, 'and the hours are reasonable. Hurrah for the RAF.'

The Dambusters Squadron, 617, was fortunate enough to be located at Woodhall Spa, south-east of Lincoln where wealthy Victorians and Edwardians once went to take the waters. On the edge of the town stood a house called Petwood, built at the beginning of the century in half-timbered neo-Elizabethan style by the Maples furniture-manufacturing family. It was there, in a low-beamed, oak-panelled parlour that 617 established its officers' mess. A photograph taken in 1943 shows a smiling Guy Gibson standing on the terrace alongside fellow officers, gins and tonics and 'half cans' of beer in hand. This was the sort of life many trainee airmen imagined they might enjoy when they finally reached an operational squadron. In most places the facilities on offer would turn out to be far more basic.

Most stations had a cinema which showed up-to-date films. There were attempts to raise the cultural tone with serious plays and concerts. Bomber Command was a rich social mixture and there were some who appreciated these occasions. Michael Scott, a schoolmaster before he joined up, listened to at least one piece of classical music virtually every day of his short career as well as devouring every book he could find. His cultural intake is listed, touchingly, in the pages of his Charles Letts Office Desk Diary. In four days in January 1941, during his flying training, he listened to Schubert's *Alfonso and Estrella* Overture and C Major Symphony, Bizet's Symphony No. 1, Haydn's Symphony No. 97, Schubert's Unfinished Symphony, Tchaikovsky's Suite in G, Humperdinck's *Hansel and Gretel* Overture and Schumann's Symphony No. 4. He also managed to read three books.

Many of those who kept diaries had literary ambitions. The life of a writer held a surprising appeal to the men of action who volunteered for Bomber Command. When at the end of the war the restless Leonard Cheshire was looking for something to do his first thought was that he should become an author. Scott found space in his limited off-duty time to work away at short stories. On the first day of 1941, he listed his hopes for the New Year. 'I would like to know where I was going to stand on December 31st,' he wrote. 'Let us look forward in a spirit of hope. In twelve months I hope to be back home with 500 hours [of flying], a demobilized Flying Officer about to return to schoolmastering. To have flown is one of the greatest joys of my life, but I want to return to my life's work.

I hope to have thirty short stories in my notebook, two of them published and a novel half-finished.'

The entries in Scott's diary get shorter and shorter as his training progresses and the prospect of action grows nearer. The literary references and nostalgia for his old life at Cheam prep school dwindle and there is a mounting tone of excitement. The last entry, for 18 May reads: 'A very heavy day, all formation flying. I found this very hard work at first, but it was a bit easier towards the end. We went over to Wotton to join up with 21 and 89. Apparently we are to do a show on Tuesday morning with fighter escort. May the Gods be with us! Formation flying is the most companionable of pursuits.' Six days later he was reported missing after he failed to return from a sweep over the North Sea on 24 May. It was his first operation. He left behind a poem, written just as spring broke in the countryside he loved.

> Why do I weep the follies of my kind?
> Larks are still merry, sing the birth of day
> Eagles still soar their proud majestic way
> The April coppices are primrose-lined
> Why do I weep?
>
> Why do I weep this man-made frenzied strife
> Mountains still sweep to heaven their rock-scarred crests
> Lakes are still blue as sunlit amethysts
> Nature is changeless, Earth is full with life
> Why do I weep . . .[12]

The Australians cultivated a reputation for hard-living philistinism. Don Charlwood and his well-read, thoughtful friends rather contradicted the image. In the evenings he would as soon listen to a classical concert on the radio as go to the bar. His friend Johnnie Gordon was a 'scholar of Latin and Greek who read *Oedipus* and *The Medea* because he "liked the murders in them" [an] accomplished violinist who "knew nothing about music but enjoyed the noise it made."'[13]

Even so, it could not be said that high culture was a major preoccupation among the crews and those who supported them. One night George Hull tried to forget the horrors of Wigsley at an orchestral concert put on at the base by RAF musicians. 'It was pretty good,' he wrote to Joan, 'although there was rather an interruption when I "ordered" two WAAFs and an airman outside for making a lot of unnecessary noise.'[14] Sometimes the entertainment was the best the country could offer. One night Robert Donat, Edith Evans, Joan Greenwood and Francis Lister, who worked for ENSA six weeks a year as their contribution to the war effort, arrived at Holme to perform a play by George Bernard Shaw. To the fastidious eyes of Reg Fayers, the reactions of the ground staff present somewhat lowered the tone. 'Everyone was darned grateful for the show they'd given us, especially under rather trying circumstances,' he wrote. 'Shaw's wit and ideas are hardly written for a gang of erks whose literary standards are mostly pornographic or James Hadley Chase.'[15]

The democratic, popular nature of Bomber Command meant that undemanding literature and light music held more appeal than the rather earnest entertainments preferred by Hull and Fayers. Hadley Chase's *No Orchids for Miss Blandish* was perhaps the most widely-read book of the war. Soldiers, sailors and airmen loved this pulp thriller whose *risqué* passages marked a new frontier of daringness in popular literature. It earned the prim disapproval of George Orwell who claimed it bordered on the obscene. To its many readers in uniform it provided a merciful diversion from the boredom interspersed with anxiety that characterized service life.

The music that affected them most were the bittersweet ballads and dance tunes that summoned thoughts of distant homes and longed-for girls who held the promise of happiness and fulfilment but who might never be seen again. The potency of these songs and melodies was at its most emotionally devastating just before ops. John Dobson, the 218 Squadron sergeant pilot who took part in the disastrous Berlin operation of 7 November 1941, remembered how before they set off, the mess echoed to the sounds of the crews' favourite records. 'Even the swingiest of them could almost evoke tears from the listener as it is impossible not to be moved by the most blatant passage of jazz when it tangibly recalls a memory that had been stored away in the innermost recesses which men who fear death keep hidden away for ever. I remember one very vividly, it began: "I dreamed that my lover had gone for a moonlight walk, I spoke to the moon, but the moon wouldn't talk."'[16]

To those who went out in bombers at night, the moon was a powerful presence. Its waxing and waning set the rhythms of their lives. They flew in its light. The sight of it hanging mysteriously in the purple blackness filled even the most unfeeling airman with wonder. It was beautiful and it was treacherous. It helped them on their way as the bombers trundled towards their targets, but it also swept away the darkness that shielded them from the night-fighters. It was easy to see why *No Moon Tonight* was an unofficial anthem of Bomber Command.

The messes provided the station's social hub. There, off-duty airmen could go for a quiet drink or a full-scale piss-up as the mood took them. The RAF took a relaxed view about alchohol consumption. Harris felt the need to justify the frequent mention of drink contained in Guy Gibson's memoirs. 'It may well be that references to "parties" and "drunks" in this book will give rise to criticism and even to outbursts of unctuous rectitude,' he wrote in the introduction. 'I do not attempt to excuse them if only because I entirely approve of them . . . remember that these crews, shining youth on the threshold of life, lived under circumstances of intolerable strain.' Anyway, he argued, the booze-ups were 'mainly on near-beer and high rather than potent spirits.'[17] This was not strictly true. Wartime restrictions meant that the beer available in the NAAFI and local pubs was notoriously flat and watery. But whisky was available and gin, which when mixed with lime cordial was supposed to have a liberating effect on the morals of WAAFs.

As Harris acknowledged, parties were a necessary part of Bomber Command life. On some occasions drunkenness and high jinks were almost obligatory. George Hull described to Joan a typical Saturday-night dance at Coningsby. 'Many people were drunk or merry (your humble servant was not among them although he drank all night at someone else's expense!). The Station Warrant Officer did an Apache dance with a redhaired bit of stuff from the orderly room. Two Squadron Leaders played rugger with a squashed bun and finished up under the billiards table. Two F/Sgts fought a bloody battle on the stairs over something they had both forgotten. We shot horrible lines to the girls we had invited from Boston, two of whom missed the bus back and spent the night in the WAAFs' quarters. The Group Captain danced a beautiful solo tango with his wife (despite his bulk) and even the Air Officer Commanding had a good time.'

Ken Dean, the flight engineer in Hull's crew and still only eighteen years old, could not stand the pace and had to be helped to bed by George and Jack Green. 'He insisted on kissing us both four times before going to sleep and this morning was filled with alcoholic remorse.'[18]

As the Coningsby dance showed, the best commanders understood it was important to occasionally reveal a less dignified side. One of the most evocative photographs of the war shows Wing Commander John Voyce, a popular and notably courageous officer in 635 Squadron, in black tie and braces leading a chorus of a mess favourite entitled 'Please Don't Burn Our Shithouse Down'.[19] Charles Patterson remembered one squadron commander from 2 Group who had to be replaced 'after an unfortunate accident . . . not a very gallant accident for such a gallant man. He fell out of the first-floor window of Weasenham Hall which was our mess after a party and had to be carted off to Cambridge hospital.'[20]

The licensed boisterousness was thought to build the team spirit which sustained the whole business of bombing. The well-oiled good fellowship that pervaded air force life could be overwhelming to a quiet men like Frank Blackman. He complained from Topcliffe to his girlfriend Mary that his attempts to concentrate on a classical music broadcast on the radio in the mess had been defeated by a dozen officers, 'mug in hand and obviously having huge fun but nevertheless making such a disturbance that music was out of the question for the three or four of us who would have liked to listen.

And these were not all your heathen Canadians but partly English squadron leaders and Flight Lieuts of the type you might personally meet anywhere.' Frank was obviously sensitive to teasing about his high-mindedness, asking 'do you not see how much more childlike are these bluff playmates than those of us who rely perhaps more upon intellect for interest and amusement?'[21]

But people like Frank Blackman were in a minority. Most members of Bomber Command were too young to be very worldly and most came from unsophisticated backgrounds. It was just as well. The bomber bases were located in parts of the country where the opportunities for pleasure were limited. Bomberland lay in the eastern half of England. It started where the pregnant belly of East Anglia juts towards the Lowlands and Germany, and stretched northwards to Lincolnshire and Yorkshire. It is a land of watery steppes and huge skies. Martha Gellhorn thought it looked 'cold . . . and dun-coloured. The land seems unused and almost not lived in.' George Hull was not impressed. 'It's flat,' he wrote, 'monotonously flat, petering out to a forlorn seashore grudgingly giving way to the sea. Windmills are the distinctive feature, great brick towers of placidity with their sturdy sweeps turning as they have done for two hundred years.'

Where the ground rises it exposes itself to the easterly winds slicing in from the North Sea. It is scattered with well-preserved small towns and villages, full of fine buildings reflecting the area's mediaeval wealth. The industrial revolution largely passed it by. The county towns are rich in old-world charm. But historical tourism was not what most of the airmen had in mind when they left the base to look for fun.

They were looking for a cinema, a dance-hall, a pub. Cities like Lincoln, York, Nottingham, Norwich and Cambridge had enough of each to cope with peacetime demand but were stretched by the influx of men in blue. On off-duty nights they would set off by bus or bike to the nearest town or metropolis, full of the romantic optimism of youth. The provincial streets and dingy bars held the prospect of fun and even romance. That, at least, was how the evenings started.

Don Charlwood described a night out in Scunthorpe, a popular destination with the Elsham airmen. It was typical winter weather. Cloud had settled on the low fields and the wind howled in from the east driving the rain and flocks of seagulls before it. It was a night to get drunk and many were intent on doing so. Ops had been scrubbed and in Charlwood's huts there were deaths to mourn. Two of the occupants had failed to return the previous night. The authorities had laid on buses. 'As we clambered in at the back, hurrying to get out of the rain, a dim blue light was switched on. It blanched the faces of twenty or thirty men who had begun singing with steaming breaths . . .'

They stopped at the Barnetby crossroads to pick up a dozen rain-soaked WAAFs, then raced towards Scunthorpe through wet, invisible countryside, the tyres hissing on the roads. The delights of the town were limited. 'One could get drunk at the "Crosby", or see a floor show and get drunk at the "Oswald" or dance and get drunk at the "Berkeley". And in the event of missing the bus back, it was always possible to stay the night at Irish Maggie's and return to camp by train in the morning.'

When the bus light was switched on, Charlwood realized he was sitting a few seats away from his friend Keith Webber. Scunthorpe was sunk in darkness. They groped their way through the Stygian streets to the Berkeley. 'We stepped out of the rain and darkness into the sudden brilliance of a large dance floor. RAF men, Poles, Americans, Canadians and Australians circled and swayed under a pall of tobacco smoke.'

They were vying for the attention of a far smaller number of WAAFs and local girls. The serious drinkers withdrew from the competition and clustered at the bar. The buses left again at 10 p.m. The one Charlwood boarded was packed solid and he found himself hanging out of the back. As it lurched off 'the singing increased in volume. Sometimes three or four different songs were being sung together, the most tuneless now shouted to the skies . . . with each expulsion of the singers' breaths, the smell of regurgitated beer became stronger.' As the journey lengthened, the distress of the drinkers mounted. The bus stopped by the WAAF camp.

Leading from the front: WC John Voyce.

'Somewhere among the tangle of bodies a voice shouted hoarsely, "Lemme out. I gotta get out or I'll bust!" . . . a dozen men stumbled to the roadside.' Finally the bus reached Charlwood's hut. He and Webber stepped out of the fog of stale beer, cigarette fumes, perfume and wet coats into the icy night. The rain had stopped and the skies shone with frigid brilliance. The clear weather did nothing to lift their spirits. It meant that tomorrow, ops would be on for sure.[22]

The nights out described by George Hull were rather more sedate. 'The crew ambled into Lincoln on Wednesday evening,' he wrote to Joan. 'We [didn't have] much money so after a few beers and eyeing a few doubtful-looking women, we went to a local dance-hall for a session. Now only a few us can dance much, [I'm] amongst the majority, so we looked over the place, met a great many old friends from other stations, and contented ourselves with a waltz or so, a shuffle, and a cycle home – sans lights.'

The important thing was to get off the base. The nearest pub provided a welcome taste of the civilian lives they had left behind. While based at Tuddenham in Suffolk, Arthur Taylor and his crew headed whenever they had the chance for the Bull, a pub at Barton Mills. It was a 'comfortable and roomy Georgian coaching inn . . . there was a cheerful air about the place and it became the haunt of RAF personnel as it was situated close to three aerodromes. There was a good fire going when it was cold and the air was full of cigarette smoke, loud talk and laughter. To get off your bike on a black night and enter this building was a heartening experience.'[23] Jack Currie and his crew frequented a similarly welcoming pub on the northern boundary of their base in Derbyshire. There, they were 'privileged to share . . . the landlady's favours, which included the use of her kitchen for bacon, eggs and sausages after hours, and the company of her daughters. The eldest of these was a big, untidy, cuddlesome girl whose efforts to keep her relations with us on a sisterly basis weren't always successful.'

The pub had a piano, as most did in the days when jukeboxes were still a novelty. 'For the last half-hour or so before closing time . . . downing the clear, bitter ale they brew beside the Trent, we liked to sing . . . while the village postmistress pounded an accompaniment. Her repertoire was limited to hymn tunes and a few songs of the day, of which we favoured "Roll Out the Barrel", "Bless 'em All" and, for the Australians' sake, "Waltzing Matilda".'[24]

The ability to play the piano was a great social advantage. Before he was killed, an Australian sergeant, J. A. Bormann, left behind a list of eighty tunes he could bash out in mess and pub. It includes 'Over the Rainbow', ''Till The Lights of London Shine', 'Blackout Stroll', 'South of the Border', 'Beer Barrel Polka', 'Rose Marie' and 'Lily of Laguna'. These songs are old and new, sentimental and rousing, upbeat and slow but they all have one thing in common – a melody that even the tone-deaf could sing along to.

The men clustered around the piano were doing a job that would harrow the most hardened veteran, but in many ways they behaved like the adolescents they had so recently been. George Hull reported that he and the crew had 'discovered a wizard pastime . . . we call it "scrub riding". On our way to and from the mess we miss the road, turn into a muddy barren field, dive into ditches, over the plank crossing a stream and crash the wire-netting into the mental home for aircrew. Funny isn't it what you have to do for a bit of excitement. Tonight we did it in the dark – most of our cycles returned safely, but ditchwater dun half taste peequleeah.'[25]

Writing from his training camp at Yatesbury, Wiltshire, Edwin Thomas described to his mother the evening's entertainment. 'The main attraction in the ENSA concert tonight in the camp theatre is George Formby. Tomorrow night we are all going on a binge to celebrate the end of the course – and I expect it will end with a terrific pillow fight about eleven o'clock.'

At this time Thomas was a few months past his twentieth birthday but still rooted in the pleasures of childhood. 'I had fun last Wednesday at our Wing Dance which Tony and I gatecrashed,' he reported home. 'We buttonholed a cross-eyed LAC who was standing outside the NAAFI canteen, and he advised us to try to make our entry by a door at the back of the building marked "Corporals". We took this advice but the door wouldn't budge an inch. We battered at the bally thing for ages then it finally "gave" with a noise that seemed almost to bring the building down. It had been held fast with a chair. We entered a small room in pitch darkness, barking our shins, laughing and crashing into one another. We found another door leading into the Sergeants' Cloakroom. We plucked up courage, put on a bold front and simply walked through into the dance-hall. Of course, most of the WAAFs were bagged by then . . . but we enjoyed ourselves. We drank cider and NAAFI beer. The latter is as flat as a pancake, and doesn't deserve the name beer.' Edwin's innocence appears to have survived untarnished until he was killed.[26]

It is easy to imagine what lay behind all the drinking and the boisterousness. The crews, as Harris had pointed out, were facing imminent death. It was natural that they should want to fill their lives to the brim during whatever time was left to them. The privations of air force life meant that the opportunities for sensual enjoyment were limited. This was particularly true of sex. Wartime had loosened the strict limitations on sexual behaviour imposed on most of society by the *mores* of the 1930s. But the number of women who were willing to engage in brief, non-committal encounters was still very limited, especially in the provincial, unsophisticated towns where the airmen went to unwind.

At work they were surrounded with females, the women of the WAAF, who made up a large proportion of the ground staff of the bases. The fact that they had joined up rather than being drafted for war work suggested an adventurous nature. But their tendency to independence did not necessarily indicate a free-and-easy moral approach. Most of the WAAFs were women of their time. They believed in love and found it hard to imagine sex without it. If they succumbed, it was in the expectation that marriage would follow.

There were, of course, exceptions, who earned the disapproval of their more strait-laced peers. Pip Beck, a radio telephony officer at Waddington had little time for a colleague called Jane who was 'a different type entirely' from the other WAAFs. She had 'short bleached-blond hair and eyebrows plucked to a thin line and pen-cilled black; deep blue eyes with black mascared lashes; eyes, as rapidly became evident, wise in the ways of men.' It was her habit to bring her embroidery to the watch office and work on it on a quiet evening. She would spread her 'hanks of coloured silk about the desk – and wait. Sooner or later an aircrew officer would appear, and Jane would add a stitch or two to her pattern and flash her blue eyes in his direction. After a brief word with the FCO [Flying Con-trol Officer] – his excuse for the visit – he would slip into a chair beside her and chat for a while, then leave. This was followed by a discreet exit on Jane's part – and no Jane for a while.'

One night an exasperated senior officer had had enough. Pip was startled to hear a senior officer 'say, in great indignation, "what does she think this is – a bloody knocking shop!" I hadn't heard the expresssion before but was wary of asking what it meant. I had the glimmering of an idea.'[27]

The best hope for those seeking casual sex lay with the 'saloon bar sirens' who frequented the pubs of Bomberland. Some were bruised women whose husbands were away at the war or dead or imprisoned. They offered the prospect of a few free drinks and some laughter and companionship. 'A few of the ladies were pretty but most were just acceptably plain,' Brian Frow wrote. 'All were out for a good happy time with the chaps, whose days in most cases were numbered. Some did, some didn't and many just teased.'[28]

There was another category of females, much disapproved of by clean-living young men like George Hull, whom he came across in the pubs of Lincoln, 'young girls of seventeen and eighteen, offering themselves for the price of a dance ticket or a glass of port.'[29]

The desire not to die a virgin was very strong. Willie Lewis, despite many dates, had yet to lose his innocence when he was informed by a Canadian gunner that an ATS girl who Lewis had spotted him with in a Lincoln pub the previous night was 'a certain bang'. When he ran into her a week later he decided to act. 'Plump and slothful in her brown uniform she sat with a companion in the corner of the snug sipping a half-pint of bitter.' Lewis's target was called Betty. He complimented her on her hair even though it was 'fuzzed about her ears in an untidy fashion' and offered her and her friend Eva a drink – a short, he insisted, because he hated buying women beer.

They accepted two gins. It turned out that Betty's husband, like Willie, was a flight engineer. Fortunately he was thousands of miles away in India. As the small talk dwindled Lewis asked Betty if she wanted to fit in a dance at Bridgen's dance-hall before it closed. According to his slightly fictionalized account, Betty was enthusiastic.

'"Yes," she said. "I'd like a dance. You don't mind, do you, Eva?"

'"You're always doing this to me, Betty," snapped the other girl. "This is the last time I'm going to come out with you."

'As soon as they got outside they started kissing. When they finally reached Bridgen's it was full up. "What shall we do now?" she said. It was an idle question, answered as she spoke, for they had already started in the direction of the East Gate, and were under slow progress, kissing, and cuddling, every few yards, towards the town playing fields.'

It was drizzling and the fields were sodden. They took refuge in an air-raid shelter. Lewis gallantly spread his coat on the dank concrete floor. After it was over they lay there 'locked together, dozing, until the clock struck twelve in the main square.'

He walked her back to her ATS billet where they hugged for a final time. '"Wait here a moment, Willie," Betty whispered. "I've got a photograph of my husband in my room. I'll go and get it. It's quite possible you might know him."'

Lewis was appalled at the thought. He hurried away before she returned. He knew he ought to feel ashamed. Instead the experience had 'filled his thoughts with joy. "I am a man at last," he said to himself. "I am a man at last." And those words danced a pulsing, happy, feeling in his mind on the journey back to the 'drome.'[30]

This was perhaps not the most sophisticated introduction to sex. If you were in search of something more refined it was better to visit London. Jack Currie took advantage of a short leave to go there with his rear gunner, Charlie Lanham. They lunched at Australia House and took the train to Maidenhead where they stayed at Skindles on the river. The following day Currie played cricket for his old boys' side, then they took the Metropolitan Line into town for an evening of fun. Lanham had laid on a couple of girls for the evening. The first came to meet them at their Sloane Square hotel. 'She walked into the . . . bedroom, swinging her wide hips and her long, coarse hair. Lanham introduced us, and her soft, cool fingers rested in my hand. She raised her pencilled eyebrows and looked me up and down, still undulating slowly.

'"So you're his skipper, that I've heard too much about. OK let's see you skipper something, like a drink maybe?"

'"What will you have?"

'"A fainting fit if I don't sit down soon. And Scotch on the rocks . . ."'

This vampish repartee delighted Currie as Lanham was quick to notice. '"What did I tell you Jack? Isn't she a beaut? Come on, let's hit the town."'[31]

It took considerable courage to flaunt sexual differences in this fiercely heterosexual society. 'Rory', a mid-upper gunner at Wickenby felt strong enough to do so, perhaps because his toughness was never in doubt. Currie described him as 'neat and well-groomed, with a face like that of a contented cat. He spoke with a lisp and a lilting, feminine diction, and he used scented soaps and lotions.

He occasionally dabbed his nose with a small, silk hankerchief. However he was well advanced on his second tour of operations, and he wore a DFM ribbon and a wound stripe, so his manner escaped the abuse which it might have otherwise attracted, in the aggressively masculine society in which he moved.'

One night in the mess Rory was describing the damage a German bomb had done to the *objets d'art* in his London flat during the Blitz. Among the listeners were 'several robust Australians whose aesthetic interests it would not be too harsh to term philistine, embracing as they did little beyond the world of sport and "Sheilas".'

Rory's usual good humour collapsed under the weight of prolonged Australian mockery. He threw himself at his two biggest tormentors and had to be restrained. Peace was restored after the philistines apologized and Rory allowed them to buy him a gin and lime.[32]

Gay airmen were more likely to keep their preferences to themselves and pretend to be heterosexual. Drink, though, had a way of dissolving the deception. Willie Lewis remembered an occasion when an American crew that had been rescued from the Channel after ditching spent the night with his squadron on their way home. 'The three officers were made very welcome in the officers' mess, and we stood shouting, and howling, through the usual list of nice songs, and then filthy ones, and back to nice ones again. And then the incredible happened. One of our chaps continued to keep holding the hands of one of the Americans. And yet I'd never thought he was a nancy boy before . . . The American was terribly distressed . . . We grabbed our man and took him back to his bedroom and said "Don't come back." And that was that.'[33]

The British airmen may have had the good fortune to be fighting from their own country. But that was not the same as being at home. In Bomberland, the natives were not always friendly. Some of the locals resented the influx of airmen and women, and the disruption that they had brought in their wake. Farmers complained about the damage to their crops and disturbance to their flocks caused by the arrival of Bomber Command. This attitude was resented by the men who were risking their lives on their behalf. Returning to Wigsley from a night-time cross-country training flight Hull and his crew 'got the wind under our port wing and and ran off the runway at a hell of a pace, passing the end of the runway lights at a fairly good speed and finally leaving through a vegetable field near a farmhouse to come to rest with about sixty yards of fencing wrapped around the fuselage. We were a bit shaken but soon hopped out. A few short minutes later out came the farmer and grumbled that we had made a mess of the vegetables. "Next time," he said, "someone will hit the farm." My God! The damn audacity. We could easily . . . have been seriously injured at least if the 'plane had turned over, yet all he could think about was his measly cabbage patch.'

This was not his first run-in with ungrateful civilians. 'Yesterday evening,' he wrote to Joan on 17 November 1943,

> we got a rare evening off and cycled into Lincoln . . . a garage attendant . . . as good as told me to get the hell out of the way while I was fixing a flickering rear lamp. The hate I've been storing up for the last fortnight came to the boil. I rather let rip with my opinion of Lincoln and his garage in particular . . . Admittedly we are a little boisterous in Lincoln on occasions – it's a case of letting off steam or bursting – but I think a little toleration on the population's part is required. Would you believe that in certain cafés the RAF are pointedly refused service when the place is crowded or civilians are waiting also? I've experienced it often, but rowing with the staff has little effect – they tell us we should only use the canteens.[34]

The aircrews often had a fractious relationship with local policemen who seemed to take a perverse pleasure in picking on them for petty infringements of the blackout.

For most of the British airmen, joining the RAF was their first experience of spending a long time away from home and when leave was granted, home was the first place they headed. The question of leave caused more frustration than almost any other aspect of RAF life. It was supposed to come every four weeks or after every six ops but the rules were often altered. It was granted, then snatched away, wrecking carefully-laid plans and nascent romances. When it finally arrived it was often disappointingly short. A '48' in most cases left barely enough time to go anywhere given the snail's pace of wartime transportation. When the opportunity to return to the world they left behind did come it was a strangely disconcerting experience. By the time they reached their squadrons they had spent around two years in a parallel society that duplicated many of the functions of family life. The small minority with wives and children could plunge into a brief, blissful respite of love-making and domesticity. For the rest, re-entering the past could be dislocating. The comforts and rhythms of civilian life seemed odd and the old, familiar faces seemed altered. They found themselves talking about comrades whom those at home had only read about in letters and places they had only heard of from the radio. The confusion wore off eventually, but usually just before the return to base loomed.

The question they asked themselves, as they walked the familiar streets to their front doors, was how much to say of what they had seen and done. Granted a welcome seven days' leave after completing eight ops, Harry Yates made his way from Wolverton station to his home in Stony Stratford and decided he would tell his mother nothing. 'She would not have thanked me if, in the quiet of the evening when she was alone in the house, she had cause to ponder corkscrews and scarecrows, flaming onions and blue master beams.' His father, however, was anxious for every detail, as were the regulars in the local pub, The Case is Altered. There, he discovered, he was a celebrity, not least for having flown low over the village, a 'beat up' in RAF parlance, on a couple of occasions to show off his piloting skills. The 'regular clientele of crib and dart players and grizzled old characters who would nurse a pint of mild for an entire evening was a bit short on recent operational experience. They gave us no privacy or peace . . .' They were proud of their local hero and bought him drinks all evening.[35]

Bernard Dye left a laconic account of a six-day leave in February

1944, detailing the homely pleasures that after the dreadfulness of operational flying must have tasted as sweet as anything the peace-time world could offer. On Friday the eleventh he recorded he 'had tea at Arnold's with Trevor, Charlie and Jimmy. It was like old times.' The next day he 'went to the pictures with Mum, Dad and David. Went to the ATC social. Had a good time.' On Monday he 'had a good day in Yarmouth.' On the fourteenth he 'went to the pictures with Geoff and Grace.'

Then it was back to Mildenhall and stark reality. Four days after returning from leave and his crew were chalked up on the battle order for Stuttgart. 'Navigator and bomb-aimer refuses to fly,' he wrote. 'We were all ready in the kite to take off. [They] were then put under armed escort & put into clink, expect it will mean a court-martial for them.' The crew was subsequently reformed and posted to 622 Squadron at Lakenheath.[36]

The overseas crews had no homes to go to. Some of them were taken under the wing of kindly locals or invited back to the families of their British colleagues. Others drifted to London where places like the Kangaroo Club offered homesick men a whiff of Australia or at least the chance to get drunk with different fellow-countrymen. The Canadians had the Beaver Club in Trafalgar Square. Ralph Wood would start his London leaves there before setting off to pubs like the Captain's Cabin and a favourite RCAF watering-hole in Denman Street in the West End called the Crackers Club. Then there were afternoon dances at the Hammersmith Palais where 'young girls were plentiful . . . too young to work, but not too young to dance.' Nightlife for all servicemen was centred on Piccadilly Circus where 'about the only civilians you could see were the prostitutes, and they were numerous. They were called the Piccadilly Commandoes.'[37]

Leave was unsettling. The airmen were desperate to reconnect with the world they had left. Harry Yates, back home in Stony Stratford, took comfort in 'discussing the (for me) entirely irrelevant goings on along the street or in McCorquodale's print works or the church, the hostelries or any of the odd corners that blessed our town with its singular character and its sense of continuity.' Coming home after the manic world of the bomber base was 'like taking a four-weekly moral bath and I was ever sorry when the moment came to leave.'[38]

Contact with home could induce a desperate nostalgia for a universe that, even if they survived, had gone, banished by the annihilation of innocence that went with their work. George Hull reminisced in a letter to Joan of departed bank holidays, 'good old Hampstead on a Whit Monday, gay colourful caravans and sideshows with their bedlam of cries, steam organs and laughter. Brass bands murdering overtures in the distance, couples strolling arm-in-arm through leafy lanes, picnics in the woods with cold chicken salad and bananas and cream, tongue sandwiches with sliced, sugared tomatoes, honey and biscuits, flasks of tea and coffee. Good days taken so much for granted.'[39]

The first letters and diary entries written by airmen after their return are touched with melancholy and regret. They had caught a glimpse of the life they would lose if they went the way of so many of their friends. And the biggest loss of all would be the chance to find lasting love.

15

Love in Uniform

Love flourished in wartime. Doubts and inhibitions withered in the heat of instant attraction and the knowledge that time might be short. Starting a romance was relatively easy. The problem was how to keep it going. The road to happiness was blocked by many practical and bureaucratic obstacles. Bomberland was a conglomeration of backwaters and was badly served by trains. Unless your girl was in Lincoln or Norwich or York, you faced a long and erratic journey getting to see her on leaves. Speaking on the phone was almost more frustrating than not speaking at all. The maximum length of a trunk call was six minutes and it could take hours to get a line. Often one party or the other would find themselves tongue-tied as they struggled to find the words that would make the most of the brief opportunity. At least the mail worked. It was a reasonable assumption that letters written one day would arrive the next, no matter where they were coming from or going to. But they too brought their problems. It was tricky conducting a love affair by correspondence. Feelings were pitched high and the words often tumbled on to the paper, unrevised. Burning sentiment might have cooled in the grey light of a Lincolnshire morning, or a cautious or hesitant remark seem ungallant after a few drinks in the mess. Either way it would take another letter and another delay for the first impression to be corrected.

Frank Blackman fell for Mary Mileham in the early summer of 1943. He was a flying officer with 429 RCAF (Bison) Squadron and she was working at the Admiralty in London. They came from very different backgrounds. She was the eldest of six children, the daughter of a prosperous solicitor who lived in bourgeois comfort in Boxmoor, Hertfordshire. There was enough money to send all the children to fee-paying schools and to St Moritz to ski in the winter.

Frank Blackman's father had been killed in the First World War and never saw his son. His mother worked as a housekeeper to provide for her two boys. He wanted to become a doctor but had to settle for training as a pharmacist. Before joining the RAF he had a post with a big pharmaceutical company and lived in a flat in London where he took care of his mother. Mary's family had servants. Frank was the son of one. 'In peacetime in no way would we have been on the same road,' Mary wrote later. 'But in war it is different. We became friends as we were both on an escape path and the companionship was comforting to us both.' Mary was recovering from 'a long unsatisfactory relationship'. Frank was seeking some relief from the 'fire of landing in a bomber squadron'.

According to Mary he was 'a gentle person', 'well-informed' and 'knowledgeable'. He was sensitive and literate, knew some German and Russian and was teaching himself Italian. She considered herself 'wild', loved the country and sport, but was 'academically completely dim'.[1] This made no difference to Frank. In the ten months they knew each other, Mary and he wrote to each other constantly, sometimes twice a day. For Blackman, the relationship became the central point of his precarious life. 'Forgive me,' he wrote one June night shortly after he had spent a leave with her, 'if just for one moment before I close I send you again my love and tell you – as I began to do on the phone before people started coming through the hall – that as a direct result of that one short week the whole tenor of my existence seems to have altered. Life is now an infinitely sweet thing and the thoughts of all the things we have yet to do or see and hear – music, holidays, fun in crowds and joy alone – are the things which my mind turns constantly towards . . . blast this war darling.'

At that point their story was only a few weeks old. They appear to have first met properly on 26 May 1943 when Frank visited her office at the Admiralty. He recorded the encounter in verse.

> I bless the day I wandered in
> To see you – and still full of doubt
> Asked bashfully to take you out
> For truth to tell I always knew
> I'd like to come to mean to you
> No mere acquaintance but a friend.[2]

The following day they went for a drink. Two days later they had supper together. On 1 June they saw *Arsenic and Old Lace* and dined at the Waldorf. Just before he returned to Blyton where he was in the throes of converting to Halifaxes, he took her to meet his mother. After that they spent every leave together. Letters and phone calls flew between them during the long spaces apart. Mary's correspondence has not survived but she kept all of Frank's letters. They brim with gratitude and delight. 'Life has come to mean much more than all the year that went before,' ran one of his couplets.

Love breeds optimism. In the beginning, Frank allowed himself to believe that he might survive. One summer morning, sitting in a garden in the grounds of East Moor, the squadron base, he wrote her a letter while he waited to hear whether or not ops were on that night. 'In such surroundings on such a lovely day, one's thoughts turn to the sweet things of life,' it said. 'Truly this moment is so peaceful that the prospect of the next hours seems like an evil dream.'

The romance was proceeding at a hectic wartime pace, but he, at least, did not care. 'Don't worry Mary about the rushing of fences,' he reassured her a few days later. 'I do have sense in this matter – nevertheless I don't think any of us can be quite happy without some little dream tucked away in his mind, even in self-deception. Without it existence for most of us would be a barren experience. Probably most of us has his idea of the sought-for peace. Mine could not be complete without – indeed depends on – someone to idealize and love.' He believed he had found in her 'that tiny sheet anchor upon sanity and faith' that would enable him to keep going.

Frank's love affair seems to have become more real to him than the 'evil dream' of flying over Germany at night. He wanted the nightmare to end as quickly as possible, and his waking life to begin properly. In the middle of June he was alarmed by a rumour that the squadron might be posted 'to the Middle East which God forbid.' The relative safety of the Mediterranean theatre held no attraction if it meant he was away from Mary. Yet weighed against the optimism was a fatalism that he had learned from cold experience. 'You ask if I believe one has any control over one's destiny,' he wrote. 'Darling, much as I would like to believe it – I don't.'

Frank and Mary were baring their souls to each other on the basis of a very short acquaintance. Sometimes it worried her. 'I hope that you don't quite mean it when you say sometimes you are writing to a stranger,' he fretted. 'I understand the feeling that must go through your mind. Nevertheless, I do hope and believe that we are beginning to understand each other.'

The next proper leave was a long way away. Frank recorded gloomily that 'with the present rather grievous losses in the squadron I see our 48s receding further and further in the background.' The Battle of the Ruhr was at its height and 429 Squadron had lost seven aircraft, nearly a third of its strength, in the previous few nights in major attacks on Krefeld, Mülheim and Wuppertal.

He suggested she come north to visit him, even though there was a high likelihood that he would be flying most nights. At least she would be able to watch him depart. He gave her directions to the airfield. 'If you care to walk along the road past the telephone box and turn right you will come to the edge of the 'drome and can, if you want to, see us take off. If you do, I can't wave to you exactly – but you can be sure that that mile between us will be positively sizzling with telepathic activity.' On 25 June she travelled to York then north to East Moor, near the village of Sutton-on-the-Forest. Frank was indeed on ops. Despite its recent mauling the squadron was detailed for an attack on Gelsenkirchen in the Ruhr. The raid was not a success and losses were heavy. Thirty aircraft failed to return, more than 6 per cent of the force.

Mary arrived too late to meet him before he left but was able to watch him take off and stayed up all night to see him safely home. After he woke they enjoyed one of the days they had fantasized about. 'Frank came round just before lunch,' she wrote in her abbreviated diary. 'Lunched, walked sunbathed dinner talked early to bed.'[3] He had arranged for her to stay with a Mrs Skinner who lived near the base. The following day he picked her up in the morning. They had a blissful Sunday before going into York for dinner. He put her on the 9.30 train and she arrived back in London at 3 a.m.

The visit reinforced his desire 'to get this business done.' In the days after her departure he flew operations by night and wrestled with his feelings by day. On Wednesday 30 June he wrote that he had 'been trying to analyse my own state of mind since the weekend. I'm not being really introspective about it – I've been too busy for one thing – but emotions have been so mixed that I had to give it some thought.' On Monday he had been 'excited – perhaps even intoxicated and much of this has survived.' But overlaying this elation was 'a strong feeling of resentment that so much sweetness is so near and yet so far. I think this last day or two – since you opened once again my eyes to such boundless happiness – I have hated this war more . . . than at any time since it began.'

The righteousness of the fight seemed of lesser importance than the fact that he was in love for the first time. He now knew what he wanted and was sure he could attain it 'but for this wretched stupid war.' Viewed in this light, Frank saw little that was noble about his work. What lay ahead were 'possibly months of bitter, destructive, death-dealing labour.' He was 'not able to hate enough to feel otherwise.' He was suddenly gripped by fear, but 'not of dying. That must be . . . usually at least, thank God, oh so simple – but fear of losing the good things of life.' And by far the most important of these was Mary Mileham.

By the end of July the Battle of the Ruhr was over and Harris turned his attention to Hamburg and then Berlin. The squadron converted from Wellingtons to Halifaxes. Its losses declined dramatically and only thirty-seven men were killed in the last five months of the year, seven fewer than had died in three nights in June.

Mary went to see Frank again at East Moor early in August and spent a 'lovely weekend'.[4] Back in London she visited his mother and was waiting for him when he came to London on leave on

14 August for a few days. In September he had a '48' and they spent it together dining one night at Quaglino's.

On 22 October she made the arduous journey north again to visit him at his new base, Leeming, in Yorkshire. Afterwards he wrote to Mary in some confusion. 'You know, Mary that I cannot yet ask you to marry me. Indeed if I did you would be afraid to say yes – being far, perhaps, from knowing your own wish. Yet Mary you must know that I wish it above all things and I am supremely happy even in the hope and anticipation of it.' By that stage they had spent only seven short spells of time together. Frank's hesitation appears to have been selfless. He wanted her to be his wife. But he knew that the squadron's good luck could not last for ever and the chances remained high that if they did marry, Mary would soon be a widow. Despite the time they had spent together, which was considerable by wartime standards, she seems to have been much less certain about her feelings and more hesitant about committing herself. Her emotions were tender. As well as the 'unsatisfactory' romance she had lost her brother Denys, a fighter pilot who had fought in the Battle of Britain, who was shot down over the Channel in April 1942. Nonetheless they showed every sign of being a couple on the two leaves that Frank took in London in what was left of the year. They played bridge, visited his mother and ate out at the Liaison-Slavia Club and the Argentina.

On 20 January 1944 Frank had a week's leave and came to London. For once he did not call her immediately, provoking in Mary a pang of suspicion. 'Out with his other girlfriend?' she wondered in her diary. No one reading his love-struck letters could believe him capable of any romantic deception. The more likely explanation is that he felt his first duty was to attend to his mother. He rang on the twenty-second and the following day they went to the country and spent the afternoon playing bridge. On the last night of their leave they went to dinner at the Argentina then to the cinema to see *Jane Eyre*. 'Felt disturbed,' Mary wrote in her diary.[5] The following day he dropped by her office to say goodbye and took the train north to Leeming.

Frank always kept his hope warm, searching for positive signs in the swirling confusion of the war. Late in October 1943 he had written that 'the beginning of the end is in sight . . . with the Soviets doing these incredible things . . . there is no doubt that a point is coming when tremendous air armadas will operate day and night with at first great losses perhaps – but with an effect that may finish the war without invasion.' He was well aware of his ignorance of the big picture. 'I have no knowledge of these things at all of course,' he admitted. But it was 'obvious that this is the next step – and God help the Hun.'

His prediction was already coming true. As he wrote, the Battle of Berlin was beginning and 429 Squadron were part of it. On the snowy night of 19 February 1944 they went on one of the bloodiest raids of Bomber Command's war. Altogether 823 aircraft set off. The target was Leipzig. Frank's aircraft was among the force of 255 Halifaxes. A diversion towards Kiel aimed at drawing away the German night-fighters was unsuccessful and the bomber stream was under attack all the way to the target. The wind was stronger than forecast and pushed the bombers along so fast that many got there early and were forced to orbit until the Pathfinders arrived. Four bombers were destroyed in collisions and twenty shot down by flak. Leipzig was covered by cloud and the Pathfinders had to mark blind. Immediately there 'was a wild scramble as several hundred bombers came in from all directions, anxious to bomb quickly and get out of the area.'[6] The raid was considered a success in that more than 50,000 Germans were bombed out. But the price was appallingly high. Bomber Command recorded its worst night of the war to date with seventy-nine aircraft lost. Almost 15 per cent of the Halifaxes that reached enemy territory never returned. Many had turned back before crossing the enemy coast. Thereafter Halifax IIs and Vs, the older types, were withdrawn from operations to Germany. The raid had been a disaster.

Frank's Halifax was shot down by a night-fighter near Berlin. All on board were killed. It was Mary who received the telegram telling her that he was missing. He had listed her, rather than his mother or elder brother as his next of kin. Then came a last letter, postmarked 21 February and presumably posted by a comrade. There is no indication of when it was written. After the passion and enthusiasm of his other letters the tone seems flat and stilted and there is a feeling of resignation behind the unconvincing optimism.

> Well Mary, dear.
>
> This will tell you if something unfortunate has happened. I shall hope in due course to be writing to you again either from some Oflag or other – or with any luck from England on return.
>
> In the meantime it is hard to know what to say. You have meant so much to me – and been so very charming to me during these last few months that it is hard to say 'Goodbye' even if only for a while.
>
> God bless you darling and thank you again – a million times. Lots of luck and my deepest and sincerest wishes.

Despite the chaos of wartime, Frank and Mary had at least managed to have something like a fulfilling courtship. They had met and flirted, fallen for each other, though he clearly more heavily than she. They had shared rich experiences leaving memories that lasted Mary the rest of her life. They revealed themselves to each other with a rare frankness and traded more sincere endearments than many couples do in a lifetime.

George Hull's relationship with Joan Kirby was less satisfying. He met her at the funeral of her brother who had been killed in a training accident in July 1943. George had made friends with John Kirby in Canada where they were both training to be navigators.

He was brought up in Stepney, east London, the only son of Jack and Margaret Hull. As a boy he was interested in science and once rigged up an electric sign that flashed 'Happy Christmas' to visitors when they stepped on the doormat. George belonged to a category of young men who grew up in the nineteen-thirties that was particularly well represented in the ranks of Bomber Command. He came from an ordinary background and received an ordinary education. But the walls of deference were crumbling, a process that was hastened by the war, and he was eager to plunge into the world of

'Silver wings in the moonlight / Flying high up above
While I'm patiently waiting / Please take care of my love.'

high culture that had previously been the domain of the wealthy.
He loved good books and good music as well as the ordinary pleasures of the British male. His idea of a perfect evening was a visit
to the Proms followed by a few pints and a game of darts. He

had, Joan remembered, a strong social conscience. 'He was a great believer in social justice,' she said. 'He would have been a leader in some form.' His initial ambitions were simple enough. If he got through the war alive he planned, like Frank, to be a pharmacist. He was, in a quiet way, a patriot who felt his Englishness with a poetic intensity. Nazism represented everything that repelled him and he had joined the RAF Volunteer Reserve as soon as the war began.

George disguised an attractive naivety behind a show of sophistication and pragmatism and there was enough of the lingering legacy of Victorianism in his make-up for him to affect a dislike of overt displays of feeling. 'He was a very jolly sort of chap,' Joan said, 'an optimist full of plans for getting the war over and getting on with life. Yet he had a very serious side to him and was quite unsentimental. I got a bit mawkish one time, I remember, and he more or less said, don't be ridiculous. Sentiment is fine but sentimentality is not.'[7]

Coming from George this was mildly hypocritical. His letters vibrate with emotion. The correspondence began after he and his friend Philip Kitto, known to everyone as Mac, travelled back with Joan when she returned to her WRNS base, HMS *Cabbala* at Lowton near Warrington after her brother's funeral. The journey was fun and lifted some of the gloom imposed by John's death. His loss seemed particularly pointless. His aircraft had been diverted from his home base at Wigsley to another airfield after a training exercise and crashed on landing. The Kirbys were a tight-knit, dutiful English middle-class family. Mr Kirby was in charge of the Air Raid Precautions area. His wife was a hardworking Red Cross nurse. The death cast a shadow over the family's happiness which never quite cleared.

Being with her brother's best friends cheered her up. 'What do you think? – George and Mac came right the way up here with me,' she wrote home. 'I was terribly pleased because instead of the horrible journey I anticipated, it was very pleasant. You would have laughed to see us; we were sitting around a desolated refreshment room on one of the platforms with my sandwiches and three cups of tea trying to work out how to get through the barrier without paying.'[8]

On 8 July the long pursuit began. He was, he wrote to her, waiting for his new crew to finish off their training and for once had some time on his hands. 'With a bit of luck and a cunning tongue, I may be able to pop up and see you for a weekend – that is if you get any time to yourself during Saturdays and Sundays.' George was completing his training at Bruntingthorpe in Leicestershire, not so very far from Warrington. But this apparently simple ambition turned out to be maddeningly difficult to achieve.

As George schemed to make a rendezvous, Joan was getting acquainted with a new and exotic species of servicemen; the Americans. One Sunday in the middle of July, dressed up in her new uniform she 'went to an American Red X dance in Warrington. The dance itself was awful – it was an afternoon affair but we got taken to tea at the American Club and had "Coke" which John used to talk about so much.' At the end of the month the prospect of leave was once again dangled tantalizingly in front of George, and then whipped away. 'Well it happened again,' he wrote to her. 'I don't know what you are thinking about all this but I would have given a week's pay not to have had to send that telegram on Friday evening. I felt sure I would get that "48" this weekend. All Friday morning I talked to the rest of the navigators about asking for a "48" until they could think of nothing else. The course leader was approached and he saw the OC of our flight. The decision was rather vague. "Perhaps, eh. We'll see." At 10 a.m. that morning we found ourselves building a road with picks and shovels under the impression that if we did enough we might get it. Needless to say nobody really believed it. That's a common instance of official craftiness.'[9]

While George fumed, Joan was making the most of the rich social opportunities available to an attractive young woman in a country crammed with men in uniform who were starved of female company. Returning by train from a leave spent at the family home in Oxhey near Watford she and her friend Jan 'met some Americans – I've got a date with a Captain McClees on Friday – wrote me a complicated phone number and got me a table and carried my bag and said "please ring me up tomorrow as I can't ring you." . . . I might go – be fun for a few weeks – he's a doctor so he should be alright, but he's married!'

Joan did indeed go out with the captain, three times in a row. 'He takes me out to dinner etc. & is quite nice,' she wrote to her family on 17 August. 'Unfortunately he's going south this week but wants to see me on my leave in four weeks' time & all kinds of things. I came back . . . laden up with cigarettes etc., it's really quite amusing.'

Nearly two months after their first encounter, George and Joan had still not managed to meet. 'I hope we can see something of each other within the next few weeks,' he wrote plaintively. 'I am eager to see this winsome Wren in uniform.' When he did finally get some leave he went to London to see his family but was able to keep his memories of Joan fresh by visiting her parents at 'Shirley', the Kirbys' house. 'I went to see your folks on Friday evening,' he wrote. 'Mac came along too. Your Dad met us at Carpenters Park around five thirty and we walked to Shirley.' They then set off to the Load of Hay, the local pub which was to lodge in George's mind as a symbol of the cosy Englishness that comforted and sustained him. There, he was 'as usual beaten in two darts matches' and settled down to drink pints for the rest of the evening.

George had something far more significant to report but modestly left the news to well down the page. 'Did I tell you that I did my first ops trip last week? Well I did! We made a good job of it apparently. As you can guess we had our doubts at the beginning but soon we were on our way and I was too busy to think about anything but navigation.' This appears to be a reference to a raid on a long-range gun battery at Boulogne on 8/9 September 1943 in which crews from Operational Training Units took part. It was a relatively easy debut. Little damage was done to the emplacements but no aircraft were lost.

By now Joan was finding the novelty of Americans was wearing off. She wrote home to complain about a dance at the American Red Cross in Warrington. 'Jan went out with a Yank. I had one as well but didn't fancy going out with him. They bore me. All they talk about is themselves non-stop with just enough breaks now and then to say "gee I like your legs" or "how far is your camp from here honey?" Makes you sick!'

Towards the end of October, George finally managed to be reunited with the girl who had haunted his thoughts for nearly four months. Joan wrote to her parents with the news. 'On Saturday afternoon I was waiting at the local bus stop about 1.15 p.m. for a bus to the station when a Warrington bus stopped at the other side of the road and who should get out but George! Evidently he and his bomb aimer – Ray [Stones] – had mizzled off from camp Friday night and come up to Manchester where Ray lives. He had taken a 100–1 chance & come to Lowton to see if he could see me. By tremendous luck I had just ignored a lorry as being too dirty and was still in the queue with Jill. We went to Chester and had a very nice time . . . it's a lovely old town full of old-fashioned tea places etc. We had a look round for a present for Jan, then had tea, then went to the pictures, then went to a lovely hotel called "The Blossoms" for dinner.'

Joan had arranged to go to Liverpool that Sunday to visit a ship but put it off in order to meet George in Manchester. 'He was terribly pleased to see me and marched me off to "the most palatial place in town" viz the Midland Hotel where you pay 2/6 to wipe your feet. We were safely ensconced in a corner of the lounge with a silver teapot when Jan drifted in. Her date had let her down so she made for the Midland and us. George rang up Ray who was out to tell [his mother to tell him] to come down town . . . the boy's train went at 5.30 p.m. so we went to the station and met said bombaimer there – a very nice boy indeed – and saw them off midst great giggles & kisses and promises of "be up next weekend." Jan and I killed ourselves laughing and then went and had a lavish dinner at the Queen's. The coffee was 2/- a cup so we left it & went down to the YM[CA] for a cuppa tea!! We laughed all the more then – Queen's to the YM!'

George, by now, was completely smitten. 'You may not believe this but the last two days were the best I've spent ever,' he wrote on his return. Even desolate Wigsley, which lay under a thick autumn mist seemed 'easier to endure now'. The mood did not last long. Less than a week later he was missing her badly and taking out his frustration on Bomber Command. 'I hate the RAF, this camp in particular. I hate the job we do, not for myself but for those who are lost in the gamble.'

By the middle of November his crew were making their final preparations before starting their full operational tour. 'Tonight is a special occasion,' he wrote to Joan on the thirteenth. 'It's the first night for eight in a row that we can get to bed at a reasonable hour. We've flown twenty-five hours in three days! Both night and day. We ought to be on a squadron in a few days, then you can really sing "Silver Wings in the Moonlight", say a prayer or two and get worried.' The weather had got even worse. He was writing the letter 'huddled over the radio in the mess waiting to be told to get airborne. It's hellish cold, there's about five hundred bods, about a square foot of glowing coals and there's more heat from my cigarette than from the fire at this range.'

The approach of operations coincided with the news that Joan would soon be moving on from Warrington, a thought that filled George with anxiety. 'One of the chief reasons for my being completely cheesed is the realization in my more pessimistic moods what with going from the Manchester area after Christmas and our leaves never coinciding we are unlikely to be seeing each other at all again – grim isn't it, or don't you think so?'

Death was edging closer all the time. The names of those he had trained with in Canada were starting to appear on the casualty lists. 'Do you remember my raving about John Beebe, one of the Winnipeg and Harrogate boys?' he asked her. 'He is posted as 'missing' on his thirteenth 'op'. Two more went the same way last week. God! How right you are on the world's unnecessary suffering.'

George finally reached 207 Squadron in mid-December, 1943. The Battle of Berlin was at its height. Like many, he found that after all the training it came as something of a relief to finally be fighting and the anxiety was overcome by the professional satisfaction of doing what he set out to do. 'Strike One!' he wrote exultantly to

Joan. 'Hull opens his offensive on Germany. Last night bombers of considerable strength Bombed Berlin – you can surely guess the rest!' His squadron had been part of a force of 483 Lancasters which struck the capital on the night of 16/17 December. Little industrial damage was done. Most of the bombs hit houses and railways, killing more than 700 people.

It had been a hard night. The bomber stream flew straight, without diversions, and night-fighters harried them all the way to Berlin and over the target area. Twenty-five Lancasters were lost. When they returned they found heavy cloud smothering many of the bases. Another twenty-nine Lancasters either crashed or were abandoned by their crews. Nearly 150 men were killed in the confusion. Altogether 283 men died on the raid, a casualty rate of 9.3 per cent. George's squadron had got off lightly. Only one aircraft belonging to 207 Squadron was shot down, the victim of a night-fighter. Two of the crew were killed and five subsequently reported to be prisoners of war.

Ten days later the good mood had worn off. By now he had three squadron operations under his belt, one to Frankfurt and another trip to Berlin on the night of 23/24 December. Two days after Christmas he wrote that the holiday had been 'a mixture of work and play, Noel over Unter Den Linden . . . we were so damned tired on our return after close on thirty-six hours without sleep that we were fit for nothing.' He felt curiously dispassionate about the raids. 'I cannot say that I have much emotion. I appreciate their extreme danger but also their necessity. It has a cancelling-out effect. Physically they call for all you have. On return I feel wretchedly tired and depressed and to sleep through a glorious morning when I should like to be walking through the countryside in the crisp, clean air depresses me further.'

George surveyed the coming year in a mood of cold realism. He had grown very close to the Kirby family during his visits to 'Shirley' and 'The Load'. He had put Mr Kirby's name on his 'death form' as someone who was to be informed in the event of bad news. Later he changed his mind and took it off, reckoning that 'it would be unfair to ask him to be subjected to what might amount to a great shock . . . he's had enough already.' He now accepted that his feelings for Joan were not, at least for the moment, reciprocated. She was, he told her semi-facetiously, the third woman in his life, coming after his 'kite', A-Able, and his mother. Joan was the 'girl from whom I draw inspiration to give battle against those who violate peace and God's wish to succour humble mankind. If fate deems me unfortunate in unrequited love then that is [fate's] will.'

The chances of their meeting again were about to become even more remote. At the end of January Joan learned where she was to be posted next. She was going to a Fleet Air Arm base at Machrihanish on the Mull of Kintyre and 'one of the loneliest parts of the Scottish coast you'd ever find.' This was unwelcome for a number of reasons as she explained in a letter to her family. She would be unable to get home for the weekends as she had at Warrington and only one of the friends she had made at HMS *Cabbala* was coming with her. Worst of all it meant 'leaving all my boyfriends, viz Bob and Dennis (my sailor) and getting further away from George.'

Joan was in great demand. Bob was the American who had bought her lobster at the Midland Hotel in Manchester. She had received, she reported 'a proposal . . . last Monday night!!! Of course I'd never marry him but it wasn't altogether a shock. The poor lad will be so miserable at me going so far away from him but I think it's a good thing as I didn't love him a scrap. Poor Dennis too will be disappointed, he's out on a trip on his corvette now but should be in port again next Friday.' And then there was Flight Sergeant Hull. 'Won't George be disappointed? Poor thing, every time we make any arrangements they are always upset. It seems like fate, doesn't it?'

George felt the same way. 'I am sure you feel quite bad enough without me adding to your unhappiness,' he wrote on 27 January 1944 from London where he spent his leave with his family as well as making his regular visit to the Kirbys. 'It seems like a plot to prevent us meeting, apart from the stolen weekend in Manchester – for which I thank God for giving me such an opportunity. We have consistently crossed each other's tracks but never coincide. Perhaps if I ask to be transferred to the Far East our chances would improve. Cheerio pet, keep that chin up. We won't always be unhappy.'

When his leave was up his mother and father saw him off at King's Cross. George found the parting upsetting. 'Nothing tries me so much as the pseudo cheerfulness that we all present to each other during those last few hours: Dad talks hurriedly about "when you come home again" and Mother's organization and preparation would be just the thing for a Polar Expedition. Then in the last few minutes remaining we say goodbye with lightness that certainly finds no echo in our hearts. Mother stands bravely at the gate striving to hide those tears . . . King's Cross . . . a long, boring journey, and the familiar face of a Station Policeman who assumes the role of jailer for another six weeks of uncertainty.'

Joan's worries about Machrihanish did not last long. On the ferry to the Mull of Kintyre she was 'entertained by two sub-lieutenants – one a radio officer at Campbeltown who wanted me to meet him tonight but I wasn't having any.' The other, a Fleet Air Arm pilot called Bill was 'just her dream man'. He reminded her of her brother John, who had always been the ideal she sought, 'tall and a bit thin with a thin face and sandy-coloured hair, not really good looking but ooooo! He's terribly cynical on top because he was shot up over Salerno and they won't let him fly at sea any more but underneath he's grand.'

Clearly Joan was concerned about the effect that the guilelessly reported news of her busy social life would have at home. She sent a letter bursting with frank pleasure at the joy of being an optimistic and pretty young woman enjoying every minute of the new freedom that the war had brought in its wake. 'Really and truly I am fed up as hell. Bill is flying most nights so I can't even see him, but we had a lovely time last week. We walked our shoes off almost going up the hills and among the heather!! Happy days – I'm not a flirt Dad, you can't help liking them, they're such good fun and so crazy. I love them all a little.'

She had just received George's latest letter, telling of his visit to the Kirbys. 'He does like coming up to Shirley doesn't he – it's his second home almost, The Load being the third. I wish I could come home for a day or two. I'd love to stroll up to The Load this evening.' Mrs Kirby had clearly been intrigued by the elbowing of Bob. 'How did I convey to Bob that I didn't love him mummy? Well I just told him!! I told him I liked him an awful lot but I didn't love him the way he loved me – I couldn't marry him! He talked a bit about "love coming later" but I know different by now and I wasn't having any! I feel terribly sorry for him as he's going through hell I know but callous though it seems I can't do anything about it. He'll just have to go away and forget me. It's been done before.'

Whether or not he knew about the new developments in Joan's romantic life, George's pursuit remained as dogged as ever. He sent a plaintive letter from Coningsby. 'It does seem that Fate takes a hand in all our plans but my reaction is to fight her,' he wrote. 'I could get a great deal fonder of you if I saw you more often – I remember that weekend in Manchester all too vividly – and perhaps it would not be fair. Not fair to me because it disturbs my peace of mind, unfair to you because what little interest you may have in me might be one day a grief to you equal almost to that which you have lately suffered. I don't want to labour the question of danger in this job like a little tin hero but I do want you to know that what I said . . . about the girl who inspires me still holds. What I really mean is that when I think of you I want to hold on to life with both hands and get out of the War somehow and live in certainty – a dangerous idea when it is for people like you that I will fight this to the end.'

Joan appears to have given a cautious response to this declaration for in his next letter he accepted that it would better to take things more slowly. 'Thank you for the many sweet things you talk about in your letter,' he wrote. 'I appreciate your feelings and reluctantly agree with them. I had already made my mind up before I wrote that letter I would not trespass on your feelings to the extent of making a major issue of it. It is, as you suggest, a strange thing that our correspondence during the last months has developed an understanding. It's such a limited medium for thoughts, things could hardly go beyond the present stage. I doubt whether writing less often would have much effect. For my part I should miss your frequent letters more than anyone else.' He now seemed resigned to the unlikelihood of their meeting in the near future. 'Since . . . only a miracle of chance could bring us together we simply must mark it down to the debit side of the War . . .'

By now 61 Squadron, with whom George had flown most of his operations, was firmly in the front line of the Battle of Berlin. All together, it dispatched 242 Lancasters on twenty raids on the Big City. By the middle of February, as Bomber Command was heading for defeat, George wrote that he was 'very tired, cold, hungry, thirsty and deafened.' He had just returned from a huge raid on the night of 15/16 in which forty-three aircraft were lost. 'When I think back to what happened over there last night I am sure that this morning we are living on borrowed time!'

George was now flying so often that there was little time for writing letters. As the flow of correspondence slackened Joan started to become alarmed. 'I'm terribly worried about George,' she wrote home on 11 March 1944. 'He's never left it as long as this ever between letters & it's now over a week since I heard. I'm sure something must be up. So sure in fact that I sent him a telegram but so far haven't heard a word back. I don't know what to do next. Maybe I'm worrying needlessly but there's something strange going on I'm sure.' Her concern prompted both her mother and father to send letters of their own to Coningsby, asking if anything was the matter.

The following day George wrote to say he had received the telegram and two letters. 'I am very sorry to have caused you so much anxiety but there was nothing I could do about it. We have flown day and night in all weathers on all sorts of missions during the past few weeks and had barely enough sleep quite often, let alone spare time. I am afraid a satisfactory explanation would entail telling more than I am permitted to talk about – I ain't trying to be all mysterious like, it's a fact.'

The war and his determination to fulfil his part of it had pushed all other thoughts aside. His doubts melted in the heat of the fight and his criticisms of the RAF were forgotten. He told her proudly how he and his comrades had been honoured with one of the photographs showing spot-on bombing that Harris signed and awarded as a prize to successful crews. The squadron had been switched temporarily to French targets. The moonlit night before, they had taken part in a smallish raid directed at four factories and George's crew were expecting another aiming point photograph. 'I believe we are earning our keep,' he wrote with satisfaction. He was trying not to think about the leave that would soon fall due. 'It looks like the twenty-fourth more or less for certain. I am so fed up with haggling that I do not really care if we go on leave or not.'

That was the last letter. Six days later George and his crew were part of a force of 846 aircraft that took off for Frankfurt. The marking was accurate and the city suffered heavily. Some 420 civilians were killed and 55,500 bombed out. The damage to Bomber Command was light. Only twenty-two aircraft were lost, 2.6 per cent of the force. It was some time before it was discovered how George met his death. After taking off from Coningsby at 19.17 hours on 18 March nothing more was heard of the aircraft or crew. An investigation by the Missing Research and Enquiry Service discovered that their Lancaster had been hit by anti-aircraft fire and crashed into the outskirts of Biegwald Forest near Frankfurt. All on board died but only George and Jack Green were allotted identifiable graves. They were buried first at the Frankfurt Main Cemetery by the German authorities. After the war their bodies were moved to the Bad Tölz British Military Cemetery.

George was not as resigned about his lack of progress with Joan as his last letters suggest. A few days before he was killed he telephoned Mr Kirby to say that he thought he might be able to make it back for Joan's birthday which was on 20 March. He had some important news. '[He] said that he was going to ask me to marry him though things hadn't got to that stage,' Joan recalled. She was at home when the telegram came. She thought at first that it was yet another disappointing communication from George announcing that his leave had been cancelled. Jack and Margaret Hull telephoned and came to Shirley at the weekend and the families grieved together for their lost sons.

It was only later that Joan came to really appreciate the magnitude of the loss. 'Reading those letters it stands out a mile . . . he never really had a chance to press his case.' When his effects were collected a wedding ring was found in one of his pockets.[10]

The bomber stations were emotional incubators. There was no attempt to integrate wives and families into the social structure of the base. Spouses were seen as a nuisance and a distraction. Shortly after Harris took over he banned all wives from a forty-mile radius of their husbands' bases. The order came through when Guy Gibson had just taken over 106 Squadron at Coningsby. Only those airmen who already lived out were exempted. There were only four in the squadron. Gibson, who was married himself, approved. 'This was the best news I had heard for a long time. You cannot fight a war and live at home.'[11]

Yet on the stations, men and women lived and served side by side in a proximity that would have seemed unimaginable to the generation who had fought the previous war. Romances were inevitable. Some were uncomplicated boy-meets-girl stories. Others were not. Fidelity, it has been said, is the second casualty of war. Frances Scott was one of only three WAAF officers on a Cambridgeshire bomber station. Their presence was resented by some of the older male officers but appreciated by everyone else. In their brief time at the base, she felt they had 'showed we could offer companionship and sympathy as well as friendliness, and perhaps a deeper relationship to a chosen few.'[12] The bomber crews were unlike any men she had encountered before. 'Most of the men who flew looked older than they were. It seemed as though they suddenly changed from adolescents to mature men, missing the carefree years of the early twenties.'

In December 1943 she was setting off with a group to a dance at a neighbouring station when they were joined by a twenty-eight-year-old wing commander called Clive with a DFC ribbon on his tunic. He 'spent most of the evening talking and dancing with me, brought me back in his car and – we fell in love.' They spent Christmas at the base. The celebrations started with a dance in the mess on Christmas Eve. Regulations forbade the WAAFs to wear civilian clothes. They tried to brighten up their severe 'best blue' uniforms with silk stockings and the lightest footwear they could get away with. Clive was a 'looker' and knew it. He had a 'generous supply of black hair, giving a rakish air. His face was long with high forehead, beneath which deep set, dark blue eyes looked out on a world which offered him danger, disillusionment, love. His mouth was firm and he had a dark moustache . . .'

Clive was president of the mess committee and one of the hosts of the evening but he often 'left his guests for longer than he should. We ate and drank and laughed and found each other.' When everyone had departed they ended the evening in front of the dying fire, wrapped chastely in each other's arms. The following day there was a service in the station church, a simple wooden hut. Afterwards the officers served Christmas dinner to non-commissioned men and women before retiring to their own mess for a buffet lunch. Somebody produced some mistletoe and one of the officers urged Clive to give Frances a kiss. This remark 'though made in fun, had an unintentional effect on some of those present who put the proverbial "2 and 2" together and tongues wagged, male tongues and malicious tongues for Clive was not popular at that time on the squadron.'

That night there was a dinner in the mess which went on until the early hours. Clive took her back to the little sitting room which served as the WAAF officers' mess. It was out of bounds to male visitors after 11 p.m. but they ignored the rules, sitting on the floor by the fire and drinking wine. Clive seemed subdued. It turned out he was on ops the following day. As a senior commander he was not expected to go on every trip but that did not reduce the agony of anticipation. '"I suppose you think wing commanders with DFCs don't know fear?"' he asked her bitterly. He appeared thoughtful and on the point of saying something important. 'He seemed to want to talk, to get at something in his life that puzzled him, and it put a shadow across his face. "If only there was something more to come back to," he said, "something to hold on to like so many of the [others] have."'

Frances's spirits rose. She began to hope that there could be more between them than an awkward infatuation. She decided to reveal her feelings. She had known him for just forty-eight hours but already felt she loved him, and told him so. Clive's tender expression turned 'to a gloom bordering on anger'. Frances immediately regretted her boldness and tried to reassure him. She understood his reticence. He was afraid of starting an affair that would only end in pain and grief, if he was killed.

Clive seemed suddenly relieved. '"Yes," he said, "yes that's it," as if struggling for a reason and glad I had provided it for him. "I shall hurt you if I love you any more and you must not get hurt." But I knew that this wasn't his reason. I was aware of the streak of selfishness, and I knew, as surely as I knew that dawn would come, that I would get hurt, but I let it go at that for it didn't seem to matter.'

In fact it was several days before Clive flew again. They went out for supper one evening to a riverside hotel, the Pike and Eel, at St Ives, Cambridgeshire, where there was good food and wine. Two of Clive's RAF acquaintances from the neighbouring station were there when they walked in, together with their wives. 'Clive spoke to them and introduced me casually and seemed very on edge. They were politely interested and no doubt found ample gossip in our relationship once our backs were turned.'

Frances believed that their liaison aroused particular comment because she was a junior WAAF and he was an important man. She worried that she had got a reputation for 'cold-shouldering any officer beneath the rank of squadron leader,' which was, she felt, 'a malicious untruth.' One night she complained to Clive about the injustice of it. '"Just because I go about with a wing commander . . ." I stormed, "I am classed as a 'ring-chaser' and flirt of the highest order, and yet, if you were a pilot officer, people wouldn't notice us, it makes me livid, why is it?" "They're jealous, my sweet, I expect," he answered absentmindedly, but I knew that this was not the real reason.'

On the morning of 30 January 1944 Frances woke to find the base humming with activity. Ops were on that night. Clive came to see her in the office where she worked as assistant to the station adjutant. He was an altered man. He stayed only long enough to ensure that she would look after Jasper, his golden retriever, while he was away.

Later, as the orange winter sun sank in the west and the rumble of the engines vibrated through the station she watched Clive and his crew climb into their Lancaster, 'their figures awkward and bulging with the weight of their flying kit.' She got a lift to a vantage point near the runway and watched them take off before going back to sleep. She was woken at 1 a.m. by a phone call telling her the squadron was back. She dressed and ran to the interrogation hut where 'a familiar scene greeted us – a cheery scene, brightly lit, it breathed good news at once. We always knew when they had all returned safely; the CO, MO, and the Padre would smile benignly at us; but if they were awaiting some news they would probably scowl absentmindedly . . . the first crew had arrived, tired, grubby-faced and dishevelled, but with a ready smile for us, who brought them what they most longed for at that moment, tea and cigarettes.'

Clive was some time showing up. Jasper started barking before he reached the door. Frances 'felt a pang of envy as I watched him snuggle close to his master and receive an affectionate caress, which doubtless I would have had under different circumstances.' Clive managed to exchange a few words with her when he slipped into the kitchen where she was making more tea. She saw him the following day at lunch. He had some news. He had just been given command of a squadron based at a neighbouring station. The reason for his promotion, he explained, was that its CO had failed to return the previous night. He 'announced this horrifying news with about as much emotion as if he'd been telling me that cabbages grew in the kitchen garden.' That night he took her to a New Year's Eve dance at his new station. After midnight chimed and 'Auld Lang Syne' had been sung, Clive grabbed her arm to lead her away to a quieter spot. Suddenly, they came face to face with a couple whose faces were familiar. It was one of the couples they had run into at the Pike and Eel just before Christmas. 'How they must have been waiting for this opportunity and how quickly they came to the point. He wore that "it's for your own good" expression on his face, and she was smugly silent. "Hallo Buck, Happy New Year," called Clive, as completely happy and carefree as I had ever known him. I felt wonderfully pleased with life and we had promised each other that a separation of five miles would do nothing to stop our relationship.

'"Same to you," answered Buck . . . "What a pity your wife isn't here, Clive, we four could have had some fun together," he said turning to his wife and regarding me as if I were the direct descendant of a slug.' Clive looked panic-stricken. The 'expression on his face was terrible; he looked like a caged animal looking around frantically for some escape as he mumbled excuses for his wife's absence.'

That explained everything. Frances's first reaction was to walk away but she found herself being steered outside and into Clive's car. They drove for a while in silence. There were tears in his eyes. Then they parked up and he began a long rambling speech, half a defence of his actions and half a declaration of love. He had been married to his wife for only three years but they had already drifted apart. Frances, to her surprise, found herself looking for reasons to believe him. She should, she knew, stop it now, painful though that might be. On the other hand, she reasoned, if she did so, 'he'll soon find someone else.' She told him, somewhat to his surprise, that she would accept the situation and 'be to you what I've been in the past, something for you to hold on to, to live for, and to come back to until we can see another way out.'

Clive had a few days to settle business on the base before he moved up the road. The story was now in the open. Frances went to his leaving lunch which was supposed to be a stag affair, and endured some knowing banter from the CO. She drove with him to the new station, a pre-war base with well-built roads, laid-out gardens and brick buildings with hot water and central heating.

He left her at the WAAF office while he talked to the station commander. When he returned his mood had darkened. Both of them realized that the story was over.

> The coming days were bound to be different; things would not be the same again, no matter how hard we tried. For one thing we would not be bumping into each other several times a day in the casual way we had . . .

I would not know if Clive was flying and I wouldn't be able to see him when he came back . . . Clive's entire position had changed. He had become what was often termed 'A Little Tin God' . . . everything he did and said would be criticized and heard by the whole station. His private life would surely come into the limelight too, especially if there was something like an 'affair' attached to it. This would be unearthed, examined and enlarged by all who indulged in . . . gossip.

Frances decided to go to London for a few days to see her parents. Clive phoned the day after she returned and that evening they went to the pictures. Afterwards he drove her back to her quarters and he sat by the fire while she cooked an omelette on the electric stove. The girls she shared with were absent. Mary, the senior officer, was on leave and Leslie was unlikely to bother them when she returned. But the warm domestic scene was interrupted when Leslie did show her face. She disapproved of liaisons with married men. Frances was unrepentant, telling her, 'I've fallen in love with him and at the moment I don't give a damn if he has ten wives.' Now Leslie had come to deliver a warning. She had been talking to the CO and he had asked what time the WAAF officers ejected their male visitors from their quarters. She replied that they were always out by 11 p.m., as the rules dictated. The CO seemed unconvinced. He hinted that he might spring a surprise visit on the girls one night, to check that the regulations were being obeyed.

It seemed to Frances like a bad omen. The next day, however, her doubts evaporated when Clive called to remind her of a mess party in a nearby aerodrome to which they had both been invited. They spent a 'very happy if somewhat boisterous evening.' She danced with a few old admirers but noticed how quickly they slipped away afterwards as soon as Clive appeared to take her off to the buffet or for a drink. She glimpsed, for a moment 'how lonely and miserable I would be without him.'

Almost immediately the premonition became real. The morning after the dance she was summoned to the CO's office. She was told that she was to leave the base immediately for a new post at Bomber Command HQ in High Wycombe. There was no attempt to disguise the reasons for the order. It was her relationship with Clive. News of it had 'reached the ears of senior WAAF officers who considered it "undesirable".' She would be allowed to say goodbye to Clive. After that she was not to communicate with him in any way. The CO claimed to have tried to stop the posting. But, in the circumstances, he told her, he felt it was probably for the best. At least it would give Clive a chance to mend his marriage. The last meeting was too painful for Frances to record. The next six months for her were the unhappiest time of her four years in the WAAF. She 'missed Clive unbearably, and the busy, warm atmosphere of life on a bomber station.' At HQ she 'worked mainly with women and social life was almost nil.' Eventually the misery came to an end. She was posted to RAF Scampton where she met the man who was to become her husband. When love and war collided, the interests of the RAF were always going to prevail. And in the spring of 1944, Bomber Command was as busy as it had ever been.

16

D-Day Diversion

The approach of *Overlord* gave Bomber Command a new purpose. Its efforts up until the spring of 1944 had been titanic but they had failed to achieve the promised results. The attack on Berlin had been the ultimate test of Harris's theories. But the Big City, though bleeding, was still functioning and the spirit of its citizens was bruised but not crushed.

Bombing France was less dangerous than bombing Germany and the switch to preparing the ground for D-Day was welcomed by the crews. Their primary task was to disrupt the transportation links that would play a vital part in shifting enemy troops around the battlefield once the invasion began. This meant a radical change in their *modus operandi*. They were now engaged in widespread attacks on a number of objectives rather than a concentration of force against one. This change of tactics created problems for the German defences, and particularly the night-fighters. Bombers flying in a stream up to 150 miles long, six miles wide and two miles deep made a big, vulnerable target. Once the radar had located them, the interceptors could harry them almost at their leisure, knowing they had little to fear from their guns. The Luftwaffe now had to juggle its resources to deal with several diverse threats. They had less time to get into an attacking position, for the bomber bases were much closer to the targets they wanted to bomb.

The new conditions meant a significant reduction in losses. Between April and June, Bomber Command flew operations on fifty-seven nights and lost 525 aircraft. This was a considerable improvement on the 1,128 machines, almost all four-engined bombers, destroyed during the Battle of Berlin period when only 18 per cent more sorties were flown. Even when Bomber Command resumed its onslaught on Germany it would never again face such dreadful odds as it had endured during the winter of 1943/44.

Harris thought of the new work as a diversion, but one that he accepted was both inevitable and desirable. The Casablanca and Pointblank directives of a year before had given the combined American and British bomber forces the job of creating conditions for the main Allied invasion of Europe to begin. Harris had largely ignored the spirit of Pointblank. He had chosen to misinterpret the instruction to concentrate on a system of precise war industry targets, in particular both the equipment and infrastructure of the German air force. Instead, he persisted with bombing towns.

As *Overlord* approached, this contrariness could no longer be tolerated. To obtain the tightest possible co-ordination between the key elements in the operation, Bomber Command was placed under the direction of the Supreme Allied Commander, General Dwight Eisenhower. For once Harris was subordinated to an authority that was impervious to his bluster and he came to heel with surprising grace. He may also have felt the need to behave following the manifest failure of the Berlin campaign, which had threatened to destroy his command.

The principal objective was the dislocation of the railways of northern Europe and in particular northern France. Harris doubted whether his men had the ability to deliver the concentration and accuracy needed for the attacks to be effective but he went ahead and ordered their execution. They began in March with raids on marshalling yards at important junctions like Le Mans, Amiens, Trappes and Courtrai. Between the beginning of April and the end of June, a hundred major operations were flown. There were constant attacks against any target that could interfere with the success of the landing. They included the flying bomb launching sites which threatened the forming-up areas across the Channel, coastal batteries, the synapses of the enemy signalling system, ammunition dumps and military camps. For a while German place names were heard only occasionally at briefings. Between April and D-Day there were only twelve major attacks and eight minor ones on German targets. Instead, to the satisfaction of the crews, they were now directed to specific targets which had an obvious bearing on the progress of the war.

The activities of Bomber Command were, for the time being at least, in tune with American perceptions as to how the air war should be fought. Having entered the war first, the RAF naturally assumed that its methods were the best but the pre-war theories about bombing practice had rapidly been chewed up in the jaws of experience. Commanders had begun the campaign in the belief that bombers, flying in disciplined formations, could defend themselves with their onboard armament. According to this thinking fighter escorts, although desirable, were not essential. There were none available in any case. At the start of the war, designers had yet to come up with a machine with the range and speed to accompany and defend bomber fleets on long-distance raids.

The myth of self-protection had been shattered in the winter of 1939 and spring of 1940 when German fighters, flak and radar made it impossible for Bomber Command to operate in daylight. Instead it sought the cover of darkness. Its survival depended on invisibility, and developing equipment and techniques to outwit the German defences. The Germans in turn devised counter-measures and refined their aeroplanes to deal with each new threat, culminating in the high point of their success, the introduction of the radar-equipped night-fighter.

The RAF tried to pass on its hard-won tactical wisdom to the USAAF. The Americans were reluctant to listen. In the first place they had little faith in the value of of night bombing. They had some evidence of its lack of success through the reports of professional observers, the American diplomats and journalists who stayed in Germany until the United States entered the war in December 1941. By the time the first units of the Eighth Air Force arrived in Britain in 1942 they already had in place the foundations of a bomber fleet which they believed fitted their strategic vision of how an air war should be conducted.

The Americans' preference was, as they constantly reiterated, for precision bombing carried out in daylight. The emphasis they placed on this formula seemed at times a reproach to Bomber Command. The implication was that American methods were superior to the indiscriminate nocturnal blunderings of the British. The American approach was meant to be cleaner, both militarily and morally. In daylight, the theory ran, they could see what they were doing. In addition their bombers were equipped with the Norden bombsight, which was believed to be marvellously accurate. With all these advantages they stood a far better chance of hitting their targets and missing innocent civilians than their amiable, but to American minds, misguided allies. This belief turned out to be something of an illusion, though it sustained American thinking for some time.

As for the risks of operating in daylight, the USAAF planners discounted the British experiences of the early war. Their two main aircraft, the B17 Flying Fortress and the Liberator, were well equipped with heavy .50 machine guns firing from five turrets. In theory at least, a tidily-held formation should enable the gunners to provide a field of fire of such breadth, height and depth to deter all but the most foolhardy German fighter pilot. To add to their defences, they had the support of fighter escorts which began arriving in numbers in Britain in the autumn of 1943. Their reach though, was limited. The Lightnings and Thunderbolts could not range more than 300–400 miles from base if they were forced to weave or to dogfight.

The Americans were intent on hitting specific targets which had a direct and unarguable bearing on the Germans' ability to prosecute the war. That meant factories, oil installations, ports, submarine pens and the like. Operations began in the late summer of 1942. Initially they concentrated on objectives in France but in January 1943 moved into Germany itself. In keeping with Pointblank, their particular intention was to fatally weaken German air power by destroying aircraft while they were still in production. This ambition was undiminished by the fact that the aircraft industry was widely dispersed and its factories hard to find. By the late summer they were suffering severe losses but remained convinced that they were nonetheless inflicting serious damage on the enemy. On 17 August

An early version of the American P-51 long-range escort.

1943, the anniversary of the beginning of operations from England, two large groups of Fortresses set off to bomb the Messerschmitt factory at Regensburg and the ball-bearing factories at Schweinfurt, a particular favourite with those who believed in surgical operations to cut out vital components of the machinery of war. The 147 aircraft from Fourth Bomb Wing heading for Regensburg were to carry on after their attack to land in bases in North Africa. Those from First Wing bound for Schweinfurt were to return to England. The two groups were supposed to leave together in order to divert the attentions of the waiting fighters. First Wing were held up by thick ground mist. The delay meant that the chance that the enemy would be confused by the two-pronged assault was lost. The first group crossed the Dutch coast at 10 a.m. in formations of twenty-one. There was barely a cloud in the sky. Two clusters of Thunderbolt fighters met up with them over Holland to provide a patchy escort for as long as their petrol supply allowed.

The ordeal started when Focke-Wulf fighters began attacking the unprotected tail of the stream, south-east of Brussels. At the German frontier, the fuel indicator needles of the Thunderbolts were dipping ominously and they were obliged to turn back. As the Fortresses headed into Germany the attack began in earnest. Relay after relay of Focke-Wulfs and Messerschmitt 109s drove into the formations, often in head-on attacks and one by one the bombers began to burn and fall. An observer riding with the 100th group reported later that 'the sight was fantastic; it surpassed fiction.' A historian of the Eighth Air Force described the battle moving over Germany, 'its course marked by flashes, flames, smoke, the debris of disintegrating aircraft, parachutes and men; the noise indescribable . . .'[1] This running combat went on for ninety minutes. By the time the Americans reached Regensburg seventeen Fortresses had been destroyed. Nonetheless the force, led by the famously aggressive Colonel Curtis Le May, still managed to attack with exemplary determination and precision. On arrival in Africa, Le May cabled London: 'Objective believed totally destroyed.' The belief was justified. The result turned out to be even better than he imagined. Unbeknown to him, the bombs had obliterated a workshop housing the fuselage jigs for a secret jet fighter.

First Wing had met equally ferocious opposition. From Antwerp to Schweinfurt and back it was under continuous attack from a swarm of fighters vectored in from virtually every Luftwaffe fighter base in the West. The bombers beat on with extraordinary bravery and achieved respectable results. The cost of the operation, though, was shockingly high. At the end thirty-six B-17s and 370 crew were missing. Many other aircraft limped home with dead and wounded aboard.

Altogether sixty aircraft were lost. This was more than double the previous high of twenty-six recorded in a raid the previous 13 June. Was it worth it? The claims made by the air gunners suggested it might be. They reported downing an astonishing 288 enemy aircraft. This figure almost matched the entire Luftwaffe force involved in the interception. The figure was later reduced to 148, still an impressive score and one which some senior officers appeared to find credible. The true figure, it emerged later, was twenty-seven.[2]

The Schweinfurt factories continued to exert a fatal attraction for the Eighth Air Force planners. Destroying ball-bearing production would not only do fundamental damage to the German military machine. It would also vindicate the air chiefs' claims. On 14 October 1943 the bombers went back in an operation that was to settle the question of whether air operations could continue as conceived.

A force of about 300 set off from bases in central and eastern England. The German fighters waited for their escorts to drop away before attacking in earnest. Then the assaults were relentless all the way to and from the target. The attack was a success. Three of the five main plants were hit heavily. But so too were the bombers, especially as they ran for home. At the final count, sixty aircraft were lost and five others crashed in England as a result of damage sustained in the fight.

The operation was nonetheless hailed as a significant victory. Portal was particularly fulsome. It could well, he claimed, 'have saved countless lives by depriving the enemy of a great part of his means of resistance.'[3] The lives that were demonstrably saved by the operation, as it turned out, were those of American airmen as a result of the change of tactics that the incident had brought about. The overall losses of 14 October were nearly twice the figure of 5 per cent of the force, considered as the maximum that could be sustained for a protracted period before operations became too costly to endure. The Americans could not mount similar operations on a regular basis without a catastrophic loss of both effectiveness and morale. Despite the extravagant claims of the gunners it was clear that their efforts were having no appreciable effect on eroding the means and the will of the Luftwaffe to resist. Inevitably, as any professional and motivated air force could be expected to do, the Germans had devised tactics that blunted the formations' ability to defend themselves. They had learned to concentrate on one formation at a time, unleashing salvoes of rockets from beyond the range of the American guns so that the pilots were unable to hold station, then swooping in on the dispersed components.

There was clearly an urgent need to think again. In the space of six days 148 American bombers had failed to return home. It was obvious that until they gained control of the air and succeeded in dominating the enemy's skies, they would never achieve their strategic goals.

The American air force staff, despite its proud modernity, was sometimes afflicted by stiffness of thought and an arrogant outlook. Its members could, on occasion, be as mulish as the most conservative French or British general of the First World War, preferring to reinforce failure than to admit error or the fallibility of the rule book. The obvious thing to consider, when it became clear that the British warnings about daylight operations were well-founded, was whether to follow their example and shift to bombing by night. Indeed the idea was explored tentatively in the late summer of 1943 when 422 Bomb Squadron carried out a handful of night operations alongside the RAF. But the experiment was discontinued. The American crews had been prepared for only one task. A shift from daylight to darkness would mean enormous upheaval and the effective discontinuation of the American effort for an unacceptable period. Portal reckoned the process would take two years. The American crews were highly trained in the formation tactics that sustained day bombing. But that was of little use at night. What was needed primarily was an ability to navigate in the dark, which few American navigators possessed. In the absence of that option, intensive thought was given to the question of how the bombers could be better protected. The need for an effective long-range fighter escort was more obvious than ever.

The Americans' occasional inflexibility was counterbalanced by a redeeming national virtue. Faced with a crisis, they could react effectively and fast. In this case the hunt for the solution was greatly helped by the application of British technical ingenuity. Underlying the transformation in the Allies' fortunes was the arrival of a new aeroplane which completely altered the nature of the air war. This was the long-range fighter which could accompany the bomber fleets all the way to distant targets and escort them home again. The value of the long-range escort had long been understood but until the winter of 1943 the technology was not available to provide one.

In the history of aviation no single aircraft tipped the strategic balance as effectively as the P-51 Mustang. Its arrival on the battle-field resuscitated the Eighth Air Force and accelerated the Luftwaffe's terminal decline. The aircraft began life in the most unpromising circumstances. It was designed by North American Aviation in 1940 in answer to a request from the RAF's Air Commission who were desperate to obtain aircraft from any quarter. Britain bought a number. The Americans, whose needs were less urgent, were unim-pressed however. The Mustang was slowish and its performance fell off sharply at altitude. Its optimal height was only 15,000 feet where it strained to reach 366 mph. By the time it arrived at the RAF in November 1941 the aircraft shortage was over and it was shunted off to army co-operation duties. There the Mustang's undistinguished operational career might have ended but for the diligence of some Rolls-Royce engineers. The problem, they decided, was a lack of power. As an experiment they installed their own Merlin 61 engines in five aircraft and put them through air tests. The initial results were unpromising. They decided to persist, modifying the airframe and trying again with a new power plant, a Packard-Merlin hybrid. This technological cross-breeding worked brilliantly. The humdrum genes produced a machine which shattered the existing supposition that long-range and a sparkling peformance could not be combined in the same machine.

The new Mustang went faster as it got higher. At 15,000 feet it could only manage 375 mph. At 35,000 feet it could reach 440 mph. This made it quicker than both the Focke-Wulf 190 and the Messerschmitt 109. Even more importantly, it could turn more tightly than its two main adversaries, thus giving it a crucial edge in the most important manoeuvre in dogfighting. But speed and nimbleness were of limited use without range. By September 1943 Thunderbolts fitted with drop tanks were covering 1,500 miles in test flights, with the extra weight of fuel only marginally reducing performance. This was soon stretched yet further so that by the spring of 1944 they could accompany the Fortresses and Liberators from their bases in the Midlands and East Anglia deep into eastern Germany.

After Schweinfurt, Mustangs began to pour off the production lines. They started operations with the Eighth Air Force in December 1943. Thanks to their arrival, the effectiveness of the short-range fighters was also substantially increased. Until now the Luftwaffe could, if it chose, ignore the presence of Lightnings and Thunderbolts. It was simply a matter of waiting for their fuel to run low and their noses to turn homewards. Then the German fighters had the freedom of their own skies. Now the luxury of waiting for their prey to come to them, unescorted, had vanished. The aerial front line was pushed forward and henceforth they were forced to attack wherever they could, exposing themselves to the attentions of the conventional Allied fighters. The demands the new circumstances imposed also meant that German night-fighter units were now landed with the extra duty of going to the support of their daytime colleagues.

The extraordinary difference the Mustangs would make to the balance of the air war became apparent in a few days in February 1944, which became known as Big Week. Between 20 and 25 February the Eighth Air Force carried out thirteen major strikes against fifteen centres of the German air industry. The 1,000 bombers had with them an almost equal number of fighter escorts. Faced with the destruction of their infrastructure, the Luftwaffe, as General Carl Spaatz, commander of the American strategic air forces in Europe had calculated, had no choice but to come up to meet them. In the fighting, the Americans claim to have destroyed more than 600 German interceptors for losses on their side of 210 bombers and thirty-eight fighters. These figures were of course extremely unreliable but whatever the precise details one thing was undeniable. American operations may not have devastated the German aircraft industry which showed astonishing resilience in continuing to produce machines. But the punishment they inflicted on the existing machines and the men flying in them could not be sustained. The grinding attrition continued through March as the Eighth expanded its operations to Berlin. The American bombers suffered heavily in the process but the huge increase in the number of crews and aircraft pouring into the theatre meant the losses could be more easily absorbed. After Big Week the Luftwaffe's daytime ascendancy was finished and the force in general gradually and inexorably lost control of the skies.

Looking back, General Joseph 'Beppo' Schmid, who commanded the fighter group 1 Jagdkorps from September 1943 to November 1944, recorded that as early as March 'the numeric superiority of enemy fighters had become so great that fighting became most difficult for our own units.' The supply of aircraft and men could not keep up with the losses so that 'the alacrity or fighting spirit of the [airmen] was generally below the average.' Germany was fighting an air war on three fronts, in Russia and the Mediterranean as well as Western Europe, with limited and declining resources. The Luftwaffe pilots were courageous and highly motivated but they were often poorly trained compared with their Allied counterparts. Many of their casualties were caused by crashes. The Luftwaffe General Adolf Galland calculated that in the first quarter of 1944, more than 1,000 pilots were lost from the day-fighter force including some their finest. He concluded that 'each incursion of the enemy is costing us some fifty aircrews. The time has come when our weapon is in sight of collapse.'[4]

The success of the Mustangs raised the question of whether Bomber Command should follow the Americans' example. By switching to daylight bombing the RAF could benefit from the air superiority established by the American escorts and reinforce it with their own short-range fighters. The Air Staff thought seriously about this dramatic change of course. Harris, however, was opposed to the idea. The new American methods retained the tight formation and the defensive field of fire as the basis of its tactics. The great advance was that now each group had the additional protection of a phalanx of aggressive, free-ranging fighters buzzing around it ready to swoop on any enemy aircraft that dared to approach.

Harris argued that the system only worked because of the higher operational ceiling of the American aircraft, which allowed them both to hold station and avoid the worst of the German ground artillery. The British bombers were different. Even the easy-handling Lancasters were incapable of keeping formation at heights above nineteen thousand feet. At that altitude they would be vulnerable to flak and any savings gained from the protection offered by the fighter escort would be cancelled out by losses from ground fire. In any case, if such an important decision was implemented, the preparations needed would mean it would be a very long time before it started producing results. The arguments now seem glib and flimsy. No effort was made to put his assertion to the test. Far greater difficulties had been encountered and overcome. Harris may not have set Bomber Command on its original course. But once established, he followed it relentlessly and distrusted ideas that seemed to take it in a different direction. The shift from night to day was far too radical a change for him to accept without protest. Inevitably, he came up with some suggestions of his own.

His solution was to establish during the hours of darkness the same degree of air superiority that the Americans had achieved by day. Harris had been appealing for a force of long-range night-fighters to support his command since the summer of 1943 but had been consistently turned down by the Air Staff. Harris believed that Mosquitoes could do the same job as the American escorts and asked that ten squadrons of them should be supplied to Bomber Command. In April 1944, he was allowed three. They proved to be far less effective than their American counterparts. In the seventeen months from December 1943 to the end of the war, the fighter squadrons of 100 Group, which escorted Bomber Command, destroyed less than 270 enemy aircraft. Equipment was part of the problem. The onboard radar they carried had difficulty tracking any aircraft and when it did, could not distinguish between friend or foe.

The Mosquito was many things but it was not a long-range escort fighter. The absence of such a machine from the RAF's front-line force was due, in part at least, to the obstinacy of Portal. From the start of the war he had stuck to his view that stamina could only be increased at the expense of performance and agility. Once a long-range fighter met its German short-range opponent, the German was bound to win. The Americans had tried to persuade him other-wise, even modifying some Spitfires so they could fly the Atlantic. Portal's usually agile mind was unmoved. Pressure to switch to day bombing slackened but it never went away. But in the spring of 1944, the debate was shunted aside by the approach of D-Day.

In March Bomber Command began preparatory operations in France. The targets were small compared to those that it was used to attacking in Germany, and often lightly defended. The emphasis now was on avoiding civilian casualties. Churchill the Francophile was particularly distressed at the thought of spilling French blood, which he feared might 'smear the good name of the Royal Air Force across the world.' But try as they might to spare the innocent, it could not always be done. The civilian death toll proved tragically the argument that even with the best intentions and the greatest care, in a bombing war non-combatants inevitably died.

On the night of 9 April, 239 aircraft, most of them Halifaxes, arrived over Lille, an important road and rail crossroads in northern France. Their mission was to destroy the Lille-Délivrance goods station. There was a full moon. The bombs devastated the railway complex, destroying most of the wagons lying in the sidings and tearing up the tracks. But they also fell in the narrow streets housing the *cheminots* who worked on the railways, which lined the yards. The bloodshed was on the scale inflicted in an area attack, with 456 dead and many wounded. In the district of Lomme, 5,000 houses were destroyed or damaged. To those searching through the smoking rubble for loved ones the drone of the bombers overhead did not seem like the sound of liberation. Less than ten days later another sizeable raid was mounted on marshalling yards at Noisy-Le-Sec. Again great damage was done to the complex but again friendly civilians paid for the success with 464 killed and 370 injured.

Despite these horrible but inevitable mistakes, the crews felt uplifted by the work they were doing. The prospect of the invasion cheered everyone. An end, no matter how remote, was at last in sight. Now they really could start to believe that each mission accelerated victory. Their bombs would help to liberate France and save the lives of many of their own soldiers. As the casualty figures declined and the number of operations carried out without loss grew, their hopes rose that they might be there to celebrate victory.

The operations they were engaged in reminded them of why they had joined. There were some spectacular successes that suggested that Bomber Command, for so long a blunt weapon, was at last evolving into a sharp instrument of efficient and useful destruction. On the night of 5/6 April, 144 Lancasters of 5 Group attacked and completely destroyed an aircraft factory at Toulouse. The accuracy of the attack was attributed to the precision of the marking which for the first time had been carried out by a Mosquito flying at low level. The pilot was Leonard Cheshire who had been applying his innovative intelligence and considerable energy to improving bombing accuracy. The problem at this stage was less with bomb-aiming than with marking. Much of the latter was being carried out by Mosquitoes equipped with the *Oboe* blind-bombing radar device, which told the pilot where the target indicator should be dropped. This was an advance on earlier methods but still far from infallible. Cheshire's idea was to cast the Mosquito in yet another role. Using its great speed and nimbleness it would be possible, he claimed, to fly in very low and drop the marker by sight alone, eschewing radar and relying only on the bombsight.

At Toulouse he put his theory to the test. He and his co-pilot Flying Officer Pat Kelly made two passes over the factory before releasing red spot markers. Lancaster crews higher in the sky dropped more indicators, which now burned brightly from the heart of the target. The main force then went in, demolishing or heavily damaging nearly all the buildings in the target area. Even with all the care and skill this was not a surgical strike. Bombs struck about a hundred houses near the factory killing twenty-two.

These successes did not come without cost. On the night of 3 May, a force of 346 Lancasters lead by Mosquitoes went to bomb a German military camp near the village of Mailly, south of Châlons-en-Champagne. The target was well marked by Cheshire but the order for the main force to attack was drowned out by an American forces broadcast and in the delay caused by the confusion German fighters arrived. In the ensuing carnage forty-two Lancasters were lost.

As *Overlord* opened, Bomber Command's might was displayed in the southern skies of England. On the night of 5/6 June, the inhabitants of the south of England looked up to watch an apparently seamless carpet of bombers rolling overhead towards the beaches and cliffs of Normandy. Harris had amassed more than a thousand aircraft, Lancasters, Halifaxes and Mosquitoes, laden with bombs to pulverize the coastal batteries sunk into the dunes behind the tranquil, low-built fishing villages that for centuries had managed to avoid Europe's swirling wars. The weather favoured Hitler. Only two of the ten targets, Ouistreham and La Pernelle, were free of cloud. The rest were bombed blind using *Oboe*. In the course of the night 5,000 tons of bombs were dropped, the greatest quantity in the war so far. A thousand bombers were in the air again the following night smashing railway and road junctions to prevent the Germans rushing troops to the beach-heads.

So it went on. The destructive power of the Allies was enhanced by the deployment of a new super-bomb, the Tallboy, another invention of Professor Barnes Wallis whose bouncing bomb had made the Dams Raid possible. It weighed 12,000 pounds and was sleekly designed to drive deep into the earth before exploding, creating an earthquake effect that produced a crater that needed 5,000 tons of earth to fill. On the night of 8/9 June 617 Squadron, led by Leonard Cheshire, set off to attack a railway tunnel near Saumur, in the Loire valley. A German Panzer force was expected to pass through heading towards the Normandy beach-head from its garrison in the south. The area was marked by flares by four Lancasters, then Cheshire and two other outstanding master bombers, Squadron Leader David Shannon and Flight Lieutenant Gerry Fawke, dived in low to place their red spot markers at the mouth of the tunnel. The subsequent bombing was reasonably accurate. The reconnaissance photographs show two direct hits on the railway lines that gouged out enormous craters in the cutting leading to the tunnel. Even greater devastation was caused by a bomb which speared through the roof of the tunnel entrance, bringing down an avalanche of rock and dirt. This took a major effort to clear and the progress of the Panzers to Normandy was, for the time being, halted.

The role of the British and American air forces was crucial to the success of *Overlord*. In the space of a few months Bomber Command had gone from the wretched and harrowing business of pounding cities to the cleaner work of destroying an army in the field. For once they were dropping bombs on an enemy that was wearing uniform. More and more, they were operating in daylight. Between the invasion and the middle of August, 17,580 out of the command's 46,824 sorties were outside the hours of darkness.

Their activities transformed the battlefield. On 18 June they successfully carried out a huge attack on five villages east of Caen which lay across the British line of advance. Twelve days later at Villers-Bocage they obliterated a crucial road junction through which two Panzer divisions were expected to pass on their way to launching a counterattack at the point in the line where the British and American armies met. As a result, the German operation was abandoned. Offering close support to the men on the ground carried inevitable dangers. Confusion, inaccuracy and human error combined to create some black incidents when British and American bombs fell on Allied troops. But given the colossal scale of the enterprise, perhaps the real surprise was that there were not more of them.

The crews now felt an engagement with the battlefield that they had never experienced before. On 30 July, Ken Newman set off to bomb six German positions in the Villers-Bocage-Caumont area which were holding up the American advance. He was forced down to 2,000 feet to get below the cloud. The low altitude made him nervous, and the fact that 'the twenty-four of us from Wickenby were all trying to get into the same small airspace at the same time and I had to keep moving the aircraft around to avoid a collision.' But then the markers went down and he witnessed a phenomenon which he 'had never seen before, or ever saw again. We were so low that I was able to see the pressure wave of every exploding bomb – a bright red ring expanding rapidly outwards like ripples on the surface of the water.' Newman decided to risk staying low to witness the spectacle and the navigator and wireless operator came forward to share the experience. It was 'exciting to see the hundreds of Allied tanks, their crews waving madly at us . . . I waggled our wings in acknowledgement.' At that moment 'we all felt that we had done something to help our Army colleagues in Normandy and wished them every good fortune.'[5]

Despite the care taken over civilian casualties the bloodshed continued. On one particularly appalling occasion, the catastrophe was due to incompetence rather than accident. On 5 September, Bomber Command was sent to Le Havre. The retreating Germans had left garrisons in several Channel ports with orders to hold them for as long as they could stand and fight. When Harry Yates and his crew heard that 75 Squadron were on the raid their first reaction was relief. They had expected to be briefed for Dortmund, a particularly daunting target in their experience. By comparison 'a brief excursion to occupied France was a cakewalk.'

They were further cheered by the assurance that the raid 'would trigger the liberation of Le Havre and save the lives of countless British soldiers.' The local population had been warned by leaflet drops to vacate the town. The only ones underneath their bombs would be the diehard German soldiers. Later Yates was to reflect on the 'total trust we put in the facts as they were presented to us. I doubt if anybody had a single insubordinate thought about them or about the safety of the local populace. Our competence did not extend to such matters. That was the preserve of high-flying staff officers at Bomber Command and the Group HQs.'

The operation went off smoothly. The bombs fell with remarkable accuracy. In the Plough and Harrow, the Mepal local, that night Yates and his crew all 'thought the same. It was a job well done. We wouldn't be going back.'[6]

It fact the intelligence had been disastrously wrong. Few Germans were left in the target area. Much worse, the French population were concentrated in the old part of town, the district in which most of the 6,000 bombs that were dropped fell. Three thousand men, women and children died.

As well as their contribution to the success of the Normandy landings the crews were also helping to make the Home Front safer. Throughout the high summer they flew missions against V1 flying bomb sites and stores, reducing the Germans' ability to bombard London and other British cities. The sites were small and hard to hit and despite the enormous expenditure of effort the Germans still managed to launch bombs in significant numbers long after D-Day. By 15 July, 2,579 had fallen on England, about half of them on London. The determination of the crews, British and American, to stop them was measured by the casualties. About 3,000 airmen were killed in attacks on V-weapon targets. Leonard Cheshire's last operational mission was against a site at Mimoyecques on 6 July. After that he was ordered to take a rest, along with three other leading 617 Squadron officers, all of them veterans of the Dams Raid.

They were withdrawing from a battlefield that was becoming decreasingly dangerous for airmen. As the Allied beach-head widened, German day-fighters faded from the Normandy skies. On some days major operations on land and in the air proceeded without a German aircraft being seen. Bomber Command continued to suffer casualties. Flak was still lethal, especially over the ports. Ralph Briars, a gunner with 617 Squadron, was happy to note that there were no fighters near Le Havre when they went to drop Tallboys on the E-boat pens on 14 June. 'Target quiet until a few minutes before dropping,' he wrote in his diary. 'Then they let loose bags of light and medium flak . . . as bomb left, flak hit starboard inner engine and top turret, gunner OK, engine had to be feathered.' The danger, he recorded with satisfaction, was worth it. 'U-boat pens, twenty-five feet thick, were hit. Good bombing.'

There were still night-fighters to worry about. During a number of operations mounted against synthetic oil plants in Germany during June, July and August, the normal levels of losses obtained. But overall the trend was heartening. During the period the casualty rate fell to a level that the crews would have considered trifling six months before. Only 1.6 per cent of the force dispatched were lost. Nonetheless, that still amounted to 727 aircraft.

Germany had fallen to the back of the minds of the Bomber Boys during their welcome French diversion. Only one major operation had been launched against a German city, when Stuttgart was laid waste in three nights in late July. But as the nights lengthened and the Allies moved eastwards, the respite drew to a close. Once again Bomber Command turned back to its task of destroying the Reich.

17

Tallboys and Tirpitz

The great advances in methods and technology Bomber Command had achieved meant it was now able to strike targets that had previously eluded it. At the top of this list came the battleship *Tirpitz*. In the autumn of 1944, it was lying in Kaa Fjord in northern Norway, threatening the vital Arctic convoys that supplied the Soviet war effort. It was the most powerful warship in the Western Hemisphere. It could steam at nearly 40 mph and was armed with eight fifteen-inch guns, twelve six-inch guns and about eighty flak guns. In the course of the war it had survived more than thirty aerial attacks, largely thanks to its heavy armour, which seemed proof against the bombs of the Fleet Air Arm and RAF. In September, two squadrons, 9 and 617, were ordered to the Soviet Union to launch their attack. The trip made an interesting diversion for Ralph Briars, who left with 617 from Woodhall on the evening of 11 September, crossing Norway and Sweden and landing at an island airfield near Archangel. The crews were put up in an old river steamer. While they waited for suitable weather, they were fed on eggs and spam. Mutual incomprehension did not stop them making friends with the Russians, who swapped their cap badges for cigarettes. The authorities laid on entertainment for the three nights they were there; films, concerts and dances. The movies were earnest sagas with interminable battle scenes. The dances were better. The band could even play 'The Lambeth Walk'.

It was all very different from Woodhall Spa. They were looked after by local staff who lived in primitive huts around the airfield. The women were baffled by requests for hot water to shave in. The men spent much of the time playing cards, breaking off occasionally to supervise their wives' labour as they lugged away logs that floated down the river and chopped them up for firewood. The crews found the Russians 'kindly, generous hosts' and good sportsmen, too. They played football and the base side trounced them seven–nil.[1] On 15 September the weather cleared and the Lancasters, loaded with 12,000-pound Tallboy bombs and 'Johnny Walker' mines designed to blow up under the battleship's hull, took off. Tony Iveson remembered seeing the battleship clearly outlined, 'black against the cliff and the snowy mountains,' but at the same time I saw the smoke generators start up all round the cliffs and by the time we got to bombing height there was just a sea of cloud beneath us.' The *Tirpitz* was badly damaged but still afloat. Two months later the RAF went back again. By now the *Tirpitz* had moved to the sheltered waters of Tromsø on the west coast of Norway. One attempt at the end of October was thwarted by low cloud. On 12 November they tried again. The thirty Lancasters of 9 and 617 squadrons that mounted the attack had been specially modified so as to be able to reach Tromsø from Lossiemouth in the north of Scotland. All armour plating as well as the mid-upper and front gun turrets were removed. They were also fitted with improved-performance Merlin T24 engines. Loaded with a Tallboy, they were just capable of making the twelve-and-a-half-hour round trip.

Tony Iveson and seventeen other 617 Squadron crews were set to take off at 2 a.m. They lined up while the hoarfrost was swept from the wings then 'off we went, up past the Orkneys and the Shetlands to about 65 north, seven east when we turned towards Norway.' As dawn came up he 'saw another Lancaster, silhouetted, so I formated on him.' It was his CO, James Tait. They headed for a lake that had been designated as the rendezvous point. As they circled it, 'Lancaster after Lancaster came out of the dark western sky and joined us.' Tait fired a Verey light, the signal for the last leg of the operation to begin and they set off for Tromsø. As morning broke 'it was absolutely gin clear. You could see for miles and below the white-topped mountains and the blue, blue sea.' Their first thought was that the conditions could not have been more perfect for bombing. Their second was that they were equally favourable for the German fighter unit that was believed to be stationed in the area.

When they arrived, the *Tirpitz* appeared to have been taken by surprise. There was no smokescreen. It was a Sunday and many of the crew were ashore. Iveson and the rest of 617 Squadron dropped their bombs within the space of four minutes from 15,000 feet. Their Lancasters were fitted with a new, computer-assisted bomb-sight. The Tallboys fell away 'on a beautiful, steady course. After the fourteenth bomb they weren't able to plot any more because there was so much smoke and muck around.' The accuracy was extraordinary. There were two direct hits on the battleship and three near misses. Within six minutes of the first strike she was on her side. Within eleven minutes she had capsized but was unable to sink completely because of the shallowness of the water. Nearly a thousand sailors were killed or injured out of the ship's company of 1,900 men, including the captain and most of the officers. The attackers suffered only one casualty. A Lancaster of 9 Squadron, which arrived shortly after 617, was damaged by flak but landed safely in Sweden. The German fighters that Iveson had feared took off too late to intercept the bombers.[2]

By now the Tallboys were a key element in Bomber Command's arsenal, allowing them to hit important strategic targets with devastating effect and at reduced risk. Unlike the 'cookie' which resembled a giant oil-drum, the Tallboy looked like a proper bomb. It was twenty-one feet long, made out of special steel casing, and was shaped aerodynamically with four stabilizer fins that made it spin on its axis as it fell. It was designed for deep penetration, so that on detonation it set up a ripple of shock waves that destroyed the target from its foundations.

Tallboys had been dropped first by Leonard Cheshire and David Shannon in their celebrated attack on the railway tunnel at Saumur during the Normandy landings. Their effectiveness was demonstrated again on the night of 23/24 September against the Dortmund–Ems canal, a vital waterway. The banks of both branches of the canal were breached and a six-mile stretch of it was drained. Most of the damage was done by bombs dropped by 617 Squadron. Ralph Briars took part in the raid and his diary entry for the night is a reminder that although the Luftwaffe was severely weakened

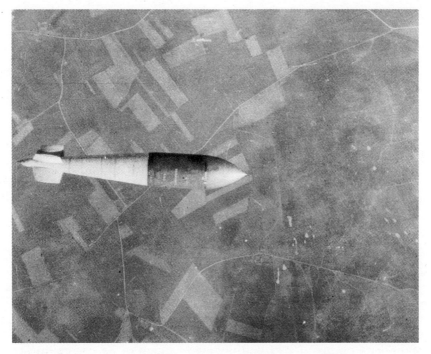

A Tallboy, seconds after release.

Bomber Command's operations were very far from being risk free. 'Had first shaking when two kites collided off coast,' he wrote in his diary. 'Queer things, red, green and yellow flares, enormous flak bursts, kites going down without combat – no tracer used by fighters, I guess. Spot fire just under cloud, had several tries to bomb, but it became covered just before release so we brought it back. Felt tired and shaken on return, curse the darkness.' Reading this entry many years later he thought he detected in it 'just a hint of bother'. It revealed, he suspected, the advent of 'the Twitch', which he had noticed in airmen who had been flying too long.[3] Fourteen Lancasters, more than 10 per cent of the force, failed to make it back from this operation.

By the end of 1944 the Allied airforces had achieved virtual mastery of the skies of Europe. But despite the efforts of the bombers against the German aircraft industry, it was still managing to function, and at a remarkably brisk pace. In September the production of single-engined fighters reached a new high. By the end of the year the overall number of aircraft had climbed to 3,300. As Germany by then had a much smaller area to defend, this force, in theory at least, could be used with more concentration and therefore with more effect.

These statistics disguised the hopeless situation facing the Luftwaffe. There was no shortage of aircraft. But there was a desperate lack of fuel to propel them and men to fly them. As summer faded, the shortage of petrol made a mockery of the abundance of equipment. In August 1944, Germany was still managing to meet 65 per cent of its aviation spirit needs. By February 1945 the figure had fallen to 5 per cent. Starved of fuel, ground down by relentless attrition, the Luftwaffe could no longer exert any control over the direction of events in the air or on the ground.

It seemed obvious that the Allies' air power would best be used in trying to turn off the fuel tap completely. This was how the Americans saw it. They had been bombing oil targets since March. Bomber Command also had dedicated much of its energy during the Normandy campaign to hitting synthetic oil plants in the Ruhr. Oil had been a favourite target of RAF planners since the start of the war, and continued to be until they were persuaded that the difficulty of finding and hitting installations and the losses this entailed outweighed the results. Now the tactical landscape held far fewer perils.

The new approach was spelled out in a directive of 25 September 1944. It listed, in order of priority, Bomber Command's targets. The first was the 'petroleum industry, with special emphasis on petrol (gasoline) including storage.' Next came the German rail, river and canal systems, followed by tank and lorry factories.

The emphasis on oil had the approval of Portal and the Air Staff. It did not please Harris, whose independence had been restored after Bomber Command was detached from Eisenhower's control in September. The new realities appeared to have done nothing to modify his belief that the continued bombing of cities was the fastest way to end the war. He had always derided the 'oily boys' who preached that cutting the fuel pipeline was the key to victory.

There had been many occasions when he had enjoyed the satisfaction of being able to point out that their theories, however logical, were easier to expound than to put into practice. Now the goal seemed within reach. Harris, though, remained deeply and aggressively sceptical.

He was, he recorded in his memoir, 'altogether opposed to this further diversion, which, as I saw it, would only prolong the respite which the German industrial cities had gained from the use of the bombers in a tactical role [i.e. in the Normandy campaign]. I did not think we had any right to give up a method of attack which was indisputably doing the enemy enormous harm, for the sake of prosecuting a new scheme the success of which was far from assured.' He admitted in retrospect that, as it turned out, the offensive against oil was a 'complete success', and shamelessly claimed credit on behalf of Bomber Command for its contribution to the result. Nonetheless, he was determined to have the last word. The advocates of the strategy may have been right, he argued, but they were right for the wrong reasons. At the time he had raised his objections, 'it was [not] reasonable . . . to expect that the campaign would succeed.' What the Allied strategists had done was to 'bet on an outsider, and it happened to win the race.'[4]

Like it or not, the oily boys had carried the argument. Harris hated losing, but he knew the advantages of a tactical withdrawal. He proceeded against a list of oil targets but managed by imaginative interpretation of the directive to carry on battering cities at the same time, achieving, he boasted, 'a destruction rate of two and a half a month'. He also maintained his aversion to day operations, even though they were now both effective and comparatively trouble-free, and seemed to order them only reluctantly.

The Luftwaffe, though apparently dying, was still capable of causing lethal damage with its last kicks. On 16 December the German army launched its desperate counter-offensive through the Ardennes. On New Year's Day 1945, the Luftwaffe made its contribution to the action. Somehow it scraped together more than 750 fighters and enough fuel to get them into battle. The operation was mounted in complete secrecy and there was astonishment when they arrived at seventeen Allied airfields in the Lowlands and France. They destroyed 150 aircraft and killed forty-six people, most of whom were working on the ground. It was an impressive act of defiance but in the long term achieved nothing. The German losses were disastrous; 270 aircraft lost and 260 aircrew killed. Adolf Galland regarded this as the last gasp of his beloved air force. 'The Luftwaffe received its death blow at the Ardennes offensive,' he wrote.[5]

Even before this catastrophe German aircraft were decreasingly seen in the skies. On their way to Cologne at the end of October 1944, Harry Yates and his crew in S-Sugar were startled to see an unfamiliar silhouette flash in front of them, climbing out of nowhere at an impossible speed and angle. It was an Me 262 jet, one of the few that the Luftwaffe managed to get airborne. This was the only visual sighting of any German aircraft by 75 Squadron in the forty-six sorties it had flown in the previous four days. The main enemy now was flak. Shortly before this encounter and just as they approached the target Yates watched the end of two aircraft ahead of him in the stream. 'One of them carved a fiery trail down into the cloud. There seemed to be a reasonable chance that one of them would get out. The other . . . took a direct hit in the bomb bay and in the blink of an eye was a ball of shocking white and orange, expanding violently outwards across a large area of sky and then petering out into a sickeningly slow drift to earth.' He looked away, reflecting that 'sometimes the cynical view was right. It was all a matter of luck. Every kite had its bomb doors open. One small splinter of flak hitting S-Sugar's cookie or incendiaries would bring the same end to us.'

As they went into the bombing run they 'entered a furious hailstorm of red-hot metal. An instant later there was an explosion between us, unseen but no distance away.' The aircraft convulsed and Yates felt something solid and fast-moving smash into it. The Perspex panel above the pilot's seat blew out, blasting freezing air through the fuselage. Yates felt a 'flood tide of fear'. The thing he dreaded was finally happening to him. But the Lancaster flew on unperturbed and Yates's pounding heart subsided.[6]

Bomber Command's work rate was extraordinary. In the last three months of 1944 it dropped 163,000 tons of bombs and would drop even more in 1945. This deluge would have been even heavier if the munitions could have kept up with demand. The thought, energy and sacrifice of the early years had produced a creation of terrifying power and efficiency. Harris was determined that it should go on being put to the use for which he believed it was intended.

Despite the 25 September directive, 53 per cent of Bomber Command's effort in the last three months of 1944 had gone into flattening cities. Oil targets accounted for 14 per cent while the rest was expended on railways and canals, enemy troops and fortifications and naval and other objectives. Some of the targets were old Bomber Command favourites. So far they had escaped total destruction. But now, in its new might, the RAF was returning to finally cross them off its list. On the night of 6/7 October it was Bremen's turn. It had been visited on the first night of the war when a handful of Whitley bombers scattered a harmless cargo of leaflets over its rooftops. It was attacked about seventy times thereafter and had been the objective of a 'thousand' raid. This time only 262 Lancasters took part, dropping 1,021 tons of bombs. What was left of Bremen's war industry went up in flames, including the two Focke-Wulf factories. Sixty-five people were killed and 766 wounded, a low figure that suggests that most people had fled. Bremen was effectively dead. The bombers had no need to go back again.

The name of Essen had once induced dread in the crews. Now they could attack it with virtual impunity and did so in two huge attacks thirty-six hours apart at the end of October. By now incendiaries did not always make up the bulk of the bomb loads. In some towns, it was reckoned that everything that could burn, had burned in previous raids and high explosive was more effective. By the time the raids were over, Essen had ceased to be an important centre of war production, though this was not the end of its ordeal.

These attacks were easy to justify. Germany had patently lost the war yet still could not bring itself to surrender. Every extra day meant more Allied casualties. The attacks on oil targets were proceeding but the beneficial results were not yet visible. Anything that persuaded Germans of the hopelessness of their situation was worth doing. In the Ruhr, which lay in the path of the Allied armies, dogged workers and their directors were continuing to try to make weapons for a struggle that had already been lost. Operation *Hurricane* was devised by the Allied planners to address that problem. Its purpose was spelled out in a directive of 13 October 1944 to Harris. It read: 'In order to demonstrate to the enemy in Germany generally the overwhelming superiority of the Allied Air Forces in this theatre . . . the intention is to apply within the shortest practical period the maximum effort of the Royal Air Force Bomber Command and the VIIIth United States Bomber Command against objectives in the densely populated Ruhr.' The object was, in the words of the official history, 'to cause mass panic, havoc and disorganization in the Ruhr Valley, to disrupt the immediate German front-line communications by driving the railheads back east of the Rhine and to demonstrate to the Germans the futility of further resistance.'

This was not intended to replace oil targets as the principal object of the American and British air forces' attentions. However it did mark a further advance in another plan which had been under consideration as the Allies pondered how to use their massive superiority to its best advantage.

Portal had asked the Air Staff in July 1944 for their thoughts on how the bombing war should proceed. They had ceased to believe that bombing on its own could create a decisive collapse of German morale. However a 'blow of catastrophic force' delivered at the right moment, and taken in conjunction with defeats on other fronts, might persuade the population that there was no further point in holding out. That right moment would only come when Germans generally believed that the Nazi system was collapsing and total defeat was imminent. The object of the attack would not be to destroy Germany entirely but to preserve what little remained. In other words, it was to hasten surrender rather than induce defeat. An orderly surrender would avert the risk of the breakdown of central military and civil authority with all the problems that would create for the invading Allies. The memorandum gave a cautiously

optimistic appraisal of the effects of a 'catastrophic blow' against
Berlin, which as the centre of government and the home of 5 per
cent of the population was the obvious target. But it also suggested
that 'immense devastation could be produced if the entire attack
was concentrated on a single big town other than Berlin and the
effect would be especially great if the town was one hitherto relatively undamaged.' This proposal, which became known as the
Thunderclap plan, was passed on to the Chiefs of Staff. It was received
unenthusiastically by their planners who did not feel it 'likely to
achieve any worthwhile degree of success' at that time. They did,
however, recommend that it should be placed before the Chiefs of
Staff when conditions seemed more promising.

In the meantime Harris went about implementing *Hurricane*,
starting with a massive raid on Duisburg. He put together more
than a thousand bombers, accompanied by a fighter escort. The
Americans sent 1,251 heavy bombers and 749 fighters to Cologne.
They attacked during the day and saw not a single Luftwaffe fighter.
That night yet another 1,000 RAF aircraft went back to Duisburg.
The raids did not have the effect wished for by the *Hurricane* planners and the town would be bombed several times more before the
war was ended.

Such was the wealth of Harris's resources that he could also
mount an attack on Brunswick the same evening. This was the fifth
raid on the town that year and there was no need of another.
Bomber Command was running out of urban targets. Its attentions
were now turned to places that had not previously seemed worth
attacking. Until now Bonn, a small well-preserved town on the
banks of the Rhine, had been left alone. It had no importance to
the German war effort or to Allied plans. That changed when Air
Vice-Marshal R. Harrison, the commander of 3 Group, requested
permission to raid it. Some of the Lancasters in Harrison's force had
been fitted with a new radar blind-bombing device called G-H,
which in theory enabled bombing to continue even in the worst
weather.

The conditions on 18 October were cloudy enough to test this
proposition. Harrison sent 128 Lancasters to Bonn accompanied by

Mustang and Spitfire escorts. They flew in 'vics' of three, each formation headed by a G-H equipped aircraft. Only one German fighter was seen on the journey but its pilot prudently veered away. The raid was a success. It was an exaggeration to say, as one post-operational report did, that the attack 'practically wiped out the town'. But it had certainly done severe damage. The university and many public buildings were burned out. The house in which Beethoven lived and composed was saved by the heroism of its caretakers. Seven hundred houses were destroyed and many more damaged; 313 people were killed. The bomb damage was easy to assess. As Bonn had never been targeted before there was no previous wreckage to obscure the picture when the reconnaissance photographs came back. This, it was believed, was one of the reasons why it had been chosen.

Towns which presented any kind of threat or hindrance to the Allied advance were now in peril. Freiburg, on the banks of the upper Rhine near the French border, had never been attacked by the RAF before. It had no industry to speak of but was the site of a minor rail junction. At the pre-op briefing, Ken Newman and the rest of the crews were told that 'it had not previously been regarded as a worthwhile target but it had an important railway junction. Moreover . . . it had been reported that the town was full of German troops poised to repel any Allied attempt to cross the Rhine in that area.' Allied troops were approaching from the west. Freiburg was protected only by light flak batteries. About 350 aircraft attacked on the night of 27/28 November. They dropped 1,900 tons of bombs which failed to hit the rail junction. They fell instead on the main town, killing 2,088 civilians. Another 858 were reported missing. The soldiers in the town were either well-protected or few in number. Only seventy-five of them were killed. On the run into the target, Newman had seen 'no opposition whatsoever'. The highlight of the trip for him was the St Elmo's Fire which flickered over the propellers as they crossed the Channel for home.[7]

Anything that lay in the Allied path could now expect annihilation. The historic town of Heilbronn was even more militarily insignificant than Freiburg. It had the misfortune to lie on a main north–south railway line. On the night of 4/5 December, 282 Lancasters of 5 Group dropped 1,254 tons of bombs in the space of a few minutes. The density of the bombardment produced a firestorm which devoured the wooden-framed buildings and killed 7,000 people.

During the autumn and winter Harris once again came under pressure to broaden the scope of Bomber Command's attacks. Sir Arthur Tedder, the Deputy Supreme Allied Commander, argued for an integrated approach so that 'various operations should fit into one comprehensive pattern.' That meant attacks on everything that kept the German war effort going; oil, yes, but also road, rail and river communications and 'political targets'.[8]

Portal supported his view. It was translated into a directive from the Combined Chiefs of Staff on 1 November 1944. Again it listed the petroleum industry as the first priority with the German lines of communication as the second. 'Important industrial areas' were only mentioned in third place. This left little room for imaginative interpretation.

The directive could be seen as an implicit criticism of Harris's singular approach. That was certainly how he took it. Until now he had taken care to avoid a head-on confrontation with Portal. He appears to have reckoned that as long as Bomber Command kept up a reasonable rate of attacks against oil, he would be left alone to pursue his course of wiping out Germany's largest cities.

In doing so, he was flouting the wishes of every commander with a say in how the air war should proceed. Harris, though, was undeterrred. His reply to the directive was brusque and unapologetic. He repeated his conviction that targeting individual objectives could never be as effective as area attacks. The dramatically changed situation which gave the Allies command of the air seemed to have had no effect on his prescription of blanket destruction. It only needed the obliteration of twelve more cities, including Berlin, for the job to be done. 'Are we now to abandon this vast task . . . just as it nears completion?' he demanded.[9]

This sort of disagreement was intolerable at a crucial stage of the war. If it was allowed to persist the great advantage of air superiority could be dissipated and the opportunity to bring a swift end to the war squandered. Portal, with his customary combination of steeliness and emollience, moved to deflect his turbulent subordinate from a collision course.

'I have, I must confess at times wondered [he wrote in a letter of 12 November] whether the magnetism of the remaining German cities has not in the past tended as much to deflect our bombers from their primary objectives as . . . tactical and weather difficulties . . . I would like you to reassure me that this is not so. If I knew you to be as wholehearted in the attack of oil as you have in the past been in the matter of attacking cities I would have little to worry about.'[10]

This smooth rebuke produced some results, but they were only temporary. The proportion of operations against oil targets climbed from 6 per cent in October to 24 per cent in November. Harris had responded to the tug on his chain. But he had by no means changed his mind, and did not pretend that he had. On 12 December he wrote a sulky letter to Portal deriding the scientific experts of the Ministry of Economic Warfare for their faith in 'panacea targets', his favourite term for specific industrial targets such as the famous ball-bearing works at Schweinfurt whose destruction they claimed would hasten German defeat.

Portal replied in a tone of weary disappointment. Harris's belief that oil was another 'panacea' was to be regretted. 'Naturally,' he wrote, 'while you hold this view you will be unable to put your heart into the attack on oil.' The exchanges went on into the New Year with Portal struggling to get his subordinate to do what he was told. It was no good. Harris was immovable; he brought the dispute to a head in mid-January 1945 when he offered his resignation. In his letter he declared he had 'no faith' in selective bombing and 'none whatever in the present oil policy'. But he protested that despite his misgivings he had never failed 'in any *worthwhile* efforts to achieve even those things which I knew from the start to be impracticable, once they had been decided upon.'[11]

The temptation to call his bluff must have been enormous. Portal resisted it. In his reply he blandly accepted Harris's assurance. 'I am very sorry that you do not believe in it,' he wrote 'but it is no use my craving for what is evidently unattainable. We must wait until after the end of the war before we can know for certain who was right.' He went on: 'I sincerely hope that until then you will continue in command of the force which has done so much towards defeating the enemy and has brought such credit and renown to yourself and to the Air Force.' Thus Portal not only missed his chance to sack Harris. He had also guaranteed him tenure of his job until the end of war.

How was Harris able to get away with this extraordinary behaviour, which bordered on insubordination? In his time at the head of Bomber Command he had achieved a gilding of prestige that shone as brightly as that emanating from Montgomery and approached the aura of glory that surrounded Churchill himself. He had arrived at the head of Bomber Command when it was sunk in failure and was beginning to be tainted by despair. His effect on the organization had been extraordinary. His aggression and sense of showmanship restored in the crews a faith in their own abilities and a sense of worth about what they were doing. He impressed the public with his obvious confidence and pride in his command's achievements. Harris had a strong understanding of what propaganda could do for him and his men in the internal bureaucratic battles he fought with as much ferocity and tenacity as he showed towards the Germans.

He was helped by his proximity to the prime minister. Whether Churchill liked him or not was questionable. But in the end it did not matter. Far more importantly he trusted him and judged him to be the man to do the job. The qualities needed to pursue the biggest bombing campaign ever seen in history were not necessarily attractive or endearing. The task required an ability to inure oneself to death, whether that of an airman or a German civilian. It needed someone who could take in minutes, decisions that merited a year of reflection, and once taken, stick to them, even when the initial evidence suggested that they might be wrong.

Harris was able to do these things. He belonged outside the normal confines of time and place. Those around him, his staff and his family, maintained loyally that there was a warm and affectionate side to Harris. If so, it is hard to discern in his writings and his actions. The crews who never saw him had a better understanding of who he was. To them, he was remote and unemotional, untouched by the climate of sentimentality that flourished in wartime as a respite from the uncertainties and harshness of existence. That did not mean that they did not trust him or respect him. But nobody would say they loved him.

Portal's reaction was probably inevitable. Sacking someone of Harris's standing at that stage of the war would have disrupted the smooth running of Bomber Command at a crucial period in the campaign. It was still an unfortunate decision. Harris had outlived his usefulness. He had never, as Webster and Frankland drily pointed out, been famous for his farsightedness.

'Sir Arthur Harris's prestige did not depend on a reputation for good judgement,' they wrote. 'He had, after all, opposed the introduction of the incendiary technique, the creation of the Pathfinder Force and the development of the bomb with which the Möhne and Eder dams were breached. He had confidently supposed that the Battle of Berlin could win the war, and he had declared that Bomber Command would be operationally incapable of carrying out the French railway campaign. In all these, and many other judgements, he had been shown to be, or at least by his superiors been supposed to be, wrong and he had repeatedly been overruled, in theory if not always in practice.'[12]

Despite all Portal's pleading and cajoling, Harris continued to direct most of Bomber Command's efforts against cities. In the remaining months of the war, it devoted only just over a quarter of its energy to attacking oil targets. Attacks on cities, however, made up 36.6 per cent of its effort. In that time it showered 66,482 tons on built-up areas, drenching them in high explosive in a literal demonstration of overkill that often brought minimal military advantage.

It was an irony that the raid that did most to damage the reputation of Bomber Command after the war was far easier to justify than operations such as those against sleepy, mediaeval backwaters like Freiburg and Heilbronn.

The attack on Dresden was one of the most carefully considered of Bomber Command's war. It had its origins in the *Thunderclap* plan of August 1944 which the official historians judged could 'be regarded, if only indirectly, as the title deeds' of the operation.[13] By the time it was back on the table for consideration the Allies and the Soviet Union had moved even closer to victory, though how long the end would be in coming was impossible to predict. The operation was carried out in the belief that a major attack on a city that had hitherto escaped serious bombardment would significantly hasten the end of the war. It was essentially devised to create mayhem in the German front-line areas as they faced the Russian offensive developing in the east.

What was needed, Portal wrote to his deputy Norman Bottomley at the end of January 1945, was 'one big attack on Berlin and attacks on Dresden, Leipzig, Chemnitz, or any other cities where a severe blitz will not only cause confusion in the evacuation from the East but will also hamper the movement of troops from the West.'[14] The object was to destroy infrastructure and create panic, forcing non-combatant men, women and children on to the roads, creating conditions that would stop German soldiers getting to and from the battlefield. It was not a pretty idea. But by this stage of the war it was well within the boundaries which the Allies, and those in whose name they were fighting, thought acceptable.

18

Götterdämmerung

On the morning of Monday, 13 February 1945, Roy Lodge, a twenty-one-year-old bomb-aimer with 51 Squadron and the rest of his crew learned that they were on operations that night. Their job was to mark a target that was as yet unannounced. 'The normal preparations for an op went ahead,' he remembered. In the afternoon they heard where they were going. 'The CO addressed us with, "Gentlemen, your target for tonight is . . . Dresden," and the curtain over the map was drawn aside.' The news caused some whistles and groans. It was the depth of winter and 'Dresden seemed to be halfway across the world, an eight-and-a-half-hour trip there and back.'

Lodge, a Cambridge undergraduate before volunteering, read afterwards that some of those who took part in the raid had experienced beforehand 'a sense of foreboding as though they felt some terrible act was about to be committed.' For him and his crew, however, 'Dresden was just another target, though a long, long way away.'

The normal routine had differed in only one respect. Unusual detail was given about the purpose of the mission. 'We were told that the Russian armies advancing towards Dresden had been held up; that Dresden was the main base for the German army on that front; that though normally it was not an important industrial town, it would be crammed with German troops and transport; that the Russians had asked Bomber Command to help break German resistance.'[1]

Until now Dresden had escaped serious bombardment. But it had been in the Allies' sights for some months and its attraction as a target had increased as the Russian advance ground westward. During the second half of January, Soviet troops crossed Poland

and breached Germany's eastern border. Germany was now fighting hard on two fronts inside its own territory.

The Allies gave urgent thought to how their air power could be used to clear the way for the Red Army. It was apparent that the speed of the Soviet advance would have a decisive effect on the length of the war. The view of the influential Joint Intelligence Committee (JIC), where all the main intelligence services came together, was that the assault on oil targets should remain the main priority. But they also proposed that a major effort should be made to come to the aid of the Russians. Portal shared their opinion.

The Russians' progress was by no means assured. Their advance was threatened by the arrival of German reinforcements from the west. A JIC assessment had predicted that almost half a million men could be moved from Germany's rapidly shrinking territories to reinforce the Eastern Front. For Hitler, stemming the tide from the east was the overwhelming priority. Of all the Germans' many enemies it was the Russians who struck real terror into their hearts.

Churchill was eager to hear the RAF's ideas for hounding the Germans as they were pushed back. He considered Berlin and 'other large cities in East Germany' to be 'especially attractive targets'. On 27 January, Portal issued orders to Harris and Bomber Command to prepare for an attack. Portal considered that an all-out assault on Berlin would not produce decisive results. His pessimism was justified a week later when the Americans took on that task. Almost a thousand Fortresses bombarded the capital in daylight in what was effectively a classic area attack. Over two thousand tons of bombs were dropped, half of which were incendiaries. Huge destruction was done to the fabric of the city and nearly three thousand people were killed. But there was no surrender and Berlin staggered on.

In view of the prime minister's preferences, it was placed on Bomber Command's target list. The cities of Dresden, Leipzig and Chemnitz were also added. A few days later, the Vice-Chief of the Air Staff, Sir Douglas Evill, told the Chiefs of Staff Committee what the RAF were planning. His report placed great emphasis on the potential for exploiting the disruption caused by the large number of evacuees streaming westward through Berlin, Dresden and

Leipzig from the German and German-occupied areas that were falling before the advancing Soviet troops. The administrative problems in dealing with them were 'immense'. The strain on the authorities was doubled by the need to handle the military reinforcements arriving to shore up the crumbling Eastern Front. 'A series of heavy attacks by day and night upon those administrative and control centres,' he wrote, 'is likely to create considerable delays in the deployment of troops . . . and may well result in establishing a state of chaos in some or all of these centres.'² Such operations would serve the dual purpose of speeding the Russians' progress westwards as well as perhaps fulfilling the objective mooted in *Thunderclap* of creating sufficient panic and despair to persuade the German nation that further resistance was futile.

On 4 February, four days after this assessment was delivered, Churchill, Stalin and Roosevelt met in the ballroom of the Livadia Palace, the summer residence of the Tsars near Yalta in the Crimea, to discuss the war's next, crucial phase. On the subject of bombing, the Red Army made a request for air action to hinder the enemy from moving troops to the Eastern Front.

Four days later this had been translated into the basis of an order. On 8 February, the Air Staff's targets committee informed Bomber Command, the US Strategic Air Force Command and Supreme Headquarters Allied Expeditionary Force (SHAEF) that 'the following targets have been selected for their importance in relation to the movements of Evacuees from, and of military forces to, the Eastern Front.' On the list were Berlin, Dresden and Chemnitz. But it was Dresden that was to be dealt with first.

The crews, on the whole, were pleased to be doing something to help their Russian allies. The members of the newly-formed 227 Squadron heard about it at the afternoon briefing from their CO, Wing Commander Ernest Millington, who went on to become a Labour MP. In the audience was Freddie Hulance, who had just completed eight operations as a pilot. 'He announced with some relish,' he said later, 'that the target of Dresden had been nominated at the Yalta conference by the Russians who wanted support for their front, which was then about 100 miles to the east.'

Hulance 'got a certain amount of satisfaction about supporting the Russians.' They had 'born the brunt of the land forces offensive at the time and suffered the worst casualties . . . not that I in any way had Communist feelings, but they were allies, doing a good job, bringing the war to a more hasty conclusion.' The rest of the squadron, he believed, felt the same way.[3]

The Americans had agreed to help and were scheduled to open the attack on 13 February but the operation was scrubbed due to bad weather. In the end, Bomber Command did most of the work, dispatching 796 Lancasters and nine Mosquitoes in two separate raids that came three hours apart.

The first wave of 244 bombers, all from 5 Group, took off shortly after 6 p.m. Despite the weakness of the Luftwaffe night-fighter force they took a tortuous route, turning first towards the Ruhr, then along a jinking path designed to keep the German defences constantly guessing as to where they were heading. These deceptions meant the journey was 500 miles longer than the direct route.

The 5 Group Pathfinders began marking at 10 p.m. local time. Green marker flares were dropped to define the bounds of the city centre, followed by a thousand white magnesium flares to illuminate the ground. Then Mosquitoes swooped down to 2,000 feet to deliver 1,000-pound target indicator canisters whose red flares lit up the aiming point. The planners had chosen the stadium of the city's most popular football club, just to the west of the River Elbe, as the focus of the attack. There was nothing to put the markers off their aim. Most of the city's limited anti-aircraft artillery had been moved to sites deemed to be more important and there were only ten night-fighters stationed in the area.

The main force Lancasters came in at different heights and slightly different approaches to create a zone of destruction that fanned out south and east of the aiming point. The 400 tons of bombs they dropped were a mixture of high explosive which blew down walls and blasted away roofs, and 4-pound incendiaries which set the ruins alight. As the last of the 5 Group aircraft turned away towards home, the fires seemed to be taking hold well.

Roy Lodge was in the second wave of 529 Lancasters. He was still a hundred miles from the target when the glow from Dresden became visible. 'As I drew closer I saw the cause of the glow,' he wrote. 'Ahead was the most enormous fire. Ahead, and then below us were great patches, pools, areas of flame.' Lodge's crew had been detailed to further mark the target but it hardly seemed necessary. 'We added our own long line of flares to those already across the target . . . I saw white flashes of bomb explosions and more splashes of sparkling incendiaries. As we completed our run across the target and turned away on our homeward journey, I could see that the pools of flame were joining up into one huge inferno.'

This was not an exaggeration. The attack had created a firestorm that was to engulf the old city centre. The morning brought no reprieve. More than 300 American Fortresses dropped 771 tons of bombs, aiming at the railway yards which had been outside the RAF's bombing area. At the same time, to intensify the chaos, some of their Mustang fighter escorts shot up road traffic. When the ordeal finally ended, according to the latest best estimate, between 25,000 and 40,000 people had been killed.[4]

The scenes the crews had witnessed were impressive but not necessarily indicative of enormous loss of life. Looking back, Lodge chiefly remembered he and his comrades as afterwards feeling 'tired, of course, excited by what we had seen and done, awed by the enormous destructive power that we had demonstrated.' But it did not seem to him that they had taken part in 'an especially historic event'. Bill Farquharson, who was flying with 115 Squadron, arrived in the middle of the main force when the target was already ablaze. 'At the time it didn't strike me as being a heavy raid,' he said.[5]

Dresden was unusual only in that it went off so well. It was, as it turned out, a disastrous success. The death toll was on a par with that resulting from the first firestorm, created some eighteen months previously at Hamburg, which was regarded at the time as a great victory. But by the time the war was over Hamburg was only a memory to a few non-Germans. The horror of Dresden was still fresh and raw when the last shot was fired. Such a devastating act so close to the dawning of peace seemed particularly brutal and gratuitous. How could killing on such a scale be justified when the end was in sight? The simple answer was that the end was not in sight. No one could know when the war would finish and in the middle of February 1945 there was no indication that the Germans would not fight on until the death of the last Nazi.

Even while fires still burned in the ruins of the old city, unease was mounting about the raid. On 17 February a report by Associated Press, the main American news agency, from Supreme Allied Head-quarters stated that the 'Allied Air Chiefs' had made a decision to 'adopt deliberate terror bombing of German population centres as a ruthless expedient to hastening Hitler's doom.' It cited recent attacks on 'residential sections' of Dresden, as well as Berlin and Chemnitz as evidence that the campaign was already under way. This dispatch was widely distributed and broadcast and though quickly suppressed it made a strong impression. It was especially disturbing to American audiences who had received continual official assurances that their air force was a precision instrument which was applied only to select targets. The stir the story created was thought sufficiently damaging to merit a clarification from the US Secretary of War, General George C. Marshall, who issued a counter-statement emphasizing that the attack on Dresden had taken place at the request of the Russians.

The controversy, initially at least, made little impression on the crews. They were anxious to press on. Although the final date of the war was unguessable it was clear that the Germans were beaten. There were odd, cheering signs that lifted their spirits. Flying over Sweden, Dennis Steiner and his crew were buoyed to see below them lines of tracer hosing up in the form of a V for Victory sign.

When a crew finished a tour they could now reasonably hope that they would not have to do another. Harry Yates's thirtieth op was a trip to a place he had never heard of before, Vohwinkel in the Ruhr, where the target was the marshalling yards. Crews were specially apprehensive on their last trip. The loss rate may have dropped to just below 1 per cent. But inside a squadron, the deaths of friends and comrades were as real and painful as ever, and despite the weakness of the Luftwaffe, people were still dying.

Essen, May 1945.

At the briefing before Yates's final trip, the route map was heavily spattered with red blobs indicating the whereabouts of flak batteries. Over the target they met sustained and accurate anti-aircraft fire which disrupted the bomber stream, breaking up its coherence. They 'rocked through the dirty air, anxious like everybody about our proximity to other kites.' The bombing was ragged and the high wind further diluted the concentration. The bombs missed the rail junctions, even largely failed to hit the town.

Yates and his friends did not care. 'We came away with joy and relief bubbling up as irresistibly as champagne from a shaken bottle . . . no words were wasted on the bombing we had just witnessed. The time had come to celebrate the fact of being alive.' As they headed home 'a party atmosphere swept through the aircraft. We crossed Holland at 5,000 feet while the boys bawled a gloriously crass ditty into the intercom. The coffee came out.' His New Zealander navigator, Bill Birnie, proposed a toast: 'To us.' Yates offered his own. ' "To our future," I said, realizing as I pronounced the word that I had not allowed myself such unqualified optimism for the last twenty weeks.' They came to a halt at the end of the runway at Mepal to 'wild, triumphant cheering.' Yates had climbed aboard his aircraft 'proud of who we were and what we were doing.' This was how most of the men in Bomber Command felt.[6]

Peter Johnson was one of the few who had contemporaneous doubts about the morality of carrying on the bombing. By March 1945 he was commanding 97 (Pathfinder Force) Squadron. On the sixteenth he woke up in his room at Coningsby feeling that the 'smell of victory was in the air.' Operations were on that night and he assumed that he would be marking an oil target in eastern Germany or Czechoslovakia. At the briefing he learned that they were in fact going to Würzburg, which had not until then been subjected to a major attack. He asked the squadron intelligence officer what was the significance of the target and was told 'nothing very much'. There were 'no big factories', just 'a bit of a railway junction'.

Johnson was too busy making preparations to give the matter much thought. He and his crew, using sophisticated blind-bombing techniqes, would be first on the target, dropping primary indicators. Soon after, magnesium flares would light up the bombing area for seven or eight minutes allowing Mosquitoes to swoop in low and mark the exact point for the bombing force to aim at. By now they could be reasonably assured of success. His group had 'perfected an elaborate method of bombing towns [that] ensured that bombs were evenly distributed over the target area and conducive, with the huge numbers of incendiaries used, to the production of a firestorm . . . this was the treatment we were to mete out at Würzburg.'

Johnson was a believer in the virtue of Bomber Command and

the necessity of the strategic bombing campaign, for which he had specifically volunteered. He had been untouched by the murmurs of doubt that had from time to time emanated from churchmen and the benches of parliament. 'Such criticism,' he thought, 'had come from quarters unable or unwilling to suggest new or alternative policies to win the war and they had cut little ice with the general public and went unnoticed in Bomber Command.'

Johnson had been unconcerned by the Dresden operation which he had not flown on but had helped to plan. It was, he thought, 'a potent blow in assisting our Russian allies who had borne so much of the burden of war and suffered so appallingly from German atrocities in their homeland.' But as he lay uneasily on his narrow bed that afternoon awaiting the Würzburg operation he found it 'difficult to justify the deliberated destruction of a small city whose military value to the enemy seemed negligible.' The victims would certainly include some prominent Nazis. The majority though, 'would be the young and the old, many of them refugees from other disasters, non-combatants in the truest sense.' As the minutes slipped away towards H-Hour he found he 'simply could not shut my eyes to this, nor could I convince myself that "success" in our attack would make the slightest contribution to bringing the war to an end nor to saving casualties among our armies on the continent.' Johnson decided he wanted none of it. But how could he find a way out? As squadron commander he could choose whether to fly or not. But if he felt the mission was wrong he could hardly, with a clear conscience, order others to carry it out. In addition, to refuse to give the necessary orders would constitute mutiny, followed by a court-martial, severe punishment and disgrace, and penury for his family. It would shock the squadron and possibly deflate their morale. When he finally made up his mind, the deciding factor was fear of being accused, or at least suspected, of LMF. The point he was trying to make would be blotted out by the stain of cowardice.

Sick with misgivings, he took himself to the final briefing, conducted by Air Vice-Marshal H. A. Constantine, who had taken over 5 Group in January and was anxious to make an impression. He stressed that 'the war was not over and the task of Bomber Command was as important ever.' When Constantine asked if there were any questions, Johnson spoke up. Was there, he wanted to know, any special reason for the attack? '"I've said it's an important railway centre," he said (it wasn't), "and also there are thousands of houses totally undamaged sheltering tens of thousands of Germans. I hope that will not be the case tomorrow, which will be another nail in the enemy's coffin."'

Constantine's hopes were satisfied and Johnson's fears realized. The Würzburg raid was devastating. More than 1,100 tons of bombs were dropped in a little over a quarter of an hour, landing with exemplary accuracy. The authors of Bomber Command's war diaries noted that 'Würzburg contained little industry and this was an area attack.' The historic heart of the city was burned out. Nearly nine tenths of its buildings were destroyed. The number of dead was never decided. It lay somewhere between four and five thousand.

By now Bomber Command could wreak blanket destruction virtually at will. This had been demonstrated ten days after the Dresden raid when it visited Pforzheim. Hitherto the town had not been considered important enough to attack. On the night of 23/24 February, it dropped about 1,800 tons of bombs, a huge quantity, on a compact area measuring three kilometres by one and a half. In the resulting crucible, according to the local official report, 'more than 17,000 [a quarter of the population] met their death in a hurricane of fire and explosions.' This was probably the third heaviest air raid death toll in Germany during the war after Hamburg and Dresden.[7] To the crews though, it was just another raid. They were told at the pre-operational briefing that it was being targeted because it contained a factory making clockwork mechanisms that were used by the Luftwaffe.

The raid stoked up hatred and rage against the RAF. Three weeks afterwards seven British airmen who had baled out after being shot down were marched through Pforzheim on their way to a prisoner of war camp. They were settling down for the night in a school building in a village outside the town when a mob turned up outside. They had been sent there by a senior Nazi official in Pforzheim, Hans Christian Knab, in a 'demonstration of public outrage.'

Three of the airmen managed to run away but the remaining four were dragged to a cemetery and shot dead. One of the three escapees was recaptured and held in a police station. A Major Niklas of the Volksturm (home guard) turned up and demanded he be handed over. The police complied. The prisoner was given up to a crowd that had gathered outside and was beaten, then shot by a member of the Hitler Youth. The two other airmen survived to give evidence in the subsequent military trial. Knab and Niklas were hanged.[8]

As the end grew closer, disquiet mounted at the conduct of the bombing campaign. It was Dresden that marked the stealthy change of heart. The first indication of how the aircrews would be regarded by the post-war world came from the pen of Churchill. On 28 March 1945 he sent a minute to Portal and the Chiefs of Staff Committee which questioned the usefulness of further area bombing. It is remarkable in its frank acceptance of the real purpose of such operations. It also shows a politician's worldly appreciation of how certain acts of war were likely to be viewed once the smoke had cleared from the battlefield. 'It seems to me [he wrote] that the moment has come when the question of the bombing of the German cities simply for the sake of increasing the terror, though under other pretexts, should be reviewed. Otherwise we shall come into control of an utterly ruined land.' This was common sense. Continuing to knock down German houses at this point merely added to the Allies' post-war headaches. It was they who would have to look after the welfare of the defeated nation. He might have added that flattening towns made the job of the advancing armies harder as the rubble provided cover for the defending forces.

But hidden in the middle of what was a workaday communication was a sentence that bore no relation to the surrounding subject matter. 'The destruction of Dresden,' Churchill wrote, 'remains a serious query against the conduct of the Allied bombing.'[9] With these charged words the prime minister signalled the arrival of a controversy that is still alive today.

This statement was disingenuous and hypocritical whichever way it was looked at. As the official history pointed out, it ignored the fact that Dresden had happened six weeks before, when the situation had been much more uncertain. The plan of attacking important cities in eastern Germany had been approved at all levels the previous year and had Churchill's enthusiastic backing. This was consistent with his attitude of the previous four years, whereby he had been firmly supportive of Harris's dogged mission, whatever doubts he might have from time to time as to the utility of the violence. Now he appeared to be changing his tune.

It did not take much imagination to foresee the trouble ahead. Once the war was over the world would have the chance to see what strategic bombing had done to Germany. It would shock even the most fervent advocate of revenge. Some of it was, as Churchill had admitted in the minute, terror bombing. Yet the official position was that the Allies had been engaged in no such thing. As recently as early March, Richard Stokes, the Labour MP who had persistently and bravely questioned the conduct of the campaign, had once again returned to the subject. Was terror bombing, he demanded of Sir Archibald Sinclair, the air minister, the policy of the RAF? Sinclair replied with what now seems spurious indignation. 'It does not do the Honourable Member justice to come here to this House and suggest that there are a lot of Air Marshals or pilots or anyone else sitting in a room trying to think how many German women and children they can kill,' he said.[10]

On the evening after Churchill's minute was written Portal suggested to him that he should think about it again. The prime minister took the hint and withdrew it, substituting a few days later a few mild sentences repeating his concern about the usefulness of continued area bombing but making no mention of Dresden. 'We must see to it,' he wrote on 1 April, 'that our attacks do not do more harm to ourselves in the long run than they do to the enemies' immediate war effort.'

The Air Staff was now anyway agreed that area bombing had outlived its usefulness and that 'at this advanced stage of the war no immediate additional advantage can be gained from [attacks on] the remaining industrial centres of Germany.' They wished though, to reserve the right to bomb towns near the front if German resistance revived and to strike at population centres in Thuringia if the Nazi leadership made a last stand there.

In the event, no such action was needed. Germany was tottering towards total collapse and the main work of Bomber Command was done. For the remainder of the war the force would mainly be used helping the army and blowing up roads and railways in and around Leipzig and Halle on the German line of retreat.

On 16 April Portal sent a message to Harris that he suggested should be turned into an order of the day. The last paragraph stated that 'henceforth the main tasks of the strategic air forces will be to afford direct support to the allied armies in the land battle and to continue their offensive against the sea power of the enemy which they have already done so much to destroy. I am confident that Bomber Command will maintain in these final phases of the war in the air over Europe the high standard of skill and devotion that has marked their work since the earliest days of the war.' With these words the strategic air offensive against Germany effectively came to an end.[11]

The last area bombing raid of the war had taken place the day before. Five hundred Lancasters and twelve Mosquitoes closed in on Potsdam, the imperial and military town west of Berlin. It was the first time that big bombers had entered the area since Harris had called off the Battle of Berlin in March 1944, when it was realized that they were no match for the German night-fighters. Now they could do as they pleased. The aiming point was a barracks in the centre of the town, once the home of the old Prussian guards regiments. The bombs fell all over the place and as far afield as northern and eastern districts of Berlin. Up to 5,000 people were killed, possibly because many neglected to take shelter thinking, when they heard the air-raid sirens, that the attack was bound for the capital. This was the raid that so impressed Portal when he drove through the ruins a few weeks later and felt both awed and depressed at what had been done on his orders.

The last heavy bomber raids of the war took place on 25 April. One was aimed at Hitler's Bavarian retreat at Berchtesgaden and the SS barracks nearby. Freddie Hulance, who had been at Dresden, took part. The two operations could not have been more different. Berchtesgaden was a fine example of aerial warfare, precisely applied. Setting off from Lincolnshire, Hulance felt relief that the end of the war seemed only days away, but also apprehension. The target was believed to be one of the most heavily defended in the Reich. All together 359 Lancasters and sixteen Mosquitoes of 1, 5 and 8 Groups were involved. For most of the crews, it was their last operation of the war. There was scattered cloud when they arrived over the Bavarian Alps. 'We were briefed that we shouldn't bomb unless we could see the target,' he remembered, '[then] quite suddenly the cloud cleared as I was approaching it so we bombed.' Hulance watched the ordnance slanting down towards the SS barracks which was 'pretty well saturated. There was only one building unscathed.' The crews had been told they would be blowing up the Führer himself. But Hitler was not at home.

Thirty-nine airmen died on operations that day. Most of them were killed during an attack on the coastal batteries on the Friesian island of Wangerooge, in a series of mid-air collisions between friendly aircraft. It was a reminder, if anyone needed one, of the precarious nature of life in Bomber Command.

The last German civilians died when sixty-three Mosquitoes attacked Kiel on the night of 2/3 May. It was feared that ships were waiting to carry troops to Norway to carry on the fight. Bombs fell on the town and eighteen people were killed. Flying Officer R. Catterall, DFC and Flight Sergeant D. J. Beadle were lost carrying out a low-level attack on an airfield. Shortly afterwards the remaining German soldiers left town and Kiel was declared an open city. After carrying away what they could from the central stores, the citizens went home to await the arrival of British and Canadian troops.

The war ended just before Bomber Command dropped its millionth ton of bombs. The final figure was 955,044 tons. The USAAF had delivered a further 395,000 tons. The American troops arriving in the Ruhr valley in April 1945 entered a vast ocean of rubble from which protruded the twisted girders and tortured metal that were all that was left of the factories, foundries and workshops that powered the German war machine. It was destruction on a cosmic scale.

There had been sixty large towns and cities on Harris's target list. All of them now had been substantially damaged and many almost completely destroyed. Three quarters of Hamburg was razed, 69 per cent of Darmstadt and 64 per cent of Hannover. A third of sprawling Berlin was flattened: 6,427 acres. That compared with the 400 acres of London that the Luftwaffe laid waste. In the infamous raid on Coventry, they had devasted a hundred acres. In Düsseldorf, a town of similar size, Allied bombing had wiped out an area twenty times as large.

Hidden underneath the desert of brick and dust lay the unburied dead. The figure of around 600,000 came to be accepted as the number of German civilians killed by bombing. A post-war enquiry by the German Federal Government's statistics office, published in 1962, put the total as 593,000.[12] The exact number will probably never be known. After heavy raids civil defence workers often piled up the human remains, doused them in petrol and set them on fire to reduce the risk of disease. Whole families were wiped out leaving no one to report their deaths. A further 67,000 were killed in France by air attack according to recent research. In Italy, more than 60,000 are thought to have died.

The number of combatants killed in the bombing was low. The German dead were mostly women, children and the old, those who were left at home when the men of fighting age not needed to run the factories went off to the war. Thus, for every 100 male casualties in Darmstadt, there were 181 females. Many in Britain were prepared to accept the argument that any German adult engaged in war work could be regarded as having placed himself or herself in the firing line. But no definition of what constituted a legitimate target could include children. In Hamburg, 7,000 of the dead were children or adolescent. This slaughter of the young was repeated in numerous urban centres big and small, in roughly the same proportions.

In Freiburg, in the Breisgau region, 252 boys and girls under the age of sixteen were killed, 19 per cent of the total civilian death toll.

The old died alongside the women and children, and for the same reasons. When the air war came to Germany they found themselves in the front line. In some cities they made up 22 per cent of the dead. There were many others who lost their lives because of grotesque bad luck. A substantial number of the victims were forced workers from the countries that the Allies were fighting to liberate.[13]

German history provided a comparison for death on this scale. Official figures claimed that 800,000 people had died directly or indirectly as a result of the Royal Navy's maritime blockade during the First World War. Included in the figure were the 150,000 who, it was claimed, perished as a result of undernourishment which lowered their defences against the influenza epidemic that ravaged Europe after the war.

But it was the sort of death the victims had suffered that gave the tolls their awesome quality. Death by malnourishment or disease came in stages. It was slow and organic. Death by bombing came in several forms, all of them horrible. It was violence distilled into its most nightmarish form. By the end of the war, raids had been compressed into a few horrific minutes. In Pforzheim there was just over a quarter of an hour between the first bomb falling and the last bomber departing, leaving behind a town whose centre had been turned into fire and smoke and glowing ashes. The lucky ones died immediately, from crashing masonry or the effects of blast. The less fortunate burned up, or, cowering in a shelter or cellar, suffocated as the fire consumed the oxygen in the air leaving only carbon monoxide.

The crews had mostly had few doubts about the justice of what they were doing and little sympathy for those they were doing it to. It was nonetheless a relief when, in the last days, Bomber Command was given tasks that gave life rather than took it. Operation *Manna* was launched to bring relief supplies to western Holland. The population was approaching starvation and many old people had already died. It began at the end of April and lasted until the German surrender. In that time, Lancasters and Mosquitoes flew nearly 3,000 sorties, dropping 7,000 tons of food into an area that was still under German occupation.

Another operation, *Exodus*, brought particular satisfaction. By the end of the war there were 75,000 British servicemen in German prisoner-of-war camps. It was remembered that after the previous war it had taken nearly two months before all PoWs were repatriated. The RAF offered its Lancasters to speed up the process. Leaflets were dropped over a number of camps telling them to stand by to be liberated. Between 26 April and 7 May, 469 sorties were flown without accident. Each Lancaster could take twenty-six passengers. Many were too shattered by their experience to show much gratitude. Peter Johnson flew a batch from Brussels and stood with the crew at the foot of the ladder to welcome them back home. 'They were tired and still numb from their freedom. Many were emaciated from lack of proper food. It was queer that not one of those that I brought back said "Thank You" to the crew.'[14]

Among the the PoWs were 9,838 airmen from Bomber Command, some of whom had been incarcerated since the earliest days of the war. Given the destruction that the aircrews had inflicted on the Reich, the Germans' treatment of their British and American charges was surprisingly mild and respectful. They could, undoubtedly, be ruthless when needed. No one would forget the mass murder carried out by the Gestapo in March 1944 of fifty PoWs from Stalag Luft III captured in the aftermath of the Great Escape. But unless prisoners looked for trouble, their main enemies for much of the war were boredom, frustration and the psychological chafing caused by enforced communal life.

The Germans quickly established a system of processing captured airmen. The experience of Geoffrey Willatt, whom we last heard of baling out on the night of Sunday, September 5/6 after his Lancaster was shot down by a night-fighter on the way back from Mannheim, was typical.[15] He was the only one of the crew to survive. He was soon picked up and taken to Dulag Luft, an interrogation centre near Frankfurt through which most captured aircrew personnel passed.

RAF intelligence officers painted a lurid and not unattractive picture of what could be expected there. The camp was supposed to be an oasis of leisure and luxury, where flighty women and peacetime comforts were employed to loosen the captives' tongues.

The truth, he noted in his diary, bore 'no resemblance whatsoever' to what he had been told. There were 'no parks, no booze, no women, no dances.' The intelligence was proved right in one respect however. Many prisoners reported being interrogated by sympathetic officers who spoke perfect English and startled them with questions such as 'and how are Wing Commander Gibson and Wing Commander Cheshire?' just as they had been warned.[16]

Geoffrey was then packed with other RAF prisoners into a cattle truck, whose capacity was labelled '40 hommes ou 8 chevaux' and taken by train to the place where he would spend the next eighteen months. Stalag Luft III, carved out of a pine forest at Sagan, about a hundred miles south-east of Berlin, was the hub of the prison system. When he arrived at the North Compound there was a crowd waiting to look over the new arrivals. Some shouted delightedly as they recognized old comrades but 'mostly [they were] silent, looking at us in the way old prisoners look at new ones (poor b—ers, but lucky devils to have come so recently from home).' They were a motley bunch dressed in 'anything from full uniform to loin cloths, and looked incredibly fit with brown bodies and beards.'

By now Stalag Luft III had expanded considerably. In North Compound there were fifteen sleeping huts, fifty yards long, partitioned off into twenty-four rooms. Each held up to six men who slept in bunk beds. Geoffrey made quick character assessments of his fellow-inmates. The British all seemed good types. An American navigator who had been flying with the Canadians, however, was 'inclined to be self-centred and with an all-embracing prejudice against anything English. The less said the better.'

Geoffrey had nightmares at first, reliving the terror of being shot down, but soon recorded that 'usually I sleep like a log.' He learned the camp patois. They, the inmates, were 'kriegies', taken from the German word for war prisoner. The guards were 'goons' and the English-speaking staff who tried to mingle and snoop were 'ferrets'. He learned, too quickly, the established routines of the captive's life. He was among men 'from nearly every country in the world, Holland, Norway, India, S. America, Denmark, Poland, Czecho-Slovakia.'

It was the custom to walk in twos around the circuit by the side of the warning wire, ten yards from the perimeter fence. Stepping over the wire invited a shot from a watchtower. Too many circuits were 'apt to accentuate the position of the wire and the smallness of the camp.'

As he grew accustomed to camp life he found that 'kriegies are influenced enormously by 4 things in this order – mail, weather, food and news, and it's extraordinary how our spirits are up or down all in a moment.'

The flow of mail was erratic but somehow the system worked. There would be nothing for days on end, and then a welcome flood. Geoffrey was able to keep in touch with his wife Audrey. Her first letter arrived on 11 November. 'Marvellous feeling,' he recorded. 'I can actually see her writing and the paper she wrote on.'

Reg Fayers, who ended up in Stalag Luft I near Barth on the Baltic coast, after being shot down on the night of 25/6 November 1943, received a steady stream of letters from his beloved wife Phyllis. The news of the films she had seen and the mundane goings-on in their home town of Sudbury in Suffolk provided a heartening glimpse of the longed-for life going on hundreds of miles away across the wire.

'Darling it's evening time and everywhere is smelling so perfect,' she wrote on 30 July 1944. 'I wish we were walking round Brundon [a local beauty spot] or even sitting here together with all our favourite records . . . darling I love you so very much. Why should this war have to come now?' There was no doubt in her mind that sooner or later the reunion would come. On 7 October she mentioned the latest movie she had seen, A Guy Named Joe, starring Spencer Tracy and Irene Dunne. 'I loved every minute of it,' she wrote. 'We shall just have to see it when you come home. Darling how are you after all these months? Do you still look the same and talk the same? You will never really change will you? I wished so much that you were with me this morning . . .'

There were plenty of opportunities to indulge the British preoccupation with the weather. It was sometimes extreme and often uncertain. Geoffrey was able to sunbathe on 1 November. There was more sunbathing early in April the following year but the false spring was followed by a snowfall. 'Who said the English climate is unpredictable?' he wrote. In the winter the huts were dismal. There was one stove to a room and barely any coal, which had to be eked out with potato peelings and tea leaves. The cruel east wind stripped the felt from the roof letting in the rain. One night Geoffrey and his room-mates dragged their beds into the corridor to escape the drips and slept in their clothes to keep warm.

Food was restricted to one Red Cross parcel per man per week, supplemented by meagre German rations. The cooking was centralized. Each room was given thirty-five minutes' use of the one small stove and two pots. Monty, one of Geoffrey's room-mates, had volunteered to be chef. 'Little knowing what we were in for we accept,' he wrote. 'We take it in turns to be "Joe" for a day, peeling potatoes, washing up, sweeping out, fetching hot water etc. Not very irksome in itself but tiresome when Monty criticizes all the time . . .' Food theft was a shameful crime. 'This month's bombshell,' wrote Geoffrey in September 1944. 'Someone in the room is "fiddling" bits of food. We seem to be short of milk, margarine and other things . . . This all sounds petty but is of real importance when every little scrap of food must be rationed out.' The culprit was eventually caught red-handed and expelled from the room.

The potential for getting on each other's nerves was enormous. Bad weather meant they were cooped up together, 'leading to increased friction'. Most of it, he believed, was 'caused by one person who has no sense of give and take & issues anti-British propaganda at every pore' – presumably the American navigator. His conduct drove the others 'out of the room on every possible occasion to lectures on Art, Music, Architecture, Literature & concerts in unheated lecture rooms.'

Anything that relieved the boredom was welcomed. They played football, rugby and cricket. They tried to learn languages and study for the careers they hoped to follow when the war was over. They read enormously from the libraries provided by the Red Cross and mounted dramatic productions. Sagan had a theatre which put on a stream of often ambitious shows. There was a prodigious amount of talent in the ranks of the kriegies. Denholm Elliott, the RADA student turned wireless op who was shot down in the North Sea in September 1943, ended up in Stalag VIII B, near Breslau in Upper Silesia. On learning of the theatrical possibilities he approached 'a chap called Stanley Platts who later became a professional after the war ... he used to talk "lake thet" in a rather sepulchral voice. I said to him "excuse me but I am a student from the Royal Academy and I wondered if . . ."' Platts offered him an understudy role in the Patrick Hamilton play *Rope*. Soon he had all the parts he could want, including Macbeth, and Eliza Doolittle in *Pygmalion*. Female roles were something of a speciality. He also played Viola in *Twelfth Night*. The Germans could not have been more helpful. For the latter production they lent the prisoners costumes from the Breslau Opera House. All this activity was designed to dispel the most lowering aspect of camp life. 'The unpleasant thing about being a PoW was the uncertainty,' Denholm Elliott recalled afterwards. 'When would one be released? In six weeks or sixty years. One didn't know.'[17]

Prisoners were remarkably well connected with the outside world. They listened to the BBC on home-made radios, and interrogated the friendlier goons who also supplied them with German newspapers. News of the progress of the war created wild mood swings. By April 1944 Sagan was humming with rumours of the impending invasion. Fantastic bets were struck about the date. A sergeant pledged he would allow himself to be thrown into the communal latrine if the landings did not come before a certain date. There was a craze for table-rapping séances to seek the spirit world's advice on when liberation would come. Already they could see evidence of the Allies' progress in the far-off flashes from the air raids on Berlin.

For once it seemed that the veteran kriegies' predictions that they would 'all be home by Christmas' would come true. But Christmas 1944 came and went and they were still there. Geoffrey sang in the camp choir's production of *Messiah*. The festivities were overshadowed by news of the success of the German offensive in the Ardennes. Nonetheless they managed to put together a feast of tinned turkey, sausage, and Christmas pud and 'cheer up momentarily'.

In mid-January their spirits received a real lift when they heard that the Russian offensive was gathering pace to the east. Soon they could hear the guns in the distance. On the evening of 27 January the order was given to evacuate the camp. One ordeal was over but another was beginning.

At 1 a.m. Geoffrey and his fellow prisoners passed through the camp gates and out into the freezing snow. They piled their Red Cross provisions on to makeshift sledges, which began to break up within a few hundred yards. They trudged through the night, passed by streams of refugees and white-clad troops heading towards the sound of the guns. The few guards with them abandoned any pretence of discipline. Kriegie and goon were facing the future together.

The civilians in the fearful villages they passed through seemed 'amazingly friendly'. Geoffrey, who had learned German in captivity, overheard two women discussing the prisoners as they passed. 'The older one said, "I do feel sorry for them but they *are* terror-bombers." The younger one answers, "yes but they are a lot of nice-looking young men."' The Red Cross coffee and chocolate and the cigarettes they brought with them could be traded for almost anything that was available. They slept in barns and one night in a bomb shelter.

The greatest danger seemed to be not from the Germans but from the Allied aircraft which droned frequently overhead, sometimes shooting up trains and traffic. The Russians were coming and everyone knew it. At one point, as they trailed westwards, away from the direction of the advance they watched 'small groups of old men dig pathetic little gun pits and sit in them,' waiting fatalistically for the enemy. After six days' march they were put on cattle trucks which hauled them off to another camp at Tarmstedt, near Bremen. They stood in the freezing slush outside for three hours before they were let in. It was a surreal moment. 'A few hysterical voices can be heard shouting "open the bloody gates!"' he recorded. 'Fancy shouting to be let *in*' to a prisoners' camp.

Geoffrey and his fellow-prisoners had to endure another forced march before liberation. When it finally came they were billeted in the farm buildings of a large estate not far from Lübeck. They shared it with Polish female slave workers aged from twelve to seventy who had been living and working there in appalling conditions for five years. When he woke up on 2 May the guards had gone. He ate a breakfast of egg and chips in glorious sunshine and with the sound of approaching gunfire in the background. 'Unmistakably this time tanks on both sides of us,' he wrote. 'German soldiers of all kinds start straggling along the road – all going to give themselves up . . . they are tired & bedraggled and some of them are armed but most have thrown their guns away. We give them cigarettes and they give us their belts, badges, food etc. Their chief feeling is relief that it is all over . . .'

A rumour began that British tanks were at the edge of town. At last 'a Bren carrier rushed into the camp and the Kriegies go mad. We shout, cheer and clamber all over it, shaking the crews' hands . . . we are prisoners no more . . . the wireless on the Bren carrier starts up. The driver answers "tank 19 speaking. Am in village & at PW camp. Over to you, over –" Yes. Over to you, over the English Channel & *home*.'

In the strange anarchic interlude between the Germans abandoning their posts and the arrival of their liberators, some had the chance to see the nature of the enemy they had been fighting. The Germans had seemed amiable enough to Geoffrey Willatt. Reg Fayers saw another side of them. When the Russians arrived at his camp on 2 May the inmates set out to explore the surrounding country. When they returned they told each other what they had seen. There were two concentration camps nearby. 'Thirty thousand have reputedly gone thru it,' he wrote. 'The other one, eight thousand. On two potatoes, watery soup, one seventh of a loaf, forced labour worked hard until they were useless, then they were gassed. Our army doc was, he said, almost sick when he entered rooms where living skeletons sat around tables too weak to move, to get out of their own excreta . . . the bodies stayed there, decomposing, bloated. One thousand were supposed to have been drowned in the creek on one barge. And so on . . .' All the prisoners shared his disgust. 'This has been going on within a few miles of us. Any humanitarian feelings for the German plight now is banished by all this.'[18]

Back in England the crews celebrated VE day in the way that they knew best. Dennis Steiner and his comrades went into Gainsborough to their favourite pub, the Woolsack, where they 'made a thorough nuisance of ourselves. We "borrowed" a builders barrow and loaded it with WAAFs and toured the town, on the way removing convenient bunting that had decorated the streets . . .' The following day the mayor of Gainsborough arrived to reclaim the town's decorations. Negotiations were conducted in the mess where he was 'well and truly entertained and had to be driven home, having lost all interest in his bunting.'[19]

There had been a hundred nights like it but this time there was an altered quality to the fun. There was something that was lacking, something whose absence was very welcome. For the first time in nearly five years, the thought that this party might be the last no longer hung over the celebrations. Cy March was on leave and in bed with his wife Ellen when they heard a tremendous crashing at the door. He 'went out and asked what the hell they thought they were playing at.' The neighbours told him the news. 'I can't explain the relief I felt,' he wrote later. 'No more flak or fighters, biting cold, sleepless nights.' The following night he celebrated in the local pub, all the time time wishing 'I had been on the station with all the boys.' When he got back to Syerston he took the ground crew on an aerial 'Cook's Tour' of the places they had contributed to bombing. The flight took eight hours. 'We flew quite low at times and you could see the crowds milling about in the towns, all as chuffed at the war's end as we were I suppose. One thing stuck in my mind. We flew over the Black Forest and it must have been a forester's cabin, but he and his wife and little girl were at their door waving like mad. Yesterday's enemies, I thought, just like families at home after all that.'[20]

19

Forgetting

Eight days after the end of the war Harris issued a special order of the day to Bomber Command. It was a tribute to his men and women, thanking them for all they had done for him, the country and the free world. 'To those who survive I would say this,' it ran. 'Content yourself and take credit with those who perished that now the "Cease Fire" has sounded countless homes within our Empire will welcome back a father, husband or son whose life, but for your endeavours and your sacrifices, would assuredly have been expended during long further years of agony.' He went on to list their many feats and finished by declaring his pride in having been 'your Commander-in-Chief through more than three years of your Saga . . . Famously have you fought. Well have you deserved of your country and her Allies.'[1]

The nation's thanks, though, were slow in coming. Bomber Command was both the symbol and the instrument of Britain's defiance of the Germans throughout the war. It provided an antidote to despair and sustained the hope of victory and peace. In the early years, Britain suffered serial defeats. But in the air it seemed different. Every night the bombers went out into the darkness, the searchlights and the flak to show the world that though the struggle against the Germans might appear futile, there was still someone prepared to wage it. Hearing the throb of friendly bomber engines overhead, listening to the radio bulletins or reading the reports in the papers, the nation could comfort itself with the thought that their injuries at the hands of the Luftwaffe were being repaid. With the arrival of new aircraft, new crews and new equipment and techniques, the attack ceased to be symbolic. By the middle of the war British bombers were inflicting terrible destruction and pain on the enemy.

At the end, their now enormous power helped to crush the last sparks of vitality out of Hitler's empire.

The main job carried out by the crews was amongst the worst that warfare could devise. There was little satisfaction or glory in bombing cities. Yet that was what they had been asked to do and that is what they did, unflinchingly for the most part and at enormous cost to themselves. Yet when it came time give thanks and honour to the living and the dead the official voice was muted.

Churchill broadcast his speech announcing Victory in Europe on the afternoon of 13 May. All over the country, in NAAFI and mess, sitting room and pub, citizens and servicemen clustered round the wireless to hear the prime minister thank all who had secured Britain's survival and eventual triumph. Everyone received their share of praise: the Royal Navy for keeping the sea lanes open, the Merchant Navy who gallantly manned the convoys, the Army whose victories in North Africa paved the way for the reconquest of Europe. The crews listened eagerly as he reached the part played by the RAF. He began by eulogizing Fighter Command and its victory in the Battle of Britain, asserting again that 'never before in the history of human conflict was so much owed by so many to so few.' He predicted that the name of Dowding, its commander, would 'ever be linked with this splendid event.' He spoke of the danger posed by the Germans' V weapons and the RAF's role, along with the domestic anti-aircraft batteries in suppressing them. They had not completely destroyed the menace, however. The credit for that went to the Allied armies who 'cleaned up the coast and overran all the points of discharge.' Otherwise, he went on, 'the autumn of 1944, to say nothing of 1945, might well have seen London as shattered as Berlin.'

The Bomber Boys leaned forward to enjoy their share of the praise that seemed to be coming next. But that was it. Churchill passed on to survey the post-war scene. The strategic air campaign might never have happened. As the speech ended and the radios were switched off, the airmen were left with the uncomfortable feeling that all their mighty effort, all the fear and sorrow, the stresses and sacrifices, had not been been considered worth mentioning.

The peace celebrations had barely begun but the victors were already constructing their version of history. The war had been a triumph for morality and civilized values, of light over darkness. The presence of Bomber Command loomed awkwardly over this legend. From then on, the political establishment colluded to keep it to the margins of the story. The intention seemed to be to avoid any mark of distinction that would draw attention to what Bomber Command had actually done. Harris complained to Portal that neither he nor any member of his staff was invited to any of the surrender ceremonies. When it came to awarding medals, care was taken not to identify the strategic bombing offensive as a distinct campaign. Those who served in other campaigns such as such as those in Africa, the Far East and France and Germany, were awarded their own star. Despite intense lobbying from the Air Ministry the official line held firm. These were awards for overseas service. Bomber Command had been fighting from home and would have to be content with the Defence Medal, given to all who were engaged on the home front. The aircrew, and the men on the ground who supported them were entitled to the 1939–45 Star, but that was issued to everyone. This provoked a protest from Sir Arthur Street, Permanent Undersecretary of State for Air, who represented the RAF on the Treasury committee which oversaw the grant of honours. The Star he, wrote 'is to be distributed universally . . . altogether it will not be a very worthy distinction for the aircrew of Bomber Command.' They did receive the Aircrew Europe Star. But the citation for this award was phrased with diplomatic precision. In an early draft it was described as decoration for those who had taken part in 'strategical bombing and fighter sweeps over Europe from the United Kingdom.' Later the distinction was dropped and it was given simply for 'operational flying from the United Kingdom bases over Europe.'[2]

Harris was infuriated at the perceived insult to his men. His anger was increased by his belief that it was Churchill, whom he counted as a friend as well as his most prominent supporter, who was behind the decision. On 1 June, he wrote a bitter letter to Portal and Sinclair declaring that 'if my Command are to have the Defence Medal and no "campaign" medal in the France–Germany–Italy–Naval War then I too will have the Defence Medal and no other – nothing else whatsover, neither decoration, award, rank, preferment or appointment, if any such is contemplated or intended . . . I will not stand by and see my people let down in so grossly unjust a manner without resorting to every necessary and justifiable protest which is open to me . . .'[3]

Only a fortnight after this outburst, Harris did accept a knighthood, awarded to him in the King's Birthday Honours, feeling he was unable to reject it because it came from the sovereign. The other giants of the RAF war effort, Portal and Tedder, were ennobled. The absence of a peerage excited conspiracy theories among Harris's supporters, which he was inclined to encourage. The truth was that a peerage was subsequently offered in late 1951, when Churchill returned to power. Harris decided his battle to obtain a special medal for his men was unwinnable. He declined a peerage, preferring the less cumbersome problems of duty and style presented by a baronetcy.

Why was the political establishment so reluctant to honour those who, for the duration of the war, had been cherished by the public and lionized by the government? And why was the embarrassing post-war silence when it came to marking Bomber Command's achievements not more of a public issue than it was? Harris had objected to the award of the Defence Medal on the grounds that the business of Bomber Command had been *offence*. This distinction lay at the heart of the problem. The moral rectitude of the Fighter Boys had been unquestionable. The Battle of Britain was as just a war as it was possible to fight. The pilots were defending their homes and loved ones from a cruel enemy who rejected the values of civilization. The Bomber Boys could argue that they were protecting Britain by so preoccupying the Luftwaffe that it did not have the means to continue its air offensive. But few saw this as their real purpose.

Bomber Command's task was to attack the enemy in their own homes. The British people had lived under the shadow of aerial bombardment ever since the end of the First World War. In the winter of

1940–41 they experienced the reality. They appreciated, at the time, the retribution that was delivered on their behalf. But once the war was ended they had no great desire to be reminded of the deeds that had been done in their name. That amnesia, inevitably, extended to those who had been carrying them out. Harris had summed it up with his usual harsh shrewdness: 'People didn't like being bombed and therefore they didn't like bombers on principle.'

Even those who had taken part in the campaign were filled with awe at what they had done. In May Peter Johnson was summoned by Harris to Bomber Command. 'The C-in-C drove me to his house, Springfield, for lunch wih him and Lady Harris,' he remembered. 'The journey in his Bentley, often at nearly 100 mph through Buckinghamshire lanes, was as alarming as anything on operations.' Harris offered him a post in the Bombing Research Unit being set up to gauge the level of destruction to Germany and particularly to its industry. It was small and inadequately staffed and Johnson believed its pupose was political as much as practical. 'Bert Harris knew that the Americans had an enormous bombing research unit and would be likely to claim all the credit.'[4]

He started work in the Ruhr and his first call was on what remained of Krupp's. He had already looked down on the scenes of devastation from the air. The view on the ground was even more impressive. 'Driving through Essen,' he wrote, 'I had my first close-up view of a bombed German city. As we progressed slowly down the pitted and cratered roads and streets leading to the centre of the town, the full horror of what I had seen from the air three weeks before came through to me. Every street, virtually every building, was gutted, the empty window frames showing the bare and blackened interiors, with twisted and charred remains of beds and furniture often hanging over into the streets.'

His chief, Air Commodore Claude Pelly, was similarly struck when he arrived in the Ruhr. 'There is a deadly silence, which creates a deep impression on the visitor's mind,' he reported home.[5] Johnson saw few people in the towns and most of them were old. 'Dressed mostly in black, they walked slowly, their heads bowed. The pall of their defeat was all around them and they seemed as desolate as their ruined houses.' Johnson wondered where these scarecrows lived. The answer was in cellars underground. Some of the workers who remained had lived like this for three years.

The scarecrows were finished. But there were more resilient Germans who were already pressing forward to stake their claim in the new order. Johnson was guided around the ruins by a Herr Singer, a loyal Krupp's functionary. He arrived in a large chauffeur-driven Mercedes and spoke good English. Total defeat had not crushed his spirits. 'He aimed to show that Krupp's was much more than just a firm, it was an institution which for him, outshone all the others in the Ruhr and Rhineland . . . Governments might come and go, but . . . Krupp's would last for ever.' This was the kind of German that the Allies needed to help relieve them of the burden of reconstruction. Singer, as it turned out, was right and Krupp's did indeed rise from the ashes.

The firm had kept good records. This diligence allowed the team to produce a comprehensive report. It was clear that until March 1943, the many raids launched against Essen and Krupp's had had little effect on production. That came as no surprise. The area's real ordeal began with the Battle of the Ruhr. Bomber Command launched six major raids on Essen between March and July. Two more heavy attacks were carried out in the spring of 1944. The team concluded that in the period March 1943–April 1944, Krupp's had suffered a loss of 20 per cent in output. Johnson, who flew in the battle, knew that 'this was far below what we had been led to expect by British Intelligence at the time.'

The bombing had produced some apparently spectacular benefits, such as knocking out the locomotive shop in the first raid of the Battle, and the destruction of its heavy shell-making capacity in July. But the successes were specious. Train engines and shells could be made elsewhere in the factories of the conquered territories.

After six months' hard research the team arrived at a dismaying conclusion. Over the years bombs might have destroyed or badly damaged 88 per cent of Essen's housing and killed up to seven thousand people. But in that time, the town's contribution to the war had not been substantially reduced. Essen had been defeated in the end. But that end had not come until March 1945 when the war had been substantially won. In the crucial period up to the autumn of 1944, by which time the defeat of Germany was not in doubt, Essen and Krupp's, by bravery and ingenuity, had continued to give valuable assistance to the war effort. Johnson reluctantly 'had to face the fact that no German unit had gone short of the essentials for making war because of our efforts.'

The population had suffered but they had endured. There had been breakdowns in electricity, telephones, water, gas and transport but they had been coped with. Food had been rationed but the supplies had held up almost to the end of the war. It could not even be said that morale had suffered badly. Johnson made careful enquiries. His questions met with much equivocation as the survivors were anxious to disassociate themselves from the Nazi Party. However he came to the conclusion that morale had remained unaffected and had even improved until the end of 1944 when it was becoming clear the war was lost. Even then, there was a strong determination among the population to carry on, sustained in part by the Nazis' manipulation of fears of what would happen to them if the Allies arrived. The work of the *Terrorflieger*, which lay all around, gave the strongest evidence of what they were capable of. In the end, he concluded, patriotism and a sense of duty were more powerful motivations than fear, just as they had been in Britain. He might have added that the presence of a regime that could be as cruel to its own as it was to its enemies also helped to maintain discipline and cohesion.

Johnson left Essen in a state of deep depression. 'It seemed that all that had been done in the long and often terrible summer of 1943 had been in vain. All the agonies and casualties, the numbers of the dead and missing aircrew . . . the civilian men, women and children we had killed in Germany by our rain of bombs, all this had been for nothing.'

This view started to take hold soon after the war was over, gaining ground steadily until by the late 1970s it had become for many a sort of dim truth. Anti-nuclear campaigners claimed that by launching the strategic air campaign, politicians and soldiers had crossed a moral Rubicon which had prepared the way for the use of weapons of mass destruction.

Any criticism, no matter how well meant, was unwelcome to Harris. When the official history of the strategic air offensive appeared in 1961 it brought him little comfort. It ran to four volumes and was a model of thoroughness, incisiveness and fairness. It was sympathetic and respectful towards him, taking his part in at least one of the major controversies with the Air Staff. Before publication, the authors offered to send him a draft so that he could comment, if he wished, in an unofficial capacity. Harris declined. Surely, he argued, he should have been consulted in his official role as commander-in-chief of Bomber Command. This entirely missed the point of the work which both its commissioners and authors were determined would aim for the highest peak of objectivity.

The authors believed that Bomber Command's 'contribution to victory, was, indeed a great one, though in direct terms at least . . . long delayed.' The initial attacks up to the spring of 1942 were little more than a nuisance to the Germans although they provided a great uplift to British morale. The persistence of the attacks also forced the Luftwaffe on to the defensive, which severely reduced its ability to bomb Britain. As Bomber Command's strength grew and its attacks strengthened it soaked up more and more of Germany's resources. The labour of huge numbers of German workers and foreign slaves was wasted clearing up the mayhem created by the big area attacks. Great effort was devoted to providing anti-aircraft defences and searchlight batteries for the homeland, which might otherwise have been expended on the Eastern Front. The constant attentions of the British and American bombers also hampered weapons research, severely reducing the Germans' chances of waging chemical or biological warfare.

In the last year of the war the Command, together with the USAAF, had succeeded in almost completely destroying vital segments of the oil industry, as well as virtually obliterating the communications system. These results had a decisive effect on the outcome of the war. No airman could object to these positive judgements. It was when the authors came to discuss the events of March 1943 to March 1944 that the picture grew more cloudy. The great area offensive, the authors concluded, 'did not produce direct results commensurate with the hopes once entertained and at times, indeed, feared by the Germans themselves.' Huge areas of many of Germany's great towns had been laid waste 'but the will of the German people was not broken or even significantly impaired and the effect on war production was remarkably small.' The fact was, the German economy 'was more resilient than estimated and the German people calmer, more stoical and much more determined than anticipated.' The authors' judgement on the economic effects, which stemmed from the research of the British Bombing Survey Unit, has since been convincingly challenged.

In their conclusions the authors were not attempting to make the case for those who had pressed for the selective approach rather than area bombing. 'Precision' attacks alone would not have achieved any better results. The best that could be said for the combined effort was that it had sapped some of the reserve within the German war economy and caused some factories, notably those making aircraft, to be scattered elsewhere. This made them more vulnerable to air attack later on.

Webster and Frankland's study was recognized as a landmark in military history. It was calm, finely calibrated and honest. It gave credit where it was due but did not flinch from awkward conclusions. Its judgements did not settle any arguments. But it was foolish to insist that there was only one way to fight a war. Harris did insist, however, and went on doing so until he died.

He ignored the subtleties of the authors' analysis and chose to see it as a polemic aimed against him and his men. He claimed they had presented the bombing campaign as a costly failure, an assertion they had never made. The fact that Frankland had flown thirty-six missions as a Bomber Command navigator and had been awarded a DFC did not impress him at all. He told questioners that 'he wrote it as a junior officer, and there was never a junior chief officer who didn't know better than a commander-in-chief how the show should be run.' Later though, he was to relent and pay tribute to Frankland and his work in war and in peace. By the time Harris died he had come to believe that no matter how much he might try to enlighten post-war audiences his life's great work was now seen as 'an expensive luxury' and an exercise in 'carrying out war against the civil population'.

There were few public voices to defend area bombing let alone to vaunt its achievements and inevitably his was the loudest among them. Periodically, when an anniversary or the appearance of a new publication revived the controversy, he went in to fight for his reputation and, more importantly, that of his men. There were many attempts to 'set the record straight'; by which he meant to bend public perception to his own version of events. They were expounded in a tart autobiography, *Bomber Offensive*, which bristled with criticism of his fellow wartime commanders. Any slight on himself or his men provoked a vigorous counter-attack with all the verbal violence he could muster. Harris's loyalty to those who served under him was deep and genuine. Just before he attended a dinner of 'Bomber Command Greats' at the RAF Club in 1976 he gave an interview to a researcher from the Imperial War Museum. He was in poor health, suffering from pneumonia. His doctor had advised him not to go, but Harris 'told him I was going to that show if I went on a stretcher.' He was determined, he said, 'to get the proper amount of credit awarded to my fellows who made such a tremendous contribution towards winning the war, a fact which has been acknowledged by the enemy and the senior British Army Commanders but not otherwise.'[6]

It was a difficult task, made more so by his own extravagant promises of what bombing could achieve. He claimed that the strategic air offensive could deliver victory on its own. Anything less than victory was therefore, by his own yardstick, a failure. Even so, Harris never deviated from his opinion that the bombing campaign had been a spectacular success. To support this view he leaned heavily on the evidence of Albert Speer, the German Minister of Wartime Weapon Production for much of the war. Harris seems to have admired Speer and harboured no doubts about his veracity as witness. 'He knows exactly, and better than anyone, what effect the bombing had,' he said. The old antagonists appear to have developed a mutual fascination. They corresponded after Speer's release from Spandau prison and Harris expressed a wish to meet him though the encounter never took place. Speer sent Harris a copy of *Inside the Third Reich*, his masterpiece of self-justification. According to Harris 'he said, in his own words, in the inscription of . . . the book itself, that the strategic bombing of Germany was the greatest lost battle of the war for Germany, greater than all their losses in their retreats from Russia and in the surrender of their armies at Stalingrad.'[7]

Harris's use of Speer's opinions was selective. During his post-war interrogation he said he found the attacks on city centres 'incomprehensible' and considered that 'area bombing alone would never have been a serious threat.' Civilian morale, he maintained, 'was excellent throughout, and resulted in rapid resumption of work after attacks.'[8]

In the forty-odd years of his life that remained to him after the war Harris never saw any reason to modify his views. The furore over Dresden did not impress him and in the IWM interview he defended the operation in characteristic terms. 'People are apt to say "oh poor Dresden, a lovely city solely engaged in producing beautiful little china shepherdesses with frilly skirts."' In fact, the city was the last viable governing centre of Germany as well as the last north–south corridor through which German reserves could move to reinforce resistance to both the Russian and Allied advances. What, he wanted to know, was so special about Dresden anyway? Why did no one talk of Lorient and Saint-Nazaire, which were 'destroyed to an extent where the German admiral in charge . . . said not so much as a cat remained alive to prowl the midnight ruins?' Harris suggested his own answer. 'One can only conclude that the reason is that it was ordered by the Navy and not the Air Force.'

The RAF was only doing what the senior service had been practising for centuries. 'People . . . think that when civilians get killed by bombers that it's something brand new. It's not new at all. No navy ever had a strategy except war against a nation as a whole; blockade, deprive the opposing nation of everything that made continuation of living impossible, deprive them of food as well as materials.' It was, he pointed out, 'very successful in the First War. In the 1914–18 war it was reputed to have killed about 800,000 Germans. You don't hear any criticism about that.'

He denied that Bomber Command had ever aimed 'particularly at the civilian population. We were aiming at the production of everything that made it possible for the German Armies to continue the war.' As for what constituted a legitimate human target, Harris had no doubts that munitions workers were fair game and should 'expect to be treated as active soldiers. Otherwise where do you draw the line?'[9]

Harris, as he often complained, had come to be thought of as the man chiefly responsible for the strategic bombing policy. The fact that he was its most vocal defender only intensified this identification in the public's mind. Some who were at least equally answerable avoided the post-war debates and spared themselves the hostility and opprobrium. Portal, whom Harris himself credited with being the prime mover in launching the bomber offensive, proved particularly agile in avoiding the tentacles of the controversy. In the early and middle phases of the air campaign he had been as enthusiastic as anyone in his advocacy of area bombing, only moving away from the policy once *Overlord* had changed the strategic landscape. The war was barely over when, addressing pupils at his old school, Winchester, he said he felt the need to correct 'two curious and widespread fallacies about our night bombing.' The first, he went on, was 'that our bombing is really intended to kill and frighten Germans and that we camouflaged this intention by the pretence that we would destroy industry.' This, as Portal knew better than anyone, was misleading. The intention had been to do both.

Now he told the boys that 'any such idea is completely and utterly false.' By the time he spoke the rough death toll was already known. This carnage, he maintained, 'was purely incidental and inasmuch as it involved children and women who were taking part in the war we all deplored the necessity for doing it.'[10] This struck Peter Johnson as 'hypocrisy of a fairly high order'. In a bombing war of the sort waged by the RAF innocent death was not incidental. It was inevitable. Whatever he subsequently said, Portal had even, at one point, actually thought it desirable. It was his name on the minute in November 1942 arguing the benefits of killing 900,000 Geman civilians and seriously injuring a million more.[11] Yet Portal entered the peacetime world in a shower of praise and garlanded with honours.

Harris's frequently repeated views provided his men with a set of ready-made defences when the subject of bombing came up. It is impossible to characterize the feelings of 125,000 men. But there were certain common strands of thought that ran through the reflections of the crews as they looked back on what they had done. Among the crews there were many thoughtful people, and most of them felt able to justify their actions. Surviving the experience did not induce a mood of harsh self-contemplation.

The Bomber Boys were fighting a new and never-to-be-repeated type of war. Their campaign was open-ended. It was not like a soldier gaining an objective or a sailor sinking a ship. With the advance of aerial photography their achievements became visible. But what did a rash of pockmarks in the ground and a sea of roofless houses mean to the progress of the war? To give some value to the great effort expended, the heavy losses and the great risks endured they had to believe that each trip brought the end at least an inch closer.

Even the least sensitive had some notion of the effect of their arrival over a German town. It was not hard to imagine the tension as the sirens sounded, the terrified scurry to the shelters, the din of the flak guns, the earth-trembling explosions, the smell of falling plaster and the sound of babies crying.

To give meaning to what they did they had to believe they were achieving something and that the good they were doing outweighed the bad. Some might insist that they had no concerns beyond their own survival. That was true during the duration of the operation. But on the ground there was plenty of time in which to think. It was impossible not to consider the bigger picture. Bomber Command had attracted the bravest and the brightest, forward-looking men with questioning and above all positive minds. There were few cynics inside the Lancasters and the Halifaxes. If staying alive was your first priority, why would you join Bomber Command?

So had it all been worth it? It was something that could only be asked of the living. The question of what Bomber Command had contributed to the war effort was, as Webster and Frankland had shown, complicated and never likely to be settled. The crews could comfort themselves with the unarguable fact that the campaign had seriously undermined Germany's defences and accelerated the Allies' victory. Discussion about the way force was focused, and whether different decisions would have produced quicker and better results was barren in the end. There were no lessons to be learned. Area bombing became obsolete with the first nuclear explosion.

By far the bigger issue, one that was never to go away, was the query that Churchill had raised over Bomber Command's conduct of the war. To many Bomber Boys the controversy was baffling and dismaying. They had carried out their orders with extraordinary selflessness and were now being asked to feel shame for actions for which they had once been praised. They had answered the public desire for retribution. This did not mean a measured response, proportionate to what Britain had suffered, but punishment that was relentless and merciless and that would stop the Germans from ever doing what they had done again. When it became clear exactly what the Germans had been doing, Bomber Command's slide from favour seemed all the more unjust.

There is no doubt that they felt slighted, even betrayed. Being the men they were these sentiments were submerged. The ordinary crew members were not inclined to make a fuss in public. But behind closed doors their true feelings could emerge. A speech by Marshal of the Royal Air Force Sir William Dickson, at 5 Group's first postwar reunion, thirty years after the war ended, gives an idea of their sense of hurt and a frank appreciation of what they saw as their own worth. Dickson, who had served on the Joint Planning Committee, was in a good position to put their achievements in the context of the whole struggle. Why, he asked, had the reunion been arranged after all these years? It was partly due to 'a growing feeling that time is moving on and that it is now high time . . . to celebrate the group's spirit and achievements.' But, he thought, 'it may also have something to do with a growing resentment and indignation, shared by the whole Air Force and many outside it, towards some who belittle the strategic air offensive against Germany. Some of these little people try to turn the truth upside down to sell their books or for some vested interest. We particularly resent the argument that the offensive was ineffective and caused needless casualties.'

The role given to Bomber Command after 1940, was 'a vital part of our grand strategy'. Those who criticise Bomber Command, he said, 'completely fail to appreciate the war situation or to put themselves in the place of those who bore the frightful responsibility for the conduct of the war. We were facing an enemy who was waging . . . unlimited war to gain his ends. In unlimited war it is a fight to the death between the whole of each nation. The alternative is surrender. The whole of the German nation was mobilized to destroy our nation and the Russian nation. Germany was all powerful on land, but the war-making potential of German industry was [its] Achilles' heel. Thanks to the foresight of Trenchard, and those who built on his ideas both here and in America, we had the means to attack that heel.'

Dickson then reeled off the list of the Bomber Boys' achievements. Their mission began to have decisive effect, he reckoned, early in 1942 when intensive operations forced the German High Command to concentrate on the air defence of Germany and give up hope that they could rebuild their bomber fleet and launch a new Blitz on Britain. The priority given to defending the Reich meant that outside it, the Allies eventually achieved air superiority. Without that superiority, the campaigns in Africa and Italy could not have succeeded as they did and *Overlord* would have been impossible. It also meant that on the Eastern Front, the German army was deprived of the air support to which it had been accustomed in its western campaigns. If they had the might of the Luftwaffe behind them, Russia would have been defeated. 'That,' he declared, 'should be sufficient answer to those who question the importance and achievements of the strategic air offensive.'

But there was more. Towards the end of the war, the weight and accuracy of the air offensive was such that it was close to accomplishing the Casablanca directive – the destruction and dislocation of the German military, industrial and economic system. It so weakened the enemy's military system that even with all their fighting skill, the Germans could not hold up the advance of the Allied and Russian armies. 'The Strategic Air Offensive,' he judged, 'had in fact brought about the utter defeat of Germany, and if it had not been maintained with great determination by all concerned in it, Germany must have won the war.'

There was a word about the criticism of civilian casualties. 'That criticism should not be pinned on the air offensive,' he maintained. 'It should be pinned on the horror of war itself, especially on unlimited war in which there are no non-combatants and there is no front line.' Compared with the twenty million deaths caused by the German invasion of Russia, 'the civilian casualties caused by the air offensive were astoundingly small. They were a regrettable but unavoidable necessity because the German war making potential was essentially the prime military objective of Allied strategy.'

This was a formidable array of achievements. Why then was the celebration of them so muted? Dickson had one explanation. 'It is hard,' he said, 'to convey by spoken or written word, the military glory of air operations . . . of course there were conspicuous operations which hit the headlines and stirred the nation. But neither the public then or today have any real idea of what was involved in bomber operations.'[12]

Noble Frankland had another. It was partly the fault, he believed, of the government's propagandists. 'The handling of Bomber Command by the official public relations experts had particularly unfortunate consequences,' he wrote. 'Apart from the general glossing over of all failures and the constant exaggeration of all successes . . . there was a more or less constant concealment of the aims and implications of the campaign that was being waged. Attacks on great towns were announced, but somehow or other, especially when questions were asked, the impression was given that specific targets such as armament factories and the like were being aimed at. The damage to the residential and central areas, which were in reality the main aim of the area attacks, was ascribed to what could unfortunately not be avoided if the factories and so on were to be hit.'

The result was that from an early stage in the war the impression was created that Bomber Command had the skill to target a weapons plant or some other plainly worthy target when in fact it could not. When, as occasionally happened, it was admitted that the town itself was the target, the impression was created that this had been chosen in preference to an objective that everyone would recognize as legitimate. Frankland concluded that 'from what one can only assume was a fear of moral indignation, moral indignation was created and in time more than moral indignation. The ultimate reaction was a deep feeling of shock, in the sense of surprise.'[13] It was Frankland who gave the crews the best justification for their war. 'The great immorality open to us in 1940 and 1941,' he told the Royal United Services Institution in December 1961, 'was to lose the war against Hitler's Germany. To have abandoned the only means of direct attack which we had at our disposal would have been a long step in that direction.' This sound judgement was gratefully repeated by his comrades many times in the subsequent years.

There was no great desire among the public for reminders of what had been done on its behalf. Once the reality of the war started to fade there seemed something incongruous and disturbing about the bombing campaign, something unBritish. Britain owned a great empire but its citizens like to think that it had been acquired without violence. They regarded themselves as mild and peaceable people who only took up arms when someone provoked them beyond endurance. Germany had certainly done that. But had the reaction been disproportionate?

Bomber Command was never taken to British hearts in quite the way that Fighter Command had been. It was too large for one thing and its aircraft too gargantuan. Fighter Command was of a

Noble Frankland.

cherishable size. The Spitfire was a very British aircraft. It was neat and agile without being flashy. It was small but it was powerful, like Britain itself. The Lancasters and Halifaxes were giants.

The entertainment industry sensed the public coolness. During the war there had been a series of films celebrating the Command. Movies like *Target for Tonight* (1941) which showed Britain wreaking righteous and specific vengeance on Germany and *The Way to the Stars* (1945) were great successes. The handful of post-war films tended to concentrate on the emotional damage done to the crews by their experiences rather than the damage they did to the enemy.

In the case of *Appointment in London*, which appeared eight years after the war, this owed something to the fact that the men who made it knew the reality of what they were portraying. Aubrey Baring, one of the producers, won a DFC as a fighter pilot and had gone on to fly in the Pathfinder Force. The screenplay and music were written by John Wooldridge who was a much-decorated PFF Mosquito pilot. The film starred Dirk Bogarde as Wing Commander

Tim Mason, the disciplinarian leader of a Lancaster squadron which had been sustaining heavy losses, and was set at the opening of the Battle of Berlin. Mason is on the edge of a breakdown having completed ninety operations yet is obsessively determined to carry on. The character was thought to owe much to Guy Gibson, who was Wooldridge's friend.

The best-known film about Bomber Command was *The Dambusters* which came out in 1954. Here was a subject that could wholeheartedly celebrate the skill and heroism of Bomber Command for feats which were untainted by controversy. The same was true of *633 Squadron* (1964). It was based on a novel which portrayed a fictitious Mosquito squadron in the summer of 1944, attacking a factory at the head of a Norwegian fjord which manufactured fuel needed for the Germans' V2 rocket programme. There was nothing showing fleets of bombers dropping hundreds of tons of high explosives on densely packed cities, let alone the terrible consequences on the ground.

As the years passed, Bomber Command faded from the public memory. The time of the bombers was short. In 1918 they seemed like the future of warfare. By 1946 their day had passed and would never come again. Monuments to their transience lay all over the northern and eastern counties of Britain. The runways of hastily-built aerodromes were ploughed up and the concrete carted away for hardcore. Beet and barley reclaimed the soil. Survivors returning to their old bases found only the odd humpbacked Nissen hut or hangar converted into a store or barn, or a decaying watchtower standing in the middle of a field to stir their memories.

In 1958 Don Charlwood went back to Elsham Wolds. The cement was peeling from the brick gate pillars and the guardhouse was in ruins. But from fifty yards away the mess still looked inhabited. 'I walked through the rain,' he wrote 'and went in at the open door, all at once anticipating the smell of beer and bacon and wet greatcoats, the sound of voices. But down the long room lay ploughs and harrows and bags of superphosphate ... I stood very still. Somewhere hens were clucking and rain gurgled off the roof. There were no other sounds at all. Something in the room eluded me; a deafness shut me from messages on the dusty air. I walked quickly into the rain, groping for understanding of our silenced activity, the purpose of all the courage and devotion I had once seen.'[14]

The old stations made an evocative image. The film *Twelve O'Clock High* opens with an American veteran returning four years after the war to his old base, which like Elsham has reverted to farmland. Cows graze next to the weed-infested landing strip where a tattered windsock hangs. The story that follows is set in 1942 when the American air force had just begun operations. It describes the fortunes of a bomber group which is suffering heavy losses and is undergoing a crisis in morale. The treatment is frank about the disillusioning effect of losses on the men and their commander. But essentially the film is a celebration of the Eighth Air Force and its achievements, which in the eyes of the makers were among the great American military successes of the war. The film, starring Gregory Peck, appeared in 1949.

It was produced by Darryl Zanuck, one of the great Hollywood powers of the time. It was, like all his productions, made in the expectation of commercial success. Film-makers later in the century were cautious about making movies about recently ended wars. *Twelve O'Clock High* did well at the box office. It was one sign that Americans had no qualms about the air war. A clue to the reason for their equanimity is contained in the film's opening credits, which declared: 'This motion picture is dedicated to those Americans both living and dead whose gallant effort made possible daylight precision bombing. They were the only Americans fighting in Europe in the fall of 1942. They stood alone against the enemy, and against doubts from home and abroad.'

The American insistence that they were engaged in precision bombing proved to be a magic shield against criticism. The truth was, as Frankland pointed out, that whatever they said they were doing, the effects were often much the same and the difference between an RAF area attack and a USAAF 'precision' attack could be minimal. As a senior American air force officer joked at a post-war seminar on the campaign, the RAF carried out precision attacks on area targets, while the USAAF carried out area attacks on precision targets. Nor did the American scruples extend to operations in Japan where the fire-bombing of Tokyo brought the principle of area bombing to perfection.

The Eighth Air Force suffered none of the criticism that was aimed at Bomber Command after the war. Its leaders went on to what were the most important military posts of the Cold War era, commanding the strategic bomber fleets that would wage a nuclear war. To some extent, the fact that the American air force had dropped two nuclear bombs on Japan made the debate on the validity and morality of its activities in the European theatre redundant. The American Second World War fliers continued to be honoured and their actions explained in sympathetic films like *Memphis Belle* which described the lives of one Eighth Air Force crew.

In Britain though, the controversy was never laid to rest. New books and documentaries kept the embers of the debate smouldering. As long as Harris was alive the arguments would continue. During the war he had been a remote figure to his crews and to many of those he worked with. In peacetime they began to feel protective towards him. On his ninetieth birthday he received a message from veterans of 12 and 626 Squadrons, once based at Wickenby, which must have warmed his leathery old heart. 'Few of us met you in those days,' it ran, 'but we hope you were aware that your messages which were read to us in the briefing room stirred many a young heart and strengthened many an apprehensive young airman ... We are grateful for all you have done to remind those who would prefer to forget, what we did and what we achieved and of the enormous cost.'[15]

He spoke at many Bomber Command veterans' dinners, always delivering the same message to his 'old lags' of all ranks: that they had never been given proper recognition for their decisive part in the defeat of Hitler. As long as he was alive, for good or bad, he was determined to go on making their case. During the war he had never had the time to engage in much human contact with his men. He made up for it in peacetime. After each reunion he would, as Michael Beetham remembered, 'sit late into the night with a word for everyone and outlasting most.'[16]

Harris's last great public appearance was on 4 September 1982 at the Guildhall in London to honour his presidency of the Bomber Command Association and to mark his ninetieth birthday. The evening ended with Hamish Mahaddie reciting to a spellbound hall Noel Coward's 'Lie in the Dark and Listen'. He died at his home beside the Thames at Goring on 5 April 1984, a few days before his ninety-second birthday. The presidency of the association passed to Michael Beetham, by now a senior RAF officer. 'The vilification that went on of Bert Harris was deeply resented among all of us,' he said. 'We were determined to do something about it.' St Clement Danes in the Strand is the church of the RAF. A statue of Lord Dowding, the chief of Fighter Command during the Battle of Britain, already stood before it. Beetham and and a group of other veterans decided that Harris deserved a statue of his own.

The plan was announced in September 1991. Harris was seven years dead but his reputation was as incendiary as ever. Enough time had now passed for Germans to feel they had a say in the matter. The mayor of Pforzheim was the first to protest followed by his colleagues in Cologne, Hamburg and Dresden. An attempt was made to enlist the support of the City Council of Coventry with which Dresden was twinned. The German media seized on the story and Harris's detractors in Britain publicly repeated their condemnations and criticisms. The statue was unveiled by the Queen Mother on 31 May 1992. It was, as was pointed out, the fiftieth anniversary of Harris's first spectacular, the thousand-bomber raid against Cologne. The monument cost £100,000, most of which came from ex-Bomber Boys or other past and present members of the RAF. A large group of protesters stood behind police cordons as the Queen Mother performed the ceremony. During it, a lone Lancaster flew overhead. After the ceremony was over and the crowds had dispersed, someone daubed the dull, eight-foot-high bronze with red paint. 'That was quickly cleared up,' Michael Beetham recalled. 'What I found was the most touching thing was that the following day there was a wreath from the people of the East End, in gratitude. That did more for morale than anything. They were the people who suffered and they were grateful.'[17]

The statue, like the man it represents, is open to different interpretations. Harris stands upright, his chest jutting forward and his eyes staring confidently ahead. Is it the pose of a supremely arrogant man, faithful to his own blind vision whatever the cost? Or does the stiff way he holds himself show something more admirable; fortitude, and the determination to carry out a terrible but necessary task?

The elderly men standing in the early summer sunshine fervently believed the latter. They came from all walks of life. When the war was over there was little room in the ranks of the RAF. Not many wanted to stay on. They were volunteers, civilians in uniform who had joined up to serve their country and were eager to go back to the world they had left six extraordinary years previously. A bomb-aimer's or navigator's brevet won no favours when looking for jobs. The world was full of servicemen with good wars behind them. One wing commander with a DFC could only find a job working front of house at the Odeon, Swiss Cottage.

When it came time for the Bomber Boys to say goodbye to each other, the partings were painful. Each crew was a social patchwork stitched from men of every class and background. Fear, mutual dependence and the chemistry that had attracted each to the other during crewing-up, welded them into a nucleus, bound together by respect and a form of love.

In the first decade or two of peace they drifted apart. But in late middle age as mortality once again beckoned, many felt the need to look out their old comrades. Early in 1985 Dennis Steiner learned that 170 Squadron which had shared Hemswell with his squadron, 150, were to dedicate a memorial at the base to the crews who had not returned. Through the 170 Squadron association he was able to get back in touch with three surviving crewmates and they were reunited at the service. They found each other stouter and somewhat worn by time but they could still see their old companions behind the lined faces and grey hair. Hemswell was closed and run down but intact. Like naughty schoolboys they managed to get in by forcing a side door and wandering through the old rooms, dusty and forlorn and haunted by memories.

Dennis returned to Hemswell again in 1988 for the 170 Squadron annual service with his wife and children. A Lancaster flew overhead as usual but the base was much changed. Two of the barracks blocks housed antiques centres, another was an old people's home and the officers' mess had been turned into a hotel. A market was set in the grounds at weekends. He 'walked around with some disbelief and sadness.' The market was held on the spot where many years before his room-mate had been killed when his aircraft crashed. 'I wonder if,' he wrote shortly after the visit, 'when the Lancaster had flown past in tribute to those who lost their lives, people paused in their hunt for bargains and looked up, if they knew why it had flown over and also, if they cared. I think that I shall not return.'[18]

The dead were never far away on these occasions. Between September 1939 and May 1945, Bomber Command lost 47,268 men killed on operations. Another 8,305 were killed in flying or training accidents. Another 1,570 groundcrew and WAAFs lost their lives from other causes. The total amounts to between a sixth and a seventh of all British and Commonwealth military war dead. It is a considerably higher figure than the 38,384 officers from the British Empire lost in the First World War. This toll was considered as a catastrophe, a slaughter of the paladins that blighted the post-war years. The deaths of so many Bomber Boys must be counted as another epic tragedy.

For those who came through, no peacetime experience could match the intensity of those short, terrible months when they flew and fought. The war was always there, stirring into life at the slightest nudge. 'At sixty-six, I sit looking out of my window,' wrote Cy March, forty-five years after it was all over, 'watching seagulls gliding, soaring, side-slipping and wheeling around. I think the old Lancaster could do all that . . . I also sit and watch the sunset, truly a work of God, the sheer beauty of the reds, golds and many other lovely colours. Then I think of the sunsets we created, also beautiful in a terrible way with unearthly colours flickering and brightening, the blue flashes from the cookies, the bright red bursts of flak, lit up by searchlights and fires, all created by man's inhumanity to man.'[19]

Epilogue

WENT THE DAY WELL?

With peacetime the complex human cell structure of Bomber Command dissolved. There was no need for Bomber Boys in the postwar world. They dispersed as rapidly as they had come together, settling down in every corner of the country and beyond, working at every occupation. In my early days, doing holiday jobs, I sometimes came across them in offices and factories. The war was the last thing they talked about. But somehow their experiences seemed to mark them out from the other ex-servicemen in the workforce.

Some of the survivors stayed on in the RAF. Michael Beetham had a distinguished career, retiring after forty-one years in 1982 as Marshal of the Royal Air Force and Chief of the Air Staff. He held the post longer than any of his predecessors. As a member of the Chiefs of Staff committee, he played a crucial role in the direction of the Falklands War. Ken Newman obtained a permanent commission and left, aged fifty, as a wing commander before starting a satisfying chapter of life in school and charity administration.

Most still thought of themselves as civilians and were happy to get out of uniform. Arthur Taylor shed his air force blue for a demob 'overcoat, sports coat, flannels and a pair of shoes', in January 1946. 'I felt,' he wrote, 'that when the war in Europe was over [and] the enemy had been beaten there was no longer any purpose in my staying on. . . I had had the good fortune to serve with some fine people in a fine organization and was pleased to have survived the experience.' He joined the civil service working for the Department of Employment until retiring with his wife in Norfolk, where he passed his time painting, gardening and rambling.[1]

The feat of survival brought no advantages. Dennis Steiner had to wait until July 1946 to be demobilized. He ended his RAF career as a pilot officer and by now was a married man. He went back to the office in Wimbledon he had left as a junior to be told that he would receive the same wages he was on when he joined up. 'I could not have had a clearer indication that the war was over,' he remembered.

Settling down was difficult, especially for someone like Leonard Cheshire who by the end had flown a record one hundred missions. He finished his war looking down on Nagasaki on 9 August 1945 as an atomic bomb exploded over it. In 1948 he offered his Hampshire home to a terminally-ill ex-serviceman who had nowhere to go to die. From this act of humanity grew the foundation that carries his name. It flourishes today in fifty-two countries bringing hope and help to the disabled.

Some were able to take up where they had left off when the war came along. After liberation from a German PoW camp, Reg Fayers returned to Sudbury, Suffolk, and his wife Phyllis, and joined her father in his dairy business. He resumed his old sporting career, playing football for Sudbury Town. Reg and Phyllis had a son and daughter. The family moved to west Wales. Reg took took up farming and wrote a book about it, *The Sheep of Dolgwili*. 'I suppose it was "happy ever after,"' he says now.[2]

The need to write was strong. It had been Don Charlwood's ambition since boyhood. After leaving school in the seaside town of Frankston, near Melbourne, in 1932, he approached the Australian newspaper baron Keith Murdoch for a reporter's job, but was only offered the chance to be a messenger. He managed to sell some short stories while working as a farmhand before volunteering for the RAAF in 1940.

In 1943 Don and his crew became the first in 103 Squadron in nine months to survive a tour. On returning to Australia he worked for thirty years in air-traffic control. He recorded his Bomber Command experiences movingly and perceptively in one of the finest books of the war, *No Moon Tonight*. He has written many others and now lives in happy and honoured retirement in Warrandyte, Victoria. One of the benign side effects of the strategic bombing campaign was that it produced a crop of outstanding literature, as powerful as anything that emerged from the trenches. It includes Jack Currie's *Lancaster Target* and *Luck and a Lancaster* by Harry Yates, classic memoirs which ring with authenticity.

Noble Frankland had a different kind of literary career. As well as writing the official history he became director of the Imperial War Museum and played a large part in the production of *The World At War*, the Thames Television epic, produced in the 1970s and as yet unsurpassed.

Most settled into quiet anonymity. Reg Payne went back to Kettering and a job in an engineering factory and later became a technical teacher in a local college. He took up painting evocative pictures of Lancasters in flight and rural scenes. Willie Lewis went to sea on a trawler, sailing from Hull on gruelling three-week trips to the Arctic Circle. Cy March returned to the mines.

The dead lived their unrealized lives in the memories of those they left behind. The love of George Hull's brief life, Joan Kirby, married and became Joan Hatfield. George seemed to be sitting in the corner of her cosy living room in Christchurch, Dorset, as we talked about him on an autumn Saturday afternoon. 'He was a great believer in social justice,' she said as her husband made the tea. 'Had he lived he would have been a leader in some form. It wasn't until after the war that I realized quite what marvellous material he would have been. . . he was a lovely chap. Hardly a day passes when I don't think of him.'[3]

Mary Mileham never quite forgot Frank Blackman. She destroyed most of her wartime correspondence but could not bring herself to get rid of Frank's letters. She offered them instead to the Imperial War Museum in the hope that they would give 'some idea of the pain and anguish felt by those flying boys ... the longing and wishing for peace and love'. Before she died, she wrote to a friend explaining what the relationship had meant. 'It was healing for me to be so needed and some solace to him that I was faithfully there for a few months.' But she felt that 'in peacetime it would not have been any good and had already begun to fade'.[4] After the war she married Patrick Lindsay who worked as a musical arranger at the

BBC and lived contentedly with him in an old cottage in Hampshire. She died in November 1993.

Frances Scott had a miserable few months after her broken Bomber Command romance. Then she met another Bomber Boy, became Frances Dowdeswell, and settled down to a happy married life.

Peter Johnson carried his doubts about the war he had fought into peacetime. He stayed on in the air force, taking part in the Berlin air lift and serving in the mid-fifties as civil air attaché in Bonn. He worked hard at reconciliation with the people he had once bombed and was a trustee of the Dresden Trust, which contributed to the rebuilding of the Frauenkirche, destroyed in the 1945 attack.

Virtually everyone in Bomber Command had been convinced of the justice of what they were doing while they were doing it. 'I didn't have any feelings of guilt,' Bill Farquharson said, sixty-one years after flying his last mission. 'As Harris said, you sow the wind, you reap the whirlwind. We were trying to save our country from Nazi Germany . . . my generation loved this country. We loved our way of life and we were going to keep it and fight for it. . . The majority of us felt that way.'[5]

Viewed from a Lancaster the moral perspective was clear. 'War is a brutal business,' said Tony Iveson. 'Civilization breaks down and if you're going to win, you [have to] win any way you can. Otherwise you're defeated.'[6] It was an attitude that was shared by those who were facing them. The Luftwaffe night-fighter pilot Peter Spoden felt no animosity towards those he was up against. 'We thought "we are not trying to kill the aircrew. We are trying to get the bombers who are destroying our town". . . every soldier has to do his duty... it was our duty to shoot them down. It was their duty to bomb the towns.'[7] The passage of time did little to change minds. 'I always stuck up for Bomber Command,' said Reg Fayers in December 2006. 'We did a good job and I was never ashamed of anything we did.'[8] Leonard Cheshire spent the rest of his life comforting the broken, many of them victims of the war. But he was there at the unveiling of Bomber Harris's statue outside St Clement Danes and when he was awarded a peerage he chose to remember Woodhall, the home of 617 Squadron, in his title.

As the years passed and death got closer many felt the pull of the rare intimacy of their wartime lives and sought out their old comrades. They met again in pubs in Lincolnshire and Yorkshire and Suffolk and drove out to look at their bases, many all but unrecognizable save for an old Nissen hut or a derelict watchtower. The dead were never far away and the need to commemorate them was strong. In Britain there is no public day to mark their sacrifice. But many of the dead airmen shot down over France, Belgium, Holland and Norway are still remembered on the anniversary of their deaths by local communities who regard them as liberators and heroes. In September 2006, the small town of Werkendam gave a fitting burial to the crew of a 78 Squadron Halifax that was shot down by a night-fighter and crashed into marshy ground on the night of 24/ 25 May 1944. The town council raised £85,000 towards the cost of retrieving their remains and raising the headstones. The councillor who led the campaign, Gerard Paans, declared 'we owe our freedom to these brave airmen'.[9]

The Bomber Boys conducted their own rituals of remembrance and raised their own modest memorials. A plaque in Tuddenham parish church in Suffolk commemorates a crew who died flying from the base, which has now melted back into the fields. There are only seven names on it. But the inscription could serve for all the dead Bomber Boys.

> Went the day well?
> We died and never knew.
> But well or ill, Freedom,
> We died for you.[10]

Notes

PROLOGUE

1 Interview with author.
2 W. R. Chorley, *Bomber Command Losses of the Second World War. 1939–40*, Midland Publishing, 2005.
3 ibid, 1945.
4 Jörg Friedrich, *The Fire, The Bombing of Germany 1940–45*, Columbia University Press, 2006.

INTRODUCTION

1 Quoted in Denis Richards, *Portal of Hungerford*, Heinemann 1979, pp. 294–5.
2 Peter Johnson, *The Withered Garland*, New European Publications 1995, pp. 262–3.
3 George F. Kennan, *Sketches from a Life*, W. W. Norton, 2000, p. 121.
4 Harris, IWM, 000931/01.
5 *The Strategic Air War Against Germany 1939–1945. Report of the British Bombing Survey Unit*, Frank Cass 1998, p. 68. The lowest civilian casualty is cited in the survey. The highest is given in Paul Johnson, *Modern Times*, 1983.
6 Interview with author.
7 Lobban, IWM, 88/31/1.
8 Don Charlwood, *No Moon Tonight*, Goodall 2000, p. 131.
9 Harris, Introduction to Guy Gibson, *Enemy Coast Ahead – UNCENSORED*, Crécy 2003, p. 10.
10 James Hampton, *Selected for Aircrew*, Air Research Publications, p. 343.
11 Harry Yates, *Luck and a Lancaster*, Airlife Classic 2001, p. 211.

12 Fayers, *Microfilm copy of letters and diaries.* IWM.

ONE

1 Guy Gibson, op cit, pp. 34–8.
2 The Earl of Halsbury, *1944*, Thornton Butterworth, London 1926, p. 94.
3 In the preface he cites a tract by J. B. S. Haldane, a prominent left-wing academic, to support his predictions. In *Callinicus*, published a year previously, Haldane had also dwelt on the subject of poison gas, an understandable preoccupation with someone who had suffered its effects in the trenches. Unlike Halsbury he suggested some counter-measures to avert the coming catastrophe. In the case of mustard gas, he wrote, 'the American army made a systematic examination of the susceptibility of large numbers of recruits. They found that there was a very resistant class, comprising 20% of the white men tried but no less than 80% of the negroes. This is intelligible as the symptoms of mustard gas blistering and sunburn are very similar, and negroes are pretty well immune to sunburn. It looks, therefore, as if, after a stringent preliminary test, it should be possible to obtain coloured troops who would all be resistant to mustard gas concentrations harmful to most white men. Enough resistant whites are available to officer them.'
4 Titmuss, *Problems of Social Policy*, London 1950, pp. 12–14, 41.

5 Sir John Slessor, *The Central Blue*, Cassell 1956, p. 56.
6 Recounted to Henrietta Miers by Archie Bevan.
7 Letter from Mönchengladbach City Archivist Dr Christian Wolfsburger, 12.9.2006.
8 Sir Charles Webster and Noble Frankland, *The Strategic Air Offensive Against Germany, 1939–1945*, HMSO 1961, vol. I, p. 150.
9 Webster and Frankland, vol. I, p. 47.
10 Webster and Frankland, vol. IV, p. 89.
11 Webster and Frankland, vol. I, p. 154.
12 ibid, vol. I, p. 154.

TWO

1 Memoir of D. R. Field, IWM Department of Documents, 92/29/1.
2 Tim Lewis, *Moonlight Sonata, the Coventry Blitz, 14/15 November 1940*, Tim Lewis and Coventry City Council, pp. 57–61.
3 ibid, p. 63.
4 ibid, p. 82.
5 Kris and Speier, *German Radio Propaganda*, p. 332.
6 John Shelton, *A Night in Little Park Street*, Britannicus Liber 1950.
7 Norman Longmate, *Air Raid*, Arrow 1976, p. 106.
8 Lewis, op cit, p. 128.
9 Longmate, op cit, p. 63.
10 ibid, p. 213.
11 Mass Observation Archive, Sussex University, 6/4/E.
12 ibid.
13 ibid.
14 *The Observer*, 17.11.40.
15 Lewis, op cit, p. 57.
16 MO Archive.

THREE

1 Johnson, op cit, p. 23.
2 IWM sound archive, 8204/03/01.
3 A. R. Taylor, unpublished memoir, IWM Department of Documents.
4 Public Record Office, AIR 29/603.
5 Yates, op cit, p. 15.
6 Brian Frow, unpublished memoir, RAF Museum.
7 Kenneth Jack Newman, unpublished memoir, IWM documents, 06/12/1.
8 IWM, 92/29/1.
9 IWM sound archive, 20926.
10 IWM sound archive, 008901/16.
11 Johnson, op cit, p. 12.
12 IWM, 06/12/1.
13 Ken Goodchild, unpublished memoir, IWM, 98/31/1.
14 Richard Morris, *Cheshire*, Viking 2000, p. 22.
15 Gibson, op cit, pp. 28–30.
16 Interview with author.
17 Interview with author.
18 Bruce Lewis, *Aircrew*, Cassell 2003, p. 117.
19 Interview with author.
20 IWM sound archive, 007372.
21 IWM, 06/12/1.
22 IWM, 94/37/1.
23 Morris, op cit, p. 32.
24 Ralph Wood, 'Seven is My Lucky Number', unpublished manuscript, RAF Museum.
25 Charlwood, op cit, p. 25.
26 ibid, p. 7.

FOUR

1 Webster and Frankland, op cit, vol. IV, p. 30.
2 Interview with author.
3 IWM, 92/29/1.
4 Yates, op cit, p. 59.
5 Denis Steiner, unpublished memoir, IWM, 92/79/1.
6 Hampton, op cit, p. 122.
7 Frow, op cit.
8 Cyril March, unpublished memoir, IWM, 67/281/1.

9 Bruce Lewis, op cit, p. 118.
10 Wood, op cit.
11 Henry Hughes, unpublished memoir, IWM, 99/64/1.
12 Denholm Elliott, recorded reminiscences, IWM, 98/7/1.
13 Interview with author.
14 Charlwood, op cit, p. 17.
15 Interview with author.
16 IWM sound archive, 11587/114.
17 IWM sound archive, 20914/3.
18 Jack Currie, *Lancaster Target*, Goodall 2004, pp. 9–10.
19 Yates, op cit, p. 66.
20 IWM sound archive, 2897/03.
21 IWM sound archive, 20917.
22 IWM, 06/12/1.

FIVE

1 IWM, 94/37/1.
2 PRO AIR, 14/2221.
3 Eric Woods, *While Others Slept*, Woodfield 2001, pp. 57–8.
4 Webster and Frankland, op cit, vol. IV, pp. 128–9.
5 Slessor, op cit, p. 371.
6 Webster and Frankland, op cit, vol. IV, pp. 135–41.
7 ibid, vol. IV, pp. 194–5.
8 Gibson, op cit, p. 195.
9 Slessor, op cit, p. 389.
10 PRO AIR, 21/5. The pilot appealed the verdict and his accuser was killed in action before the appeal came to court.
11 Slessor, op cit, p. 367.
12 John Patrick Dobson, unpublished memoir, IWM, 92/2/1.

SIX

1 Johnson, op cit, pp. 150–151.
2 Arthur Harris, *Bomber Offensive*, Pen and Sword 2005, pp. 88–9.
3 Currie, op cit, p. 91.
4 Interview with author.
5 IWM sound archive, 20926.
6 IWM, 88/22/2.
7 Henry Probert, *Bomber Harris*, Greenhill 2003, p. 204.
8 Wood, op cit.

9 Harris, op cit, p. 83.
10 ibid, p. 85.
11 ibid, p. 105.
12 Quoted in Frederick Taylor, *Dresden*, Bloomsbury 2005, p. 143.
13 Harris, op cit, p. 107.
14 James Fyfe, *The Great Ingratitude*, GC Book Publishers 1993, p. 323.
15 Frow, unpublished memoir, RAF Museum.
16 IWM sound archive, 2897/03.
17 IWM sound archive, 9378/5/2.
18 IWM, 98/7/1.
19 IWM sound archive, 007298/04.
20 IWM, 99/14/1.

SEVEN

1 Quoted in Anja vom Stein, *Unser Köln. Erinnerungen 1910–1960. Erzählte Geschichte*, Sutton Verlag, pp. 111, 116–18.
2 ibid.
3 ibid.
4 ibid.
5 R. M. Ellscheid, *Erinnerungen von 1896–1987*, Stadt Köln, 1988.
6 Quoted in Martin Rüther, *Köln im Zweiten Weltkrieg. Alltag und Erfahrungen zwischen 1939 und 1945*, Emons 2005.
7 Quoted in Bernd Haunfelder and Markus Schmitz, *Humanität und Diplomatie. Die Schweiz in Köln*, Aschendorff Münster, pp. 202–3.
8 Stein, op cit.
9 ibid.
10 ibid.
11 Heinz Pettenberg, *Starke Verbände im Anflug auf Köln. Eine Kriegschronik in Tagebuchnotizen 1939–1945*, Verlag JP Bachem 1981, pp. 162–8.
12 Quoted in Hans-Willi Hermans, *Köln im Bombenkrieg 1942–1945*, Wartberg, Gudensberg-Gleichen 2004, pp. 30, 32.
13 Hans Sester, *Als Junge im sogenannten Dritten Reich*, H-A Herchen Verlag 1986, pp. 47–52.
14 Martin Rüther, op cit.
15 Pettenberg, op cit.

16 Dr P. Simon, *Köln im Luftkrieg. Ein Tatsachenbericht über Fliegeralarme und Fliegerangriffe*, Köln 1954.
17 Stein, op cit.
18 *Die geheinem Lageberichte des Sicherheitsdienst der SS, 1938–45*, ed. Heinz Boberach, Herrsching 1984, vol. 14.
19 Webster and Frankland, op cit, vol. IV, p. 310.

EIGHT

1 Johnson, op cit, p.165.
2 Newman, op cit.
3 IWM, 74/93/1.
4 IWM, 88/22/2.
5 IWM, 93/5/1.
6 IWM sound archive, 209/23/2.
7 IWM, 85/6/1.
8 Hull, op cit.
9 IWM sound archive, 20926.
10 Newman, op cit.
11 Johnson, op cit.
12 IWM, 67/281/1.
13 IWM sound archive, 20917.
14 Yates, op cit, p. 90.
15 IWM, 209147.
16 IWM, 67/281/1.
17 ibid.
18 IWM sound archive, 8901/16/14.
19 IWM, 98/30/1.
20 IWM, 88/47/1.
21 Johnson, op cit, pp. 191–3, 173–4.
22 Parliamentary Debates, Commons, vol. 380, pp. 178–9.
23 ibid, vol. 385, p. 685.
24 ibid, vol. 388, p.155.
25 Quoted in Max Hastings, *Bomber Command*, p. 177.
26 Parliamentary Debates, Lords, vol. 130, pp. 737–46.
27 Parliamentary Debates, Commons, vol. 380, p. 1378.
28 Parliamentary Debates, Lords, vol. 130, pp. 748–9.
29 *The Secret Beast*, quoted in Fyfe, op cit, p. 216.
30 IWM, 88/31/1.
31 Correspondence of Rev. G. Martin, IWM, 93/48/2.
32 IWM sound archive, 2164.

33 Martha Gellhorn, *The Face of War*, p. 166.
34 IWM sound archive, 2170.
35 Terence Rattigan, *Flare Path*, Hamish Hamilton 1942.
36 Currie, op cit, p. 130.

NINE

1 Charlwood, op cit, p. 90.
2 IWM sound archive, 20923/2.
3 IWM, 88/22/2.
4 Johnson, op cit, p. 177.
5 IWM, 80/46/1.
6 Charlwood, op cit, p. 111.
7 Flying Personnel Research Committee, 412 (f) 17.
8 Charlwood, op cit, p. 32.
9 IWM sound archive, 20923/2.
10 Yates, p. 125.
11 Gibson, op cit, p. 174.
12 IWM, 92/29/1.
13 Yates, op cit, p. 101.
14 IWM sound archive, 20926.
15 Woods, op cit.
16 Newman, op cit.
17 John Pudney, *Ten Summers: Poems 1933–43*, Bodley Head 1944, p. 48.
18 Willie Lewis, unpublished memoir, IWM, 67/28/1.
19 ibid.
20 IWM, 67/281/1.
21 IWM, 92/29/1.
22 IWM sound archive, 11587/4.
23 Quoted in Theo Boiten, *Nachtjagd*, The Crowood Press 1997. Pietrek claimed three crewmen managed to bale out successfully. The incident does not appear in British records.
24 IWM, 67/281/1.
25 IWM, 20929/2.
26 Webster and Frankland, op cit, vol. IV, p. 433.
27 IWM, 94/37/1.
28 Johnson, op cit, p. 166.
29 IWM, 94/37/1.
30 IWM sound archive, 20926/2.
31 Charlwood, op cit, p. 44.
32 IWM sound archive, 20923/2.
33 Johnson, op cit, pp. 175–6.
34 IWM, 67/28/1.
35 Currie, op cit, p. 97.

36 IWM, 88/47/1.
37 IWM, 92/10/1.
38 *Militärgeschichtliches Forschungsamt, Das Deutsche Reich und der II Weltskrieg*, vol. 9.
39 PRO WO 235/153.
40 IWM, 98/31/1.
41 Yates, op cit, p. 122.
42 Currie, op cit, p. 86.

TEN

1 IWM, 94/37/1.
2 IWM, 88/22/2.
3 IWM sound archive, 007372/04/02.
4 IWM, 67/281/1.
5 Newman, op cit.
6 IWM, 67/28/1.
7 Interview with author.
8 IWM sound archive, 007372/04/02.
9 Charlwood, op cit, p. 121.
10 IWM, 88/22/2.
11 IWM, 92/29/1.
12 IWM, 94/37/1.
13 Interview with author.
14 IWM sound archive, 007373/04/02.
15 Newman, op cit.
16 *The Second World War Letters of G. J. Hull*, Imperial War Museum Department of Documents.
17 IWM, 67/281/1.
18 IWM sound archive, 007298/04.
19 IWM sound archive, 007372/04/02.
20 Interview with author.
21 IWM, 67/28/1.
22 Charlwood, op cit, p. 53.
23 Newman, op cit.
24 IWM, 94/37/1.
25 Frow, op cit.
26 IWM, 67/28/1.
27 IWM, 88/22/2.
28 Charlwood, op cit.

ELEVEN

1 Webster and Frankland, op cit, vol. IV, p. 155.
2 PRO AIR, 14/3507.

3 Quoted in John Terraine, *The Right of the Line*, Hodder & Stoughton 1985, p. 547.
4 Harris, op cit, p. 176.
5 IWM sound archive, 209182.
6 Webster and Frankland, op cit, vol. II, pp. 201–2.
7 Harris, op cit, p. 187.
8 Interview with author.
9 *The Berlin Diaries of Marie Vassiltchikov*, The Folio Society, London 1991, pp. 97–9.
10 Hans-Georg von Studnitz, *Diarium der Jahre 1943–45*, pp. 137–9.
11 Hans-Dieter Schäfer, *Berlin im Zweiten Weltkrieg*, pp. 144–59.
12 PRO, *Bang On*, 31 December 1943.
13 Freeman Dyson, *Disturbing the Universe*, pp. 19–20.
14 Interview with author.
15 Noble Frankland, *The Bombing Offensive Against Germany*, p. 72.

TWELVE

1 Interview with author.
2 IWM, 94/37/1.
3 Gibson, op cit, p. 127.
4 IWM, 88/22/2.
5 Frow, op cit.
6 Charlwood, op cit, p. 63.
7 IWM, 67/281/1.
8 Letters of Edwin Thomas, IWM Department of Documents.
9 Interview with author.
10 IWM sound archive, 209/23/2.
11 Terraine, op cit, p. 527.
12 IWM sound archive, 8901/16/9.
13 Webster and Frankland, op cit, vol. IV, p. 445.
14 Jonathan Falconer, *Bomber Command Handbook*, Sutton Publishing 2003, p. 51.
15 Hampton, op cit, p. 263.
16 Dyson, op cit, p. 21.
17 Martin Middlebrook, *The Berlin Raids*, Cassell 1988, p. 378.
18 Newman, op cit, p. 110.
19 Dyson, op cit, pp. 25–6.
20 Newman, op cit, p. 70.
21 ibid, p. 184.

22 IWM, 88/22/2.
23 Gibson, op cit, p. 273.
24 Interview with author.
25 Yates, op cit, p. 227.
26 Flying Personnel Research Committee, p. 10.
27 IWM sound archive, 20718/5.
28 IWM sound archive, 8901/16/9.
29 Interview with author.
30 IWM sound archive, 20718/5.

THIRTEEN

1 IWM, 92/29/1.
2 Currie, op cit, p. 114.
3 See Allan D. English, 'A Predisposition to Cowardice? Aviation Psychology and the Genesis of "Lack of Moral Fibre" ', *War and Society*, vol. 13, no. 1, May 1995.
4 PRO AIR, 2/8591, AM Pamphlet 100.
5 PRO, Symonds and Williams, *Investigation of Psychological Disorders in Flying Personnel*, FPRC 412(f).
6 ibid.
7 IWM sound archive, 20718/5.
8 Dyson, op cit, pp. 23–4.
9 Currie, op cit, p. 139.
10 PRO AIR, 2.
11 English, op cit, p. 26.
12 Mark K. Wells, *Courage and Air Warfare*, Frank Cass 2000, p. 204.
13 PRO Air Ministry memo, 1 March 1945, S 61141/S7(d).
14 Lawson memorandum, RAF Air Historical Branch.
15 Quoted in Wells, op cit, p. 200.
16 Johnson, op cit, p. 246.
17 Currie, op cit, p. 136.
18 Interview with author.
19 PRO AIR.
20 PRO AIR.
21 Flying Personnel Research Committee, op cit.
22 IWM, 94/37/1.
23 Wells, op cit, p. 205.

FOURTEEN

1 Dyson, op cit, p. 19.
2 Hull, op cit.
3 IWM, 92/29/1.
4 IWM, 88/22/2.
5 Charlwood, op cit, p. 54.
6 IWM, 80/46/1.
7 Newman, op cit.
8 Woods, op cit.
9 IWM, 85/6/1.
10 IWM, 94/37/1.
11 IWM, 92/29/1.
12 IWM, 74/93/1.
13 Charlwood, op cit, pp. 153, 156.
14 Hull, op cit.
15 IWM, 88/22/2.
16 IWM, 92/2/1.
17 Gibson, op cit, p. 10.
18 Hull, op cit.
19 See Lewis, op cit, p. 36.
20 IWM sound archive, 8901/16/14.
21 IWM, 80/46/1.
22 Charlwood, op cit, pp. 59–61.
23 IWM, 99/14/1.
24 Currie, op cit, p. 12.
25 Hull, op cit.
26 Letters of E. G. Thomas, IWM, 67/277/1.
27 Pip Beck, *Keeping Watch*, Crécy 2004, pp. 27–8.
28 Frow, op cit.
29 Hull, op cit.
30 IWM, 67/28/1.
31 Currie, op cit, pp. 73–4.
32 ibid, pp. 163–4.
33 IWM, 67/28/1.
34 Hull, op cit.
35 Yates, op cit, p. 132.
36 IWM, 85/6/1.
37 Woods, op cit.
38 Yates, op cit.
39 Hull, op cit.

FIFTEEN

1 Letters of Mary Mileham. Mileham family papers.
2 Following correspondence taken from Letters of Flying Officer F. H. Blackman, IWM Documents Department, 80/46/1.

3 ibid.
4 Mileham papers.
5 ibid.
6 Martin Middlebrook and Chris Everitt, *The Bomber Command War Diaries*, Penguin 1990, p. 271.
7 Interview with author.
8 Following correspondence taken from Letters of Joan Kirby, IWM, Department of Documents.
9 Following correspondence taken from the Letters of George Hull, IWM, Department of Documents.
10 Interview with author.
11 Gibson, op cit.
12 Frances Dowdeswell, *The Path*, unpublished memoir, IWM.

SIXTEEN

1 Roger Freeman, *The Mighty Eighth*, Cassell 2000, pp. 67–9.
2 ibid.
3 ibid, p. 78.
4 Terraine, op cit, p. 620.
5 Newman, op cit.
6 Yates, op cit, p. 135.

SEVENTEEN

1 Ralph Briars, unpublished memoir, IWM, 67/385/1.
2 Interview with author.
3 IWM, 67/385/1.
4 Harris, op. cit, p. 220.
5 Terraine, op cit, p. 676.
6 Yates, op cit, pp. 179–80.
7 Newman, op cit.
8 Quoted in Terraine, op cit, p. 673.
9 Quoted in Webster and Frankland, op cit, vol. III, p. 82.
10 ibid, p. 84.
11 ibid, p. 93.
12 ibid, p. 80.
13 ibid, p. 55.
14 ibid, p. 101.

EIGHTEEN

1 Roy Lodge, unpublished memoir.
2 Quoted in Frederick Taylor, *Dresden*, Bloomsbury 2004, pp. 214–15. The most thorough and lucid work on the subject as well as the most balanced.
3 Interview with author.
4 See Taylor, op cit, pp. 503–9 for discussion of the controversy over the death toll.
5 Interview with author.
6 Yates, op cit, pp. 235–6.
7 Middlebrook and Everitt, op cit, p. 669.
8 PRO WO 235/235.
9 Quoted in Webster and Frankland, op cit, vol. III, p. 112.
10 Quoted in Johnson, op cit, p. 243.
11 Webster and Frankland, op cit, vol. III, p. 119.
12 Statistisches Bundesamt, *Wirtschaft und Statistik*, vol. III, pp. 139–42.
13 Hans Rumpf, *The Bombing of Germany*, Muller 1963, pp. 154–65. The statistics for civilian deaths in France are taken from Eddy Florentin, *Quand les Alliés bombardaient la France*, Perrin 1997.
14 Johnson, op cit, p. 260.
15 Following account from IWM, 88/47/1.
16 IWM, 92/10/1.
17 IWM, 98/7/1.
18 Fayers, op cit.
19 IWM, 92/29/1.
20 IWM, 67/281/1.

NINETEEN

1 Quoted in Henry Probert, *Bomber Harris*, Greenhill 2003, p. 343.
2 PRO, letter from Sir Arthur Street to Sir Robert Knox, 17 January 1945.
3 Probert, op cit, p. 348.
4 Quoted in *The Many*, WH Smith 1995.
5 Quoted in Richards, op cit, p. 335.
6 IWM, 931/01.
7 Quoted in Probert, op cit, p. 410.
8 Webster and Frankland, op cit, p. 375.
9 IWM, 931/01.
10 Richards, op cit, p 339.
11 Terraine, op cit, pp. 505, 684.

12 IWM Documents Department, Misc, 10.202.
13 Frankland, op cit.
14 Charlwood, op cit, p. 218.
15 Quoted in Probert, op cit, p. 411.
16 ibid, p. 411.
17 Interview with author.
18 IWM, 42/29/1.
19 IWM, 67/281/1.

4 IWM 80/46/1.
5 Interview with author.
6 Interview with author.
7 IWM 20/91/8.
8 Conversation with author.
9 *Daily Mail*, 28 September 2006.
10 The lines are usually attributed to the English classicist John Maxwell Edmonds, 1875–1958.

EPILOGUE

1 IWM 99/14/1.
2 Conversation with author.
3 Interview with author.

Bombers

The specifications below are average for each aircraft. Modifications were constantly being made as design and capacity were changed, and the plans overleaf show a precise version ('Mark') of our five most important bombers of World War II.

WELLINGTON
Long-range night bomber

Wingspan:	86 ft
Length:	61 ft
No & type of engines:	2 Merlin X
Crew:	6
Bomb loading:	4,500 lb
Armament:	4 machine guns
Max speed:	255 mph
Average height:	12,500 ft
Range:	1540 miles (loaded)

LANCASTER
Heavy bomber

Wingspan:	102 ft
Length:	69.5 ft
No & type of engines:	4 Merlin
Crew:	7
Bomb loading:	14,000 to 22,000 lb
Armament:	10 machine guns
Max speed:	287 mph
Average height:	1400 ft
Range:	1660 miles

HALIFAX
Heavy bomber

Wingspan:	104 ft
Length:	70 ft
No & type of engines:	4 Hercules XVI
Crew:	7
Bomb loading:	13,000 lb
Armament:	9 machine guns
Max speed:	282 mph
Average height:	13,000 ft
Range:	1260 miles (loaded)

STIRLING
Heavy bomber

Wingspan:	99 ft
Length:	87 ft
No & type of engines:	4 Hercules II
Crew:	7 or 8
Bomb loading:	14,000 lb
Armament:	8 machine guns
Max speed:	270 mph
Average height:	14,000 ft
Range:	2010 miles

MOSQUITO
Fighter bomber

Wingspan:	54 ft
Length:	40 ft
No & type of engines:	2 Merlin 21
Crew:	2
Bomb loading:	2000 lb
Armament:	machine guns or cannon
Max speed:	380 mph
Average height:	21,000 ft
Range:	1220 miles

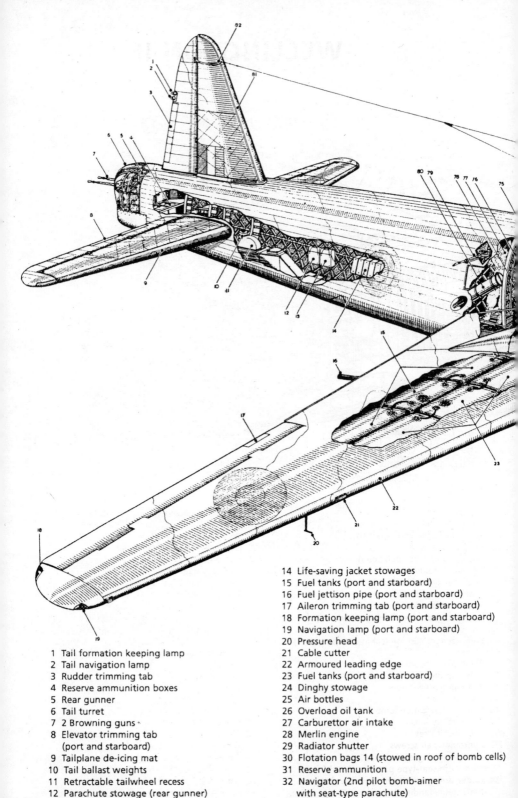

1 Tail formation keeping lamp
2 Tail navigation lamp
3 Rudder trimming tab
4 Reserve ammunition boxes
5 Rear gunner
6 Tail turret
7 2 Browning guns
8 Elevator trimming tab
   (port and starboard)
9 Tailplane de-icing mat
10 Tail ballast weights
11 Retractable tailwheel recess
12 Parachute stowage (rear gunner)
13 Parachute stowage (mid gunner)

14 Life-saving jacket stowages
15 Fuel tanks (port and starboard)
16 Fuel jettison pipe (port and starboard)
17 Aileron trimming tab (port and starboard)
18 Formation keeping lamp (port and starboard)
19 Navigation lamp (port and starboard)
20 Pressure head
21 Cable cutter
22 Armoured leading edge
23 Fuel tanks (port and starboard)
24 Dinghy stowage
25 Air bottles
26 Overload oil tank
27 Carburettor air intake
28 Merlin engine
29 Radiator shutter
30 Flotation bags 14 (stowed in roof of bomb cells)
31 Reserve ammunition
32 Navigator (2nd pilot bomb-aimer
    with seat-type parachute)
33 Bombs

WELLINGTON II

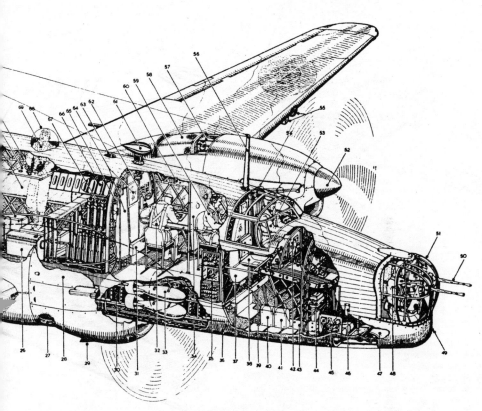

34 Armour plate
35 Main electrical panel
36 Bomb doors (extending aft to
   mid-gun position)
37 Door (sound-proof bulkhead)
38 2nd pilot's folding seat
   (with seat-type parachute)
39 Cabin heating duct
40 Parachute stowage (bomb-aimer)
41 Parachute stowage (front gunner)
42 Pilot's instrument panel
43 Bomb-aimer's cushion (cabin entrance door)
44 Camera
45 Bomb-aimer's control panel
46 Thermometer fairing
47 Bomb-aimer's window
48 Front gunner
49 Forward navigation lamp
50 2 Browning guns
51 Nose gun turret
52 Hydromatic air screws
   (with anti-icing equipment)
53 Pilot (with seat-type parachute)
54 Undercarriage positioning warning horn
55 Retractable landing lamps
56 Aerial mast

57 Oil tank (port and starboard nacelle)
58 Fuel tank (port and starboard nacelle)
59 Wireless operator
60 Navigator's instrument panel
61 D.F. loop
62 Map stowage
63 Upward identification lamp
64 Doors (sound-proof bulkhead)
65 Hand fire extinguisher
66 Oxygen bottles (port and starboard)
67 Reconnaisancre flares
68 Observation dome
69 Navigator (in sextant reading position)
70 Compass
71 Sextant steady
72 Rest bunk
73 Parachute stowage
74 Thermos flasks stowage
75 Mid gun hatch (port and starboard)
76 Elsan closet
77 Mid-gunner's position
78 Flame floats or sea markers
79 Vickers 'K' gun (starboard mid-gun position)
80 Flare chute
81 Fin de-icing mat
82 Rudder mass balance

LANCASTER I

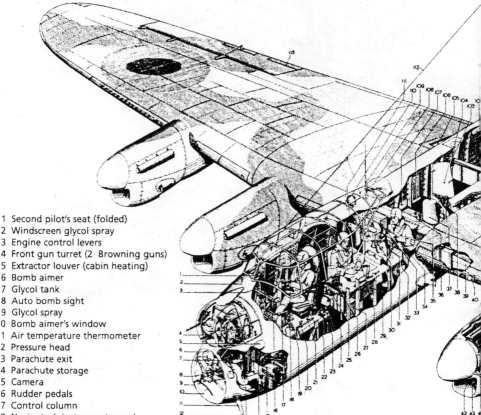

1 Second pilot's seat (folded)
2 Windscreen glycol spray
3 Engine control levers
4 Front gun turret (2 Browning guns)
5 Extractor louver (cabin heating)
6 Bomb aimer
7 Glycol tank
8 Auto bomb sight
9 Glycol spray
10 Bomb aimer's window
11 Air temperature thermometer
12 Pressure head
13 Parachute exit
14 Parachute storage
15 Camera
16 Rudder pedals
17 Control column
18 Navigator's instrument panel
19 Pilot's glycol hand pump
20 Fuel jettison control .
21 Intake control
22 Seat adjusting lever
23 Bomb door controlvalue
24 Pilot
25 Pilot's armour plating
26 A.R.I. 5033
27 A.R.I. 5033
28 Navigator
29 T.R.9.F. wireless
30 Navigator's D.F. receiver
31 W.I. operator's receiver
32 Trailing aerial winch
33 T.1154 transmitter
34 Amplifier
35 W.T.operator
36 Signal pistol
37 Hydraulic reservoir
38 Hydraulic hand pump
39 Cabin heating duct
40 Cabin heating inlet

41 B.B.P. plate
42 Oil cooler
43 Radiator (coolant)
44 Header tank
45 Merlin XX engine
46 Oil tank
47 No 1 fuel tank
48 Undercarriage doors
49 Landing wheel
50 Undercarriage jack
51 No 2 fuel tank
52 Flame damper
53 Carburettor air intake
54 No 3 fuel tank
55 B.B.P. plate
56 B.B. cable cutter
57 Navigation lamp

58 Formation keeping lamps
59 Aileron
60 Aileron balance tab
61 Flaps
62 Whip aerial (beam approach)
63 Flare chute
64 Mid gunner
65 Mid lower turret (2 Browning guns)
66 Vacuum flasks
67 Entrance door
68 Downward identification lamps
69 Stepover ammunition chutes
70 Dip-sticks stowage
71 Fireman's axe
72 First aid stowage
73 Dipole aerial
74 Sanitary pan

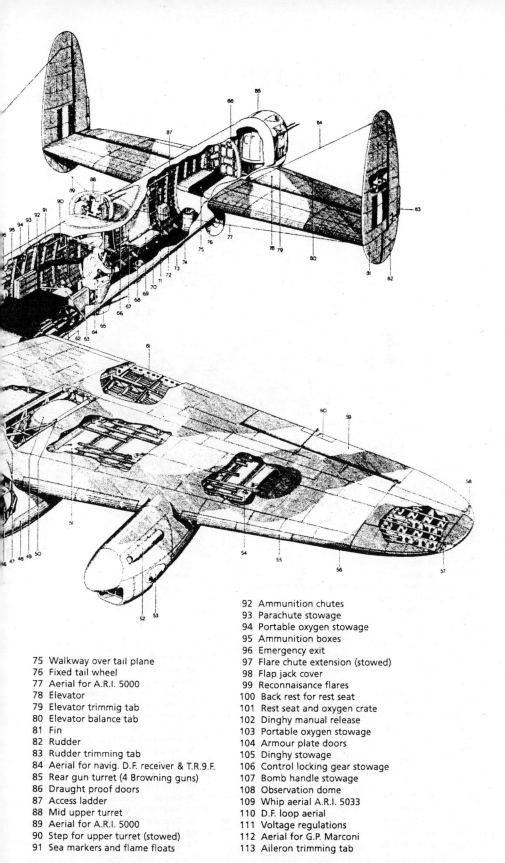

92 Ammunition chutes
93 Parachute stowage
94 Portable oxygen stowage
95 Ammunition boxes
96 Emergency exit
97 Flare chute extension (stowed)
98 Flap jack cover
99 Reconnaisance flares
100 Back rest for rest seat
101 Rest seat and oxygen crate
102 Dinghy manual release
103 Portable oxygen stowage
104 Armour plate doors
105 Dinghy stowage
106 Control locking gear stowage
107 Bomb handle stowage
108 Observation dome
109 Whip aerial A.R.I. 5033
110 D.F. loop aerial
111 Voltage regulations
112 Aerial for G.P. Marconi
113 Aileron trimming tab

75 Walkway over tail plane
76 Fixed tail wheel
77 Aerial for A.R.I. 5000
78 Elevator
79 Elevator trimmig tab
80 Elevator balance tab
81 Fin
82 Rudder
83 Rudder trimming tab
84 Aerial for navig. D.F. receiver & T.R.9.F.
85 Rear gun turret (4 Browning guns)
86 Draught proof doors
87 Access ladder
88 Mid upper turret
89 Aerial for A.R.I. 5000
90 Step for upper turret (stowed)
91 Sea markers and flame floats

HALIFAX II

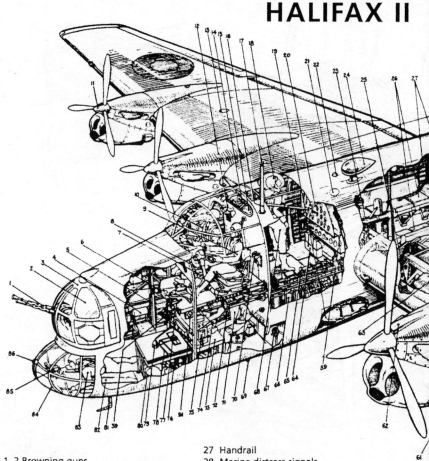

1 2 Browning guns
2 Front gunner's position
3 Nose gun turret
4 Navigator's seat
5 Flexible heating pipes to crew positions
6 Cabin heating
7 Pilot's compass
8 Pilot's panel
9 First pilot
10 Second pilot
11 Airscrews for de-icing equipment
12 Fuel cock controls (pilot operated)
13 Fuel tanks air vent
14 Engine starter buttons
15 Armoured glass
16 Aerial mast de-icing
17 Aerial mast
18 Astral dome
19 Bombs (fuselage bomb bay)
20 Flight engineer's instrument panel
21 Very light signal pistol aperture
22 Upward identification lamp
23 Emergency hand pump
   (hydraulic system)
24 D.F. loop
25 Engine control runs
26 Crew's rest position

27 Handrail
28 Marine distress signals
29 Bombs (in wing bomb bays)
30 Reconnaissance flares
31 Rear escape hatch
32 Dinghy stowage
33 Mid gun turret
34 2 Browning guns
35 Ammunition boxes
36 Ammunition tracks
37 Crash axe stowage
38 D.R. compass
39 Astrograph
40 Tail wheel shock absorber cover
41 Rear gunner's parachute stowage
42 Rear gunner'r instrument panel
43 Rear gunner's rest seat
44 Rear gunner
45 Rear gun turret
46 Four Browning guns
47 Rear identification lamp
48 Rudder tab
49 Rear armour plated bulkhead
50 Entrance door
51 Fuel tanks
52 Oil tank (outboard engine)
53 Aileron tab
54 Formation keeping lamps (port and starboard)

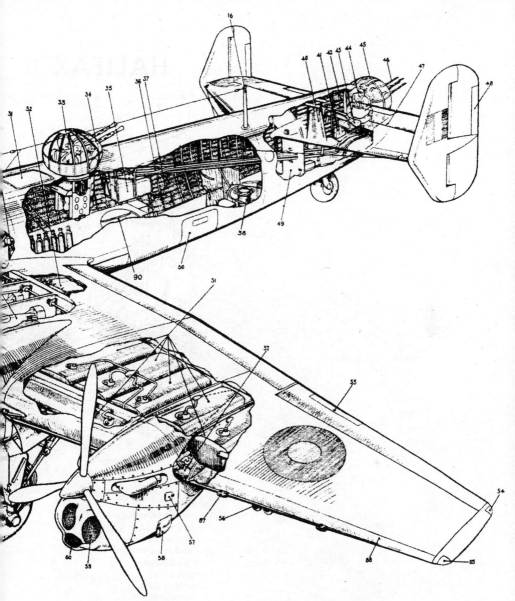

55 Navigation lamp (port and starboard)
56 Retractable landing lamps
57 Access to engine priming cocks
58 Carburettor air intake
59 Cooling system radiator
60 Oil cooler radiator
61 Radiator flap
62 Heater system air intake
63 Oil tank (inboard engine)
64 Flight engineer's parachute stowage
65 Automatic controls
66 Oxygen bottles
67 Spare trailing aerial reel stowage
68 Flight engineer
69 Trailing aerial
70 Controls for emergency flares
71 Radio operator
72 Main electrical panel

73 Radio operator's table
74 R.O. parachute stowage
75 Transmitting and receiving sets
76 Camera
77 Map stowage
78 Navigator's table and chart plotter
79 Navigator's table lamp
80 Navigator's parachute stowage
81 Pressure head
82 Bomb-aimer's prone ramp
83 Bomb-aimer
84 Bomb-aimer's window
85 Bomb sight
86 Forward navigation lamp
87 Cable cutters
88 Armoured leading edge
89 Armour plated bulkhead and door
90 Provision for lower gun turret
91 Navigator's compass repeater

1 Fuel tanks (outboard inter-spar)
2 Fuel tanks (inboard inter-spar)
3 Fuel tanks (rear)
4 Upward identification lamp
5 Fuel tank (leading edge)
6 Aerial mast
7 Aerial mast de-icing equipment
8 Charging and distribution panel
9 D.F. loop
10 Heating system handwheel
11 Airframe de-icing control handwheel
12 Charging cable stowage
13 Oxygen bottles
14 Fuel cock controls
15 Bunk (rest station)
16 Central service accumulators
17 Oxygen bottles
18 Airscrew anti-icing fluid tank

19 Observation dome (stowed)
20 Fire extinguisher
21 Fuselage heating pipe
22 Ground signalling strips
23 Escape ladder
24 Mid-upper turret (2 Browning guns)
25 Flame floats or sea markers
26 Four reconnaissance flares
27 Fuel filler extension
28 Fin de-icing equipment
29 Rudder balance tab
30 Navigation lamp (tail)
31 Rudder trimming tab
32 Rear turret (4 Browning guns)
33 Parachute stowage (rear turret)
34 Elevator trimming tab
35 Tail plane de-icing equipment
36 Bulkhead door

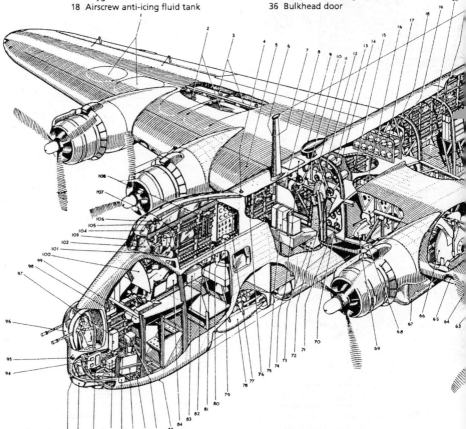

37 Elsan closet
38 Fuselage entrance door
39 Parachute stowage (flare launcher)
40 Parachute stowage (mid-gunner)
41 Four reconnaissance flares
42 Forced-landing flare chute
43 Reconnaissance flare chute
44 Maintenance trestles
45 Maintenance trestle struts
46 Tool roll
47 Ammunition conveyor (to rear turret)
48 Ammunition (rear turret)

49 Reserve ammunition
50 Dinghy stowage
51 Flap
52 Fuel tanks (inboard inter-spar)
53 Fuel tanks (outboard inter-spar)
54 Aileron trimming strip
55 Port formation-keeping lamp
56 Port navigation lamp
57 Twin landing lamps (retractable)
58 Oil tank
59 Carburettor air intake
60 Engine cooling gills

STIRLING I

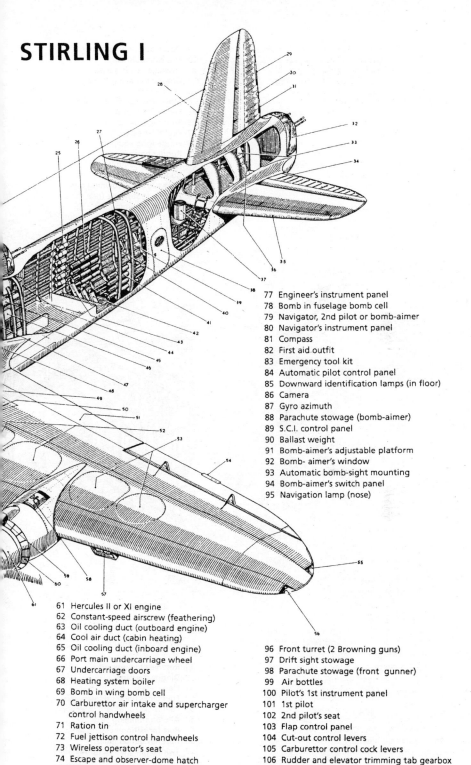

77 Engineer's instrument panel
78 Bomb in fuselage bomb cell
79 Navigator, 2nd pilot or bomb-aimer
80 Navigator's instrument panel
81 Compass
82 First aid outfit
83 Emergency tool kit
84 Automatic pilot control panel
85 Downward identification lamps (in floor)
86 Camera
87 Gyro azimuth
88 Parachute stowage (bomb-aimer)
89 S.C.I. control panel
90 Ballast weight
91 Bomb-aimer's adjustable platform
92 Bomb- aimer's window
93 Automatic bomb-sight mounting
94 Bomb-aimer's switch panel
95 Navigation lamp (nose)

61 Hercules II or XI engine
62 Constant-speed airscrew (feathering)
63 Oil cooling duct (outboard engine)
64 Cool air duct (cabin heating)
65 Oil cooling duct (inboard engine)
66 Port main undercarriage wheel
67 Undercarriage doors
68 Heating system boiler
69 Bomb in wing bomb cell
70 Carburettor air intake and supercharger
   control handwheels
71 Ration tin
72 Fuel jettison control handwheels
73 Wireless operator's seat
74 Escape and observer-dome hatch
75 Wireless equipment
76 Fire extinguisher

96 Front turret (2 Browning guns)
97 Drift sight stowage
98 Parachute stowage (front gunner)
99 Air bottles
100 Pilot's 1st instrument panel
101 1st pilot
102 2nd pilot's seat
103 Flap control panel
104 Cut-out control levers
105 Carburettor control cock levers
106 Rudder and elevator trimming tab gearbox
107 Compass mounting
108 Flying control locking gear stowage

MOSQUITO IV

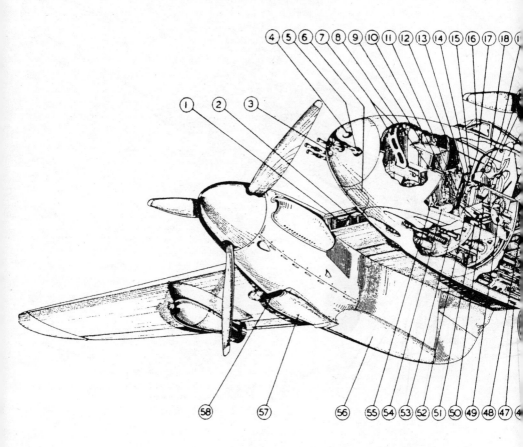

1 Oil cooler	21 Cockpit lamp
2 Coolant radiator	22 Pilot's seat and harness
3 Navigation headlamp	23 Flame-trap exhaust
4 Camera gun spot	24 Outboard fuel tanks
5 Four 303 guns	25 Landing lamp
6 Cover to used cartridge-case chamber	26 500 lb bomb
7 Ammunition boxes and feed chutes for 303 guns	27 Navigation lamp
8 Hinge for gun loading door	28 Resin lamp
9 Inspection door for instrument panel	29 Pitot head (pressure)
10 Folding ladder	30 Aerial for R.1155
11 Ventilator control	31 Tail navigation lamp
12 Compass	32 Tail-wheel (retracted)
13 Control column	33 Oxygen bottles
14 Brake lever	34 Accumulators
15 Firing switches	35 Inboard fuel tanks
16 Sliding window	36 Long range fuel tank bearers
17 Trailing aerial winch	37 Downward identification lamp
18 Emergency exit	38 Bomb winch and hawser
19 Engine and propeller control box	39 Ventral compartment lamp
20 Observer's seat and harness	40 Bomb carriers

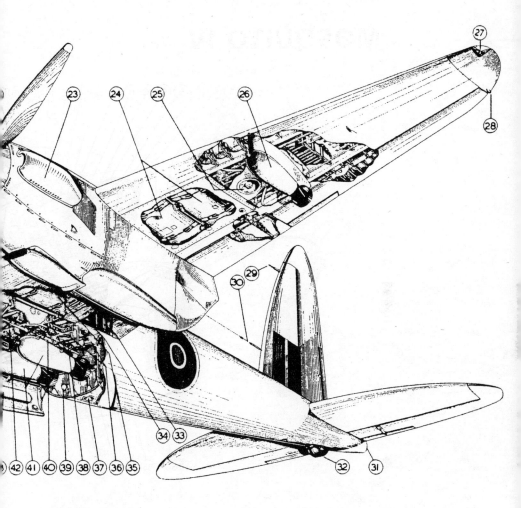

41 500 lb bombs
42 Bomb racks
43 Bomb doors showing trough
   for clearance of 500 lb bomb
44 Central tanks
45 Hydraulic jacks (4)
46 Ammunition boxes and feed chutes
   for 20mm guns
47 Link and c artridge chute cases
48 De- icing tank
49 Elevator trim hand-wheel
50 Pilot's seat adjusting lever
51 Sanitary container
52 First aid box
53 20mm guns (4)
54 Entrance door (starboard)
55 Rudder pedals
56 Undercarriage wheel doors
57 Air intake
58 Ice guard

Acknowledgements

A book like this owes its existence to the generosity of those who took part in the events described. This paperback edition has also benefited from the contributions of readers, many of them veterans of Bomber Command or with relations who served in it, who have put me right on points of fact and detail. I would like to thank everyone who gave so freely of their time and their memories, spoken and written. I owe a special debt to Tony Iveson, Doug Radcliffe and Sir Michael Beetham of the Bomber Command Association for supporting *Bomber Boys*. I am also grateful to the following for allowing me to quote from their memoirs: Reg Fayers, Dennis Field (whose fascinating *Boy, Blitz and Bombers* will shortly be published), Roy Lodge, Cyril March, Ken Newman, Dennis Steiner and Harry Yates. Geoffrey Willat gave me permission to quote from his illuminating book, *Bombs and Barbed Wire, My War in the RAF and Stalag Luft III* (Upfront Publishing), and Mark Briars from the memoir of his late father, Ralph. Thanks to Bruce Lewis for permission to quote from *Aircrew: The Story of the Men Who Flew the Bombers*. Kind permission to quote from Jack Currie's *Lancaster Target* and Don Charlwood's *No Moon Tonight* (both Goodall paperbacks) was granted by Crécy Publishing. Thanks also are due for permission to quote from Harry Yates's *Luck and a Lancaster: Chance and Survival in World War II* (The Crowood Press Ltd, new edition, ISBN 1–84037291-5). New European Publications likewise kindly granted permission to quote from Peter Johnson's *The Withered Garland: Doubts and Reflections of a Bomber*. I have failed in my attempts to contact Arthur Taylor and Doug Mourton, whose memoirs are held at the Imperial War Museum. Please accept my apologies.

I am particularly grateful for the encouragement I received from Edward Hearn of 50 Squadron at the start of my research. Also for the help and hospitality offered by Frances Dowdeswell, Bill Farquharson, Joan Hatfield, Fred Hulance, Philip Mileham and Reg Payne. The great Noble Frankland and his worthy successor Sebastian Cox, Chief Historian of the RAF, were generous with their wisdom. The staff at the Imperial War Museum and the RAF Museum were, as always, friendly and helpful. Arabella Pike, Annabel Wright, Melanie Haselden, Vera Brice and the rest of the team at HarperCollins were the best an author could hope for. A heartfelt vote of thanks, too, to my agent David Godwin. I am grateful to Angelica von Hase for her excellent research on the bombing of Germany. Kate Connolly kindly provided information about the early bombing of Germany. Thanks too, to Felicity Hawkins, Annabel Merullo and Tim Harris for their friendship when the going got tough. I would also like to record my gratitude to my old teacher, Richard Milward, head of history at Wimbledon College, who died last year after a lifetime inspiring generations of boys with his love of history. I cannot thank Henrietta Miers enough. But I will try, in another place in another way.

Index

Page numbers in *italics* denotes an illustration